Gilbert
Hernandez **HEARTBREAK SOUP**

A LOVE AND ROCKETS BOOK

FANTAGRAPHICS BOOKS

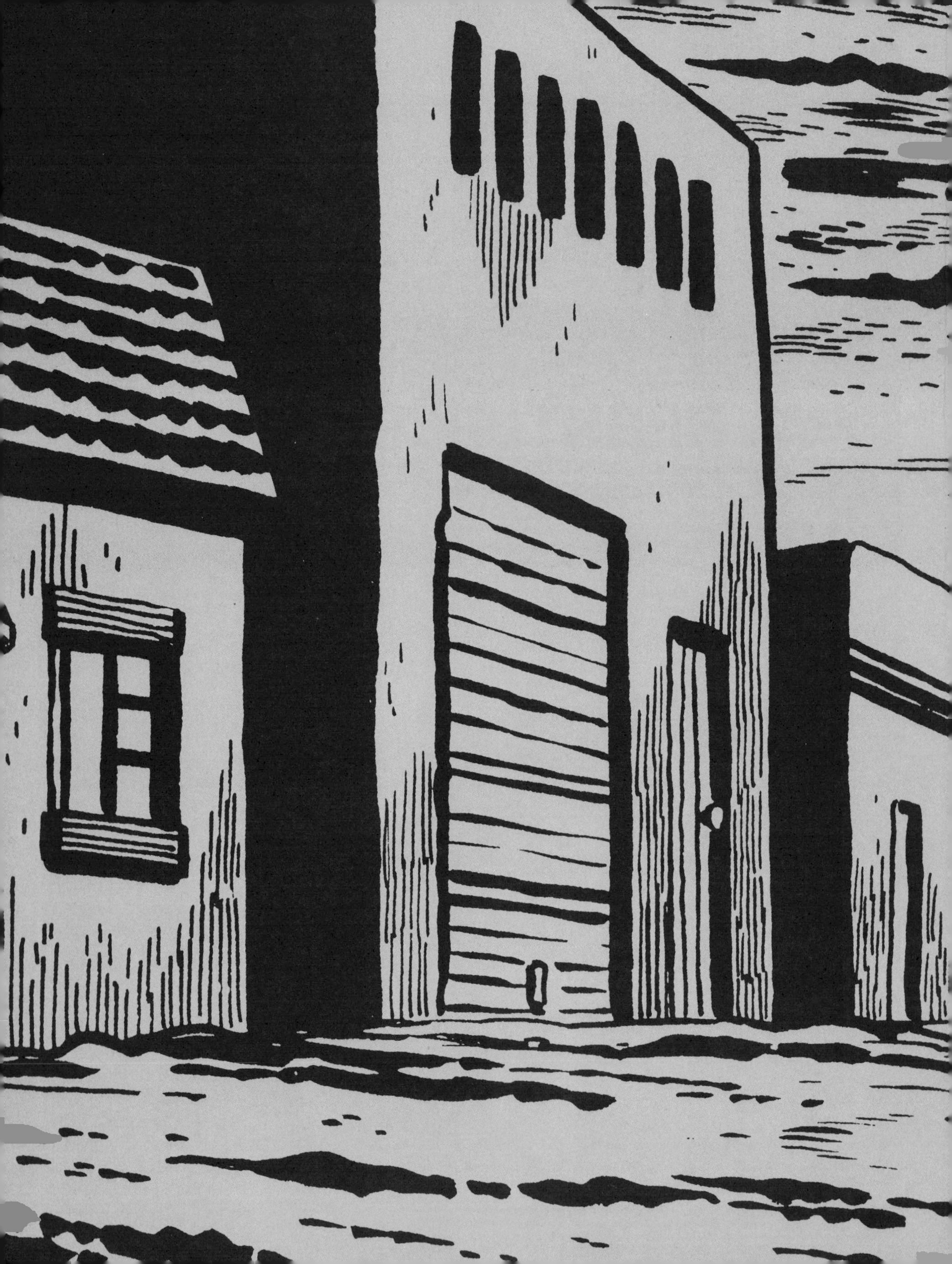

HEARTBREAK SOUP

A LOVE AND ROCKETS BOOK

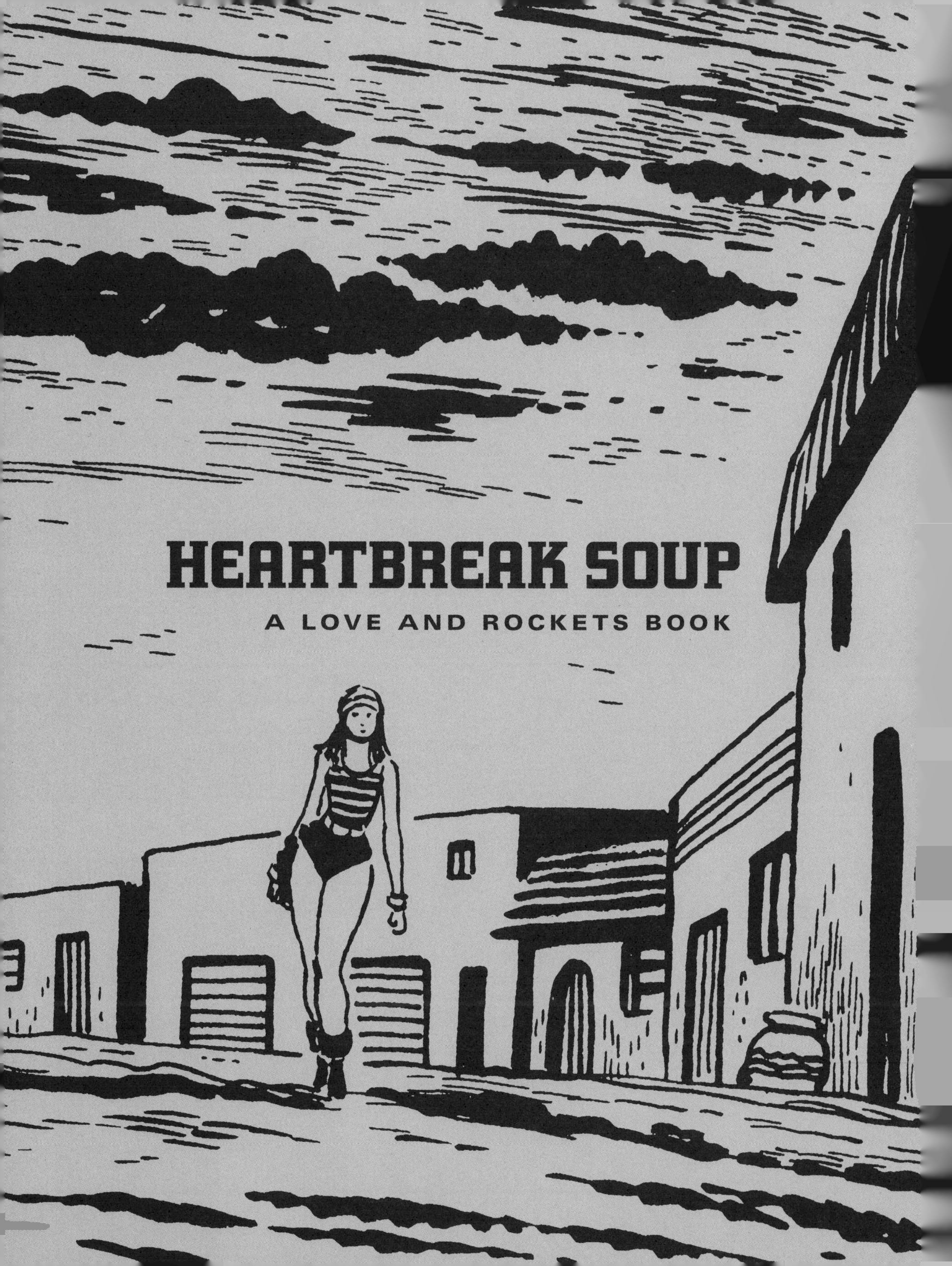

HEARTBREAK SOUP:
THE LOVE AND ROCKETS LIBRARY Vol. 2

Fantagraphics Books
7563 Lake City Way NE
Seattle, WA 98115

www.fantagraphics.com

Edited by Kim Thompson
Original comics edited by Gary Groth
Design and art direction by Jacob Covey
Production by Paul Baresh
Associate Publisher: Eric Reynolds
Publisher: Gary Groth

Fourth printing: February 2017
ISBN 978-1-56097-783-4

Printed in Hong Kong

These stories originally appeared in *Love and Rockets* Vol. I #3–10, #12 –20, *Love and Rockets* Vol. II #6, and *The Complete Love and Rockets* Vols.1 –2.

THE LOVE AND ROCKETS LIBRARY:

Vol. 1 *Maggie the Mechanic* by Jaime Hernandez
Vol. 2 *Heartbreak Soup* by Gilbert Hernandez
Vol. 3 *The Girl from H.O.P.P.E.R.S.* by Jaime Hernandez
Vol. 4 *Human Diastrophism* by Gilbert Hernandez
Vol. 5 *Perla La Loca* by Jaime Hernandez
Vol. 6 *Beyond Palomar* by Gilbert Hernandez
Vol. 7 *Amor Y Cohetes* by Gilbert, Jaime & Mario Hernandez
Vol. 8 *Penny Century* by Jaime Hernandez
Vol. 9 *Esperanza* by Jaime Hernandez
Vol. 10 *Luba and Her Family* by Gilbert Hernandez
Vol. 11 *Ofelia* by Gilbert Hernandez
Vol. 12 *Comics Dementia* by Gilbert Hernandez
Vol. 13 *Angels and Magpies* by Jaime Hernandez

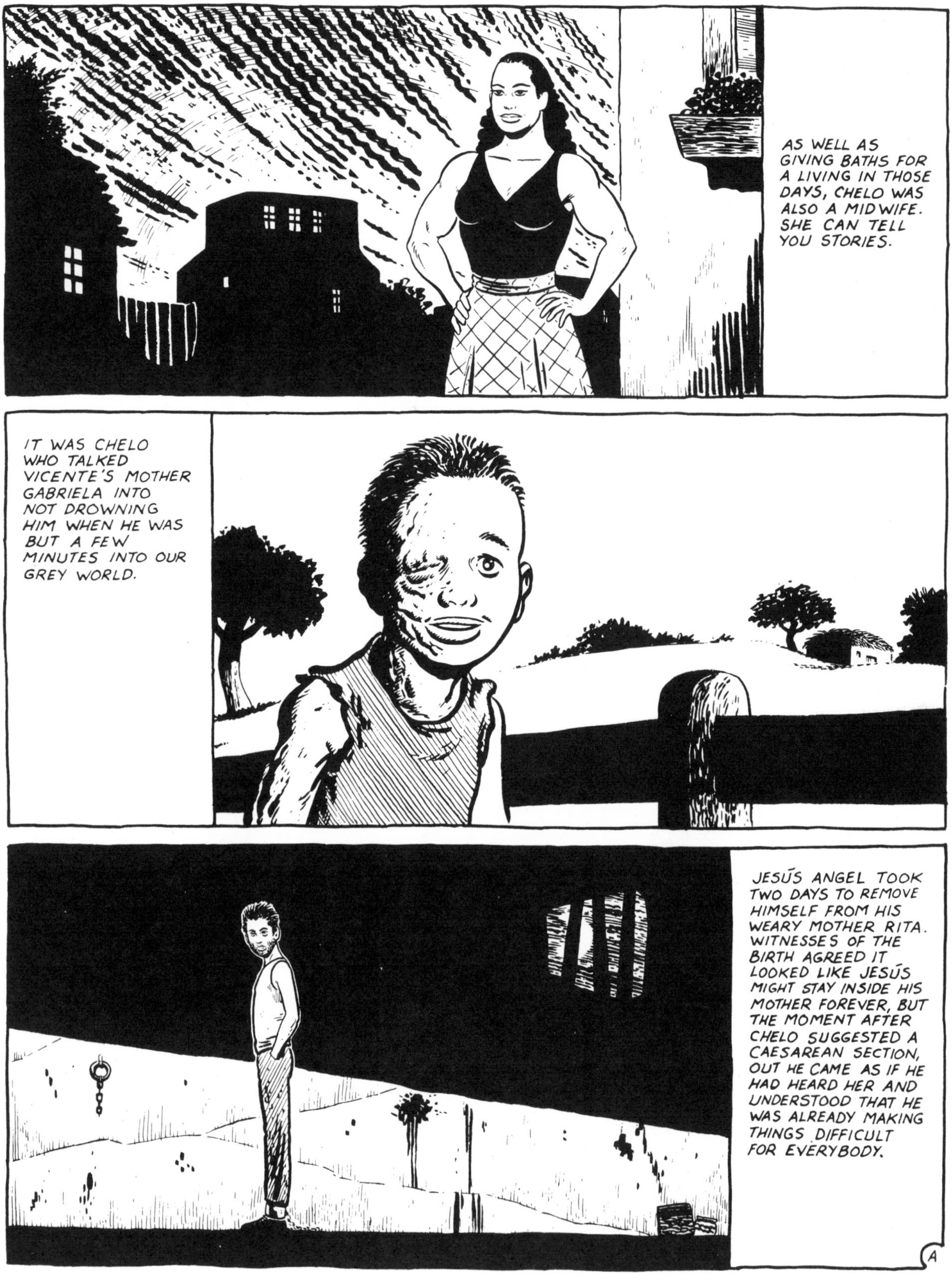
AS WELL AS GIVING BATHS FOR A LIVING IN THOSE DAYS, CHELO WAS ALSO A MIDWIFE. SHE CAN TELL YOU STORIES.
IT WAS CHELO WHO TALKED VICENTE'S MOTHER GABRIELA INTO NOT DROWNING HIM WHEN HE WAS BUT A FEW MINUTES INTO OUR GREY WORLD.
JESÚS ANGEL TOOK TWO DAYS TO REMOVE HIMSELF FROM HIS WEARY MOTHER RITA. WITNESSES OF THE BIRTH AGREED IT LOOKED LIKE JESÚS MIGHT STAY INSIDE HIS MOTHER FOREVER, BUT THE MOMENT AFTER CHELO SUGGESTED A CAESAREAN SECTION, OUT HE CAME AS IF HE HAD HEARD HER AND UNDERSTOOD THAT HE WAS ALREADY MAKING THINGS DIFFICULT FOR EVERYBODY.

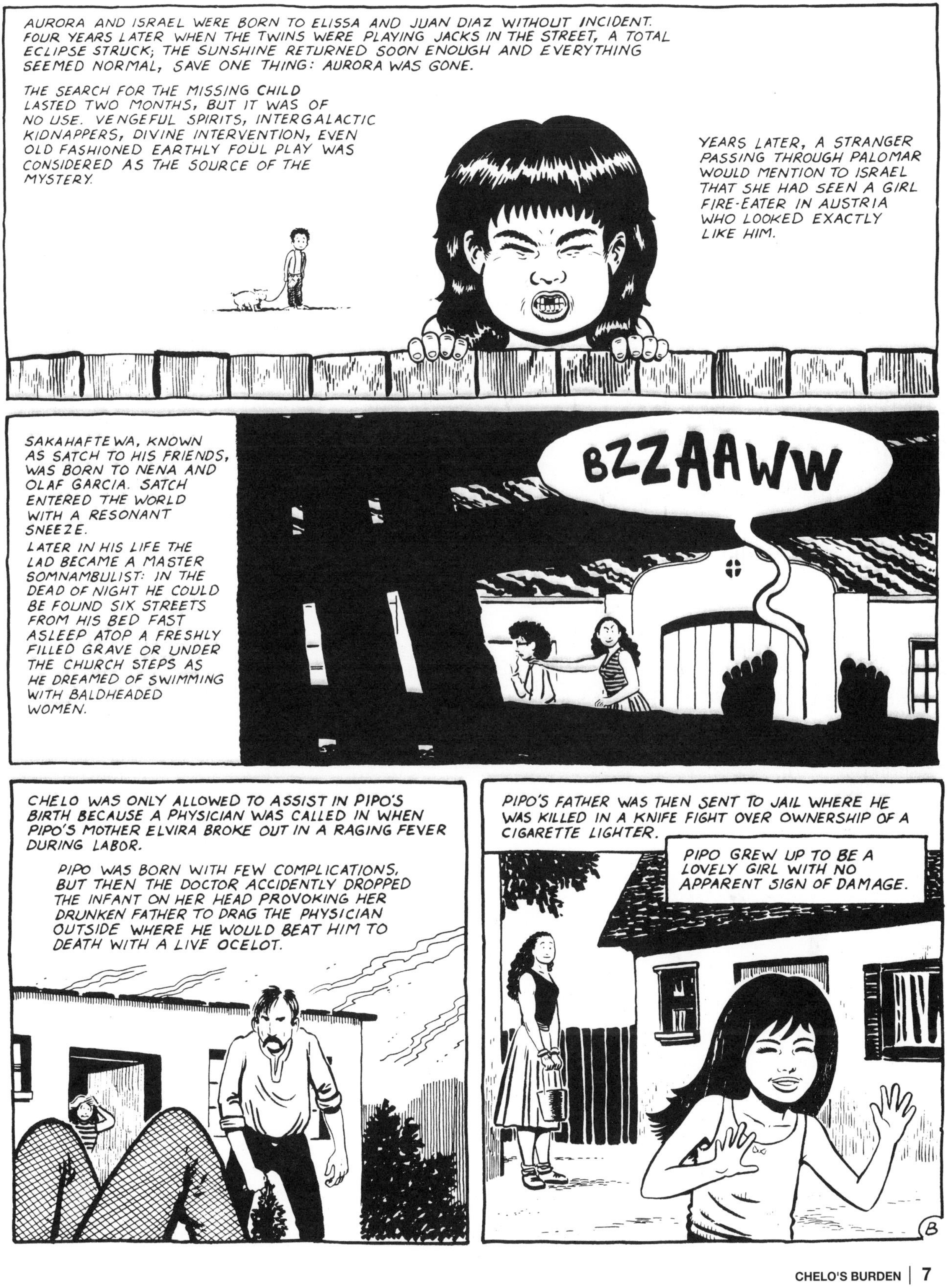
AURORA AND ISRAEL WERE BORN TO ELISSA AND JUAN DIAZ WITHOUT INCIDENT. FOUR YEARS LATER WHEN THE TWINS WERE PLAYING JACKS IN THE STREET, A TOTAL ECLIPSE STRUCK; THE SUNSHINE RETURNED SOON ENOUGH AND EVERYTHING SEEMED NORMAL, SAVE ONE THING: AURORA WAS GONE.
THE SEARCH FOR THE MISSING CHILD LASTED TWO MONTHS, BUT IT WAS OF NO USE. VENGEFUL SPIRITS, INTERGALACTIC KIDNAPPERS, DIVINE INTERVENTION, EVEN OLD FASHIONED EARTHLY FOUL PLAY WAS CONSIDERED AS THE SOURCE OF THE MYSTERY.
YEARS LATER, A STRANGER PASSING THROUGH PALOMAR WOULD MENTION TO ISRAEL THAT SHE HAD SEEN A GIRL FIRE-EATER IN AUSTRIA WHO LOOKED EXACTLY LIKE HIM.
SAKAHAFTEWA, KNOWN AS SATCH TO HIS FRIENDS, WAS BORN TO NENA AND OLAF GARCIA. SATCH ENTERED THE WORLD WITH A RESONANT SNEEZE.
LATER IN HIS LIFE THE LAD BECAME A MASTER SOMNAMBULIST: IN THE DEAD OF NIGHT HE COULD BE FOUND SIX STREETS FROM HIS BED FAST ASLEEP ATOP A FRESHLY FILLED GRAVE OR UNDER THE CHURCH STEPS AS HE DREAMED OF SWIMMING WITH BALDHEADED WOMEN.
BZZAAWW
CHELO WAS ONLY ALLOWED TO ASSIST IN PIPO'S BIRTH BECAUSE A PHYSICIAN WAS CALLED IN WHEN PIPO'S MOTHER ELVIRA BROKE OUT IN A RAGING FEVER DURING LABOR.
PIPO WAS BORN WITH FEW COMPLICATIONS, BUT THEN THE DOCTOR ACCIDENTLY DROPPED THE INFANT ON HER HEAD PROVOKING HER DRUNKEN FATHER TO DRAG THE PHYSICIAN OUTSIDE WHERE HE WOULD BEAT HIM TO DEATH WITH A LIVE OCELOT.
PIPO'S FATHER WAS THEN SENT TO JAIL WHERE HE WAS KILLED IN A KNIFE FIGHT OVER OWNERSHIP OF A CIGARETTE LIGHTER.
PIPO GREW UP TO BE A LOVELY GIRL WITH NO APPARENT SIGN OF DAMAGE.
B

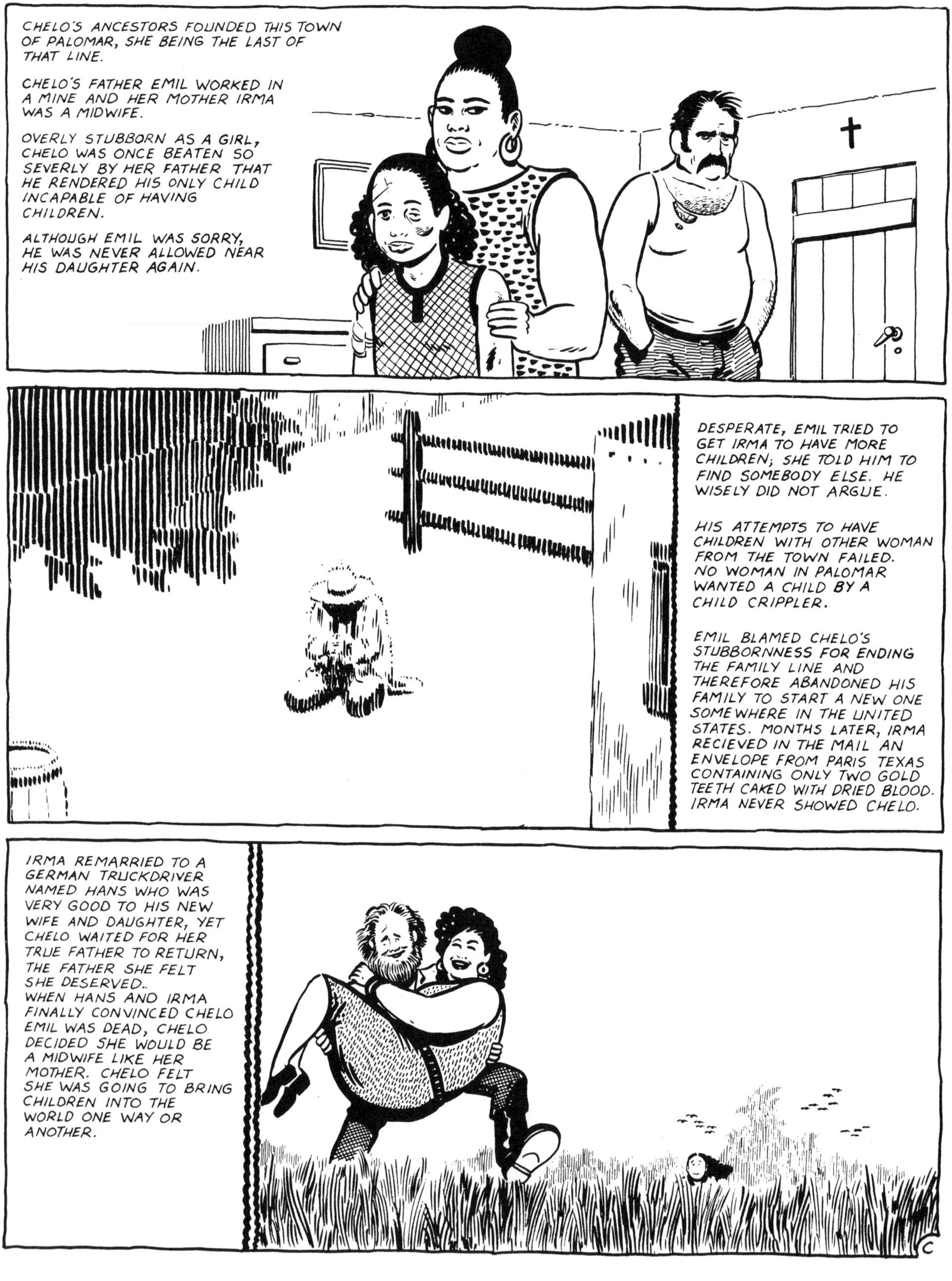
CHELO'S ANCESTORS FOUNDED THIS TOWN OF PALOMAR, SHE BEING THE LAST OF THAT LINE.
CHELO'S FATHER EMIL WORKED IN A MINE AND HER MOTHER IRMA WAS A MIDWIFE.
OVERLY STUBBORN AS A GIRL, CHELO WAS ONCE BEATEN SO SEVERLY BY HER FATHER THAT HE RENDERED HIS ONLY CHILD INCAPABLE OF HAVING CHILDREN.
ALTHOUGH EMIL WAS SORRY, HE WAS NEVER ALLOWED NEAR HIS DAUGHTER AGAIN.
DESPERATE, EMIL TRIED TO GET IRMA TO HAVE MORE CHILDREN; SHE TOLD HIM TO FIND SOMEBODY ELSE. HE WISELY DID NOT ARGUE.
HIS ATTEMPTS TO HAVE CHILDREN WITH OTHER WOMAN FROM THE TOWN FAILED. NO WOMAN IN PALOMAR WANTED A CHILD BY A CHILD CRIPPLER.
EMIL BLAMED CHELO'S STUBBORNNESS FOR ENDING THE FAMILY LINE AND THEREFORE ABANDONED HIS FAMILY TO START A NEW ONE SOMEWHERE IN THE UNITED STATES. MONTHS LATER, IRMA RECIEVED IN THE MAIL AN ENVELOPE FROM PARIS TEXAS CONTAINING ONLY TWO GOLD TEETH CAKED WITH DRIED BLOOD. IRMA NEVER SHOWED CHELO.
IRMA REMARRIED TO A GERMAN TRUCKDRIVER NAMED HANS WHO WAS VERY GOOD TO HIS NEW WIFE AND DAUGHTER, YET CHELO WAITED FOR HER TRUE FATHER TO RETURN, THE FATHER SHE FELT SHE DESERVED..
WHEN HANS AND IRMA FINALLY CONVINCED CHELO EMIL WAS DEAD, CHELO DECIDED SHE WOULD BE A MIDWIFE LIKE HER MOTHER. CHELO FELT SHE WAS GOING TO BRING CHILDREN INTO THE WORLD ONE WAY OR ANOTHER.

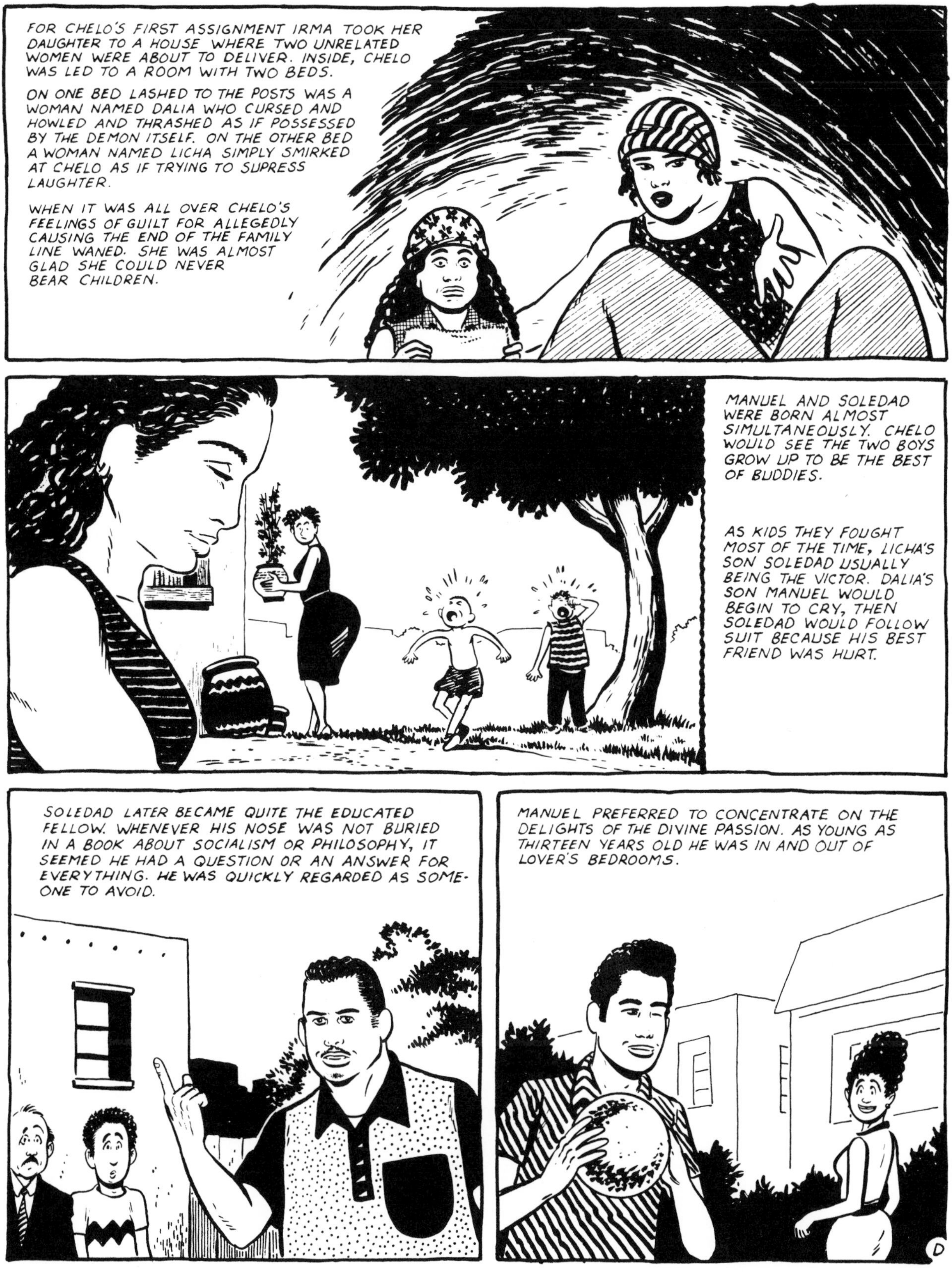
FOR CHELO'S FIRST ASSIGNMENT IRMA TOOK HER DAUGHTER TO A HOUSE WHERE TWO UNRELATED WOMEN WERE ABOUT TO DELIVER. INSIDE, CHELO WAS LED TO A ROOM WITH TWO BEDS.
ON ONE BED LASHED TO THE POSTS WAS A WOMAN NAMED DALIA WHO CURSED AND HOWLED AND THRASHED AS IF POSSESSED BY THE DEMON ITSELF. ON THE OTHER BED A WOMAN NAMED LICHA SIMPLY SMIRKED AT CHELO AS IF TRYING TO SUPRESS LAUGHTER.
WHEN IT WAS ALL OVER CHELO'S FEELINGS OF GUILT FOR ALLEGEDLY CAUSING THE END OF THE FAMILY LINE WANED. SHE WAS ALMOST GLAD SHE COULD NEVER BEAR CHILDREN.
MANUEL AND SOLEDAD WERE BORN ALMOST SIMULTANEOUSLY. CHELO WOULD SEE THE TWO BOYS GROW UP TO BE THE BEST OF BUDDIES.
AS KIDS THEY FOUGHT MOST OF THE TIME, LICHA'S SON SOLEDAD USUALLY BEING THE VICTOR. DALIA'S SON MANUEL WOULD BEGIN TO CRY, THEN SOLEDAD WOULD FOLLOW SUIT BECAUSE HIS BEST FRIEND WAS HURT.
SOLEDAD LATER BECAME QUITE THE EDUCATED FELLOW. WHENEVER HIS NOSE WAS NOT BURIED IN A BOOK ABOUT SOCIALISM OR PHILOSOPHY, IT SEEMED HE HAD A QUESTION OR AN ANSWER FOR EVERYTHING. HE WAS QUICKLY REGARDED AS SOME-ONE TO AVOID.
MANUEL PREFERRED TO CONCENTRATE ON THE DELIGHTS OF THE DIVINE PASSION. AS YOUNG AS THIRTEEN YEARS OLD HE WAS IN AND OUT OF LOVER'S BEDROOMS.

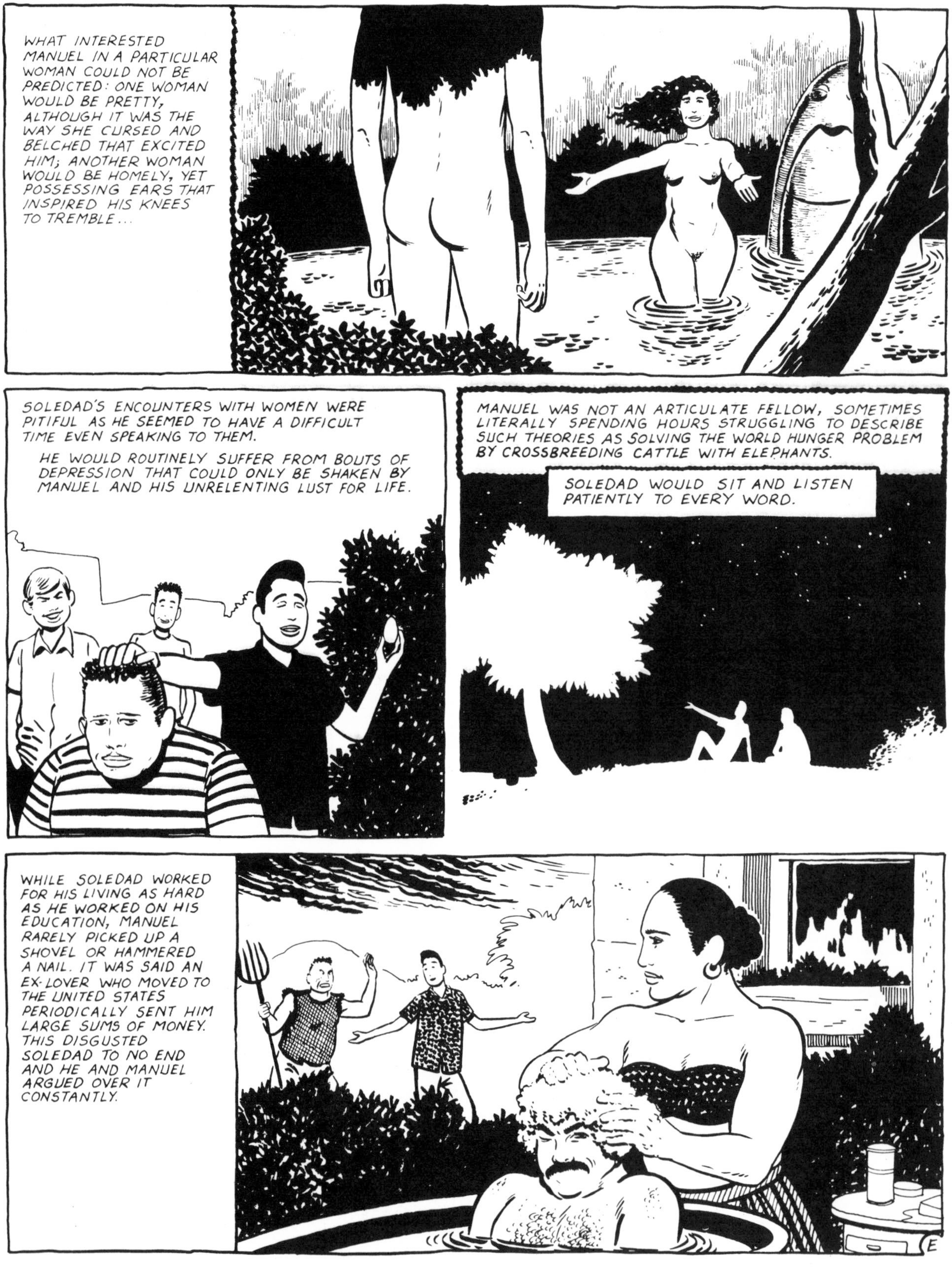
WHAT INTERESTED MANUEL IN A PARTICULAR WOMAN COULD NOT BE PREDICTED: ONE WOMAN WOULD BE PRETTY, ALTHOUGH IT WAS THE WAY SHE CURSED AND BELCHED THAT EXCITED HIM; ANOTHER WOMAN WOULD BE HOMELY, YET POSSESSING EARS THAT INSPIRED HIS KNEES TO TREMBLE...
SOLEDAD'S ENCOUNTERS WITH WOMEN WERE PITIFUL AS HE SEEMED TO HAVE A DIFFICULT TIME EVEN SPEAKING TO THEM.
HE WOULD ROUTINELY SUFFER FROM BOUTS OF DEPRESSION THAT COULD ONLY BE SHAKEN BY MANUEL AND HIS UNRELENTING LUST FOR LIFE.
MANUEL WAS NOT AN ARTICULATE FELLOW, SOMETIMES LITERALLY SPENDING HOURS STRUGGLING TO DESCRIBE SUCH THEORIES AS SOLVING THE WORLD HUNGER PROBLEM BY CROSSBREEDING CATTLE WITH ELEPHANTS.
SOLEDAD WOULD SIT AND LISTEN PATIENTLY TO EVERY WORD.
WHILE SOLEDAD WORKED FOR HIS LIVING AS HARD AS HE WORKED ON HIS EDUCATION, MANUEL RARELY PICKED UP A SHOVEL OR HAMMERED A NAIL. IT WAS SAID AN EX-LOVER WHO MOVED TO THE UNITED STATES PERIODICALLY SENT HIM LARGE SUMS OF MONEY. THIS DISGUSTED SOLEDAD TO NO END AND HE AND MANUEL ARGUED OVER IT CONSTANTLY.

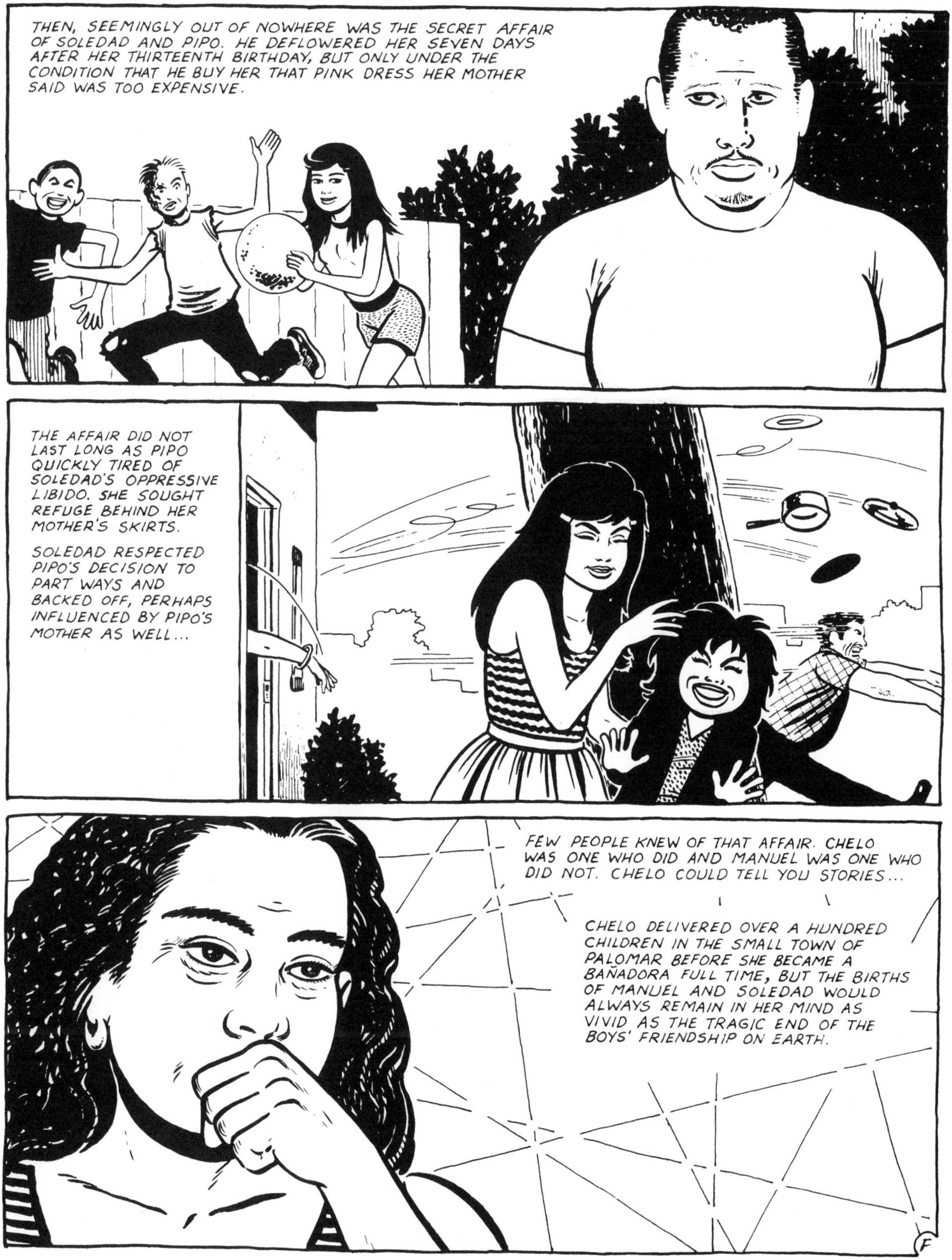
THEN, SEEMINGLY OUT OF NOWHERE WAS THE SECRET AFFAIR OF SOLEDAD AND PIPO. HE DEFLOWERED HER SEVEN DAYS AFTER HER THIRTEENTH BIRTHDAY, BUT ONLY UNDER THE CONDITION THAT HE BUY HER THAT PINK DRESS HER MOTHER SAID WAS TOO EXPENSIVE.
THE AFFAIR DID NOT LAST LONG AS PIPO QUICKLY TIRED OF SOLEDAD'S OPPRESSIVE LIBIDO. SHE SOUGHT REFUGE BEHIND HER MOTHER'S SKIRTS.
SOLEDAD RESPECTED PIPO'S DECISION TO PART WAYS AND BACKED OFF, PERHAPS INFLUENCED BY PIPO'S MOTHER AS WELL...
FEW PEOPLE KNEW OF THAT AFFAIR. CHELO WAS ONE WHO DID AND MANUEL WAS ONE WHO DID NOT. CHELO COULD TELL YOU STORIES...
CHELO DELIVERED OVER A HUNDRED CHILDREN IN THE SMALL TOWN OF PALOMAR BEFORE SHE BECAME A BAÑADORA FULL TIME, BUT THE BIRTHS OF MANUEL AND SOLEDAD WOULD ALWAYS REMAIN IN HER MIND AS VIVID AS THE TRAGIC END OF THE BOYS' FRIENDSHIP ON EARTH.
F

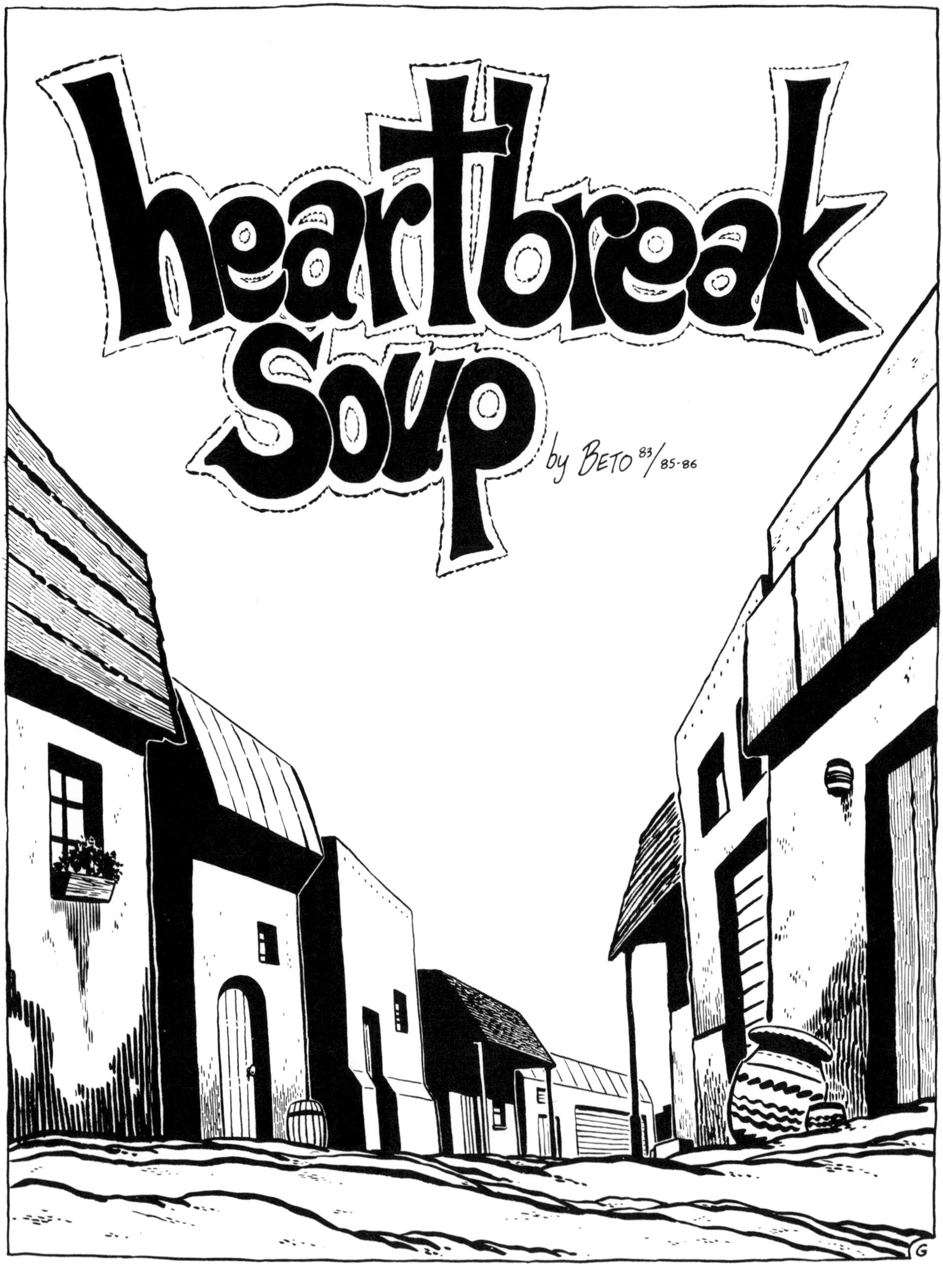
heartbreak
Soup
by BETO 83/85-86
G

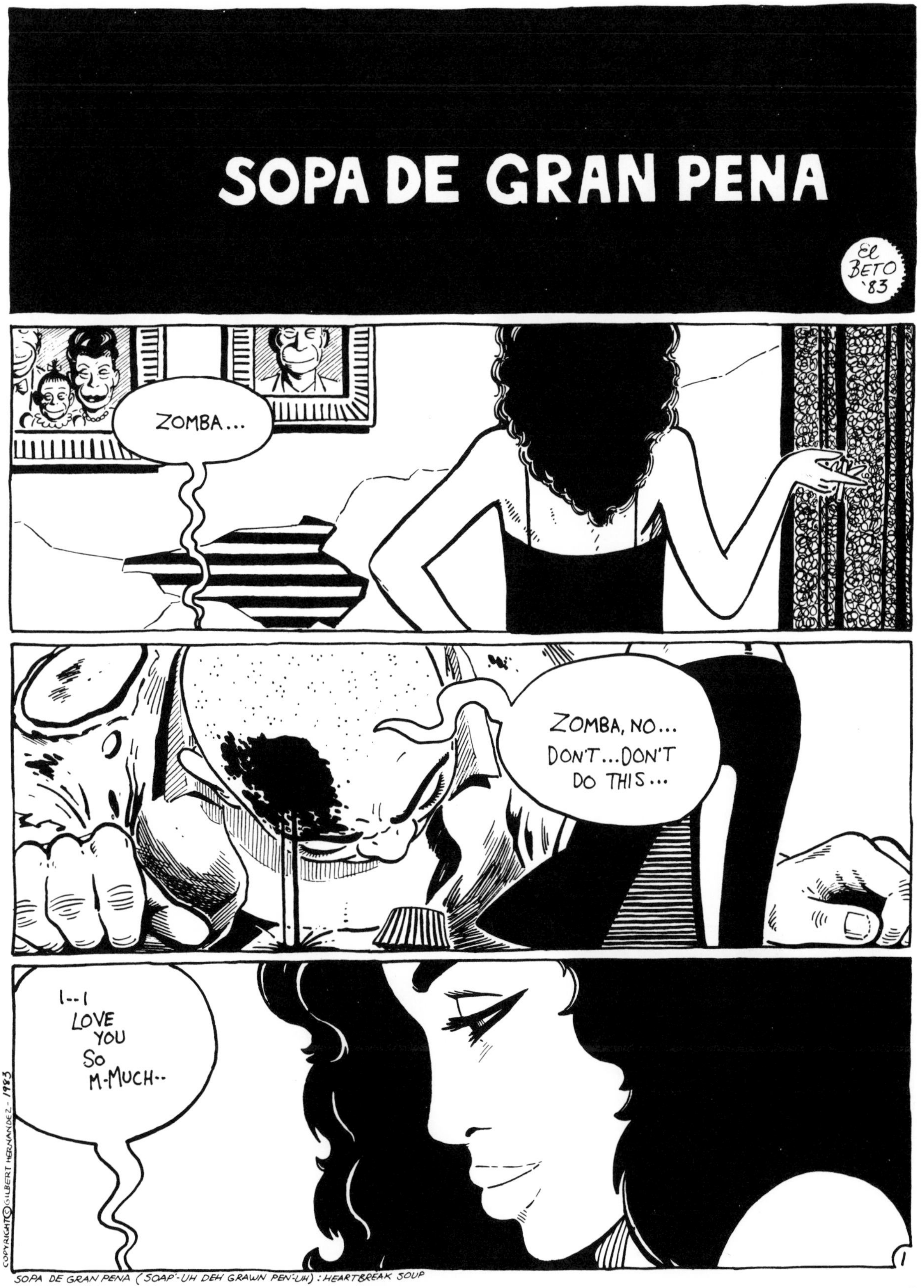
SOPA DE GRAN PENA
El BETO '83
ZOMBA...
ZOMBA, NO... DON'T...DON'T DO THIS...
I--I LOVE YOU So M-MUCH--
COPYRIGHT © GILBERT HERNANDEZ - 1983
1
SOPA DE GRAN PENA (SOAP'-UH DEH GRAWN PEN'-UH): HEARTBREAK SOUP

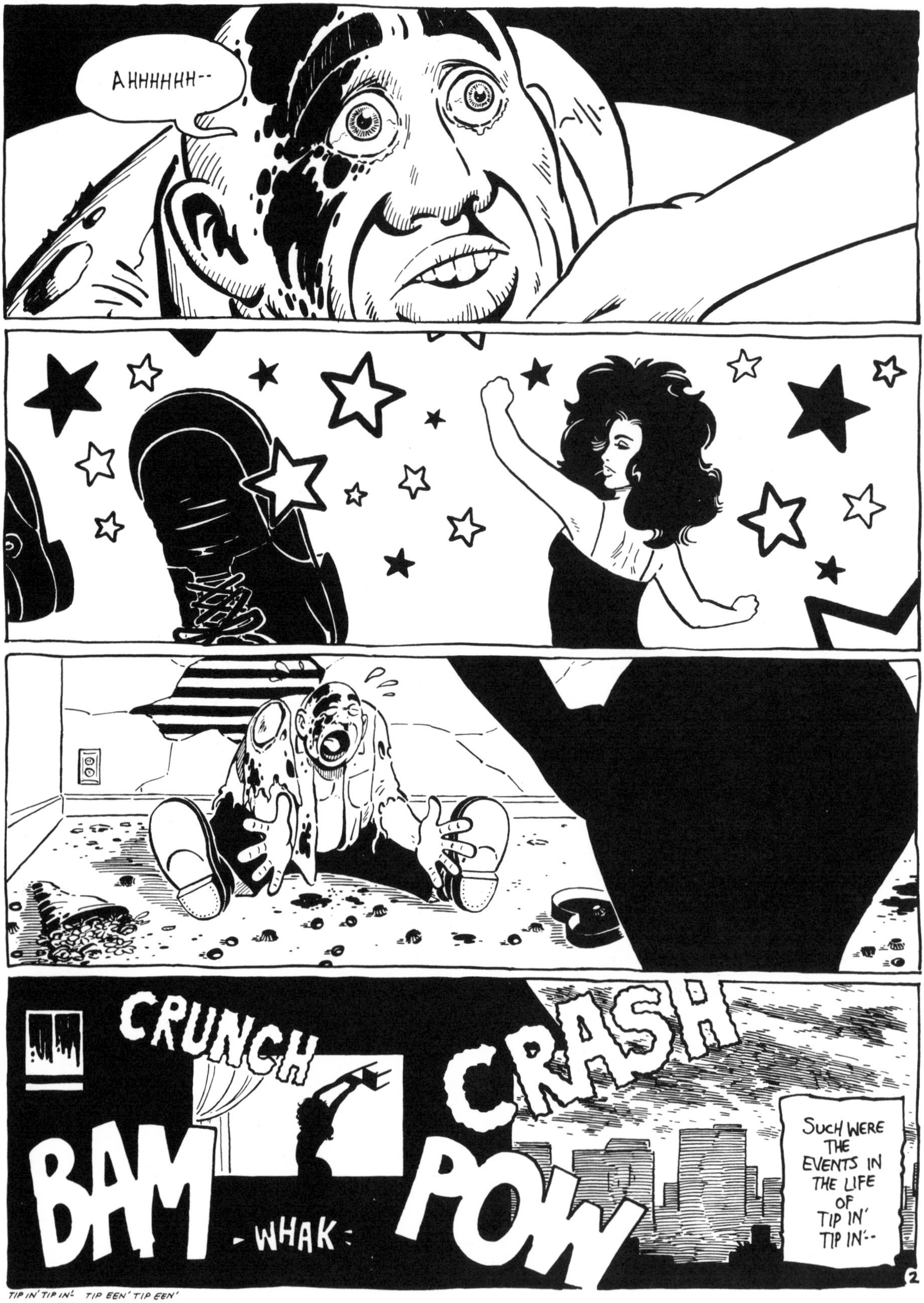
AHHHHHH--
CRUNCH
CRASH
BAM
-WHAK-
POW
SUCH WERE THE EVENTS IN THE LIFE OF TIP IN' TIP IN'--
2

TIP IN' TIP IN'- TIP EEN' TIP EEN'

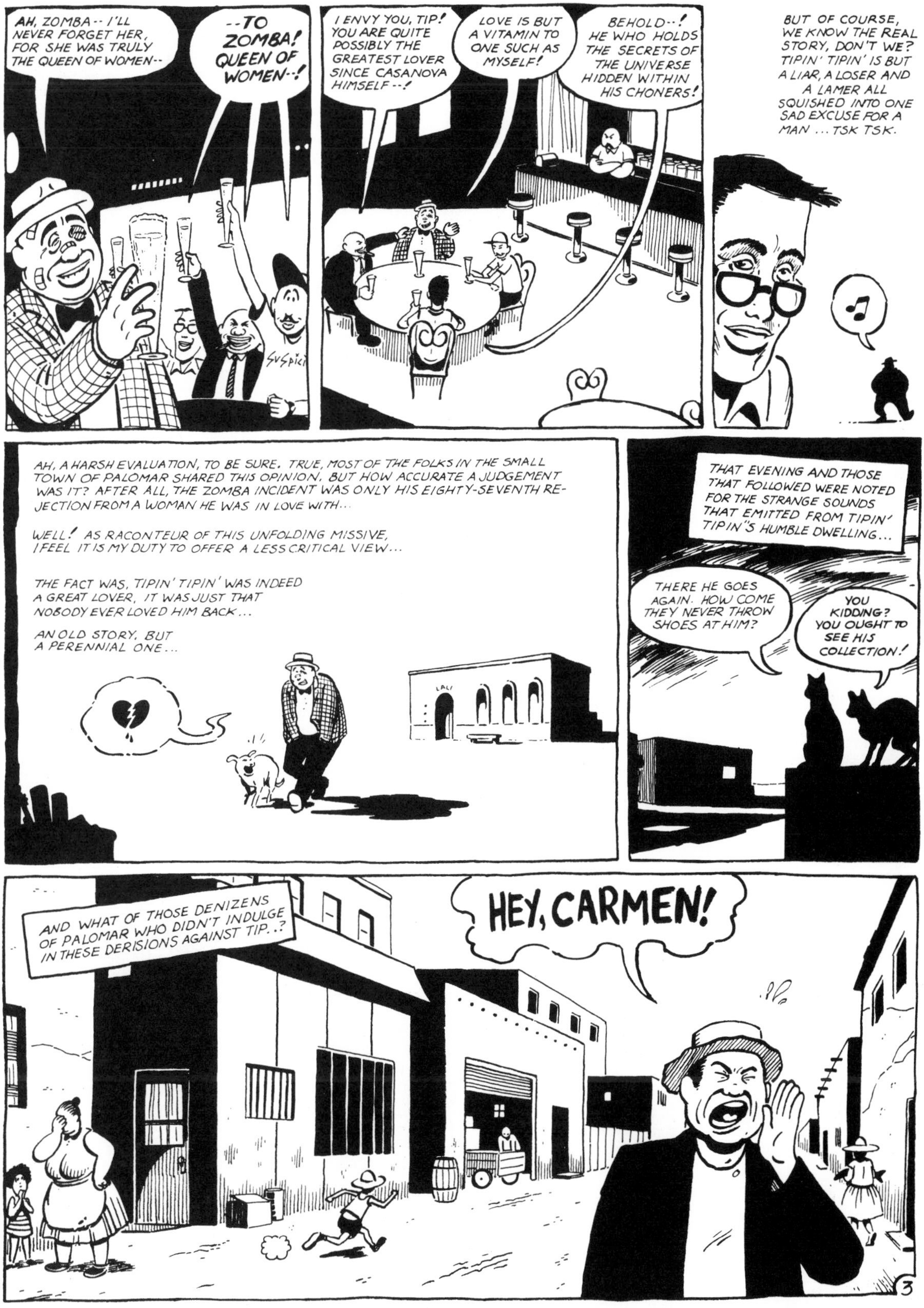
AH, ZOMBA -- I'LL NEVER FORGET HER, FOR SHE WAS TRULY THE QUEEN OF WOMEN--
--TO ZOMBA! QUEEN OF WOMEN--!
I ENVY YOU, TIP! YOU ARE QUITE POSSIBLY THE GREATEST LOVER SINCE CASANOVA HIMSELF--!
LOVE IS BUT A VITAMIN TO ONE SUCH AS MYSELF!
BEHOLD--! HE WHO HOLDS THE SECRETS OF THE UNIVERSE HIDDEN WITHIN HIS CHONERS!
BUT OF COURSE, WE KNOW THE REAL STORY, DON'T WE? TIPIN' TIPIN' IS BUT A LIAR, A LOSER AND A LAMER ALL SQUISHED INTO ONE SAD EXCUSE FOR A MAN ... TSK TSK.
AH, A HARSH EVALUATION, TO BE SURE. TRUE, MOST OF THE FOLKS IN THE SMALL TOWN OF PALOMAR SHARED THIS OPINION. BUT HOW ACCURATE A JUDGEMENT WAS IT? AFTER ALL, THE ZOMBA INCIDENT WAS ONLY HIS EIGHTY-SEVENTH REJECTION FROM A WOMAN HE WAS IN LOVE WITH...
WELL! AS RACONTEUR OF THIS UNFOLDING MISSIVE, I FEEL IT IS MY DUTY TO OFFER A LESS CRITICAL VIEW...
THE FACT WAS, TIPIN' TIPIN' WAS INDEED A GREAT LOVER, IT WAS JUST THAT NOBODY EVER LOVED HIM BACK...
AN OLD STORY, BUT A PERENNIAL ONE...
LALI
THAT EVENING AND THOSE THAT FOLLOWED WERE NOTED FOR THE STRANGE SOUNDS THAT EMITTED FROM TIPIN' TIPIN''S HUMBLE DWELLING...
THERE HE GOES AGAIN. HOW COME THEY NEVER THROW SHOES AT HIM?
YOU KIDDING? YOU OUGHT TO SEE HIS COLLECTION!
AND WHAT OF THOSE DENIZENS OF PALOMAR WHO DIDN'T INDULGE IN THESE DERISIONS AGAINST TIP..?
HEY, CARMEN!
3

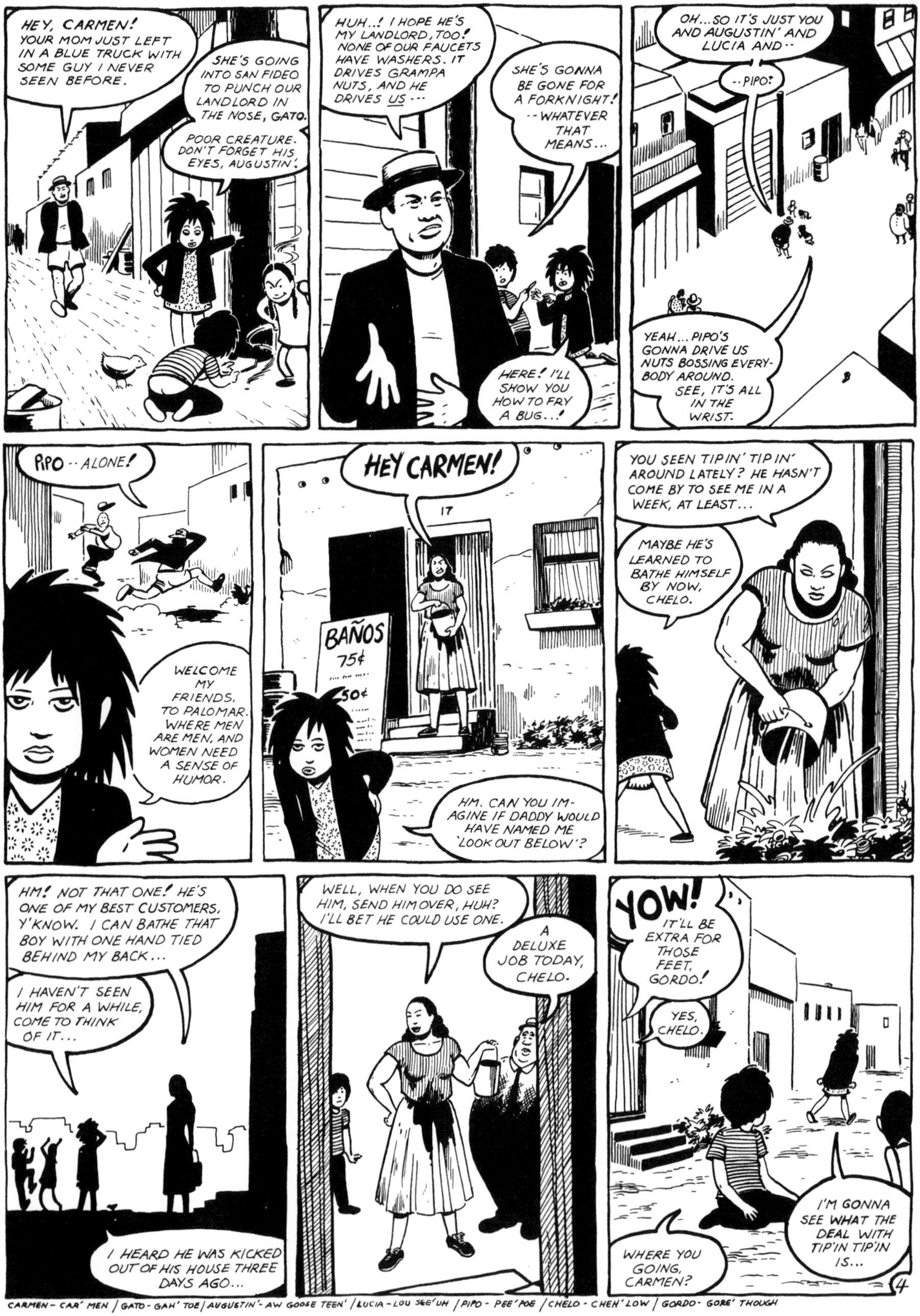
HEY, CARMEN! YOUR MOM JUST LEFT IN A BLUE TRUCK WITH SOME GUY I NEVER SEEN BEFORE.
SHE'S GOING INTO SAN FIDEO TO PUNCH OUR LANDLORD IN THE NOSE, GATO.
POOR CREATURE. DON'T FORGET HIS EYES, AUGUSTIN'.
HUH..! I HOPE HE'S MY LANDLORD, TOO! NONE OF OUR FAUCETS HAVE WASHERS. IT DRIVES GRAMPA NUTS, AND HE DRIVES US ···
SHE'S GONNA BE GONE FOR A FORKNIGHT! --WHATEVER THAT MEANS...
HERE! I'LL SHOW YOU HOW TO FRY A BUG...!
OH...SO IT'S JUST YOU AND AUGUSTIN' AND LUCIA AND--
--PIPO?
YEAH... PIPO'S GONNA DRIVE US NUTS BOSSING EVERYBODY AROUND.
SEE, IT'S ALL IN THE WRIST.
PIPO--ALONE!
WELCOME MY FRIENDS, TO PALOMAR. WHERE MEN ARE MEN, AND WOMEN NEED A SENSE OF HUMOR.
HEY CARMEN!
17
BAÑOS 75¢ 50¢
HM. CAN YOU IMAGINE IF DADDY WOULD HAVE NAMED ME 'LOOK OUT BELOW'?
YOU SEEN TIP'IN' TIP'IN' AROUND LATELY? HE HASN'T COME BY TO SEE ME IN A WEEK, AT LEAST...
MAYBE HE'S LEARNED TO BATHE HIMSELF BY NOW, CHELO.
HM! NOT THAT ONE! HE'S ONE OF MY BEST CUSTOMERS, Y'KNOW. I CAN BATHE THAT BOY WITH ONE HAND TIED BEHIND MY BACK...
I HAVEN'T SEEN HIM FOR A WHILE, COME TO THINK OF IT...
I HEARD HE WAS KICKED OUT OF HIS HOUSE THREE DAYS AGO...
WELL, WHEN YOU DO SEE HIM, SEND HIM OVER, HUH? I'LL BET HE COULD USE ONE.
A DELUXE JOB TODAY, CHELO.
YOW!
IT'LL BE EXTRA FOR THOSE FEET, GORDO!
YES, CHELO.
I'M GONNA SEE WHAT THE DEAL WITH TIP'IN TIP'IN IS...
WHERE YOU GOING, CARMEN?
4
CARMEN - CAR' MEN / GATO - GAH' TOE / AUGUSTIN' - AW GOOSE TEEN' / LUCIA - LOU SEE' UH / PIPO - PEE' POE / CHELO - CHEH' LOW / GORDO - GORE' THOUGH

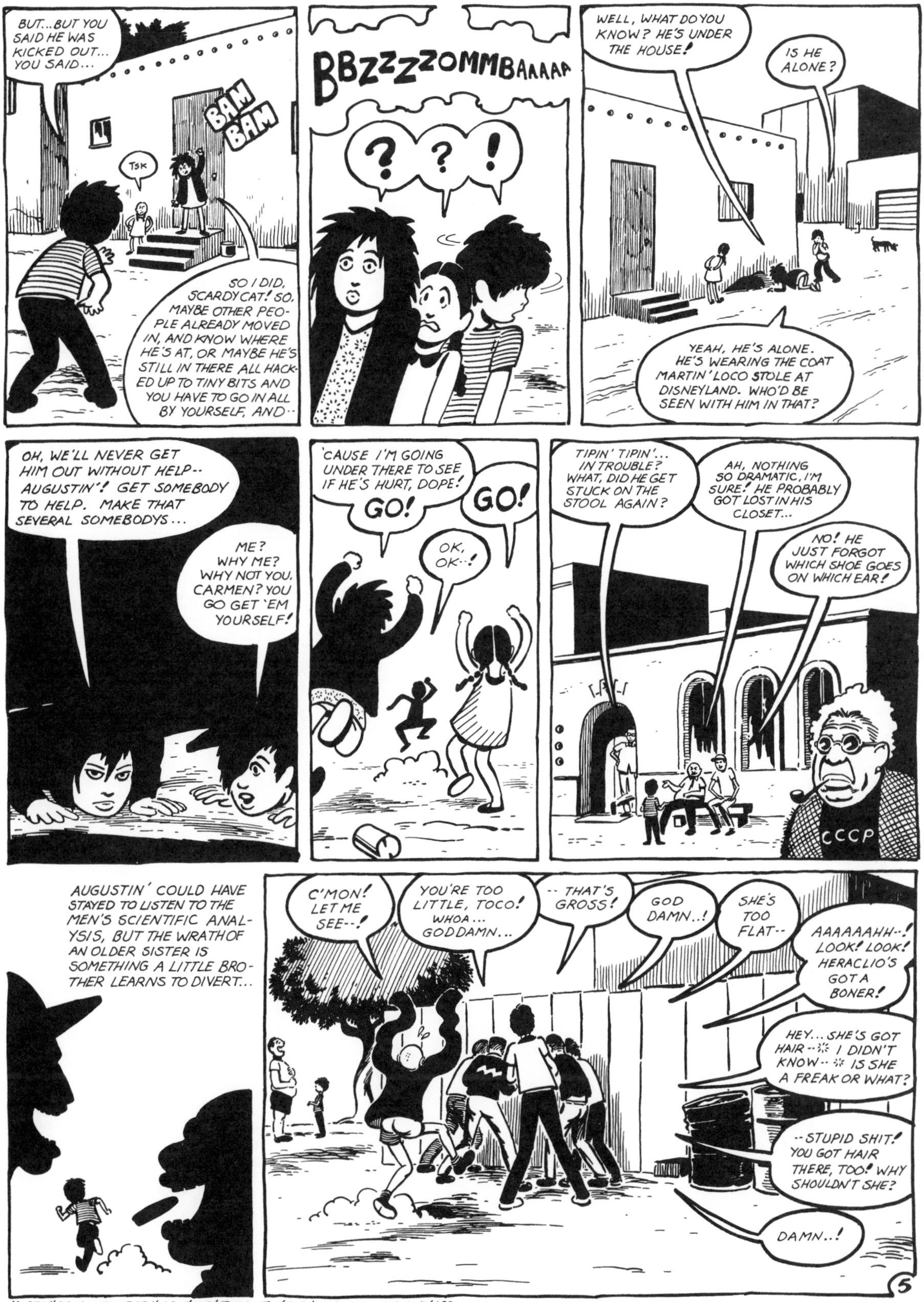
BUT...BUT YOU SAID HE WAS KICKED OUT... YOU SAID...
BAM BAM
TSK
SO I DID, SCARDY CAT! SO, MAYBE OTHER PEOPLE ALREADY MOVED IN, AND KNOW WHERE HE'S AT, OR MAYBE HE'S STILL IN THERE ALL HACKED UP TO TINY BITS AND YOU HAVE TO GO IN ALL BY YOURSELF, AND··
BBZZZZOMMBAAAAA
? ? !
WELL, WHAT DO YOU KNOW? HE'S UNDER THE HOUSE!
IS HE ALONE?
YEAH, HE'S ALONE. HE'S WEARING THE COAT MARTIN' LOCO STOLE AT DISNEYLAND. WHO'D BE SEEN WITH HIM IN THAT?
OH, WE'LL NEVER GET HIM OUT WITHOUT HELP-- AUGUSTIN'! GET SOMEBODY TO HELP. MAKE THAT SEVERAL SOMEBODYS...
ME? WHY ME? WHY NOT YOU, CARMEN? YOU GO GET 'EM YOURSELF!
'CAUSE I'M GOING UNDER THERE TO SEE IF HE'S HURT, DOPE! GO!
GO!
OK, OK··!
TIPIN' TIPIN'... IN TROUBLE? WHAT, DID HE GET STUCK ON THE STOOL AGAIN?
AH, NOTHING SO DRAMATIC, I'M SURE! HE PROBABLY GOT LOST IN HIS CLOSET...
NO! HE JUST FORGOT WHICH SHOE GOES ON WHICH EAR!
CCCP
AUGUSTIN' COULD HAVE STAYED TO LISTEN TO THE MEN'S SCIENTIFIC ANALYSIS, BUT THE WRATH OF AN OLDER SISTER IS SOMETHING A LITTLE BROTHER LEARNS TO DIVERT...
C'MON! LET ME SEE--!
YOU'RE TOO LITTLE, TOCO! WHOA... GODDAMN...
-- THAT'S GROSS!
GOD DAMN..!
SHE'S TOO FLAT--
AAAAAAHH--! LOOK! LOOK! HERACLIO'S GOT A BONER!
HEY... SHE'S GOT HAIR -- I DIDN'T KNOW -- IS SHE A FREAK OR WHAT?
--STUPID SHIT! YOU GOT HAIR THERE, TOO! WHY SHOULDN'T SHE?
DAMN..!
5

MARTIN' LOCO - MAR TEEN' LOW'COE / TOCO - TOE'COE / HERACLIO - AIR AWK' LEO

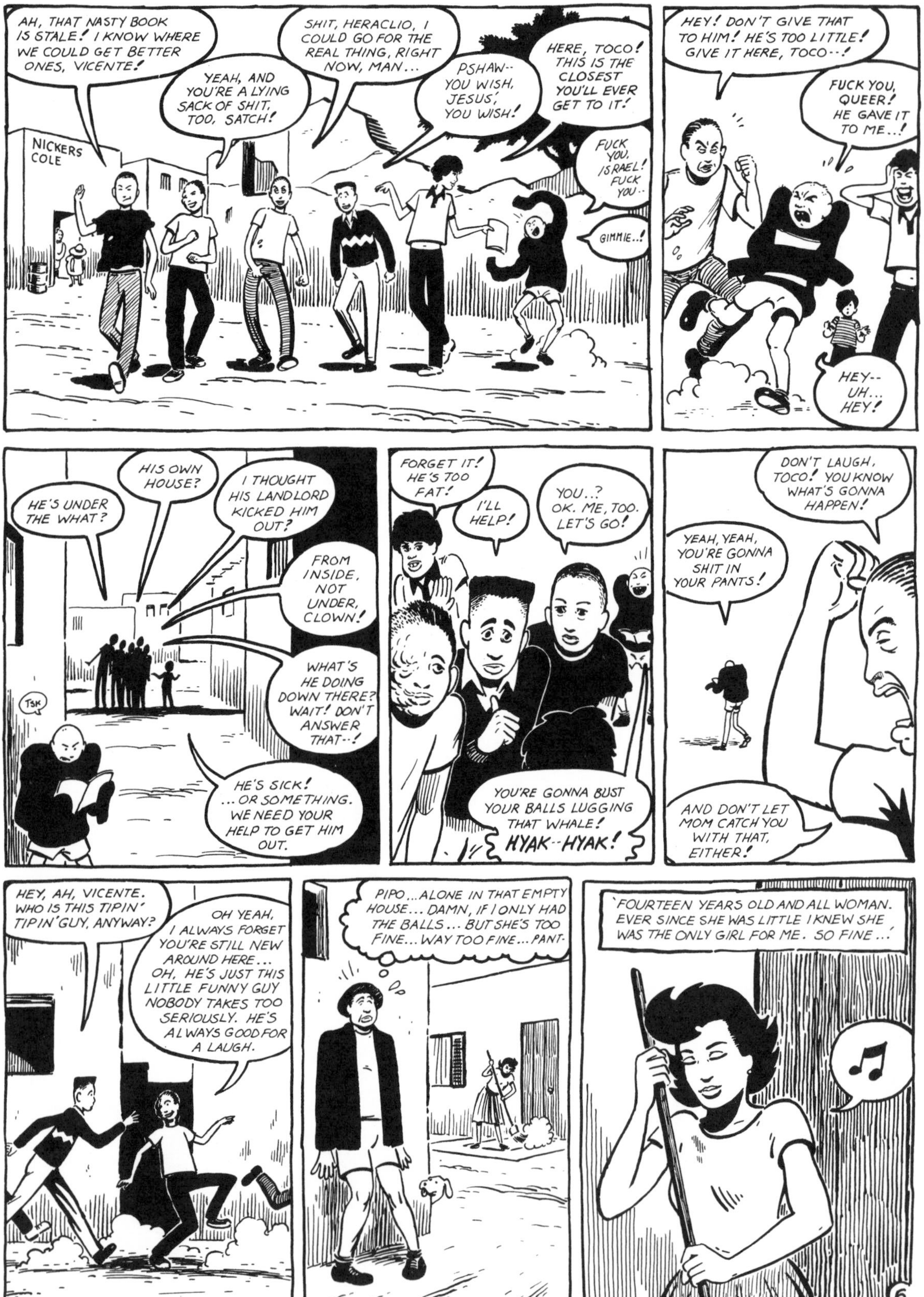

AH, THAT NASTY BOOK IS STALE! I KNOW WHERE WE COULD GET BETTER ONES, VICENTE!
YEAH, AND YOU'RE A LYING SACK OF SHIT, TOO, SATCH!
SHIT, HERACLIO, I COULD GO FOR THE REAL THING, RIGHT NOW, MAN...
PSHAW-- YOU WISH, JESUS, YOU WISH!
HERE, TOCO! THIS IS THE CLOSEST YOU'LL EVER GET TO IT!
NICKERS COLE
FUCK YOU, ISRAEL! FUCK YOU..
GIMMIE..!
HEY! DON'T GIVE THAT TO HIM! HE'S TOO LITTLE! GIVE IT HERE, TOCO--!
FUCK YOU, QUEER! HE GAVE IT TO ME..!
HEY-- UH... HEY!
HE'S UNDER THE WHAT?
HIS OWN HOUSE?
I THOUGHT HIS LANDLORD KICKED HIM OUT?
FROM INSIDE, NOT UNDER, CLOWN!
WHAT'S HE DOING DOWN THERE? WAIT! DON'T ANSWER THAT--!
TSK
HE'S SICK! ...OR SOMETHING. WE NEED YOUR HELP TO GET HIM OUT.
FORGET IT! HE'S TOO FAT!
I'LL HELP!
YOU..? OK. ME, TOO. LET'S GO!
YOU'RE GONNA BUST YOUR BALLS LUGGING THAT WHALE! HYAK--HYAK!
DON'T LAUGH, TOCO! YOU KNOW WHAT'S GONNA HAPPEN!
YEAH, YEAH, YOU'RE GONNA SHIT IN YOUR PANTS!
AND DON'T LET MOM CATCH YOU WITH THAT, EITHER!
HEY, AH, VICENTE. WHO IS THIS TIPIN' TIPIN' GUY, ANYWAY?
OH YEAH, I ALWAYS FORGET YOU'RE STILL NEW AROUND HERE... OH, HE'S JUST THIS LITTLE FUNNY GUY NOBODY TAKES TOO SERIOUSLY. HE'S ALWAYS GOOD FOR A LAUGH.
PIPO... ALONE IN THAT EMPTY HOUSE... DAMN, IF I ONLY HAD THE BALLS... BUT SHE'S TOO FINE... WAY TOO FINE... PANT-
'FOURTEEN YEARS OLD AND ALL WOMAN. EVER SINCE SHE WAS LITTLE I KNEW SHE WAS THE ONLY GIRL FOR ME. SO FINE...'
6

VICENTE - VEE ZEN'TEH / JESUS' - HEH SOOS' / ISRAEL - EES' RYE EL

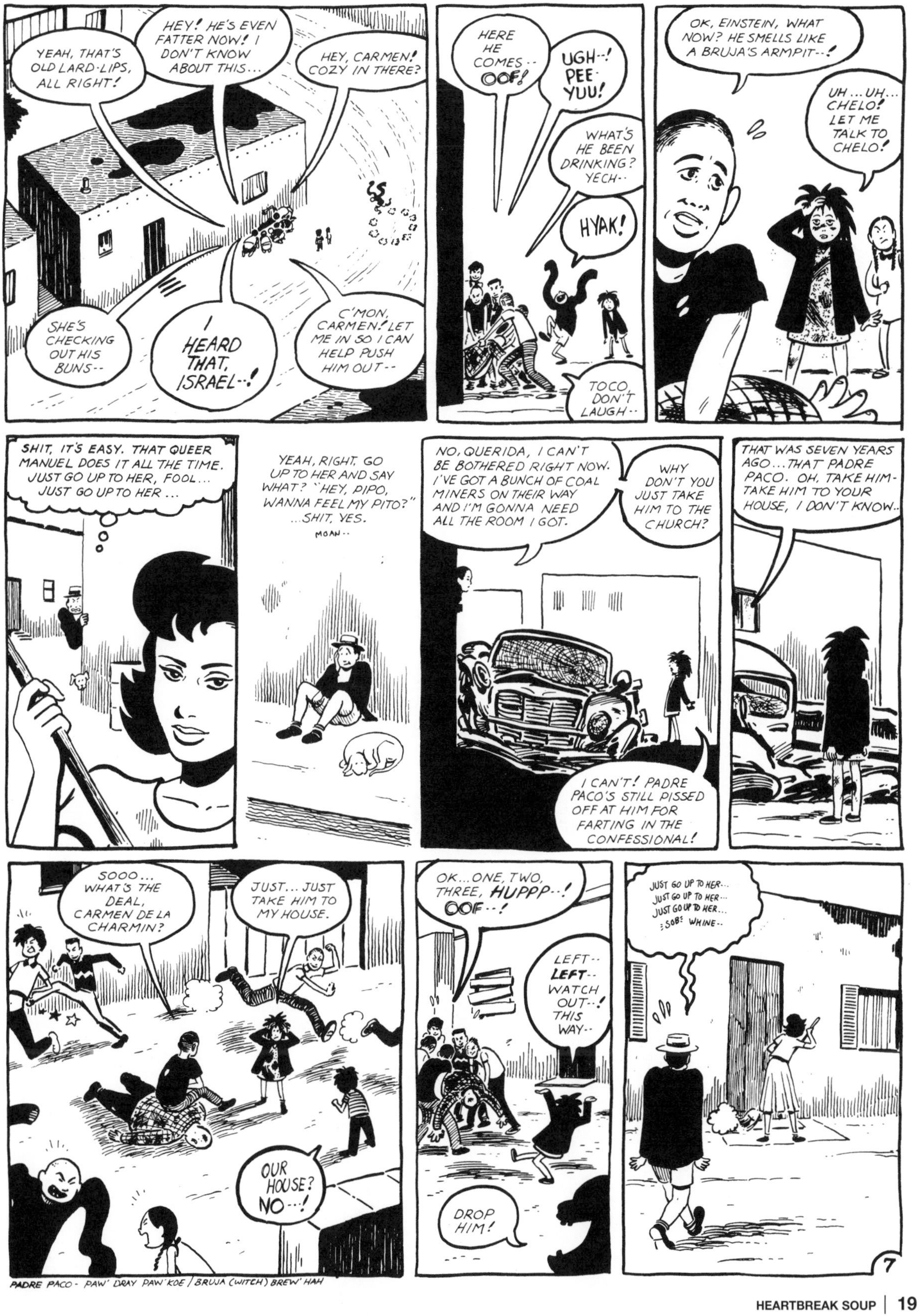
YEAH, THAT'S OLD LARD-LIPS, ALL RIGHT!
HEY! HE'S EVEN FATTER NOW! I DON'T KNOW ABOUT THIS...
HEY, CARMEN! COZY IN THERE?
SHE'S CHECKING OUT HIS BUNS--
I HEARD THAT, ISRAEL--!
C'MON, CARMEN! LET ME IN SO I CAN HELP PUSH HIM OUT--
HERE HE COMES-- OOF!
UGH--! PEE-YUU!
WHAT'S HE BEEN DRINKING? YECH--
HYAK!
TOCO, DON'T LAUGH--
OK, EINSTEIN, WHAT NOW? HE SMELLS LIKE A BRUJA'S ARMPIT--!
UH...UH... CHELO! LET ME TALK TO CHELO!
SHIT, IT'S EASY. THAT QUEER MANUEL DOES IT ALL THE TIME. JUST GO UP TO HER, FOOL... JUST GO UP TO HER...
YEAH, RIGHT. GO UP TO HER AND SAY WHAT? "HEY, PIPO, WANNA FEEL MY PITO?" ...SHIT, YES.
MOAN--
NO, QUERIDA, I CAN'T BE BOTHERED RIGHT NOW. I'VE GOT A BUNCH OF COAL MINERS ON THEIR WAY AND I'M GONNA NEED ALL THE ROOM I GOT.
WHY DON'T YOU JUST TAKE HIM TO THE CHURCH?
I CAN'T! PADRE PACO'S STILL PISSED OFF AT HIM FOR FARTING IN THE CONFESSIONAL!
THAT WAS SEVEN YEARS AGO...THAT PADRE PACO. OH, TAKE HIM-TAKE HIM TO YOUR HOUSE, I DON'T KNOW..
SOOO... WHAT'S THE DEAL, CARMEN DE LA CHARMIN?
JUST... JUST TAKE HIM TO MY HOUSE.
OUR HOUSE? NO--!
OK...ONE, TWO, THREE, HUPPP--! OOF--!
LEFT-- LEFT-- WATCH OUT--! THIS WAY--
DROP HIM!
JUST GO UP TO HER... JUST GO UP TO HER... JUST GO UP TO HER...
SOB! WHINE--
7

PADRE PACO - PAW' DRAY PAW' KOE / BRUJA (WITCH) BREW' HAH

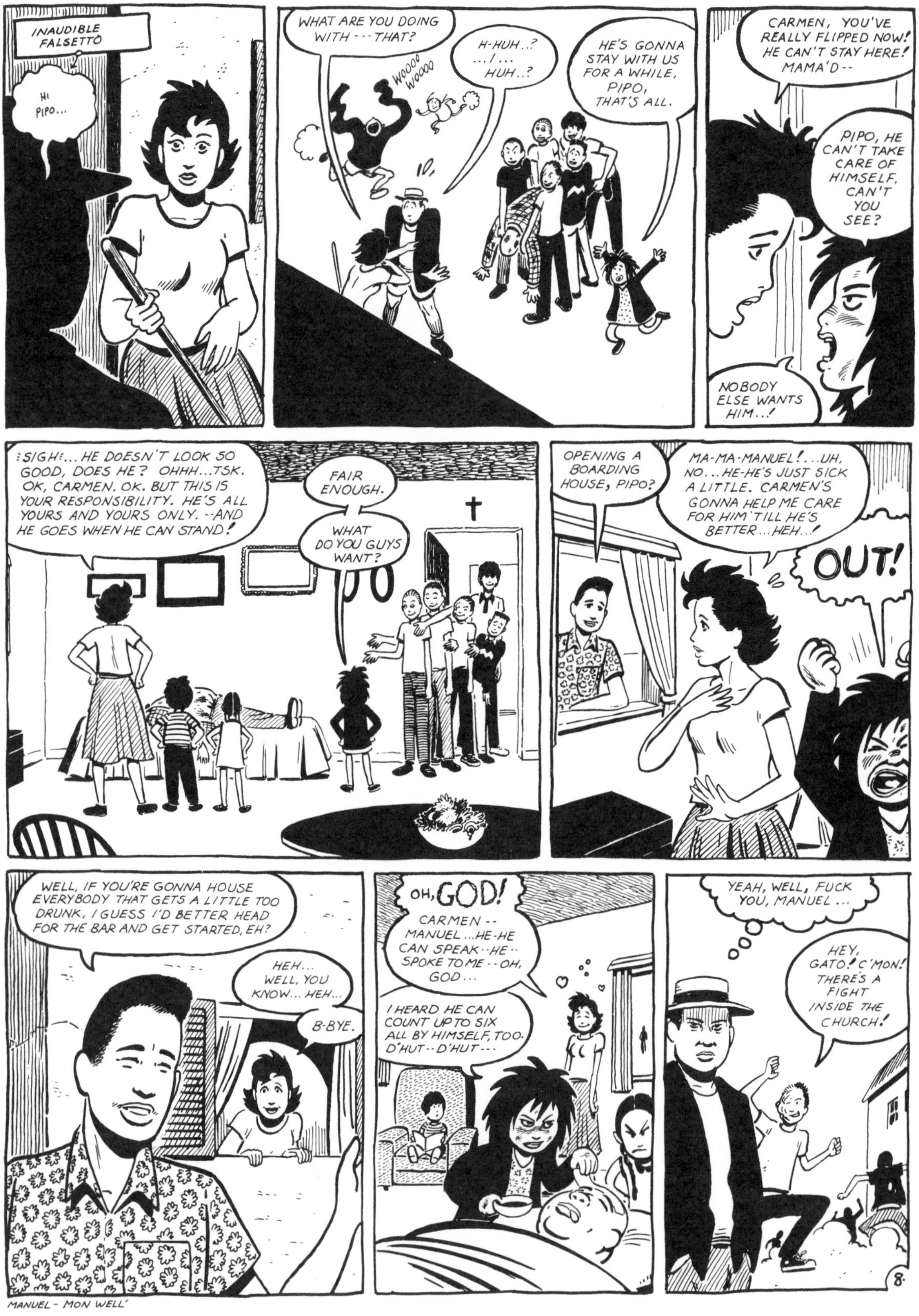
INAUDIBLE FALSETTO
HI PIPO...
WHAT ARE YOU DOING WITH --- THAT?
WOOOO WOOOO
H-HUH..? ...I... HUH..?
HE'S GONNA STAY WITH US FOR A WHILE, PIPO, THAT'S ALL.
CARMEN, YOU'VE REALLY FLIPPED NOW! HE CAN'T STAY HERE! MAMA'D --
PIPO, HE CAN'T TAKE CARE OF HIMSELF, CAN'T YOU SEE?
NOBODY ELSE WANTS HIM..!
:SIGH:... HE DOESN'T LOOK SO GOOD, DOES HE? OHHH...TSK. OK, CARMEN. OK. BUT THIS IS YOUR RESPONSIBILITY. HE'S ALL YOURS AND YOURS ONLY. --AND HE GOES WHEN HE CAN STAND!
FAIR ENOUGH.
WHAT DO YOU GUYS WANT?
OPENING A BOARDING HOUSE, PIPO?
MA-MA-MANUEL!...UH, NO... HE-HE'S JUST SICK A LITTLE. CARMEN'S GONNA HELP ME CARE FOR HIM 'TILL HE'S BETTER...HEH..!
OUT!
WELL, IF YOU'RE GONNA HOUSE EVERYBODY THAT GETS A LITTLE TOO DRUNK, I GUESS I'D BETTER HEAD FOR THE BAR AND GET STARTED, EH?
HEH... WELL, YOU KNOW... HEH...
B-BYE.
OH, GOD!
CARMEN -- MANUEL...HE-HE CAN SPEAK--HE-- SPOKE TO ME--OH, GOD...
I HEARD HE CAN COUNT UP TO SIX ALL BY HIMSELF, TOO. D'HUT--D'HUT---
YEAH, WELL, FUCK YOU, MANUEL...
HEY, GATO! C'MON! THERE'S A FIGHT INSIDE THE CHURCH!
8.
MANUEL - MON WELL'

THAT EVENING...

YOW!

NO WAY! NO WAY! EEEE-YOW!

AUGUSTIN, WHAT'S WRONG?!

CARMEN!! SHE WON'T LET ME SLEEP WITH HER AND LUCIA! SHE 'SPECTS ME TO SLEEP WITH-- WITH--HIM!!

AUGUSTIN' MOVES AROUND TOO MUCH. I FIGURE TIPIN' TIPIN' WOULDN'T NOTICE...

OK, OK. YOU'LL SLEEP WITH ME, AUGUSTIN.

AND CARMEN, IF TIPIN' TIPIN' SNORES...!

LOUDER'N YOU? THAT'S A HOT ONE. --GOOD NIGHT.

AH, PALOMAR. HERACLIO HAD BEEN LIVING THERE FOR ONLY THREE MONTHS, BUT THE TOWN FIT HIM LIKE A PAIR OF FAVORITE TROUSERS...

HE NEVER COUNTED ON ANYTHING TO CONFUSE THAT SENSE OF SECURITY...

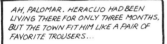

LIKE THE TIME HE CAME UPON THE OLDER GUYS: ARTURO, SOLEDAD, MANUEL AND GUERO HANGING OUT... HERACLIO THOUGHT MANUEL WAS THE COOLEST BECAUSE MANUEL NEVER TREATED HIM LIKE A KID...

UH... HOW'S IT GOING GUYS?

GRUNT..

HOY, HERCULES! WHERE'S YOUR GANG?

OH, ALMOST EVERYONE'S AT SCHOOL, I GUESS. I DON'T START HIGH SCHOOL 'TILL NEXT SEMESTER.

YEAH? HEY, WELL, I ENVY YOU, BUDDY. LOTS OF REAL BEAUTIES IN HIGH SCHOOL...

AH-- THERE HE IS.

WHO? OH...

WHO'S THAT?

IT'S PINTOR. GO AHEAD. WAVE. HE WON'T MIND.

HEY, UH, HOW COME THAT GUY PINTOR SITS ALONE THERE? DOESN'T HE LIKE YOU GUYS OR SOMETHING?

OH... HE'S GONE.

OH, WELL, PINTOR USED TO SIT ON THAT BENCH EVERY AFTERNOON 'BOUT THIS TIME BEFORE HIS ACCIDENT...

I'M GONNA SEE YOU GUYS LATER, HUH?

LATER, MANNY.

LATER, 'EY.

9

ARTURO- ARE TWO' ROW | SOLEDAD- SO LEH DAHD' | PINTOR- PEEN TOR' | GUERO- WHED'OH (BLOND)

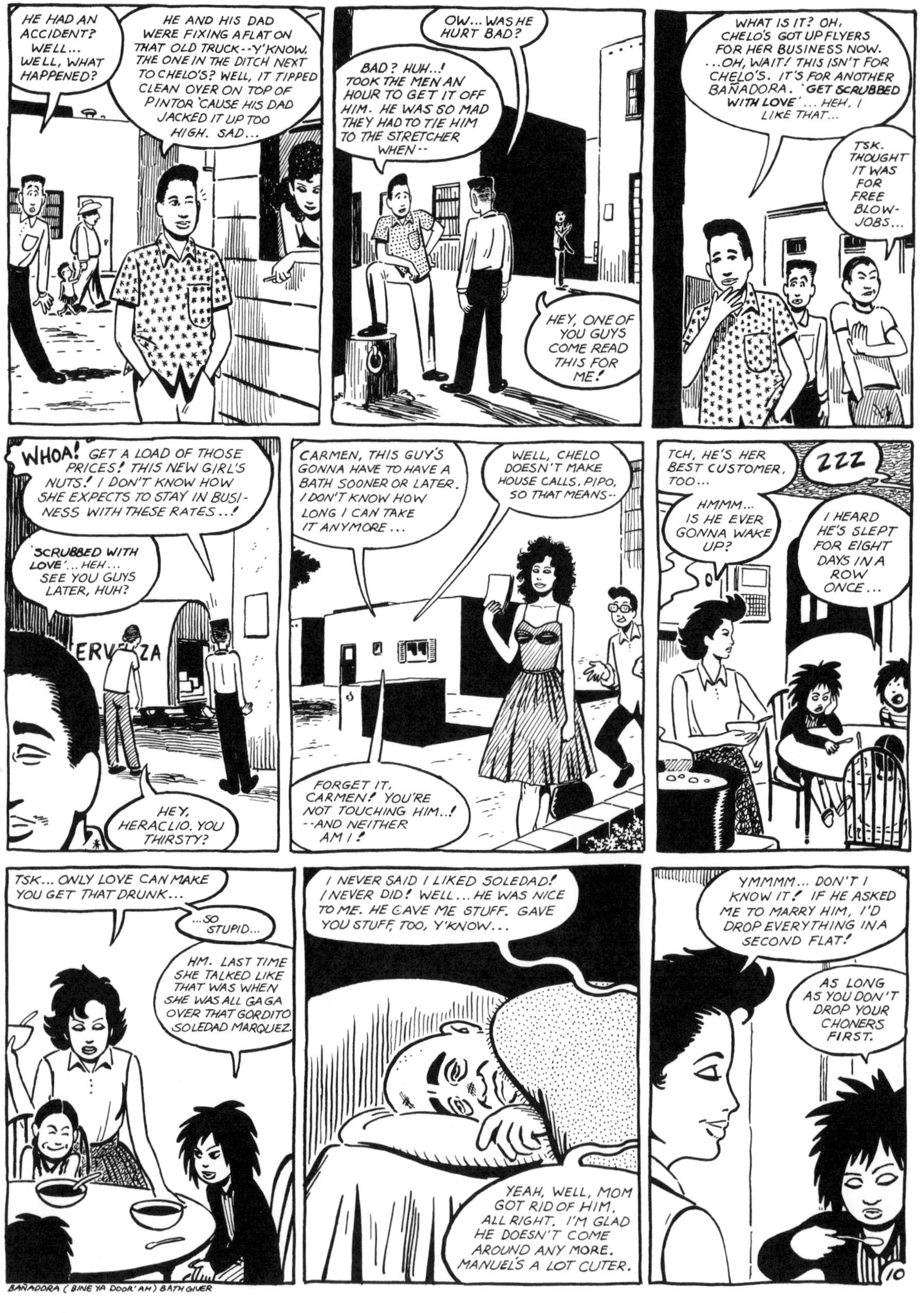
HE HAD AN ACCIDENT? WELL... WELL, WHAT HAPPENED?
HE AND HIS DAD WERE FIXING A FLAT ON THAT OLD TRUCK--Y'KNOW, THE ONE IN THE DITCH NEXT TO CHELO'S? WELL, IT TIPPED CLEAN OVER ON TOP OF PINTOR 'CAUSE HIS DAD JACKED IT UP TOO HIGH. SAD...
OW... WAS HE HURT BAD?
BAD? HUH..! TOOK THE MEN AN HOUR TO GET IT OFF HIM. HE WAS SO MAD THEY HAD TO TIE HIM TO THE STRETCHER WHEN--
HEY, ONE OF YOU GUYS COME READ THIS FOR ME!
WHAT IS IT? OH, CHELO'S GOT UP FLYERS FOR HER BUSINESS NOW. ...OH, WAIT! THIS ISN'T FOR CHELO'S. IT'S FOR ANOTHER BAÑADORA. 'GET SCRUBBED WITH LOVE'... HEH, I LIKE THAT...
TSK. THOUGHT IT WAS FOR FREE BLOW-JOBS...
WHOA! GET A LOAD OF THOSE PRICES! THIS NEW GIRL'S NUTS! I DON'T KNOW HOW SHE EXPECTS TO STAY IN BUSINESS WITH THESE RATES..!
'SCRUBBED WITH LOVE'... HEH... SEE YOU GUYS LATER, HUH?
ERV ZA
HEY, HERACLIO. YOU THIRSTY?
CARMEN, THIS GUY'S GONNA HAVE TO HAVE A BATH SOONER OR LATER. I DON'T KNOW HOW LONG I CAN TAKE IT ANYMORE...
WELL, CHELO DOESN'T MAKE HOUSE CALLS, PIPO, SO THAT MEANS--
FORGET IT, CARMEN! YOU'RE NOT TOUCHING HIM..! --AND NEITHER AM I!
TCH, HE'S HER BEST CUSTOMER, TOO...
ZZZ
HMMM... IS HE EVER GONNA WAKE UP?
I HEARD HE'S SLEPT FOR EIGHT DAYS IN A ROW ONCE...
TSK... ONLY LOVE CAN MAKE YOU GET THAT DRUNK...
...SO STUPID...
HM. LAST TIME SHE TALKED LIKE THAT WAS WHEN SHE WAS ALL GAGA OVER THAT GORDITO SOLEDAD MARQUEZ.
I NEVER SAID I LIKED SOLEDAD! I NEVER DID! WELL... HE WAS NICE TO ME. HE GAVE ME STUFF. GAVE YOU STUFF, TOO, Y'KNOW...
YEAH, WELL, MOM GOT RID OF HIM, ALL RIGHT. I'M GLAD HE DOESN'T COME AROUND ANY MORE. MANUEL'S A LOT CUTER.
YMMMM... DON'T I KNOW IT! IF HE ASKED ME TO MARRY HIM, I'D DROP EVERYTHING IN A SECOND FLAT!
AS LONG AS YOU DON'T DROP YOUR CHONERS FIRST.
10
BAÑADORA (BINE YA DOOR' AH) BATH GIVER

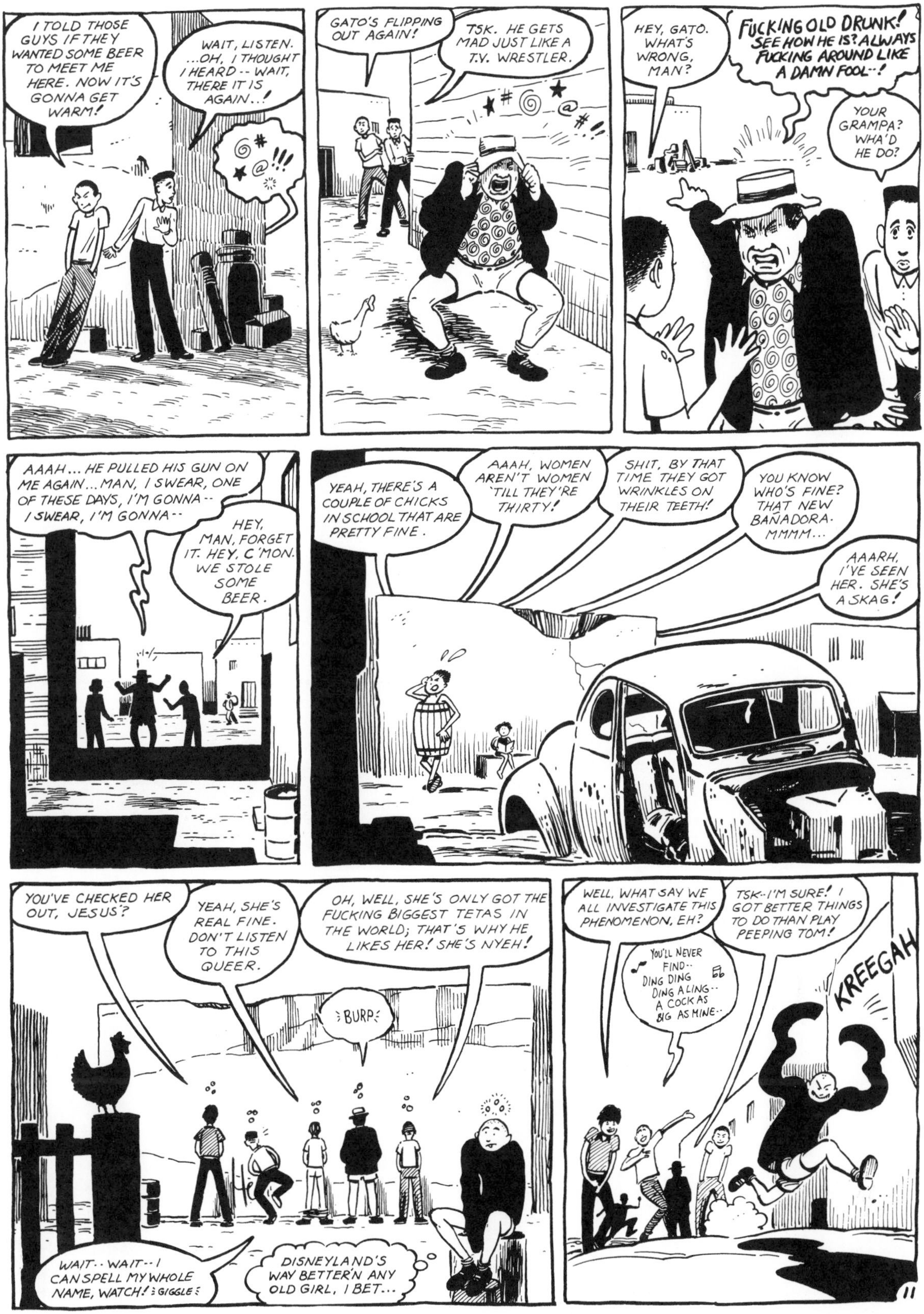

I TOLD THOSE GUYS IF THEY WANTED SOME BEER TO MEET ME HERE. NOW IT'S GONNA GET WARM!
WAIT, LISTEN. ...OH, I THOUGHT I HEARD -- WAIT, THERE IT IS AGAIN..!
GATO'S FLIPPING OUT AGAIN!
TSK. HE GETS MAD JUST LIKE A T.V. WRESTLER.
HEY, GATO. WHAT'S WRONG, MAN?
FUCKING OLD DRUNK! SEE HOW HE IS? ALWAYS FUCKING AROUND LIKE A DAMN FOOL--!
YOUR GRAMPA? WHA'D HE DO?
AAAH... HE PULLED HIS GUN ON ME AGAIN... MAN, I SWEAR, ONE OF THESE DAYS, I'M GONNA-- I SWEAR, I'M GONNA--
HEY, MAN, FORGET IT. HEY, C'MON. WE STOLE SOME BEER.
YEAH, THERE'S A COUPLE OF CHICKS IN SCHOOL THAT ARE PRETTY FINE.
AAAH, WOMEN AREN'T WOMEN 'TILL THEY'RE THIRTY!
SHIT, BY THAT TIME THEY GOT WRINKLES ON THEIR TEETH!
YOU KNOW WHO'S FINE? THAT NEW BAÑADORA. MMMM...
AAARH, I'VE SEEN HER. SHE'S A SKAG!
YOU'VE CHECKED HER OUT, JESUS?
YEAH, SHE'S REAL FINE. DON'T LISTEN TO THIS QUEER.
OH, WELL, SHE'S ONLY GOT THE FUCKING BIGGEST TETAS IN THE WORLD; THAT'S WHY HE LIKES HER! SHE'S NYEH!
BURP
WAIT-- WAIT-- I CAN SPELL MY WHOLE NAME, WATCH! GIGGLE
DISNEYLAND'S WAY BETTER'N ANY OLD GIRL, I BET...
WELL, WHAT SAY WE ALL INVESTIGATE THIS PHENOMENON, EH?
YOU'LL NEVER FIND-- DING DING DING A LING-- A COCK AS BIG AS MINE--
TSK--I'M SURE! I GOT BETTER THINGS TO DO THAN PLAY PEEPING TOM!
KREEGAH
11

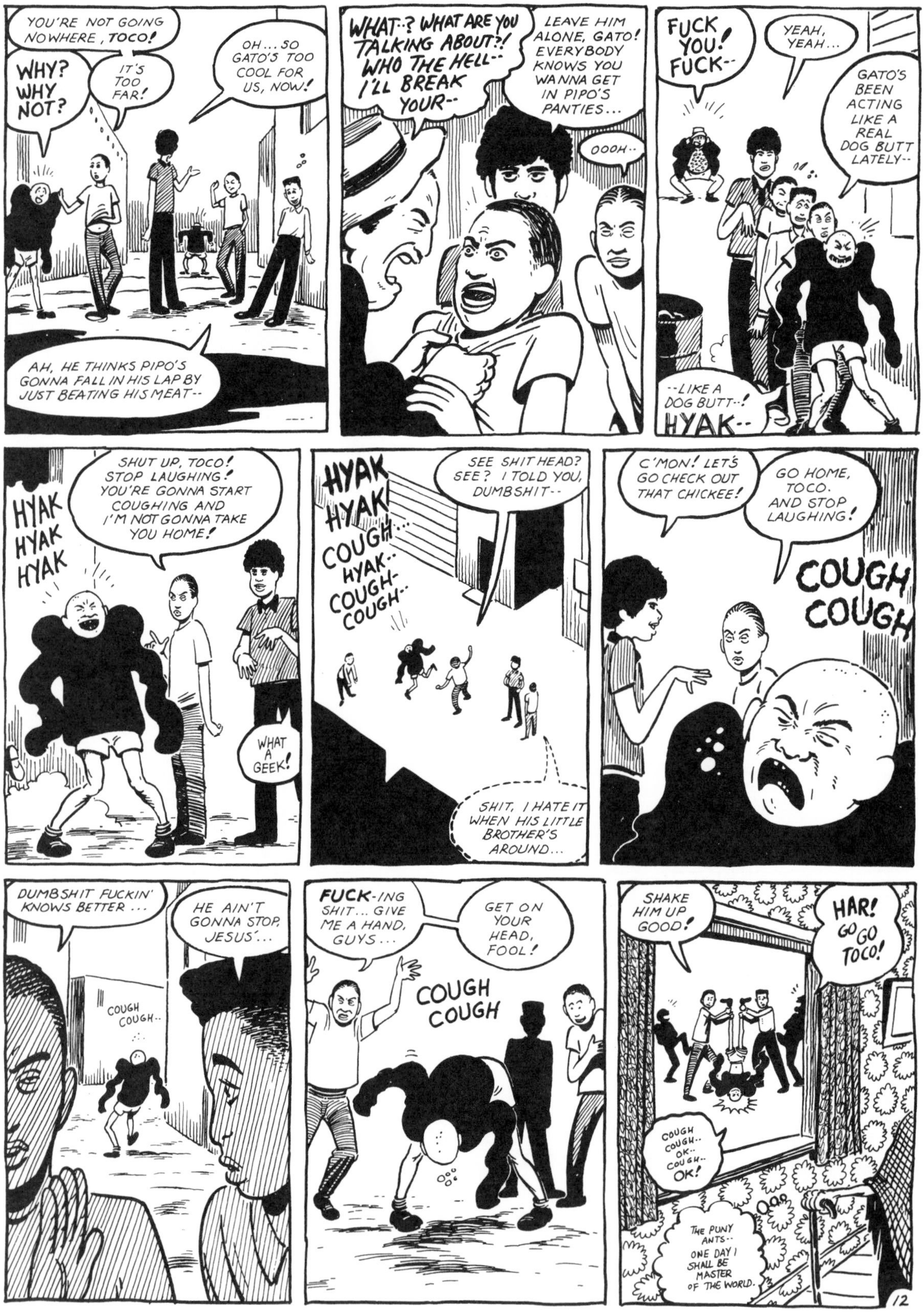
YOU'RE NOT GOING NOWHERE, TOCO!
WHY? WHY NOT?
IT'S TOO FAR!
OH... SO GATO'S TOO COOL FOR US, NOW!
AH, HE THINKS PIPO'S GONNA FALL IN HIS LAP BY JUST BEATING HIS MEAT--
WHAT..? WHAT ARE YOU TALKING ABOUT?! WHO THE HELL-- I'LL BREAK YOUR--
LEAVE HIM ALONE, GATO! EVERYBODY KNOWS YOU WANNA GET IN PIPO'S PANTIES...
OOOH--
FUCK YOU! FUCK--
YEAH, YEAH...
GATO'S BEEN ACTING LIKE A REAL DOG BUTT LATELY--
--LIKE A DOG BUTT--! HYAK--
HYAK HYAK HYAK
SHUT UP, TOCO! STOP LAUGHING! YOU'RE GONNA START COUGHING AND I'M NOT GONNA TAKE YOU HOME!
WHAT A GEEK!
HYAK HYAK COUGH... HYAK.. COUGH-COUGH..
SEE SHIT HEAD? SEE? I TOLD YOU, DUMBSHIT--
SHIT, I HATE IT WHEN HIS LITTLE BROTHER'S AROUND...
C'MON! LET'S GO CHECK OUT THAT CHICKEE!
GO HOME, TOCO. AND STOP LAUGHING!
COUGH COUGH
DUMBSHIT FUCKIN' KNOWS BETTER...
HE AIN'T GONNA STOP, JESUS'...
COUGH COUGH..
FUCK-ING SHIT... GIVE ME A HAND, GUYS...
GET ON YOUR HEAD, FOOL!
COUGH COUGH
SHAKE HIM UP GOOD!
HAR! GO GO TOCO!
COUGH COUGH.. OK.. COUGH.. OK!
THE PUNY ANTS-- ONE DAY I SHALL BE MASTER OF THE WORLD.
12

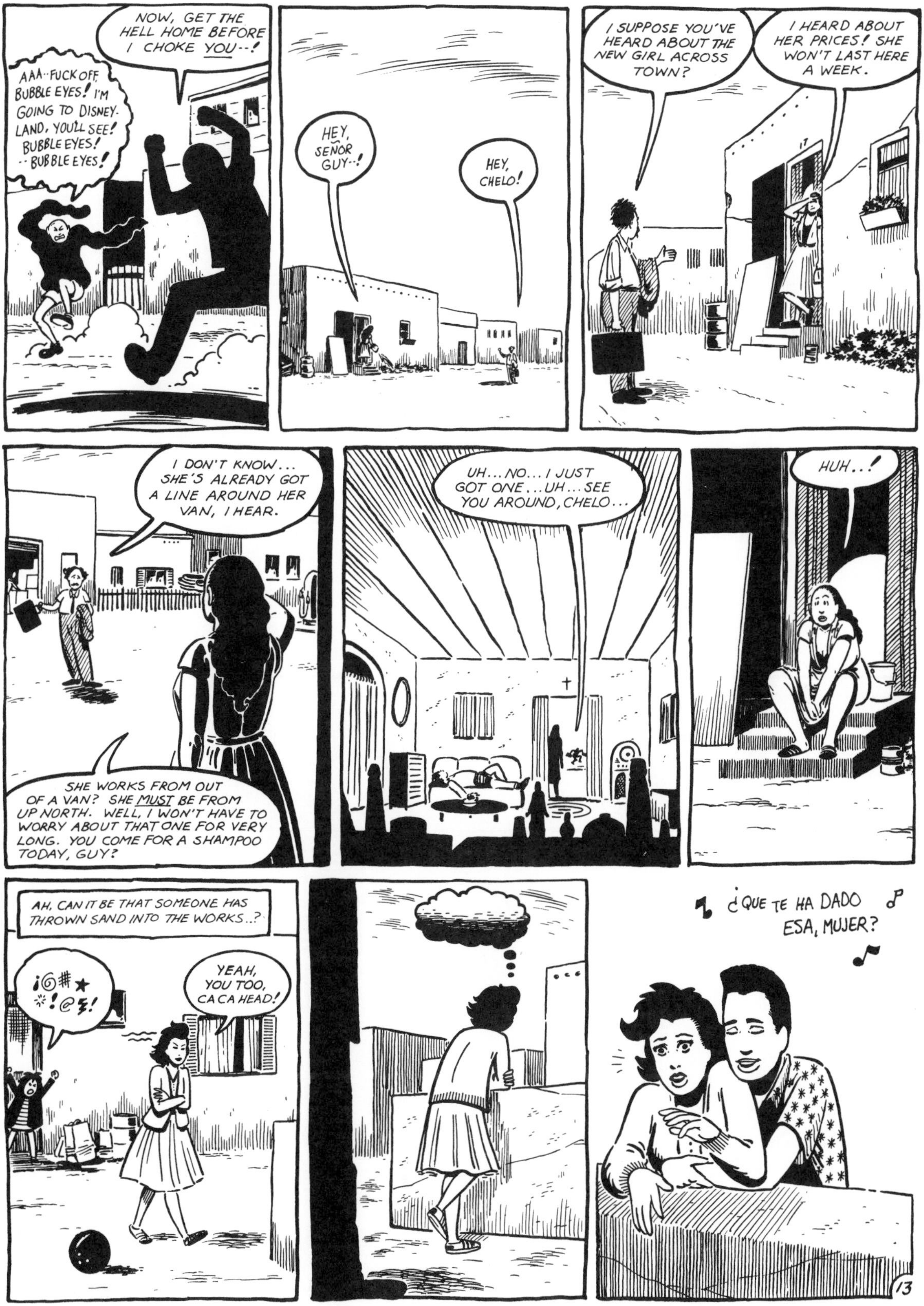
NOW, GET THE HELL HOME BEFORE I CHOKE YOU--!
AAA--FUCK OFF, BUBBLE EYES! I'M GOING TO DISNEY-LAND, YOU'LL SEE! BUBBLE EYES! --BUBBLE EYES!
HEY, SEÑOR GUY--!
HEY, CHELO!
I SUPPOSE YOU'VE HEARD ABOUT THE NEW GIRL ACROSS TOWN?
I HEARD ABOUT HER PRICES! SHE WON'T LAST HERE A WEEK.
I DON'T KNOW... SHE'S ALREADY GOT A LINE AROUND HER VAN, I HEAR.
SHE WORKS FROM OUT OF A VAN? SHE MUST BE FROM UP NORTH. WELL, I WON'T HAVE TO WORRY ABOUT THAT ONE FOR VERY LONG. YOU COME FOR A SHAMPOO TODAY, GUY?
UH... NO... I JUST GOT ONE... UH... SEE YOU AROUND, CHELO...
HUH..!
AH, CAN IT BE THAT SOMEONE HAS THROWN SAND INTO THE WORKS..?
¡@#★*!@$!
YEAH, YOU TOO, CACA HEAD!
¿QUE TE HA DADO ESA, MUJER?
13

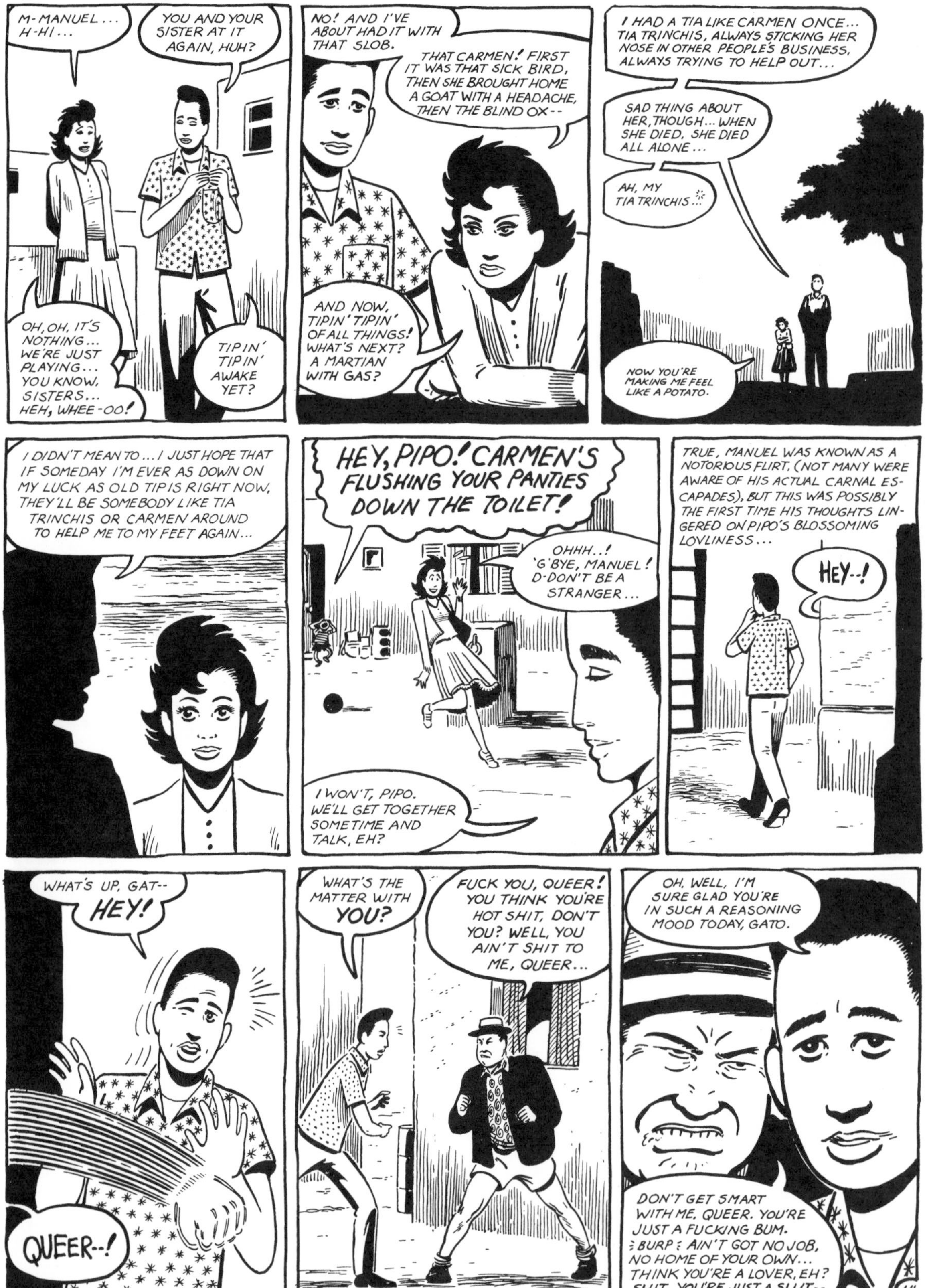
M-MANUEL... H-HI...
YOU AND YOUR SISTER AT IT AGAIN, HUH?
OH, OH, IT'S NOTHING... WE'RE JUST PLAYING... YOU KNOW, SISTERS... HEH, WHEE-OO!
TIPIN' TIPIN' AWAKE YET?
NO! AND I'VE ABOUT HAD IT WITH THAT SLOB.
THAT CARMEN! FIRST IT WAS THAT SICK BIRD, THEN SHE BROUGHT HOME A GOAT WITH A HEADACHE, THEN THE BLIND OX--
AND NOW, TIPIN' TIPIN' OF ALL THINGS! WHAT'S NEXT? A MARTIAN WITH GAS?
I HAD A TIA LIKE CARMEN ONCE... TIA TRINCHIS, ALWAYS STICKING HER NOSE IN OTHER PEOPLE'S BUSINESS, ALWAYS TRYING TO HELP OUT...
SAD THING ABOUT HER, THOUGH... WHEN SHE DIED, SHE DIED ALL ALONE...
AH, MY TIA TRINCHIS...
NOW YOU'RE MAKING ME FEEL LIKE A POTATO.
I DIDN'T MEAN TO... I JUST HOPE THAT IF SOMEDAY I'M EVER AS DOWN ON MY LUCK AS OLD TIPIS RIGHT NOW, THEY'LL BE SOMEBODY LIKE TIA TRINCHIS OR CARMEN AROUND TO HELP ME TO MY FEET AGAIN...
HEY, PIPO! CARMEN'S FLUSHING YOUR PANTIES DOWN THE TOILET!
OHHH..! 'G'BYE, MANUEL! D-DON'T BE A STRANGER...
I WON'T, PIPO. WE'LL GET TOGETHER SOMETIME AND TALK, EH?
TRUE, MANUEL WAS KNOWN AS A NOTORIOUS FLIRT, (NOT MANY WERE AWARE OF HIS ACTUAL CARNAL ESCAPADES), BUT THIS WAS POSSIBLY THE FIRST TIME HIS THOUGHTS LINGERED ON PIPO'S BLOSSOMING LOVLINESS...
HEY--!
WHAT'S UP, GAT-- HEY!
QUEER--!
WHAT'S THE MATTER WITH YOU?
FUCK YOU, QUEER! YOU THINK YOU'RE HOT SHIT, DON'T YOU? WELL, YOU AIN'T SHIT TO ME, QUEER...
OH, WELL, I'M SURE GLAD YOU'RE IN SUCH A REASONING MOOD TODAY, GATO.
DON'T GET SMART WITH ME, QUEER. YOU'RE JUST A FUCKING BUM. BURP AIN'T GOT NO JOB, NO HOME OF YOUR OWN... THINK YOU'RE A LOVER, EH? SHIT, YOU'RE JUST A SLUT--
14

TIA (AUNT) TRINCHIS (TEA'-UH TREEN' CHEESE)

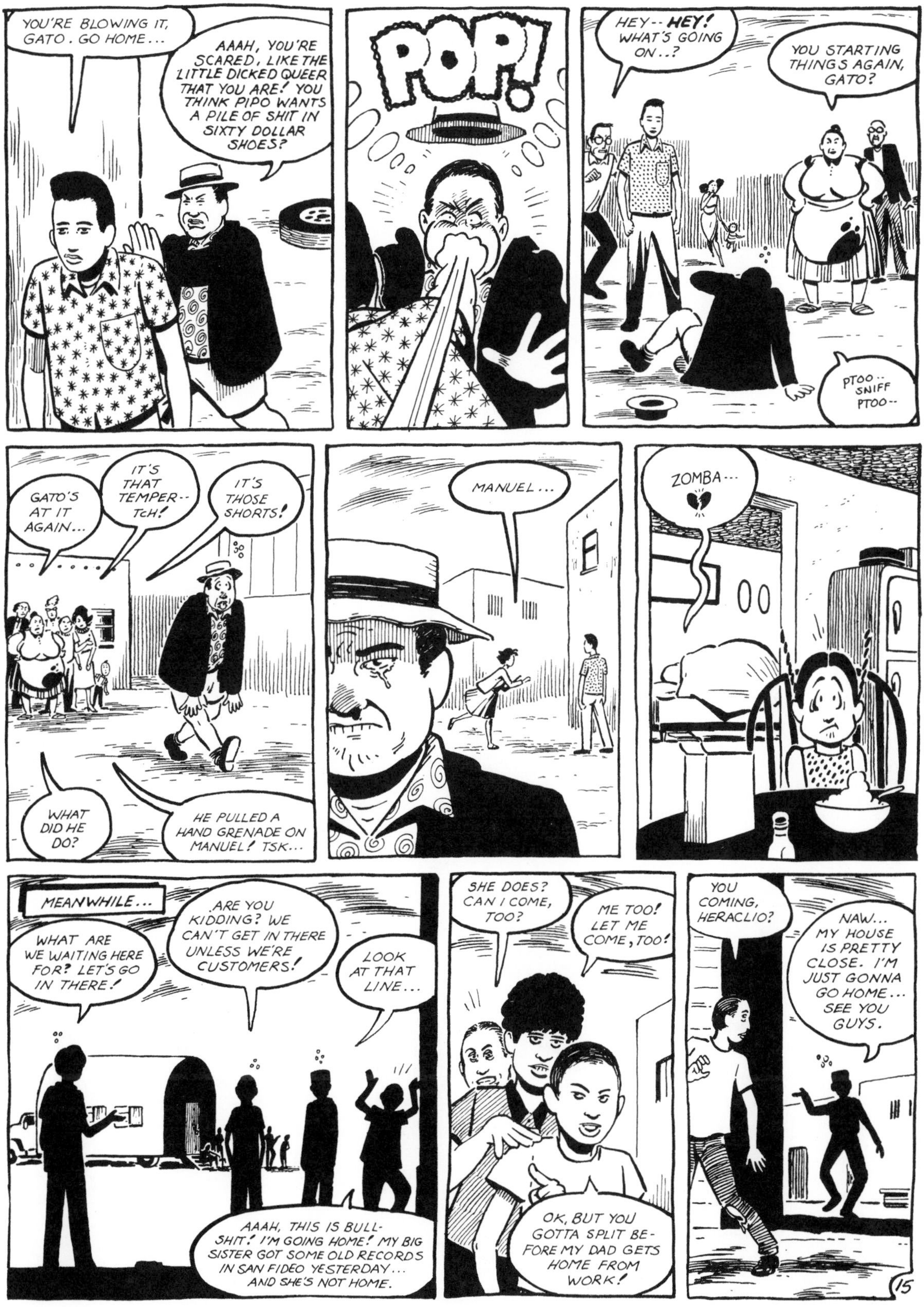

YOU'RE BLOWING IT, GATO. GO HOME...
AAAH, YOU'RE SCARED, LIKE THE LITTLE DICKED QUEER THAT YOU ARE! YOU THINK PIPO WANTS A PILE OF SHIT IN SIXTY DOLLAR SHOES?
POP!
HEY-- HEY! WHAT'S GOING ON..?
YOU STARTING THINGS AGAIN, GATO?
PTOO.. SNIFF PTOO--
GATO'S AT IT AGAIN...
IT'S THAT TEMPER-- TCH!
IT'S THOSE SHORTS!
WHAT DID HE DO?
HE PULLED A HAND GRENADE ON MANUEL! TSK...
MANUEL...
ZOMBA...
MEANWHILE...
WHAT ARE WE WAITING HERE FOR? LET'S GO IN THERE!
ARE YOU KIDDING? WE CAN'T GET IN THERE UNLESS WE'RE CUSTOMERS!
LOOK AT THAT LINE...
AAAH, THIS IS BULL-SHIT! I'M GOING HOME! MY BIG SISTER GOT SOME OLD RECORDS IN SAN FIDEO YESTERDAY... AND SHE'S NOT HOME.
SHE DOES? CAN I COME, TOO?
ME TOO! LET ME COME, TOO!
OK, BUT YOU GOTTA SPLIT BE-FORE MY DAD GETS HOME FROM WORK!
YOU COMING, HERACLIO?
NAW... MY HOUSE IS PRETTY CLOSE. I'M JUST GONNA GO HOME... SEE YOU GUYS.
15

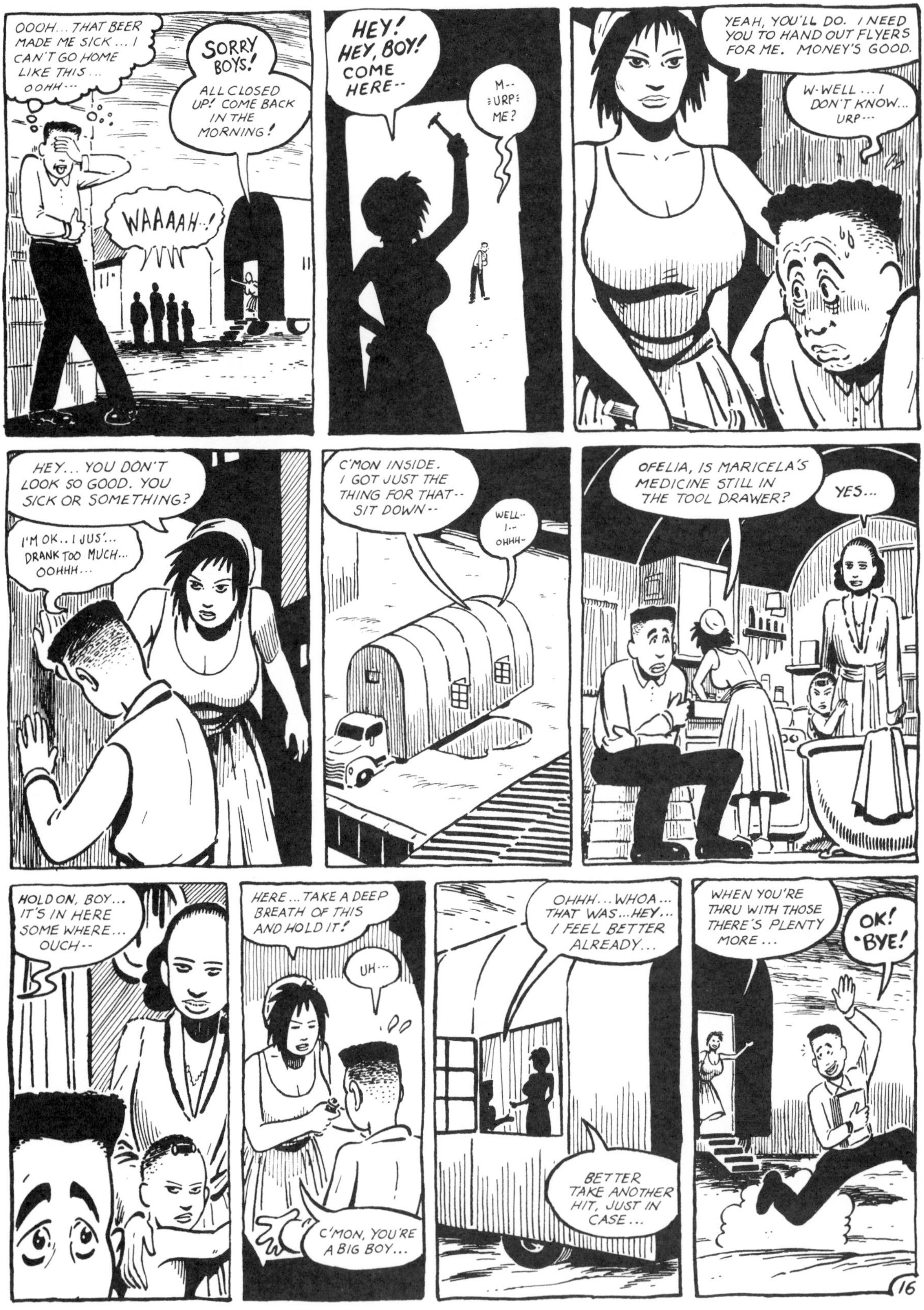
OOOH... THAT BEER MADE ME SICK... I CAN'T GO HOME LIKE THIS... OOHH...
SORRY BOYS!
ALL CLOSED UP! COME BACK IN THE MORNING!
WAAAAH..!
HEY! HEY, BOY! COME HERE--
M-- URP ME?
YEAH, YOU'LL DO. I NEED YOU TO HAND OUT FLYERS FOR ME. MONEY'S GOOD.
W-WELL... I DON'T KNOW... URP...
HEY... YOU DON'T LOOK SO GOOD. YOU SICK OR SOMETHING?
I'M OK.. I JUS'... DRANK TOO MUCH... OOHHH...
C'MON INSIDE. I GOT JUST THE THING FOR THAT-- SIT DOWN--
WELL.. I.. OHHH..
OFELIA, IS MARICELA'S MEDICINE STILL IN THE TOOL DRAWER?
YES...
HOLD ON, BOY... IT'S IN HERE SOME WHERE... OUCH--
HERE... TAKE A DEEP BREATH OF THIS AND HOLD IT!
UH...
C'MON, YOU'RE A BIG BOY...
OHHH... WHOA... THAT WAS... HEY... I FEEL BETTER ALREADY...
BETTER TAKE ANOTHER HIT, JUST IN CASE...
WHEN YOU'RE THRU WITH THOSE THERE'S PLENTY MORE...
OK! BYE!
16

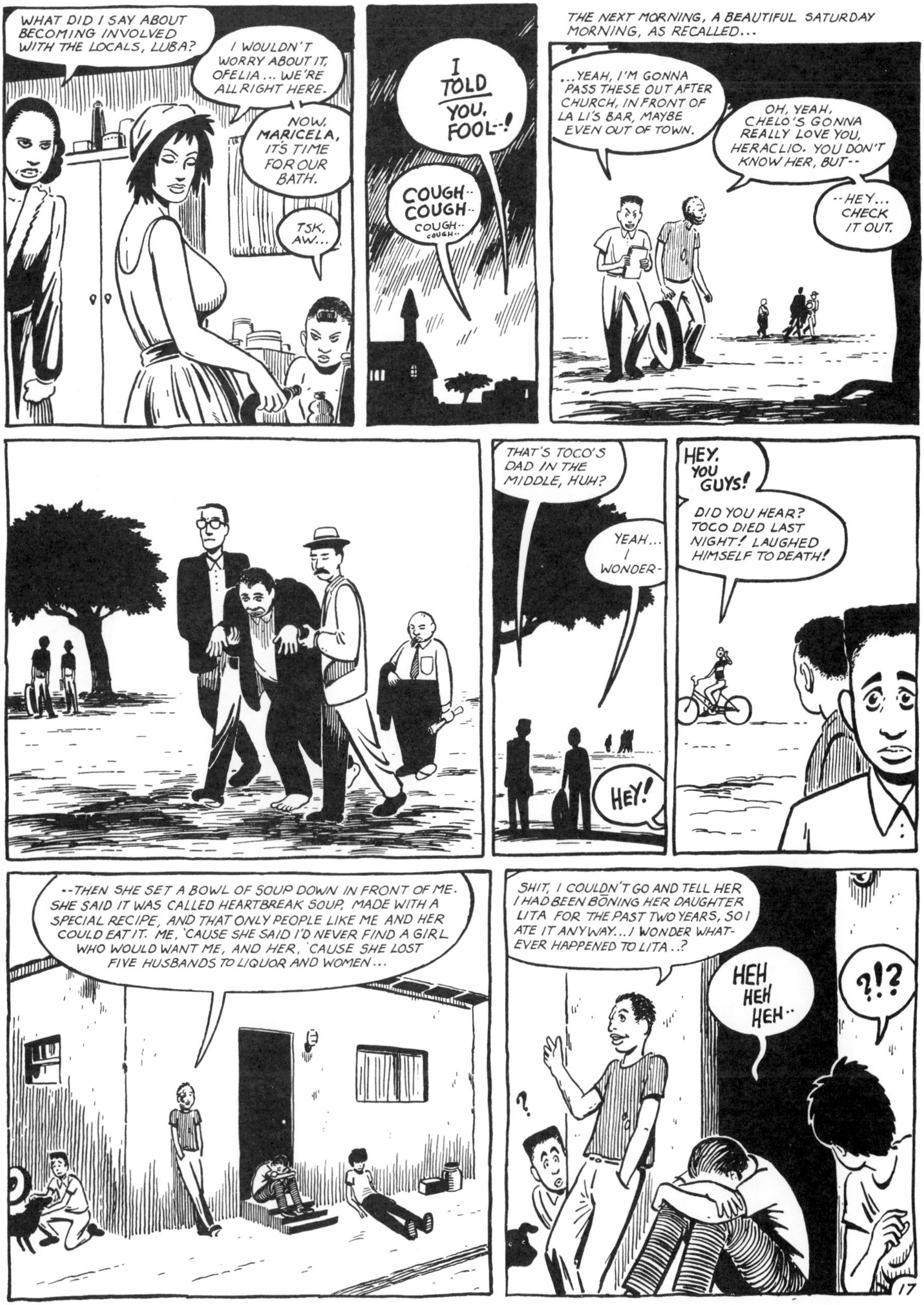
WHAT DID I SAY ABOUT BECOMING INVOLVED WITH THE LOCALS, LUBA?
I WOULDN'T WORRY ABOUT IT, OFELIA... WE'RE ALL RIGHT HERE.
NOW, MARICELA, IT'S TIME FOR OUR BATH.
TSK, AW...
I TOLD YOU, FOOL--!
COUGH.. COUGH.. COUGH.. COUGH..
THE NEXT MORNING, A BEAUTIFUL SATURDAY MORNING, AS RECALLED...
...YEAH, I'M GONNA PASS THESE OUT AFTER CHURCH, IN FRONT OF LA LI'S BAR, MAYBE EVEN OUT OF TOWN.
OH, YEAH, CHELO'S GONNA REALLY LOVE YOU, HERACLIO. YOU DON'T KNOW HER, BUT--
--HEY... CHECK IT OUT.
THAT'S TOCO'S DAD IN THE MIDDLE, HUH?
YEAH... I WONDER-
HEY!
HEY. YOU GUYS!
DID YOU HEAR? TOCO DIED LAST NIGHT! LAUGHED HIMSELF TO DEATH!
--THEN SHE SET A BOWL OF SOUP DOWN IN FRONT OF ME. SHE SAID IT WAS CALLED HEARTBREAK SOUP, MADE WITH A SPECIAL RECIPE, AND THAT ONLY PEOPLE LIKE ME AND HER COULD EAT IT. ME, 'CAUSE SHE SAID I'D NEVER FIND A GIRL WHO WOULD WANT ME, AND HER, 'CAUSE SHE LOST FIVE HUSBANDS TO LIQUOR AND WOMEN...
SHIT, I COULDN'T GO AND TELL HER I HAD BEEN BONING HER DAUGHTER LITA FOR THE PAST TWO YEARS, SO I ATE IT ANYWAY... I WONDER WHAT-EVER HAPPENED TO LITA..?
HEH HEH HEH..
?!?
?
17

"...YOU KNOW WHAT IT WAS TOCO WAS LAUGHING AT?"

"...HAR!"

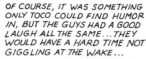

OF COURSE, IT WAS SOMETHING ONLY TOCO COULD FIND HUMOR IN, BUT THE GUYS HAD A GOOD LAUGH ALL THE SAME...THEY WOULD HAVE A HARD TIME NOT GIGGLING AT THE WAKE...

THE FUNERAL WAS SMALL AND TYPICAL (ONLY TWO FIGHTS BROKE OUT). WITHIN THE NEXT FEW DAYS THINGS WERE BACK TO BUSINESS AGAIN...

"WELL, CARMEN FINALLY GOT HIM TO EAT, BUT HE JUST SITS THERE STARING AT THE FLOOR."

"I KNOW... IT'S LIKE LIVING WITH A ZOMBIE."

"NO WAY! HIS MOUTH ISN'T ALL SEWED UP, OR..."

"AUGUSTIN'---I...OH, UH, HERE! GO GET AN ICE-CREAM, OK?"

"MANUEL...YOUR FACE! WAS IT THAT STUPID GATO..?!"

"HEY, HEY, HOLD ON... NO, ME AND SOME OF THE GUYS HAD TO GET TOCO'S DAD OUT OF LALI'S BAR..."

LUCHA LIBRE

GROTH V.S. TODO EL MUNDO

HOY

"SEVENTY FIVE CENTS FOR ICE CREAM..?"

"...HE GOT A LITTLE TOUGH, BUT THAT'S ALL. HE'S ALL RIGHT, NOW."

"OH, POOR MAN... SEEMS LIKE EVERYBODY NEEDS BABY-SITTING IN THIS TOWN THESE DAYS..."

"PIPO... COME WITH ME..."

"WHAT--?"

"COME WITH ME..."

"I JUST WANT TO ...TALK TO YOU. ALONE."

"A WHOLE SEVENTY FIVE CENTS... A WHOLE ...S...."

"SAKAHAFTEWA! WHERE THE HELL ARE YOU?"

"YOUR MOM'S CALLING YOU, SATCH."

"IGNORE HER, HERACLIO. I ALWAYS DO."

18

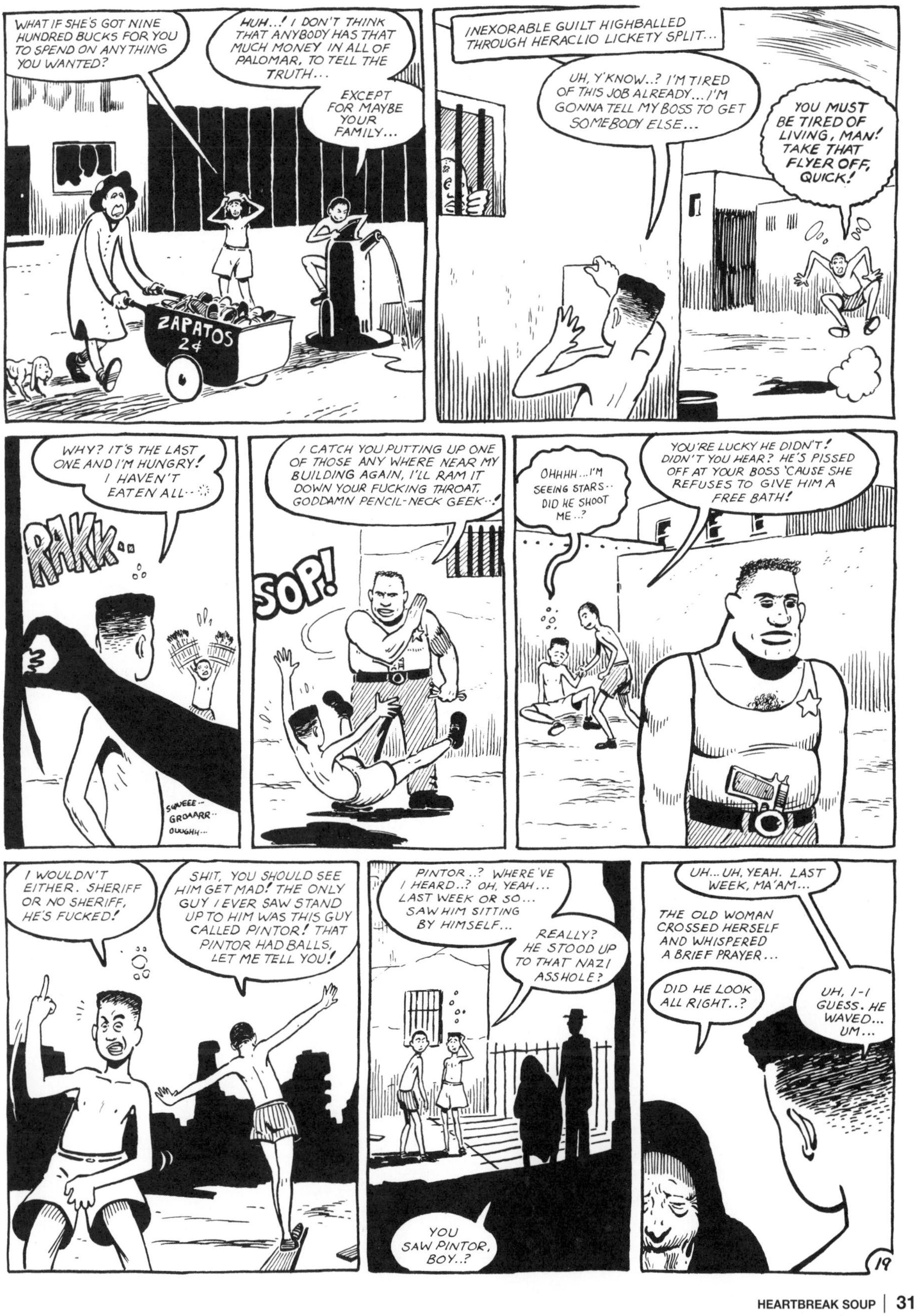
WHAT IF SHE'S GOT NINE HUNDRED BUCKS FOR YOU TO SPEND ON ANYTHING YOU WANTED?
HUH...! I DON'T THINK THAT ANYBODY HAS THAT MUCH MONEY IN ALL OF PALOMAR, TO TELL THE TRUTH...
EXCEPT FOR MAYBE YOUR FAMILY...
ZAPATOS 24
INEXORABLE GUILT HIGHBALLED THROUGH HERACLIO LICKETY SPLIT...
UH, Y'KNOW..? I'M TIRED OF THIS JOB ALREADY... I'M GONNA TELL MY BOSS TO GET SOMEBODY ELSE...
YOU MUST BE TIRED OF LIVING, MAN! TAKE THAT FLYER OFF, QUICK!
WHY? IT'S THE LAST ONE AND I'M HUNGRY! I HAVEN'T EATEN ALL··
RAKK..
SQUEEE.. GROAARR.. OUUGHH...
I CATCH YOU PUTTING UP ONE OF THOSE ANY WHERE NEAR MY BUILDING AGAIN, I'LL RAM IT DOWN YOUR FUCKING THROAT, GODDAMN PENCIL-NECK GEEK··!
SOP!
OHHHH...I'M SEEING STARS.. DID HE SHOOT ME..?
YOU'RE LUCKY HE DIDN'T! DIDN'T YOU HEAR? HE'S PISSED OFF AT YOUR BOSS 'CAUSE SHE REFUSES TO GIVE HIM A FREE BATH!
I WOULDN'T EITHER. SHERIFF OR NO SHERIFF, HE'S FUCKED!
SHIT, YOU SHOULD SEE HIM GET MAD! THE ONLY GUY I EVER SAW STAND UP TO HIM WAS THIS GUY CALLED PINTOR! THAT PINTOR HAD BALLS, LET ME TELL YOU!
PINTOR..? WHERE'VE I HEARD..? OH, YEAH... LAST WEEK OR SO... SAW HIM SITTING BY HIMSELF...
REALLY? HE STOOD UP TO THAT NAZI ASSHOLE?
YOU SAW PINTOR, BOY..?
UH... UH, YEAH. LAST WEEK, MA'AM...
THE OLD WOMAN CROSSED HERSELF AND WHISPERED A BRIEF PRAYER...
DID HE LOOK ALL RIGHT..?
UH, I-I GUESS. HE WAVED... UM...
19

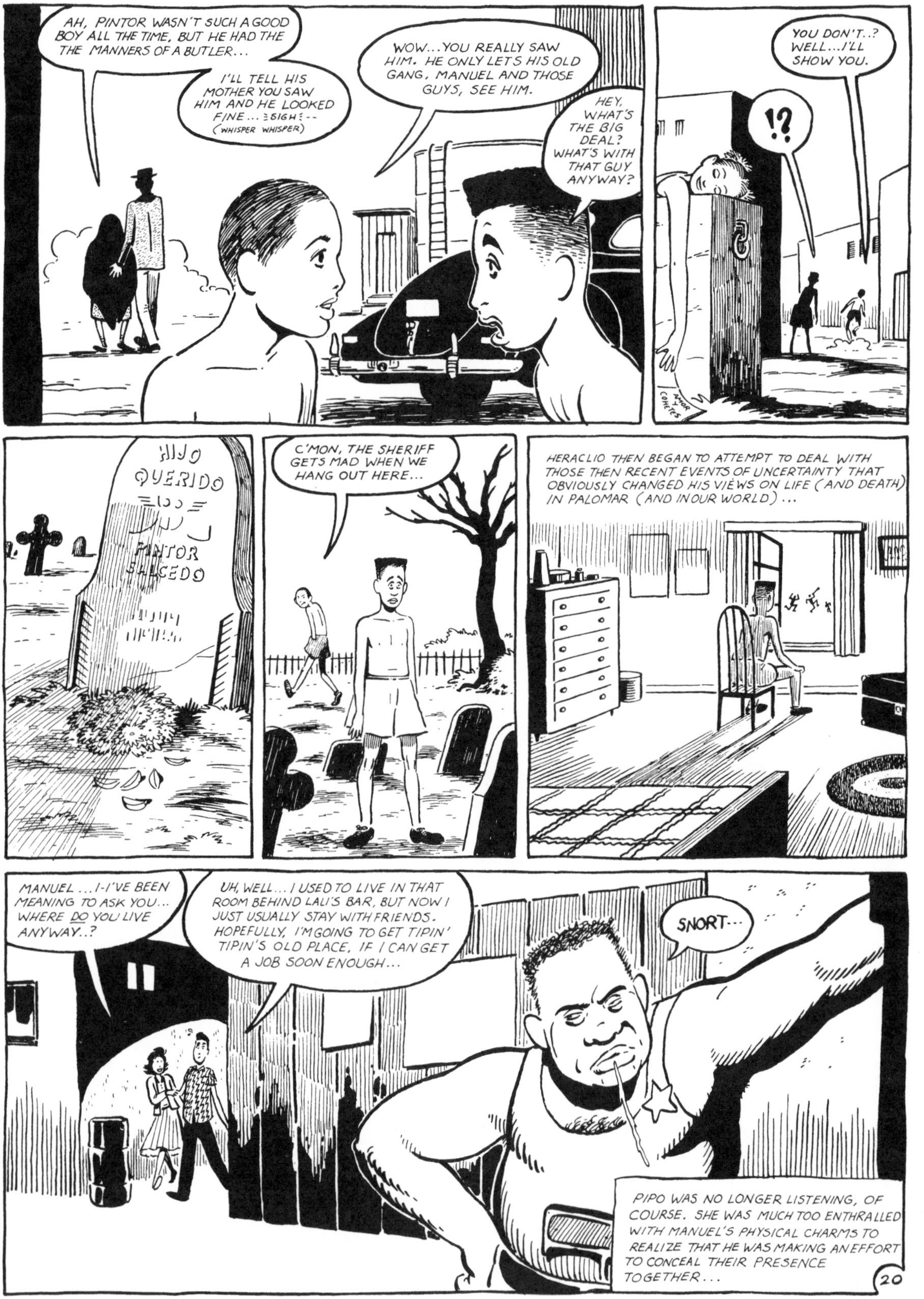

AH, PINTOR WASN'T SUCH A GOOD BOY ALL THE TIME, BUT HE HAD THE THE MANNERS OF A BUTLER...
I'LL TELL HIS MOTHER YOU SAW HIM AND HE LOOKED FINE... SIGH --
(WHISPER WHISPER)
WOW... YOU REALLY SAW HIM. HE ONLY LETS HIS OLD GANG, MANUEL AND THOSE GUYS, SEE HIM.
HEY, WHAT'S THE BIG DEAL? WHAT'S WITH THAT GUY ANYWAY?
YOU DON'T..? WELL...I'LL SHOW YOU.
!?
AMOR Y COHETES
HIJO QUERIDO
PINTOR SALCEDO
C'MON, THE SHERIFF GETS MAD WHEN WE HANG OUT HERE...
HERACLIO THEN BEGAN TO ATTEMPT TO DEAL WITH THOSE THEN RECENT EVENTS OF UNCERTAINTY THAT OBVIOUSLY CHANGED HIS VIEWS ON LIFE (AND DEATH) IN PALOMAR (AND IN OUR WORLD)...
MANUEL... I-I'VE BEEN MEANING TO ASK YOU... WHERE DO YOU LIVE ANYWAY..?
UH, WELL... I USED TO LIVE IN THAT ROOM BEHIND LALI'S BAR, BUT NOW I JUST USUALLY STAY WITH FRIENDS. HOPEFULLY, I'M GOING TO GET TIPIN' TIPIN'S OLD PLACE, IF I CAN GET A JOB SOON ENOUGH...
SNORT...
PIPO WAS NO LONGER LISTENING, OF COURSE. SHE WAS MUCH TOO ENTHRALLED WITH MANUEL'S PHYSICAL CHARMS TO REALIZE THAT HE WAS MAKING AN EFFORT TO CONCEAL THEIR PRESENCE TOGETHER...
20

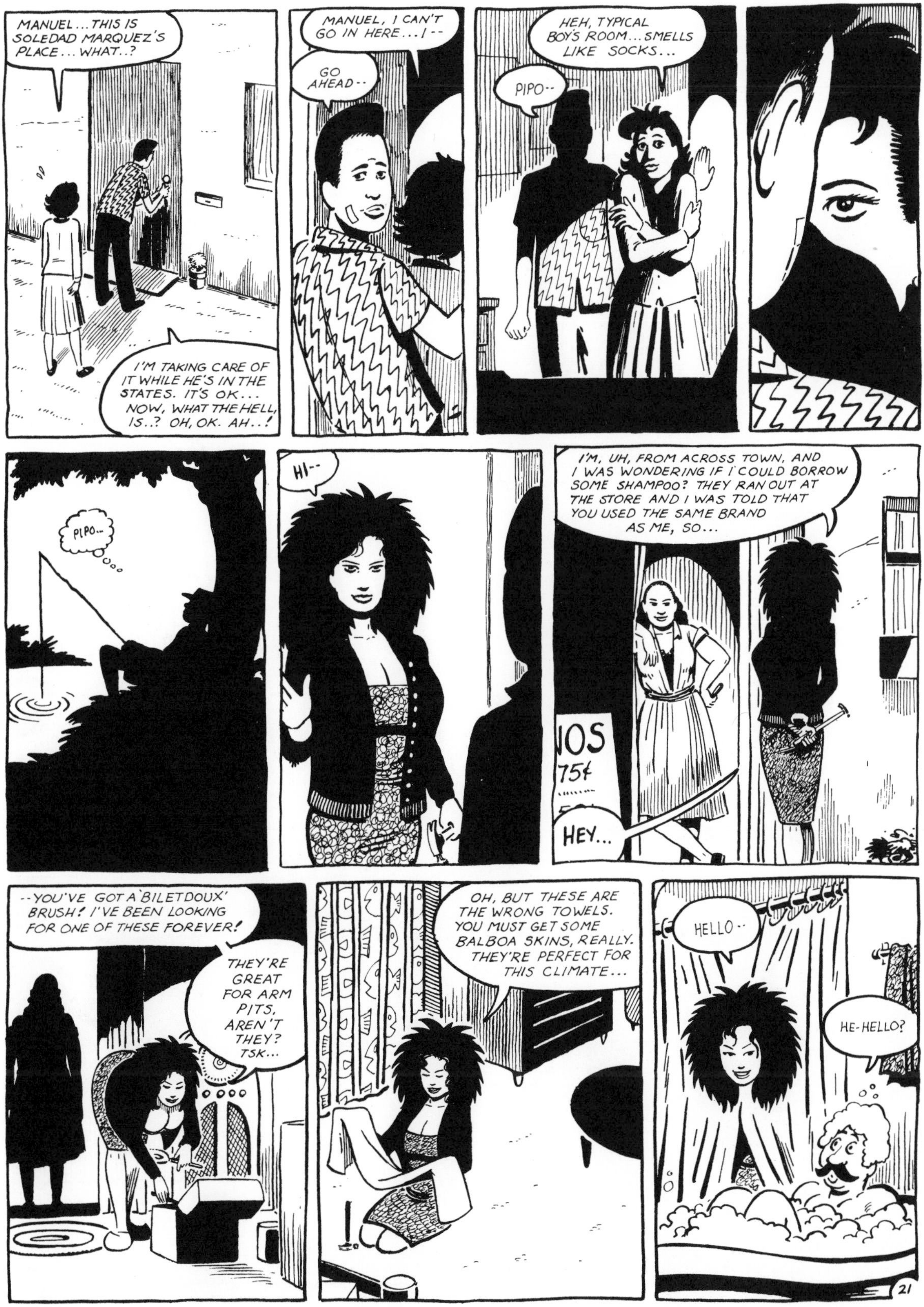

MANUEL... THIS IS SOLEDAD MARQUEZ'S PLACE... WHAT..?
I'M TAKING CARE OF IT WHILE HE'S IN THE STATES. IT'S OK... NOW, WHAT THE HELL, IS..? OH, OK. AH..!
MANUEL, I CAN'T GO IN HERE...I--
GO AHEAD--
HEH, TYPICAL BOY'S ROOM... SMELLS LIKE SOCKS...
PIPO--
PIPO...
HI--
I'M, UH, FROM ACROSS TOWN, AND I WAS WONDERING IF I COULD BORROW SOME SHAMPOO? THEY RAN OUT AT THE STORE AND I WAS TOLD THAT YOU USED THE SAME BRAND AS ME, SO...
NOS
75¢
HEY...
--YOU'VE GOT A 'BILETDOUX' BRUSH! I'VE BEEN LOOKING FOR ONE OF THESE FOREVER!
THEY'RE GREAT FOR ARM PITS, AREN'T THEY? TSK...
OH, BUT THESE ARE THE WRONG TOWELS. YOU MUST GET SOME BALBOA SKINS, REALLY. THEY'RE PERFECT FOR THIS CLIMATE...
HELLO--
HE-HELLO?
21

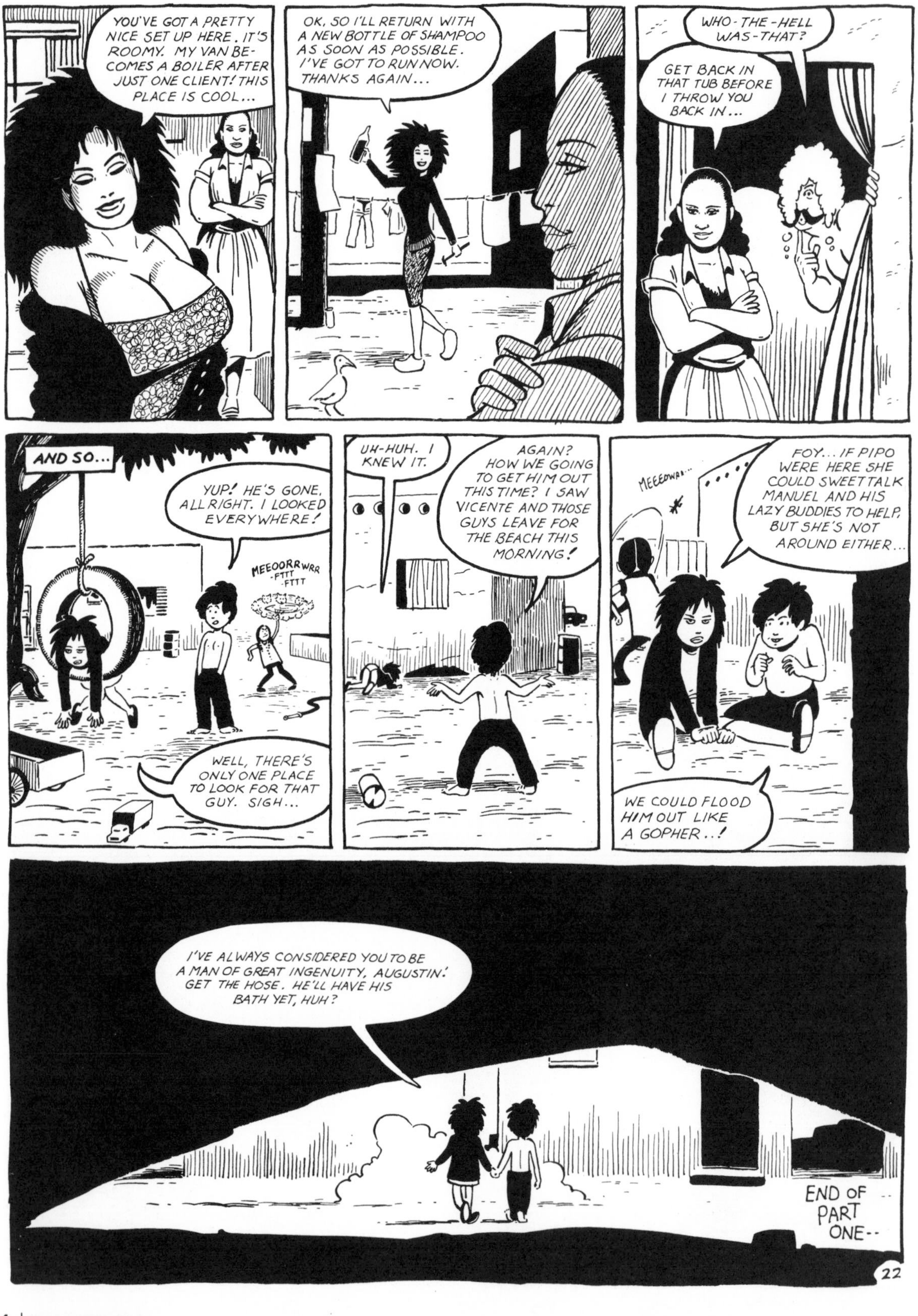
YOU'VE GOT A PRETTY NICE SET UP HERE. IT'S ROOMY. MY VAN BECOMES A BOILER AFTER JUST ONE CLIENT! THIS PLACE IS COOL...
OK, SO I'LL RETURN WITH A NEW BOTTLE OF SHAMPOO AS SOON AS POSSIBLE. I'VE GOT TO RUN NOW. THANKS AGAIN...
WHO-THE-HELL WAS-THAT?
GET BACK IN THAT TUB BEFORE I THROW YOU BACK IN...
AND SO...
YUP! HE'S GONE, ALL RIGHT. I LOOKED EVERYWHERE!
MEEOORRWRR -FTTT -FTTT
WELL, THERE'S ONLY ONE PLACE TO LOOK FOR THAT GUY. SIGH...
UH-HUH. I KNEW IT.
AGAIN? HOW WE GOING TO GET HIM OUT THIS TIME? I SAW VICENTE AND THOSE GUYS LEAVE FOR THE BEACH THIS MORNING!
FOY... IF PIPO WERE HERE SHE COULD SWEETTALK MANUEL AND HIS LAZY BUDDIES TO HELP, BUT SHE'S NOT AROUND EITHER...
WE COULD FLOOD HIM OUT LIKE A GOPHER..!
I'VE ALWAYS CONSIDERED YOU TO BE A MAN OF GREAT INGENUITY, AUGUSTIN! GET THE HOSE. HE'LL HAVE HIS BATH YET, HUH?
END OF PART ONE--
22

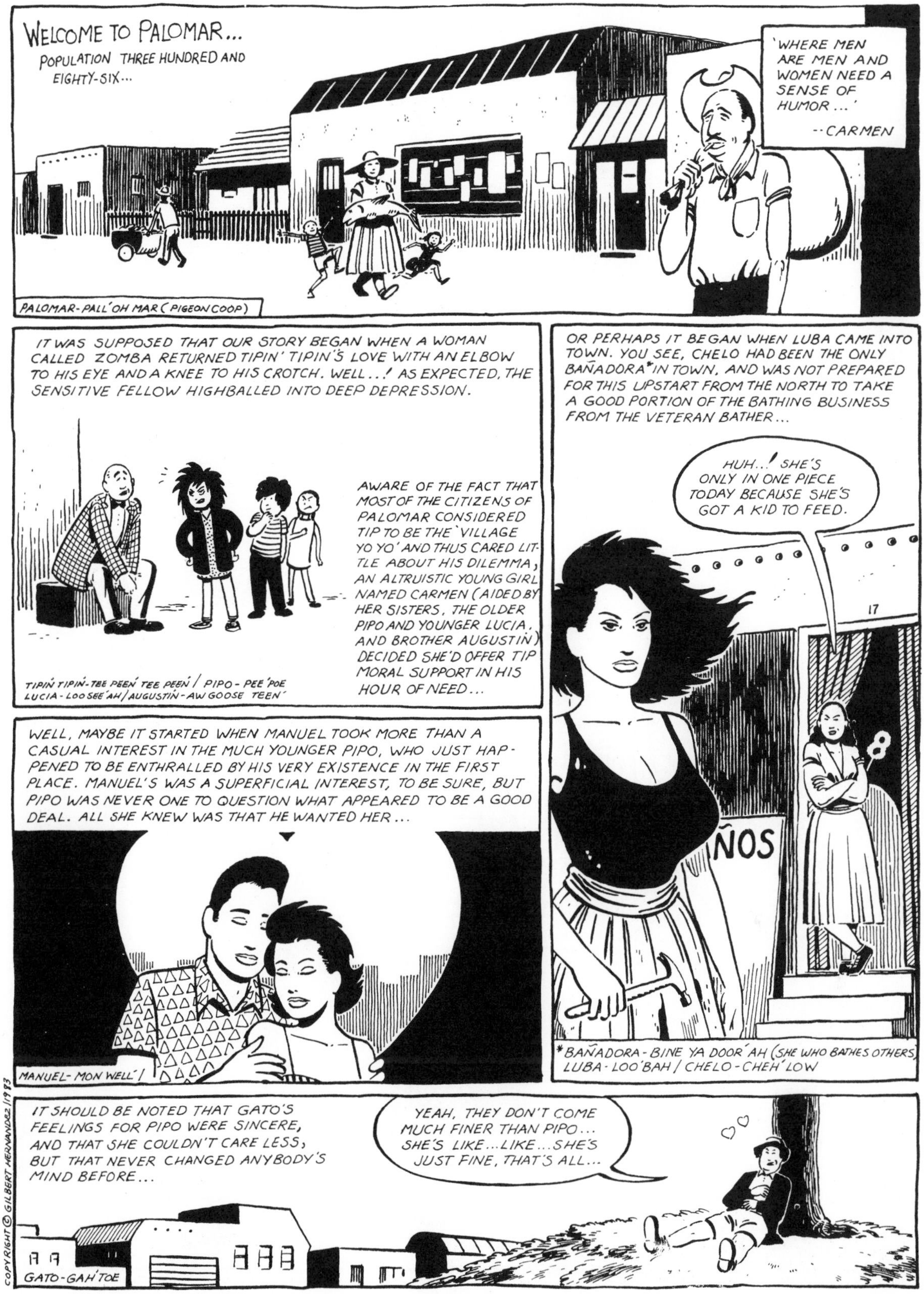
WELCOME TO PALOMAR...
POPULATION THREE HUNDRED AND EIGHTY-SIX...
'WHERE MEN ARE MEN AND WOMEN NEED A SENSE OF HUMOR...' --CARMEN
PALOMAR-PALL'OH MAR (PIGEON COOP)
IT WAS SUPPOSED THAT OUR STORY BEGAN WHEN A WOMAN CALLED ZOMBA RETURNED TIPIN' TIPIN'S LOVE WITH AN ELBOW TO HIS EYE AND A KNEE TO HIS CROTCH. WELL...! AS EXPECTED, THE SENSITIVE FELLOW HIGHBALLED INTO DEEP DEPRESSION.
AWARE OF THE FACT THAT MOST OF THE CITIZENS OF PALOMAR CONSIDERED TIP TO BE THE 'VILLAGE YO YO' AND THUS CARED LITTLE ABOUT HIS DILEMMA, AN ALTRUISTIC YOUNG GIRL NAMED CARMEN (AIDED BY HER SISTERS, THE OLDER PIPO AND YOUNGER LUCIA, AND BROTHER AUGUSTIN) DECIDED SHE'D OFFER TIP MORAL SUPPORT IN HIS HOUR OF NEED...
TIPIN TIPIN-TEE PEEN' TEE PEEN' / PIPO-PEE'POE
LUCIA-LOO SEE'AH / AUGUSTIN-AW GOOSE TEEN'
OR PERHAPS IT BEGAN WHEN LUBA CAME INTO TOWN. YOU SEE, CHELO HAD BEEN THE ONLY BAÑADORA* IN TOWN, AND WAS NOT PREPARED FOR THIS UPSTART FROM THE NORTH TO TAKE A GOOD PORTION OF THE BATHING BUSINESS FROM THE VETERAN BATHER...
HUH...! SHE'S ONLY IN ONE PIECE TODAY BECAUSE SHE'S GOT A KID TO FEED.
17
ÑOS
*BAÑADORA-BINE YA DOOR'AH (SHE WHO BATHES OTHERS)
LUBA-LOO'BAH / CHELO-CHEH'LOW
WELL, MAYBE IT STARTED WHEN MANUEL TOOK MORE THAN A CASUAL INTEREST IN THE MUCH YOUNGER PIPO, WHO JUST HAPPENED TO BE ENTHRALLED BY HIS VERY EXISTENCE IN THE FIRST PLACE. MANUEL'S WAS A SUPERFICIAL INTEREST, TO BE SURE, BUT PIPO WAS NEVER ONE TO QUESTION WHAT APPEARED TO BE A GOOD DEAL. ALL SHE KNEW WAS THAT HE WANTED HER...
MANUEL-MON WELL'
IT SHOULD BE NOTED THAT GATO'S FEELINGS FOR PIPO WERE SINCERE, AND THAT SHE COULDN'T CARE LESS, BUT THAT NEVER CHANGED ANYBODY'S MIND BEFORE...
YEAH, THEY DON'T COME MUCH FINER THAN PIPO... SHE'S LIKE... LIKE... SHE'S JUST FINE, THAT'S ALL...
GATO-GAH'TOE
COPYRIGHT © GILBERT HERNANDEZ 1983

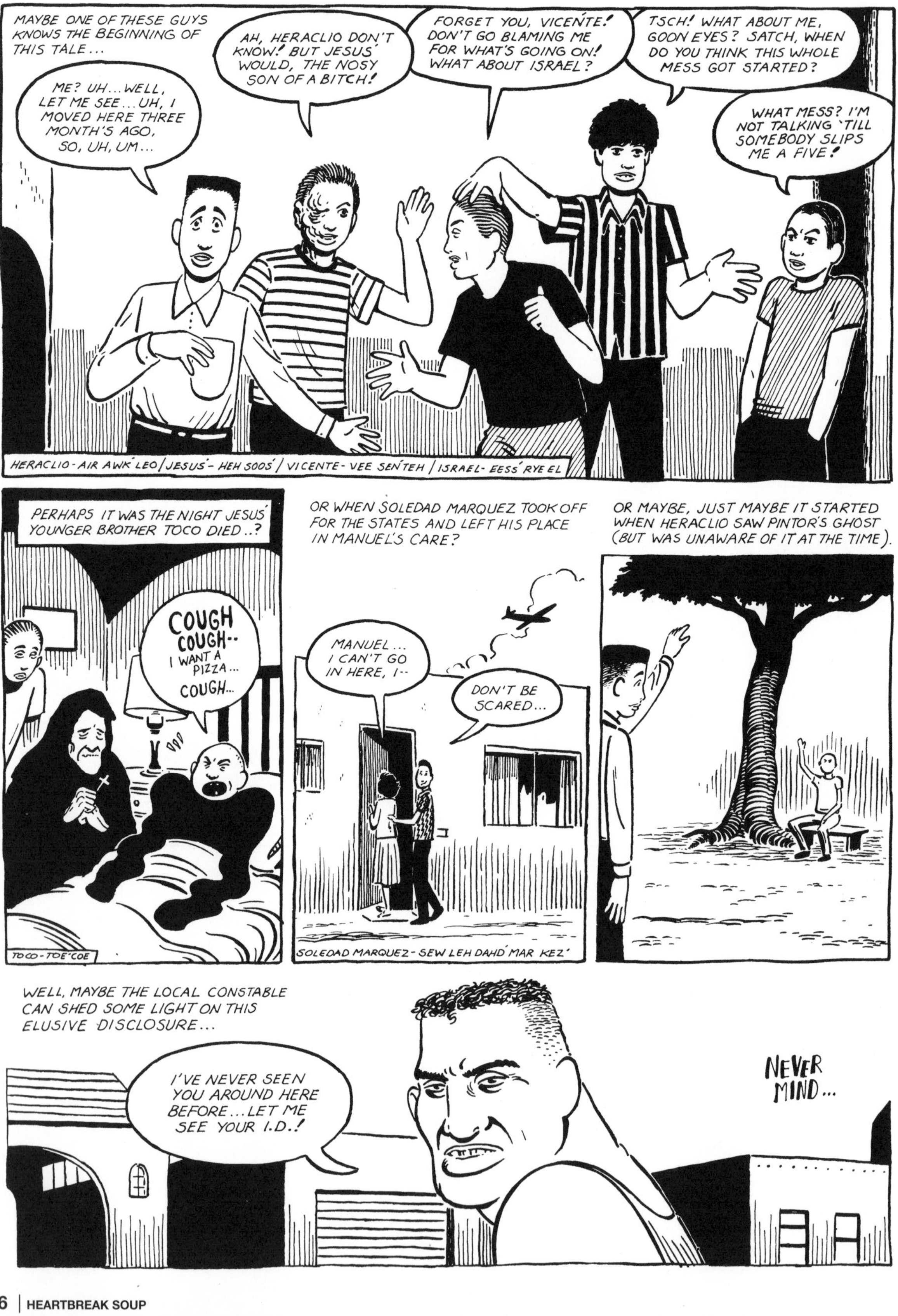
MAYBE ONE OF THESE GUYS KNOWS THE BEGINNING OF THIS TALE...
ME? UH... WELL, LET ME SEE... UH, I MOVED HERE THREE MONTH'S AGO, SO, UH, UM...
AH, HERACLIO DON'T KNOW! BUT JESUS' WOULD, THE NOSY SON OF A BITCH!
FORGET YOU, VICENTE! DON'T GO BLAMING ME FOR WHAT'S GOING ON! WHAT ABOUT ISRAEL?
TSCH! WHAT ABOUT ME, GOON EYES? SATCH, WHEN DO YOU THINK THIS WHOLE MESS GOT STARTED?
WHAT MESS? I'M NOT TALKING 'TILL SOMEBODY SLIPS ME A FIVE!
HERACLIO - AIR AWK' LEO / JESUS' - HEH SOOS' / VICENTE - VEE SEN'TEH / ISRAEL - EESS' RYE EL
PERHAPS IT WAS THE NIGHT JESUS' YOUNGER BROTHER TOCO DIED..?
COUGH COUGH.. I WANT A PIZZA... COUGH...
TOCO - TOE' COE
OR WHEN SOLEDAD MARQUEZ TOOK OFF FOR THE STATES AND LEFT HIS PLACE IN MANUEL'S CARE?
MANUEL... I CAN'T GO IN HERE, I--
DON'T BE SCARED...
SOLEDAD MARQUEZ - SEW LEH DAHD' MAR KEZ'
OR MAYBE, JUST MAYBE IT STARTED WHEN HERACLIO SAW PINTOR'S GHOST (BUT WAS UNAWARE OF IT AT THE TIME).
WELL, MAYBE THE LOCAL CONSTABLE CAN SHED SOME LIGHT ON THIS ELUSIVE DISCLOSURE...
I'VE NEVER SEEN YOU AROUND HERE BEFORE... LET ME SEE YOUR I.D..!
NEVER MIND...

SOPA DE GRAN PENA

HEARTBREAK SOUP PART TWO BY BETO '83

AMANECIDA...

AHHH...

OHHHH... ANOTHER DAY, ANOTHER PAIN...

A WOMAN'S WORK IS NEVER DONE...

GRUMBLE GRUMBLE MOAN··

HIGHER, LUCIA!!! ELEVATION! I DEMAND CULMINATION!!

IT'S ALWAYS BEEN SAID THAT CARMEN WAS MORE EFFECTIVE THAN A HUNDRED ALARM CLOCKS!

I MEAN... I WONDER WHERE TOCO IS RIGHT NOW. RIGHT NOW...

HE'S IN A BOX THREE HUNDRED YARDS FROM HERE, SIX FEET UNDER A BED OF LILACS, FOOL.

BONO SE

NO, I MEAN...TOCO! YOU KNOW...TOCO. DOES HE MIND BEING DEAD? I WONDER IF HE'S BORED ALREADY, OR WHAT... YOU KNOW WHAT I MEAN..?

WHO THE HELL GIVES A FUCKING SHIT? HE WAS WORTHLESS ANYWAY. I'M GLAD HE CROAKED. I JUST HOPE MANUEL AND HIS GOD DAMN SIXTY DOLLAR SHOES ARE NEXT--!

COPYRIGHT © GILBERT HERNANDEZ 1/1983

SEE HOW YOU ARE ?!! SEE HOW YOU FUCKING ARE?!! I CAN'T SAY SHIT TO YOU WITHOUT YOU··YOU··AAAAH!

HEY... ··HEY!

OOF·!

GET OFF, YOU FUCKIN' SKINNY··

TWENTY THREE

SOPA DE GRAN PENA - SOAP"UH DEH GRAWN PEN"UH

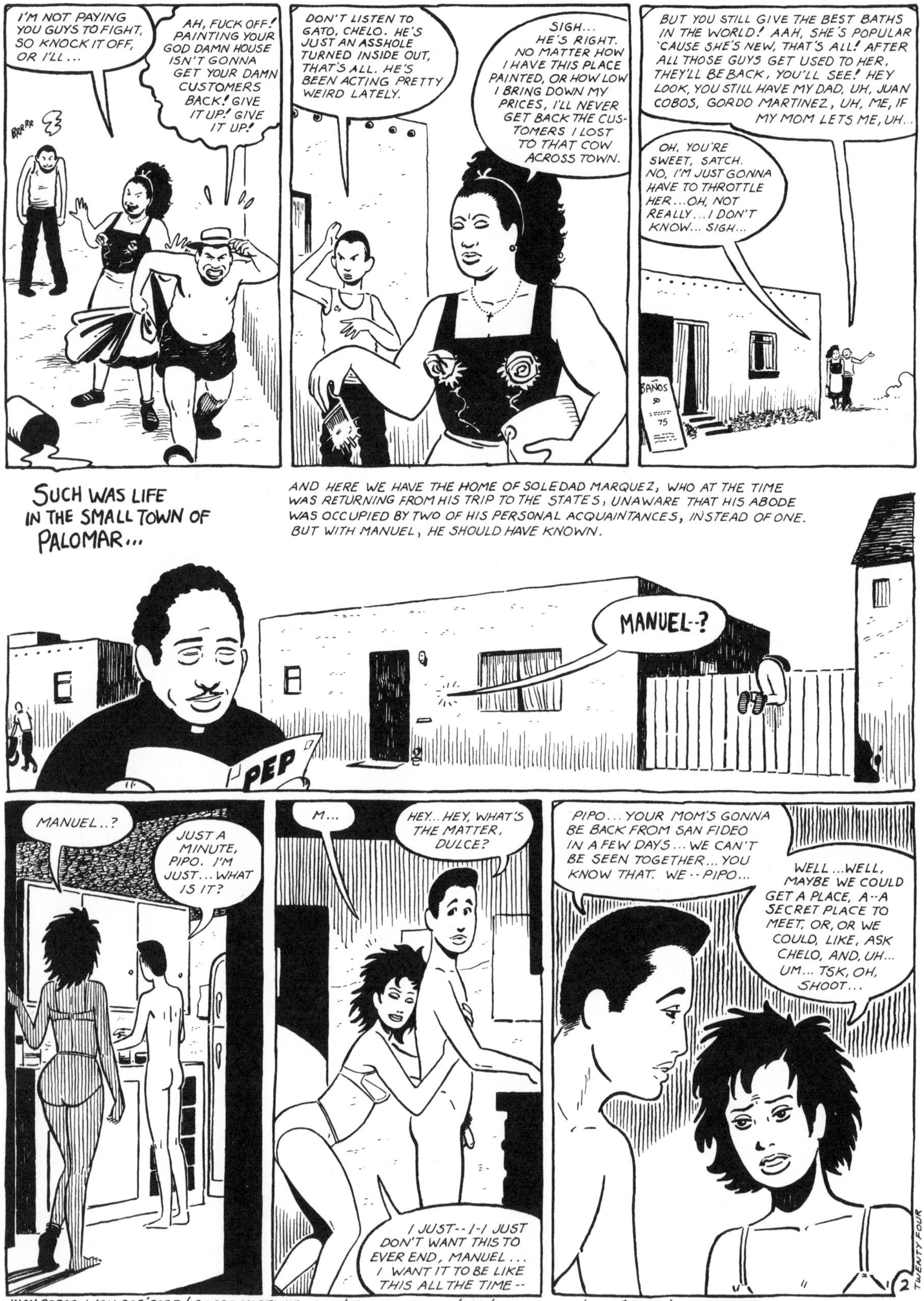
I'M NOT PAYING YOU GUYS TO FIGHT, SO KNOCK IT OFF, OR I'LL...
AH, FUCK OFF! PAINTING YOUR GOD DAMN HOUSE ISN'T GONNA GET YOUR DAMN CUSTOMERS BACK! GIVE IT UP! GIVE IT UP!
BRRRR
DON'T LISTEN TO GATO, CHELO. HE'S JUST AN ASSHOLE TURNED INSIDE OUT, THAT'S ALL. HE'S BEEN ACTING PRETTY WEIRD LATELY.
SIGH... HE'S RIGHT. NO MATTER HOW I HAVE THIS PLACE PAINTED, OR HOW LOW I BRING DOWN MY PRICES, I'LL NEVER GET BACK THE CUSTOMERS I LOST TO THAT COW ACROSS TOWN.
BUT YOU STILL GIVE THE BEST BATHS IN THE WORLD! AAH, SHE'S POPULAR 'CAUSE SHE'S NEW, THAT'S ALL! AFTER ALL THOSE GUYS GET USED TO HER, THEY'LL BE BACK, YOU'LL SEE! HEY LOOK, YOU STILL HAVE MY DAD, UH, JUAN COBOS, GORDO MARTINEZ, UH, ME, IF MY MOM LETS ME, UH...
OH, YOU'RE SWEET, SATCH. NO, I'M JUST GONNA HAVE TO THROTTLE HER... OH, NOT REALLY... I DON'T KNOW... SIGH...
BAÑOS
50
75
SUCH WAS LIFE IN THE SMALL TOWN OF PALOMAR...
AND HERE WE HAVE THE HOME OF SOLEDAD MARQUEZ, WHO AT THE TIME WAS RETURNING FROM HIS TRIP TO THE STATES, UNAWARE THAT HIS ABODE WAS OCCUPIED BY TWO OF HIS PERSONAL ACQUAINTANCES, INSTEAD OF ONE. BUT WITH MANUEL, HE SHOULD HAVE KNOWN.
MANUEL--?
PEP
MANUEL..?
JUST A MINUTE, PIPO. I'M JUST... WHAT IS IT?
M...
HEY... HEY, WHAT'S THE MATTER, DULCE?
I JUST-- I-I JUST DON'T WANT THIS TO EVER END, MANUEL... I WANT IT TO BE LIKE THIS ALL THE TIME--
PIPO... YOUR MOM'S GONNA BE BACK FROM SAN FIDEO IN A FEW DAYS... WE CAN'T BE SEEN TOGETHER... YOU KNOW THAT. WE -- PIPO...
WELL... WELL, MAYBE WE COULD GET A PLACE, A--A SECRET PLACE TO MEET, OR, OR WE COULD, LIKE, ASK CHELO, AND, UH... UM... TSK, OH, SHOOT...
TWENTY FOUR
2

JUAN COBOS- WON COE'BOZE / GORDO MARTINEZ - GORD' THOUGH MAR TEEÑ EZ / DULCE - DUEL' SEH (SWEET)

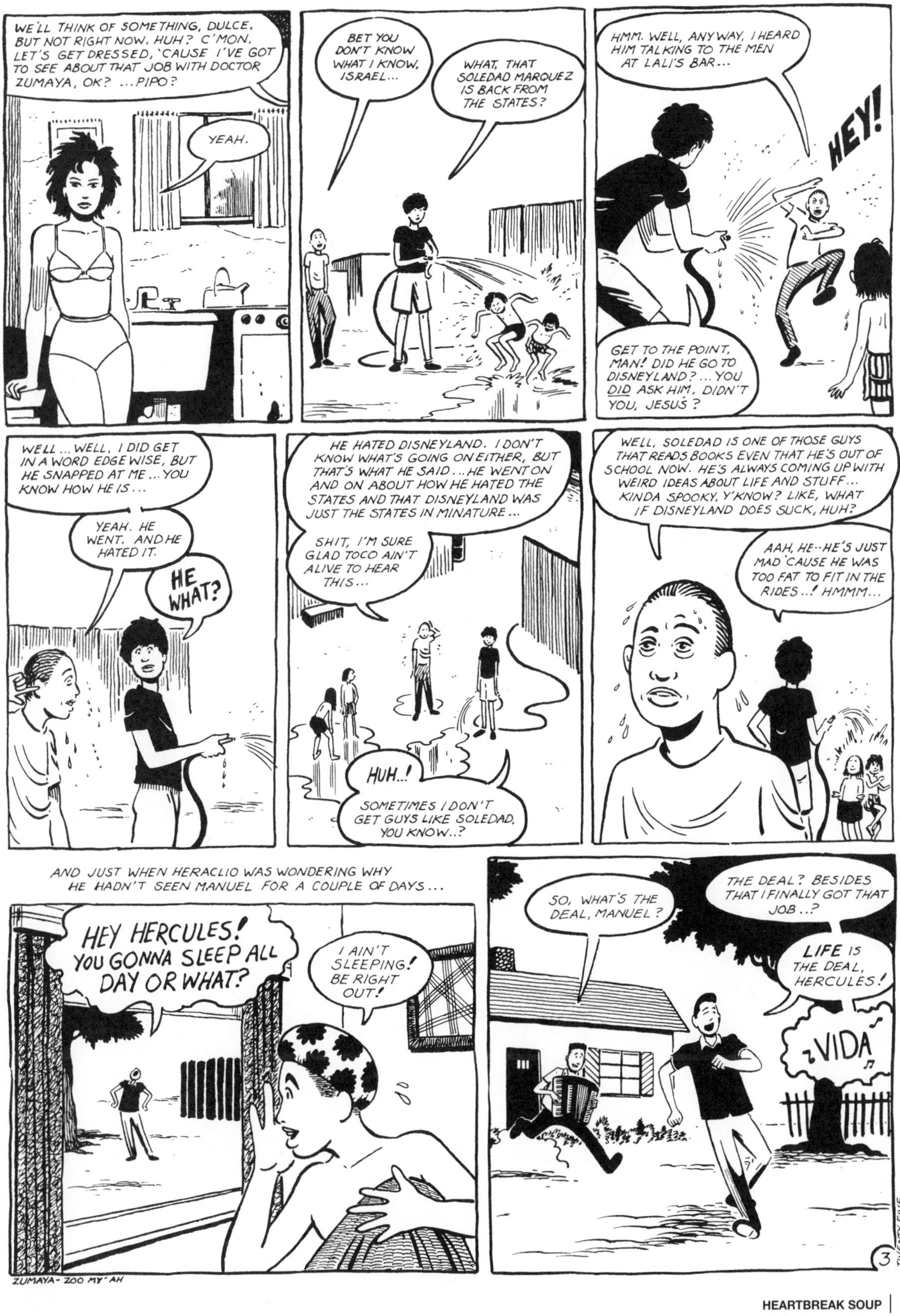
WE'LL THINK OF SOMETHING, DULCE, BUT NOT RIGHT NOW. HUH? C'MON, LET'S GET DRESSED, 'CAUSE I'VE GOT TO SEE ABOUT THAT JOB WITH DOCTOR ZUMAYA, OK? ...PIPO?
YEAH.
BET YOU DON'T KNOW WHAT I KNOW, ISRAEL...
WHAT, THAT SOLEDAD MARQUEZ IS BACK FROM THE STATES?
HMM. WELL, ANYWAY, I HEARD HIM TALKING TO THE MEN AT LALI'S BAR...
HEY!
GET TO THE POINT, MAN! DID HE GO TO DISNEYLAND? ...YOU DID ASK HIM, DIDN'T YOU, JESUS?
WELL... WELL, I DID GET IN A WORD EDGEWISE, BUT HE SNAPPED AT ME... YOU KNOW HOW HE IS...
YEAH. HE WENT. AND HE HATED IT.
HE WHAT?
HE HATED DISNEYLAND. I DON'T KNOW WHAT'S GOING ON EITHER, BUT THAT'S WHAT HE SAID... HE WENT ON AND ON ABOUT HOW HE HATED THE STATES AND THAT DISNEYLAND WAS JUST THE STATES IN MINATURE...
SHIT, I'M SURE GLAD TOCO AIN'T ALIVE TO HEAR THIS...
HUH..!
SOMETIMES I DON'T GET GUYS LIKE SOLEDAD, YOU KNOW..?
WELL, SOLEDAD IS ONE OF THOSE GUYS THAT READS BOOKS EVEN THAT HE'S OUT OF SCHOOL NOW. HE'S ALWAYS COMING UP WITH WEIRD IDEAS ABOUT LIFE AND STUFF... KINDA SPOOKY, Y'KNOW? LIKE, WHAT IF DISNEYLAND DOES SUCK, HUH?
AAH, HE··HE'S JUST MAD 'CAUSE HE WAS TOO FAT TO FIT IN THE RIDES..! HMMM...
AND JUST WHEN HERACLIO WAS WONDERING WHY HE HADN'T SEEN MANUEL FOR A COUPLE OF DAYS...
HEY HERCULES! YOU GONNA SLEEP ALL DAY OR WHAT?
I AIN'T SLEEPING! BE RIGHT OUT!
SO, WHAT'S THE DEAL, MANUEL?
THE DEAL? BESIDES THAT I FINALLY GOT THAT JOB..?
LIFE IS THE DEAL, HERCULES!
¿VIDA
3 TWENTY FIVE
ZUMAYA- ZOO MY' AH

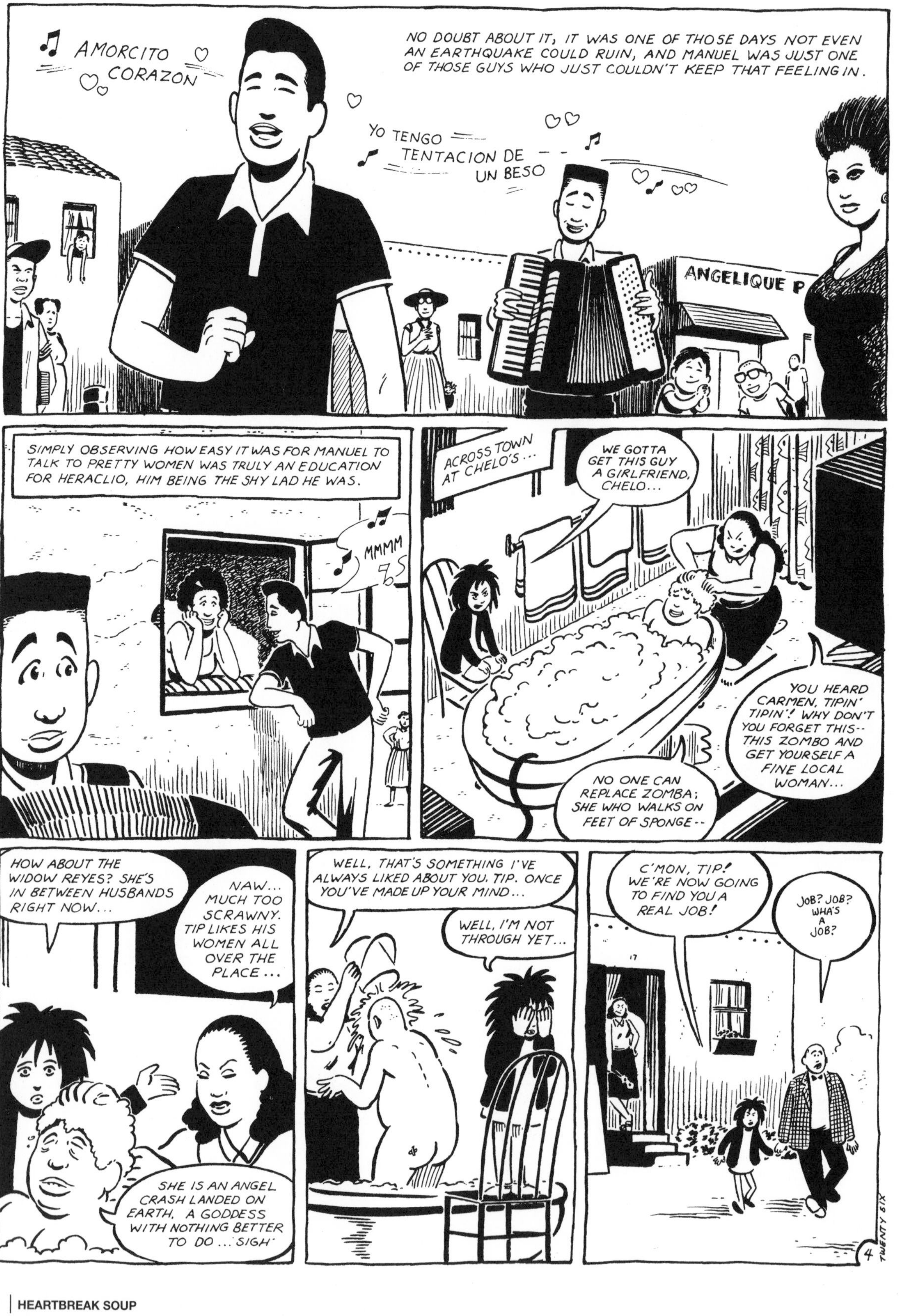
AMORCITO CORAZON
NO DOUBT ABOUT IT, IT WAS ONE OF THOSE DAYS NOT EVEN AN EARTHQUAKE COULD RUIN, AND MANUEL WAS JUST ONE OF THOSE GUYS WHO JUST COULDN'T KEEP THAT FEELING IN.
YO TENGO TENTACION DE UN BESO
ANGELIQUE P
SIMPLY OBSERVING HOW EASY IT WAS FOR MANUEL TO TALK TO PRETTY WOMEN WAS TRULY AN EDUCATION FOR HERACLIO, HIM BEING THE SHY LAD HE WAS.
MMMM
ACROSS TOWN AT CHELO'S...
WE GOTTA GET THIS GUY A GIRLFRIEND, CHELO...
YOU HEARD CARMEN, TIPIN' TIPIN'! WHY DON'T YOU FORGET THIS-- THIS ZOMBO AND GET YOURSELF A FINE LOCAL WOMAN...
NO ONE CAN REPLACE ZOMBA; SHE WHO WALKS ON FEET OF SPONGE--
HOW ABOUT THE WIDOW REYES? SHE'S IN BETWEEN HUSBANDS RIGHT NOW...
NAW... MUCH TOO SCRAWNY. TIP LIKES HIS WOMEN ALL OVER THE PLACE...
SHE IS AN ANGEL CRASH LANDED ON EARTH, A GODDESS WITH NOTHING BETTER TO DO... SIGH
WELL, THAT'S SOMETHING I'VE ALWAYS LIKED ABOUT YOU, TIP. ONCE YOU'VE MADE UP YOUR MIND...
WELL, I'M NOT THROUGH YET...
C'MON, TIP! WE'RE NOW GOING TO FIND YOU A REAL JOB!
JOB? JOB? WHA'S A JOB?
4
TWENTY SIX

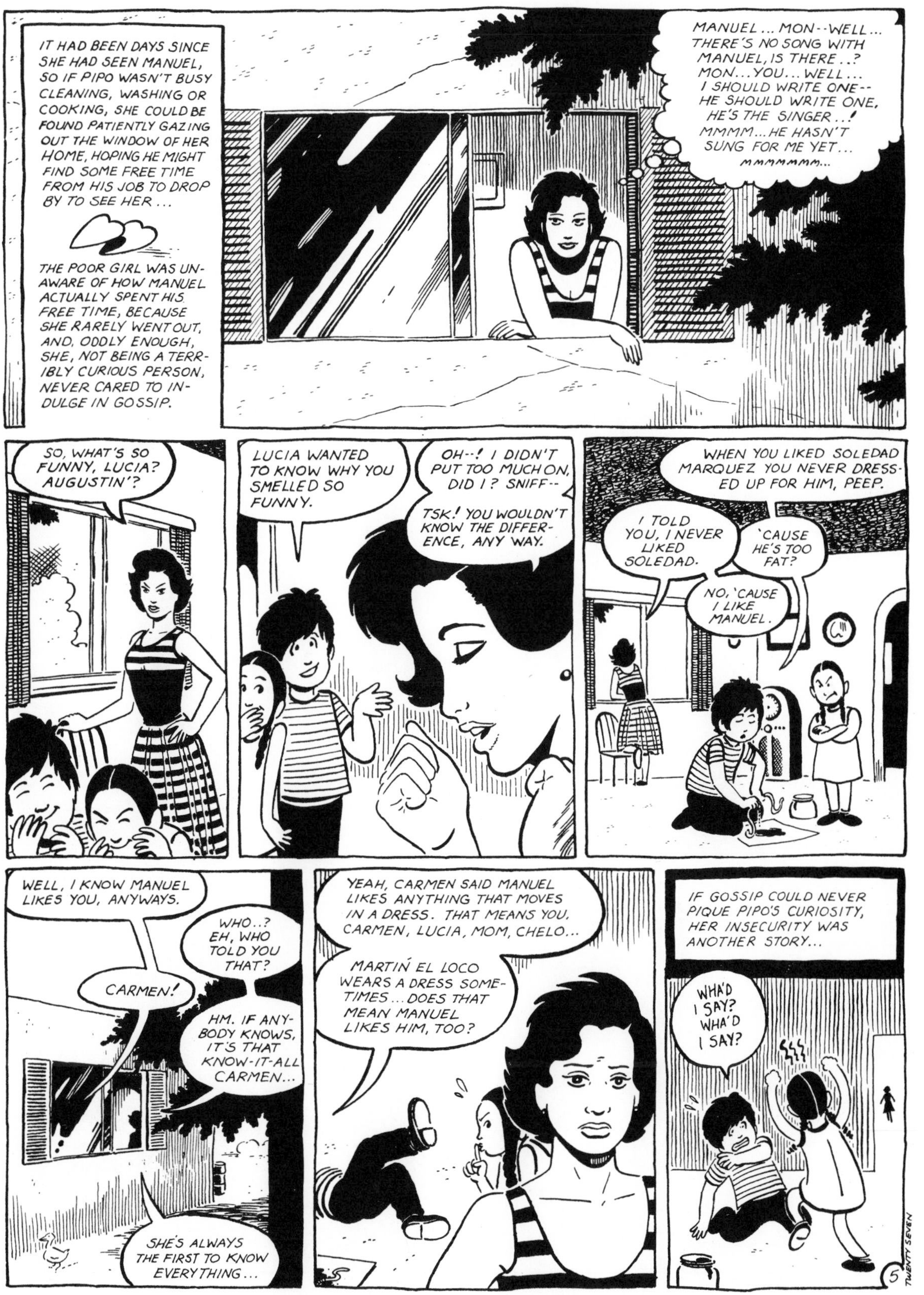
IT HAD BEEN DAYS SINCE SHE HAD SEEN MANUEL, SO IF PIPO WASN'T BUSY CLEANING, WASHING OR COOKING, SHE COULD BE FOUND PATIENTLY GAZING OUT THE WINDOW OF HER HOME, HOPING HE MIGHT FIND SOME FREE TIME FROM HIS JOB TO DROP BY TO SEE HER...
THE POOR GIRL WAS UNAWARE OF HOW MANUEL ACTUALLY SPENT HIS FREE TIME, BECAUSE SHE RARELY WENT OUT, AND, ODDLY ENOUGH, SHE, NOT BEING A TERRIBLY CURIOUS PERSON, NEVER CARED TO INDULGE IN GOSSIP.
MANUEL... MON--WELL... THERE'S NO SONG WITH MANUEL, IS THERE..? MON...YOU...WELL... I SHOULD WRITE ONE-- HE SHOULD WRITE ONE, HE'S THE SINGER..! MMMM...HE HASN'T SUNG FOR ME YET... MMMMMMM...
SO, WHAT'S SO FUNNY, LUCIA? AUGUSTIN'?
LUCIA WANTED TO KNOW WHY YOU SMELLED SO FUNNY.
OH--! I DIDN'T PUT TOO MUCH ON, DID I? SNIFF--
TSK! YOU WOULDN'T KNOW THE DIFFERENCE, ANY WAY.
WHEN YOU LIKED SOLEDAD MARQUEZ YOU NEVER DRESSED UP FOR HIM, PEEP.
I TOLD YOU, I NEVER LIKED SOLEDAD.
'CAUSE HE'S TOO FAT?
NO, 'CAUSE I LIKE MANUEL.
WELL, I KNOW MANUEL LIKES YOU, ANYWAYS.
WHO..? EH, WHO TOLD YOU THAT?
CARMEN!
HM. IF ANYBODY KNOWS, IT'S THAT KNOW-IT-ALL CARMEN...
SHE'S ALWAYS THE FIRST TO KNOW EVERYTHING...
YEAH, CARMEN SAID MANUEL LIKES ANYTHING THAT MOVES IN A DRESS. THAT MEANS YOU, CARMEN, LUCIA, MOM, CHELO...
MARTIN EL LOCO WEARS A DRESS SOMETIMES... DOES THAT MEAN MANUEL LIKES HIM, TOO?
IF GOSSIP COULD NEVER PIQUE PIPO'S CURIOSITY, HER INSECURITY WAS ANOTHER STORY...
WHA'D I SAY? WHA'D I SAY?
5
TWENTY SEVEN

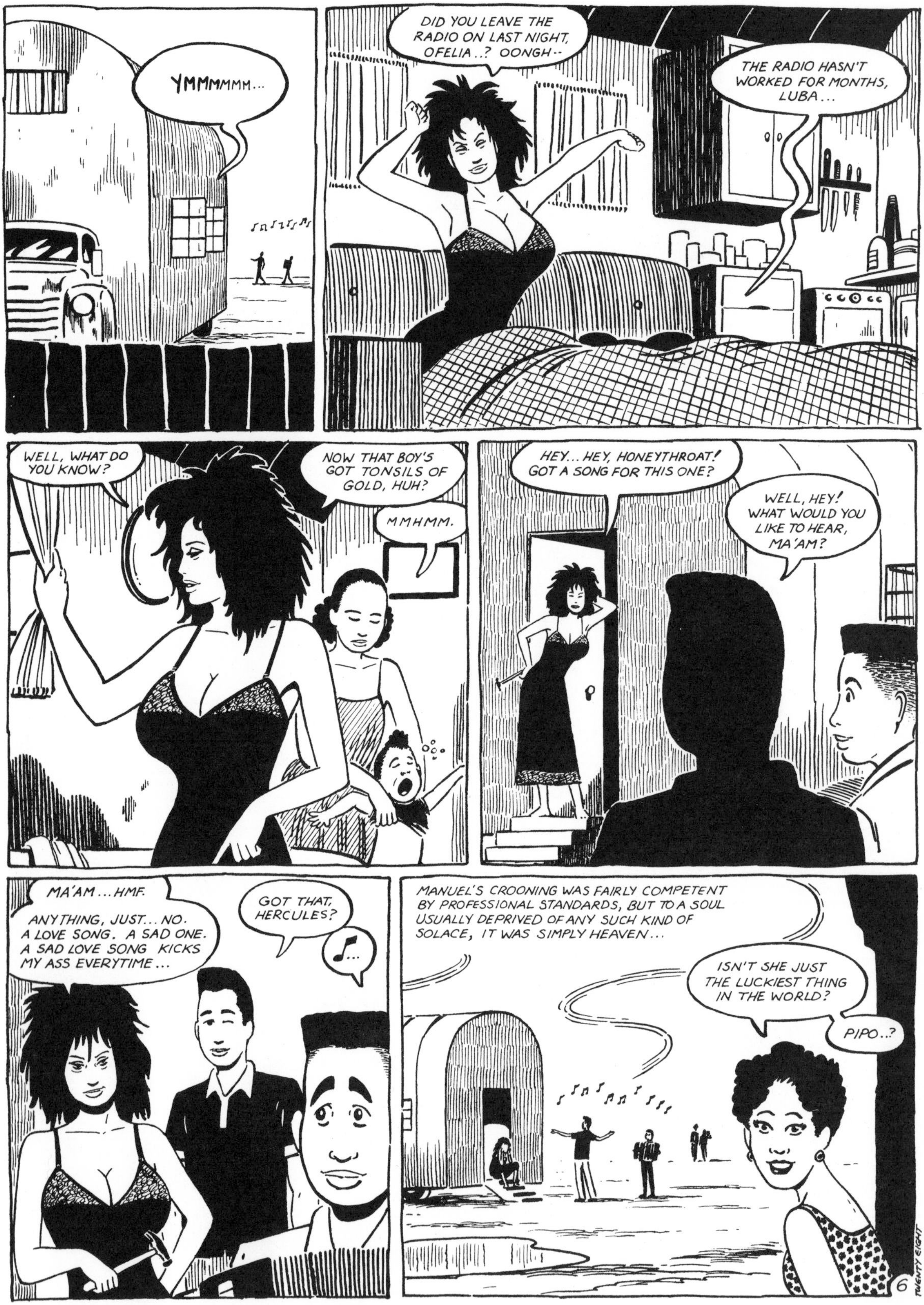
YMMMMMM...
DID YOU LEAVE THE RADIO ON LAST NIGHT, OFELIA..? OONGH--
THE RADIO HASN'T WORKED FOR MONTHS, LUBA...
WELL, WHAT DO YOU KNOW?
NOW THAT BOY'S GOT TONSILS OF GOLD, HUH?
MMHMM.
HEY... HEY, HONEYTHROAT! GOT A SONG FOR THIS ONE?
WELL, HEY! WHAT WOULD YOU LIKE TO HEAR, MA'AM?
MA'AM... HMF.
ANYTHING, JUST... NO. A LOVE SONG. A SAD ONE. A SAD LOVE SONG KICKS MY ASS EVERYTIME...
GOT THAT, HERCULES?
MANUEL'S CROONING WAS FAIRLY COMPETENT BY PROFESSIONAL STANDARDS, BUT TO A SOUL USUALLY DEPRIVED OF ANY SUCH KIND OF SOLACE, IT WAS SIMPLY HEAVEN...
ISN'T SHE JUST THE LUCKIEST THING IN THE WORLD?
PIPO..?
6
TWENTY EIGHT

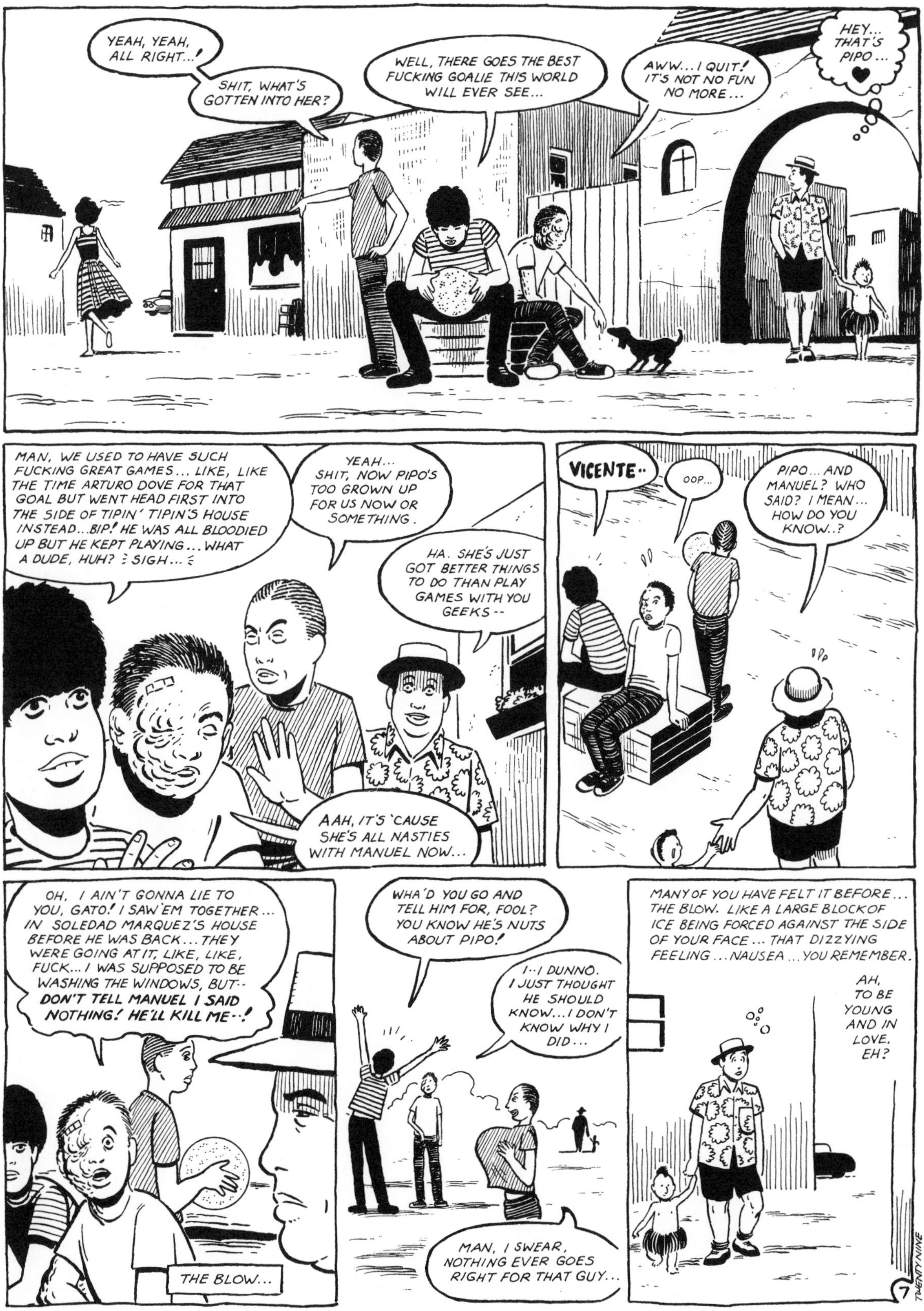
YEAH, YEAH, ALL RIGHT...!
SHIT, WHAT'S GOTTEN INTO HER?
WELL, THERE GOES THE BEST FUCKING GOALIE THIS WORLD WILL EVER SEE...
AWW... I QUIT! IT'S NOT NO FUN NO MORE...
HEY... THAT'S PIPO... ♥
MAN, WE USED TO HAVE SUCH FUCKING GREAT GAMES... LIKE, LIKE THE TIME ARTURO DOVE FOR THAT GOAL BUT WENT HEAD FIRST INTO THE SIDE OF TIPIN' TIPIN'S HOUSE INSTEAD... BIP! HE WAS ALL BLOODIED UP BUT HE KEPT PLAYING... WHAT A DUDE, HUH? SIGH...
YEAH... SHIT, NOW PIPO'S TOO GROWN UP FOR US NOW OR SOMETHING.
HA. SHE'S JUST GOT BETTER THINGS TO DO THAN PLAY GAMES WITH YOU GEEKS--
AAH, IT'S 'CAUSE SHE'S ALL NASTIES WITH MANUEL NOW...
VICENTE..
OOP...
PIPO... AND MANUEL? WHO SAID? I MEAN... HOW DO YOU KNOW..?
OH, I AIN'T GONNA LIE TO YOU, GATO! I SAW'EM TOGETHER... IN SOLEDAD MARQUEZ'S HOUSE BEFORE HE WAS BACK... THEY WERE GOING AT IT, LIKE, LIKE, FUCK... I WAS SUPPOSED TO BE WASHING THE WINDOWS, BUT-- DON'T TELL MANUEL I SAID NOTHING! HE'LL KILL ME--!
THE BLOW...
WHA'D YOU GO AND TELL HIM FOR, FOOL? YOU KNOW HE'S NUTS ABOUT PIPO!
I--I DUNNO. I JUST THOUGHT HE SHOULD KNOW... I DON'T KNOW WHY I DID...
MAN, I SWEAR, NOTHING EVER GOES RIGHT FOR THAT GUY...
MANY OF YOU HAVE FELT IT BEFORE... THE BLOW. LIKE A LARGE BLOCK OF ICE BEING FORCED AGAINST THE SIDE OF YOUR FACE... THAT DIZZYING FEELING... NAUSEA... YOU REMEMBER.
AH, TO BE YOUNG AND IN LOVE, EH?
7 TWENTY NINE

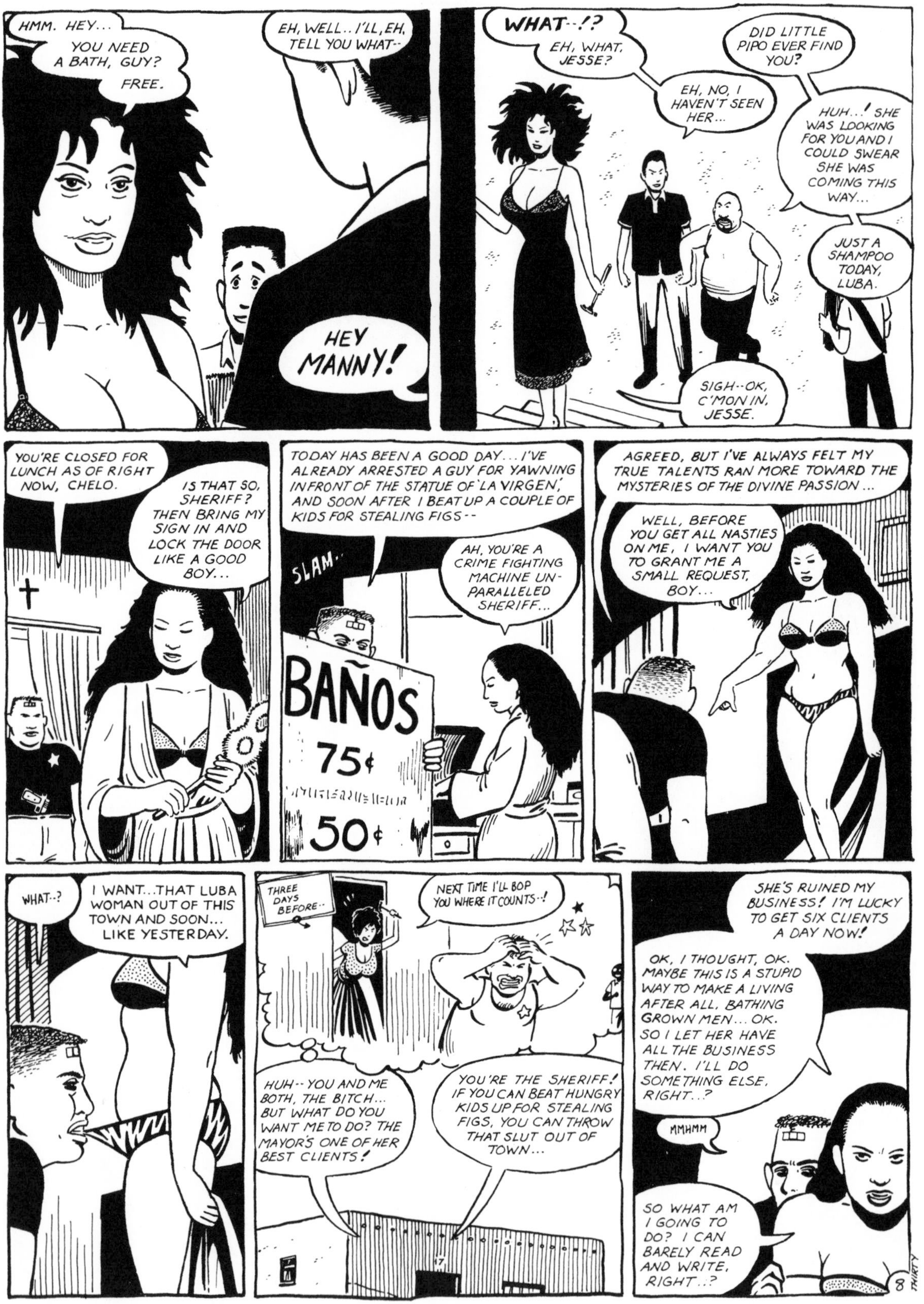
HMM. HEY... YOU NEED A BATH, GUY? FREE.
EH, WELL.. I'LL, EH, TELL YOU WHAT--
HEY MANNY!
WHAT--!?
EH, WHAT, JESSE?
DID LITTLE PIPO EVER FIND YOU?
EH, NO, I HAVEN'T SEEN HER...
HUH...! SHE WAS LOOKING FOR YOU AND I COULD SWEAR SHE WAS COMING THIS WAY...
JUST A SHAMPOO TODAY, LUBA.
SIGH--OK, C'MON IN, JESSE.
YOU'RE CLOSED FOR LUNCH AS OF RIGHT NOW, CHELO.
IS THAT SO, SHERIFF? THEN BRING MY SIGN IN AND LOCK THE DOOR LIKE A GOOD BOY...
TODAY HAS BEEN A GOOD DAY... I'VE ALREADY ARRESTED A GUY FOR YAWNING INFRONT OF THE STATUE OF 'LA VIRGEN,' AND SOON AFTER I BEAT UP A COUPLE OF KIDS FOR STEALING FIGS--
SLAM..
AH, YOU'RE A CRIME FIGHTING MACHINE UNPARALLELED SHERIFF...
BAÑOS
75¢
50¢
AGREED, BUT I'VE ALWAYS FELT MY TRUE TALENTS RAN MORE TOWARD THE MYSTERIES OF THE DIVINE PASSION...
WELL, BEFORE YOU GET ALL NASTIES ON ME, I WANT YOU TO GRANT ME A SMALL REQUEST, BOY...
WHAT--?
I WANT...THAT LUBA WOMAN OUT OF THIS TOWN AND SOON... LIKE YESTERDAY.
THREE DAYS BEFORE--
NEXT TIME I'LL BOP YOU WHERE IT COUNTS--!
HUH--YOU AND ME BOTH, THE BITCH... BUT WHAT DO YOU WANT ME TO DO? THE MAYOR'S ONE OF HER BEST CLIENTS!
YOU'RE THE SHERIFF! IF YOU CAN BEAT HUNGRY KIDS UP FOR STEALING FIGS, YOU CAN THROW THAT SLUT OUT OF TOWN...
SHE'S RUINED MY BUSINESS! I'M LUCKY TO GET SIX CLIENTS A DAY NOW!
OK, I THOUGHT, OK. MAYBE THIS IS A STUPID WAY TO MAKE A LIVING AFTER ALL, BATHING GROWN MEN... OK. SO I LET HER HAVE ALL THE BUSINESS THEN. I'LL DO SOMETHING ELSE, RIGHT..?
MMHMM
SO WHAT AM I GOING TO DO? I CAN BARELY READ AND WRITE, RIGHT..?
8 THIRTY

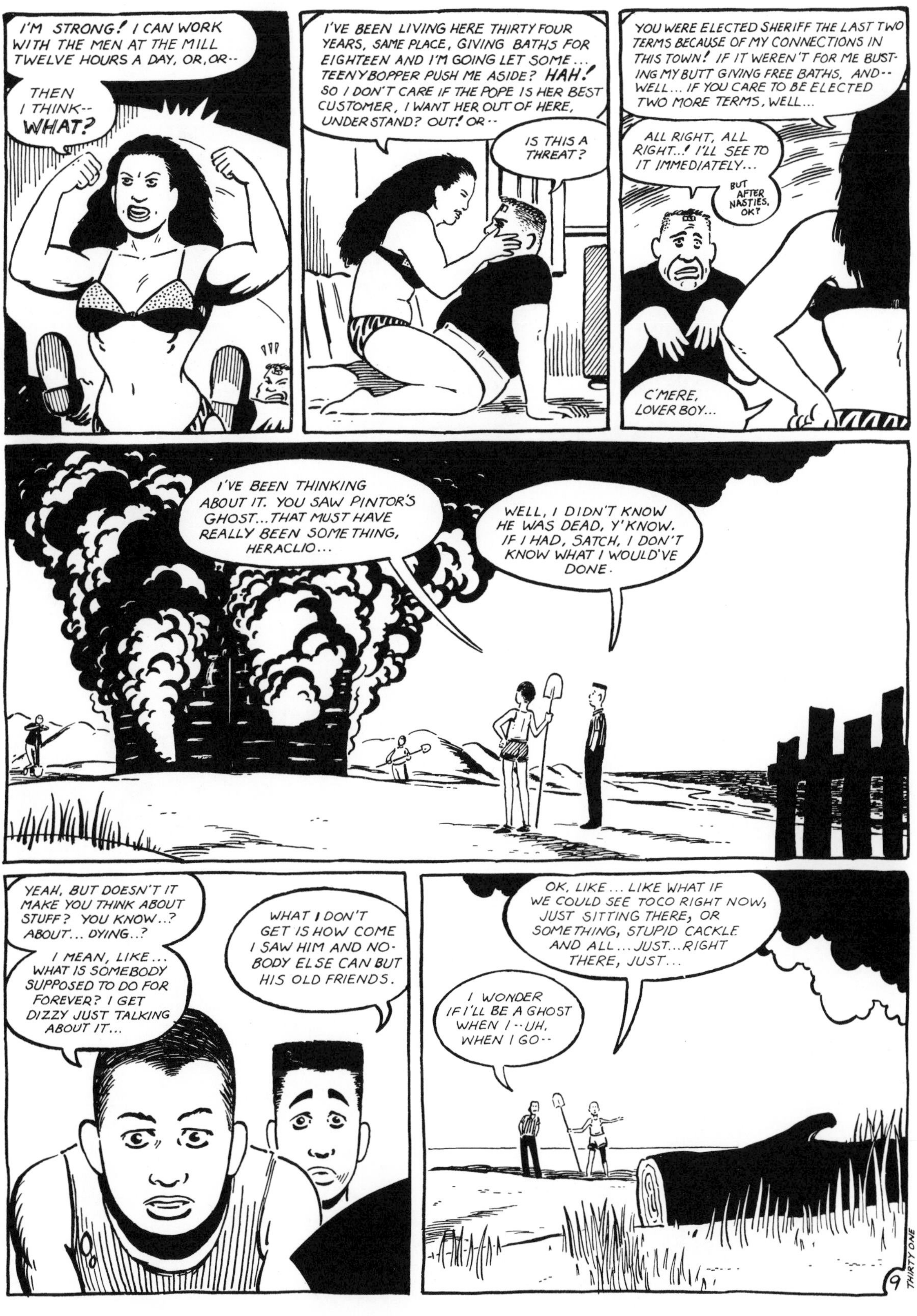
I'M STRONG! I CAN WORK WITH THE MEN AT THE MILL TWELVE HOURS A DAY, OR, OR--
THEN I THINK-- WHAT?
I'VE BEEN LIVING HERE THIRTY FOUR YEARS, SAME PLACE, GIVING BATHS FOR EIGHTEEN AND I'M GOING LET SOME... TEENYBOPPER PUSH ME ASIDE? HAH! SO I DON'T CARE IF THE POPE IS HER BEST CUSTOMER, I WANT HER OUT OF HERE, UNDERSTAND? OUT! OR--
IS THIS A THREAT?
YOU WERE ELECTED SHERIFF THE LAST TWO TERMS BECAUSE OF MY CONNECTIONS IN THIS TOWN! IF IT WEREN'T FOR ME BUSTING MY BUTT GIVING FREE BATHS, AND-- WELL... IF YOU CARE TO BE ELECTED TWO MORE TERMS, WELL...
ALL RIGHT, ALL RIGHT..! I'LL SEE TO IT IMMEDIATELY...
BUT AFTER NASTIES, OK?
C'MERE, LOVER BOY...
I'VE BEEN THINKING ABOUT IT. YOU SAW PINTOR'S GHOST... THAT MUST HAVE REALLY BEEN SOMETHING, HERACLIO...
WELL, I DIDN'T KNOW HE WAS DEAD, Y'KNOW. IF I HAD, SATCH, I DON'T KNOW WHAT I WOULD'VE DONE.
YEAH, BUT DOESN'T IT MAKE YOU THINK ABOUT STUFF? YOU KNOW..? ABOUT... DYING..?
I MEAN, LIKE... WHAT IS SOMEBODY SUPPOSED TO DO FOR FOREVER? I GET DIZZY JUST TALKING ABOUT IT...
WHAT I DON'T GET IS HOW COME I SAW HIM AND NOBODY ELSE CAN BUT HIS OLD FRIENDS.
OK, LIKE... LIKE WHAT IF WE COULD SEE TOCO RIGHT NOW, JUST SITTING THERE, OR SOMETHING, STUPID CACKLE AND ALL... JUST... RIGHT THERE, JUST...
I WONDER IF I'LL BE A GHOST WHEN I --UH, WHEN I GO--
9 THIRTY ONE

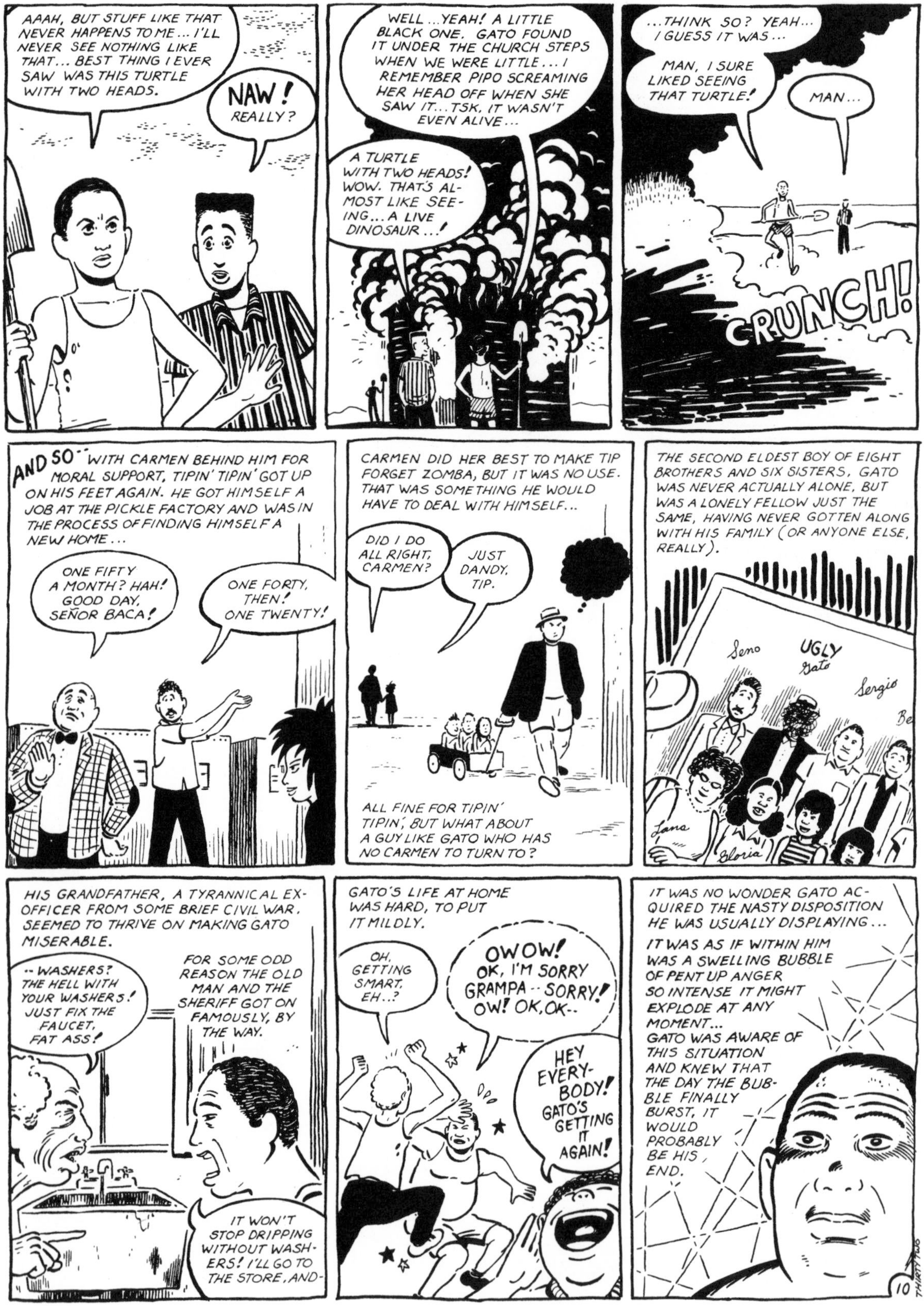
AAAH, BUT STUFF LIKE THAT NEVER HAPPENS TO ME... I'LL NEVER SEE NOTHING LIKE THAT... BEST THING I EVER SAW WAS THIS TURTLE WITH TWO HEADS.
NAW! REALLY?
WELL...YEAH! A LITTLE BLACK ONE. GATO FOUND IT UNDER THE CHURCH STEPS WHEN WE WERE LITTLE... I REMEMBER PIPO SCREAMING HER HEAD OFF WHEN SHE SAW IT... TSK, IT WASN'T EVEN ALIVE...
A TURTLE WITH TWO HEADS! WOW. THAT'S ALMOST LIKE SEEING... A LIVE DINOSAUR...!
...THINK SO? YEAH... I GUESS IT WAS...
MAN, I SURE LIKED SEEING THAT TURTLE!
MAN...
CRUNCH!
AND SO-- WITH CARMEN BEHIND HIM FOR MORAL SUPPORT, TIPIN' TIPIN' GOT UP ON HIS FEET AGAIN. HE GOT HIMSELF A JOB AT THE PICKLE FACTORY AND WAS IN THE PROCESS OF FINDING HIMSELF A NEW HOME...
ONE FIFTY A MONTH? HAH! GOOD DAY, SEÑOR BACA!
ONE FORTY, THEN! ONE TWENTY!
CARMEN DID HER BEST TO MAKE TIP FORGET ZOMBA, BUT IT WAS NO USE. THAT WAS SOMETHING HE WOULD HAVE TO DEAL WITH HIMSELF...
DID I DO ALL RIGHT, CARMEN?
JUST DANDY, TIP.
ALL FINE FOR TIPIN' TIPIN', BUT WHAT ABOUT A GUY LIKE GATO WHO HAS NO CARMEN TO TURN TO?
THE SECOND ELDEST BOY OF EIGHT BROTHERS AND SIX SISTERS, GATO WAS NEVER ACTUALLY ALONE, BUT WAS A LONELY FELLOW JUST THE SAME, HAVING NEVER GOTTEN ALONG WITH HIS FAMILY (OR ANYONE ELSE, REALLY).
Seno
UGLY Gato
Sergio
Lana
Gloria
HIS GRANDFATHER, A TYRANNICAL EX-OFFICER FROM SOME BRIEF CIVIL WAR, SEEMED TO THRIVE ON MAKING GATO MISERABLE.
--WASHERS? THE HELL WITH YOUR WASHERS! JUST FIX THE FAUCET, FAT ASS!
FOR SOME ODD REASON THE OLD MAN AND THE SHERIFF GOT ON FAMOUSLY, BY THE WAY.
IT WON'T STOP DRIPPING WITHOUT WASHERS! I'LL GO TO THE STORE, AND-
GATO'S LIFE AT HOME WAS HARD, TO PUT IT MILDLY.
OH, GETTING SMART, EH..?
OWOW! OK, I'M SORRY GRAMPA--SORRY! OW! OK, OK--
HEY EVERYBODY! GATO'S GETTING IT AGAIN!
IT WAS NO WONDER GATO ACQUIRED THE NASTY DISPOSITION HE WAS USUALLY DISPLAYING...
IT WAS AS IF WITHIN HIM WAS A SWELLING BUBBLE OF PENT UP ANGER SO INTENSE IT MIGHT EXPLODE AT ANY MOMENT...
GATO WAS AWARE OF THIS SITUATION AND KNEW THAT THE DAY THE BUBBLE FINALLY BURST, IT WOULD PROBABLY BE HIS END.
10

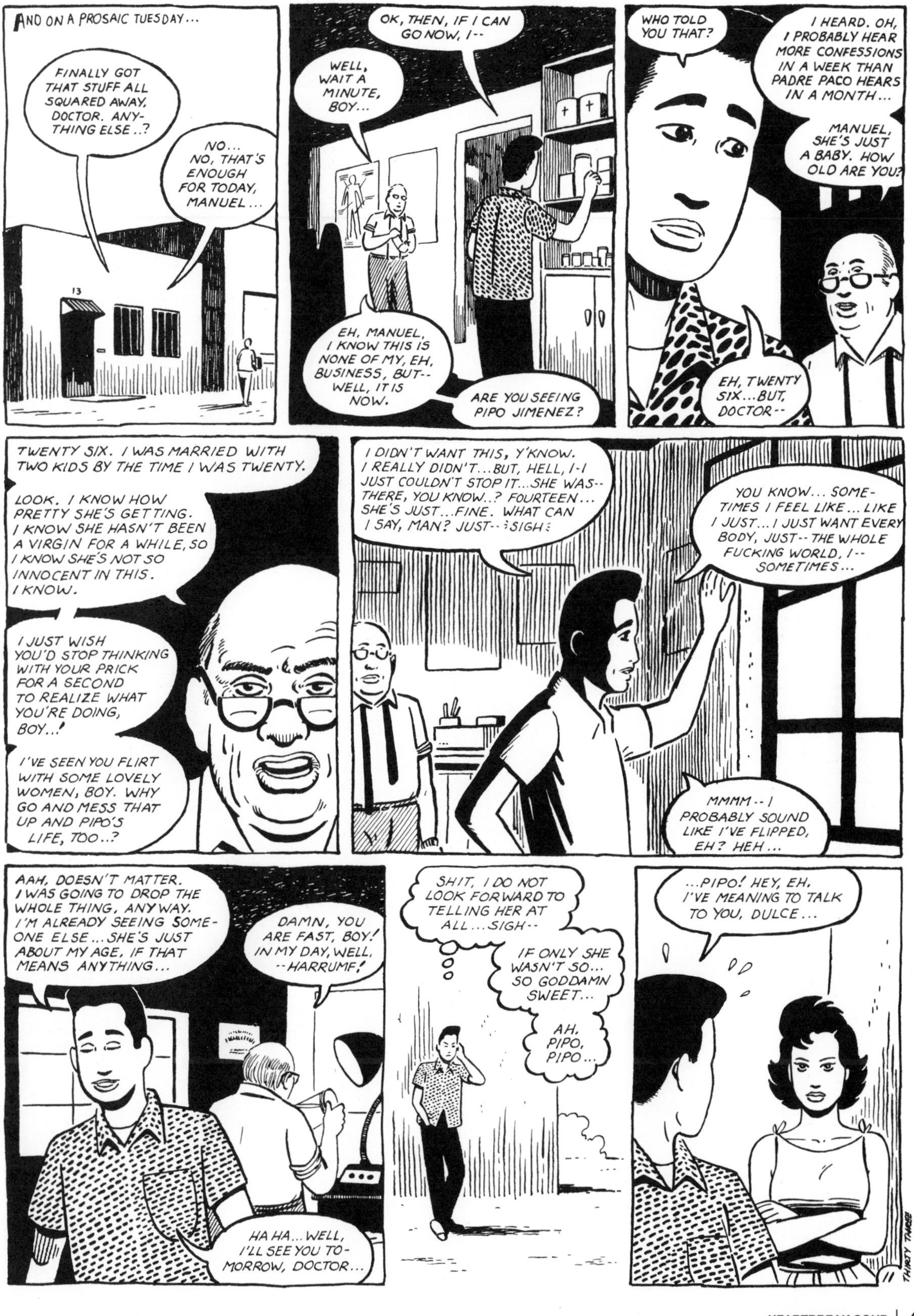
AND ON A PROSAIC TUESDAY...
FINALLY GOT THAT STUFF ALL SQUARED AWAY, DOCTOR. ANYTHING ELSE..?
NO... NO, THAT'S ENOUGH FOR TODAY, MANUEL...
13
OK, THEN, IF I CAN GO NOW, I--
WELL, WAIT A MINUTE, BOY...
EH, MANUEL, I KNOW THIS IS NONE OF MY, EH, BUSINESS, BUT-- WELL, IT IS NOW.
ARE YOU SEEING PIPO JIMENEZ?
WHO TOLD YOU THAT?
I HEARD. OH, I PROBABLY HEAR MORE CONFESSIONS IN A WEEK THAN PADRE PACO HEARS IN A MONTH...
MANUEL, SHE'S JUST A BABY. HOW OLD ARE YOU?
EH, TWENTY SIX...BUT, DOCTOR--
TWENTY SIX. I WAS MARRIED WITH TWO KIDS BY THE TIME I WAS TWENTY.
LOOK. I KNOW HOW PRETTY SHE'S GETTING. I KNOW SHE HASN'T BEEN A VIRGIN FOR A WHILE, SO I KNOW SHE'S NOT SO INNOCENT IN THIS. I KNOW.
I JUST WISH YOU'D STOP THINKING WITH YOUR PRICK FOR A SECOND TO REALIZE WHAT YOU'RE DOING, BOY...!
I'VE SEEN YOU FLIRT WITH SOME LOVELY WOMEN, BOY. WHY GO AND MESS THAT UP AND PIPO'S LIFE, TOO..?
I DIDN'T WANT THIS, Y'KNOW. I REALLY DIDN'T...BUT, HELL, I-I JUST COULDN'T STOP IT...SHE WAS-- THERE, YOU KNOW..? FOURTEEN... SHE'S JUST...FINE. WHAT CAN I SAY, MAN? JUST-- ≡SIGH≡
YOU KNOW... SOMETIMES I FEEL LIKE... LIKE I JUST... I JUST WANT EVERY BODY, JUST-- THE WHOLE FUCKING WORLD, I-- SOMETIMES...
MMMM-- I PROBABLY SOUND LIKE I'VE FLIPPED, EH? HEH...
AAH, DOESN'T MATTER. I WAS GOING TO DROP THE WHOLE THING, ANYWAY. I'M ALREADY SEEING SOMEONE ELSE...SHE'S JUST ABOUT MY AGE, IF THAT MEANS ANYTHING...
DAMN, YOU ARE FAST, BOY! IN MY DAY, WELL, --HARRUMF!
HA HA...WELL, I'LL SEE YOU TOMORROW, DOCTOR...
SHIT, I DO NOT LOOK FORWARD TO TELLING HER AT ALL...SIGH--
IF ONLY SHE WASN'T SO... SO GODDAMN SWEET...
AH, PIPO, PIPO...
...PIPO! HEY, EH. I'VE MEANING TO TALK TO YOU, DULCE...
THIRTY THREE

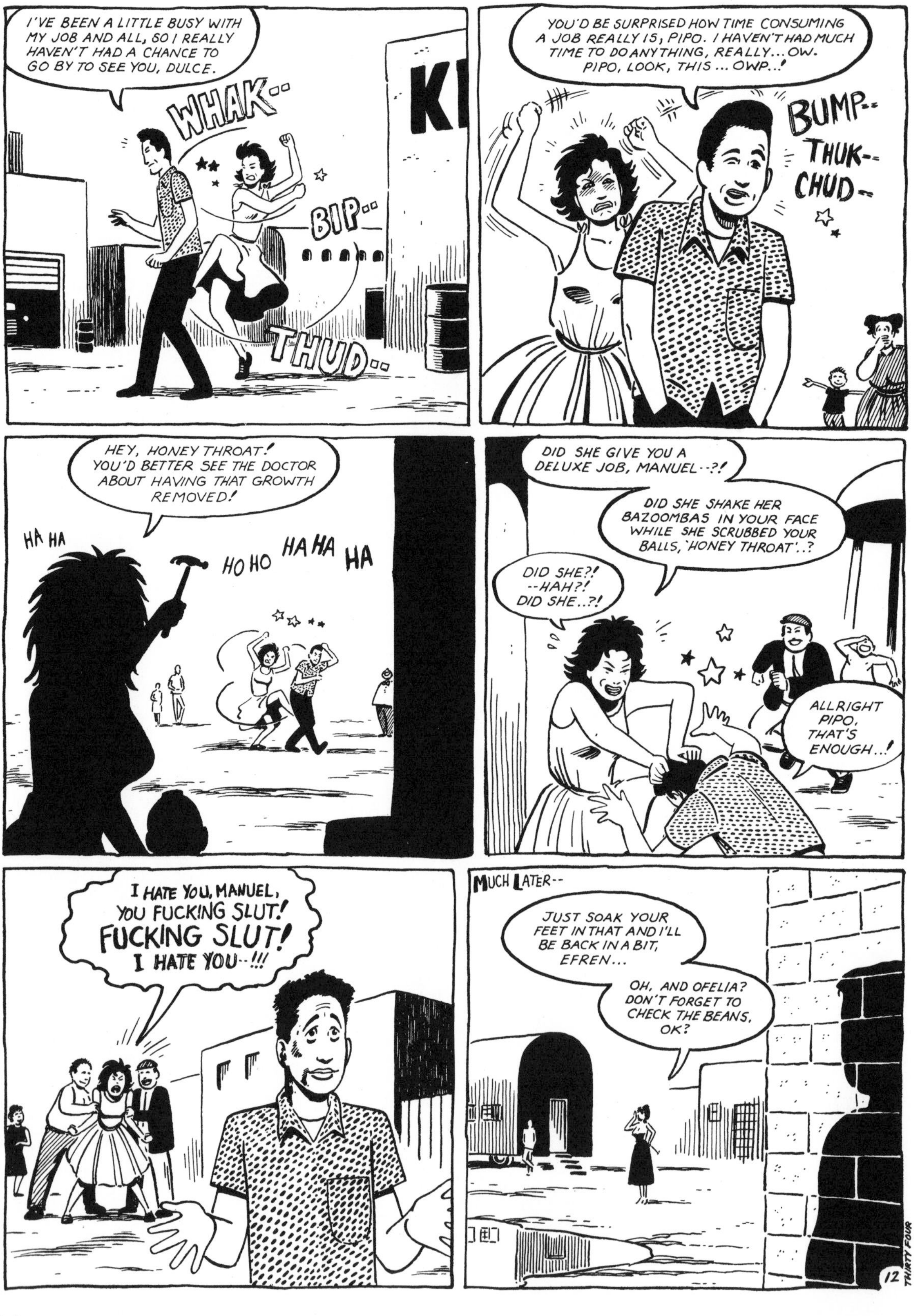

I'VE BEEN A LITTLE BUSY WITH MY JOB AND ALL, SO I REALLY HAVEN'T HAD A CHANCE TO GO BY TO SEE YOU, DULCE.
WHAK--
BIP--
THUD--
YOU'D BE SURPRISED HOW TIME CONSUMING A JOB REALLY IS, PIPO. I HAVEN'T HAD MUCH TIME TO DO ANYTHING, REALLY... OW. PIPO, LOOK, THIS ... OWP..!
BUMP--
THUK--
CHUD--
HEY, HONEY THROAT! YOU'D BETTER SEE THE DOCTOR ABOUT HAVING THAT GROWTH REMOVED!
HA HA
HO HO
HA HA
HA
DID SHE GIVE YOU A DELUXE JOB, MANUEL--?!
DID SHE SHAKE HER BAZOOMBAS IN YOUR FACE WHILE SHE SCRUBBED YOUR BALLS, 'HONEY THROAT'..?
DID SHE?! --HAH?! DID SHE..?!
ALLRIGHT PIPO, THAT'S ENOUGH..!
I HATE YOU, MANUEL, YOU FUCKING SLUT! FUCKING SLUT! I HATE YOU--!!!
MUCH LATER--
JUST SOAK YOUR FEET IN THAT AND I'LL BE BACK IN A BIT, EFREN...
OH, AND OFELIA? DON'T FORGET TO CHECK THE BEANS, OK?
THIRTY FOUR
12

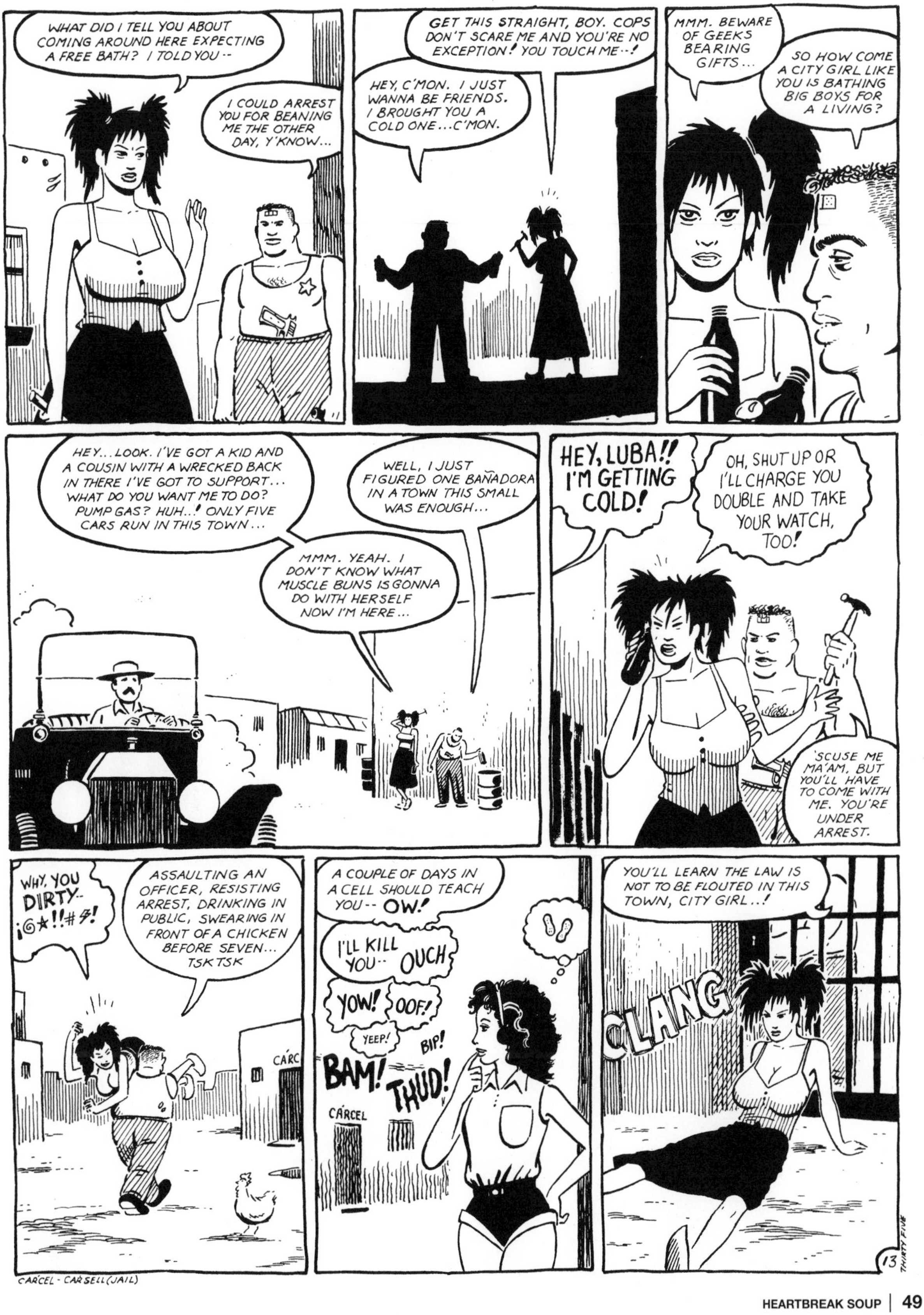
WHAT DID I TELL YOU ABOUT COMING AROUND HERE EXPECTING A FREE BATH? I TOLD YOU --
I COULD ARREST YOU FOR BEANING ME THE OTHER DAY, Y'KNOW...
GET THIS STRAIGHT, BOY. COPS DON'T SCARE ME AND YOU'RE NO EXCEPTION! YOU TOUCH ME --!
HEY, C'MON. I JUST WANNA BE FRIENDS. I BROUGHT YOU A COLD ONE... C'MON.
MMM. BEWARE OF GEEKS BEARING GIFTS...
SO HOW COME A CITY GIRL LIKE YOU IS BATHING BIG BOYS FOR A LIVING?
HEY... LOOK. I'VE GOT A KID AND A COUSIN WITH A WRECKED BACK IN THERE I'VE GOT TO SUPPORT... WHAT DO YOU WANT ME TO DO? PUMP GAS? HUH..! ONLY FIVE CARS RUN IN THIS TOWN...
WELL, I JUST FIGURED ONE BAÑADORA IN A TOWN THIS SMALL WAS ENOUGH...
MMM. YEAH. I DON'T KNOW WHAT MUSCLE BUNS IS GONNA DO WITH HERSELF NOW I'M HERE...
HEY, LUBA!! I'M GETTING COLD!
OH, SHUT UP OR I'LL CHARGE YOU DOUBLE AND TAKE YOUR WATCH, TOO!
'SCUSE ME MA'AM, BUT YOU'LL HAVE TO COME WITH ME. YOU'RE UNDER ARREST.
WHY, YOU DIRTY-- ¡@★!!#%!
ASSAULTING AN OFFICER, RESISTING ARREST, DRINKING IN PUBLIC, SWEARING IN FRONT OF A CHICKEN BEFORE SEVEN... TSK TSK
CÁRC
A COUPLE OF DAYS IN A CELL SHOULD TEACH YOU -- OW!
I'LL KILL YOU -- OUCH
YOW! OOF!
YEEP!
BIP!
BAM!
THUD!
CÁRCEL
YOU'LL LEARN THE LAW IS NOT TO BE FLOUTED IN THIS TOWN, CITY GIRL..!
CLANG
13
THIRTY FIVE
CÁRCEL - CARSELL (JAIL)

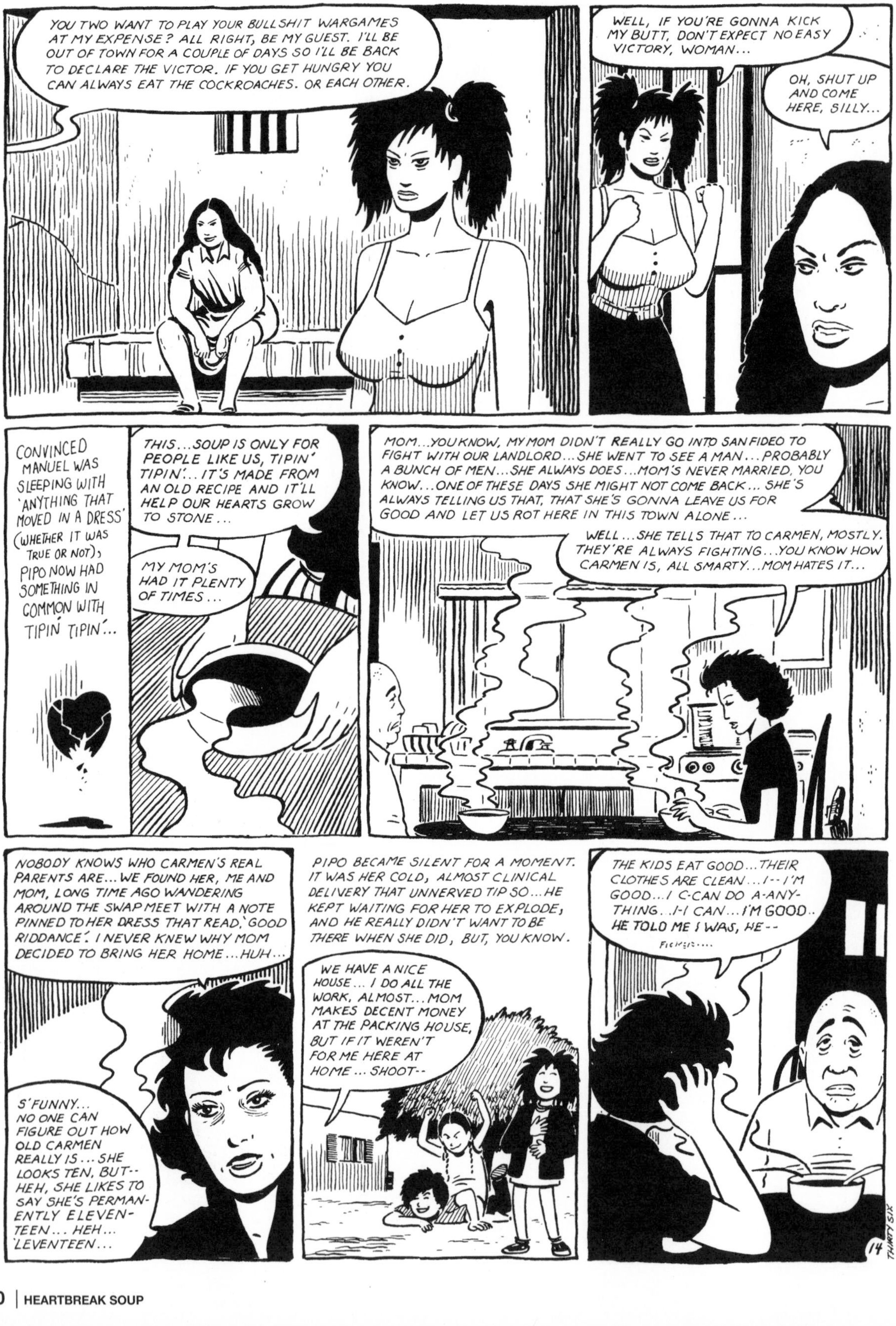

YOU TWO WANT TO PLAY YOUR BULLSHIT WARGAMES AT MY EXPENSE? ALL RIGHT, BE MY GUEST. I'LL BE OUT OF TOWN FOR A COUPLE OF DAYS SO I'LL BE BACK TO DECLARE THE VICTOR. IF YOU GET HUNGRY YOU CAN ALWAYS EAT THE COCKROACHES. OR EACH OTHER.
WELL, IF YOU'RE GONNA KICK MY BUTT, DON'T EXPECT NO EASY VICTORY, WOMAN...
OH, SHUT UP AND COME HERE, SILLY...
CONVINCED MANUEL WAS SLEEPING WITH 'ANYTHING THAT MOVED IN A DRESS' (WHETHER IT WAS TRUE OR NOT), PIPO NOW HAD SOMETHING IN COMMON WITH TIPIN' TIPIN'...
THIS... SOUP IS ONLY FOR PEOPLE LIKE US, TIPIN' TIPIN'... IT'S MADE FROM AN OLD RECIPE AND IT'LL HELP OUR HEARTS GROW TO STONE...
MY MOM'S HAD IT PLENTY OF TIMES...
MOM... YOU KNOW, MY MOM DIDN'T REALLY GO INTO SAN FIDEO TO FIGHT WITH OUR LANDLORD... SHE WENT TO SEE A MAN... PROBABLY A BUNCH OF MEN... SHE ALWAYS DOES... MOM'S NEVER MARRIED, YOU KNOW... ONE OF THESE DAYS SHE MIGHT NOT COME BACK... SHE'S ALWAYS TELLING US THAT, THAT SHE'S GONNA LEAVE US FOR GOOD AND LET US ROT HERE IN THIS TOWN ALONE...
WELL... SHE TELLS THAT TO CARMEN, MOSTLY. THEY'RE ALWAYS FIGHTING... YOU KNOW HOW CARMEN IS, ALL SMARTY... MOM HATES IT...
NOBODY KNOWS WHO CARMEN'S REAL PARENTS ARE... WE FOUND HER, ME AND MOM, LONG TIME AGO WANDERING AROUND THE SWAP MEET WITH A NOTE PINNED TO HER DRESS THAT READ, 'GOOD RIDDANCE'. I NEVER KNEW WHY MOM DECIDED TO BRING HER HOME... HUH...
S'FUNNY... NO ONE CAN FIGURE OUT HOW OLD CARMEN REALLY IS... SHE LOOKS TEN, BUT-- HEH, SHE LIKES TO SAY SHE'S PERMANENTLY ELEVENTEEN... HEH... 'LEVENTEEN...
PIPO BECAME SILENT FOR A MOMENT. IT WAS HER COLD, ALMOST CLINICAL DELIVERY THAT UNNERVED TIP SO... HE KEPT WAITING FOR HER TO EXPLODE, AND HE REALLY DIDN'T WANT TO BE THERE WHEN SHE DID, BUT, YOU KNOW.
WE HAVE A NICE HOUSE... I DO ALL THE WORK, ALMOST... MOM MAKES DECENT MONEY AT THE PACKING HOUSE, BUT IF IT WEREN'T FOR ME HERE AT HOME... SHOOT--
THE KIDS EAT GOOD... THEIR CLOTHES ARE CLEAN... I-- I'M GOOD... I C-CAN DO A-ANYTHING... I-I CAN... I'M GOOD.. HE TOLD ME I WAS, HE--
14
THIRTY SIX

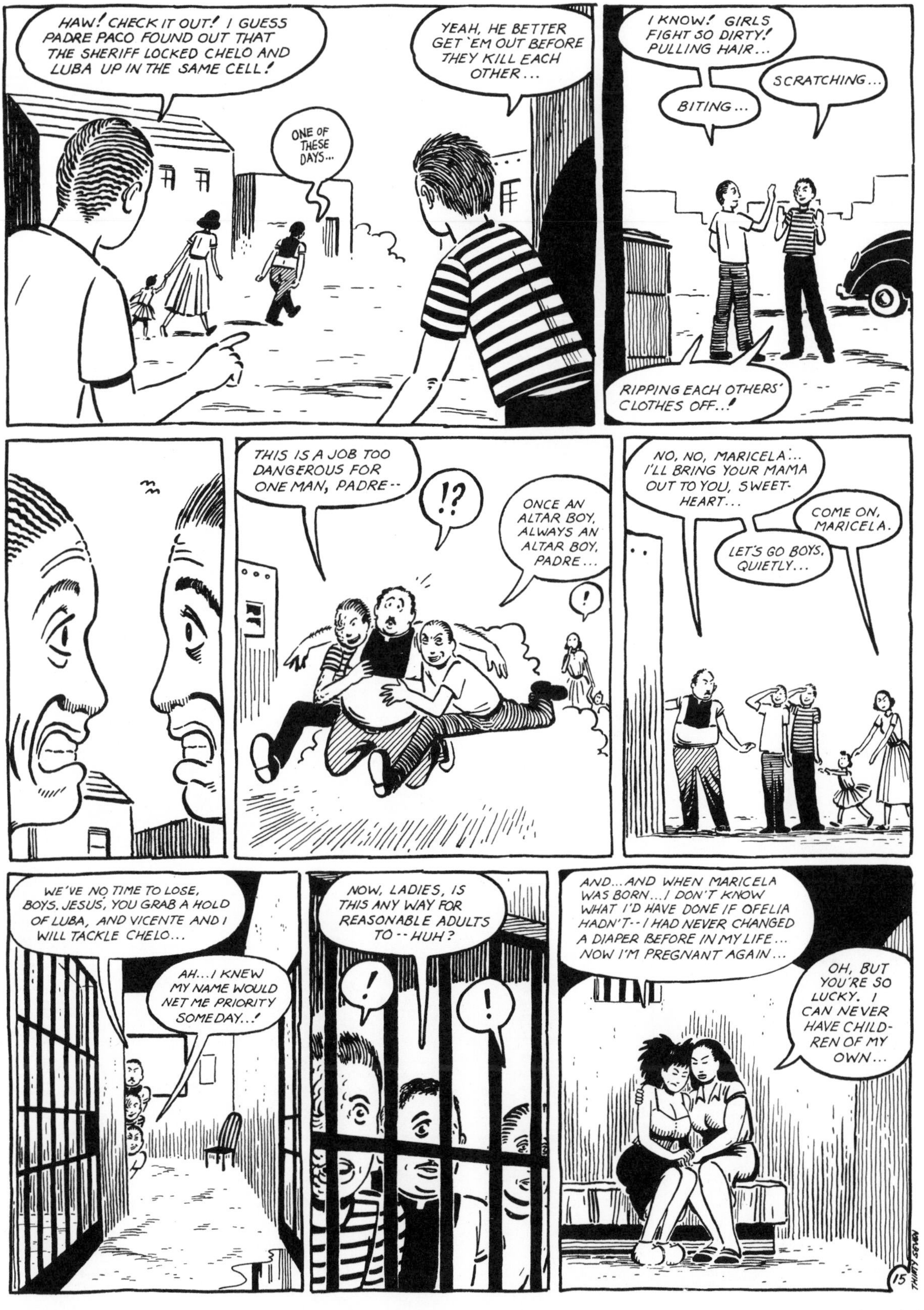
HAW! CHECK IT OUT! I GUESS PADRE PACO FOUND OUT THAT THE SHERIFF LOCKED CHELO AND LUBA UP IN THE SAME CELL!
ONE OF THESE DAYS...
YEAH, HE BETTER GET 'EM OUT BEFORE THEY KILL EACH OTHER...
I KNOW! GIRLS FIGHT SO DIRTY! PULLING HAIR...
BITING...
SCRATCHING...
RIPPING EACH OTHERS' CLOTHES OFF...!
THIS IS A JOB TOO DANGEROUS FOR ONE MAN, PADRE--
!?
ONCE AN ALTAR BOY, ALWAYS AN ALTAR BOY, PADRE...
!
NO, NO, MARICELA... I'LL BRING YOUR MAMA OUT TO YOU, SWEET-HEART...
LET'S GO BOYS, QUIETLY...
COME ON, MARICELA.
WE'VE NO TIME TO LOSE, BOYS. JESUS, YOU GRAB A HOLD OF LUBA, AND VICENTE AND I WILL TACKLE CHELO...
AH...I KNEW MY NAME WOULD NET ME PRIORITY SOMEDAY...!
NOW, LADIES, IS THIS ANY WAY FOR REASONABLE ADULTS TO -- HUH?
!
!
AND...AND WHEN MARICELA WAS BORN...I DON'T KNOW WHAT I'D HAVE DONE IF OFELIA HADN'T--I HAD NEVER CHANGED A DIAPER BEFORE IN MY LIFE... NOW I'M PREGNANT AGAIN...
OH, BUT YOU'RE SO LUCKY. I CAN NEVER HAVE CHILD-REN OF MY OWN...
15
THIRTY SEVEN

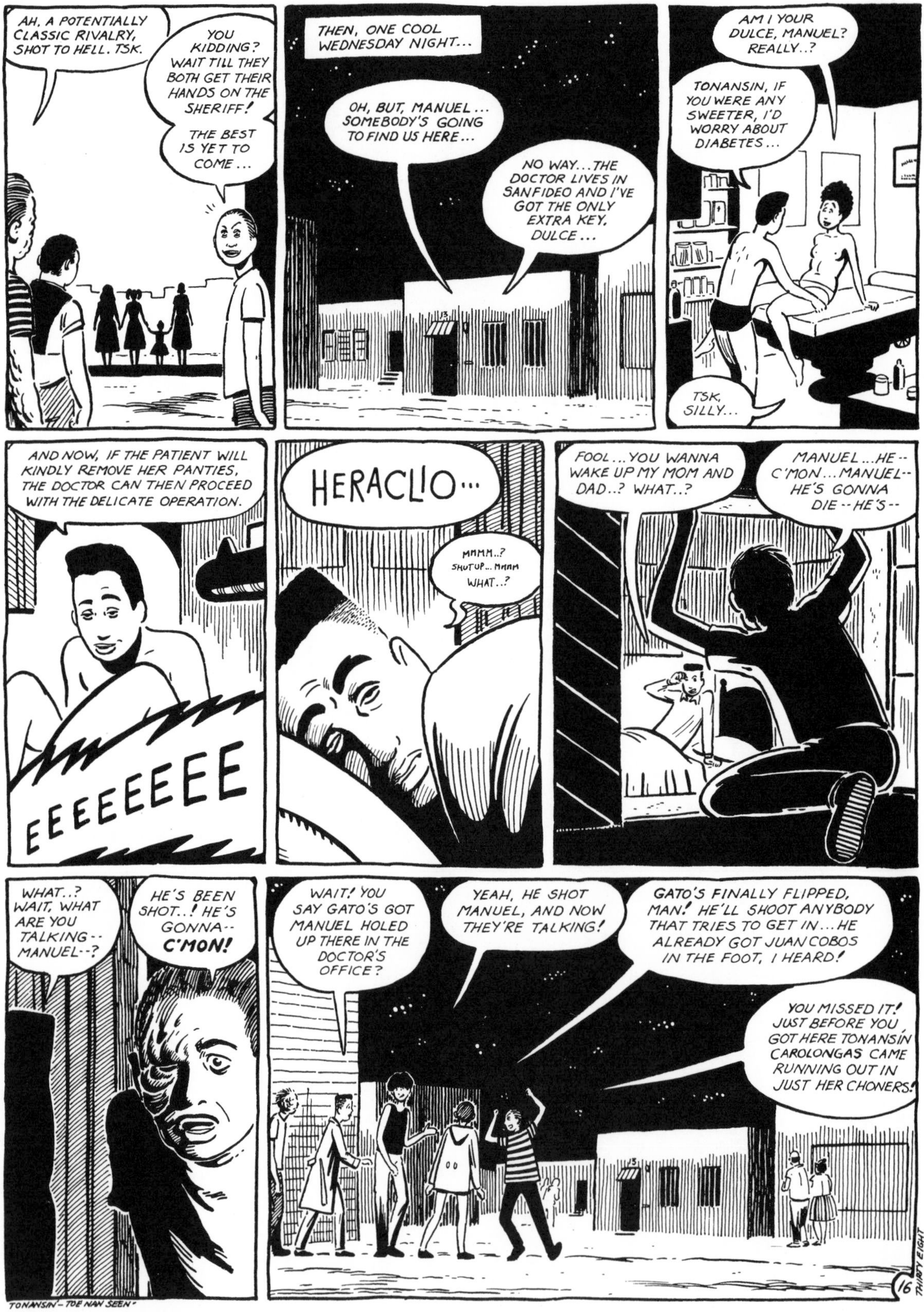
AH, A POTENTIALLY CLASSIC RIVALRY, SHOT TO HELL. TSK.
YOU KIDDING? WAIT TILL THEY BOTH GET THEIR HANDS ON THE SHERIFF!
THE BEST IS YET TO COME...
THEN, ONE COOL WEDNESDAY NIGHT...
OH, BUT, MANUEL... SOMEBODY'S GOING TO FIND US HERE...
NO WAY... THE DOCTOR LIVES IN SANFIDEO AND I'VE GOT THE ONLY EXTRA KEY, DULCE...
AM I YOUR DULCE, MANUEL? REALLY..?
TONANSIN, IF YOU WERE ANY SWEETER, I'D WORRY ABOUT DIABETES...
TSK. SILLY...
AND NOW, IF THE PATIENT WILL KINDLY REMOVE HER PANTIES, THE DOCTOR CAN THEN PROCEED WITH THE DELICATE OPERATION.
EEEEEEEE
HERACLIO...
MMMM..? SHUT UP... MMMM WHAT..?
FOOL... YOU WANNA WAKE UP MY MOM AND DAD..? WHAT..?
MANUEL... HE -- C'MON... MANUEL-- HE'S GONNA DIE -- HE'S --
WHAT..? WAIT, WHAT ARE YOU TALKING -- MANUEL--?
HE'S BEEN SHOT..! HE'S GONNA-- C'MON!
WAIT! YOU SAY GATO'S GOT MANUEL HOLED UP THERE IN THE DOCTOR'S OFFICE?
YEAH, HE SHOT MANUEL, AND NOW THEY'RE TALKING!
GATO'S FINALLY FLIPPED, MAN! HE'LL SHOOT ANYBODY THAT TRIES TO GET IN... HE ALREADY GOT JUAN COBOS IN THE FOOT, I HEARD!
YOU MISSED IT! JUST BEFORE YOU GOT HERE TONANSIN CAROLONGAS CAME RUNNING OUT IN JUST HER CHONERS!
16 THIRTY EIGHT

TONANSIN – TOE NAN SEEN

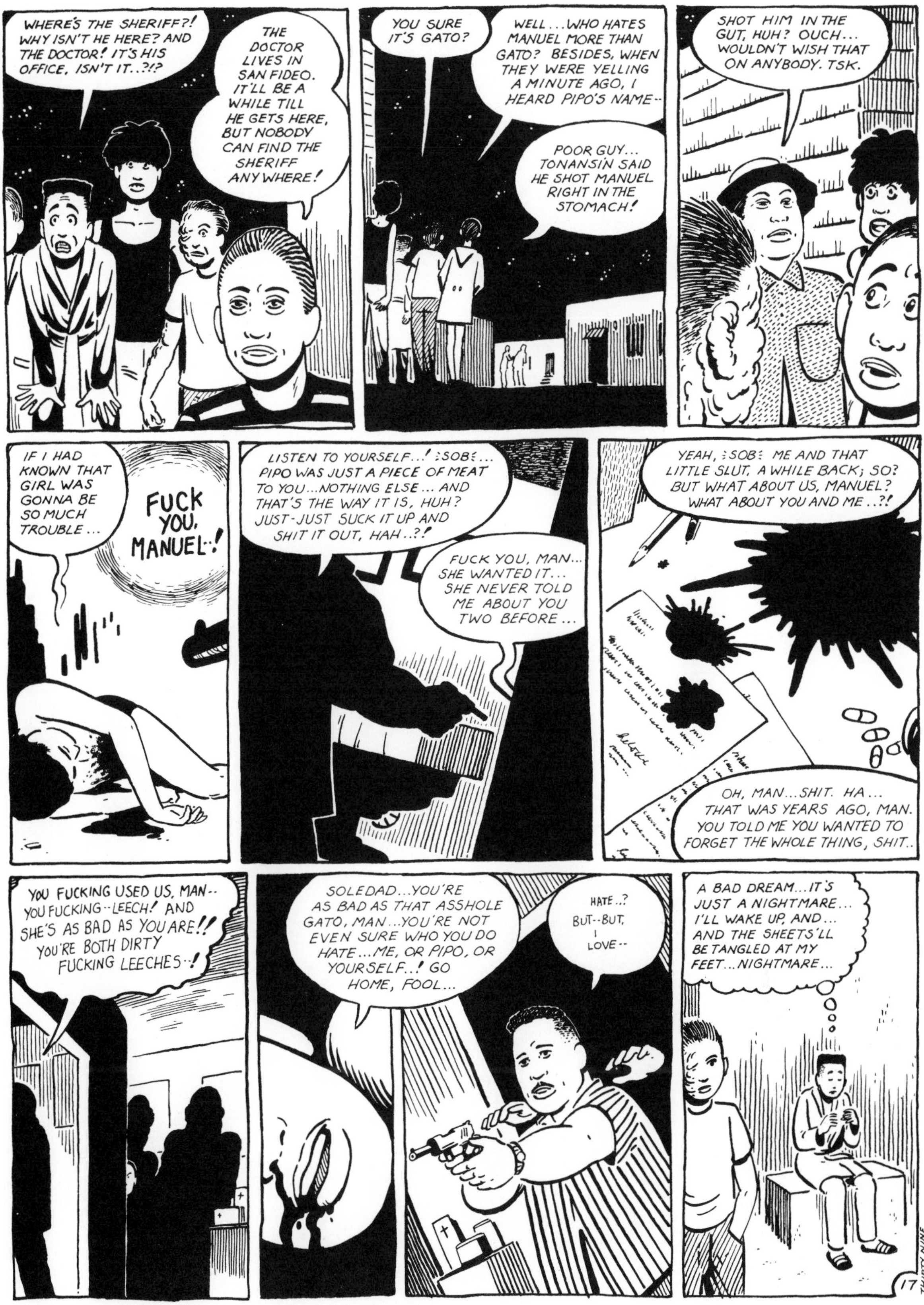
WHERE'S THE SHERIFF?! WHY ISN'T HE HERE? AND THE DOCTOR! IT'S HIS OFFICE, ISN'T IT..?!?
THE DOCTOR LIVES IN SAN FIDEO. IT'LL BE A WHILE TILL HE GETS HERE, BUT NOBODY CAN FIND THE SHERIFF ANYWHERE!
YOU SURE IT'S GATO?
WELL... WHO HATES MANUEL MORE THAN GATO? BESIDES, WHEN THEY WERE YELLING A MINUTE AGO, I HEARD PIPO'S NAME--
POOR GUY... TONANSÍN SAID HE SHOT MANUEL RIGHT IN THE STOMACH!
SHOT HIM IN THE GUT, HUH? OUCH... WOULDN'T WISH THAT ON ANYBODY. TSK.
IF I HAD KNOWN THAT GIRL WAS GONNA BE SO MUCH TROUBLE...
FUCK YOU, MANUEL..!
LISTEN TO YOURSELF...! :SOB:... PIPO WAS JUST A PIECE OF MEAT TO YOU... NOTHING ELSE... AND THAT'S THE WAY IT IS, HUH? JUST-JUST SUCK IT UP AND SHIT IT OUT, HAH..?!
FUCK YOU, MAN... SHE WANTED IT... SHE NEVER TOLD ME ABOUT YOU TWO BEFORE...
YEAH, :SOB: ME AND THAT LITTLE SLUT, A WHILE BACK; SO? BUT WHAT ABOUT US, MANUEL? WHAT ABOUT YOU AND ME..?!
OH, MAN... SHIT. HA... THAT WAS YEARS AGO, MAN. YOU TOLD ME YOU WANTED TO FORGET THE WHOLE THING, SHIT..
YOU FUCKING USED US, MAN-- YOU FUCKING--LEECH! AND SHE'S AS BAD AS YOU ARE!! YOU'RE BOTH DIRTY FUCKING LEECHES--!
SOLEDAD... YOU'RE AS BAD AS THAT ASSHOLE GATO, MAN... YOU'RE NOT EVEN SURE WHO YOU DO HATE... ME, OR PIPO, OR YOURSELF..! GO HOME, FOOL...
HATE..? BUT--BUT, I LOVE--
A BAD DREAM... IT'S JUST A NIGHTMARE... I'LL WAKE UP, AND... AND THE SHEETS'LL BE TANGLED AT MY FEET... NIGHTMARE...
17
THIRTY NINE

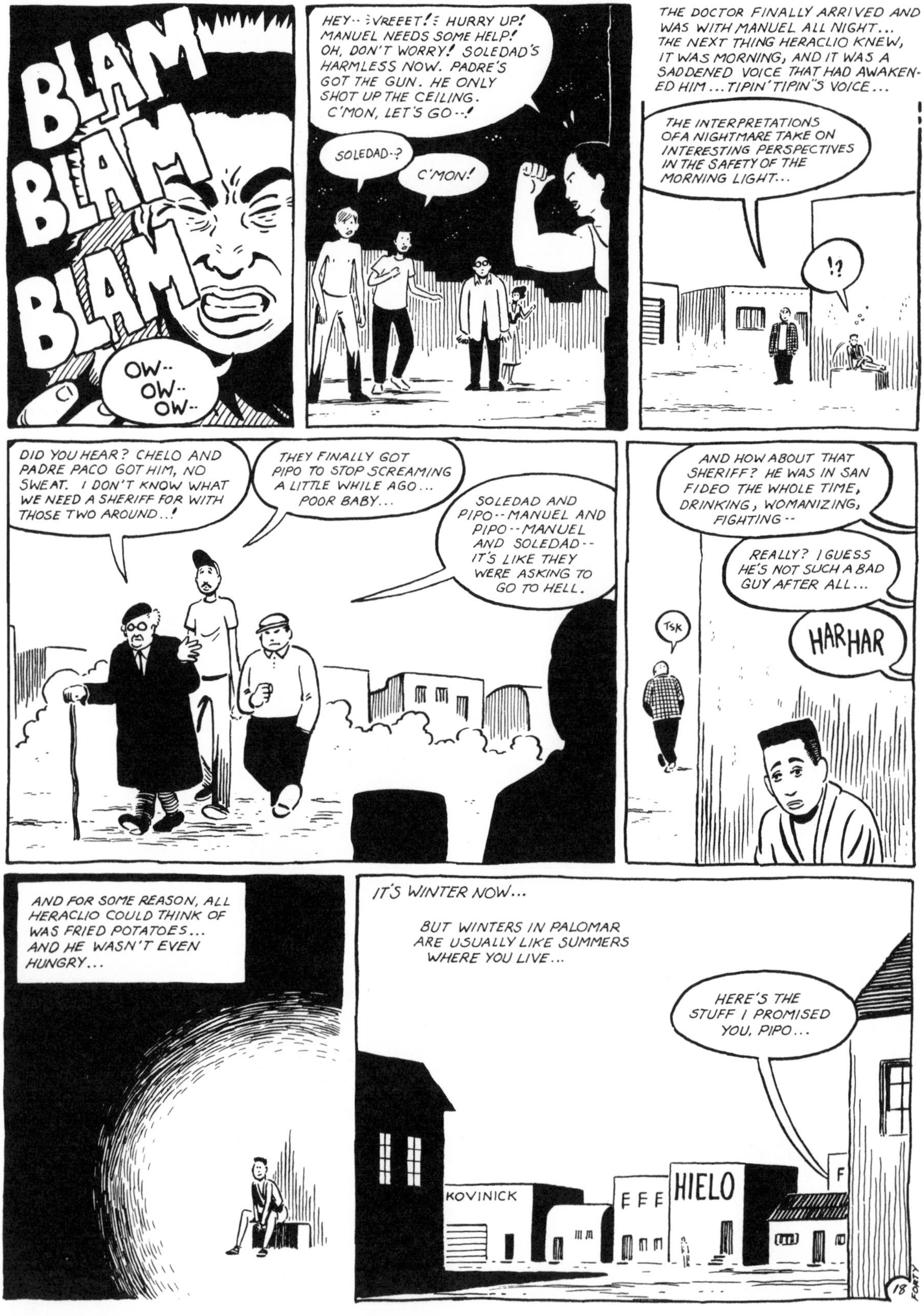
BLAM BLAM BLAM
OW.. OW.. OW..
HEY.. VREEET! HURRY UP! MANUEL NEEDS SOME HELP! OH, DON'T WORRY! SOLEDAD'S HARMLESS NOW. PADRE'S GOT THE GUN. HE ONLY SHOT UP THE CEILING. C'MON, LET'S GO..!
SOLEDAD..?
C'MON!
THE DOCTOR FINALLY ARRIVED AND WAS WITH MANUEL ALL NIGHT... THE NEXT THING HERACLIO KNEW, IT WAS MORNING, AND IT WAS A SADDENED VOICE THAT HAD AWAKENED HIM ...TIPIN' TIPIN'S VOICE...
THE INTERPRETATIONS OF A NIGHTMARE TAKE ON INTERESTING PERSPECTIVES IN THE SAFETY OF THE MORNING LIGHT...
!?
DID YOU HEAR? CHELO AND PADRE PACO GOT HIM, NO SWEAT. I DON'T KNOW WHAT WE NEED A SHERIFF FOR WITH THOSE TWO AROUND..!
THEY FINALLY GOT PIPO TO STOP SCREAMING A LITTLE WHILE AGO... POOR BABY...
SOLEDAD AND PIPO--MANUEL AND PIPO--MANUEL AND SOLEDAD-- IT'S LIKE THEY WERE ASKING TO GO TO HELL.
AND HOW ABOUT THAT SHERIFF? HE WAS IN SAN FIDEO THE WHOLE TIME, DRINKING, WOMANIZING, FIGHTING--
REALLY? I GUESS HE'S NOT SUCH A BAD GUY AFTER ALL...
TSK
HAR HAR
AND FOR SOME REASON, ALL HERACLIO COULD THINK OF WAS FRIED POTATOES... AND HE WASN'T EVEN HUNGRY...
IT'S WINTER NOW...
BUT WINTERS IN PALOMAR ARE USUALLY LIKE SUMMERS WHERE YOU LIVE...
HERE'S THE STUFF I PROMISED YOU, PIPO...
KOVINICK
HIELO
F
18
FORTY

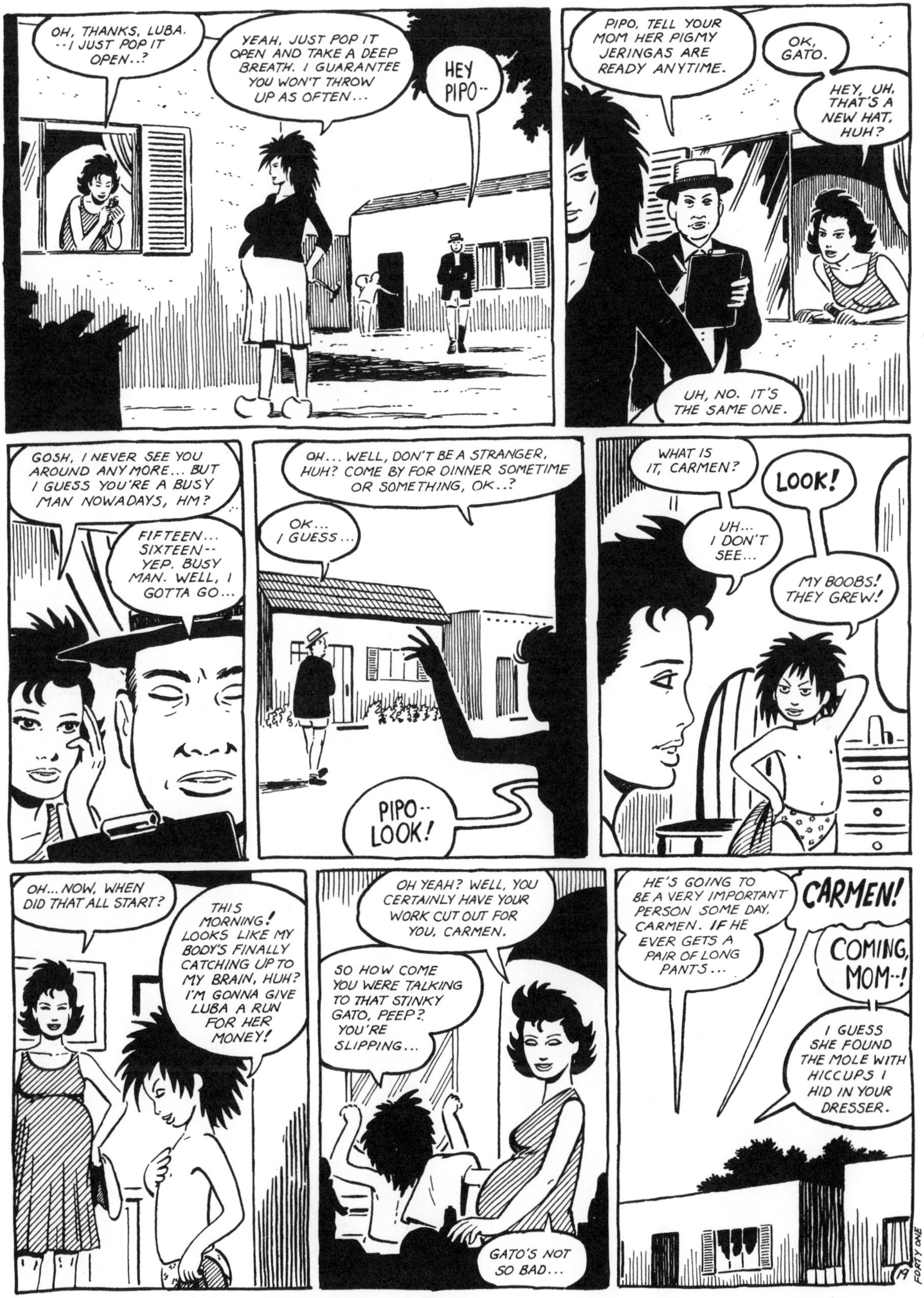
OH, THANKS, LUBA. --I JUST POP IT OPEN..?
YEAH, JUST POP IT OPEN AND TAKE A DEEP BREATH. I GUARANTEE YOU WON'T THROW UP AS OFTEN...
HEY PIPO--
PIPO, TELL YOUR MOM HER PIGMY JERINGAS ARE READY ANYTIME.
OK, GATO.
HEY, UH, THAT'S A NEW HAT, HUH?
UH, NO. IT'S THE SAME ONE.
GOSH, I NEVER SEE YOU AROUND ANY MORE... BUT I GUESS YOU'RE A BUSY MAN NOWADAYS, HM?
FIFTEEN... SIXTEEN-- YEP. BUSY MAN. WELL, I GOTTA GO...
OH... WELL, DON'T BE A STRANGER, HUH? COME BY FOR DINNER SOMETIME OR SOMETHING, OK..?
OK... I GUESS...
PIPO-- LOOK!
WHAT IS IT, CARMEN?
LOOK!
UH... I DON'T SEE...
MY BOOBS! THEY GREW!
OH... NOW, WHEN DID THAT ALL START?
THIS MORNING! LOOKS LIKE MY BODY'S FINALLY CATCHING UP TO MY BRAIN, HUH? I'M GONNA GIVE LUBA A RUN FOR HER MONEY!
OH YEAH? WELL, YOU CERTAINLY HAVE YOUR WORK CUT OUT FOR YOU, CARMEN.
SO HOW COME YOU WERE TALKING TO THAT STINKY GATO, PEEP? YOU'RE SLIPPING...
GATO'S NOT SO BAD...
HE'S GOING TO BE A VERY IMPORTANT PERSON SOME DAY, CARMEN. IF HE EVER GETS A PAIR OF LONG PANTS...
CARMEN!
COMING, MOM--!
I GUESS SHE FOUND THE MOLE WITH HICCUPS I HID IN YOUR DRESSER.
FORTY ONE

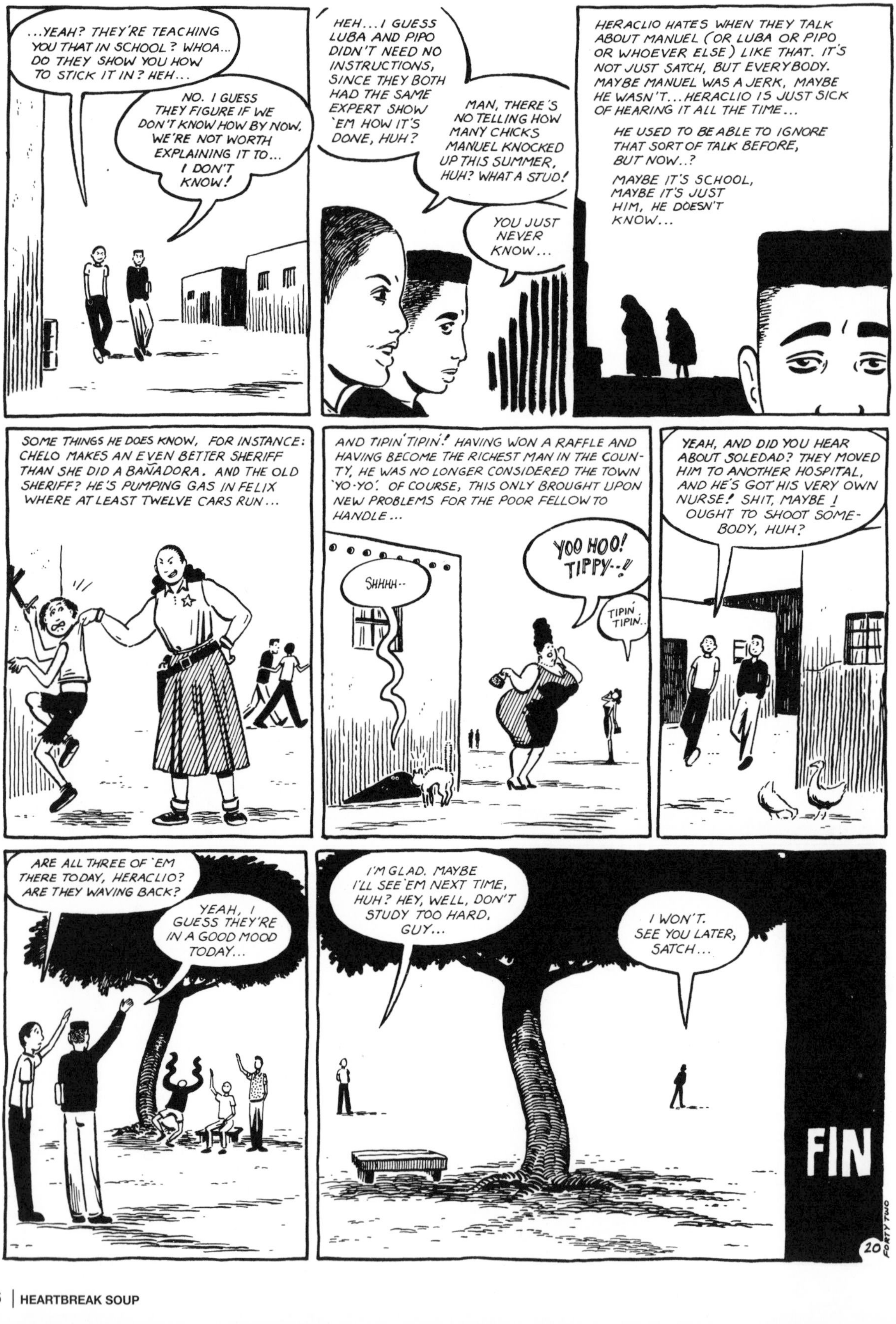
...YEAH? THEY'RE TEACHING YOU THAT IN SCHOOL? WHOA... DO THEY SHOW YOU HOW TO STICK IT IN? HEH...
NO. I GUESS THEY FIGURE IF WE DON'T KNOW HOW BY NOW, WE'RE NOT WORTH EXPLAINING IT TO... I DON'T KNOW!
HEH... I GUESS LUBA AND PIPO DIDN'T NEED NO INSTRUCTIONS, SINCE THEY BOTH HAD THE SAME EXPERT SHOW 'EM HOW IT'S DONE, HUH?
MAN, THERE'S NO TELLING HOW MANY CHICKS MANUEL KNOCKED UP THIS SUMMER, HUH? WHAT A STUD!
YOU JUST NEVER KNOW...
HERACLIO HATES WHEN THEY TALK ABOUT MANUEL (OR LUBA OR PIPO OR WHOEVER ELSE) LIKE THAT. IT'S NOT JUST SATCH, BUT EVERYBODY. MAYBE MANUEL WAS A JERK, MAYBE HE WASN'T... HERACLIO IS JUST SICK OF HEARING IT ALL THE TIME...
HE USED TO BE ABLE TO IGNORE THAT SORT OF TALK BEFORE, BUT NOW..?
MAYBE IT'S SCHOOL, MAYBE IT'S JUST HIM, HE DOESN'T KNOW...
SOME THINGS HE DOES KNOW, FOR INSTANCE: CHELO MAKES AN EVEN BETTER SHERIFF THAN SHE DID A BAÑADORA. AND THE OLD SHERIFF? HE'S PUMPING GAS IN FELIX WHERE AT LEAST TWELVE CARS RUN...
AND TIPIN' TIPIN'! HAVING WON A RAFFLE AND HAVING BECOME THE RICHEST MAN IN THE COUNTY, HE WAS NO LONGER CONSIDERED THE TOWN 'YO-YO'. OF COURSE, THIS ONLY BROUGHT UPON NEW PROBLEMS FOR THE POOR FELLOW TO HANDLE...
SHHHH--
YOO HOO! TIPPY--!
TIPIN' TIPIN'..
YEAH, AND DID YOU HEAR ABOUT SOLEDAD? THEY MOVED HIM TO ANOTHER HOSPITAL, AND HE'S GOT HIS VERY OWN NURSE! SHIT, MAYBE I OUGHT TO SHOOT SOMEBODY, HUH?
ARE ALL THREE OF 'EM THERE TODAY, HERACLIO? ARE THEY WAVING BACK?
YEAH, I GUESS THEY'RE IN A GOOD MOOD TODAY...
I'M GLAD. MAYBE I'LL SEE 'EM NEXT TIME, HUH? HEY, WELL, DON'T STUDY TOO HARD, GUY...
I WON'T. SEE YOU LATER, SATCH...
FIN
20
FORTY TWO

A LITTLE STORY...

BY GILBERT "GODFATHER of SOUL" HERNANDEZ-85

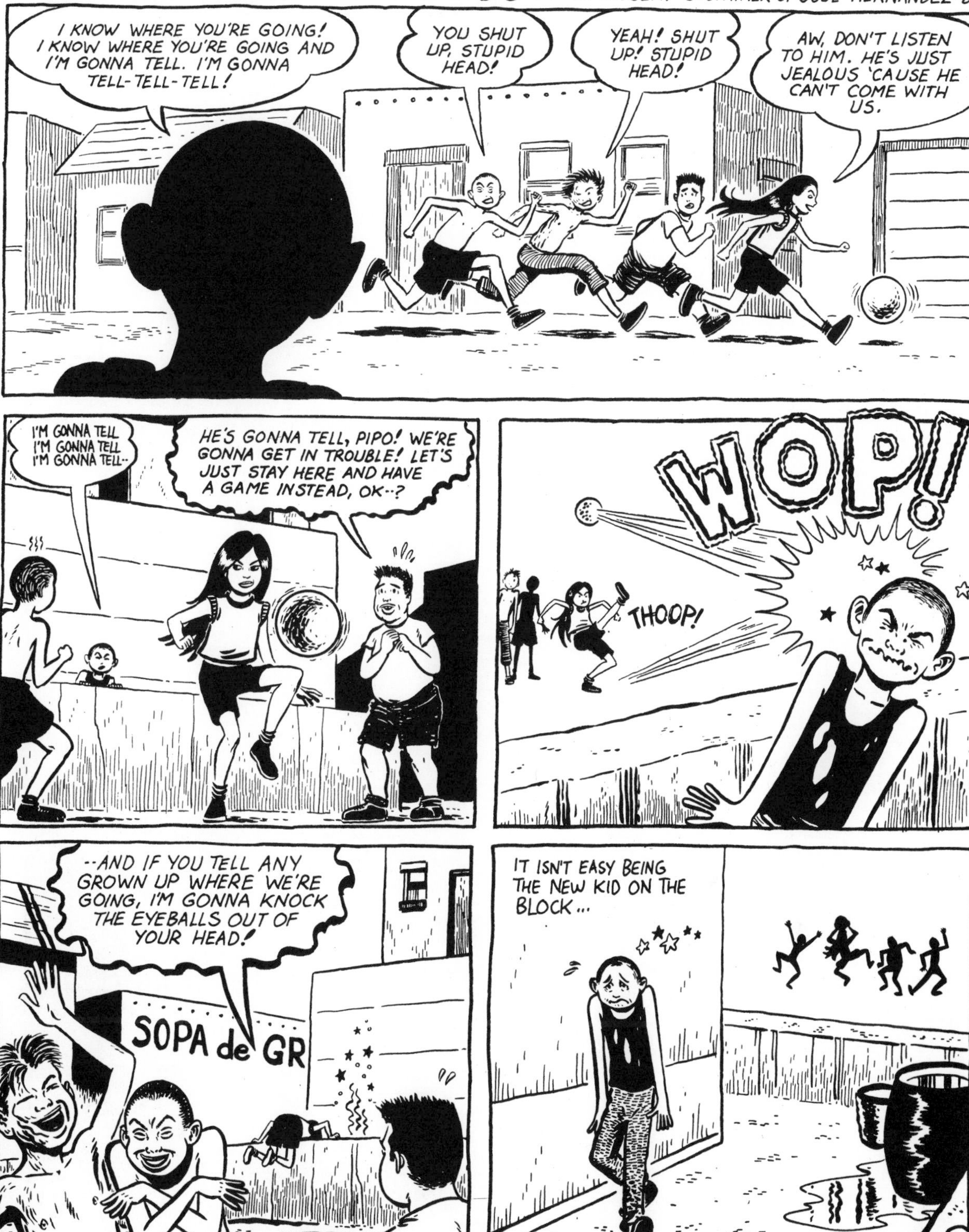

I KNOW WHERE YOU'RE GOING! I KNOW WHERE YOU'RE GOING AND I'M GONNA TELL. I'M GONNA TELL-TELL-TELL!
YOU SHUT UP, STUPID HEAD!
YEAH! SHUT UP! STUPID HEAD!
AW, DON'T LISTEN TO HIM. HE'S JUST JEALOUS 'CAUSE HE CAN'T COME WITH US.
I'M GONNA TELL I'M GONNA TELL I'M GONNA TELL..
HE'S GONNA TELL, PIPO! WE'RE GONNA GET IN TROUBLE! LET'S JUST STAY HERE AND HAVE A GAME INSTEAD, OK..?
WOP!
THOOP!
--AND IF YOU TELL ANY GROWN UP WHERE WE'RE GOING, I'M GONNA KNOCK THE EYEBALLS OUT OF YOUR HEAD!
SOPA de GR
COPYRIGHT © GILBERT HERNANDEZ · 1985
IT ISN'T EASY BEING THE NEW KID ON THE BLOCK...
1

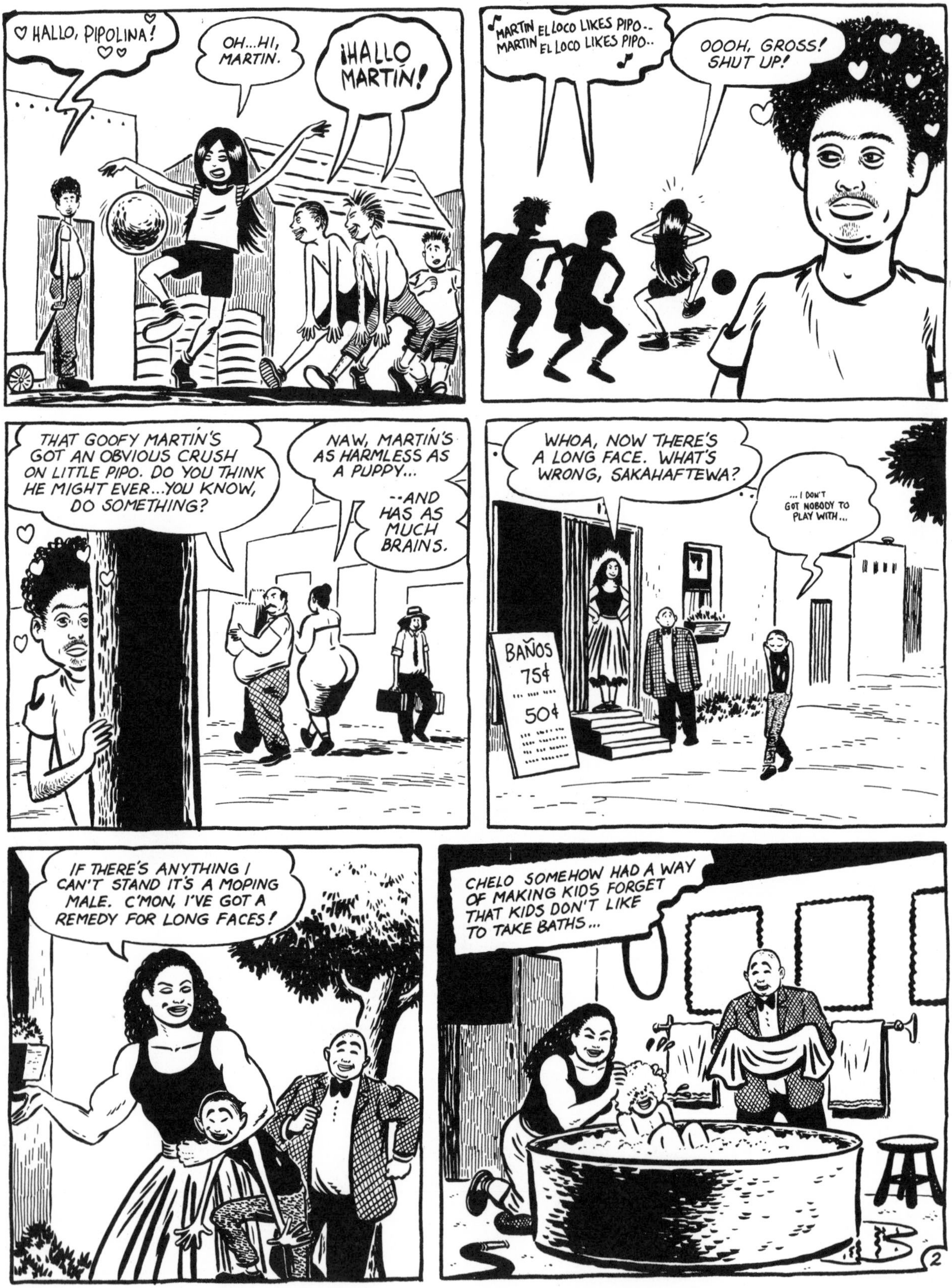
HALLO, PIPOLINA!
OH...HI, MARTIN.
¡HALLO MARTÍN!
MARTIN EL LOCO LIKES PIPO.. MARTIN EL LOCO LIKES PIPO..
OOOH, GROSS! SHUT UP!
THAT GOOFY MARTÍN'S GOT AN OBVIOUS CRUSH ON LITTLE PIPO. DO YOU THINK HE MIGHT EVER...YOU KNOW, DO SOMETHING?
NAW, MARTÍN'S AS HARMLESS AS A PUPPY...
--AND HAS AS MUCH BRAINS.
WHOA, NOW THERE'S A LONG FACE. WHAT'S WRONG, SAKAHAFTEWA?
...I DON'T GOT NOBODY TO PLAY WITH...
BAÑOS 75¢ 50¢
IF THERE'S ANYTHING I CAN'T STAND IT'S A MOPING MALE. C'MON, I'VE GOT A REMEDY FOR LONG FACES!
CHELO SOMEHOW HAD A WAY OF MAKING KIDS FORGET THAT KIDS DON'T LIKE TO TAKE BATHS...
2

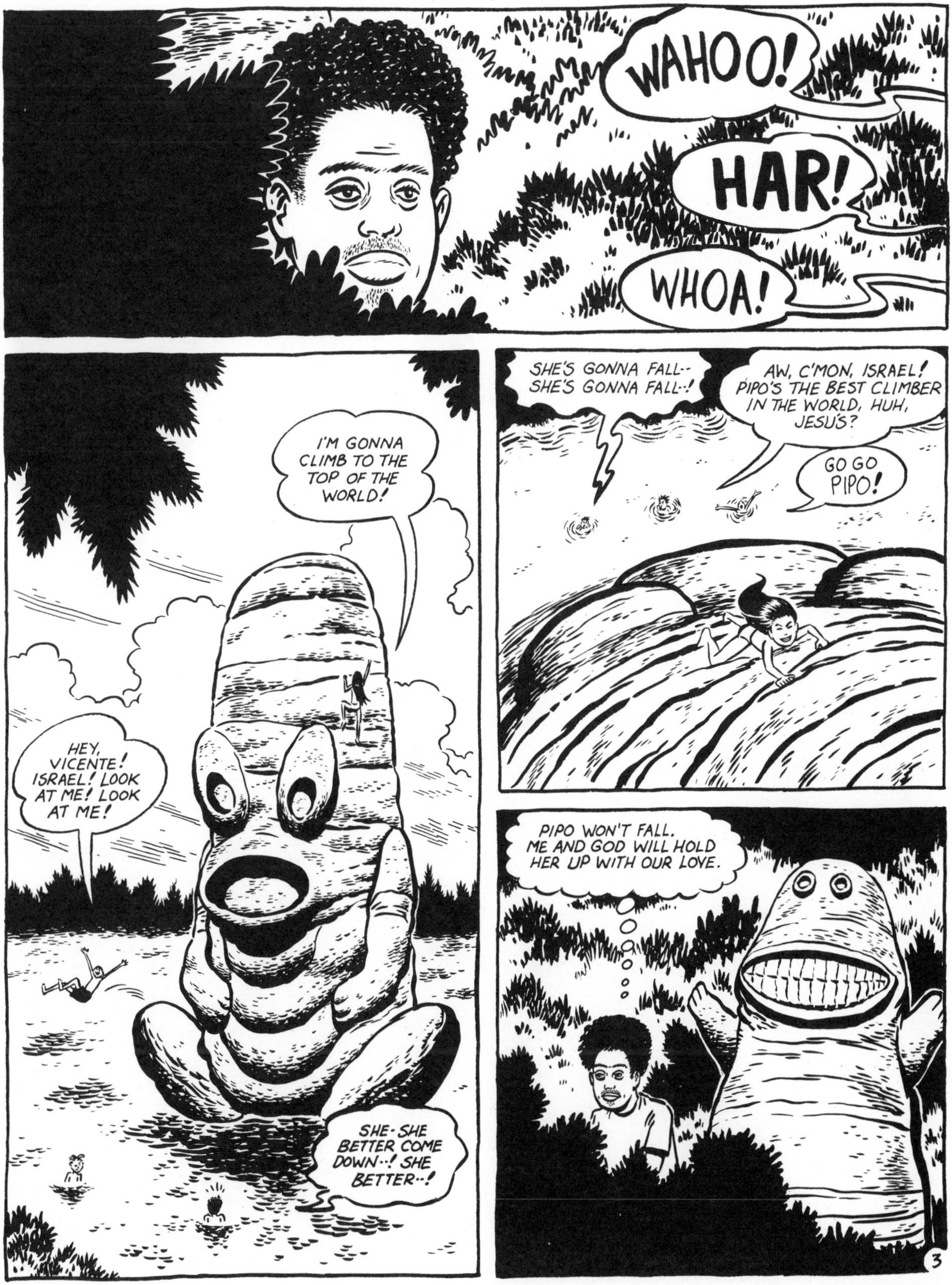
WAHOO!
HAR!
WHOA!
I'M GONNA CLIMB TO THE TOP OF THE WORLD!
HEY, VICENTE! ISRAEL! LOOK AT ME! LOOK AT ME!
SHE-SHE BETTER COME DOWN--! SHE BETTER--!
SHE'S GONNA FALL-- SHE'S GONNA FALL--!
AW, C'MON, ISRAEL! PIPO'S THE BEST CLIMBER IN THE WORLD, HUH, JESUS?
GO GO PIPO!
PIPO WON'T FALL. ME AND GOD WILL HOLD HER UP WITH OUR LOVE.
3

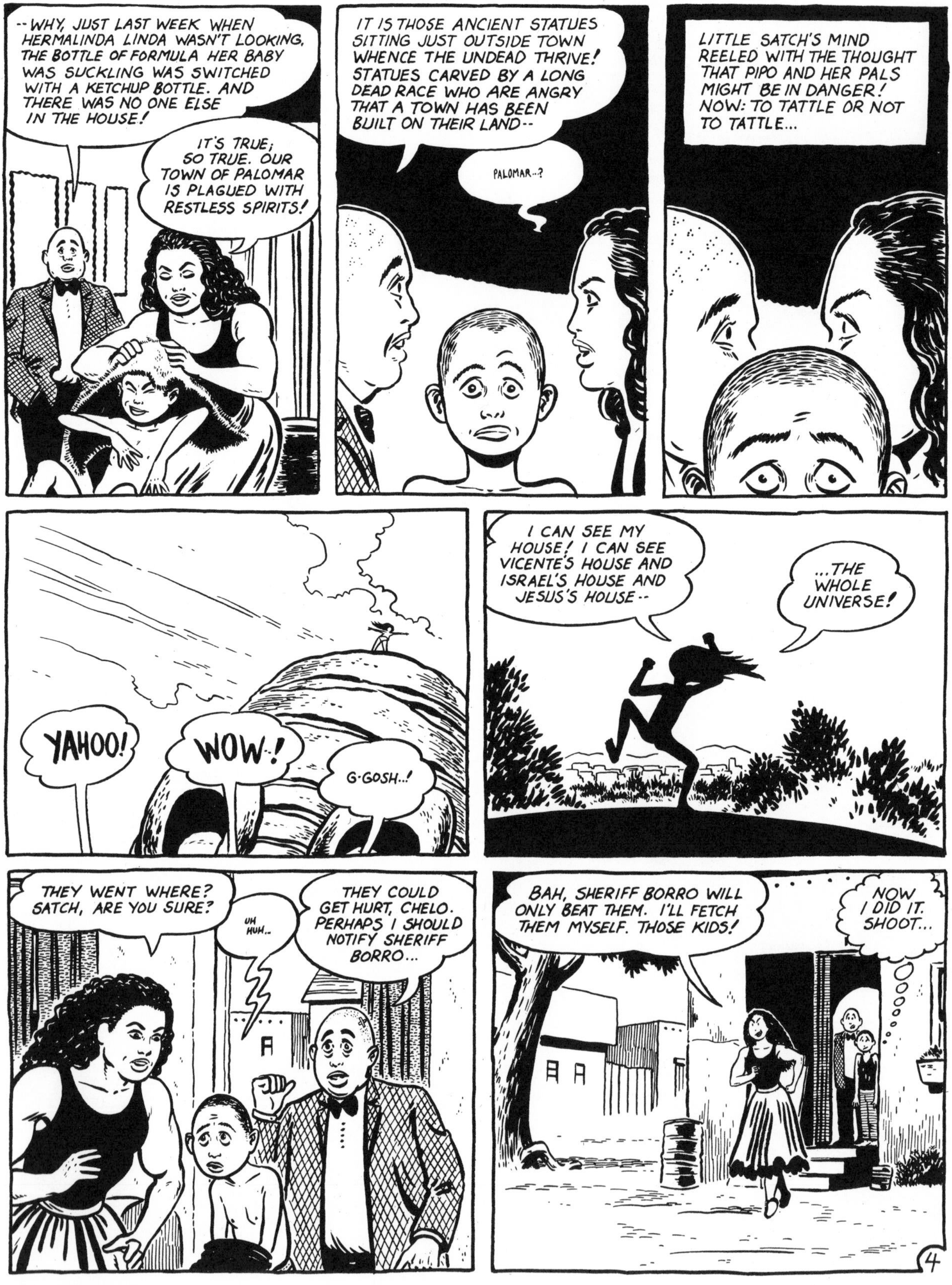
--WHY, JUST LAST WEEK WHEN HERMALINDA LINDA WASN'T LOOKING, THE BOTTLE OF FORMULA HER BABY WAS SUCKLING WAS SWITCHED WITH A KETCHUP BOTTLE. AND THERE WAS NO ONE ELSE IN THE HOUSE!
IT'S TRUE; SO TRUE. OUR TOWN OF PALOMAR IS PLAGUED WITH RESTLESS SPIRITS!
IT IS THOSE ANCIENT STATUES SITTING JUST OUTSIDE TOWN WHENCE THE UNDEAD THRIVE! STATUES CARVED BY A LONG DEAD RACE WHO ARE ANGRY THAT A TOWN HAS BEEN BUILT ON THEIR LAND--
PALOMAR...?
LITTLE SATCH'S MIND REELED WITH THE THOUGHT THAT PIPO AND HER PALS MIGHT BE IN DANGER! NOW: TO TATTLE OR NOT TO TATTLE...
YAHOO!
WOW!
G-GOSH..!
I CAN SEE MY HOUSE! I CAN SEE VICENTE'S HOUSE AND ISRAEL'S HOUSE AND JESUS'S HOUSE--
...THE WHOLE UNIVERSE!
THEY WENT WHERE? SATCH, ARE YOU SURE?
UH HUH..
THEY COULD GET HURT, CHELO. PERHAPS I SHOULD NOTIFY SHERIFF BORRO...
BAH, SHERIFF BORRO WILL ONLY BEAT THEM. I'LL FETCH THEM MYSELF. THOSE KIDS!
NOW I DID IT. SHOOT...
4

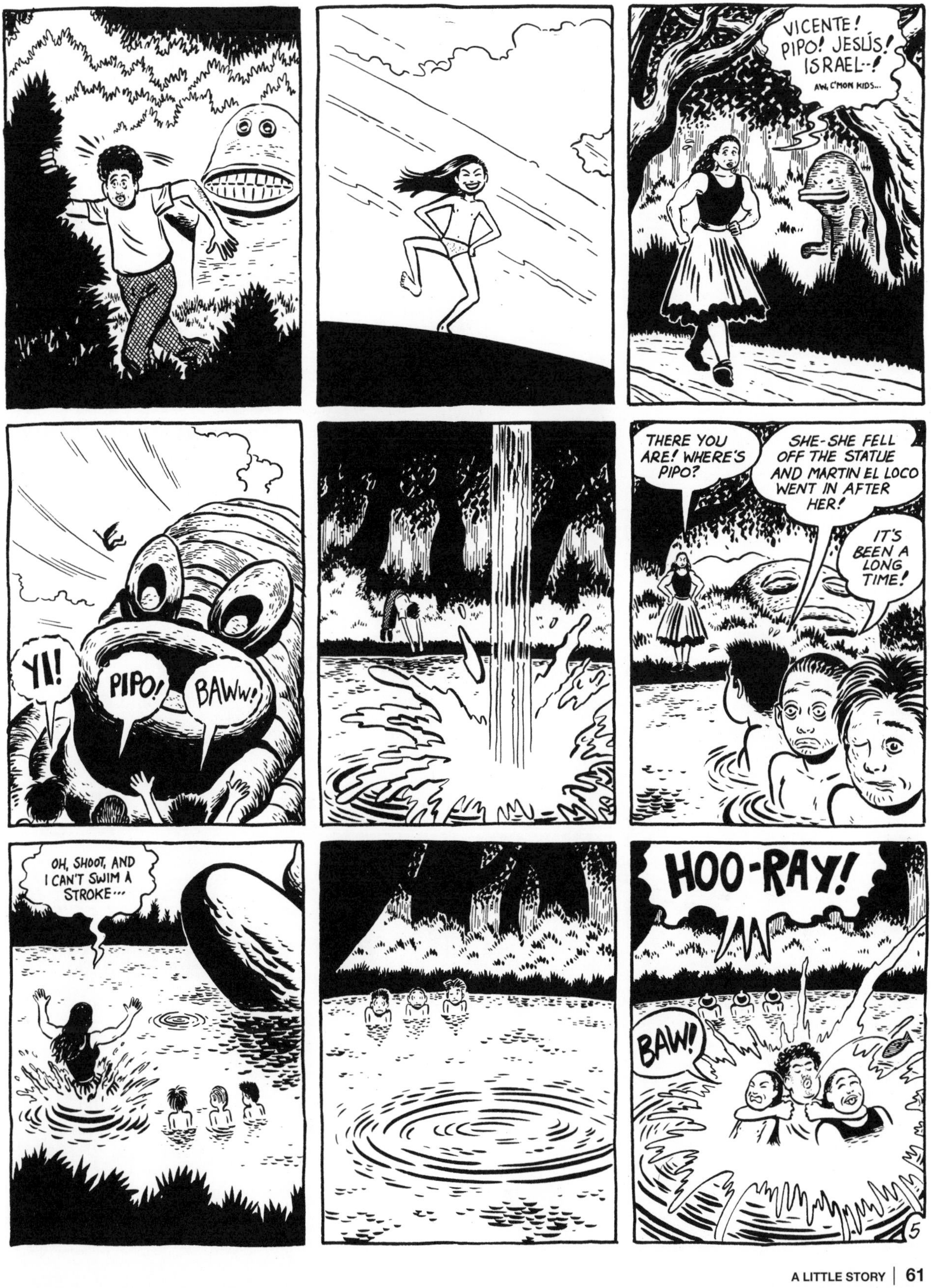
VICENTE! PIPO! JESÚS! ISRAEL--!
AW, C'MON KIDS...
YI!
PIPO!
BAWW!
THERE YOU ARE! WHERE'S PIPO?
SHE-SHE FELL OFF THE STATUE AND MARTIN EL LOCO WENT IN AFTER HER!
IT'S BEEN A LONG TIME!
OH, SHOOT, AND I CAN'T SWIM A STROKE...
HOO-RAY!
BAW!
5

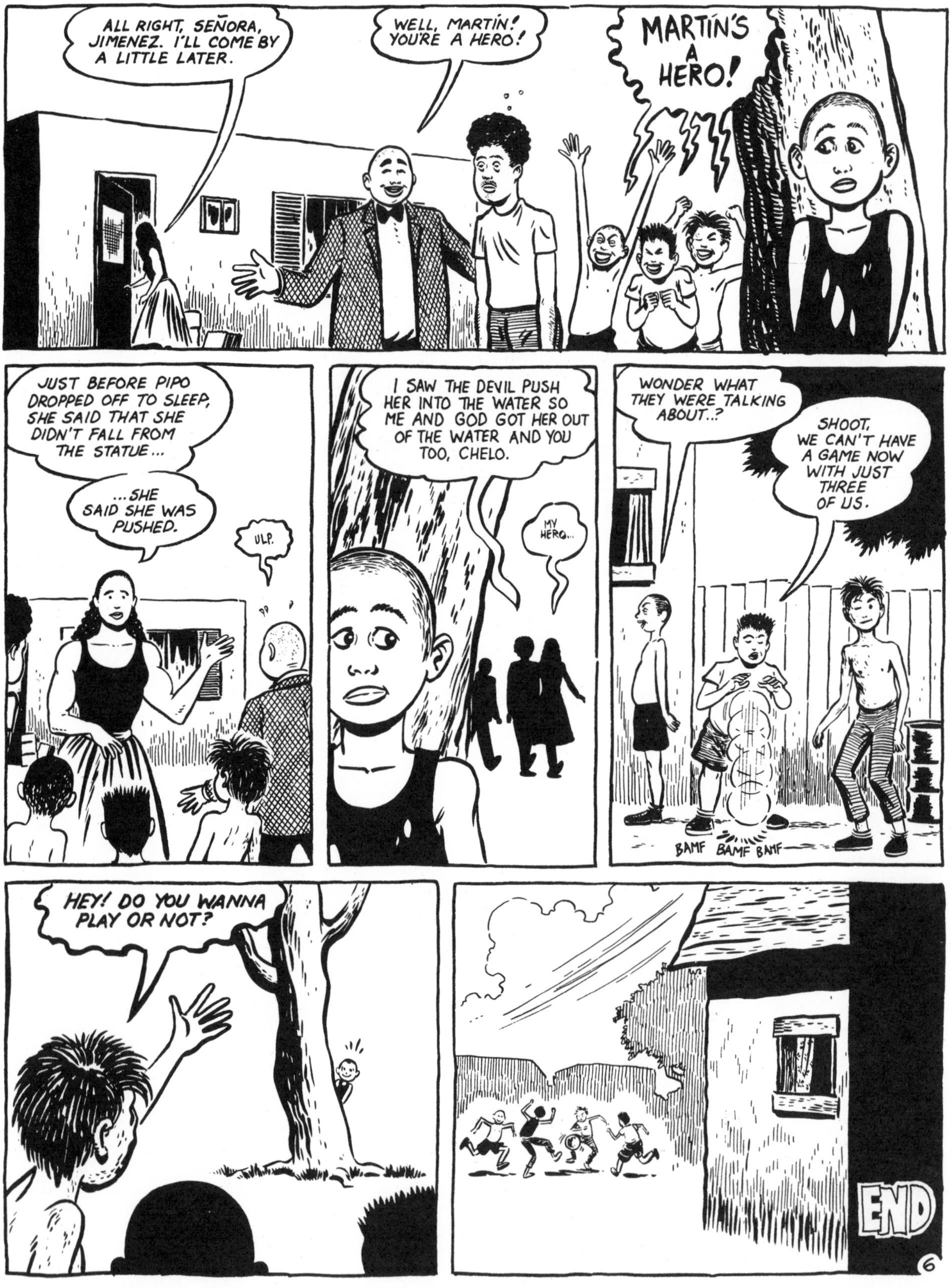
ALL RIGHT, SEÑORA, JIMENEZ. I'LL COME BY A LITTLE LATER.
WELL, MARTÍN! YOU'RE A HERO!
MARTÍN'S A HERO!
JUST BEFORE PIPO DROPPED OFF TO SLEEP, SHE SAID THAT SHE DIDN'T FALL FROM THE STATUE...
...SHE SAID SHE WAS PUSHED.
ULP.
I SAW THE DEVIL PUSH HER INTO THE WATER SO ME AND GOD GOT HER OUT OF THE WATER AND YOU TOO, CHELO.
MY HERO...
WONDER WHAT THEY WERE TALKING ABOUT..?
SHOOT, WE CAN'T HAVE A GAME NOW WITH JUST THREE OF US.
BAMF BAMF BAMF
HEY! DO YOU WANNA PLAY OR NOT?
END
6

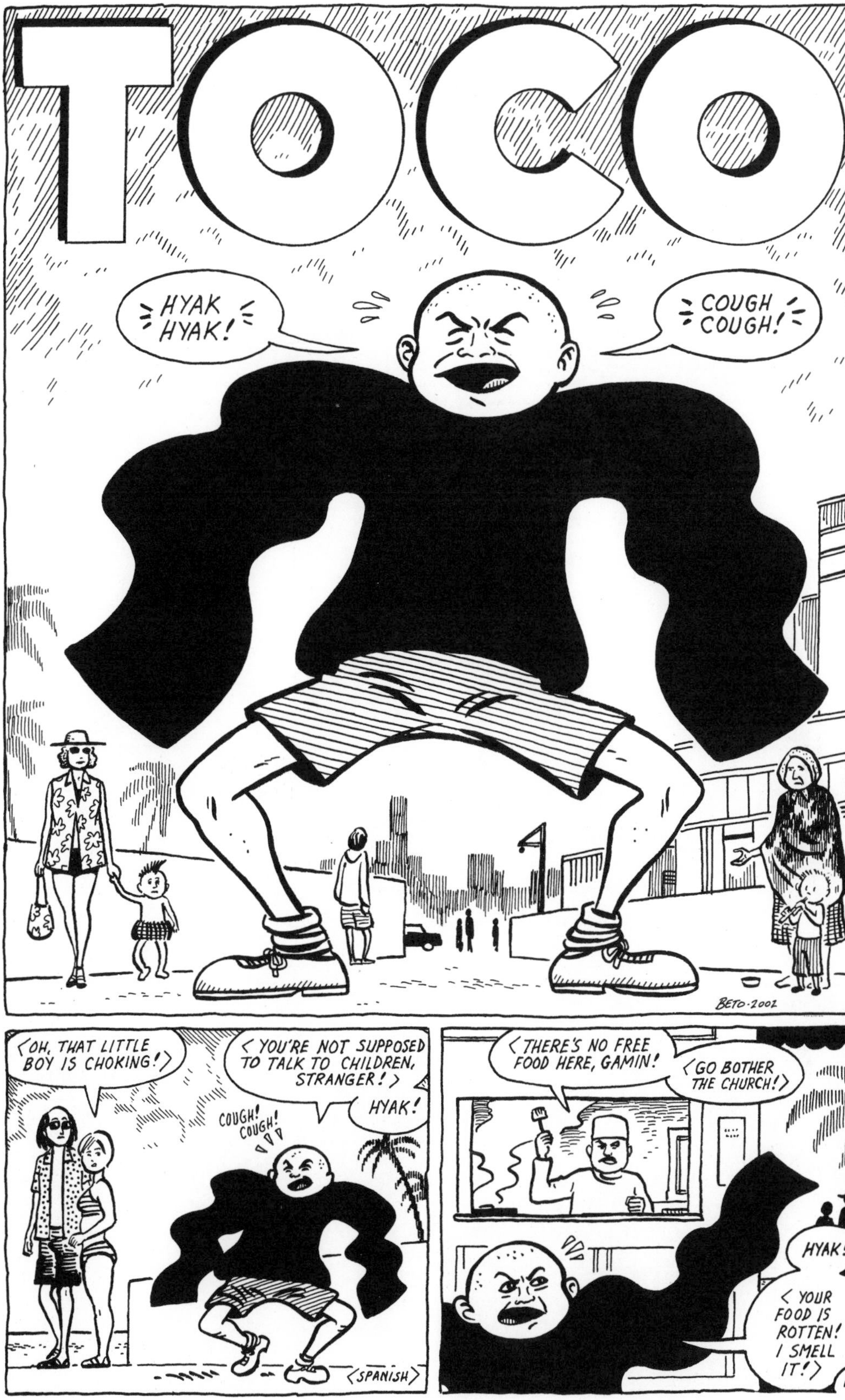
TOCO
HYAK HYAK!
COUGH COUGH!
BETO·2002
<OH, THAT LITTLE BOY IS CHOKING!>
<YOU'RE NOT SUPPOSED TO TALK TO CHILDREN, STRANGER!>
HYAK!
COUGH! COUGH!
<SPANISH>
<THERE'S NO FREE FOOD HERE, GAMIN!
<GO BOTHER THE CHURCH!>
HYAK!
<YOUR FOOD IS ROTTEN! I SMELL IT!>
1

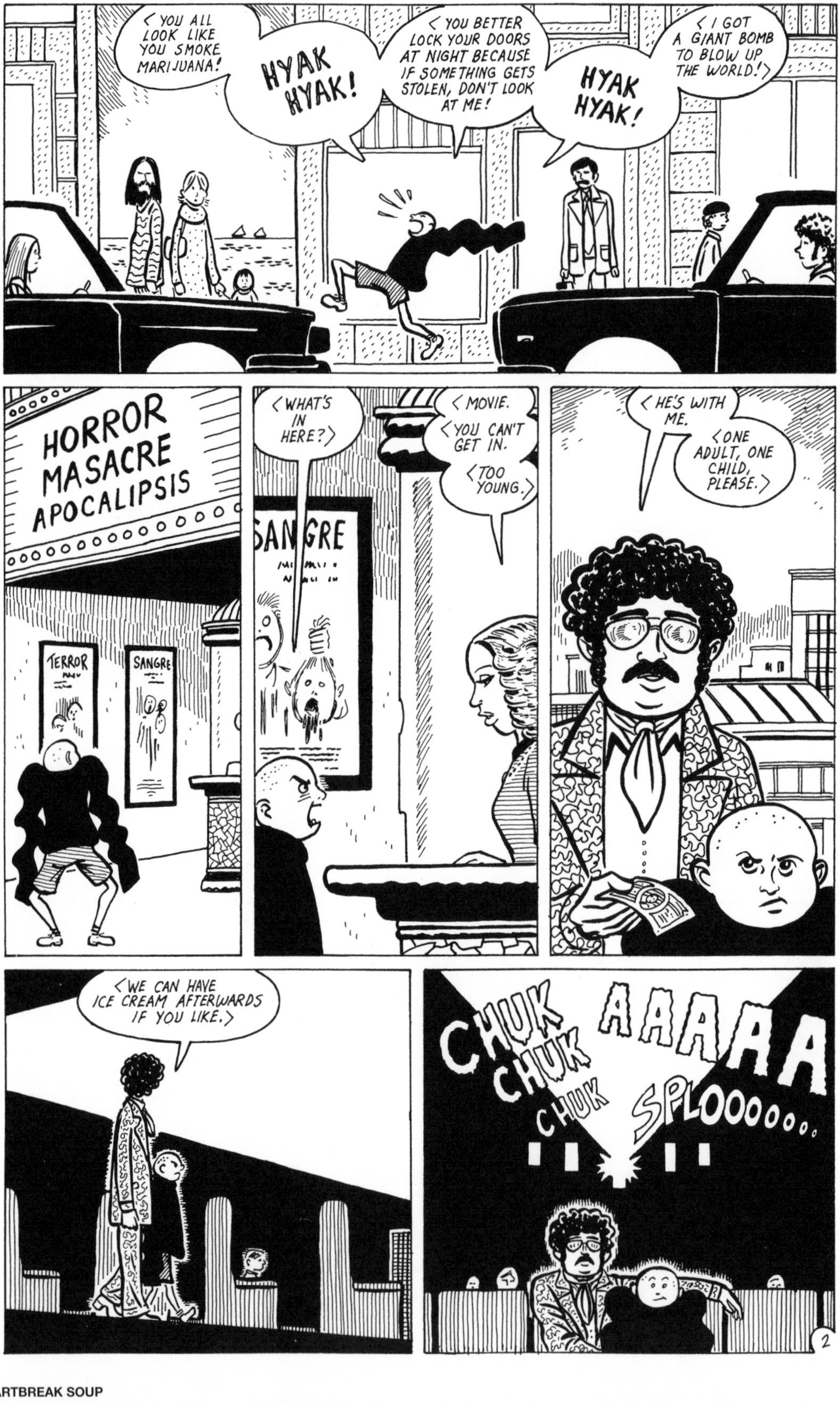

<YOU ALL LOOK LIKE YOU SMOKE MARIJUANA!
HYAK HYAK!
<YOU BETTER LOCK YOUR DOORS AT NIGHT BECAUSE IF SOMETHING GETS STOLEN, DON'T LOOK AT ME!
HYAK HYAK!
<I GOT A GIANT BOMB TO BLOW UP THE WORLD!>
HORROR MASACRE APOCALIPSIS
TERROR
SANGRE
<WHAT'S IN HERE?>
SANGRE
<MOVIE.
<YOU CAN'T GET IN.
<TOO YOUNG.>
<HE'S WITH ME.
<ONE ADULT, ONE CHILD, PLEASE.>
<WE CAN HAVE ICE CREAM AFTERWARDS IF YOU LIKE.>
CHUK CHUK CHUK
AAAAA
SPLOOOOOOO
2

< AFTER ICE CREAM WE'LL GO TO THE TOY STORE, ALL RIGHT?
<SUCH A A NICE BOY.>
< THAT'S HIM! >
<CHILD MOLESTER! >
< DON'T LET HIM GET AWAY! >
< SWINE! >
TOCO!
< WE TOLD YOU NOT TO WANDER AWAY! >
< WHERE'VE YOU BEEN FOR SO LONG? >
HYAK!
< I WENT TO THE MOVIES! I NEVER SEEN ONE BEFORE! >
< LIAR!
<REALLY?
< WHAT DID YOU SEE? THAT NEW SCARY ONE? WAS IT BLOODY? >
< HE'S GOING TO BE ALL BLOODY WHEN HIS BIG BROTHER GETS HIS HANDS ON HIM, PIPO! >
3

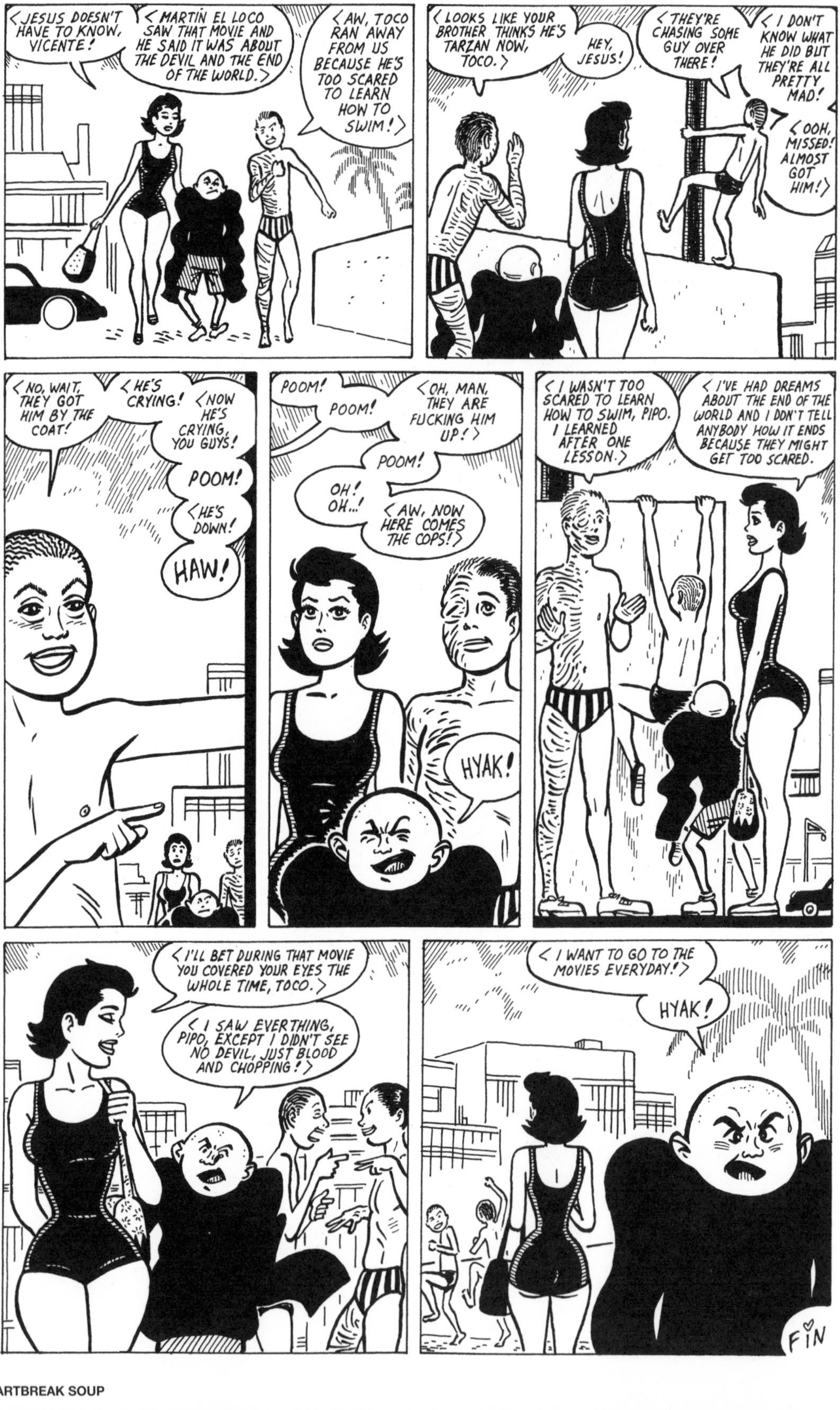

< JESUS DOESN'T HAVE TO KNOW, VICENTE! >
< MARTÍN EL LOCO SAW THAT MOVIE AND HE SAID IT WAS ABOUT THE DEVIL AND THE END OF THE WORLD. >
< AW, TOCO RAN AWAY FROM US BECAUSE HE'S TOO SCARED TO LEARN HOW TO SWIM! >
< LOOKS LIKE YOUR BROTHER THINKS HE'S TARZAN NOW, TOCO. >
HEY, JESUS!
< THEY'RE CHASING SOME GUY OVER THERE! >
< I DON'T KNOW WHAT HE DID BUT THEY'RE ALL PRETTY MAD! >
< OOH, MISSED! ALMOST GOT HIM! >
< NO, WAIT, THEY GOT HIM BY THE COAT! >
< HE'S CRYING! >
< NOW HE'S CRYING, YOU GUYS! >
POOM!
< HE'S DOWN! >
HAW!
POOM!
POOM!
< OH, MAN, THEY ARE FUCKING HIM UP! >
POOM!
OH! OH..!
< AW, NOW HERE COMES THE COPS! >
HYAK!
< I WASN'T TOO SCARED TO LEARN HOW TO SWIM, PIPO. I LEARNED AFTER ONE LESSON. >
< I'VE HAD DREAMS ABOUT THE END OF THE WORLD AND I DON'T TELL ANYBODY HOW IT ENDS BECAUSE THEY MIGHT GET TOO SCARED. >
< I'LL BET DURING THAT MOVIE YOU COVERED YOUR EYES THE WHOLE TIME, TOCO. >
< I SAW EVERTHING, PIPO, EXCEPT I DIDN'T SEE NO DEVIL, JUST BLOOD AND CHOPPING! >
< I WANT TO GO TO THE MOVIES EVERYDAY! >
HYAK!
FIN

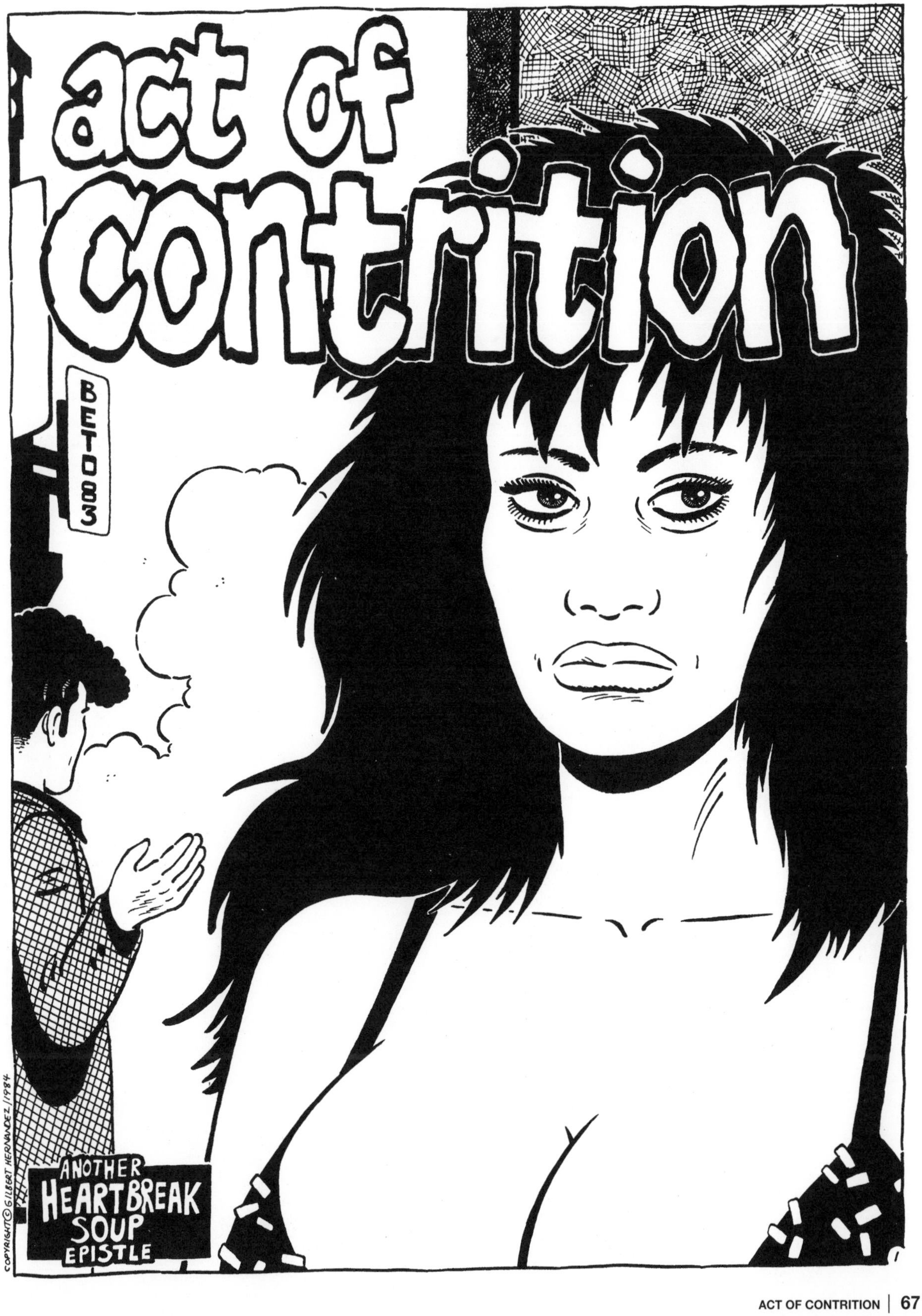
act of contrition
BETO 83
ANOTHER HEARTBREAK SOUP EPISTLE
COPYRIGHT © GILBERT HERNANDEZ / 1984

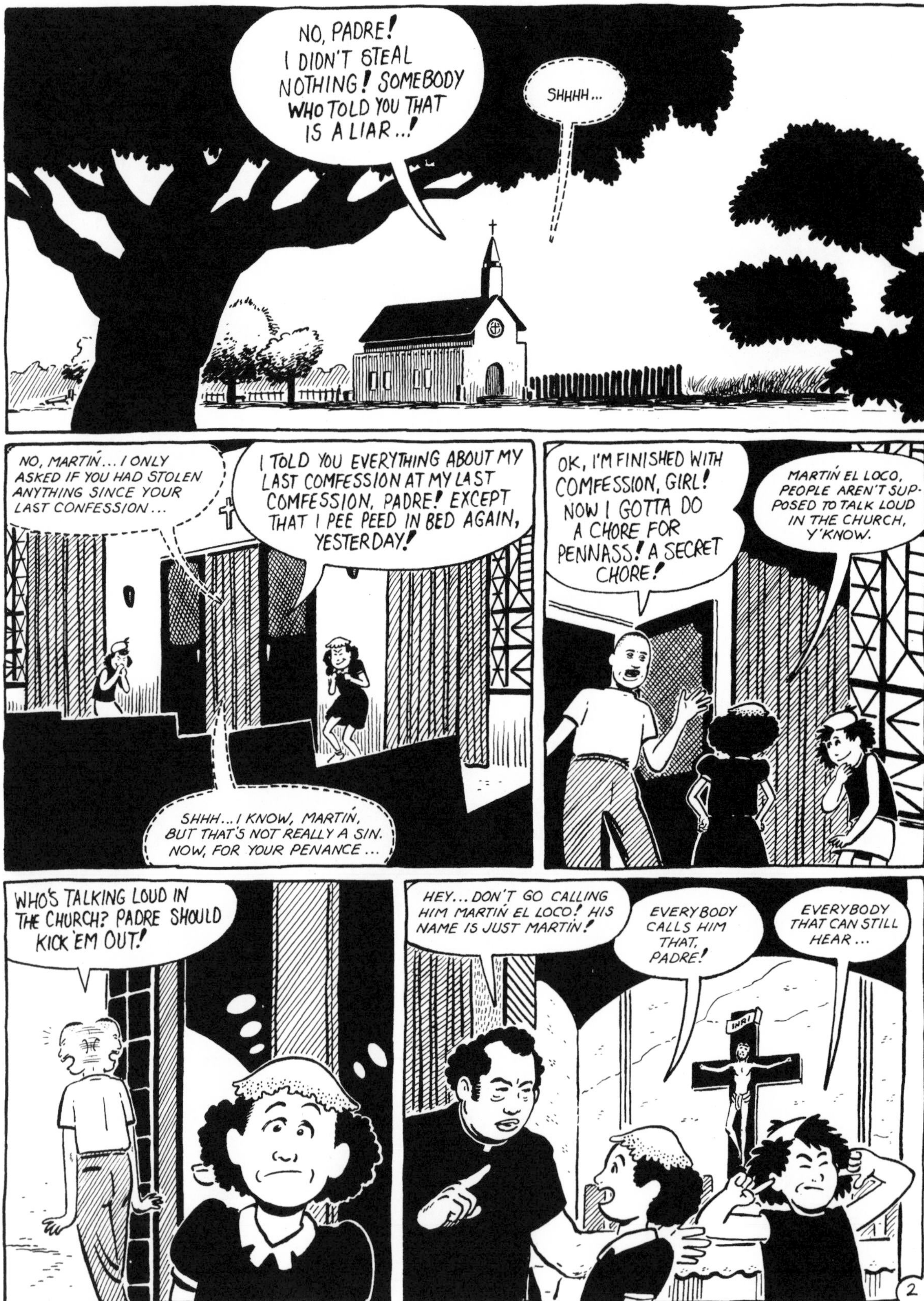
NO, PADRE! I DIDN'T STEAL NOTHING! SOMEBODY WHO TOLD YOU THAT IS A LIAR...!
SHHHH...
NO, MARTIŃ... I ONLY ASKED IF YOU HAD STOLEN ANYTHING SINCE YOUR LAST CONFESSION...
I TOLD YOU EVERYTHING ABOUT MY LAST COMFESSION AT MY LAST COMFESSION, PADRE! EXCEPT THAT I PEE PEED IN BED AGAIN, YESTERDAY!
SHHH... I KNOW, MARTIŃ, BUT THAT'S NOT REALLY A SIN. NOW, FOR YOUR PENANCE...
OK, I'M FINISHED WITH COMFESSION, GIRL! NOW I GOTTA DO A CHORE FOR PENNASS! A SECRET CHORE!
MARTIŃ EL LOCO, PEOPLE AREN'T SUPPOSED TO TALK LOUD IN THE CHURCH, Y'KNOW.
WHO'S TALKING LOUD IN THE CHURCH? PADRE SHOULD KICK 'EM OUT!
HEY... DON'T GO CALLING HIM MARTIŃ EL LOCO! HIS NAME IS JUST MARTIN!
EVERYBODY CALLS HIM THAT, PADRE!
EVERYBODY THAT CAN STILL HEAR...
INRI
2

MARTÍN EL LOCO - MAR TIN EL LOE COE (THE CRAZY)

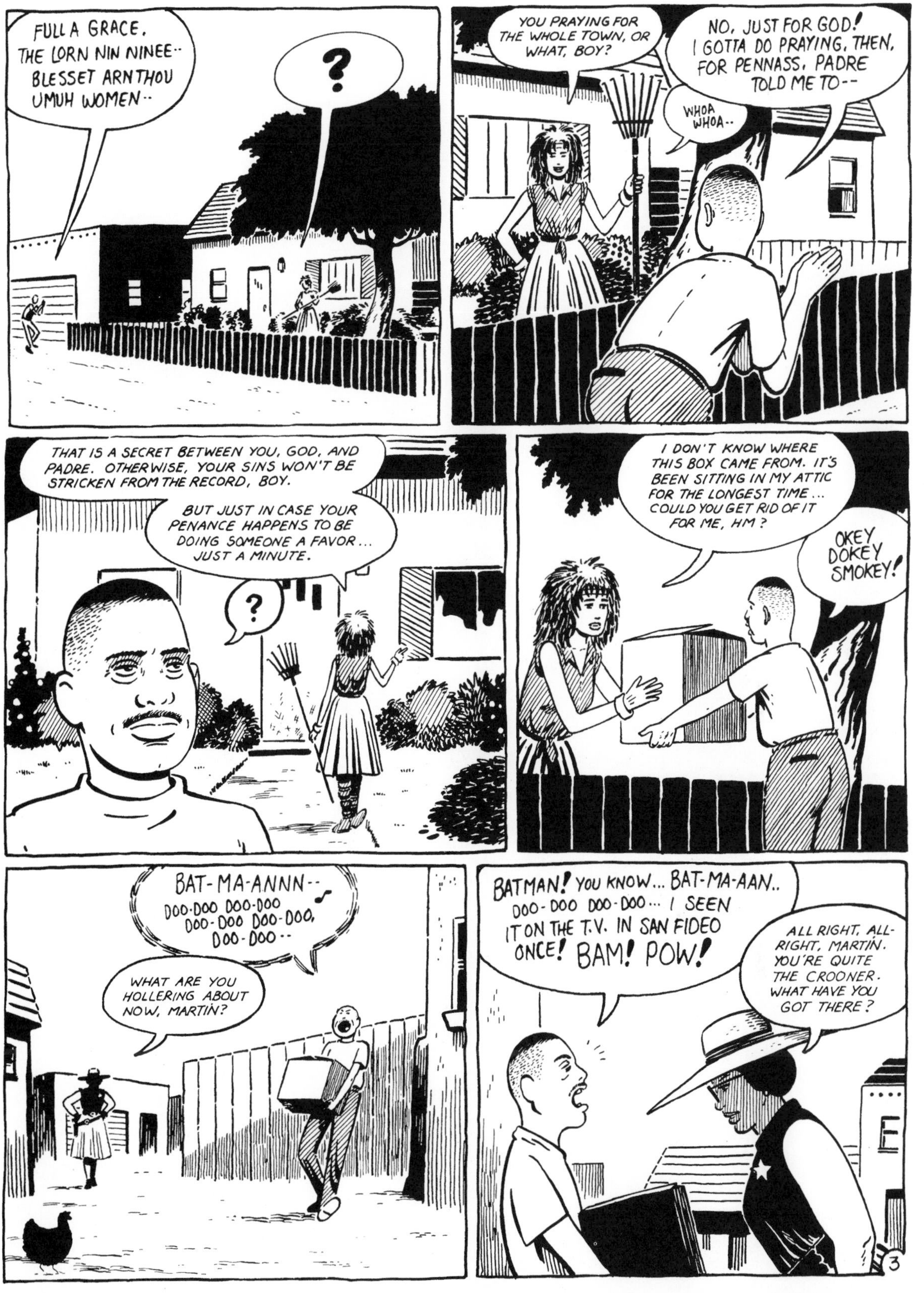
FULL A GRACE. THE LORN NIN NINEE·· BLESSET ARN THOU UMUH WOMEN··
?
YOU PRAYING FOR THE WHOLE TOWN, OR WHAT, BOY?
NO, JUST FOR GOD! I GOTTA DO PRAYING, THEN, FOR PENNASS, PADRE TOLD ME TO--
WHOA WHOA..
THAT IS A SECRET BETWEEN YOU, GOD, AND PADRE. OTHERWISE, YOUR SINS WON'T BE STRICKEN FROM THE RECORD, BOY.
BUT JUST IN CASE YOUR PENANCE HAPPENS TO BE DOING SOMEONE A FAVOR... JUST A MINUTE.
?
I DON'T KNOW WHERE THIS BOX CAME FROM. IT'S BEEN SITTING IN MY ATTIC FOR THE LONGEST TIME... COULD YOU GET RID OF IT FOR ME, HM?
OKEY DOKEY SMOKEY!
BAT-MA-ANNN-- DOO-DOO DOO-DOO DOO-DOO DOO-DOO, DOO-DOO--
WHAT ARE YOU HOLLERING ABOUT NOW, MARTÍN?
BATMAN! YOU KNOW... BAT-MA-AAN.. DOO-DOO DOO-DOO... I SEEN IT ON THE T.V. IN SAN FIDEO ONCE! BAM! POW!
ALL RIGHT, ALL-RIGHT, MARTÍN. YOU'RE QUITE THE CROONER. WHAT HAVE YOU GOT THERE?
3

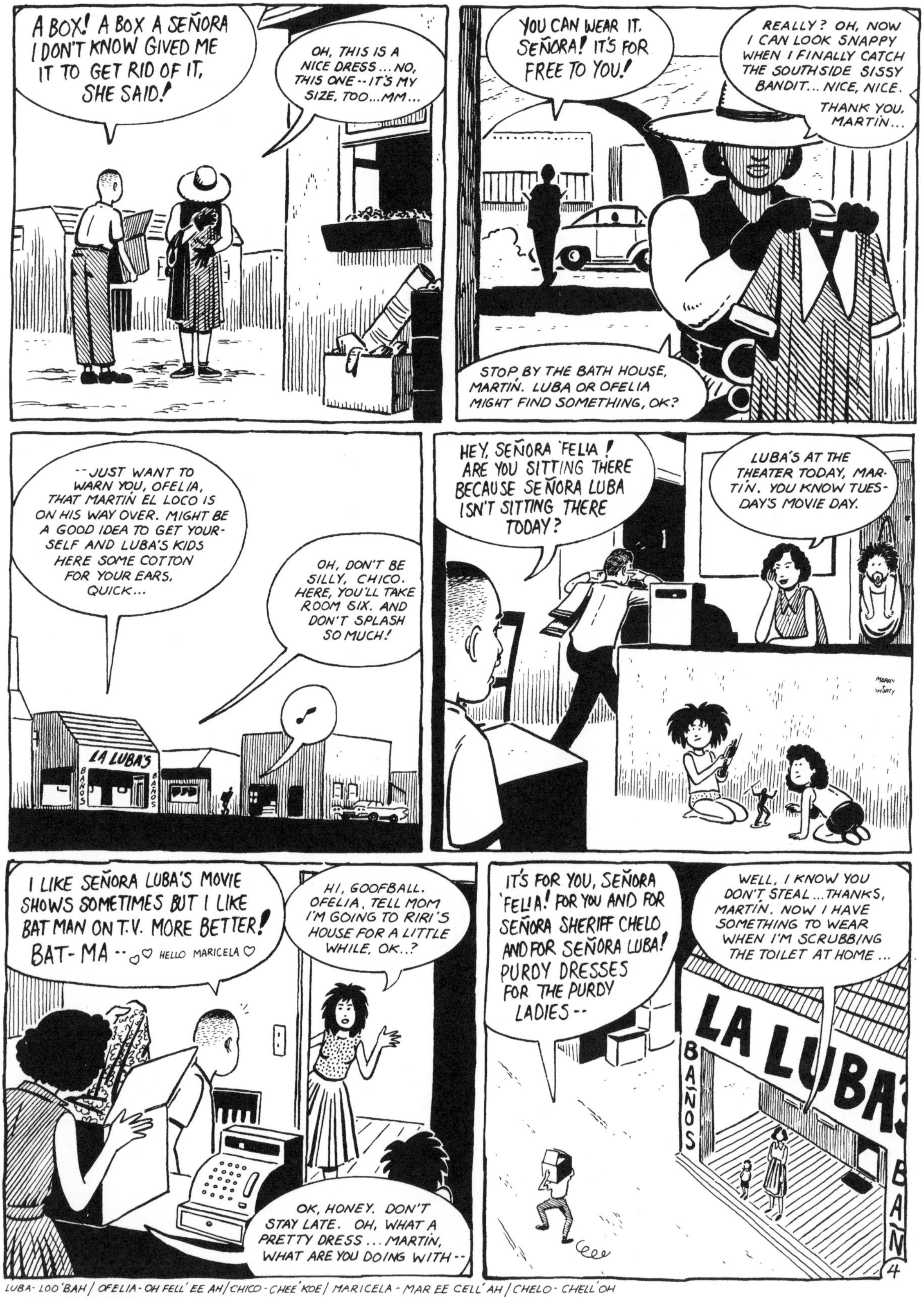
A BOX! A BOX A SEÑORA I DON'T KNOW GIVED ME IT TO GET RID OF IT, SHE SAID!
OH, THIS IS A NICE DRESS... NO, THIS ONE--IT'S MY SIZE, TOO...MM...
YOU CAN WEAR IT, SEÑORA! IT'S FOR FREE TO YOU!
REALLY? OH, NOW I CAN LOOK SNAPPY WHEN I FINALLY CATCH THE SOUTHSIDE SISSY BANDIT... NICE, NICE.
THANK YOU, MARTÍN...
STOP BY THE BATH HOUSE, MARTÍN. LUBA OR OFELIA MIGHT FIND SOMETHING, OK?
--JUST WANT TO WARN YOU, OFELIA, THAT MARTÍN EL LOCO IS ON HIS WAY OVER. MIGHT BE A GOOD IDEA TO GET YOURSELF AND LUBA'S KIDS HERE SOME COTTON FOR YOUR EARS, QUICK...
OH, DON'T BE SILLY, CHICO. HERE, YOU'LL TAKE ROOM SIX. AND DON'T SPLASH SO MUCH!
LA LUBA'S
BAÑOS
BAÑOS
HEY, SEÑORA 'FELIA! ARE YOU SITTING THERE BECAUSE SEÑORA LUBA ISN'T SITTING THERE TODAY?
LUBA'S AT THE THEATER TODAY, MARTÍN. YOU KNOW TUESDAY'S MOVIE DAY.
I LIKE SEÑORA LUBA'S MOVIE SHOWS SOMETIMES BUT I LIKE BAT MAN ON T.V. MORE BETTER! BAT-MA--
HELLO MARICELA
HI, GOOFBALL. OFELIA, TELL MOM I'M GOING TO RIRI'S HOUSE FOR A LITTLE WHILE, OK..?
OK, HONEY. DON'T STAY LATE. OH, WHAT A PRETTY DRESS... MARTÍN, WHAT ARE YOU DOING WITH--
IT'S FOR YOU, SEÑORA 'FELIA! FOR YOU AND FOR SEÑORA SHERIFF CHELO AND FOR SEÑORA LUBA! PURDY DRESSES FOR THE PURDY LADIES--
WELL, I KNOW YOU DON'T STEAL...THANKS, MARTÍN. NOW I HAVE SOMETHING TO WEAR WHEN I'M SCRUBBING THE TOILET AT HOME...
LA LUBA'S
BAÑOS
BAÑ
4

LUBA- LOO'BAH / OFELIA - OH FELL' EE AH / CHICO - CHEE'KOE / MARICELA - MAR EE CELL' AH / CHELO - CHELL'OH

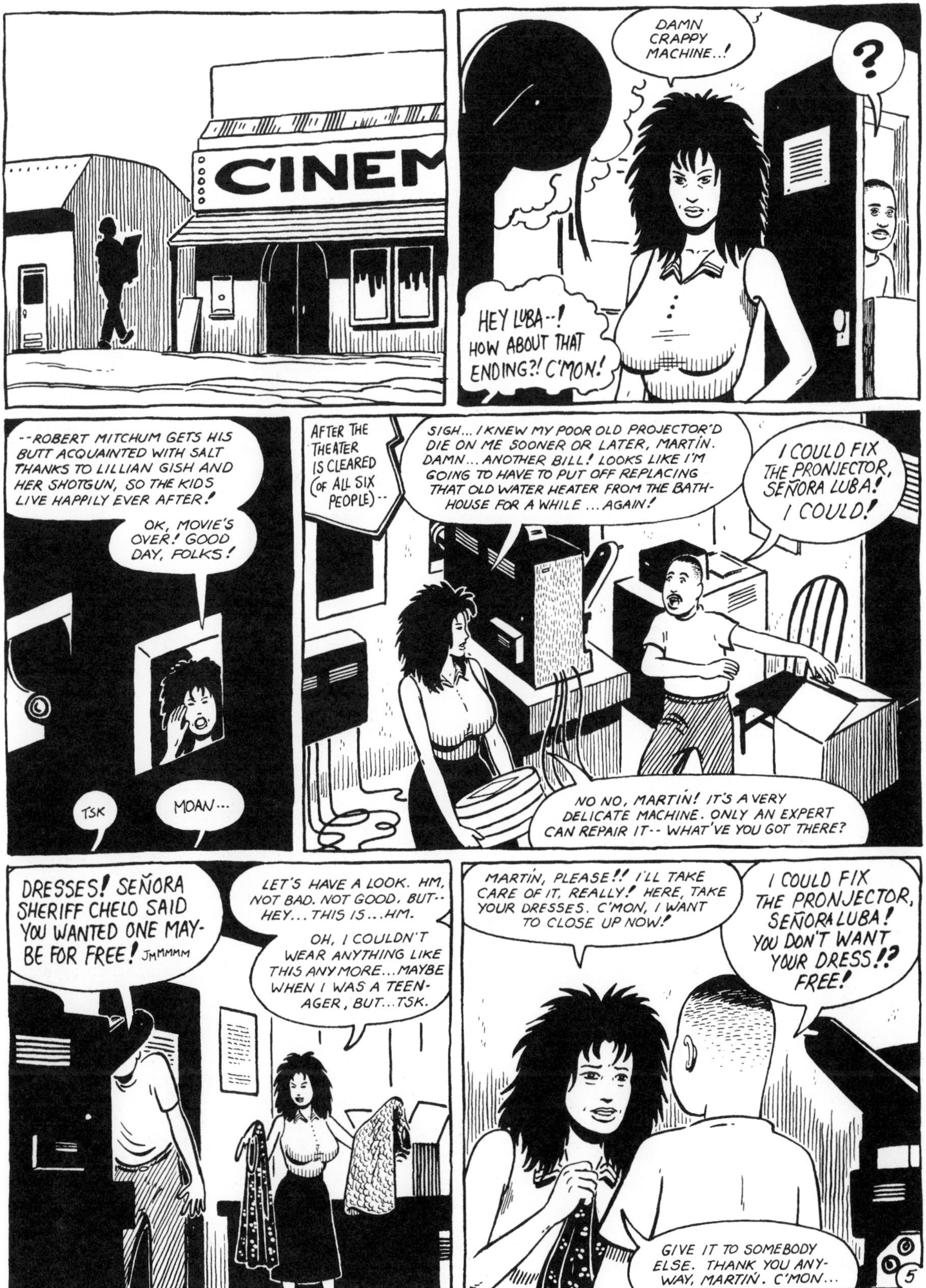
CINEM
DAMN CRAPPY MACHINE..!
?
HEY LUBA--! HOW ABOUT THAT ENDING?! C'MON!
--ROBERT MITCHUM GETS HIS BUTT ACQUAINTED WITH SALT THANKS TO LILLIAN GISH AND HER SHOTGUN, SO THE KIDS LIVE HAPPILY EVER AFTER!
OK, MOVIE'S OVER! GOOD DAY, FOLKS!
TSK
MOAN...
AFTER THE THEATER IS CLEARED (OF ALL SIX PEOPLE)--
SIGH... I KNEW MY POOR OLD PROJECTOR'D DIE ON ME SOONER OR LATER, MARTÍN. DAMN... ANOTHER BILL! LOOKS LIKE I'M GOING TO HAVE TO PUT OFF REPLACING THAT OLD WATER HEATER FROM THE BATH-HOUSE FOR A WHILE ... AGAIN!
I COULD FIX THE PRONJECTOR, SEÑORA LUBA! I COULD!
NO NO, MARTÍN! IT'S A VERY DELICATE MACHINE. ONLY AN EXPERT CAN REPAIR IT-- WHAT'VE YOU GOT THERE?
DRESSES! SEÑORA SHERIFF CHELO SAID YOU WANTED ONE MAY-BE FOR FREE! JMMMM
LET'S HAVE A LOOK. HM, NOT BAD. NOT GOOD, BUT-- HEY... THIS IS...HM.
OH, I COULDN'T WEAR ANYTHING LIKE THIS ANYMORE... MAYBE WHEN I WAS A TEEN-AGER, BUT...TSK.
MARTÍN, PLEASE!! I'LL TAKE CARE OF IT, REALLY! HERE, TAKE YOUR DRESSES. C'MON, I WANT TO CLOSE UP NOW!
I COULD FIX THE PRONJECTOR, SEÑORA LUBA! YOU DON'T WANT YOUR DRESS!? FREE!
GIVE IT TO SOMEBODY ELSE. THANK YOU ANY-WAY, MARTÍN. C'MON...
5

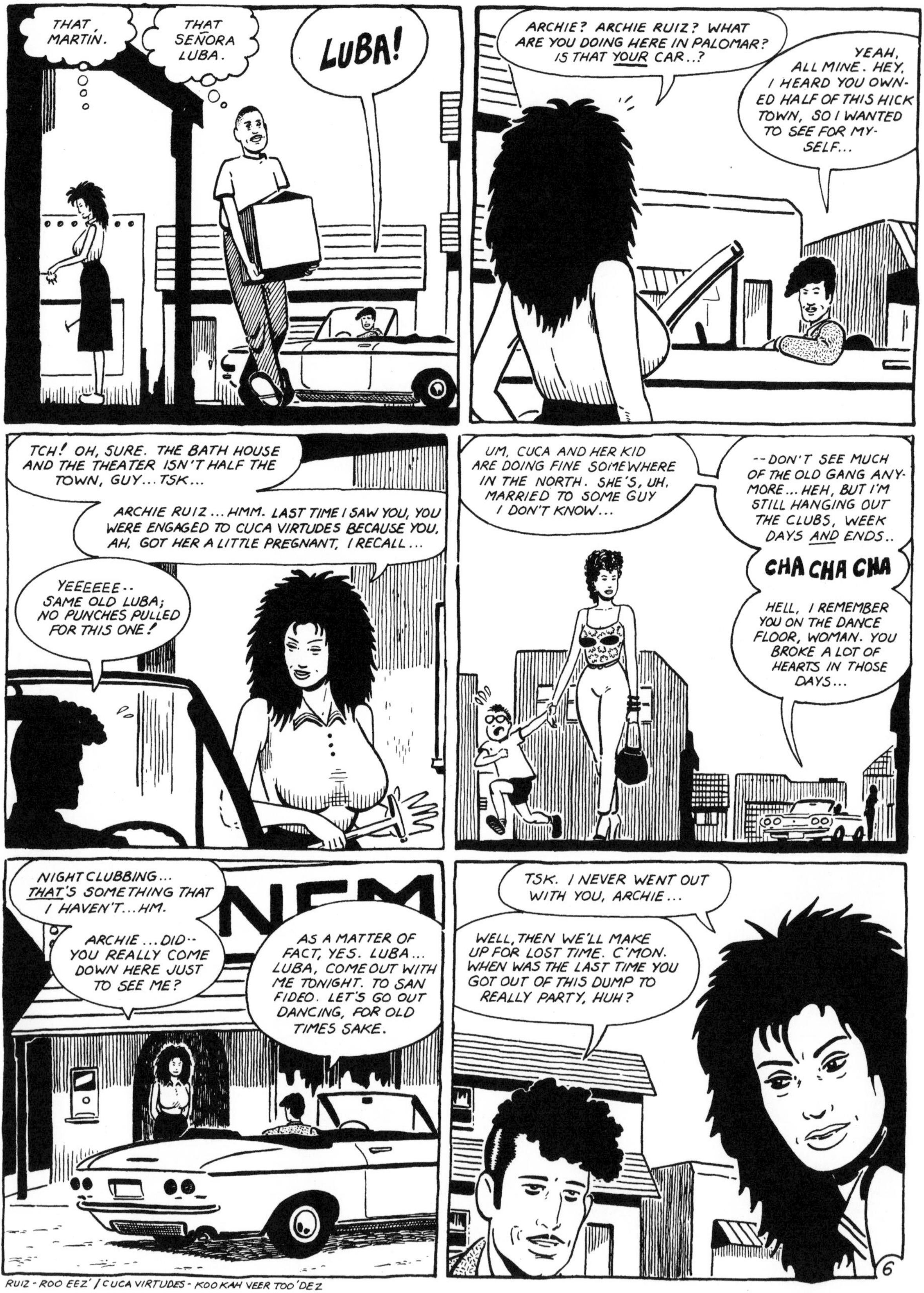
THAT, MARTÍN.
THAT SEÑORA LUBA.
LUBA!
ARCHIE? ARCHIE RUIZ? WHAT ARE YOU DOING HERE IN PALOMAR? IS THAT YOUR CAR..?
YEAH, ALL MINE. HEY, I HEARD YOU OWNED HALF OF THIS HICK TOWN, SO I WANTED TO SEE FOR MYSELF...
TCH! OH, SURE. THE BATH HOUSE AND THE THEATER ISN'T HALF THE TOWN, GUY... TSK...
ARCHIE RUIZ... HMM. LAST TIME I SAW YOU, YOU WERE ENGAGED TO CUCA VIRTUDES BECAUSE YOU, AH, GOT HER A LITTLE PREGNANT, I RECALL...
YEEEEEE-- SAME OLD LUBA; NO PUNCHES PULLED FOR THIS ONE!
UM, CUCA AND HER KID ARE DOING FINE SOMEWHERE IN THE NORTH. SHE'S, UH, MARRIED TO SOME GUY I DON'T KNOW...
--DON'T SEE MUCH OF THE OLD GANG ANYMORE... HEH, BUT I'M STILL HANGING OUT THE CLUBS, WEEK DAYS AND ENDS..
CHA CHA CHA
HELL, I REMEMBER YOU ON THE DANCE FLOOR, WOMAN. YOU BROKE A LOT OF HEARTS IN THOSE DAYS...
NIGHT CLUBBING... THAT'S SOMETHING THAT I HAVEN'T... HM.
ARCHIE... DID-- YOU REALLY COME DOWN HERE JUST TO SEE ME?
AS A MATTER OF FACT, YES. LUBA... LUBA, COME OUT WITH ME TONIGHT. TO SAN FIDEO. LET'S GO OUT DANCING, FOR OLD TIMES SAKE.
TSK. I NEVER WENT OUT WITH YOU, ARCHIE...
WELL, THEN WE'LL MAKE UP FOR LOST TIME. C'MON. WHEN WAS THE LAST TIME YOU GOT OUT OF THIS DUMP TO REALLY PARTY, HUH?
6

RUIZ - ROO EEZ' / CUCA VIRTUDES - KOO KAH VEER TOO'DEZ

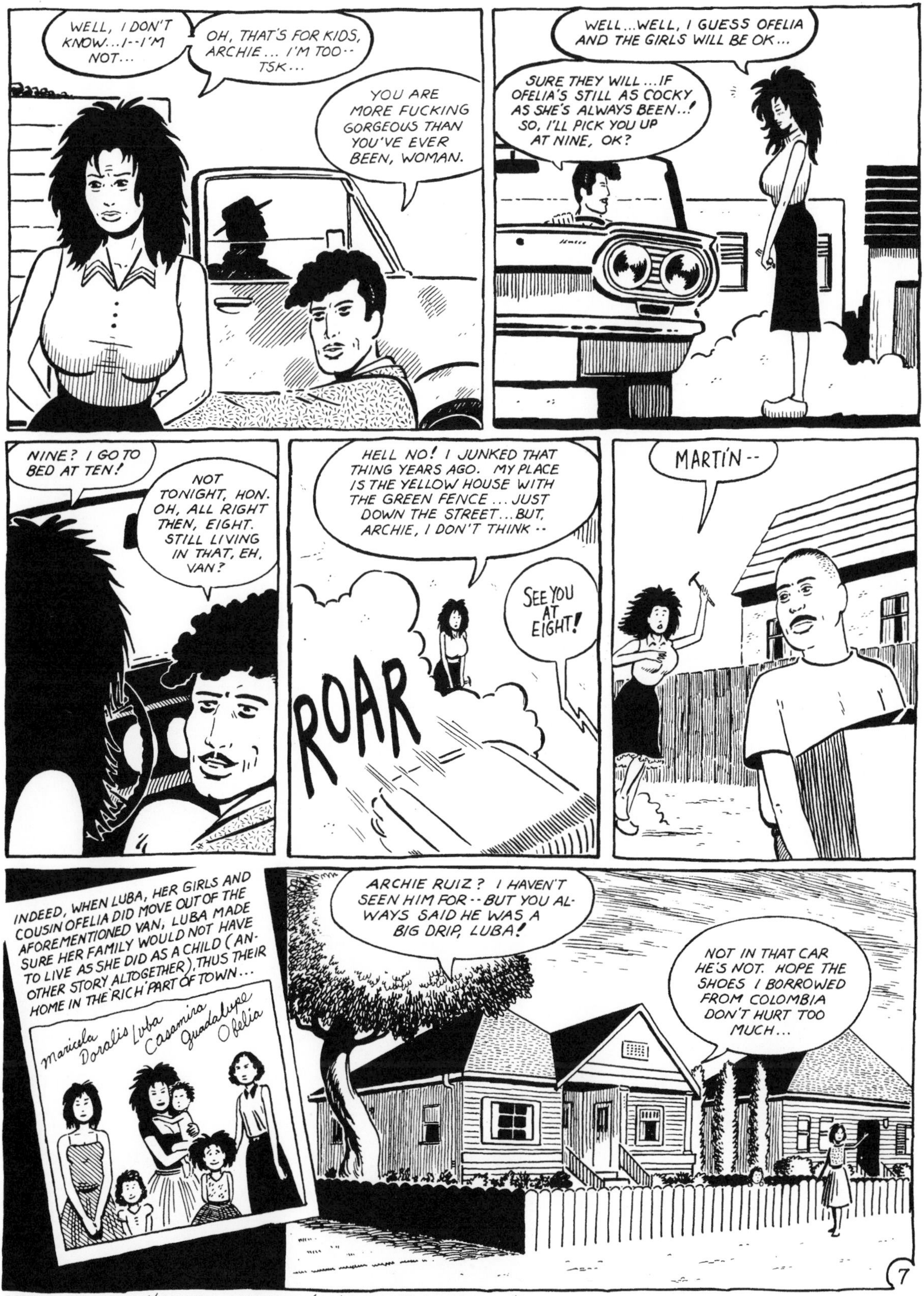
WELL, I DON'T KNOW... I--I'M NOT...
OH, THAT'S FOR KIDS, ARCHIE... I'M TOO-- TSK...
YOU ARE MORE FUCKING GORGEOUS THAN YOU'VE EVER BEEN, WOMAN.
WELL...WELL, I GUESS OFELIA AND THE GIRLS WILL BE OK...
SURE THEY WILL...IF OFELIA'S STILL AS COCKY AS SHE'S ALWAYS BEEN..! SO, I'LL PICK YOU UP AT NINE, OK?
NINE? I GO TO BED AT TEN!
NOT TONIGHT, HON. OH, ALL RIGHT THEN, EIGHT. STILL LIVING IN THAT, EH, VAN?
HELL NO! I JUNKED THAT THING YEARS AGO. MY PLACE IS THE YELLOW HOUSE WITH THE GREEN FENCE... JUST DOWN THE STREET... BUT, ARCHIE, I DON'T THINK --
SEE YOU AT EIGHT!
ROAR
MARTÍN --
INDEED, WHEN LUBA, HER GIRLS AND COUSIN OFELIA DID MOVE OUT OF THE AFOREMENTIONED VAN, LUBA MADE SURE HER FAMILY WOULD NOT HAVE TO LIVE AS SHE DID AS A CHILD (ANOTHER STORY ALTOGETHER), THUS THEIR HOME IN THE 'RICH' PART OF TOWN...
Maricela Doralis Luba Casamira Guadalupe Ofelia
ARCHIE RUIZ? I HAVEN'T SEEN HIM FOR -- BUT YOU ALWAYS SAID HE WAS A BIG DRIP, LUBA!
NOT IN THAT CAR HE'S NOT. HOPE THE SHOES I BORROWED FROM COLOMBIA DON'T HURT TOO MUCH...
7

DORALIS - DOOR AH LEES' / CASAMIRA - COSS AH MEER' AH / GUADALUPE - WAH DAH LOO'PEH

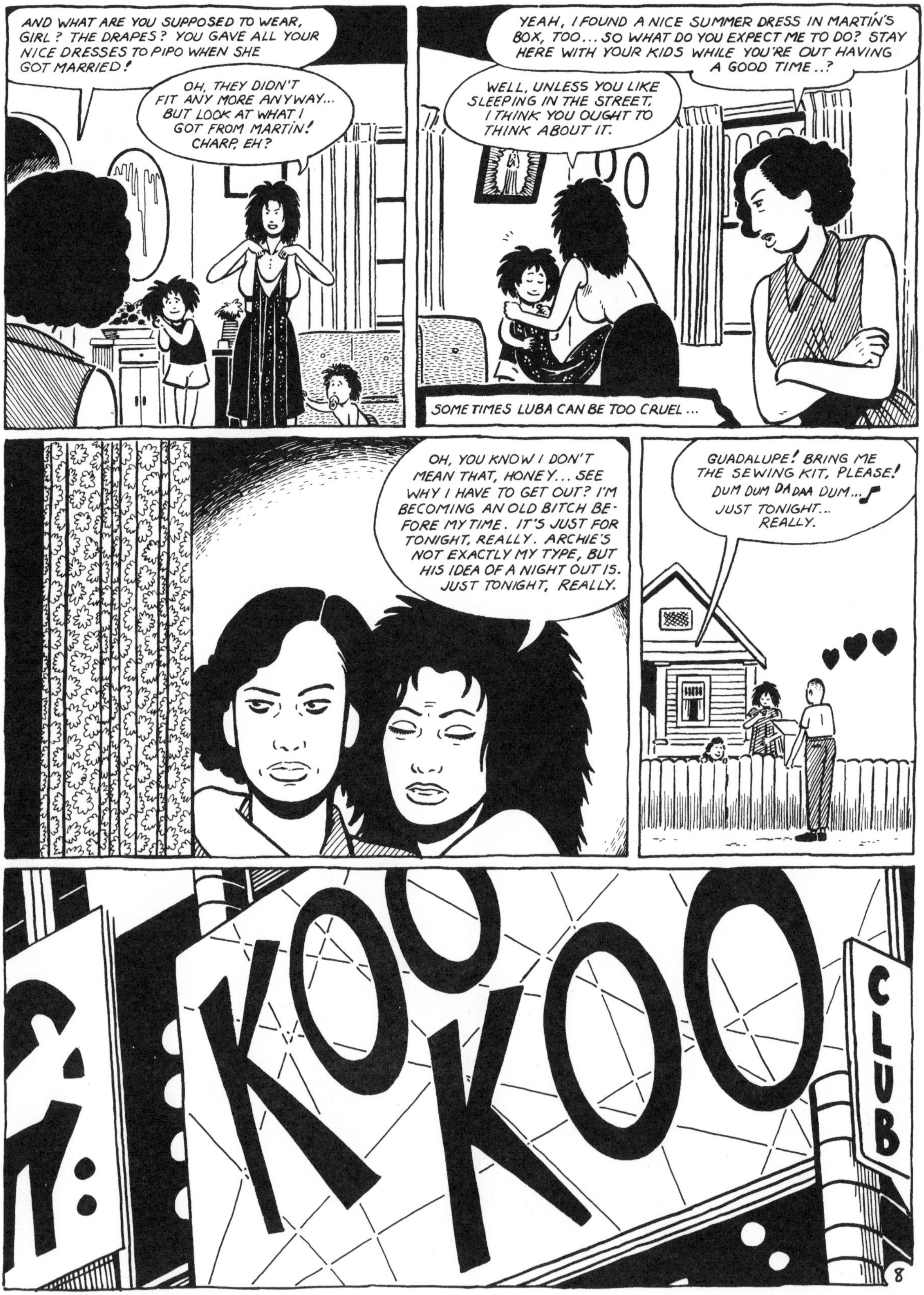
AND WHAT ARE YOU SUPPOSED TO WEAR, GIRL? THE DRAPES? YOU GAVE ALL YOUR NICE DRESSES TO PIPO WHEN SHE GOT MARRIED!
OH, THEY DIDN'T FIT ANY MORE ANYWAY... BUT LOOK AT WHAT I GOT FROM MARTÍN! CHARP, EH?
YEAH, I FOUND A NICE SUMMER DRESS IN MARTÍN'S BOX, TOO... SO WHAT DO YOU EXPECT ME TO DO? STAY HERE WITH YOUR KIDS WHILE YOU'RE OUT HAVING A GOOD TIME..?
WELL, UNLESS YOU LIKE SLEEPING IN THE STREET, I THINK YOU OUGHT TO THINK ABOUT IT.
SOME TIMES LUBA CAN BE TOO CRUEL...
OH, YOU KNOW I DON'T MEAN THAT, HONEY... SEE WHY I HAVE TO GET OUT? I'M BECOMING AN OLD BITCH BEFORE MY TIME. IT'S JUST FOR TONIGHT, REALLY. ARCHIE'S NOT EXACTLY MY TYPE, BUT HIS IDEA OF A NIGHT OUT IS. JUST TONIGHT, REALLY.
GUADALUPE! BRING ME THE SEWING KIT, PLEASE! DUM DUM DA DAA DUM... JUST TONIGHT... REALLY.
KOOKOO
CLUB
8

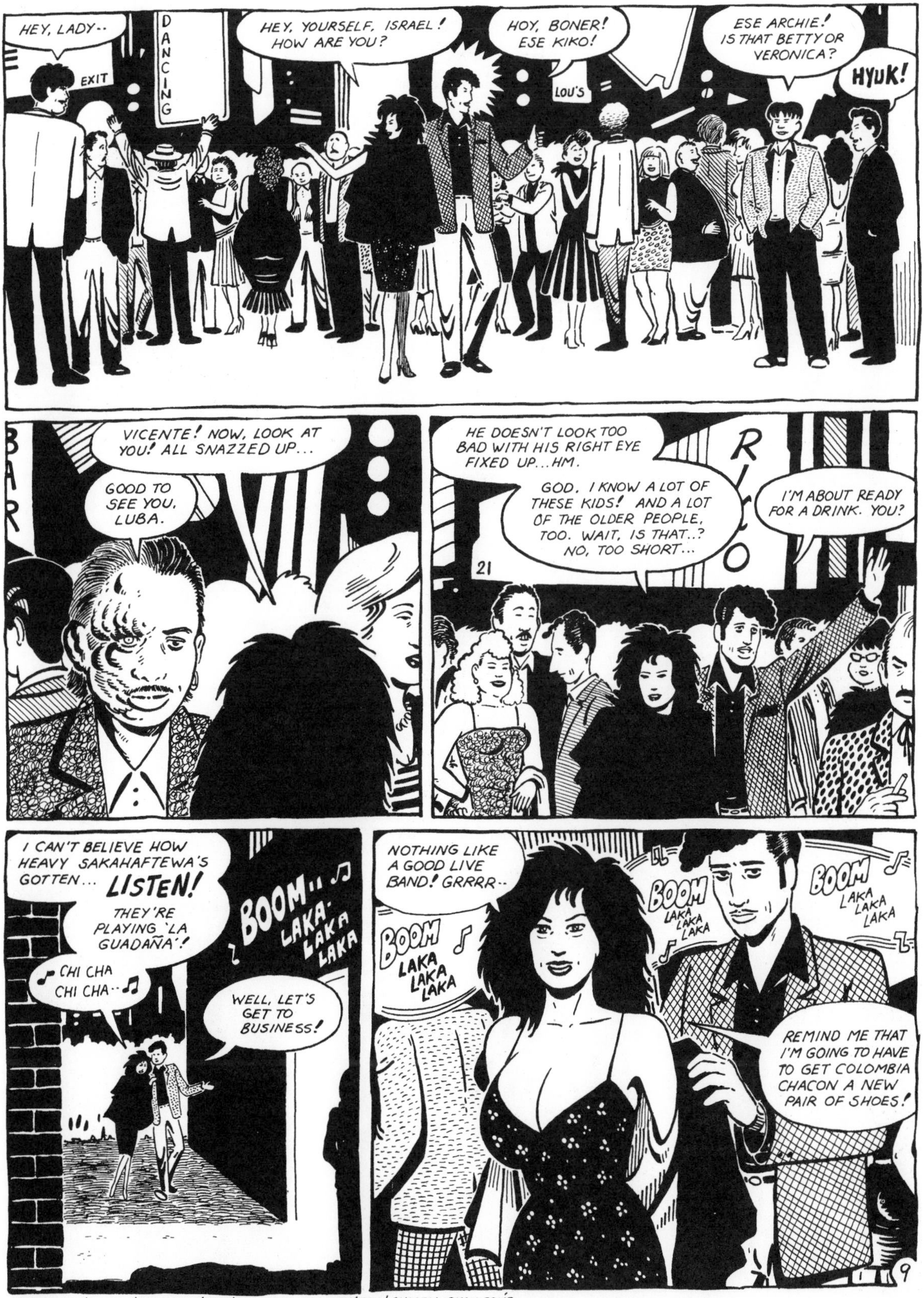
HEY, LADY..
EXIT
DANCING
HEY, YOURSELF, ISRAEL! HOW ARE YOU?
HOY, BONER! ESE KIKO!
LOU'S
ESE ARCHIE! IS THAT BETTY OR VERONICA?
HYUK!
BAR
VICENTE! NOW, LOOK AT YOU! ALL SNAZZED UP...
GOOD TO SEE YOU, LUBA.
HE DOESN'T LOOK TOO BAD WITH HIS RIGHT EYE FIXED UP...HM.
GOD, I KNOW A LOT OF THESE KIDS! AND A LOT OF THE OLDER PEOPLE, TOO. WAIT, IS THAT..? NO, TOO SHORT...
RICO
21
I'M ABOUT READY FOR A DRINK. YOU?
I CAN'T BELIEVE HOW HEAVY SAKAHAFTEWA'S GOTTEN... LISTEN!
THEY'RE PLAYING 'LA GUADAÑA'!
BOOM.. LAKA LAKA LAKA
CHI CHA CHI CHA..
WELL, LET'S GET TO BUSINESS!
NOTHING LIKE A GOOD LIVE BAND! GRRRR..
BOOM LAKA LAKA LAKA
BOOM LAKA LAKA LAKA
BOOM LAKA LAKA LAKA
REMIND ME THAT I'M GOING TO HAVE TO GET COLOMBIA CHACON A NEW PAIR OF SHOES!
9

ISRAEL - EES'RYE EL / KIKO - KEE'KOE / VICENTE - VEE SEN'TEH / CHACON - CHAH CONE

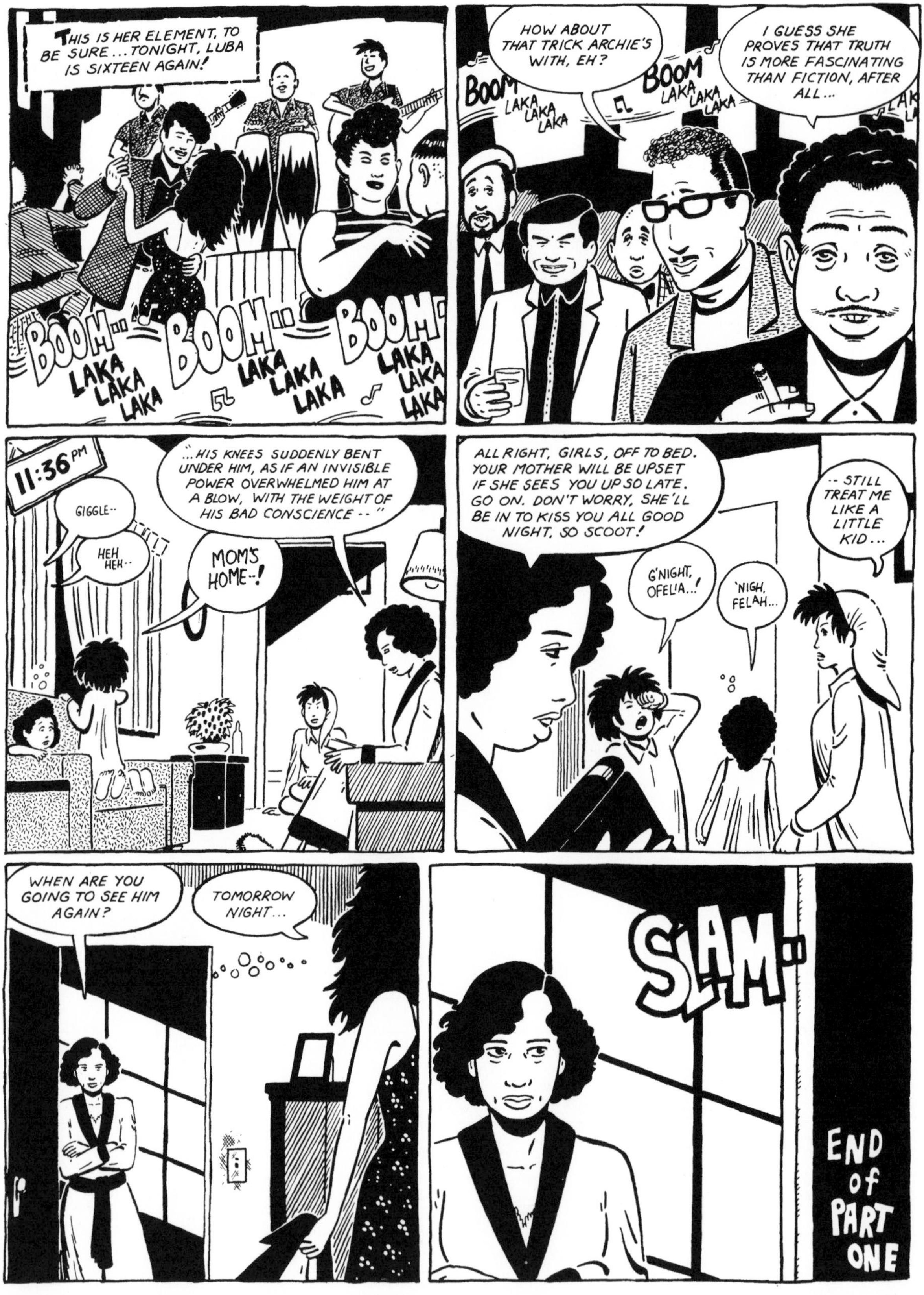
THIS IS HER ELEMENT, TO BE SURE... TONIGHT, LUBA IS SIXTEEN AGAIN!
BOOM.. LAKA LAKA LAKA
BOOM.. LAKA LAKA LAKA
BOOM.. LAKA LAKA LAKA
HOW ABOUT THAT TRICK ARCHIE'S WITH, EH?
I GUESS SHE PROVES THAT TRUTH IS MORE FASCINATING THAN FICTION, AFTER ALL...
BOOM LAKA LAKA LAKA
BOOM LAKA LAKA LAKA
11:36 PM
GIGGLE--
HEH HEH--
MOM'S HOME--!
"...HIS KNEES SUDDENLY BENT UNDER HIM, AS IF AN INVISIBLE POWER OVERWHELMED HIM AT A BLOW, WITH THE WEIGHT OF HIS BAD CONSCIENCE--"
ALL RIGHT, GIRLS, OFF TO BED. YOUR MOTHER WILL BE UPSET IF SHE SEES YOU UP SO LATE. GO ON. DON'T WORRY, SHE'LL BE IN TO KISS YOU ALL GOOD NIGHT, SO SCOOT!
G'NIGHT, OFELIA...!
'NIGH, FELAH...
-- STILL TREAT ME LIKE A LITTLE KID...
WHEN ARE YOU GOING TO SEE HIM AGAIN?
TOMORROW NIGHT...
SLAM..
END of PART ONE

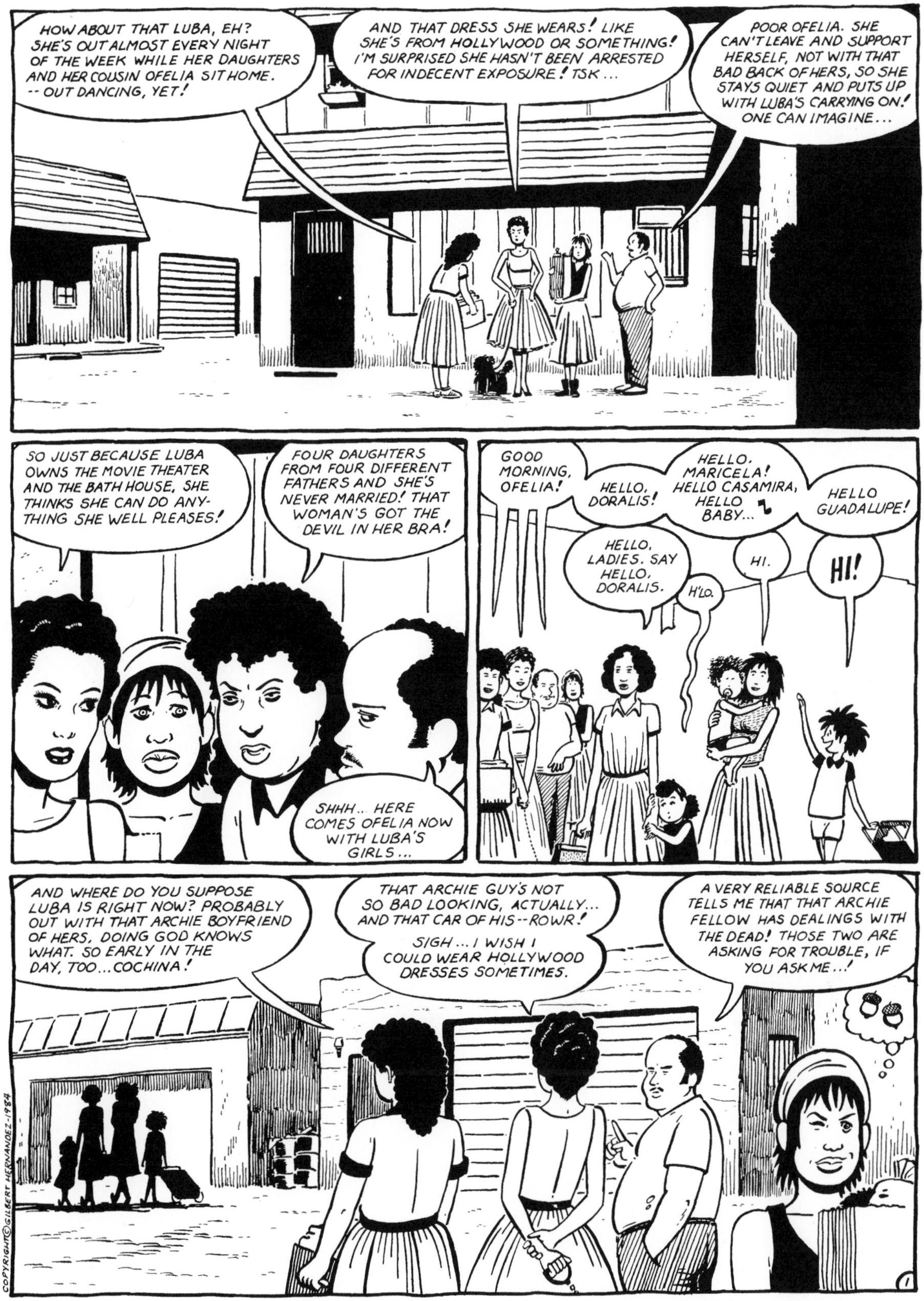

HOW ABOUT THAT LUBA, EH? SHE'S OUT ALMOST EVERY NIGHT OF THE WEEK WHILE HER DAUGHTERS AND HER COUSIN OFELIA SIT HOME. -- OUT DANCING, YET!
AND THAT DRESS SHE WEARS! LIKE SHE'S FROM HOLLYWOOD OR SOMETHING! I'M SURPRISED SHE HASN'T BEEN ARRESTED FOR INDECENT EXPOSURE! TSK ...
POOR OFELIA. SHE CAN'T LEAVE AND SUPPORT HERSELF, NOT WITH THAT BAD BACK OF HERS, SO SHE STAYS QUIET AND PUTS UP WITH LUBA'S CARRYING ON! ONE CAN IMAGINE...
SO JUST BECAUSE LUBA OWNS THE MOVIE THEATER AND THE BATH HOUSE, SHE THINKS SHE CAN DO ANYTHING SHE WELL PLEASES!
FOUR DAUGHTERS FROM FOUR DIFFERENT FATHERS AND SHE'S NEVER MARRIED! THAT WOMAN'S GOT THE DEVIL IN HER BRA!
SHHH... HERE COMES OFELIA NOW WITH LUBA'S GIRLS...
GOOD MORNING, OFELIA!
HELLO, DORALIS!
HELLO, MARICELA! HELLO CASAMIRA, HELLO BABY...
HELLO GUADALUPE!
HELLO, LADIES. SAY HELLO, DORALIS.
H'LO.
HI.
HI!
AND WHERE DO YOU SUPPOSE LUBA IS RIGHT NOW? PROBABLY OUT WITH THAT ARCHIE BOYFRIEND OF HERS, DOING GOD KNOWS WHAT. SO EARLY IN THE DAY, TOO... COCHINA!
THAT ARCHIE GUY'S NOT SO BAD LOOKING, ACTUALLY... AND THAT CAR OF HIS -- ROWR!
SIGH... I WISH I COULD WEAR HOLLYWOOD DRESSES SOMETIMES.
A VERY RELIABLE SOURCE TELLS ME THAT THAT ARCHIE FELLOW HAS DEALINGS WITH THE DEAD! THOSE TWO ARE ASKING FOR TROUBLE, IF YOU ASK ME...!
COPYRIGHT © GILBERT HERNANDEZ - 1984
1

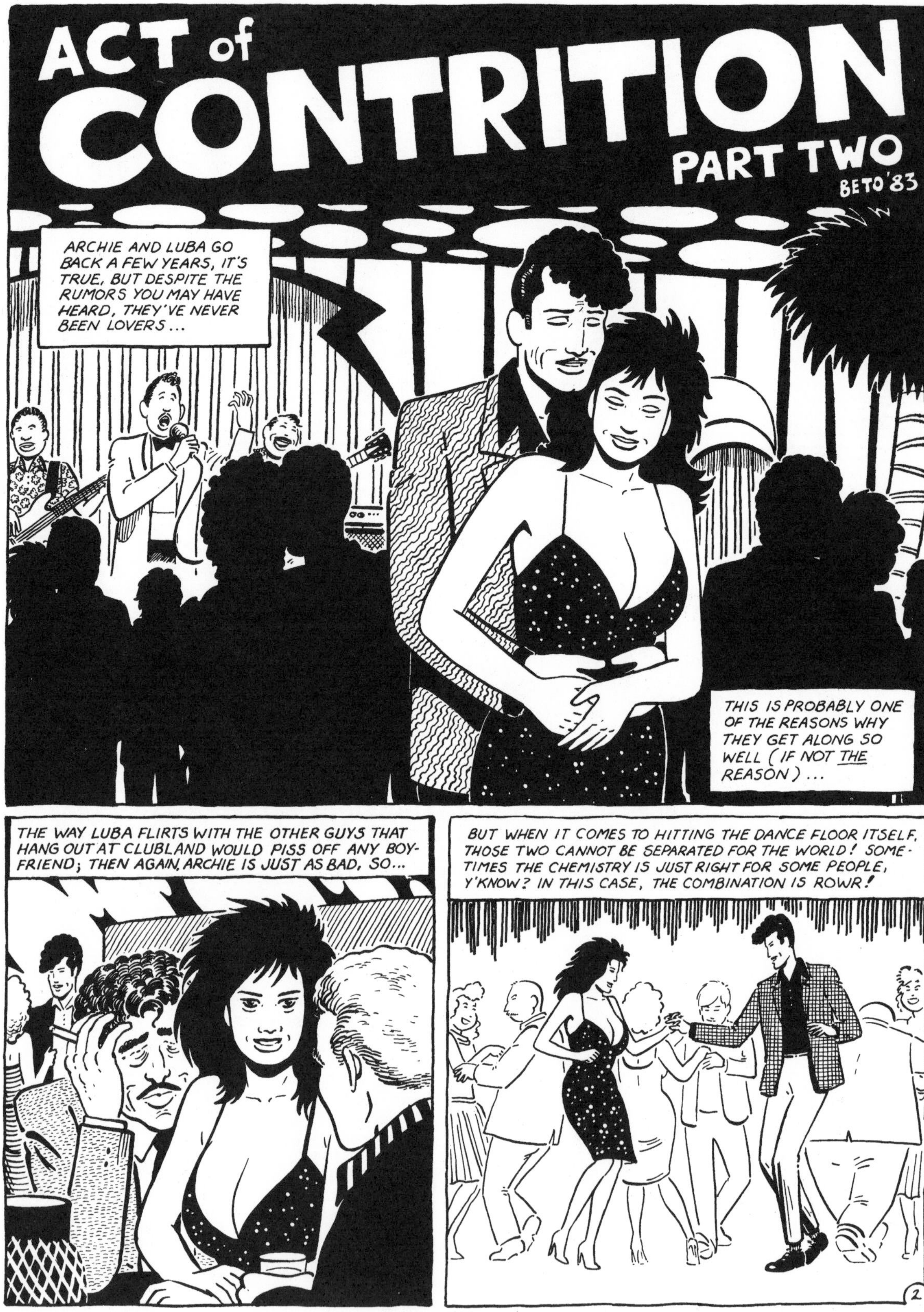
ACT of CONTRITION PART TWO
BETO '83
ARCHIE AND LUBA GO BACK A FEW YEARS, IT'S TRUE, BUT DESPITE THE RUMORS YOU MAY HAVE HEARD, THEY'VE NEVER BEEN LOVERS...
THIS IS PROBABLY ONE OF THE REASONS WHY THEY GET ALONG SO WELL (IF NOT THE REASON)...
THE WAY LUBA FLIRTS WITH THE OTHER GUYS THAT HANG OUT AT CLUBLAND WOULD PISS OFF ANY BOY-FRIEND; THEN AGAIN, ARCHIE IS JUST AS BAD, SO...
BUT WHEN IT COMES TO HITTING THE DANCE FLOOR ITSELF, THOSE TWO CANNOT BE SEPARATED FOR THE WORLD! SOME-TIMES THE CHEMISTRY IS JUST RIGHT FOR SOME PEOPLE, Y'KNOW? IN THIS CASE, THE COMBINATION IS ROWR!
2

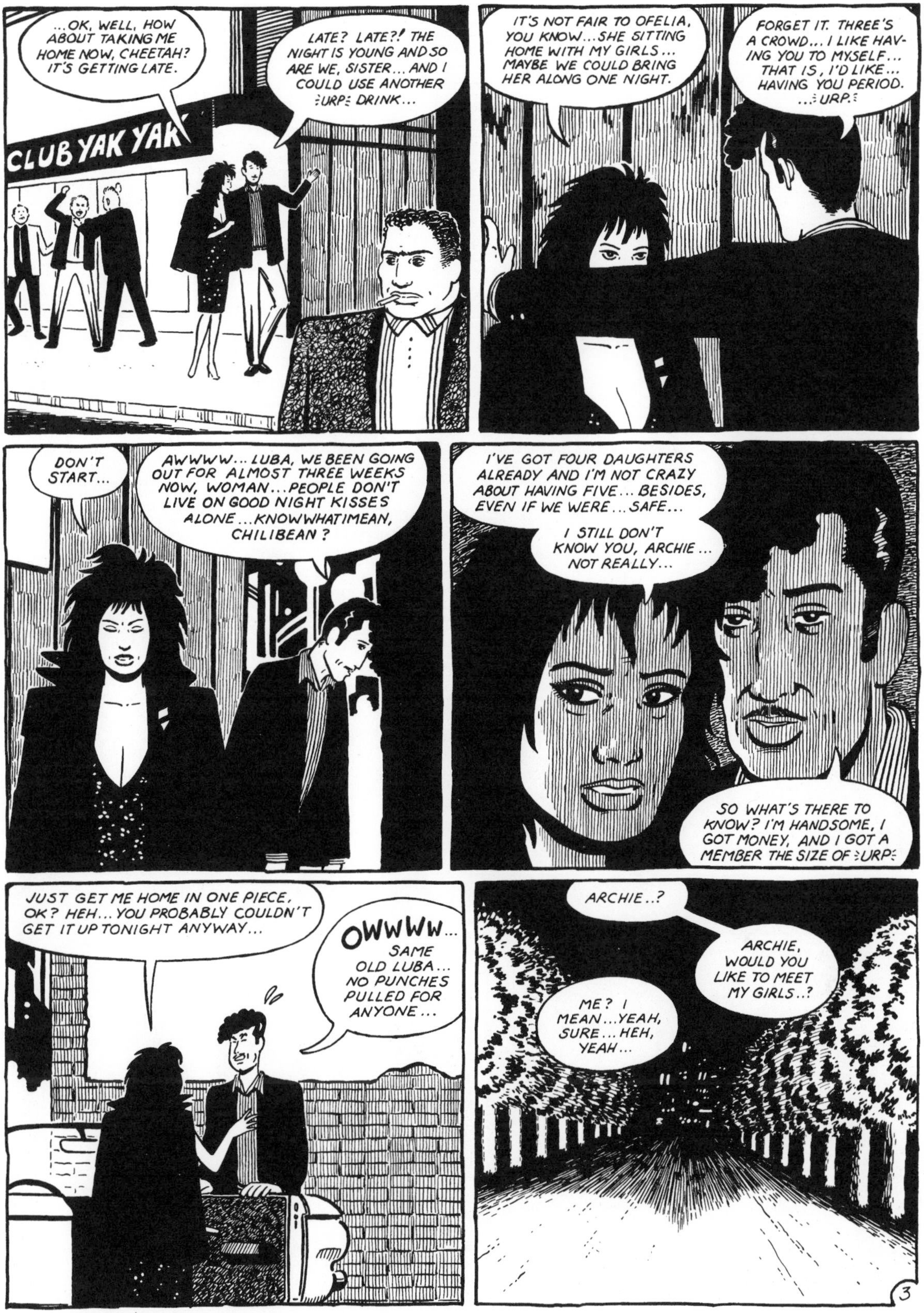
...OK, WELL, HOW ABOUT TAKING ME HOME NOW, CHEETAH? IT'S GETTING LATE.
LATE? LATE?! THE NIGHT IS YOUNG AND SO ARE WE, SISTER... AND I COULD USE ANOTHER URP DRINK...
CLUB YAK YAK
IT'S NOT FAIR TO OFELIA, YOU KNOW... SHE SITTING HOME WITH MY GIRLS... MAYBE WE COULD BRING HER ALONG ONE NIGHT.
FORGET IT. THREE'S A CROWD... I LIKE HAVING YOU TO MYSELF... THAT IS, I'D LIKE... HAVING YOU PERIOD. ...URP.
DON'T START...
AWWWW... LUBA, WE BEEN GOING OUT FOR ALMOST THREE WEEKS NOW, WOMAN... PEOPLE DON'T LIVE ON GOOD NIGHT KISSES ALONE... KNOWWHATIMEAN, CHILIBEAN?
I'VE GOT FOUR DAUGHTERS ALREADY AND I'M NOT CRAZY ABOUT HAVING FIVE... BESIDES, EVEN IF WE WERE... SAFE...
I STILL DON'T KNOW YOU, ARCHIE... NOT REALLY...
SO WHAT'S THERE TO KNOW? I'M HANDSOME, I GOT MONEY, AND I GOT A MEMBER THE SIZE OF URP
JUST GET ME HOME IN ONE PIECE, OK? HEH... YOU PROBABLY COULDN'T GET IT UP TONIGHT ANYWAY...
OWWWW... SAME OLD LUBA... NO PUNCHES PULLED FOR ANYONE...
ARCHIE..?
ARCHIE, WOULD YOU LIKE TO MEET MY GIRLS..?
ME? I MEAN... YEAH, SURE... HEH, YEAH...
3

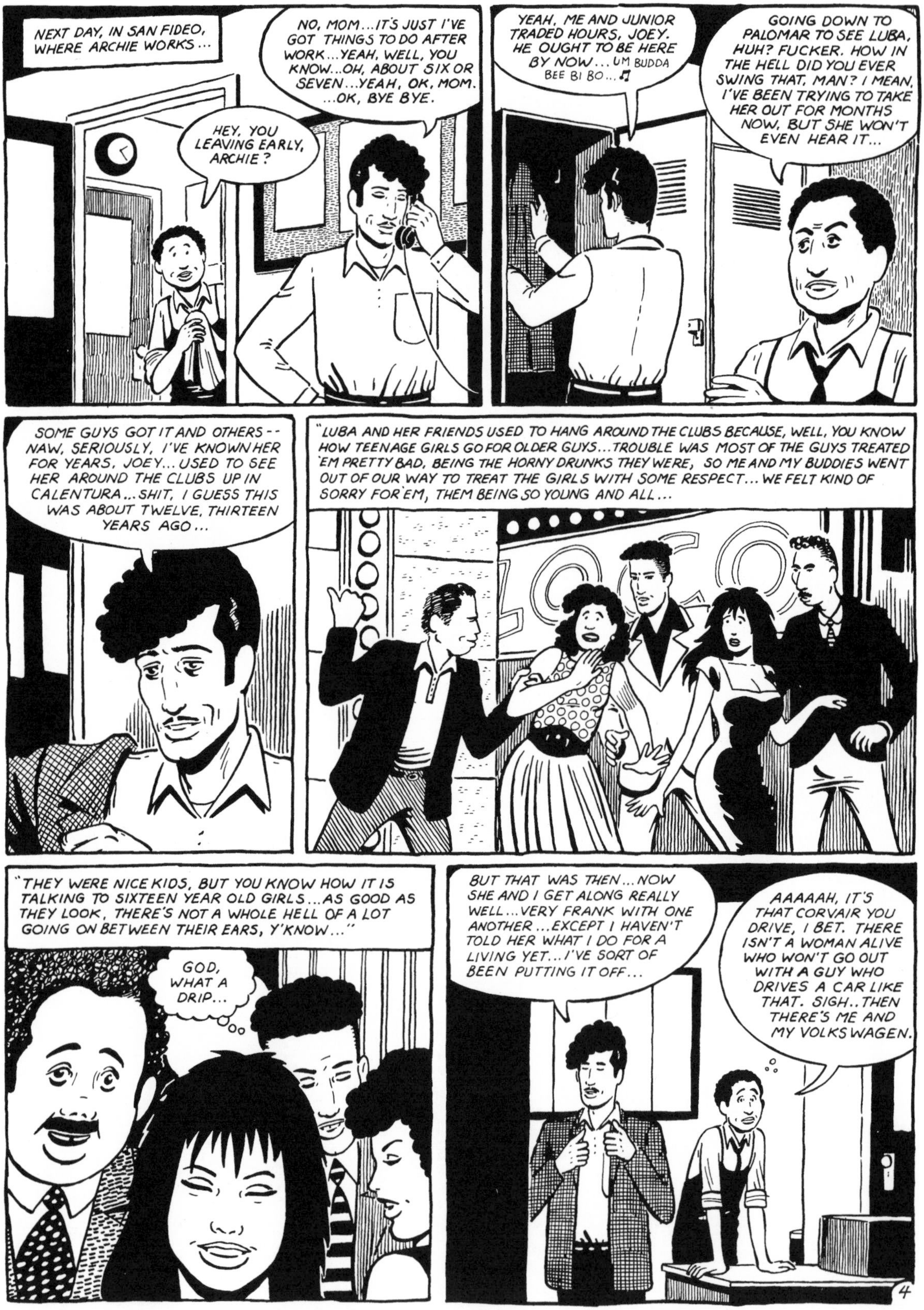
NEXT DAY, IN SAN FIDEO, WHERE ARCHIE WORKS...
NO, MOM...IT'S JUST I'VE GOT THINGS TO DO AFTER WORK...YEAH, WELL, YOU KNOW...OH, ABOUT SIX OR SEVEN...YEAH, OK, MOM. ...OK, BYE BYE.
HEY, YOU LEAVING EARLY, ARCHIE?
YEAH, ME AND JUNIOR TRADED HOURS, JOEY. HE OUGHT TO BE HERE BY NOW... UM BUDDA BEE BI BO...♫
GOING DOWN TO PALOMAR TO SEE LUBA, HUH? FUCKER. HOW IN THE HELL DID YOU EVER SWING THAT, MAN? I MEAN, I'VE BEEN TRYING TO TAKE HER OUT FOR MONTHS NOW, BUT SHE WON'T EVEN HEAR IT...
SOME GUYS GOT IT AND OTHERS-- NAW, SERIOUSLY, I'VE KNOWN HER FOR YEARS, JOEY... USED TO SEE HER AROUND THE CLUBS UP IN CALENTURA...SHIT, I GUESS THIS WAS ABOUT TWELVE, THIRTEEN YEARS AGO...
"LUBA AND HER FRIENDS USED TO HANG AROUND THE CLUBS BECAUSE, WELL, YOU KNOW HOW TEENAGE GIRLS GO FOR OLDER GUYS...TROUBLE WAS MOST OF THE GUYS TREATED 'EM PRETTY BAD, BEING THE HORNY DRUNKS THEY WERE, SO ME AND MY BUDDIES WENT OUT OF OUR WAY TO TREAT THE GIRLS WITH SOME RESPECT... WE FELT KIND OF SORRY FOR 'EM, THEM BEING SO YOUNG AND ALL...
"THEY WERE NICE KIDS, BUT YOU KNOW HOW IT IS TALKING TO SIXTEEN YEAR OLD GIRLS...AS GOOD AS THEY LOOK, THERE'S NOT A WHOLE HELL OF A LOT GOING ON BETWEEN THEIR EARS, Y'KNOW..."
GOD, WHAT A DRIP...
BUT THAT WAS THEN...NOW SHE AND I GET ALONG REALLY WELL...VERY FRANK WITH ONE ANOTHER...EXCEPT I HAVEN'T TOLD HER WHAT I DO FOR A LIVING YET...I'VE SORT OF BEEN PUTTING IT OFF...
AAAAAH, IT'S THAT CORVAIR YOU DRIVE, I BET. THERE ISN'T A WOMAN ALIVE WHO WON'T GO OUT WITH A GUY WHO DRIVES A CAR LIKE THAT. SIGH..THEN THERE'S ME AND MY VOLKSWAGEN.
4

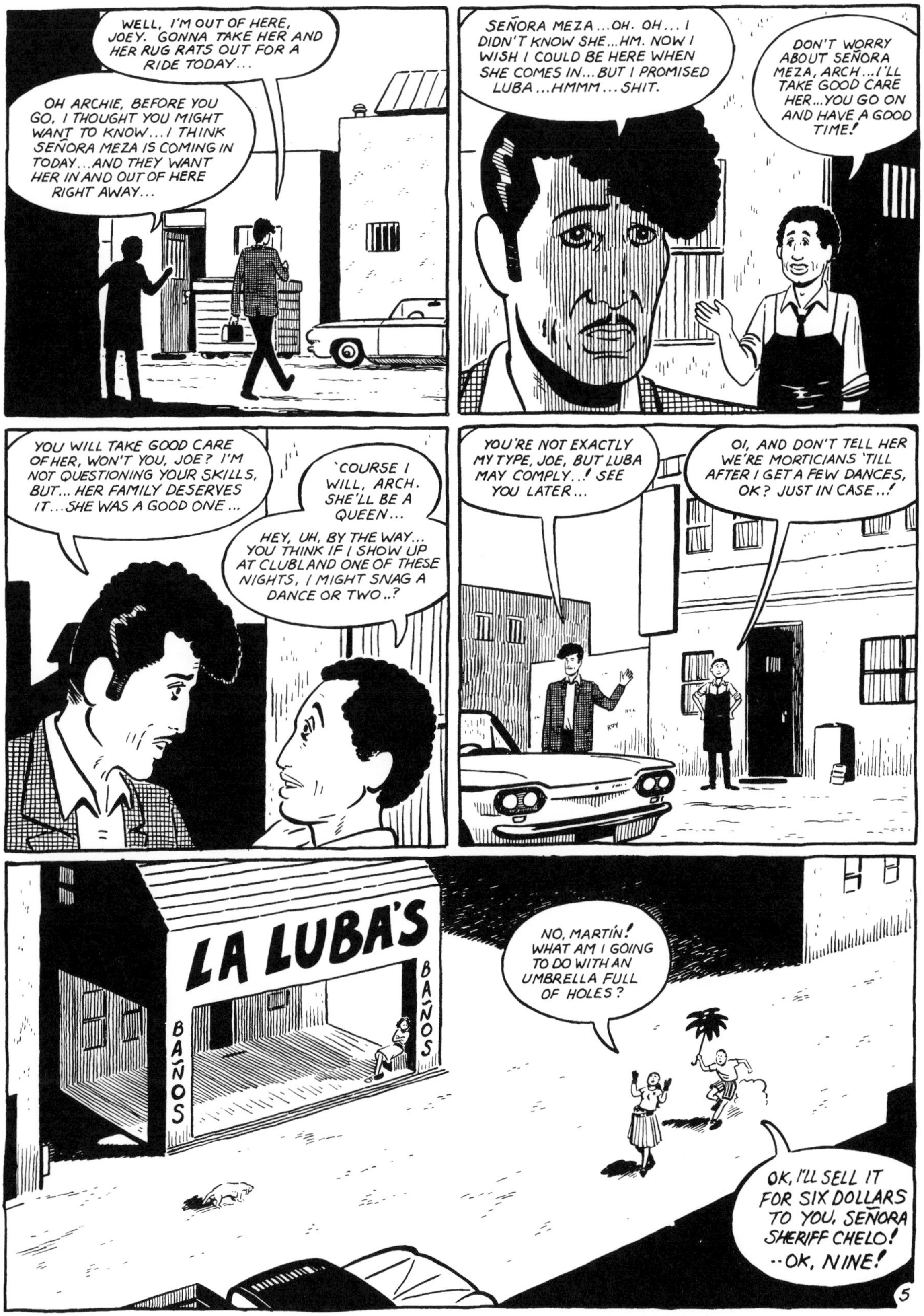
WELL, I'M OUT OF HERE, JOEY. GONNA TAKE HER AND HER RUG RATS OUT FOR A RIDE TODAY...
OH ARCHIE, BEFORE YOU GO, I THOUGHT YOU MIGHT WANT TO KNOW... I THINK SEÑORA MEZA IS COMING IN TODAY... AND THEY WANT HER IN AND OUT OF HERE RIGHT AWAY...
SEÑORA MEZA... OH. OH... I DIDN'T KNOW SHE... HM. NOW I WISH I COULD BE HERE WHEN SHE COMES IN... BUT I PROMISED LUBA... HMMM... SHIT.
DON'T WORRY ABOUT SEÑORA MEZA, ARCH... I'LL TAKE GOOD CARE HER... YOU GO ON AND HAVE A GOOD TIME!
YOU WILL TAKE GOOD CARE OF HER, WON'T YOU, JOE? I'M NOT QUESTIONING YOUR SKILLS, BUT... HER FAMILY DESERVES IT... SHE WAS A GOOD ONE...
`COURSE I WILL, ARCH. SHE'LL BE A QUEEN...
HEY, UH, BY THE WAY... YOU THINK IF I SHOW UP AT CLUBLAND ONE OF THESE NIGHTS, I MIGHT SNAG A DANCE OR TWO..?
YOU'RE NOT EXACTLY MY TYPE, JOE, BUT LUBA MAY COMPLY..! SEE YOU LATER...
OI, AND DON'T TELL HER WE'RE MORTICIANS 'TILL AFTER I GET A FEW DANCES, OK? JUST IN CASE..!
LA LUBA'S
BAÑOS
BAÑOS
NO, MARTÍN! WHAT AM I GOING TO DO WITH AN UMBRELLA FULL OF HOLES?
OK, I'LL SELL IT FOR SIX DOLLARS TO YOU, SEÑORA SHERIFF CHELO! --OK, NINE!
5

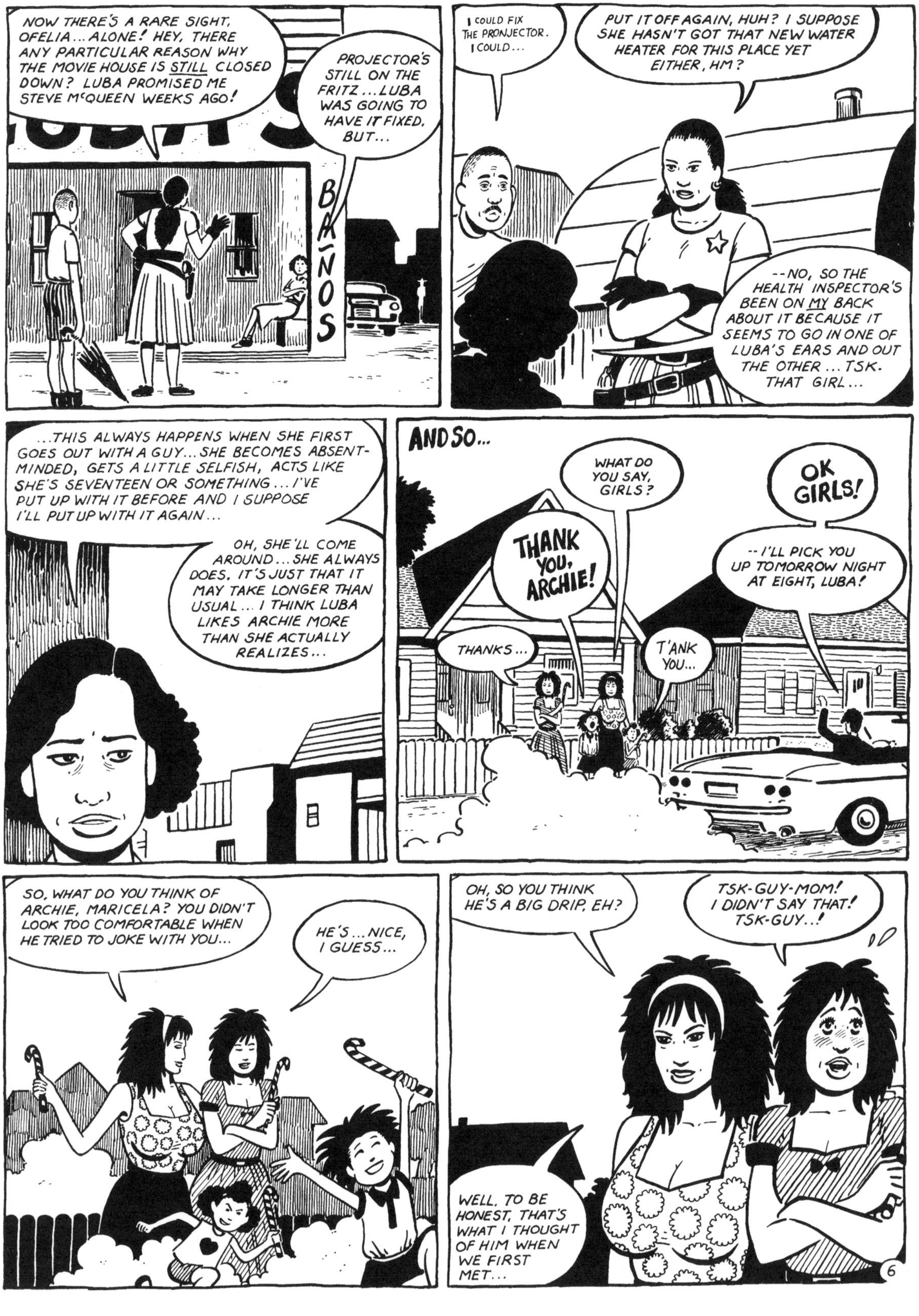
NOW THERE'S A RARE SIGHT, OFELIA... ALONE! HEY, THERE ANY PARTICULAR REASON WHY THE MOVIE HOUSE IS STILL CLOSED DOWN? LUBA PROMISED ME STEVE McQUEEN WEEKS AGO!
PROJECTOR'S STILL ON THE FRITZ... LUBA WAS GOING TO HAVE IT FIXED, BUT...
BAÑOS
I COULD FIX THE PRONJECTOR. I COULD...
PUT IT OFF AGAIN, HUH? I SUPPOSE SHE HASN'T GOT THAT NEW WATER HEATER FOR THIS PLACE YET EITHER, HM?
--NO, SO THE HEALTH INSPECTOR'S BEEN ON MY BACK ABOUT IT BECAUSE IT SEEMS TO GO IN ONE OF LUBA'S EARS AND OUT THE OTHER... TSK. THAT GIRL...
...THIS ALWAYS HAPPENS WHEN SHE FIRST GOES OUT WITH A GUY... SHE BECOMES ABSENT-MINDED, GETS A LITTLE SELFISH, ACTS LIKE SHE'S SEVENTEEN OR SOMETHING... I'VE PUT UP WITH IT BEFORE AND I SUPPOSE I'LL PUT UP WITH IT AGAIN...
OH, SHE'LL COME AROUND... SHE ALWAYS DOES. IT'S JUST THAT IT MAY TAKE LONGER THAN USUAL... I THINK LUBA LIKES ARCHIE MORE THAN SHE ACTUALLY REALIZES...
AND SO...
WHAT DO YOU SAY, GIRLS?
OK GIRLS!
THANK YOU, ARCHIE!
--I'LL PICK YOU UP TOMORROW NIGHT AT EIGHT, LUBA!
THANKS...
T'ANK YOU...
SO, WHAT DO YOU THINK OF ARCHIE, MARICELA? YOU DIDN'T LOOK TOO COMFORTABLE WHEN HE TRIED TO JOKE WITH YOU...
HE'S... NICE, I GUESS...
OH, SO YOU THINK HE'S A BIG DRIP, EH?
TSK-GUY-MOM! I DIDN'T SAY THAT! TSK-GUY..!
WELL, TO BE HONEST, THAT'S WHAT I THOUGHT OF HIM WHEN WE FIRST MET...
6

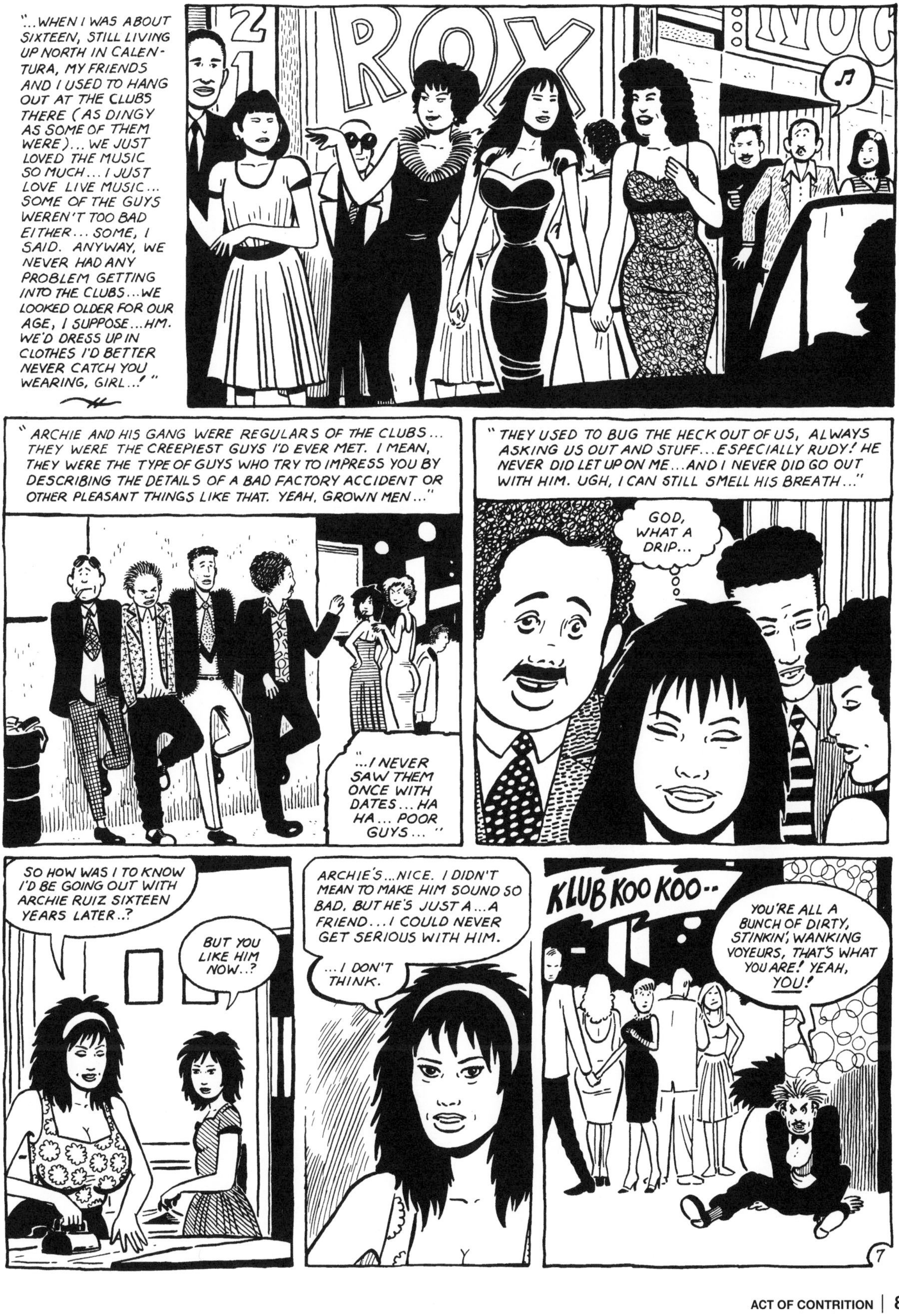
"...WHEN I WAS ABOUT SIXTEEN, STILL LIVING UP NORTH IN CALENTURA, MY FRIENDS AND I USED TO HANG OUT AT THE CLUBS THERE (AS DINGY AS SOME OF THEM WERE)... WE JUST LOVED THE MUSIC SO MUCH... I JUST LOVE LIVE MUSIC... SOME OF THE GUYS WEREN'T TOO BAD EITHER... SOME, I SAID. ANYWAY, WE NEVER HAD ANY PROBLEM GETTING INTO THE CLUBS... WE LOOKED OLDER FOR OUR AGE, I SUPPOSE... HM. WE'D DRESS UP IN CLOTHES I'D BETTER NEVER CATCH YOU WEARING, GIRL...!"
21
ROX
"ARCHIE AND HIS GANG WERE REGULARS OF THE CLUBS... THEY WERE THE CREEPIEST GUYS I'D EVER MET. I MEAN, THEY WERE THE TYPE OF GUYS WHO TRY TO IMPRESS YOU BY DESCRIBING THE DETAILS OF A BAD FACTORY ACCIDENT OR OTHER PLEASANT THINGS LIKE THAT. YEAH, GROWN MEN..."
"...I NEVER SAW THEM ONCE WITH DATES... HA HA... POOR GUYS..."
"THEY USED TO BUG THE HECK OUT OF US, ALWAYS ASKING US OUT AND STUFF... ESPECIALLY RUDY! HE NEVER DID LET UP ON ME... AND I NEVER DID GO OUT WITH HIM. UGH, I CAN STILL SMELL HIS BREATH..."
GOD, WHAT A DRIP...
SO HOW WAS I TO KNOW I'D BE GOING OUT WITH ARCHIE RUIZ SIXTEEN YEARS LATER..?
BUT YOU LIKE HIM NOW..?
ARCHIE'S... NICE. I DIDN'T MEAN TO MAKE HIM SOUND SO BAD. BUT HE'S JUST A... A FRIEND... I COULD NEVER GET SERIOUS WITH HIM.
...I DON'T THINK.
KLUB KOO KOO..
YOU'RE ALL A BUNCH OF DIRTY, STINKIN', WANKING VOYEURS, THAT'S WHAT YOU ARE! YEAH, YOU!
7

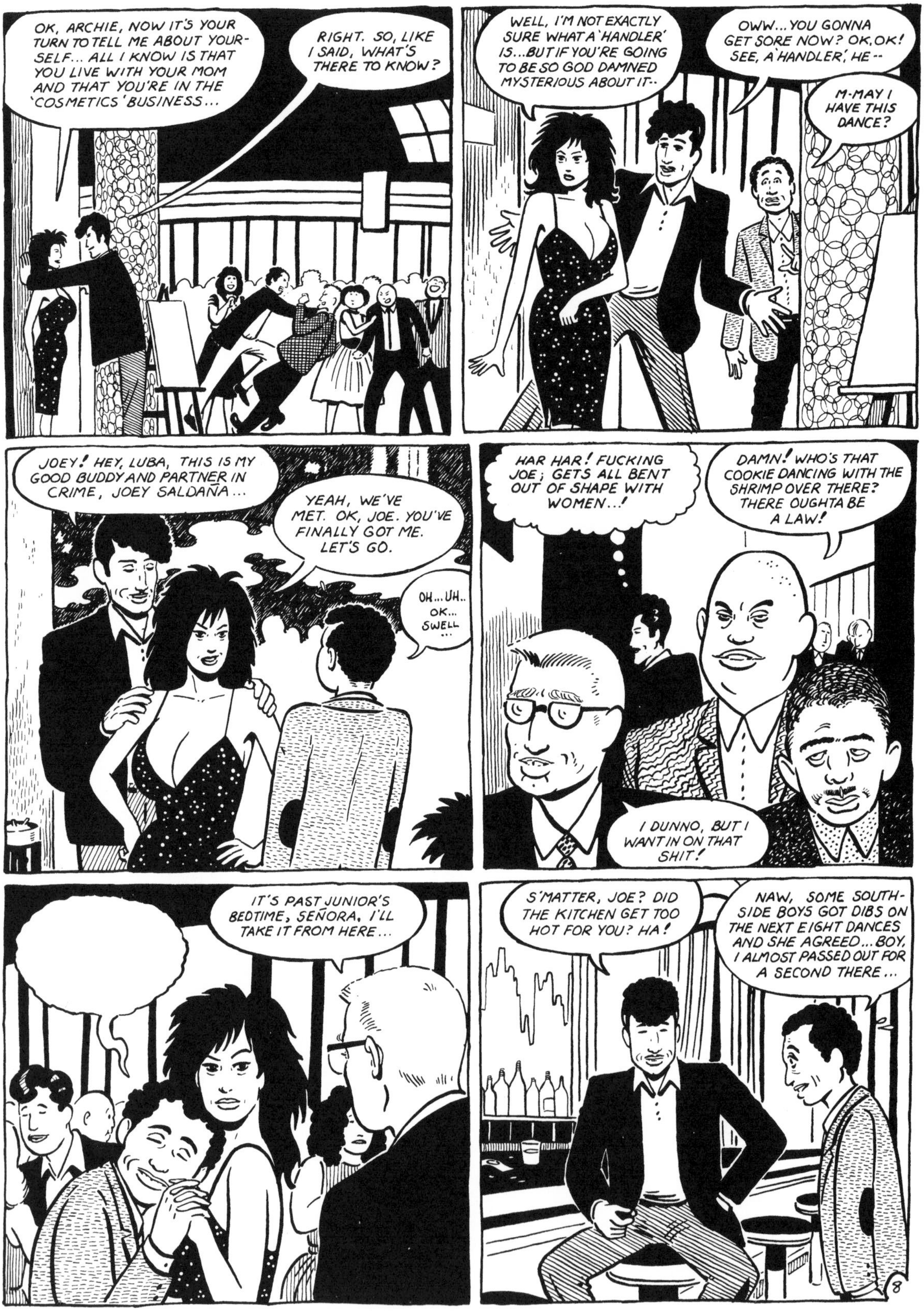

OK, ARCHIE, NOW IT'S YOUR TURN TO TELL ME ABOUT YOURSELF... ALL I KNOW IS THAT YOU LIVE WITH YOUR MOM AND THAT YOU'RE IN THE 'COSMETICS' BUSINESS...
RIGHT. SO, LIKE I SAID, WHAT'S THERE TO KNOW?
WELL, I'M NOT EXACTLY SURE WHAT A 'HANDLER' IS...BUT IF YOU'RE GOING TO BE SO GOD DAMNED MYSTERIOUS ABOUT IT--
OWW...YOU GONNA GET SORE NOW? OK, OK! SEE, A 'HANDLER', HE --
M-MAY I HAVE THIS DANCE?
JOEY! HEY, LUBA, THIS IS MY GOOD BUDDY AND PARTNER IN CRIME, JOEY SALDAÑA...
YEAH, WE'VE MET. OK, JOE. YOU'VE FINALLY GOT ME. LET'S GO.
OH...UH.. OK... SWELL ...
HAR HAR! FUCKING JOE; GETS ALL BENT OUT OF SHAPE WITH WOMEN...!
DAMN! WHO'S THAT COOKIE DANCING WITH THE SHRIMP OVER THERE? THERE OUGHTA BE A LAW!
I DUNNO, BUT I WANT IN ON THAT SHIT!
IT'S PAST JUNIOR'S BEDTIME, SEÑORA. I'LL TAKE IT FROM HERE...
S'MATTER, JOE? DID THE KITCHEN GET TOO HOT FOR YOU? HA!
NAW, SOME SOUTH-SIDE BOYS GOT DIBS ON THE NEXT EIGHT DANCES AND SHE AGREED... BOY, I ALMOST PASSED OUT FOR A SECOND THERE...
8

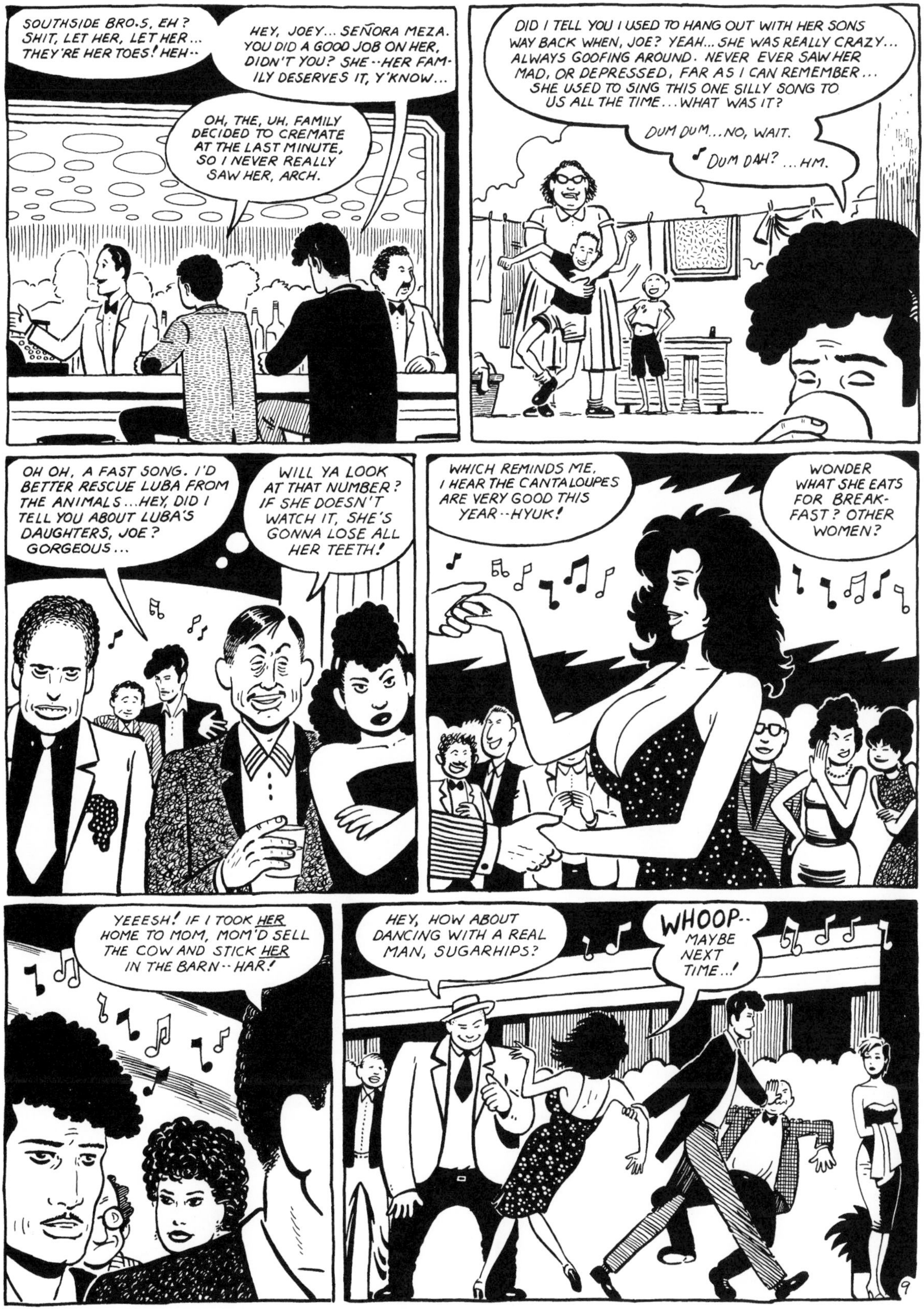
SOUTHSIDE BRO.S, EH? SHIT, LET HER, LET HER... THEY'RE HER TOES! HEH..
HEY, JOEY... SEÑORA MEZA. YOU DID A GOOD JOB ON HER, DIDN'T YOU? SHE..HER FAMILY DESERVES IT, Y'KNOW...
OH, THE, UH, FAMILY DECIDED TO CREMATE AT THE LAST MINUTE, SO I NEVER REALLY SAW HER, ARCH.
DID I TELL YOU I USED TO HANG OUT WITH HER SONS WAY BACK WHEN, JOE? YEAH... SHE WAS REALLY CRAZY... ALWAYS GOOFING AROUND. NEVER EVER SAW HER MAD, OR DEPRESSED, FAR AS I CAN REMEMBER... SHE USED TO SING THIS ONE SILLY SONG TO US ALL THE TIME... WHAT WAS IT?
DUM DUM... NO, WAIT.
DUM DAH? ...HM.
OH OH, A FAST SONG. I'D BETTER RESCUE LUBA FROM THE ANIMALS... HEY, DID I TELL YOU ABOUT LUBA'S DAUGHTERS, JOE? GORGEOUS...
WILL YA LOOK AT THAT NUMBER? IF SHE DOESN'T WATCH IT, SHE'S GONNA LOSE ALL HER TEETH!
WHICH REMINDS ME, I HEAR THE CANTALOUPES ARE VERY GOOD THIS YEAR..HYUK!
WONDER WHAT SHE EATS FOR BREAKFAST? OTHER WOMEN?
YEEESH! IF I TOOK HER HOME TO MOM, MOM'D SELL THE COW AND STICK HER IN THE BARN.. HAR!
HEY, HOW ABOUT DANCING WITH A REAL MAN, SUGARHIPS?
WHOOP..
MAYBE NEXT TIME...!
9

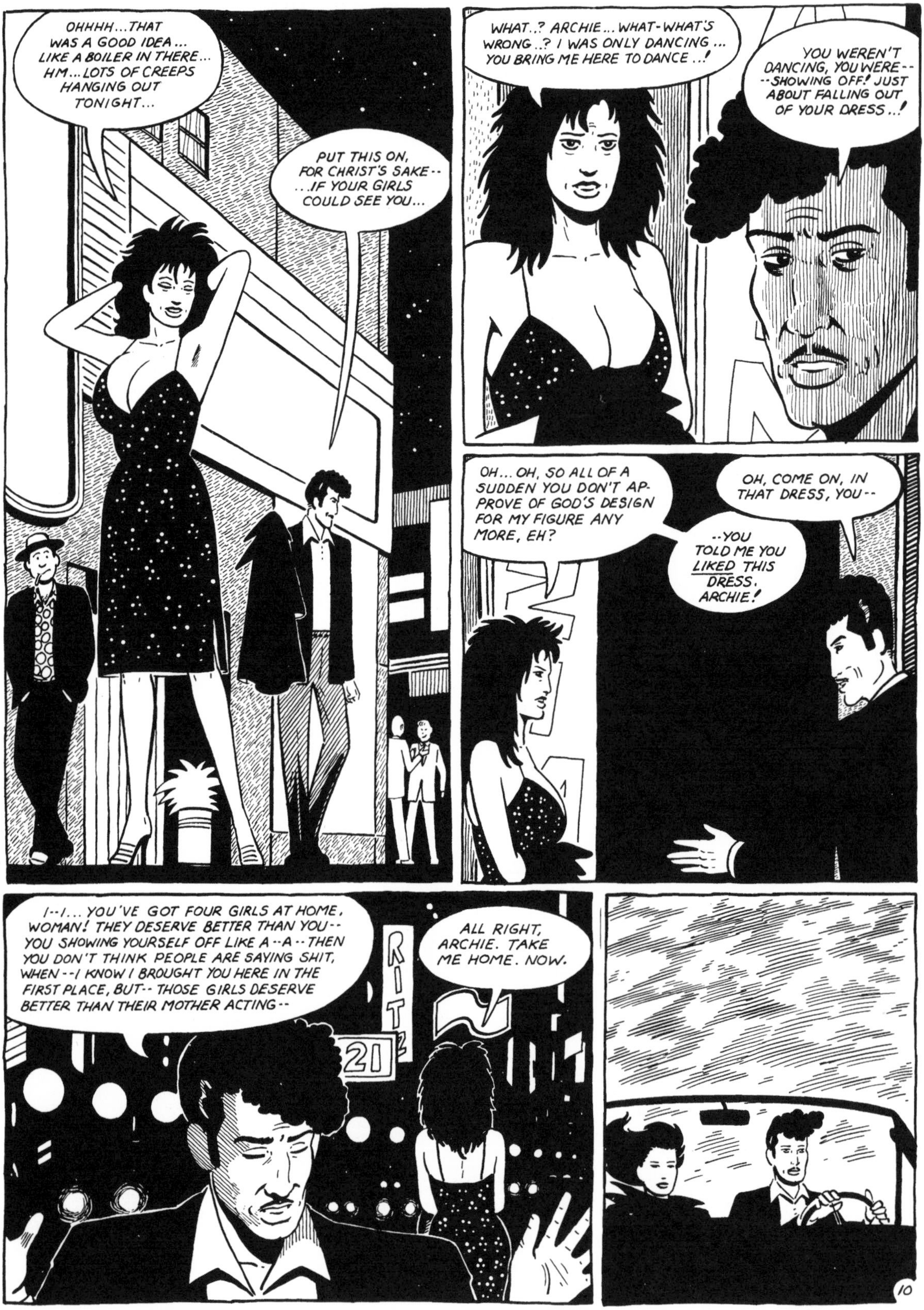
OHHHH...THAT WAS A GOOD IDEA... LIKE A BOILER IN THERE... HM...LOTS OF CREEPS HANGING OUT TONIGHT...
PUT THIS ON, FOR CHRIST'S SAKE-- ...IF YOUR GIRLS COULD SEE YOU...
WHAT..? ARCHIE...WHAT-WHAT'S WRONG..? I WAS ONLY DANCING... YOU BRING ME HERE TO DANCE..!
YOU WEREN'T DANCING, YOU WERE-- --SHOWING OFF! JUST ABOUT FALLING OUT OF YOUR DRESS..!
OH...OH, SO ALL OF A SUDDEN YOU DON'T APPROVE OF GOD'S DESIGN FOR MY FIGURE ANY MORE, EH?
OH, COME ON, IN THAT DRESS, YOU--
--YOU TOLD ME YOU LIKED THIS DRESS, ARCHIE!
I--I...YOU'VE GOT FOUR GIRLS AT HOME, WOMAN! THEY DESERVE BETTER THAN YOU-- YOU SHOWING YOURSELF OFF LIKE A--A--THEN YOU DON'T THINK PEOPLE ARE SAYING SHIT, WHEN--I KNOW I BROUGHT YOU HERE IN THE FIRST PLACE, BUT--THOSE GIRLS DESERVE BETTER THAN THEIR MOTHER ACTING--
RITZ
21
ALL RIGHT, ARCHIE. TAKE ME HOME. NOW.
10

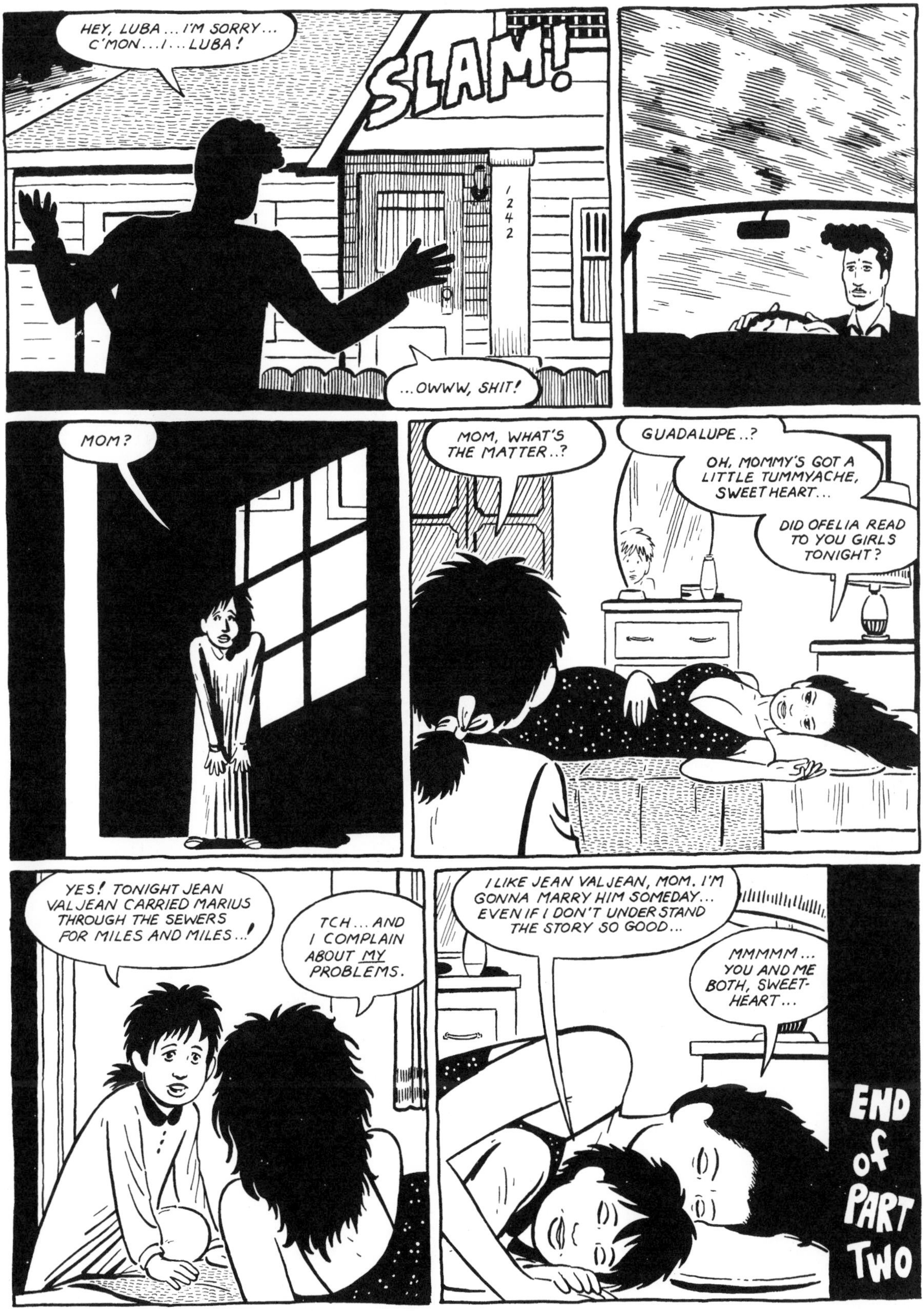
HEY, LUBA... I'M SORRY... C'MON... I... LUBA!
SLAM!
1242
...OWWW, SHIT!
MOM?
MOM, WHAT'S THE MATTER..?
GUADALUPE..?
OH, MOMMY'S GOT A LITTLE TUMMYACHE, SWEET HEART...
DID OFELIA READ TO YOU GIRLS TONIGHT?
YES! TONIGHT JEAN VALJEAN CARRIED MARIUS THROUGH THE SEWERS FOR MILES AND MILES...!
TCH... AND I COMPLAIN ABOUT MY PROBLEMS.
I LIKE JEAN VALJEAN, MOM. I'M GONNA MARRY HIM SOMEDAY... EVEN IF I DON'T UNDERSTAND THE STORY SO GOOD...
MMMMM... YOU AND ME BOTH, SWEET-HEART...
END of PART TWO

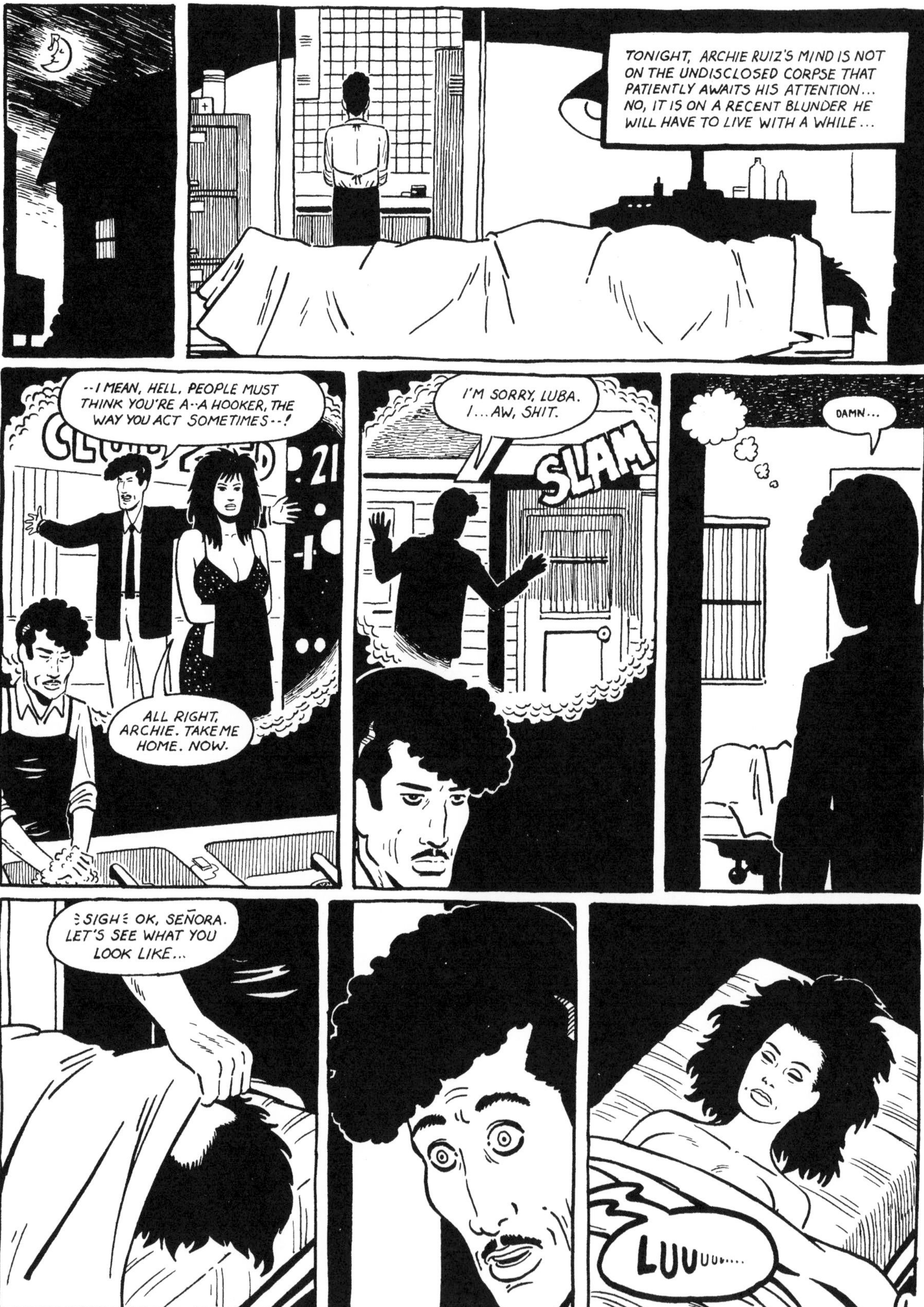
TONIGHT, ARCHIE RUIZ'S MIND IS NOT ON THE UNDISCLOSED CORPSE THAT PATIENTLY AWAITS HIS ATTENTION... NO, IT IS ON A RECENT BLUNDER HE WILL HAVE TO LIVE WITH A WHILE...
--I MEAN, HELL, PEOPLE MUST THINK YOU'RE A--A HOOKER, THE WAY YOU ACT SOMETIMES--!
ALL RIGHT, ARCHIE. TAKE ME HOME. NOW.
I'M SORRY, LUBA. I... AW, SHIT.
SLAM
DAMN...
⁝SIGH⁝ OK, SEÑORA. LET'S SEE WHAT YOU LOOK LIKE...
LUUuuu....
COPYRIGHT © GILBERT HERNANDEZ - 1984

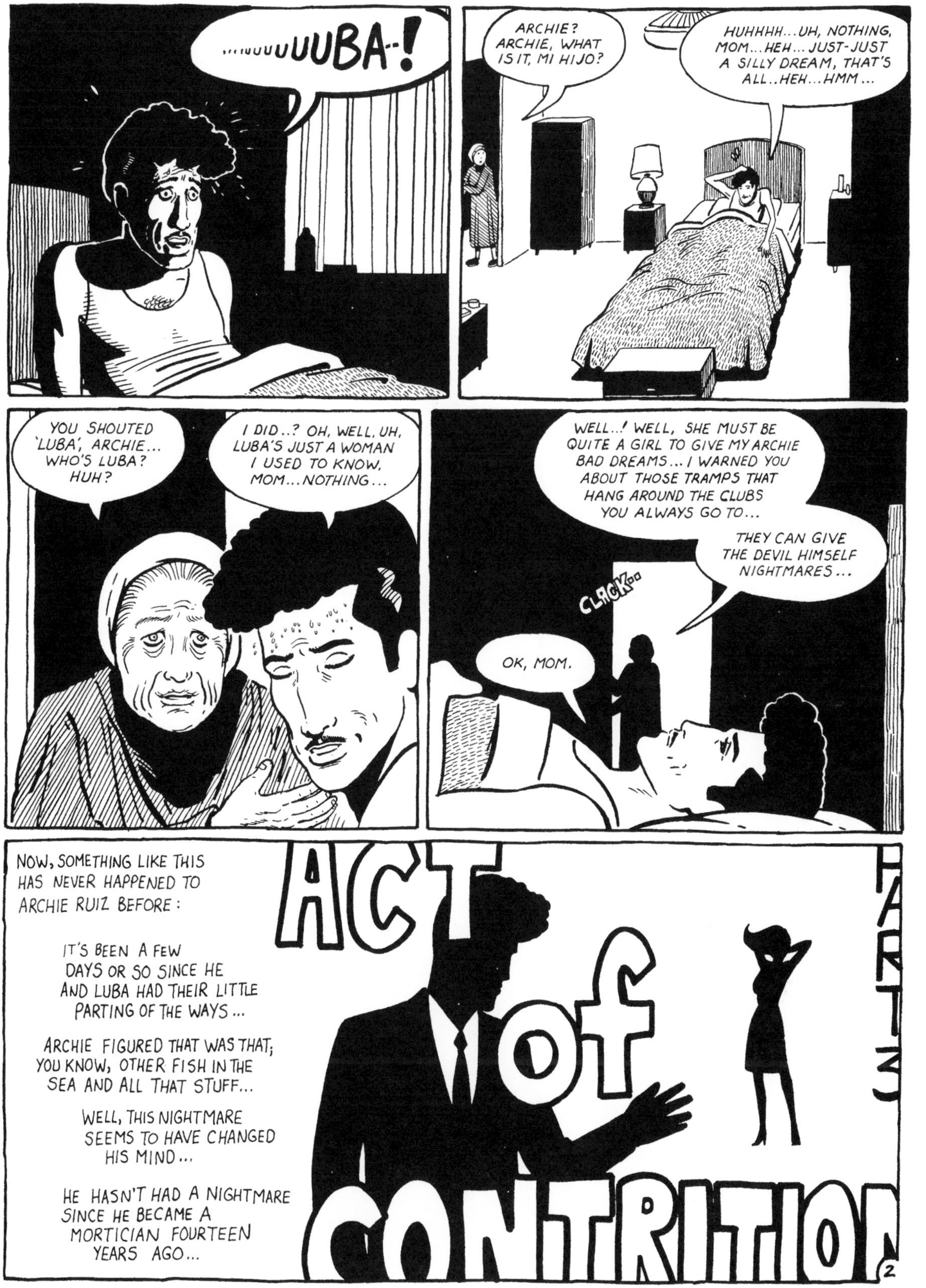
...uuuuUUBA--!
ARCHIE? ARCHIE, WHAT IS IT, MI HIJO?
HUHHHH... UH, NOTHING, MOM... HEH... JUST-JUST A SILLY DREAM, THAT'S ALL.. HEH... HMM...
YOU SHOUTED 'LUBA', ARCHIE... WHO'S LUBA? HUH?
I DID..? OH, WELL, UH, LUBA'S JUST A WOMAN I USED TO KNOW, MOM... NOTHING...
WELL..! WELL, SHE MUST BE QUITE A GIRL TO GIVE MY ARCHIE BAD DREAMS... I WARNED YOU ABOUT THOSE TRAMPS THAT HANG AROUND THE CLUBS YOU ALWAYS GO TO...
THEY CAN GIVE THE DEVIL HIMSELF NIGHTMARES...
CLACK..
OK, MOM.
NOW, SOMETHING LIKE THIS HAS NEVER HAPPENED TO ARCHIE RUIZ BEFORE:
IT'S BEEN A FEW DAYS OR SO SINCE HE AND LUBA HAD THEIR LITTLE PARTING OF THE WAYS...
ARCHIE FIGURED THAT WAS THAT; YOU KNOW, OTHER FISH IN THE SEA AND ALL THAT STUFF...
WELL, THIS NIGHTMARE SEEMS TO HAVE CHANGED HIS MIND...
HE HASN'T HAD A NIGHTMARE SINCE HE BECAME A MORTICIAN FOURTEEN YEARS AGO...
ACT of CONTRITION
PART 3
2

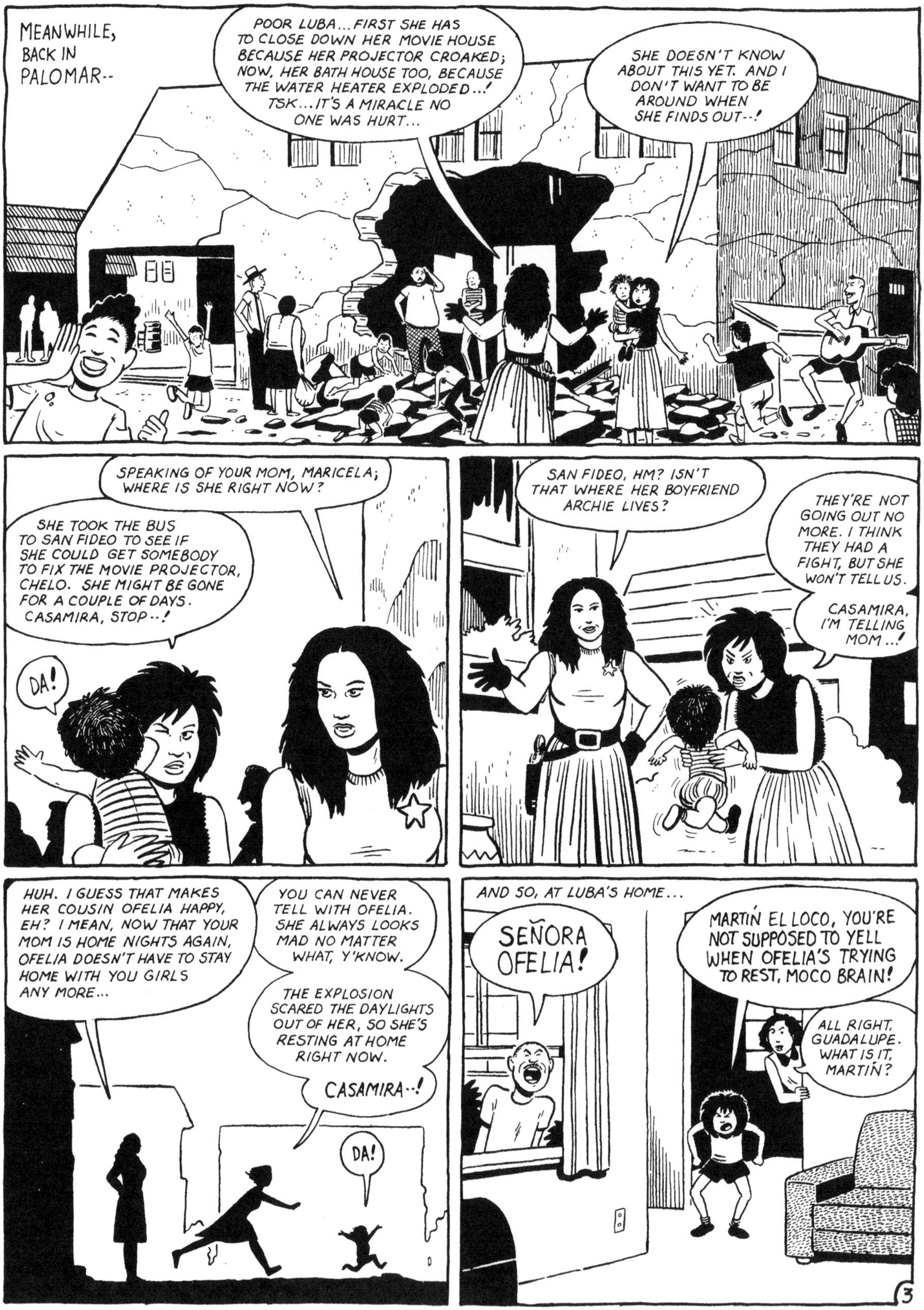
MEANWHILE, BACK IN PALOMAR--
POOR LUBA... FIRST SHE HAS TO CLOSE DOWN HER MOVIE HOUSE BECAUSE HER PROJECTOR CROAKED; NOW, HER BATH HOUSE TOO, BECAUSE THE WATER HEATER EXPLODED...! TSK... IT'S A MIRACLE NO ONE WAS HURT...
SHE DOESN'T KNOW ABOUT THIS YET. AND I DON'T WANT TO BE AROUND WHEN SHE FINDS OUT--!
SPEAKING OF YOUR MOM, MARICELA; WHERE IS SHE RIGHT NOW?
SHE TOOK THE BUS TO SAN FIDEO TO SEE IF SHE COULD GET SOMEBODY TO FIX THE MOVIE PROJECTOR, CHELO. SHE MIGHT BE GONE FOR A COUPLE OF DAYS. CASAMIRA, STOP--!
DA!
SAN FIDEO, HM? ISN'T THAT WHERE HER BOYFRIEND ARCHIE LIVES?
THEY'RE NOT GOING OUT NO MORE. I THINK THEY HAD A FIGHT, BUT SHE WON'T TELL US.
CASAMIRA, I'M TELLING MOM...!
HUH. I GUESS THAT MAKES HER COUSIN OFELIA HAPPY, EH? I MEAN, NOW THAT YOUR MOM IS HOME NIGHTS AGAIN, OFELIA DOESN'T HAVE TO STAY HOME WITH YOU GIRLS ANY MORE...
YOU CAN NEVER TELL WITH OFELIA. SHE ALWAYS LOOKS MAD NO MATTER WHAT, Y'KNOW.
THE EXPLOSION SCARED THE DAYLIGHTS OUT OF HER, SO SHE'S RESTING AT HOME RIGHT NOW.
CASAMIRA--!
DA!
AND SO, AT LUBA'S HOME...
SEÑORA OFELIA!
MARTÍN EL LOCO, YOU'RE NOT SUPPOSED TO YELL WHEN OFELIA'S TRYING TO REST, MOCO BRAIN!
ALL RIGHT, GUADALUPE. WHAT IS IT, MARTÍN?
3

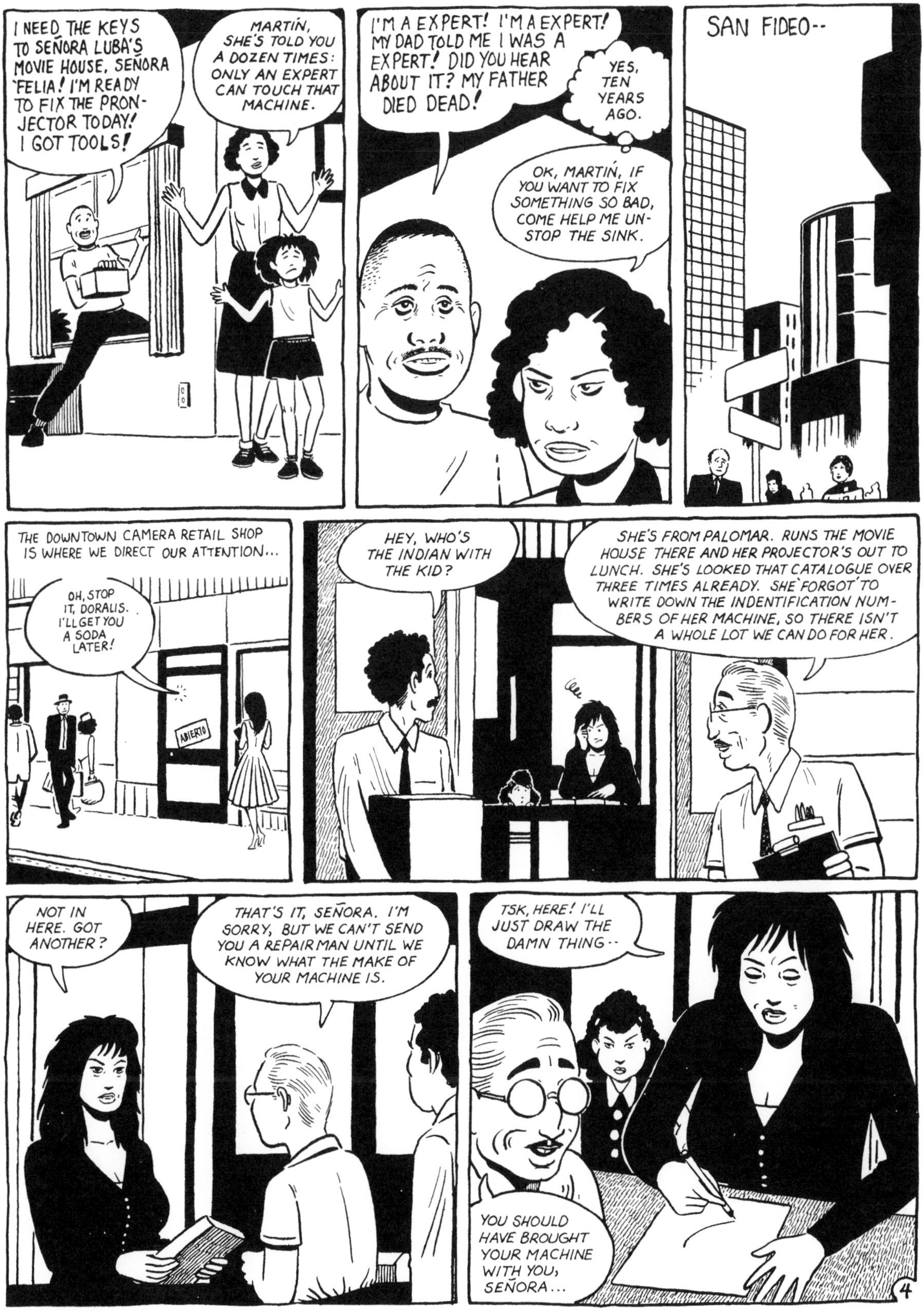
I NEED THE KEYS TO SEÑORA LUBA'S MOVIE HOUSE, SEÑORA 'FELIA! I'M READY TO FIX THE PRON-JECTOR TODAY! I GOT TOOLS!
MARTÍN, SHE'S TOLD YOU A DOZEN TIMES: ONLY AN EXPERT CAN TOUCH THAT MACHINE.
I'M A EXPERT! I'M A EXPERT! MY DAD TOLD ME I WAS A EXPERT! DID YOU HEAR ABOUT IT? MY FATHER DIED DEAD!
YES, TEN YEARS AGO.
OK, MARTÍN, IF YOU WANT TO FIX SOMETHING SO BAD, COME HELP ME UN-STOP THE SINK.
SAN FIDEO--
THE DOWNTOWN CAMERA RETAIL SHOP IS WHERE WE DIRECT OUR ATTENTION...
OH, STOP IT, DORALIS. I'LL GET YOU A SODA LATER!
ABIERTO
HEY, WHO'S THE INDIAN WITH THE KID?
SHE'S FROM PALOMAR. RUNS THE MOVIE HOUSE THERE AND HER PROJECTOR'S OUT TO LUNCH. SHE'S LOOKED THAT CATALOGUE OVER THREE TIMES ALREADY. SHE FORGOT TO WRITE DOWN THE INDENTIFICATION NUM-BERS OF HER MACHINE, SO THERE ISN'T A WHOLE LOT WE CAN DO FOR HER.
NOT IN HERE. GOT ANOTHER?
THAT'S IT, SEÑORA. I'M SORRY, BUT WE CAN'T SEND YOU A REPAIRMAN UNTIL WE KNOW WHAT THE MAKE OF YOUR MACHINE IS.
TSK, HERE! I'LL JUST DRAW THE DAMN THING--
YOU SHOULD HAVE BROUGHT YOUR MACHINE WITH YOU, SEÑORA...
4

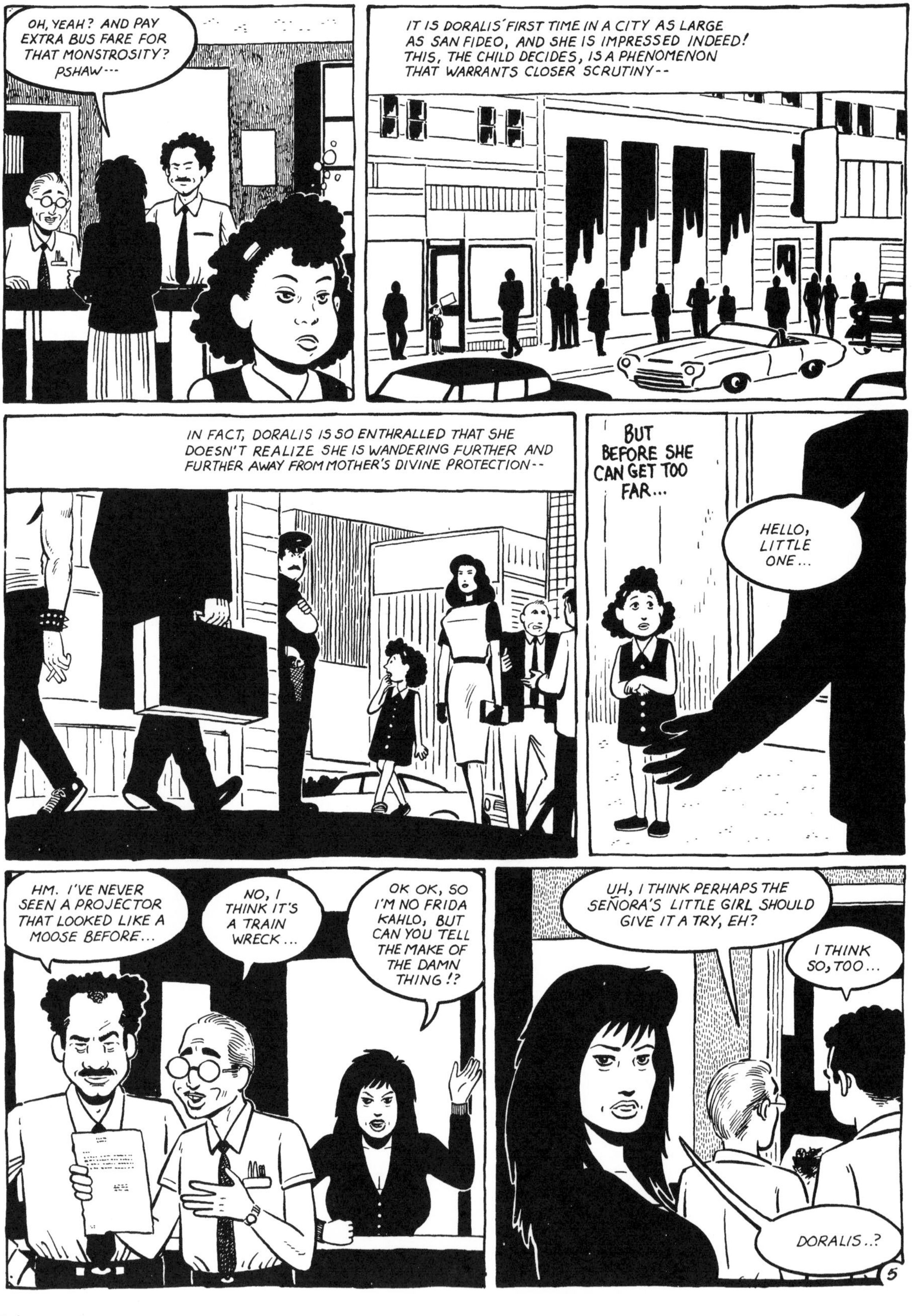
OH, YEAH? AND PAY EXTRA BUS FARE FOR THAT MONSTROSITY? PSHAW---
IT IS DORALIS' FIRST TIME IN A CITY AS LARGE AS SAN FIDEO, AND SHE IS IMPRESSED INDEED! THIS, THE CHILD DECIDES, IS A PHENOMENON THAT WARRANTS CLOSER SCRUTINY--
IN FACT, DORALIS IS SO ENTHRALLED THAT SHE DOESN'T REALIZE SHE IS WANDERING FURTHER AND FURTHER AWAY FROM MOTHER'S DIVINE PROTECTION--
BUT BEFORE SHE CAN GET TOO FAR...
HELLO, LITTLE ONE...
HM. I'VE NEVER SEEN A PROJECTOR THAT LOOKED LIKE A MOOSE BEFORE...
NO, I THINK IT'S A TRAIN WRECK...
OK OK, SO I'M NO FRIDA KAHLO, BUT CAN YOU TELL THE MAKE OF THE DAMN THING!?
UH, I THINK PERHAPS THE SEÑORA'S LITTLE GIRL SHOULD GIVE IT A TRY, EH?
I THINK SO, TOO...
DORALIS..?
5

DORALIS?
COME BACK WHEN YOU'VE GOT THOSE NUMBERS, SEÑORA. OR AT LEAST A PHOTOGRAPH!
ABIERTO
DAMN--
DORALIS...!
OX
D--
MOM!
ARCHIE...!
AND BACK IN PALOMAR...
WHERE'S MOM, OFELIA? I THOUGHT SHE AND DORALIS CAME HOME WITH ARCHIE?
SHE'S WITH HIM RIGHT NOW. I THINK THEY'RE WALKING OVER TO THE MOVIE HOUSE.
DOES SHE KNOW ABOUT THE BATH HOUSE YET?
I DON'T KNOW, MARICELA. GUADALUPE, WHERE DID MARTÍN GO OFF TO?
MARTÍN SAID HE WAS GONNA FIX MOM'S PROJECTOR ONCE AND FOR ALL!
6

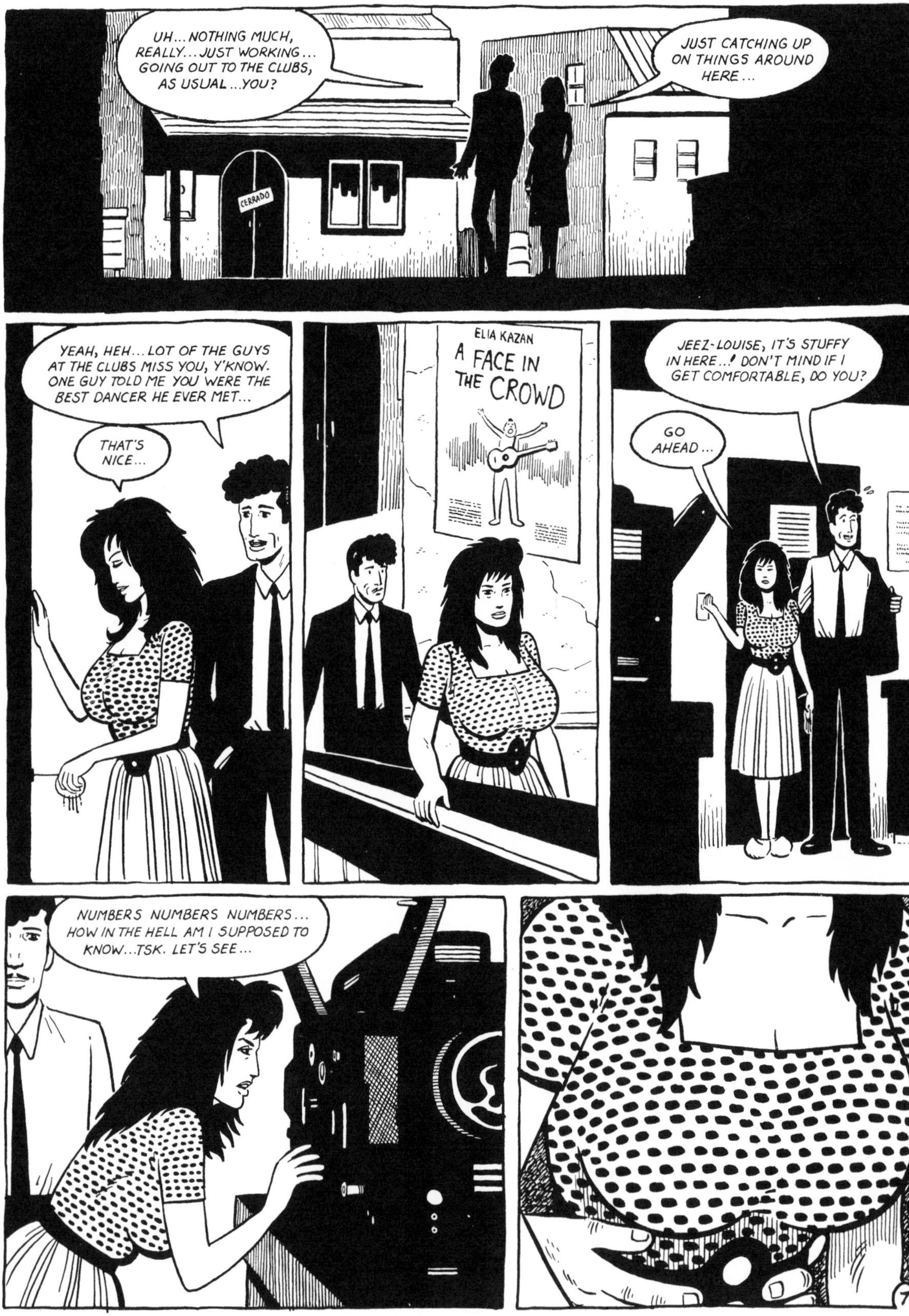
UH... NOTHING MUCH, REALLY... JUST WORKING... GOING OUT TO THE CLUBS, AS USUAL... YOU?
JUST CATCHING UP ON THINGS AROUND HERE...
CERRADO
YEAH, HEH... LOT OF THE GUYS AT THE CLUBS MISS YOU, Y'KNOW. ONE GUY TOLD ME YOU WERE THE BEST DANCER HE EVER MET...
THAT'S NICE...
ELIA KAZAN
A FACE IN THE CROWD
JEEZ-LOUISE, IT'S STUFFY IN HERE...! DON'T MIND IF I GET COMFORTABLE, DO YOU?
GO AHEAD...
NUMBERS NUMBERS NUMBERS... HOW IN THE HELL AM I SUPPOSED TO KNOW...TSK. LET'S SEE...
7

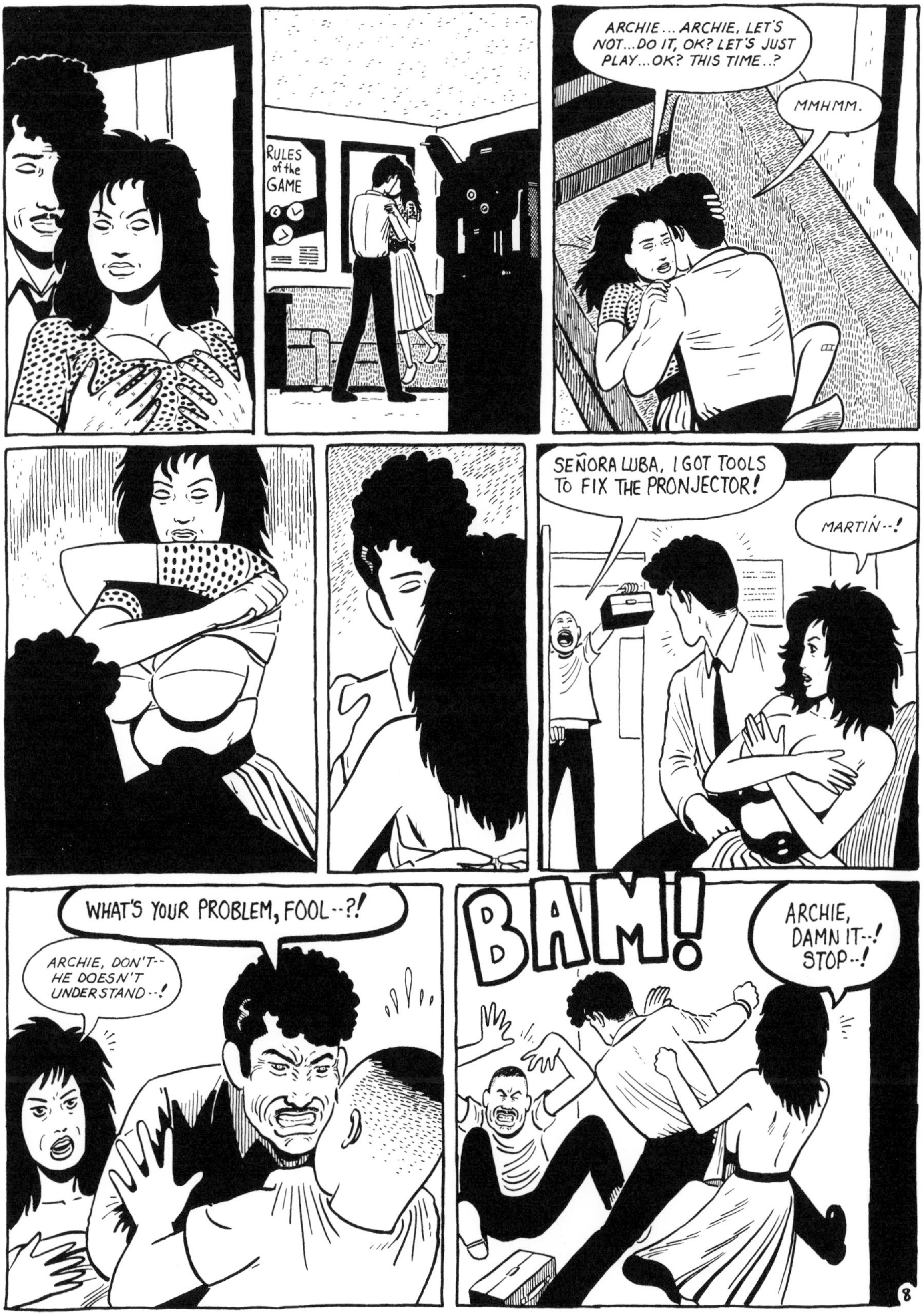
RULES of the GAME
ARCHIE... ARCHIE, LET'S NOT...DO IT, OK? LET'S JUST PLAY...OK? THIS TIME..?
MMHMM.
SEÑORA LUBA, I GOT TOOLS TO FIX THE PRONJECTOR!
MARTÍN--!
WHAT'S YOUR PROBLEM, FOOL--?!
ARCHIE, DON'T-- HE DOESN'T UNDERSTAND--!
BAM!
ARCHIE, DAMN IT--! STOP--!
8

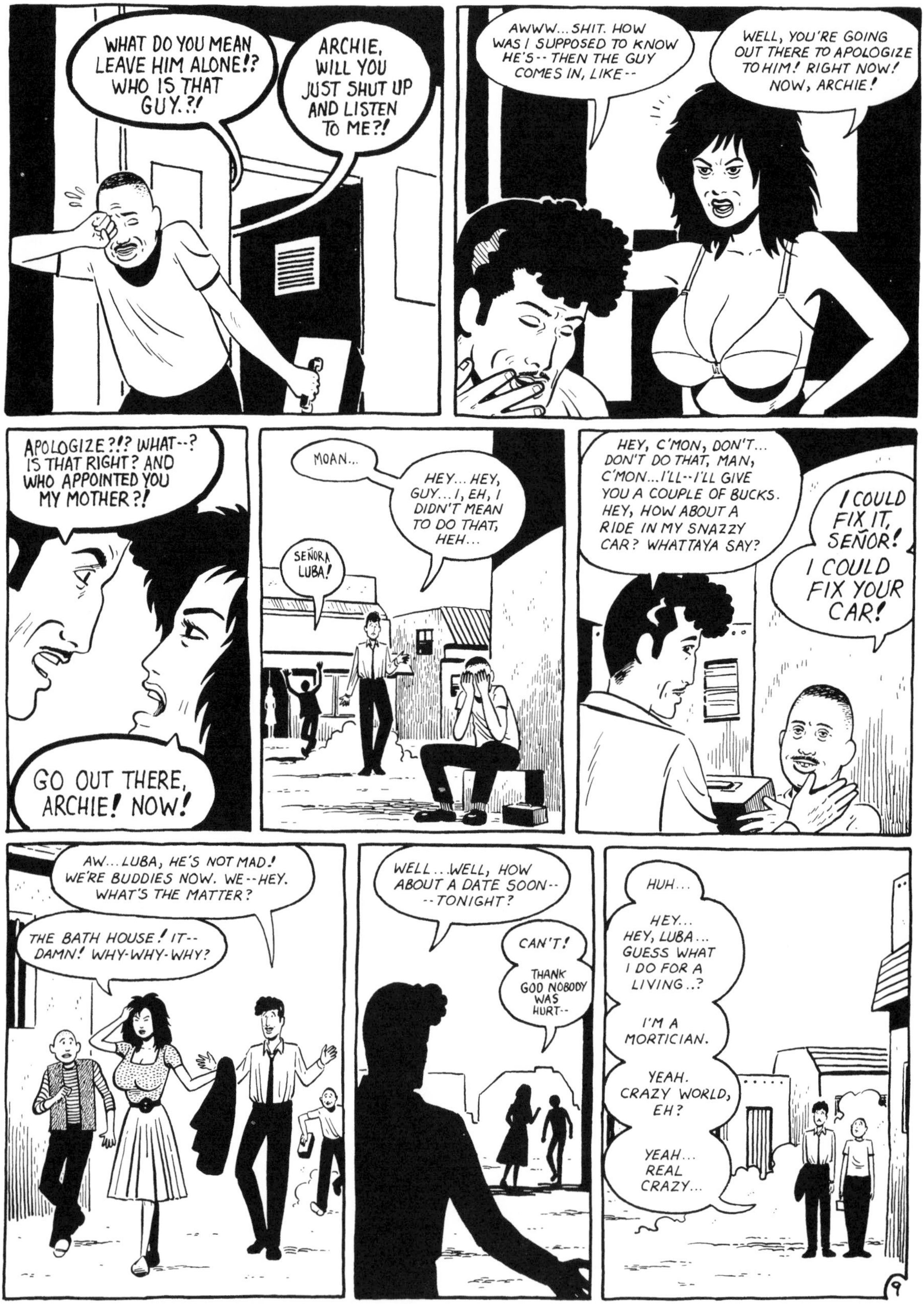
WHAT DO YOU MEAN LEAVE HIM ALONE!? WHO IS THAT GUY.?!
ARCHIE, WILL YOU JUST SHUT UP AND LISTEN TO ME?!
AWWW...SHIT. HOW WAS I SUPPOSED TO KNOW HE'S--THEN THE GUY COMES IN, LIKE--
WELL, YOU'RE GOING OUT THERE TO APOLOGIZE TO HIM! RIGHT NOW! NOW, ARCHIE!
APOLOGIZE?!? WHAT--? IS THAT RIGHT? AND WHO APPOINTED YOU MY MOTHER?!
GO OUT THERE, ARCHIE! NOW!
MOAN...
HEY...HEY, GUY...I, EH, I DIDN'T MEAN TO DO THAT, HEH...
SEÑORA LUBA!
HEY, C'MON, DON'T... DON'T DO THAT, MAN, C'MON...I'LL--I'LL GIVE YOU A COUPLE OF BUCKS. HEY, HOW ABOUT A RIDE IN MY SNAZZY CAR? WHATTAYA SAY?
I COULD FIX IT, SEÑOR!
I COULD FIX YOUR CAR!
AW...LUBA, HE'S NOT MAD! WE'RE BUDDIES NOW. WE--HEY. WHAT'S THE MATTER?
THE BATH HOUSE! IT-- DAMN! WHY-WHY-WHY?
WELL...WELL, HOW ABOUT A DATE SOON-- --TONIGHT?
CAN'T!
THANK GOD NOBODY WAS HURT--
HUH...
HEY... HEY, LUBA... GUESS WHAT I DO FOR A LIVING..?
I'M A MORTICIAN.
YEAH. CRAZY WORLD, EH?
YEAH... REAL CRAZY...
9

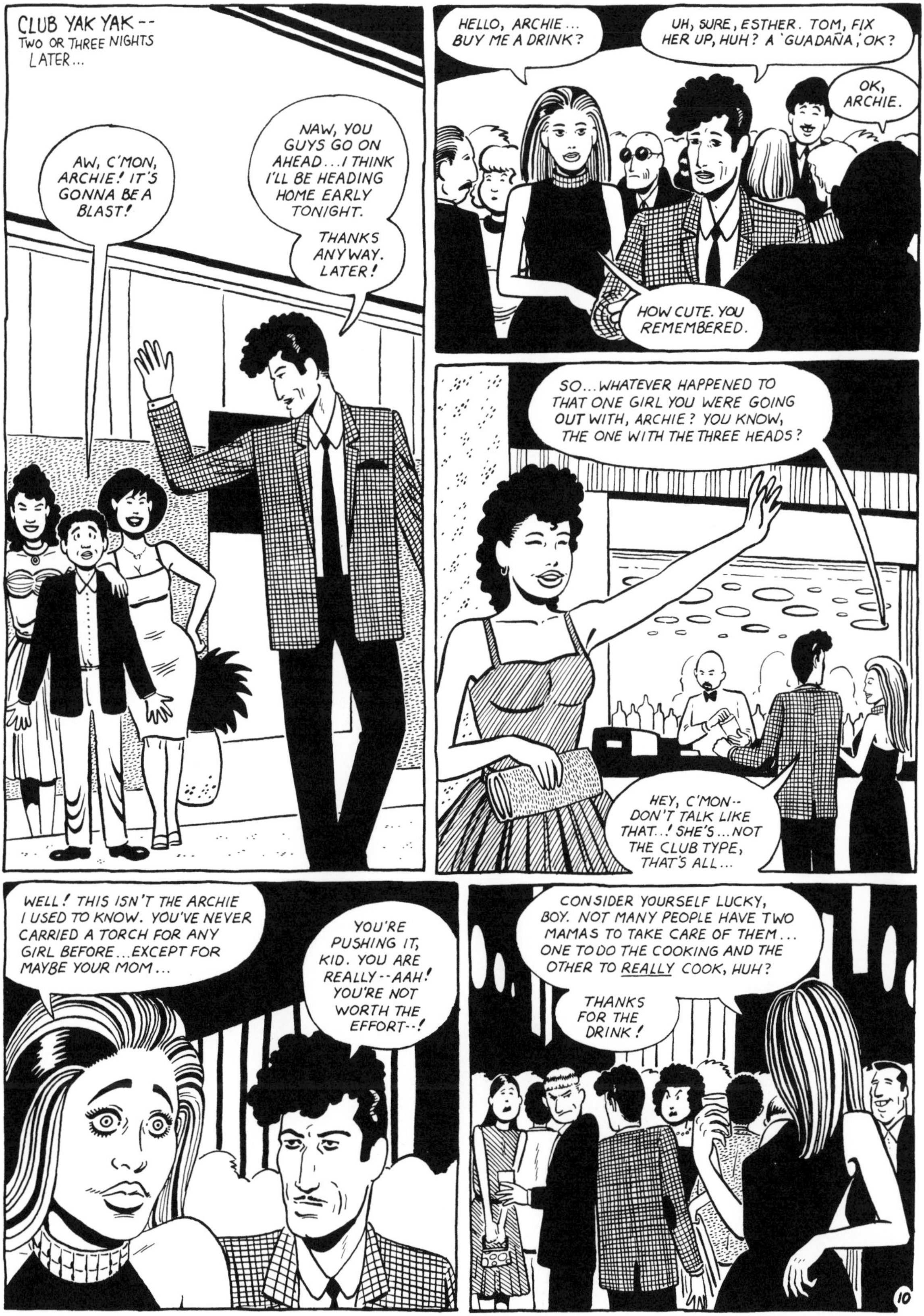
CLUB YAK YAK -- TWO OR THREE NIGHTS LATER...
AW, C'MON, ARCHIE! IT'S GONNA BE A BLAST!
NAW, YOU GUYS GO ON AHEAD... I THINK I'LL BE HEADING HOME EARLY TONIGHT.
THANKS ANYWAY. LATER!
HELLO, ARCHIE... BUY ME A DRINK?
UH, SURE, ESTHER. TOM, FIX HER UP, HUH? A 'GUADAÑA,' OK?
OK, ARCHIE.
HOW CUTE. YOU REMEMBERED.
SO... WHATEVER HAPPENED TO THAT ONE GIRL YOU WERE GOING OUT WITH, ARCHIE? YOU KNOW, THE ONE WITH THE THREE HEADS?
HEY, C'MON-- DON'T TALK LIKE THAT...! SHE'S... NOT THE CLUB TYPE, THAT'S ALL...
WELL! THIS ISN'T THE ARCHIE I USED TO KNOW. YOU'VE NEVER CARRIED A TORCH FOR ANY GIRL BEFORE... EXCEPT FOR MAYBE YOUR MOM...
YOU'RE PUSHING IT, KID. YOU ARE REALLY --AAH! YOU'RE NOT WORTH THE EFFORT--!
CONSIDER YOURSELF LUCKY, BOY. NOT MANY PEOPLE HAVE TWO MAMAS TO TAKE CARE OF THEM... ONE TO DO THE COOKING AND THE OTHER TO REALLY COOK, HUH?
THANKS FOR THE DRINK!
10

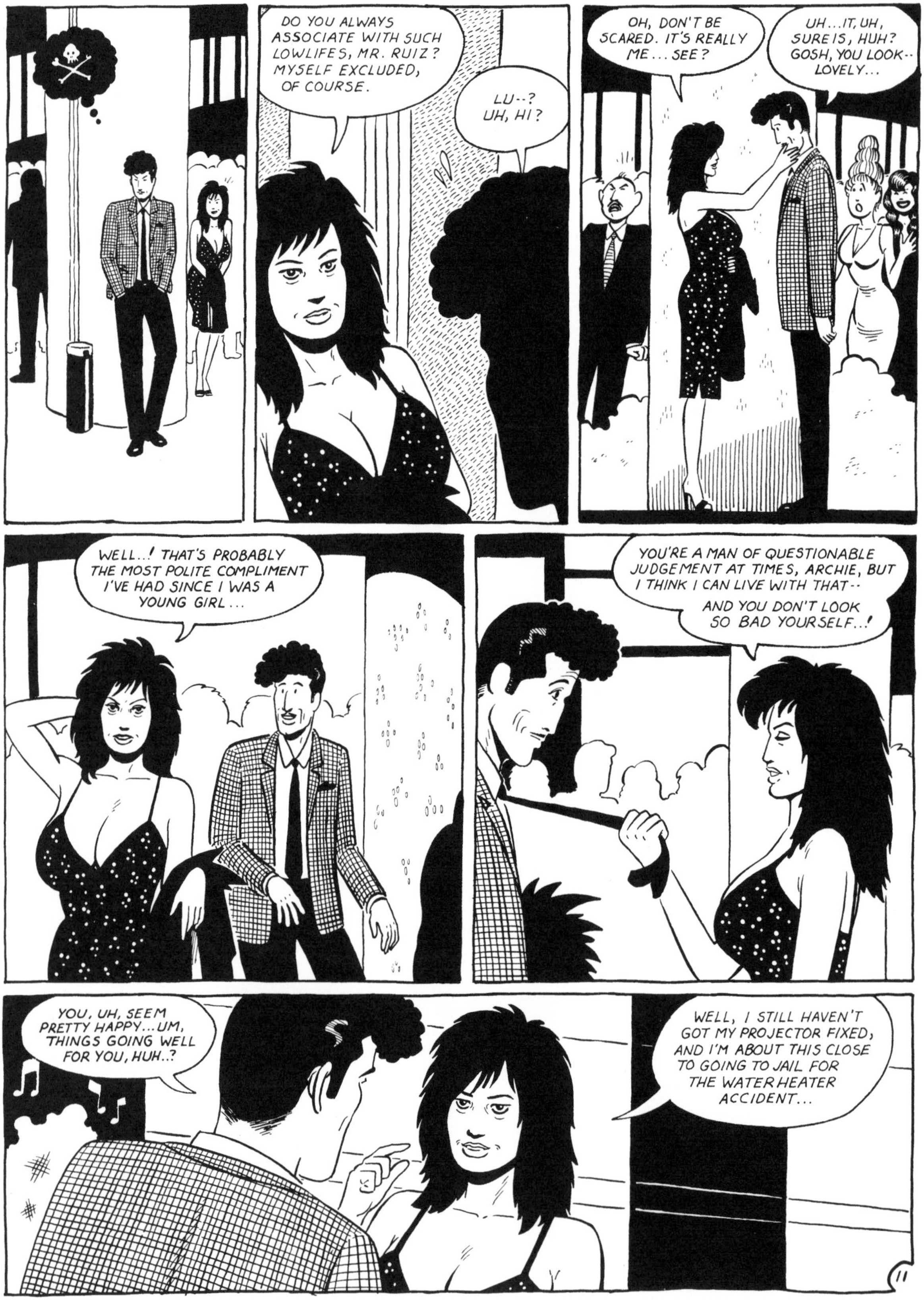
DO YOU ALWAYS ASSOCIATE WITH SUCH LOWLIFES, MR. RUIZ? MYSELF EXCLUDED, OF COURSE.
LU--? UH, HI?
OH, DON'T BE SCARED. IT'S REALLY ME... SEE?
UH... IT, UH, SURE IS, HUH? GOSH, YOU LOOK-- LOVELY...
WELL...! THAT'S PROBABLY THE MOST POLITE COMPLIMENT I'VE HAD SINCE I WAS A YOUNG GIRL...
YOU'RE A MAN OF QUESTIONABLE JUDGEMENT AT TIMES, ARCHIE, BUT I THINK I CAN LIVE WITH THAT--
AND YOU DON'T LOOK SO BAD YOURSELF...!
YOU, UH, SEEM PRETTY HAPPY... UM, THINGS GOING WELL FOR YOU, HUH..?
WELL, I STILL HAVEN'T GOT MY PROJECTOR FIXED, AND I'M ABOUT THIS CLOSE TO GOING TO JAIL FOR THE WATER HEATER ACCIDENT...
11

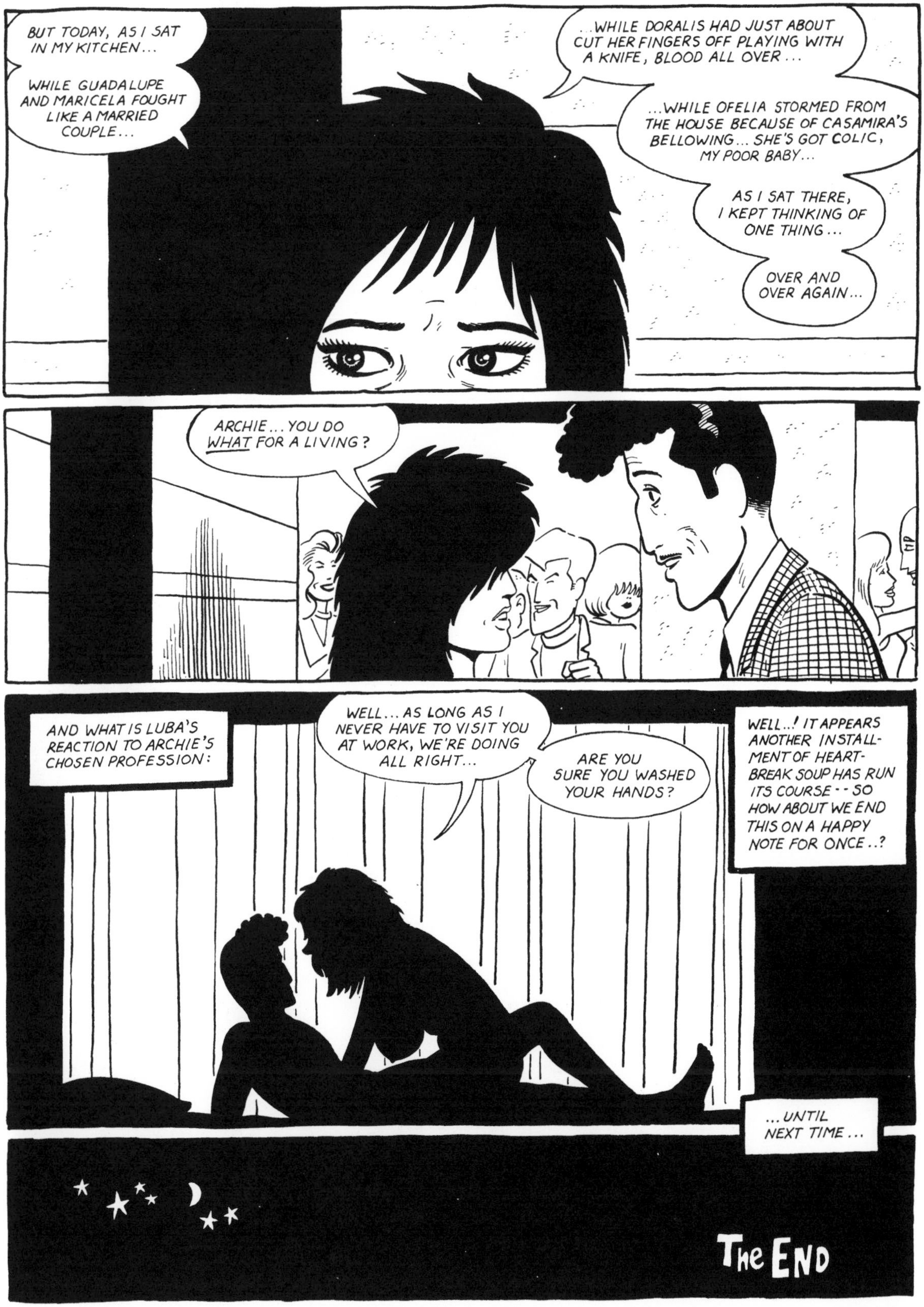
BUT TODAY, AS I SAT IN MY KITCHEN...
WHILE GUADALUPE AND MARICELA FOUGHT LIKE A MARRIED COUPLE...
...WHILE DORALIS HAD JUST ABOUT CUT HER FINGERS OFF PLAYING WITH A KNIFE, BLOOD ALL OVER...
...WHILE OFELIA STORMED FROM THE HOUSE BECAUSE OF CASAMIRA'S BELLOWING... SHE'S GOT COLIC, MY POOR BABY...
AS I SAT THERE, I KEPT THINKING OF ONE THING...
OVER AND OVER AGAIN...
ARCHIE... YOU DO WHAT FOR A LIVING?
AND WHAT IS LUBA'S REACTION TO ARCHIE'S CHOSEN PROFESSION:
WELL... AS LONG AS I NEVER HAVE TO VISIT YOU AT WORK, WE'RE DOING ALL RIGHT...
ARE YOU SURE YOU WASHED YOUR HANDS?
WELL..! IT APPEARS ANOTHER INSTALL-MENT OF HEART-BREAK SOUP HAS RUN ITS COURSE -- SO HOW ABOUT WE END THIS ON A HAPPY NOTE FOR ONCE..?
...UNTIL NEXT TIME...
The END

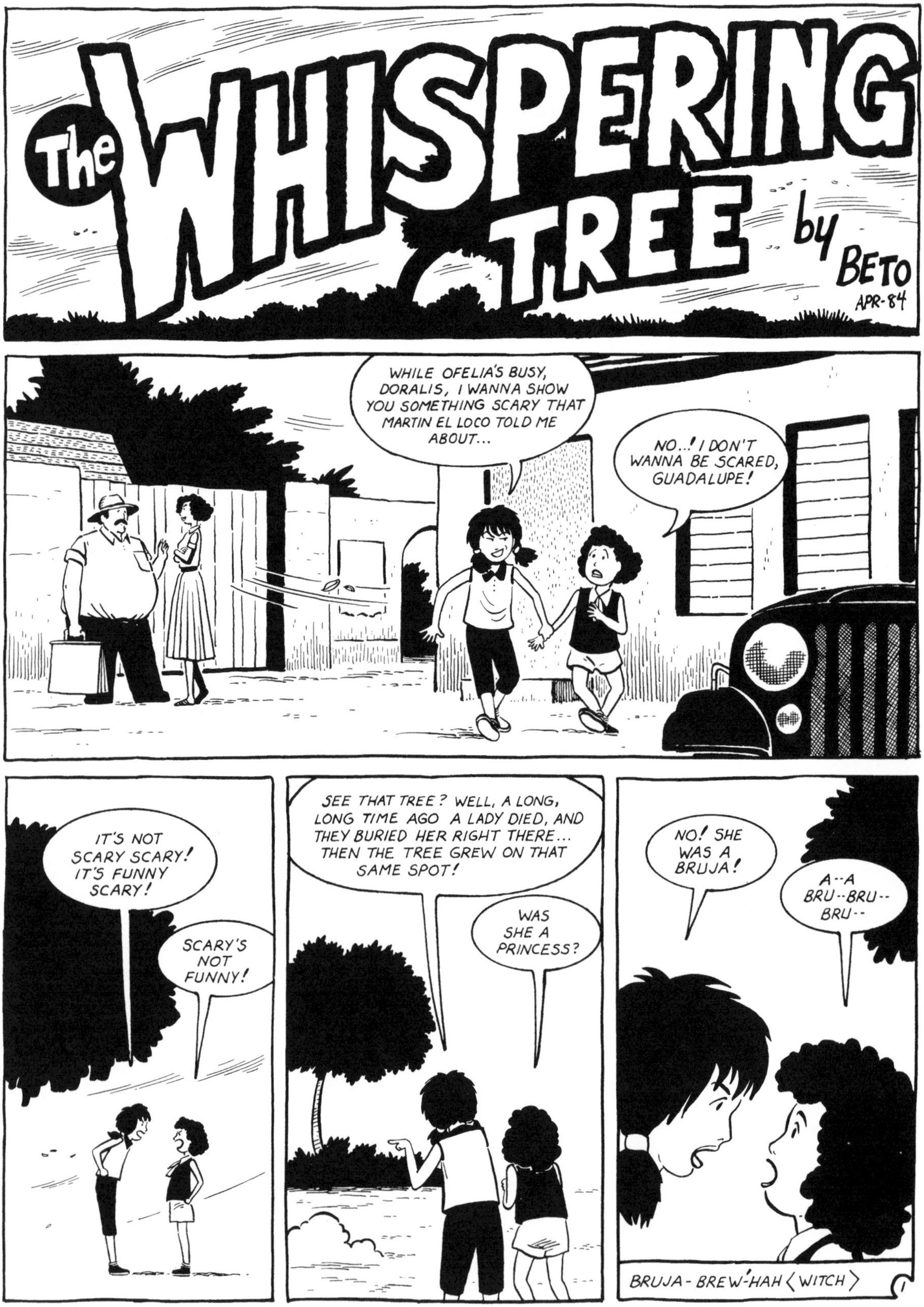
The WHISPERING TREE by BETO APR-84
WHILE OFELIA'S BUSY, DORALIS, I WANNA SHOW YOU SOMETHING SCARY THAT MARTIN EL LOCO TOLD ME ABOUT...
NO..! I DON'T WANNA BE SCARED, GUADALUPE!
IT'S NOT SCARY SCARY! IT'S FUNNY SCARY!
SCARY'S NOT FUNNY!
SEE THAT TREE? WELL, A LONG, LONG TIME AGO A LADY DIED, AND THEY BURIED HER RIGHT THERE... THEN THE TREE GREW ON THAT SAME SPOT!
WAS SHE A PRINCESS?
NO! SHE WAS A BRUJA!
A--A BRU--BRU--BRU--
BRUJA - BREW-HAH ⟨WITCH⟩
1

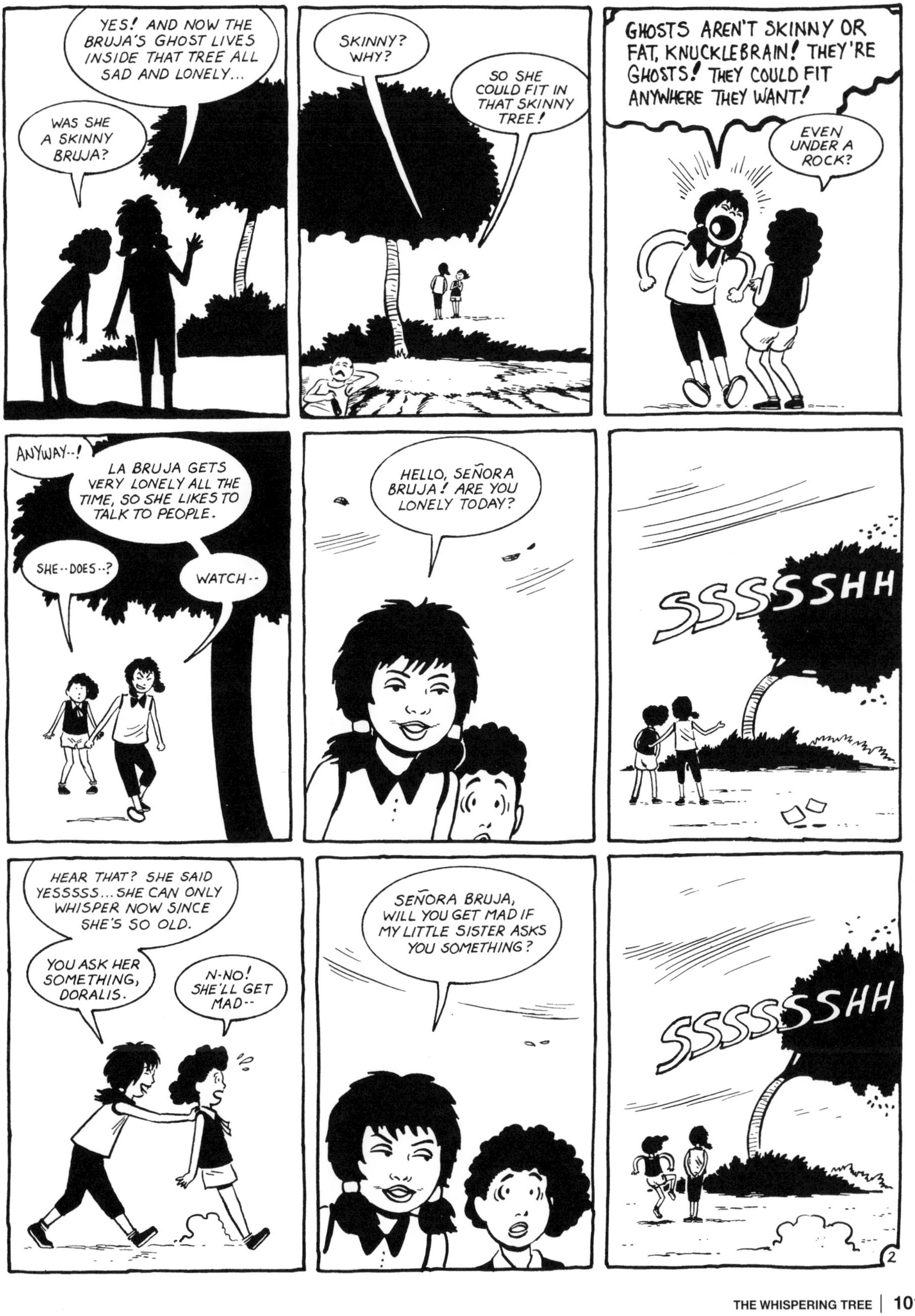
YES! AND NOW THE BRUJA'S GHOST LIVES INSIDE THAT TREE ALL SAD AND LONELY...
WAS SHE A SKINNY BRUJA?
SKINNY? WHY?
SO SHE COULD FIT IN THAT SKINNY TREE!
GHOSTS AREN'T SKINNY OR FAT, KNUCKLEBRAIN! THEY'RE GHOSTS! THEY COULD FIT ANYWHERE THEY WANT!
EVEN UNDER A ROCK?
ANYWAY--!
LA BRUJA GETS VERY LONELY ALL THE TIME, SO SHE LIKES TO TALK TO PEOPLE.
SHE--DOES--?
WATCH--
HELLO, SEÑORA BRUJA! ARE YOU LONELY TODAY?
SSSSSHH
HEAR THAT? SHE SAID YESSSSS... SHE CAN ONLY WHISPER NOW SINCE SHE'S SO OLD.
YOU ASK HER SOMETHING, DORALIS.
N-NO! SHE'LL GET MAD--
SEÑORA BRUJA, WILL YOU GET MAD IF MY LITTLE SISTER ASKS YOU SOMETHING?
SSSSSSHH
2

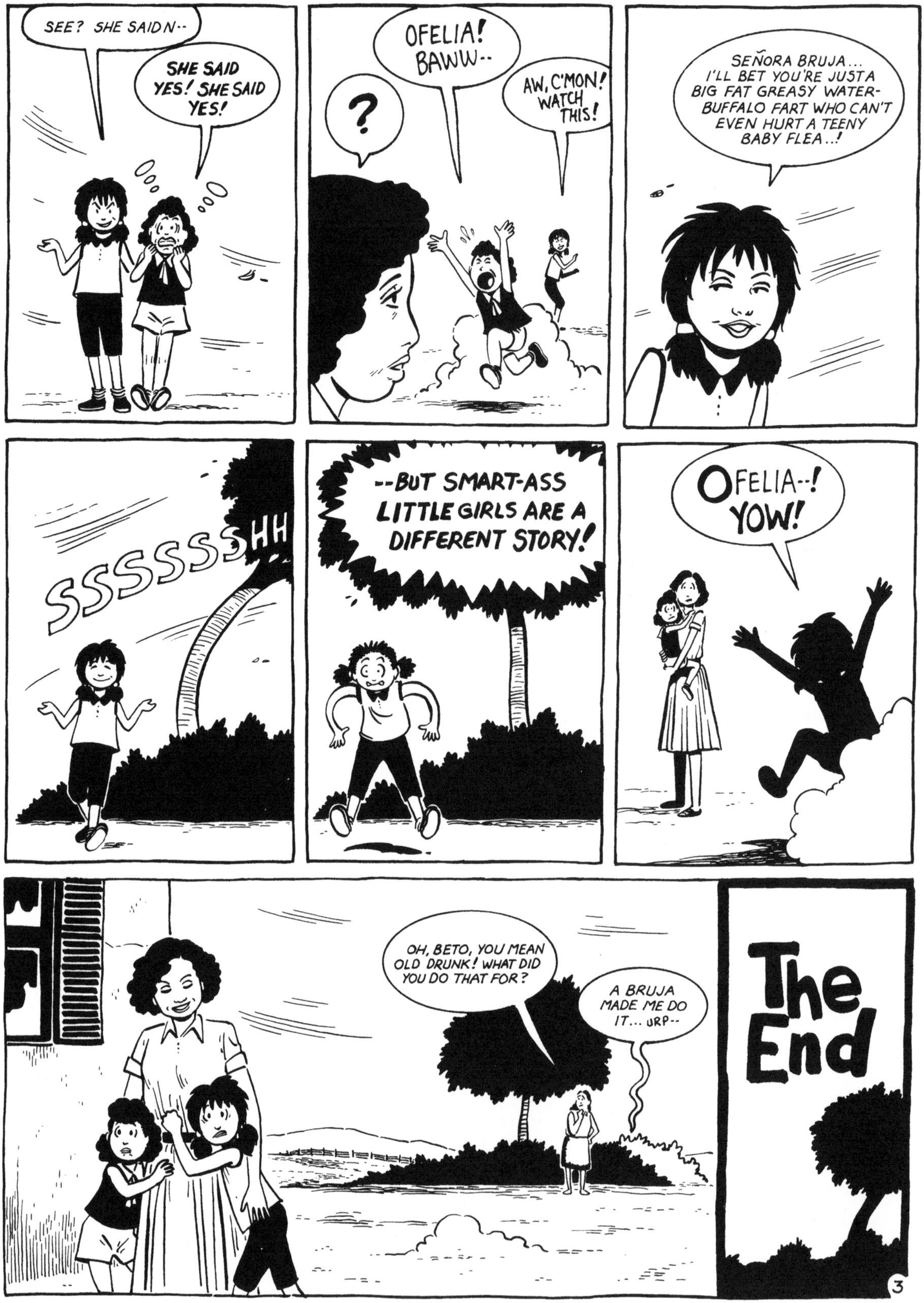
SEE? SHE SAID N--
SHE SAID YES! SHE SAID YES!
?
OFELIA! BAWW--
AW, C'MON! WATCH THIS!
SEÑORA BRUJA... I'LL BET YOU'RE JUST A BIG FAT GREASY WATER-BUFFALO FART WHO CAN'T EVEN HURT A TEENY BABY FLEA..!
SSSSSSHH
--BUT SMART-ASS LITTLE GIRLS ARE A DIFFERENT STORY!
OFELIA--! YOW!
OH, BETO, YOU MEAN OLD DRUNK! WHAT DID YOU DO THAT FOR?
A BRUJA MADE ME DO IT... URP--
The End
3

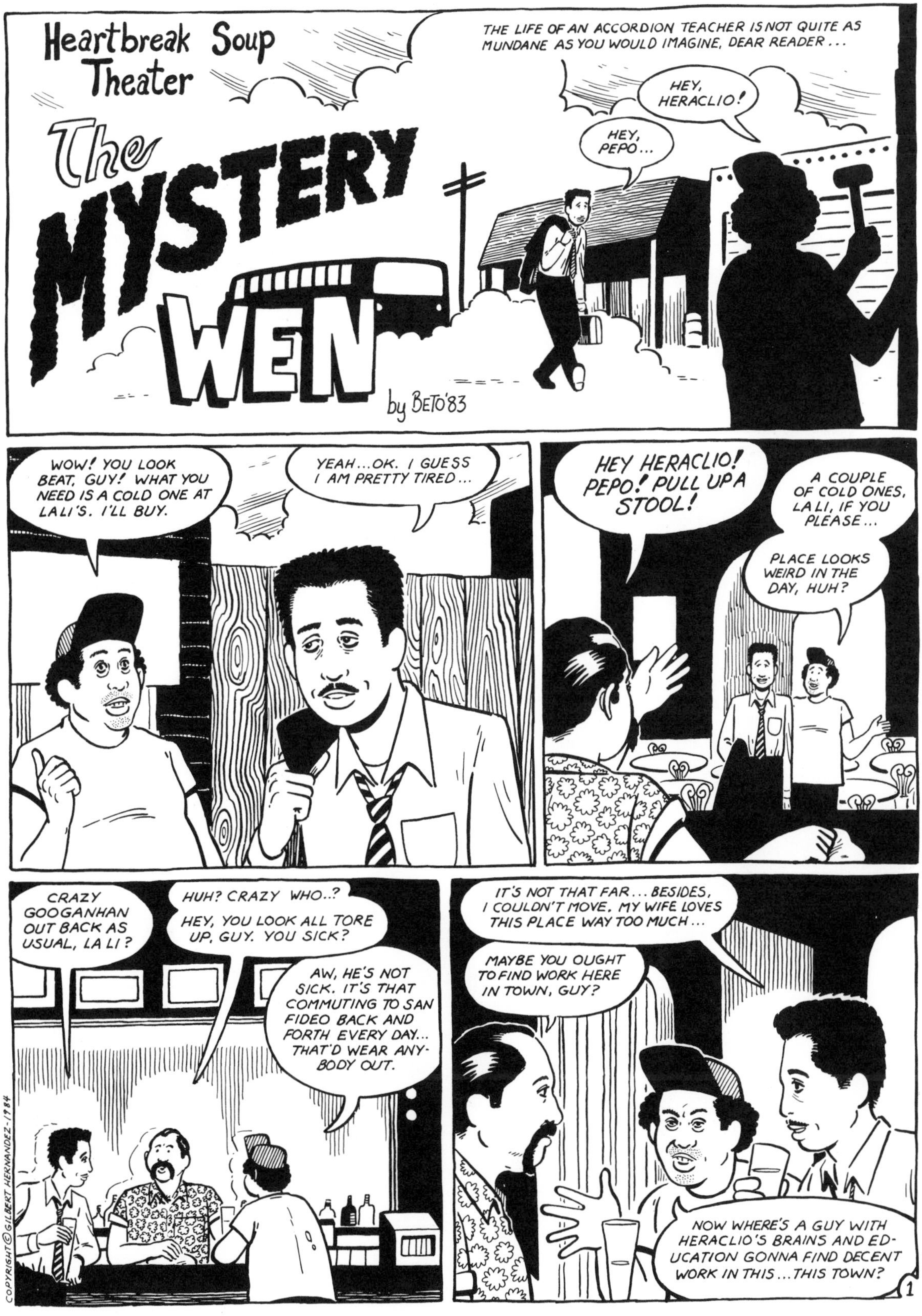
Heartbreak Soup Theater
The MYSTERY WEN
by BETO '83
THE LIFE OF AN ACCORDION TEACHER IS NOT QUITE AS MUNDANE AS YOU WOULD IMAGINE, DEAR READER ...
HEY, HERACLIO!
HEY, PEPO ...
WOW! YOU LOOK BEAT, GUY! WHAT YOU NEED IS A COLD ONE AT LALI'S. I'LL BUY.
YEAH...OK. I GUESS I AM PRETTY TIRED ...
HEY HERACLIO! PEPO! PULL UP A STOOL!
A COUPLE OF COLD ONES, LALI, IF YOU PLEASE ...
PLACE LOOKS WEIRD IN THE DAY, HUH?
CRAZY GOOGANHAN OUT BACK AS USUAL, LALI?
HUH? CRAZY WHO..?
HEY, YOU LOOK ALL TORE UP, GUY. YOU SICK?
AW, HE'S NOT SICK. IT'S THAT COMMUTING TO SAN FIDEO BACK AND FORTH EVERY DAY... THAT'D WEAR ANYBODY OUT.
COPYRIGHT © GILBERT HERNANDEZ - 1984
IT'S NOT THAT FAR ... BESIDES, I COULDN'T MOVE. MY WIFE LOVES THIS PLACE WAY TOO MUCH ...
MAYBE YOU OUGHT TO FIND WORK HERE IN TOWN, GUY?
NOW WHERE'S A GUY WITH HERACLIO'S BRAINS AND EDUCATION GONNA FIND DECENT WORK IN THIS ... THIS TOWN?
1

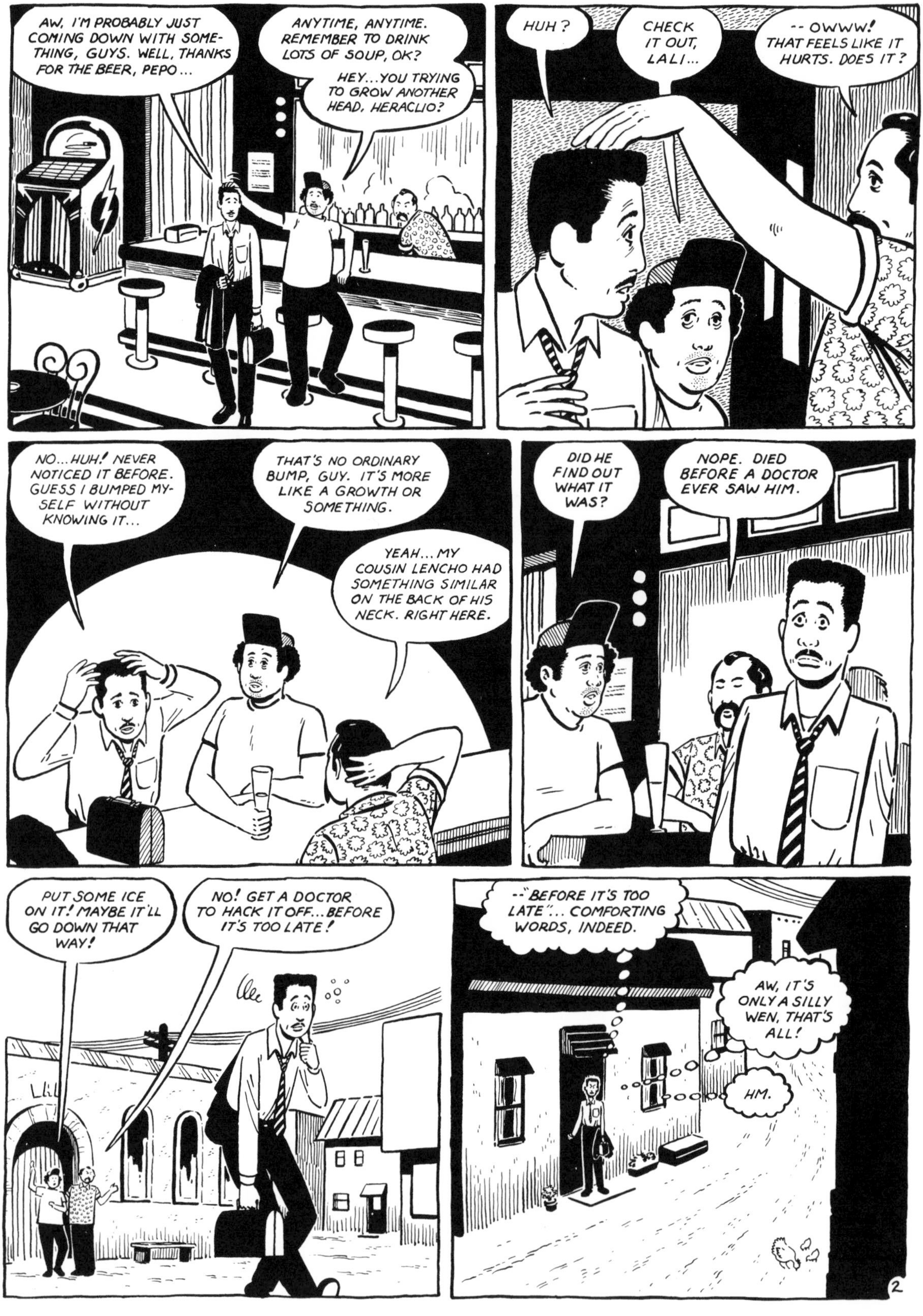
AW, I'M PROBABLY JUST COMING DOWN WITH SOMETHING, GUYS. WELL, THANKS FOR THE BEER, PEPO...
ANYTIME, ANYTIME. REMEMBER TO DRINK LOTS OF SOUP, OK?
HEY... YOU TRYING TO GROW ANOTHER HEAD, HERACLIO?
HUH?
CHECK IT OUT, LALI...
-- OWWW! THAT FEELS LIKE IT HURTS. DOES IT?
NO... HUH! NEVER NOTICED IT BEFORE. GUESS I BUMPED MYSELF WITHOUT KNOWING IT...
THAT'S NO ORDINARY BUMP, GUY. IT'S MORE LIKE A GROWTH OR SOMETHING.
YEAH... MY COUSIN LENCHO HAD SOMETHING SIMILAR ON THE BACK OF HIS NECK. RIGHT HERE.
DID HE FIND OUT WHAT IT WAS?
NOPE. DIED BEFORE A DOCTOR EVER SAW HIM.
PUT SOME ICE ON IT! MAYBE IT'LL GO DOWN THAT WAY!
NO! GET A DOCTOR TO HACK IT OFF... BEFORE IT'S TOO LATE!
--"BEFORE IT'S TOO LATE"... COMFORTING WORDS, INDEED.
AW, IT'S ONLY A SILLY WEN, THAT'S ALL!
HM.
2

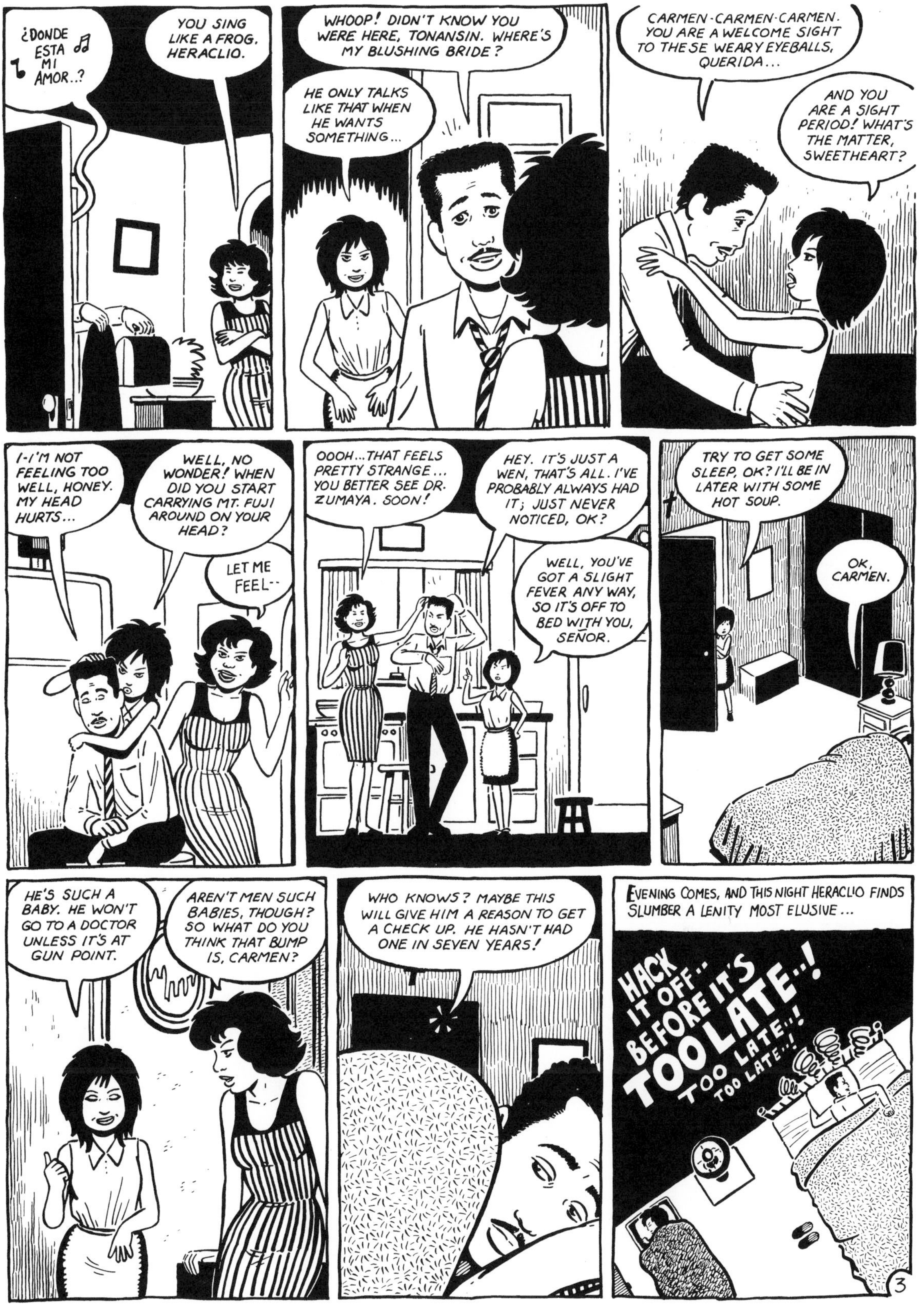
¿DONDE ESTA MI AMOR..?
YOU SING LIKE A FROG, HERACLIO.
WHOOP! DIDN'T KNOW YOU WERE HERE, TONANSIN. WHERE'S MY BLUSHING BRIDE?
HE ONLY TALKS LIKE THAT WHEN HE WANTS SOMETHING...
CARMEN-CARMEN-CARMEN. YOU ARE A WELCOME SIGHT TO THESE WEARY EYEBALLS, QUERIDA...
AND YOU ARE A SIGHT PERIOD! WHAT'S THE MATTER, SWEETHEART?
I-I'M NOT FEELING TOO WELL, HONEY. MY HEAD HURTS...
WELL, NO WONDER! WHEN DID YOU START CARRYING MT. FUJI AROUND ON YOUR HEAD?
LET ME FEEL--
OOOH...THAT FEELS PRETTY STRANGE... YOU BETTER SEE DR. ZUMAYA. SOON!
HEY. IT'S JUST A WEN, THAT'S ALL. I'VE PROBABLY ALWAYS HAD IT; JUST NEVER NOTICED, OK?
WELL, YOU'VE GOT A SLIGHT FEVER ANY WAY, SO IT'S OFF TO BED WITH YOU, SEÑOR.
TRY TO GET SOME SLEEP, OK? I'LL BE IN LATER WITH SOME HOT SOUP.
OK, CARMEN.
HE'S SUCH A BABY. HE WON'T GO TO A DOCTOR UNLESS IT'S AT GUN POINT.
AREN'T MEN SUCH BABIES, THOUGH? SO WHAT DO YOU THINK THAT BUMP IS, CARMEN?
WHO KNOWS? MAYBE THIS WILL GIVE HIM A REASON TO GET A CHECK UP. HE HASN'T HAD ONE IN SEVEN YEARS!
EVENING COMES, AND THIS NIGHT HERACLIO FINDS SLUMBER A LENITY MOST ELUSIVE...
HACK IT OFF.. BEFORE IT'S TOO LATE..! TOO LATE..! TOO LATE..!
3

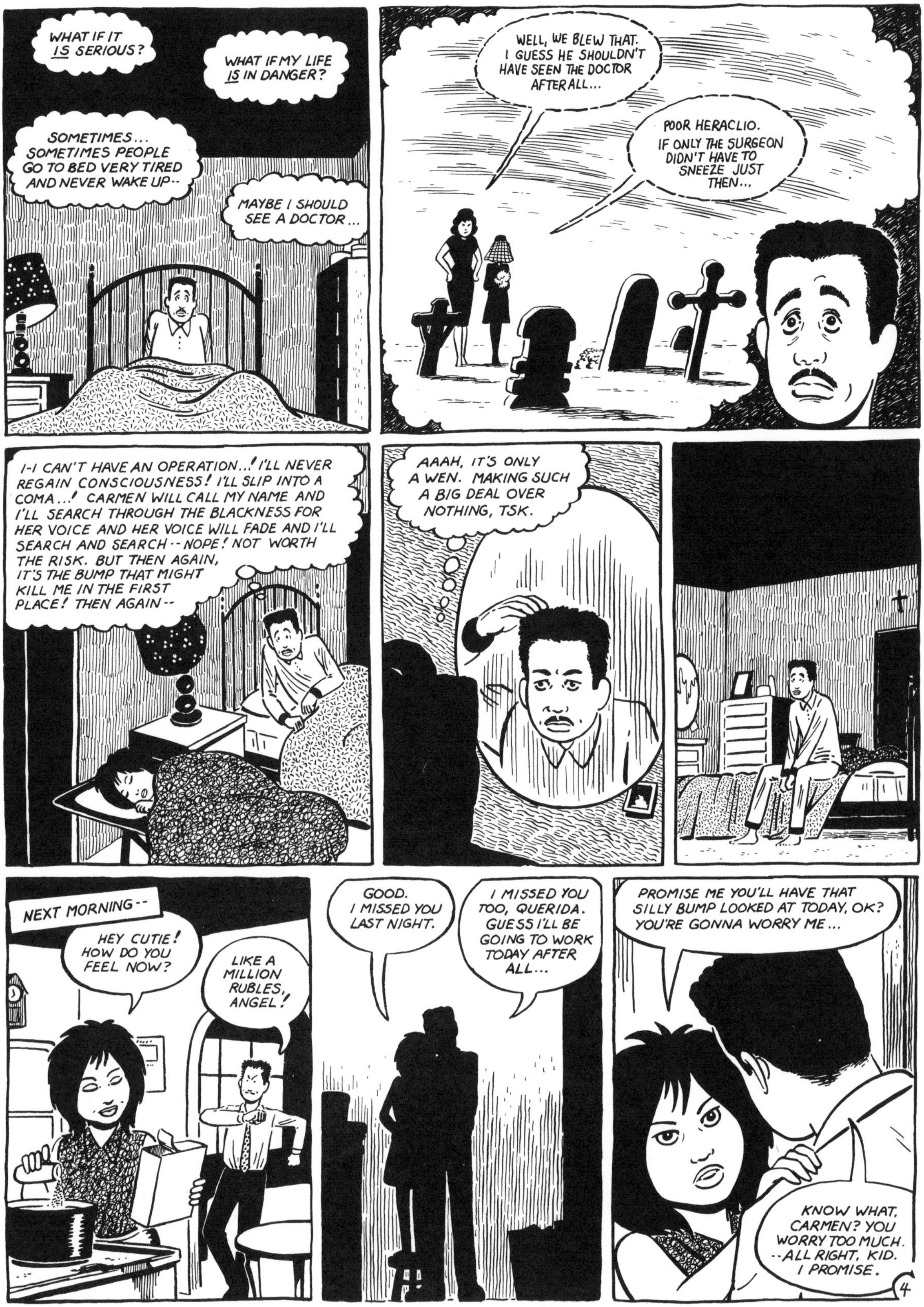
WHAT IF IT IS SERIOUS?
WHAT IF MY LIFE IS IN DANGER?
SOMETIMES... SOMETIMES PEOPLE GO TO BED VERY TIRED AND NEVER WAKE UP--
MAYBE I SHOULD SEE A DOCTOR...
WELL, WE BLEW THAT. I GUESS HE SHOULDN'T HAVE SEEN THE DOCTOR AFTER ALL...
POOR HERACLIO. IF ONLY THE SURGEON DIDN'T HAVE TO SNEEZE JUST THEN...
I-I CAN'T HAVE AN OPERATION...! I'LL NEVER REGAIN CONSCIOUSNESS! I'LL SLIP INTO A COMA...! CARMEN WILL CALL MY NAME AND I'LL SEARCH THROUGH THE BLACKNESS FOR HER VOICE AND HER VOICE WILL FADE AND I'LL SEARCH AND SEARCH--NOPE! NOT WORTH THE RISK. BUT THEN AGAIN, IT'S THE BUMP THAT MIGHT KILL ME IN THE FIRST PLACE! THEN AGAIN--
AAAH, IT'S ONLY A WEN. MAKING SUCH A BIG DEAL OVER NOTHING, TSK.
NEXT MORNING--
HEY CUTIE! HOW DO YOU FEEL NOW?
LIKE A MILLION RUBLES, ANGEL!
GOOD. I MISSED YOU LAST NIGHT.
I MISSED YOU TOO, QUERIDA. GUESS I'LL BE GOING TO WORK TODAY AFTER ALL...
PROMISE ME YOU'LL HAVE THAT SILLY BUMP LOOKED AT TODAY, OK? YOU'RE GONNA WORRY ME...
KNOW WHAT, CARMEN? YOU WORRY TOO MUCH. --ALL RIGHT, KID. I PROMISE.
4

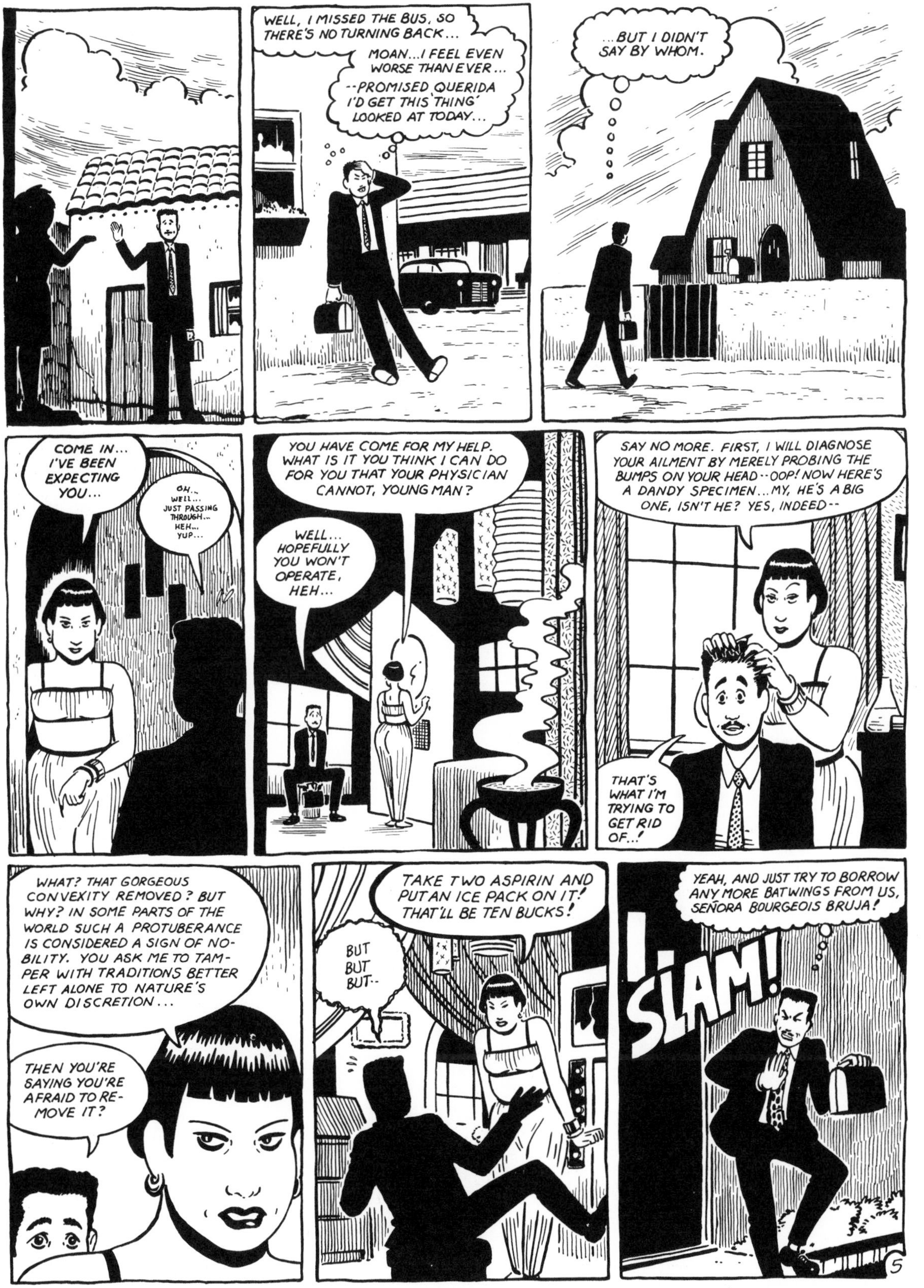

WELL, I MISSED THE BUS, SO THERE'S NO TURNING BACK...
MOAN...I FEEL EVEN WORSE THAN EVER...
--PROMISED QUERIDA I'D GET THIS 'THING' LOOKED AT TODAY...
...BUT I DIDN'T SAY BY WHOM.
COME IN... I'VE BEEN EXPECTING YOU...
OH... WELL... JUST PASSING THROUGH... HEH... YUP...
YOU HAVE COME FOR MY HELP. WHAT IS IT YOU THINK I CAN DO FOR YOU THAT YOUR PHYSICIAN CANNOT, YOUNG MAN?
WELL... HOPEFULLY YOU WON'T OPERATE, HEH...
SAY NO MORE. FIRST, I WILL DIAGNOSE YOUR AILMENT BY MERELY PROBING THE BUMPS ON YOUR HEAD--OOP! NOW HERE'S A DANDY SPECIMEN...MY, HE'S A BIG ONE, ISN'T HE? YES, INDEED--
THAT'S WHAT I'M TRYING TO GET RID OF..!
WHAT? THAT GORGEOUS CONVEXITY REMOVED? BUT WHY? IN SOME PARTS OF THE WORLD SUCH A PROTUBERANCE IS CONSIDERED A SIGN OF NOBILITY. YOU ASK ME TO TAMPER WITH TRADITIONS BETTER LEFT ALONE TO NATURE'S OWN DISCRETION...
THEN YOU'RE SAYING YOU'RE AFRAID TO REMOVE IT?
TAKE TWO ASPIRIN AND PUT AN ICE PACK ON IT! THAT'LL BE TEN BUCKS!
BUT BUT BUT--
YEAH, AND JUST TRY TO BORROW ANY MORE BATWINGS FROM US, SEÑORA BOURGEOIS BRUJA!
SLAM!

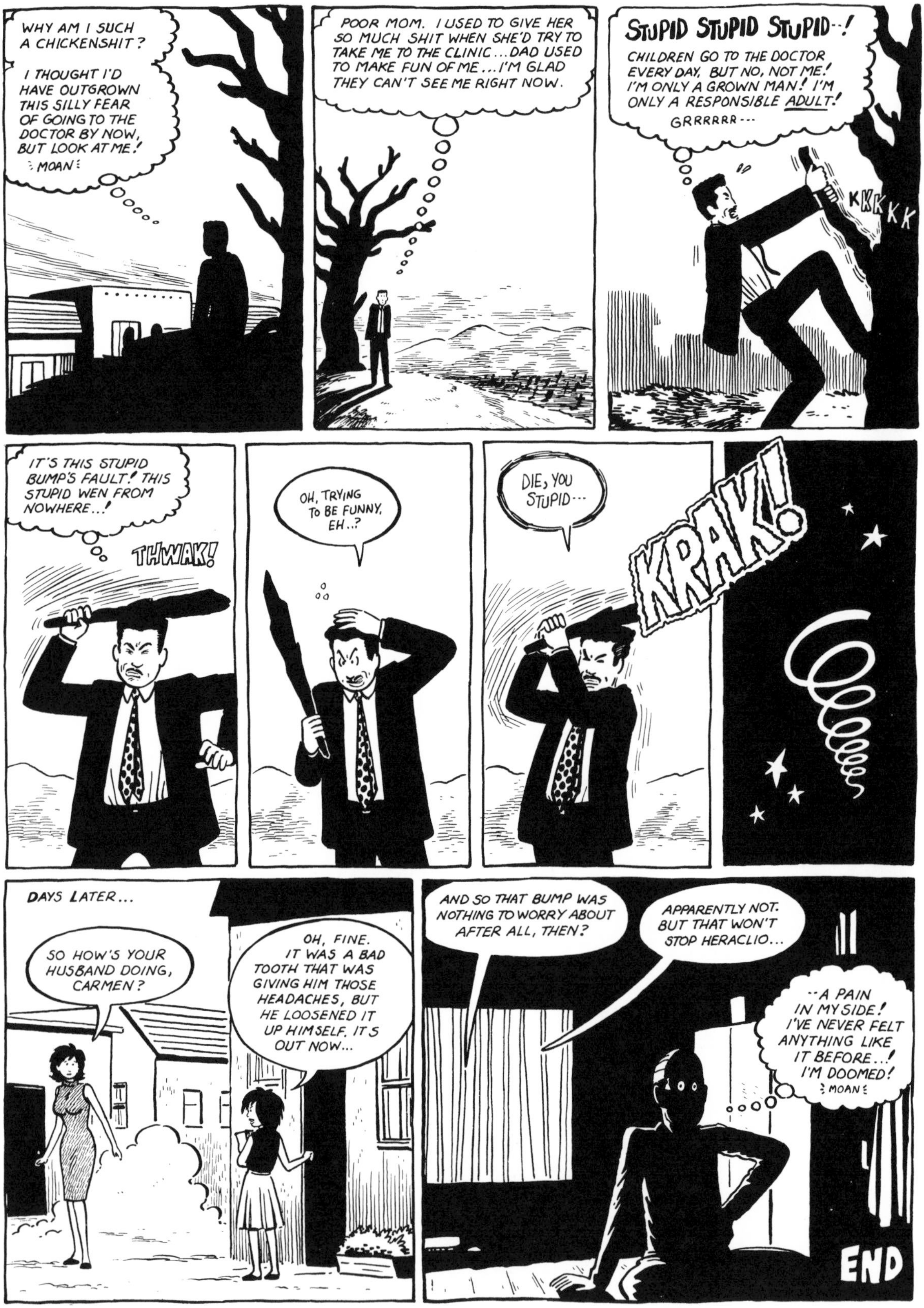
WHY AM I SUCH A CHICKENSHIT?
I THOUGHT I'D HAVE OUTGROWN THIS SILLY FEAR OF GOING TO THE DOCTOR BY NOW, BUT LOOK AT ME!
MOAN
POOR MOM. I USED TO GIVE HER SO MUCH SHIT WHEN SHE'D TRY TO TAKE ME TO THE CLINIC... DAD USED TO MAKE FUN OF ME... I'M GLAD THEY CAN'T SEE ME RIGHT NOW.
STUPID STUPID STUPID--!
CHILDREN GO TO THE DOCTOR EVERY DAY, BUT NO, NOT ME! I'M ONLY A GROWN MAN! I'M ONLY A RESPONSIBLE ADULT!
GRRRRRR---
KKKKK
IT'S THIS STUPID BUMP'S FAULT! THIS STUPID WEN FROM NOWHERE..!
THWAK!
OH, TRYING TO BE FUNNY, EH..?
DIE, YOU STUPID---
KRAK!
DAYS LATER...
SO HOW'S YOUR HUSBAND DOING, CARMEN?
OH, FINE. IT WAS A BAD TOOTH THAT WAS GIVING HIM THOSE HEADACHES, BUT HE LOOSENED IT UP HIMSELF. IT'S OUT NOW...
AND SO THAT BUMP WAS NOTHING TO WORRY ABOUT AFTER ALL, THEN?
APPARENTLY NOT. BUT THAT WON'T STOP HERACLIO...
--A PAIN IN MY SIDE! I'VE NEVER FELT ANYTHING LIKE IT BEFORE..! I'M DOOMED!
MOAN
END

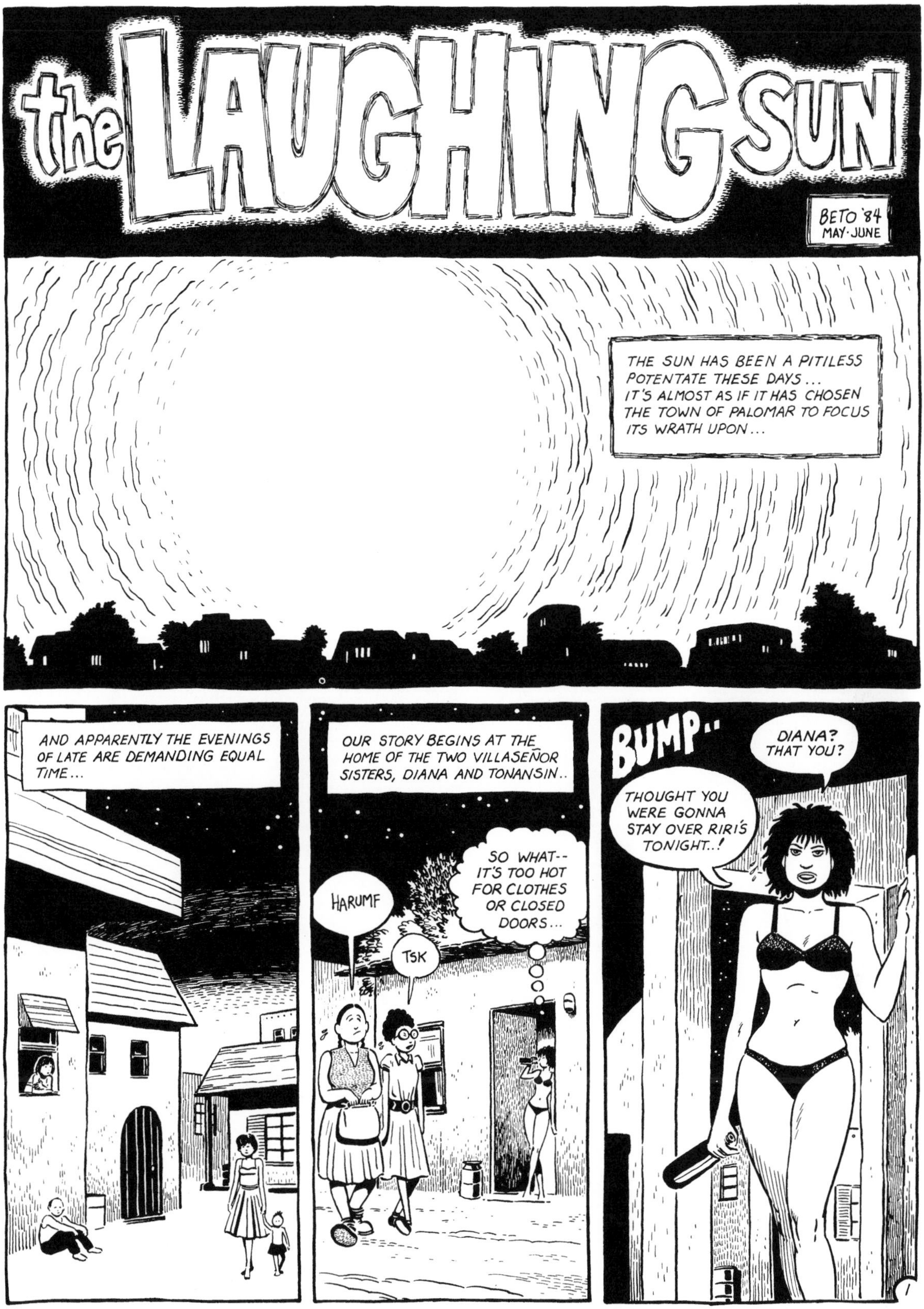
the LAUGHING SUN
BETO '84 MAY · JUNE
THE SUN HAS BEEN A PITILESS POTENTATE THESE DAYS... IT'S ALMOST AS IF IT HAS CHOSEN THE TOWN OF PALOMAR TO FOCUS ITS WRATH UPON...
AND APPARENTLY THE EVENINGS OF LATE ARE DEMANDING EQUAL TIME...
OUR STORY BEGINS AT THE HOME OF THE TWO VILLASEÑOR SISTERS, DIANA AND TONANSIN..
HARUMF
TSK
SO WHAT-- IT'S TOO HOT FOR CLOTHES OR CLOSED DOORS...
BUMP..
DIANA? THAT YOU?
THOUGHT YOU WERE GONNA STAY OVER RIRI'S TONIGHT..!
1

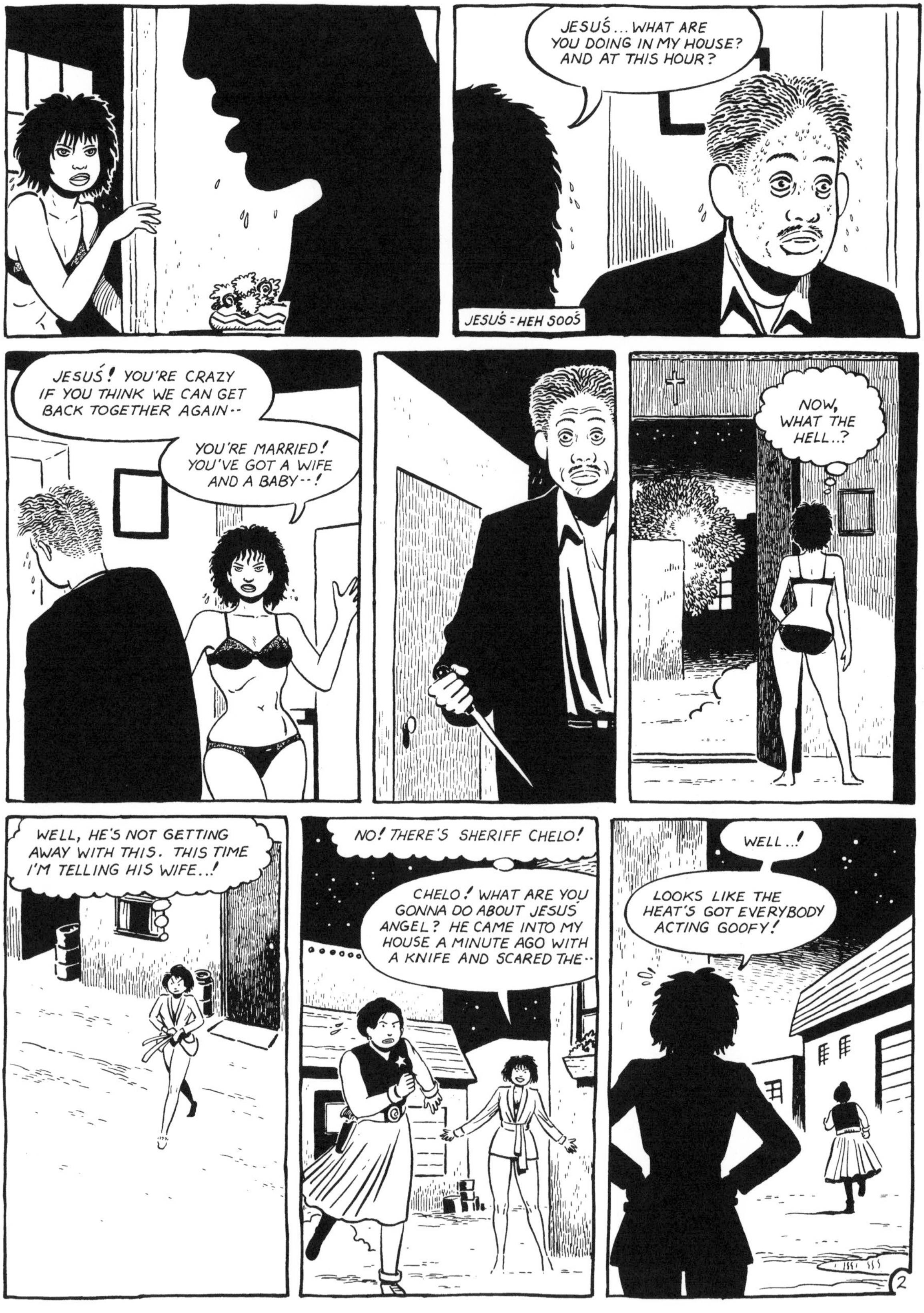
JESUŚ ... WHAT ARE YOU DOING IN MY HOUSE? AND AT THIS HOUR?
JESUŚ = HEH SOOŚ
JESUŚ! YOU'RE CRAZY IF YOU THINK WE CAN GET BACK TOGETHER AGAIN--
YOU'RE MARRIED! YOU'VE GOT A WIFE AND A BABY--!
NOW, WHAT THE HELL..?
WELL, HE'S NOT GETTING AWAY WITH THIS. THIS TIME I'M TELLING HIS WIFE...!
NO! THERE'S SHERIFF CHELO!
CHELO! WHAT ARE YOU GONNA DO ABOUT JESUŚ ANGEL? HE CAME INTO MY HOUSE A MINUTE AGO WITH A KNIFE AND SCARED THE--
WELL..!
LOOKS LIKE THE HEAT'S GOT EVERYBODY ACTING GOOFY!
2

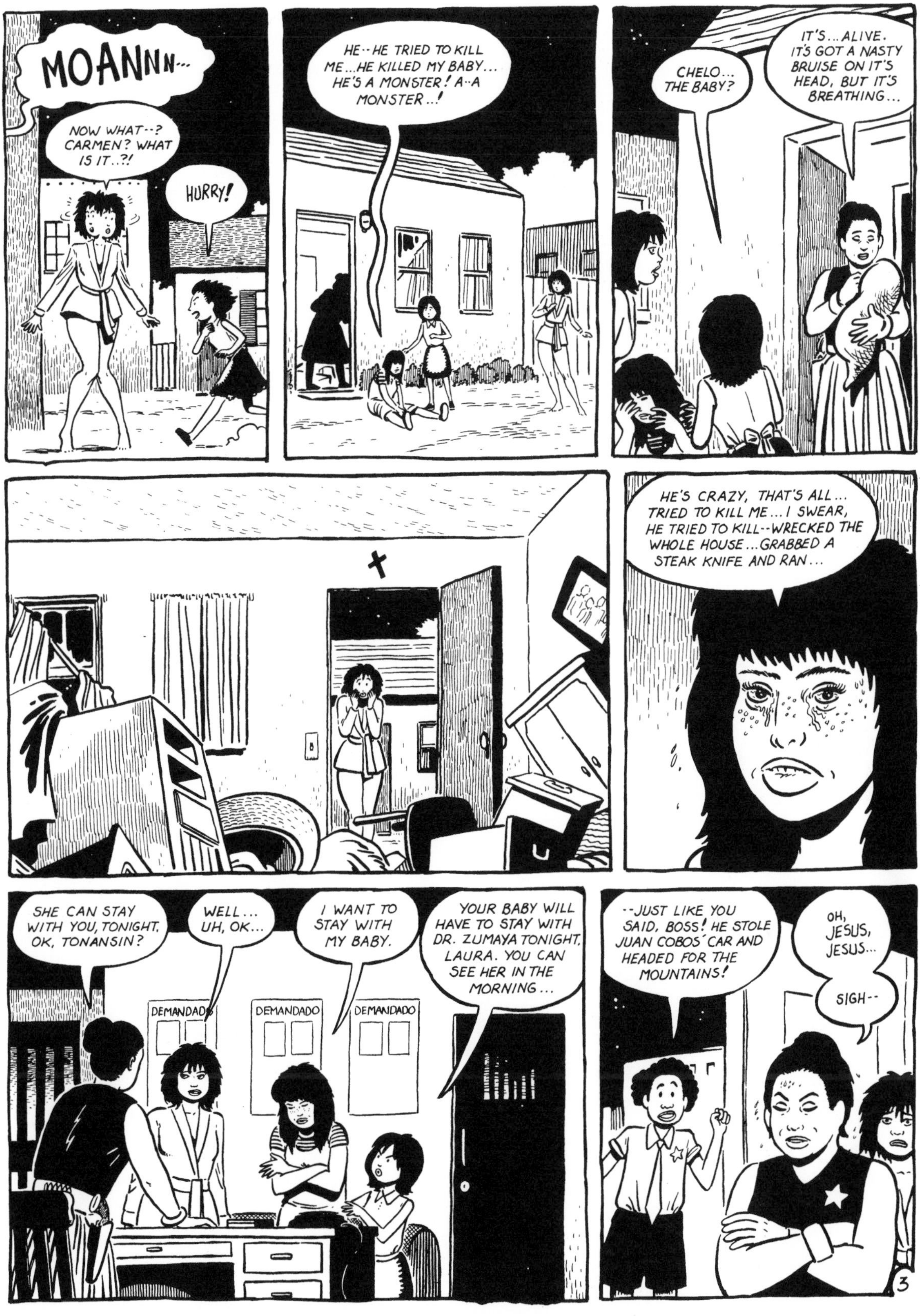
MOANNN...
NOW WHAT--? CARMEN? WHAT IS IT..?!
HURRY!
HE--HE TRIED TO KILL ME...HE KILLED MY BABY... HE'S A MONSTER! A--A MONSTER...!
CHELO... THE BABY?
IT'S...ALIVE. IT'S GOT A NASTY BRUISE ON IT'S HEAD, BUT IT'S BREATHING...
HE'S CRAZY, THAT'S ALL... TRIED TO KILL ME...I SWEAR, HE TRIED TO KILL--WRECKED THE WHOLE HOUSE...GRABBED A STEAK KNIFE AND RAN...
SHE CAN STAY WITH YOU, TONIGHT. OK, TONANSIN?
WELL... UH, OK...
I WANT TO STAY WITH MY BABY.
YOUR BABY WILL HAVE TO STAY WITH DR. ZUMAYA TONIGHT, LAURA. YOU CAN SEE HER IN THE MORNING...
DEMANDADO
DEMANDADO
DEMANDADO
--JUST LIKE YOU SAID, BOSS! HE STOLE JUAN COBOS' CAR AND HEADED FOR THE MOUNTAINS!
OH, JESUS, JESUS...
SIGH--
3

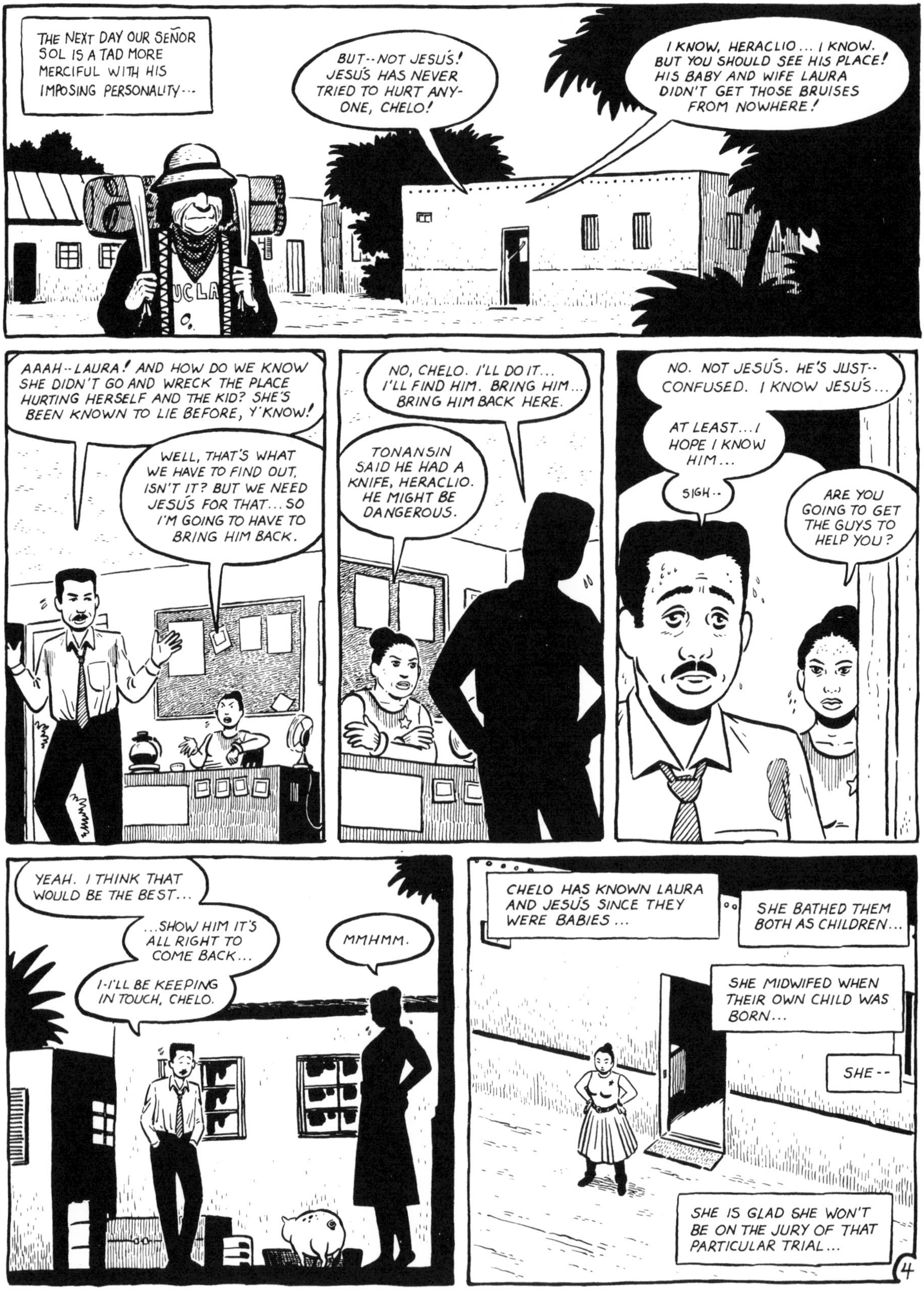
THE NEXT DAY OUR SEÑOR SOL IS A TAD MORE MERCIFUL WITH HIS IMPOSING PERSONALITY...
BUT--NOT JESÚS! JESÚS HAS NEVER TRIED TO HURT ANY-ONE, CHELO!
I KNOW, HERACLIO... I KNOW. BUT YOU SHOULD SEE HIS PLACE! HIS BABY AND WIFE LAURA DIDN'T GET THOSE BRUISES FROM NOWHERE!
UCLA
AAAH--LAURA! AND HOW DO WE KNOW SHE DIDN'T GO AND WRECK THE PLACE HURTING HERSELF AND THE KID? SHE'S BEEN KNOWN TO LIE BEFORE, Y'KNOW!
WELL, THAT'S WHAT WE HAVE TO FIND OUT, ISN'T IT? BUT WE NEED JESÚS FOR THAT... SO I'M GOING TO HAVE TO BRING HIM BACK.
NO, CHELO. I'LL DO IT... I'LL FIND HIM. BRING HIM... BRING HIM BACK HERE.
TONANSIN SAID HE HAD A KNIFE, HERACLIO. HE MIGHT BE DANGEROUS.
NO. NOT JESÚS. HE'S JUST-- CONFUSED. I KNOW JESÚS...
AT LEAST... I HOPE I KNOW HIM...
SIGH..
ARE YOU GOING TO GET THE GUYS TO HELP YOU?
YEAH. I THINK THAT WOULD BE THE BEST...
...SHOW HIM IT'S ALL RIGHT TO COME BACK...
I-I'LL BE KEEPING IN TOUCH, CHELO.
MMHMM.
CHELO HAS KNOWN LAURA AND JESÚS SINCE THEY WERE BABIES...
SHE BATHED THEM BOTH AS CHILDREN...
SHE MIDWIFED WHEN THEIR OWN CHILD WAS BORN...
SHE--
SHE IS GLAD SHE WON'T BE ON THE JURY OF THAT PARTICULAR TRIAL...
4

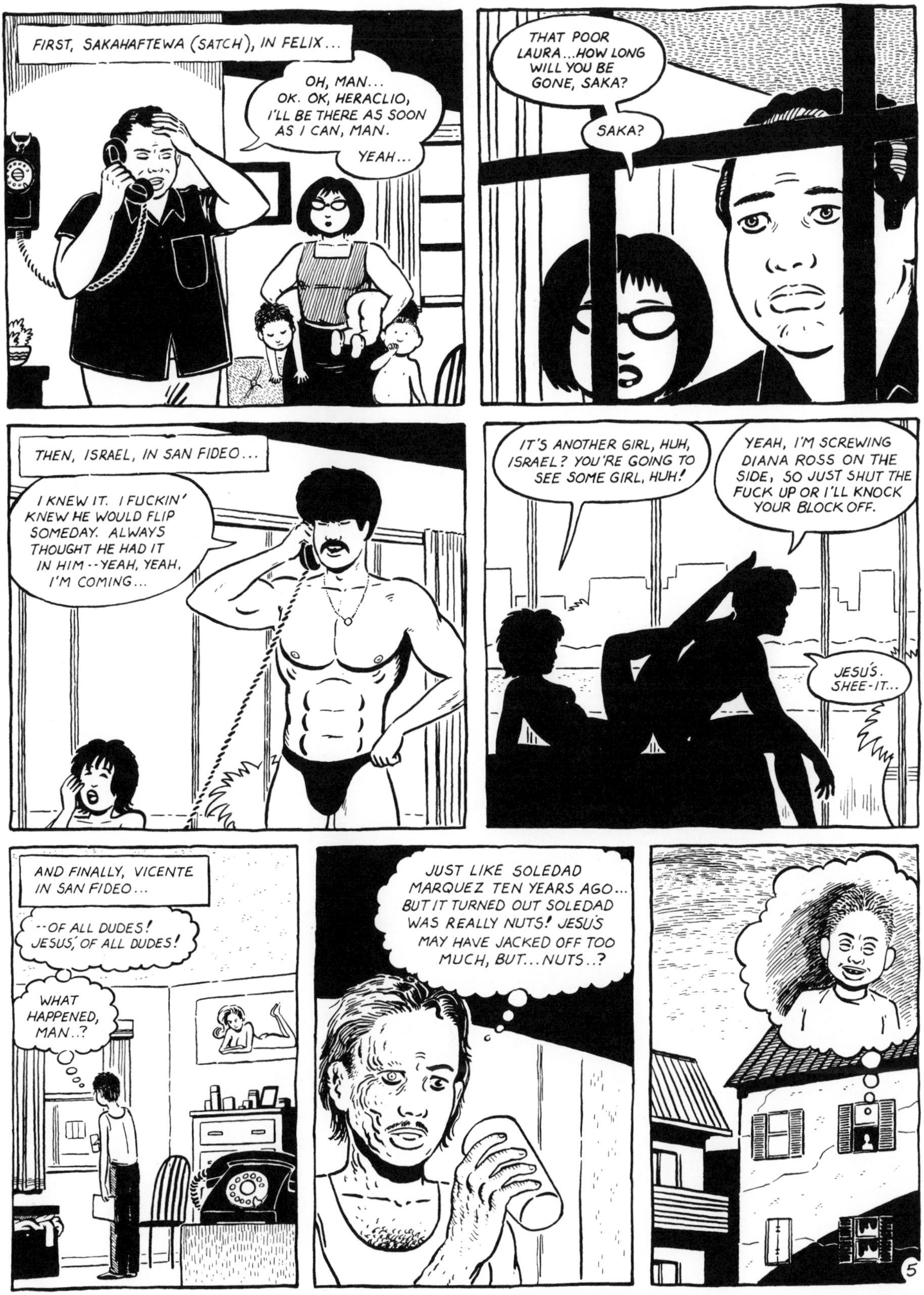
FIRST, SAKAHAFTEWA (SATCH), IN FELIX...
OH, MAN... OK. OK, HERACLIO, I'LL BE THERE AS SOON AS I CAN, MAN.
YEAH...
THAT POOR LAURA...HOW LONG WILL YOU BE GONE, SAKA?
SAKA?
THEN, ISRAEL, IN SAN FIDEO...
I KNEW IT. I FUCKIN' KNEW HE WOULD FLIP SOMEDAY. ALWAYS THOUGHT HE HAD IT IN HIM--YEAH, YEAH, I'M COMING...
IT'S ANOTHER GIRL, HUH, ISRAEL? YOU'RE GOING TO SEE SOME GIRL, HUH!
YEAH, I'M SCREWING DIANA ROSS ON THE SIDE, SO JUST SHUT THE FUCK UP OR I'LL KNOCK YOUR BLOCK OFF.
JESÚS. SHEE-IT...
AND FINALLY, VICENTE IN SAN FIDEO...
--OF ALL DUDES! JESÚS, OF ALL DUDES!
WHAT HAPPENED, MAN..?
JUST LIKE SOLEDAD MARQUEZ TEN YEARS AGO... BUT IT TURNED OUT SOLEDAD WAS REALLY NUTS! JESÚS MAY HAVE JACKED OFF TOO MUCH, BUT... NUTS..?
5

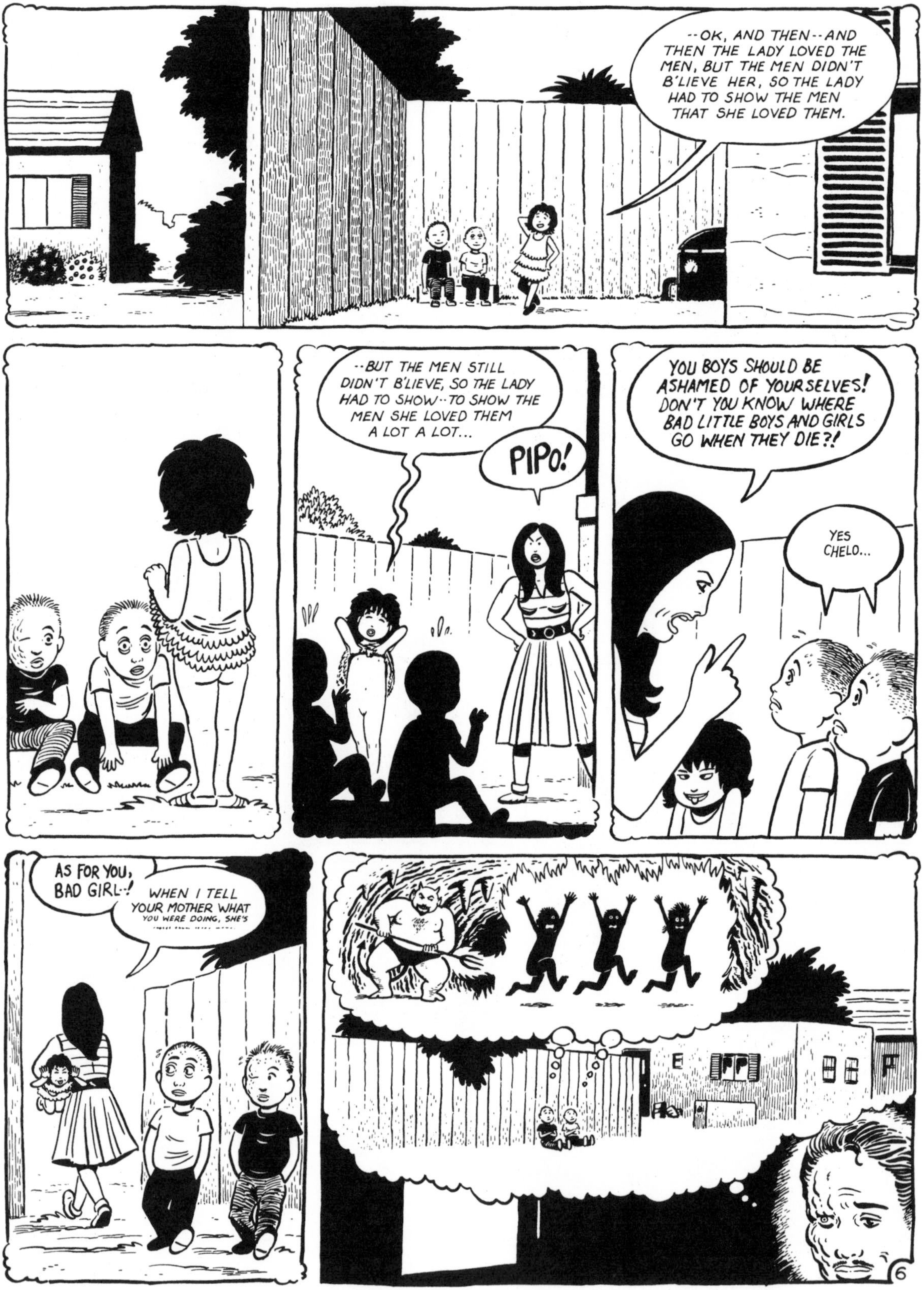
--OK, AND THEN--AND THEN THE LADY LOVED THE MEN, BUT THE MEN DIDN'T B'LIEVE HER, SO THE LADY HAD TO SHOW THE MEN THAT SHE LOVED THEM.
--BUT THE MEN STILL DIDN'T B'LIEVE, SO THE LADY HAD TO SHOW--TO SHOW THE MEN SHE LOVED THEM A LOT A LOT...
PIPO!
YOU BOYS SHOULD BE ASHAMED OF YOURSELVES! DON'T YOU KNOW WHERE BAD LITTLE BOYS AND GIRLS GO WHEN THEY DIE?!
YES CHELO...
AS FOR YOU, BAD GIRL--!
WHEN I TELL YOUR MOTHER WHAT YOU WERE DOING, SHE'S
6

FUCKIN' JESÚS...

AND SO, OLD FRIENDS ARE REUNITED, ALBEIT UNDER GRIEVOUS CIRCUMSTANCES...

SO, DID JESÚS TRY TO KILL HIS KID ON PURPOSE, OR WHAT?

WE DON'T KNOW...LAURA CLAIMS HE DID...

I DUNNO, MAN. WHAT'S THIS SHIT ABOUT HIM AND A KNIFE, HUH?

YEAH, THE FOOL'S GONNA PROBABLY ACCIDENTALLY KILL HIM-SELF BEFORE WE CAN GET TO HIM.

SO...SO, WHY ISN'T CHELO DOING THIS? SHE'S STILL SHERIFF OF THAT DUMP, ISN'T SHE?

'CAUSE WE'RE DOING IT, THAT'S WHY! IF JESÚS HAS GONE NUTS, I THINK WE SHOULD BE THE FIRST PEOPLE TO TALK TO HIM.

YEAH! WHAT'S WITH YOU, ISRAEL? IT'S JESÚS, MAN!

YEAH...JESÚS. THAT FUCKER. MAN, WHEN I GET MY HANDS ON HIM...WHY'D HE RUN FOR THE HILLS OF ALL PLACES?

NAW...! NO WAY...!

YEAH! YOU CAN ASK THESE GUYS HERE! IT'S TRUE; I SWEAR!

WHAT'S THAT, PINTOR?

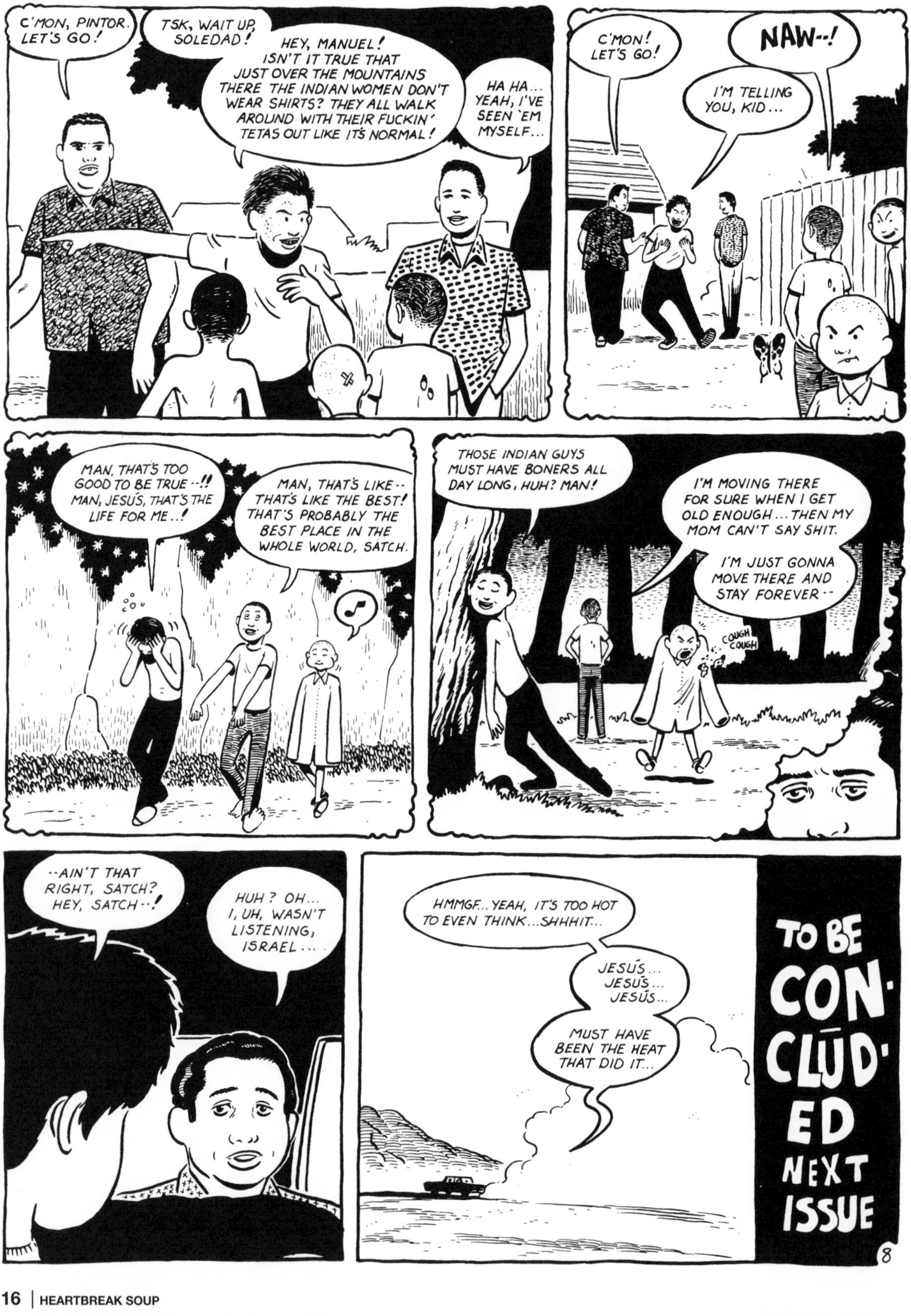
C'MON, PINTOR. LET'S GO!
TSK, WAIT UP, SOLEDAD!
HEY, MANUEL! ISN'T IT TRUE THAT JUST OVER THE MOUNTAINS THERE THE INDIAN WOMEN DON'T WEAR SHIRTS? THEY ALL WALK AROUND WITH THEIR FUCKIN' TETAS OUT LIKE IT'S NORMAL!
HA HA... YEAH, I'VE SEEN 'EM MYSELF...
C'MON! LET'S GO!
NAW--!
I'M TELLING YOU, KID...
MAN, THAT'S TOO GOOD TO BE TRUE--!! MAN, JESÚS, THAT'S THE LIFE FOR ME...!
MAN, THAT'S LIKE-- THAT'S LIKE THE BEST! THAT'S PROBABLY THE BEST PLACE IN THE WHOLE WORLD, SATCH.
THOSE INDIAN GUYS MUST HAVE BONERS ALL DAY LONG, HUH? MAN!
I'M MOVING THERE FOR SURE WHEN I GET OLD ENOUGH... THEN MY MOM CAN'T SAY SHIT.
I'M JUST GONNA MOVE THERE AND STAY FOREVER--
COUGH COUGH
--AIN'T THAT RIGHT, SATCH? HEY, SATCH--!
HUH? OH... I, UH, WASN'T LISTENING, ISRAEL...
HMMGF... YEAH, IT'S TOO HOT TO EVEN THINK... SHHHIT...
JESÚS... JESÚS... JESÚS...
MUST HAVE BEEN THE HEAT THAT DID IT...
TO BE CON-CLŪD-ED NEXT ISSUE
8

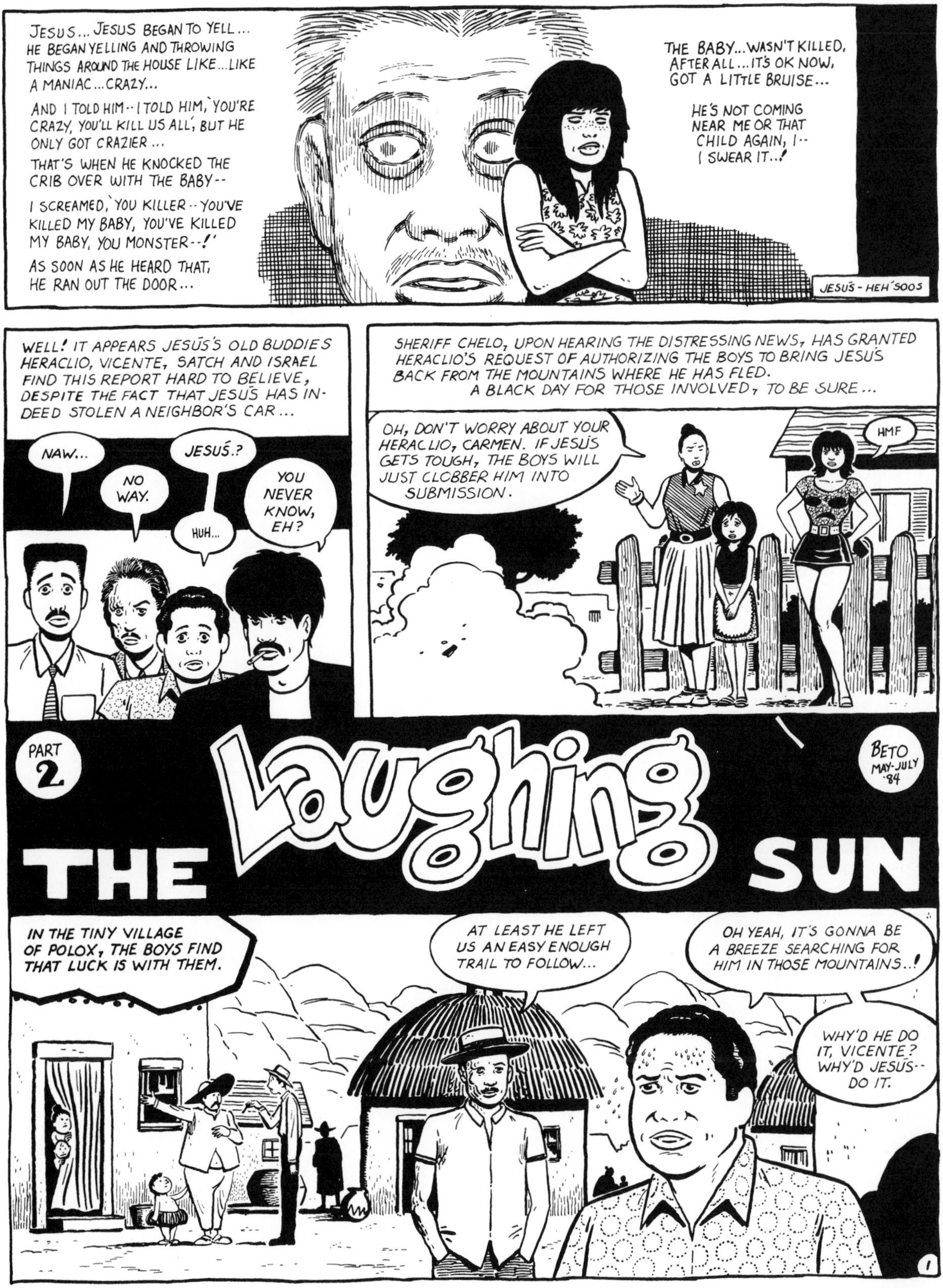

JESUS... JESUS BEGAN TO YELL... HE BEGAN YELLING AND THROWING THINGS AROUND THE HOUSE LIKE...LIKE A MANIAC...CRAZY...
AND I TOLD HIM--I TOLD HIM, 'YOU'RE CRAZY, YOU'LL KILL US ALL', BUT HE ONLY GOT CRAZIER...
THAT'S WHEN HE KNOCKED THE CRIB OVER WITH THE BABY--
I SCREAMED, 'YOU KILLER--YOU'VE KILLED MY BABY, YOU'VE KILLED MY BABY, YOU MONSTER--!'
AS SOON AS HE HEARD THAT, HE RAN OUT THE DOOR...
THE BABY...WASN'T KILLED, AFTER ALL...IT'S OK NOW, GOT A LITTLE BRUISE...
HE'S NOT COMING NEAR ME OR THAT CHILD AGAIN, I-- I SWEAR IT..!
JESÚS - HEH´SOOS
WELL! IT APPEARS JESÚS'S OLD BUDDIES HERACLIO, VICENTE, SATCH AND ISRAEL FIND THIS REPORT HARD TO BELIEVE, DESPITE THE FACT THAT JESÚS HAS INDEED STOLEN A NEIGHBOR'S CAR...
NAW...
NO WAY.
JESÚS.?
HUH...
YOU NEVER KNOW, EH?
SHERIFF CHELO, UPON HEARING THE DISTRESSING NEWS, HAS GRANTED HERACLIO'S REQUEST OF AUTHORIZING THE BOYS TO BRING JESÚS BACK FROM THE MOUNTAINS WHERE HE HAS FLED.
A BLACK DAY FOR THOSE INVOLVED, TO BE SURE...
OH, DON'T WORRY ABOUT YOUR HERACLIO, CARMEN. IF JESÚS GETS TOUGH, THE BOYS WILL JUST CLOBBER HIM INTO SUBMISSION.
HMF
PART 2
THE Laughing SUN
BETO MAY-JULY '84
IN THE TINY VILLAGE OF POLOX, THE BOYS FIND THAT LUCK IS WITH THEM.
AT LEAST HE LEFT US AN EASY ENOUGH TRAIL TO FOLLOW...
OH YEAH, IT'S GONNA BE A BREEZE SEARCHING FOR HIM IN THOSE MOUNTAINS..!
WHY'D HE DO IT, VICENTE? WHY'D JESÚS-- DO IT.
1

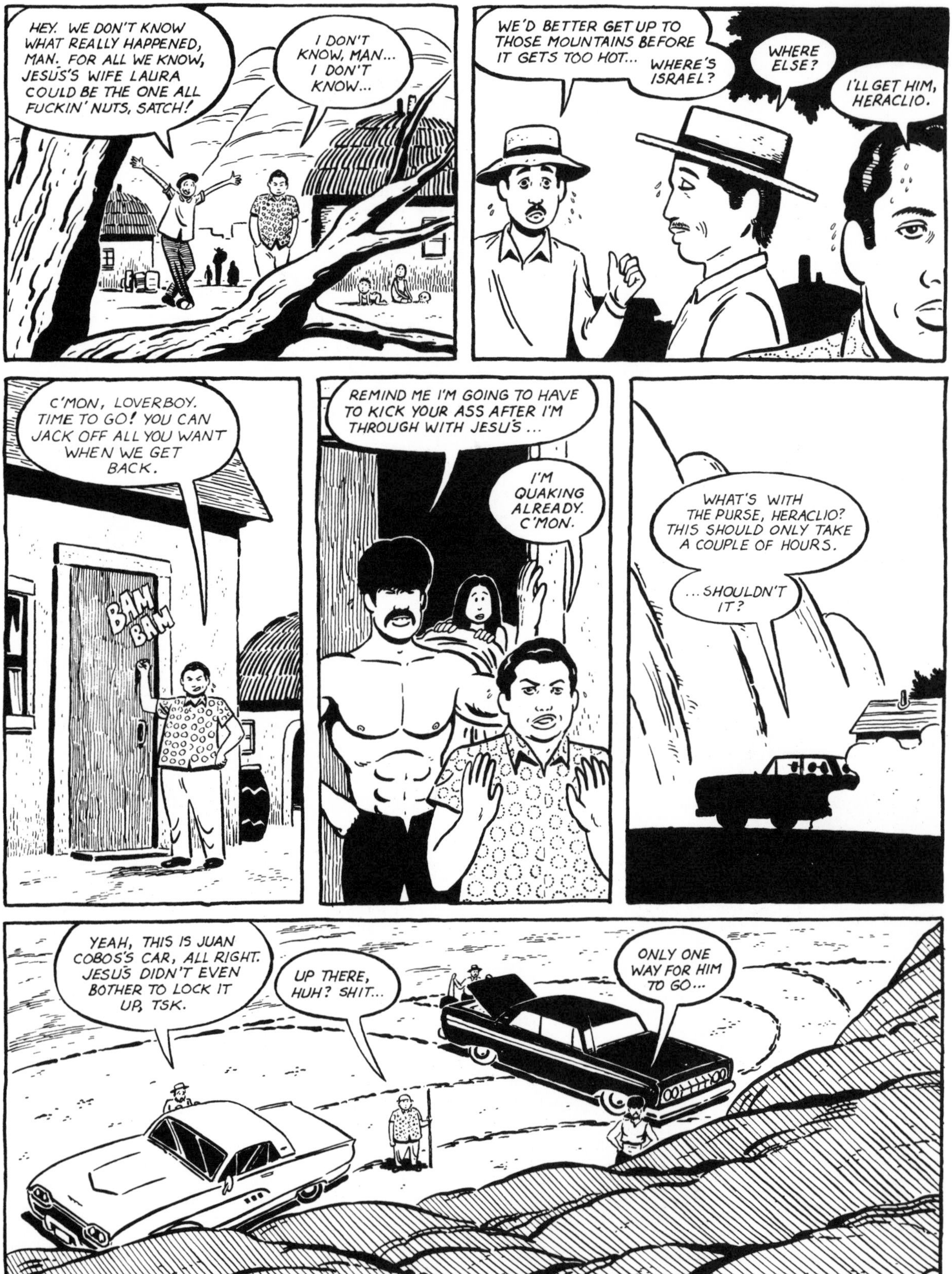
HEY. WE DON'T KNOW WHAT REALLY HAPPENED, MAN. FOR ALL WE KNOW, JESÚS'S WIFE LAURA COULD BE THE ONE ALL FUCKIN' NUTS, SATCH!
I DON'T KNOW, MAN... I DON'T KNOW...
WE'D BETTER GET UP TO THOSE MOUNTAINS BEFORE IT GETS TOO HOT... WHERE'S ISRAEL?
WHERE ELSE?
I'LL GET HIM, HERACLIO.
C'MON, LOVERBOY. TIME TO GO! YOU CAN JACK OFF ALL YOU WANT WHEN WE GET BACK.
BAM BAM
REMIND ME I'M GOING TO HAVE TO KICK YOUR ASS AFTER I'M THROUGH WITH JESÚS...
I'M QUAKING ALREADY. C'MON.
WHAT'S WITH THE PURSE, HERACLIO? THIS SHOULD ONLY TAKE A COUPLE OF HOURS.
...SHOULDN'T IT?
YEAH, THIS IS JUAN COBOS'S CAR, ALL RIGHT. JESÚS DIDN'T EVEN BOTHER TO LOCK IT UP, TSK.
UP THERE, HUH? SHIT...
ONLY ONE WAY FOR HIM TO GO...
2

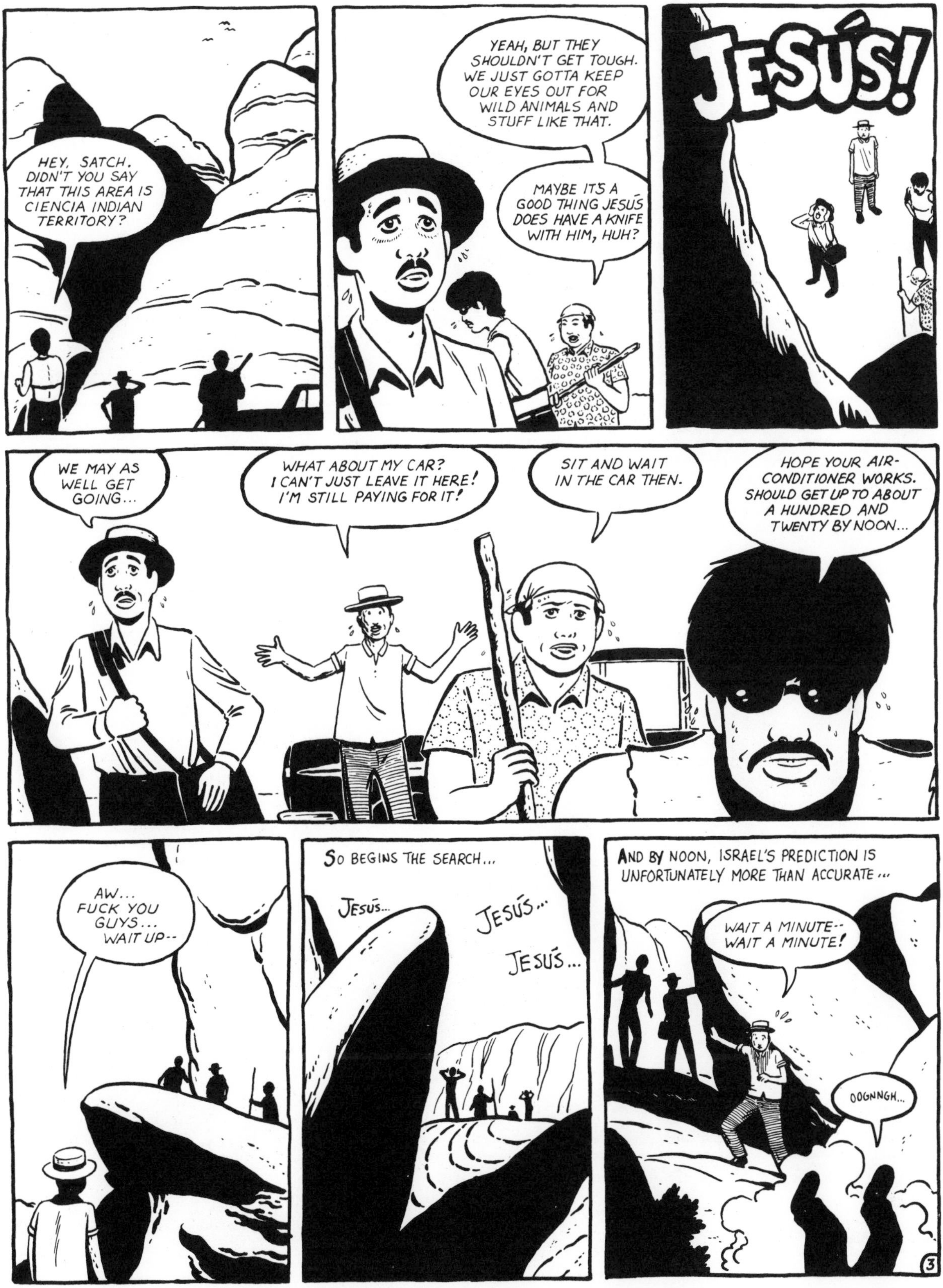
HEY, SATCH. DIDN'T YOU SAY THAT THIS AREA IS CIENCIA INDIAN TERRITORY?
YEAH, BUT THEY SHOULDN'T GET TOUGH. WE JUST GOTTA KEEP OUR EYES OUT FOR WILD ANIMALS AND STUFF LIKE THAT.
MAYBE IT'S A GOOD THING JESÚS DOES HAVE A KNIFE WITH HIM, HUH?
JESÚS!
WE MAY AS WELL GET GOING...
WHAT ABOUT MY CAR? I CAN'T JUST LEAVE IT HERE! I'M STILL PAYING FOR IT!
SIT AND WAIT IN THE CAR THEN.
HOPE YOUR AIR-CONDITIONER WORKS. SHOULD GET UP TO ABOUT A HUNDRED AND TWENTY BY NOON...
AW... FUCK YOU GUYS... WAIT UP--
SO BEGINS THE SEARCH...
JESÚS...
JESÚS...
JESÚS...
AND BY NOON, ISRAEL'S PREDICTION IS UNFORTUNATELY MORE THAN ACCURATE...
WAIT A MINUTE-- WAIT A MINUTE!
OOGNNGH...
3

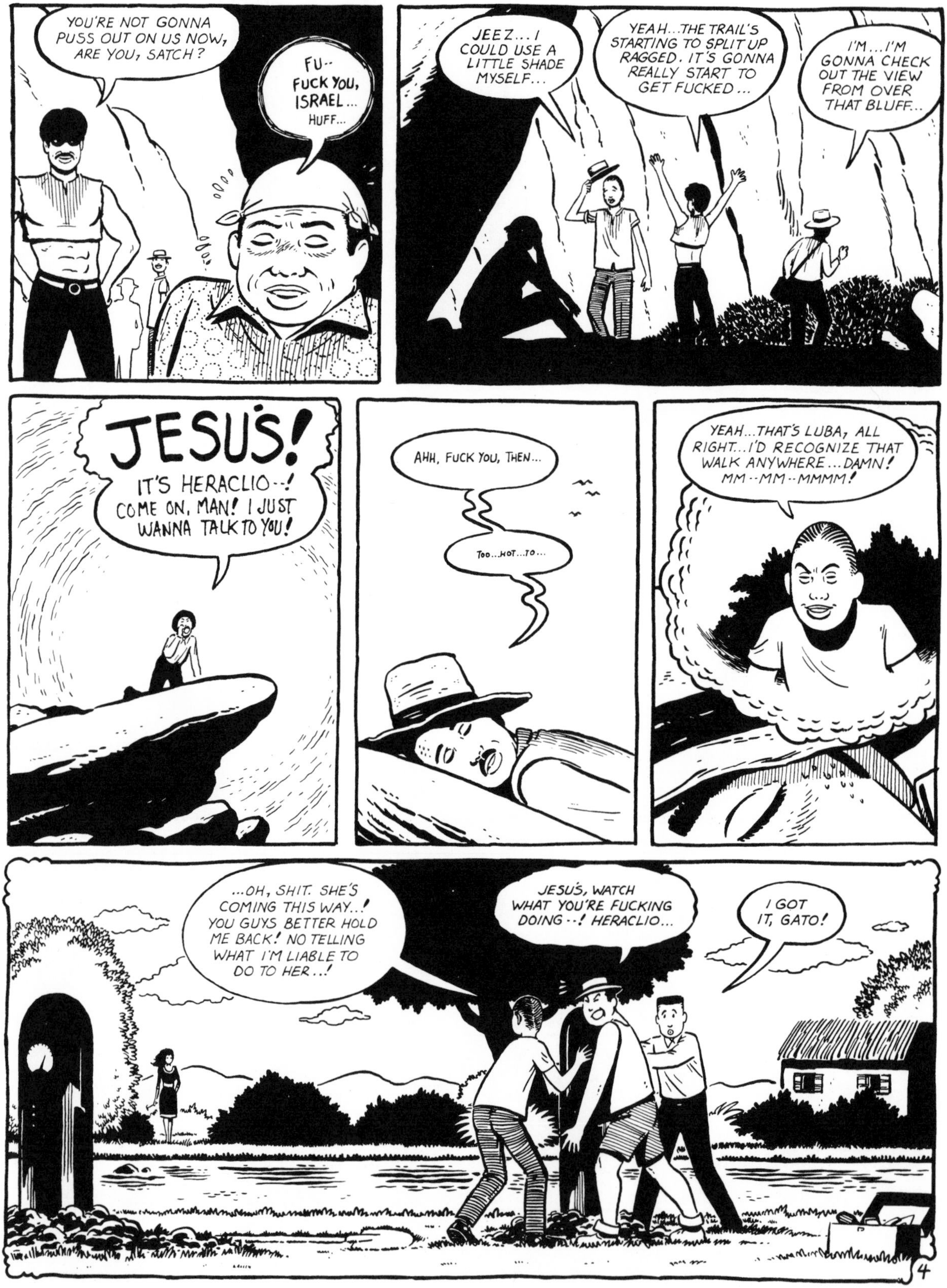
YOU'RE NOT GONNA PUSS OUT ON US NOW, ARE YOU, SATCH?
FU-- FUCK YOU, ISRAEL... HUFF...
JEEZ... I COULD USE A LITTLE SHADE MYSELF...
YEAH...THE TRAIL'S STARTING TO SPLIT UP RAGGED. IT'S GONNA REALLY START TO GET FUCKED...
I'M...I'M GONNA CHECK OUT THE VIEW FROM OVER THAT BLUFF...
JESUS!
IT'S HERACLIO--! COME ON, MAN! I JUST WANNA TALK TO YOU!
AHH, FUCK YOU, THEN...
TOO...HOT...TO...
YEAH...THAT'S LUBA, ALL RIGHT...I'D RECOGNIZE THAT WALK ANYWHERE...DAMN! MM--MM--MMMM!
...OH, SHIT. SHE'S COMING THIS WAY...! YOU GUYS BETTER HOLD ME BACK! NO TELLING WHAT I'M LIABLE TO DO TO HER...!
JESUS, WATCH WHAT YOU'RE FUCKING DOING--! HERACLIO...
I GOT IT, GATO!
4

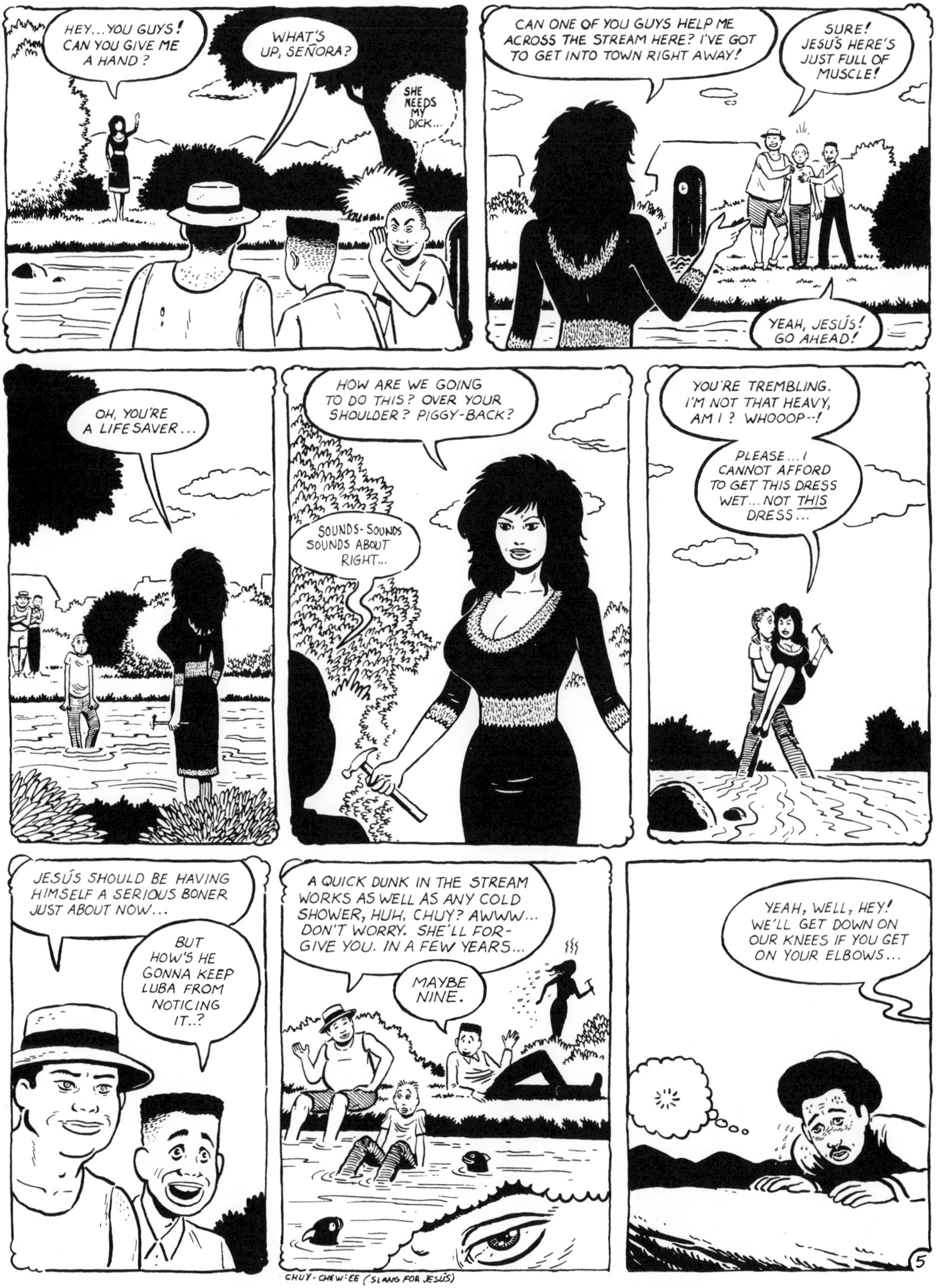
HEY... YOU GUYS! CAN YOU GIVE ME A HAND?
WHAT'S UP, SEÑORA?
SHE NEEDS MY DICK...
CAN ONE OF YOU GUYS HELP ME ACROSS THE STREAM HERE? I'VE GOT TO GET INTO TOWN RIGHT AWAY!
SURE! JESÚS HERE'S JUST FULL OF MUSCLE!
YEAH, JESÚS! GO AHEAD!
OH, YOU'RE A LIFESAVER...
HOW ARE WE GOING TO DO THIS? OVER YOUR SHOULDER? PIGGY-BACK?
SOUNDS- SOUNDS SOUNDS ABOUT RIGHT...
YOU'RE TREMBLING. I'M NOT THAT HEAVY, AM I? WHOOOP--!
PLEASE... I CANNOT AFFORD TO GET THIS DRESS WET... NOT THIS DRESS...
JESÚS SHOULD BE HAVING HIMSELF A SERIOUS BONER JUST ABOUT NOW...
BUT HOW'S HE GONNA KEEP LUBA FROM NOTICING IT..?
A QUICK DUNK IN THE STREAM WORKS AS WELL AS ANY COLD SHOWER, HUH, CHUY? AWWW... DON'T WORRY. SHE'LL FOR-GIVE YOU. IN A FEW YEARS...
MAYBE NINE.
YEAH, WELL, HEY! WE'LL GET DOWN ON OUR KNEES IF YOU GET ON YOUR ELBOWS...
5
CHUY - CHEW:EE (SLANG FOR JESÚS)

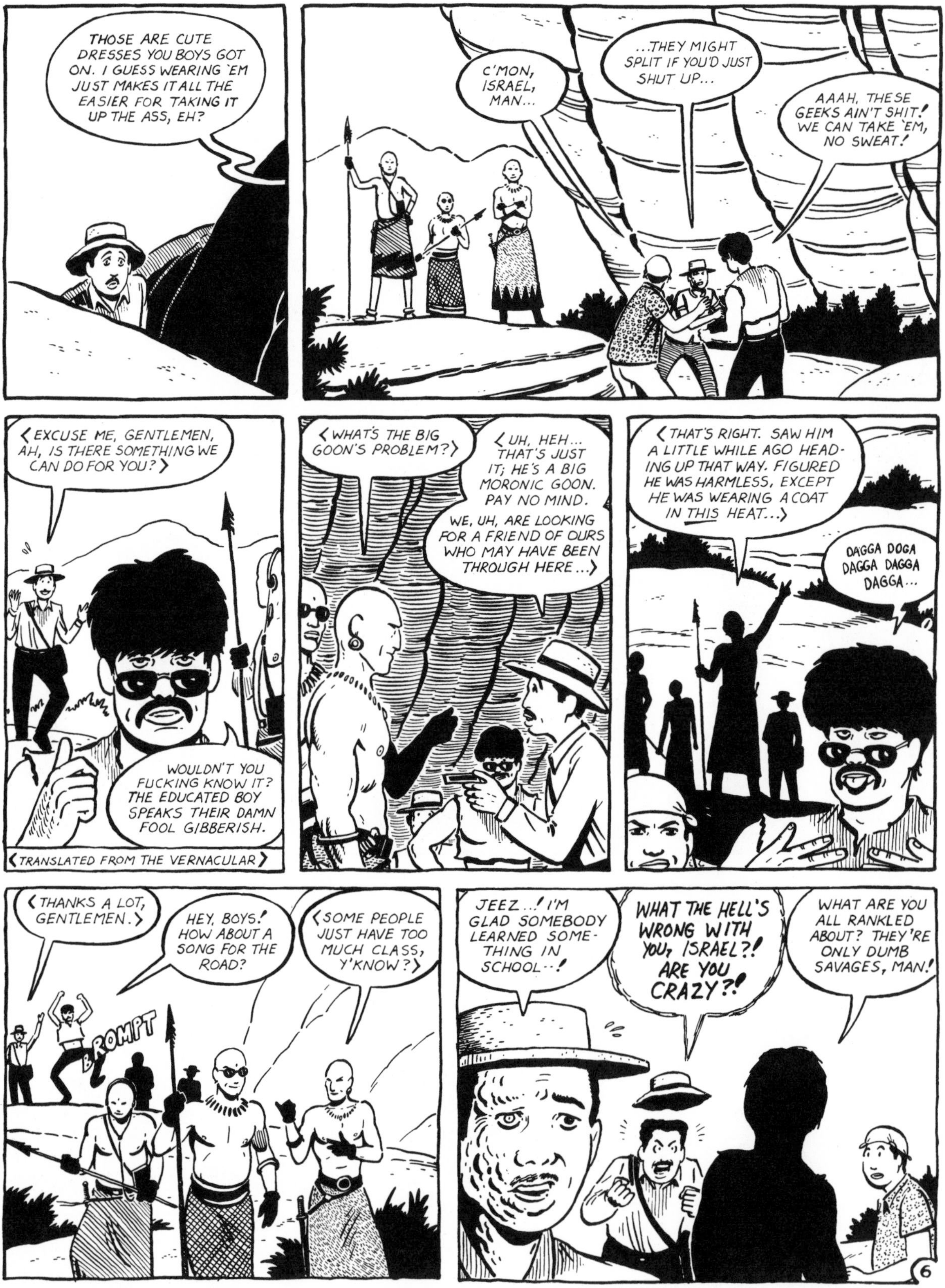
THOSE ARE CUTE DRESSES YOU BOYS GOT ON. I GUESS WEARING 'EM JUST MAKES IT ALL THE EASIER FOR TAKING IT UP THE ASS, EH?
C'MON, ISRAEL, MAN...
...THEY MIGHT SPLIT IF YOU'D JUST SHUT UP...
AAAH, THESE GEEKS AIN'T SHIT! WE CAN TAKE 'EM, NO SWEAT!
‹EXCUSE ME, GENTLEMEN, AH, IS THERE SOMETHING WE CAN DO FOR YOU?›
WOULDN'T YOU FUCKING KNOW IT? THE EDUCATED BOY SPEAKS THEIR DAMN FOOL GIBBERISH.
‹TRANSLATED FROM THE VERNACULAR›
‹WHAT'S THE BIG GOON'S PROBLEM?›
‹UH, HEH... THAT'S JUST IT; HE'S A BIG MORONIC GOON. PAY NO MIND.
WE, UH, ARE LOOKING FOR A FRIEND OF OURS WHO MAY HAVE BEEN THROUGH HERE...›
‹THAT'S RIGHT. SAW HIM A LITTLE WHILE AGO HEADING UP THAT WAY. FIGURED HE WAS HARMLESS, EXCEPT HE WAS WEARING A COAT IN THIS HEAT...›
DAGGA DOGA DAGGA DAGGA DAGGA...
‹THANKS A LOT, GENTLEMEN.›
HEY, BOYS! HOW ABOUT A SONG FOR THE ROAD?
BROMPT
‹SOME PEOPLE JUST HAVE TOO MUCH CLASS, Y'KNOW?›
JEEZ...! I'M GLAD SOMEBODY LEARNED SOMETHING IN SCHOOL..!
WHAT THE HELL'S WRONG WITH YOU, ISRAEL?! ARE YOU CRAZY?!
WHAT ARE YOU ALL RANKLED ABOUT? THEY'RE ONLY DUMB SAVAGES, MAN!
6

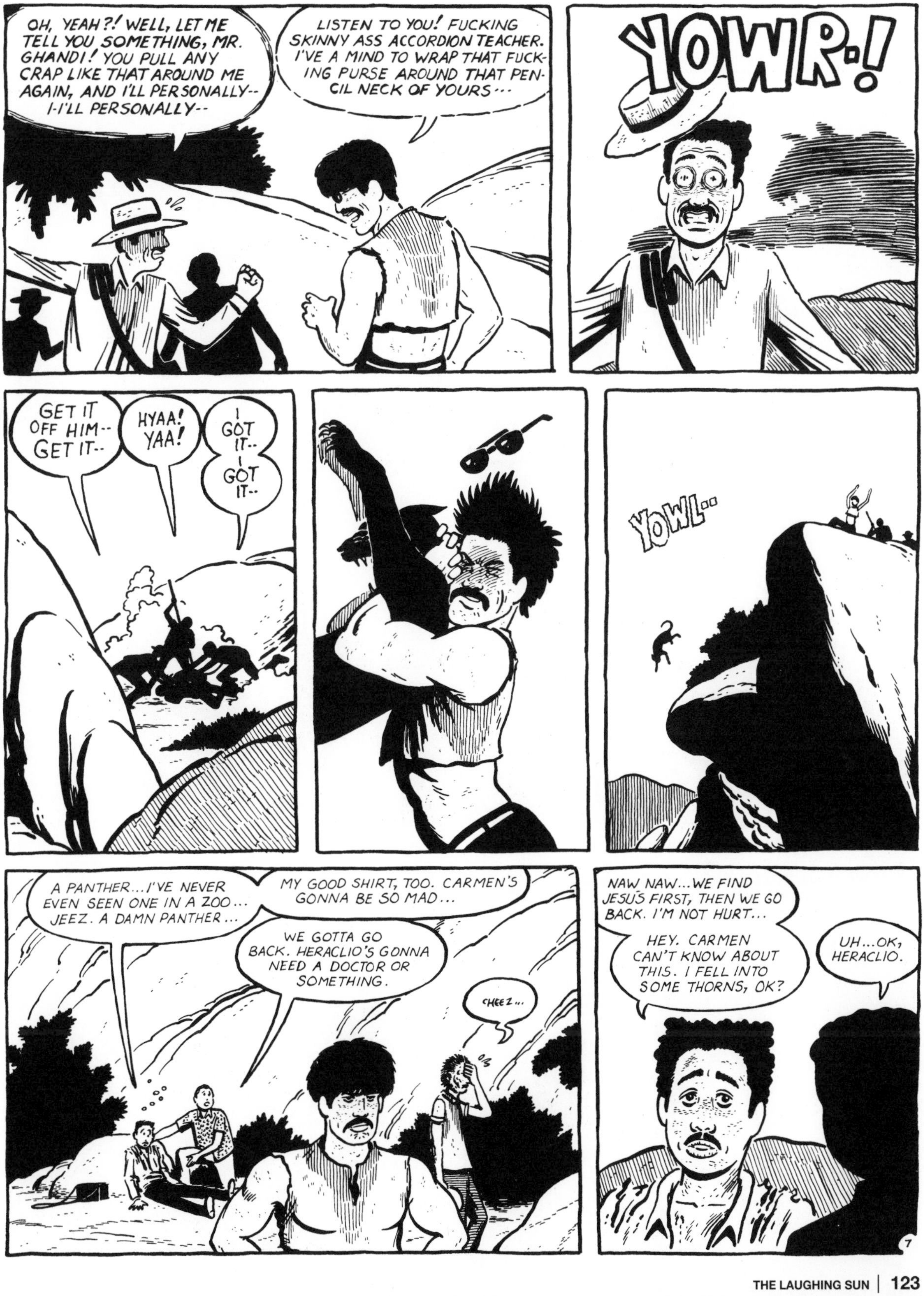
OH, YEAH?! WELL, LET ME TELL YOU SOMETHING, MR. GHANDI! YOU PULL ANY CRAP LIKE THAT AROUND ME AGAIN, AND I'LL PERSONALLY-- I-I'LL PERSONALLY--
LISTEN TO YOU! FUCKING SKINNY ASS ACCORDION TEACHER. I'VE A MIND TO WRAP THAT FUCKING PURSE AROUND THAT PENCIL NECK OF YOURS...
YOWR-!
GET IT OFF HIM-- GET IT--
HYAA! YAA!
I GOT IT-- I GOT IT--
YOWL--
A PANTHER... I'VE NEVER EVEN SEEN ONE IN A ZOO... JEEZ. A DAMN PANTHER...
MY GOOD SHIRT, TOO. CARMEN'S GONNA BE SO MAD...
WE GOTTA GO BACK. HERACLIO'S GONNA NEED A DOCTOR OR SOMETHING.
CHEEZ...
NAW NAW... WE FIND JESÚS FIRST, THEN WE GO BACK. I'M NOT HURT...
HEY. CARMEN CAN'T KNOW ABOUT THIS. I FELL INTO SOME THORNS, OK?
UH... OK, HERACLIO.
7

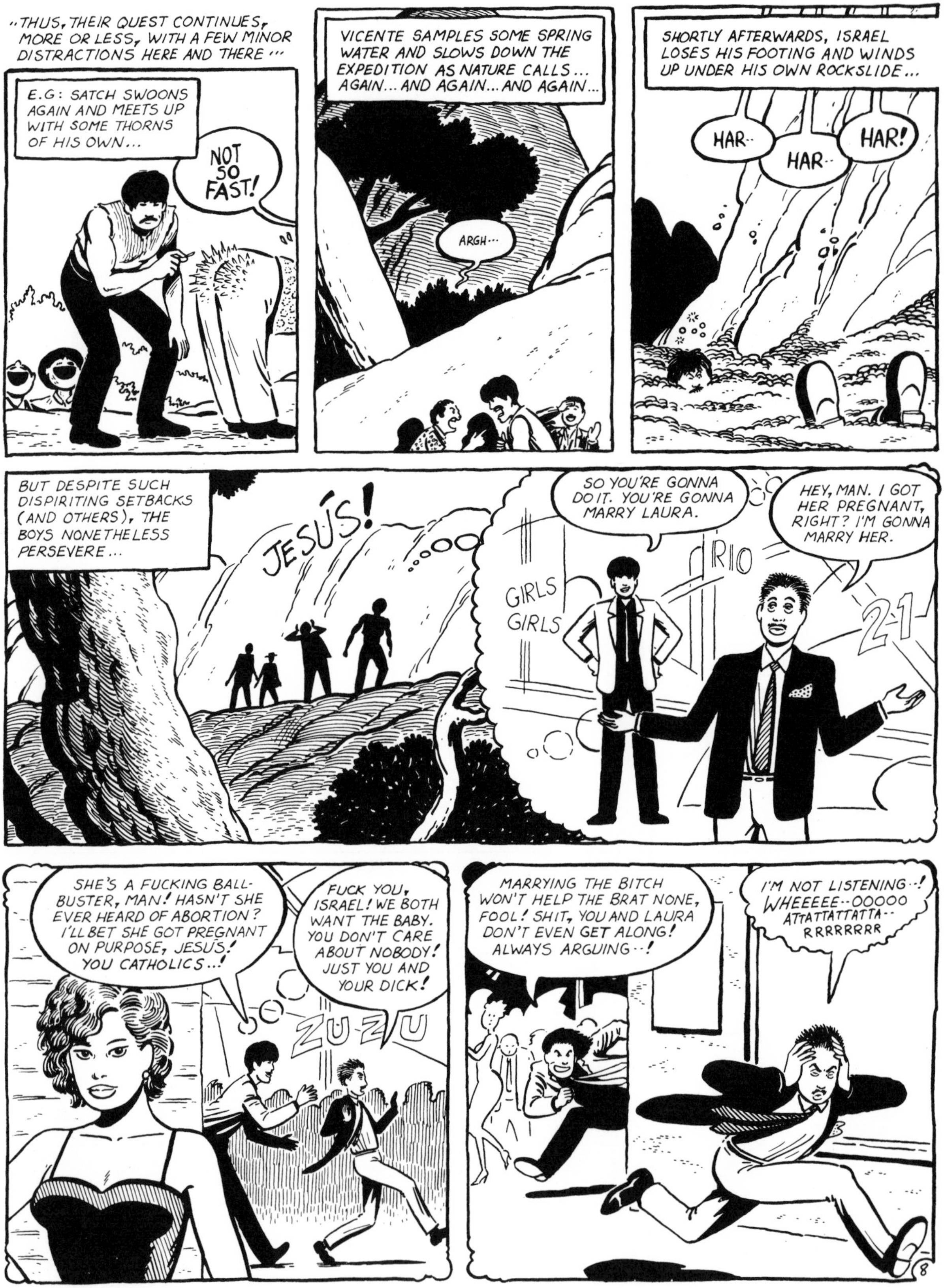

..THUS, THEIR QUEST CONTINUES, MORE OR LESS, WITH A FEW MINOR DISTRACTIONS HERE AND THERE ...
E.G: SATCH SWOONS AGAIN AND MEETS UP WITH SOME THORNS OF HIS OWN...
NOT SO FAST!
VICENTE SAMPLES SOME SPRING WATER AND SLOWS DOWN THE EXPEDITION AS NATURE CALLS... AGAIN... AND AGAIN... AND AGAIN...
ARGH...
SHORTLY AFTERWARDS, ISRAEL LOSES HIS FOOTING AND WINDS UP UNDER HIS OWN ROCKSLIDE...
HAR..
HAR..
HAR!
BUT DESPITE SUCH DISPIRITING SETBACKS (AND OTHERS), THE BOYS NONETHELESS PERSEVERE...
JESÚS!
SO YOU'RE GONNA DO IT. YOU'RE GONNA MARRY LAURA.
HEY, MAN. I GOT HER PREGNANT, RIGHT? I'M GONNA MARRY HER.
GIRLS
GIRLS
RIO
21
SHE'S A FUCKING BALL-BUSTER, MAN! HASN'T SHE EVER HEARD OF ABORTION? I'LL BET SHE GOT PREGNANT ON PURPOSE, JESÚS! YOU CATHOLICS...!
FUCK YOU, ISRAEL! WE BOTH WANT THE BABY. YOU DON'T CARE ABOUT NOBODY! JUST YOU AND YOUR DICK!
ZUZU
MARRYING THE BITCH WON'T HELP THE BRAT NONE, FOOL! SHIT, YOU AND LAURA DON'T EVEN GET ALONG! ALWAYS ARGUING..!
I'M NOT LISTENING..! WHEEEEE..OOOOO ATTATTATTATTA.. RRRRRRRR
8

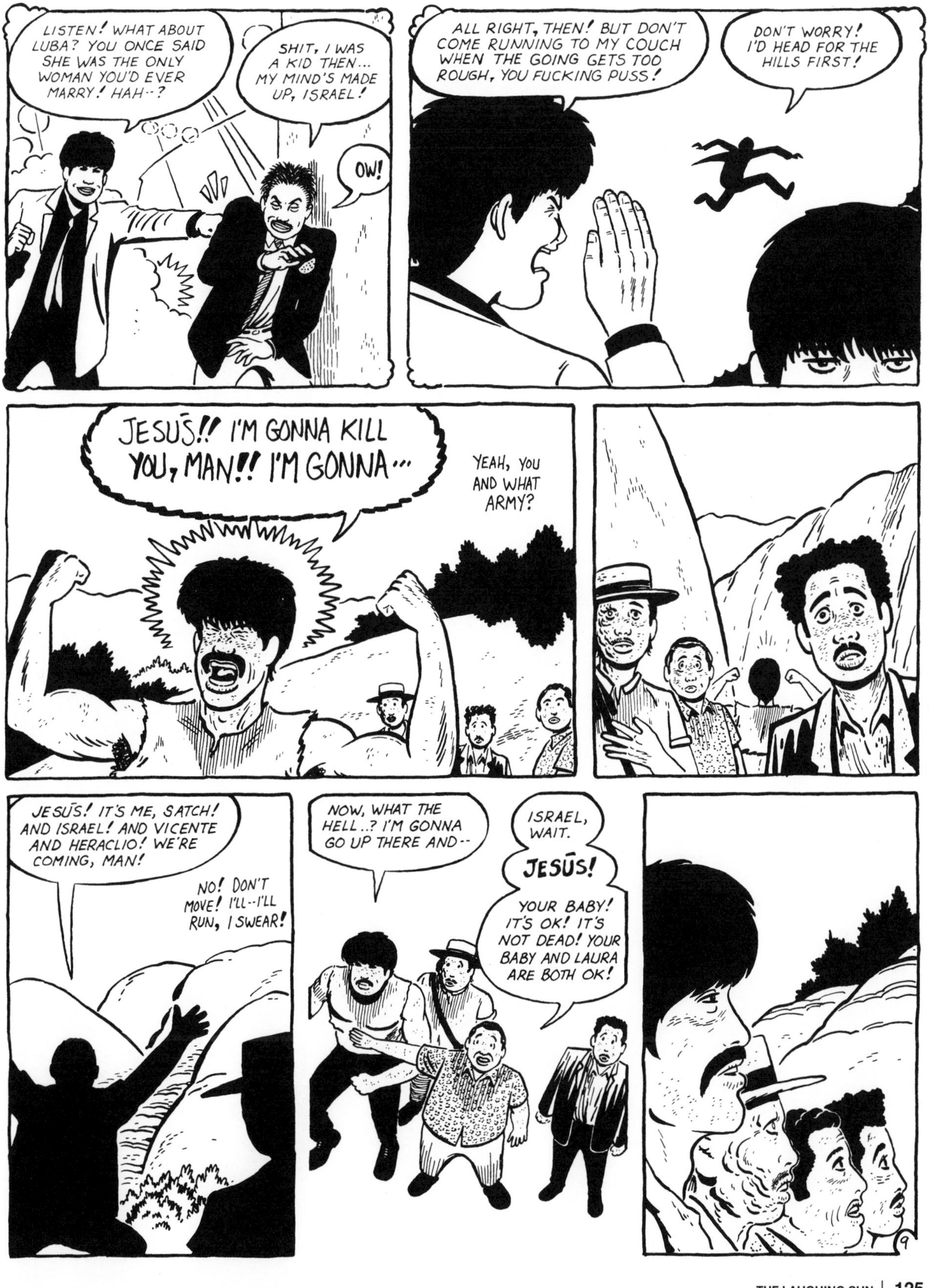
LISTEN! WHAT ABOUT LUBA? YOU ONCE SAID SHE WAS THE ONLY WOMAN YOU'D EVER MARRY! HAH--?
SHIT, I WAS A KID THEN... MY MIND'S MADE UP, ISRAEL!
OW!
ALL RIGHT, THEN! BUT DON'T COME RUNNING TO MY COUCH WHEN THE GOING GETS TOO ROUGH, YOU FUCKING PUSS!
DON'T WORRY! I'D HEAD FOR THE HILLS FIRST!
JESŪS!! I'M GONNA KILL YOU, MAN!! I'M GONNA...
YEAH, YOU AND WHAT ARMY?
JESŪS! IT'S ME, SATCH! AND ISRAEL! AND VICENTE AND HERACLIO! WE'RE COMING, MAN!
NO! DON'T MOVE! I'LL--I'LL RUN, I SWEAR!
NOW, WHAT THE HELL..? I'M GONNA GO UP THERE AND--
ISRAEL, WAIT.
JESŪS!
YOUR BABY! IT'S OK! IT'S NOT DEAD! YOUR BABY AND LAURA ARE BOTH OK!
9

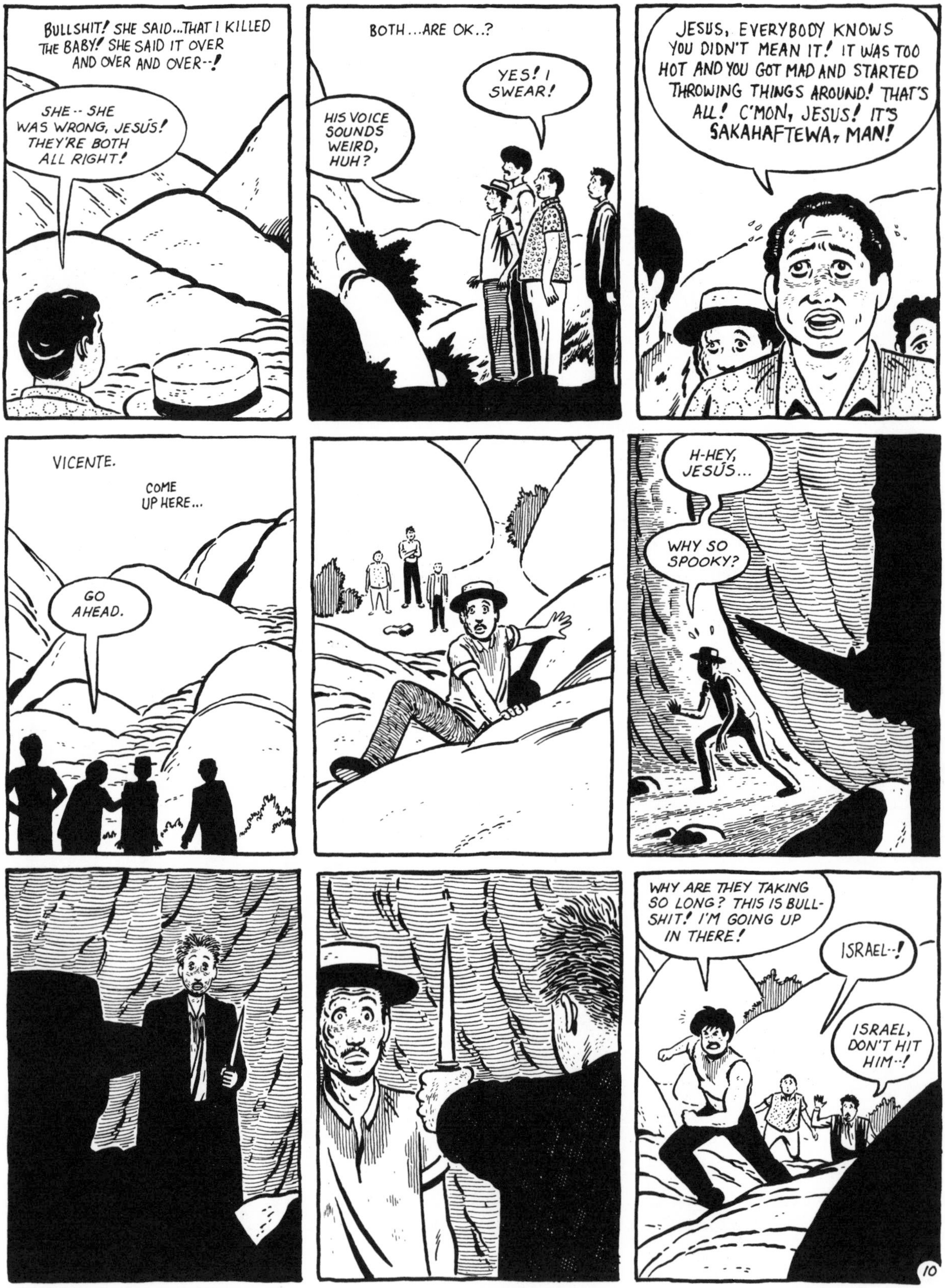
BULLSHIT! SHE SAID...THAT I KILLED THE BABY! SHE SAID IT OVER AND OVER AND OVER--!
SHE -- SHE WAS WRONG, JESÚS! THEY'RE BOTH ALL RIGHT!
BOTH...ARE OK..?
YES! I SWEAR!
HIS VOICE SOUNDS WEIRD, HUH?
JESÚS, EVERYBODY KNOWS YOU DIDN'T MEAN IT! IT WAS TOO HOT AND YOU GOT MAD AND STARTED THROWING THINGS AROUND! THAT'S ALL! C'MON, JESÚS! IT'S SAKAHAFTEWA, MAN!
VICENTE.
COME UP HERE...
GO AHEAD.
H-HEY, JESÚS...
WHY SO SPOOKY?
WHY ARE THEY TAKING SO LONG? THIS IS BULL-SHIT! I'M GOING UP IN THERE!
ISRAEL--!
ISRAEL, DON'T HIT HIM--!
10

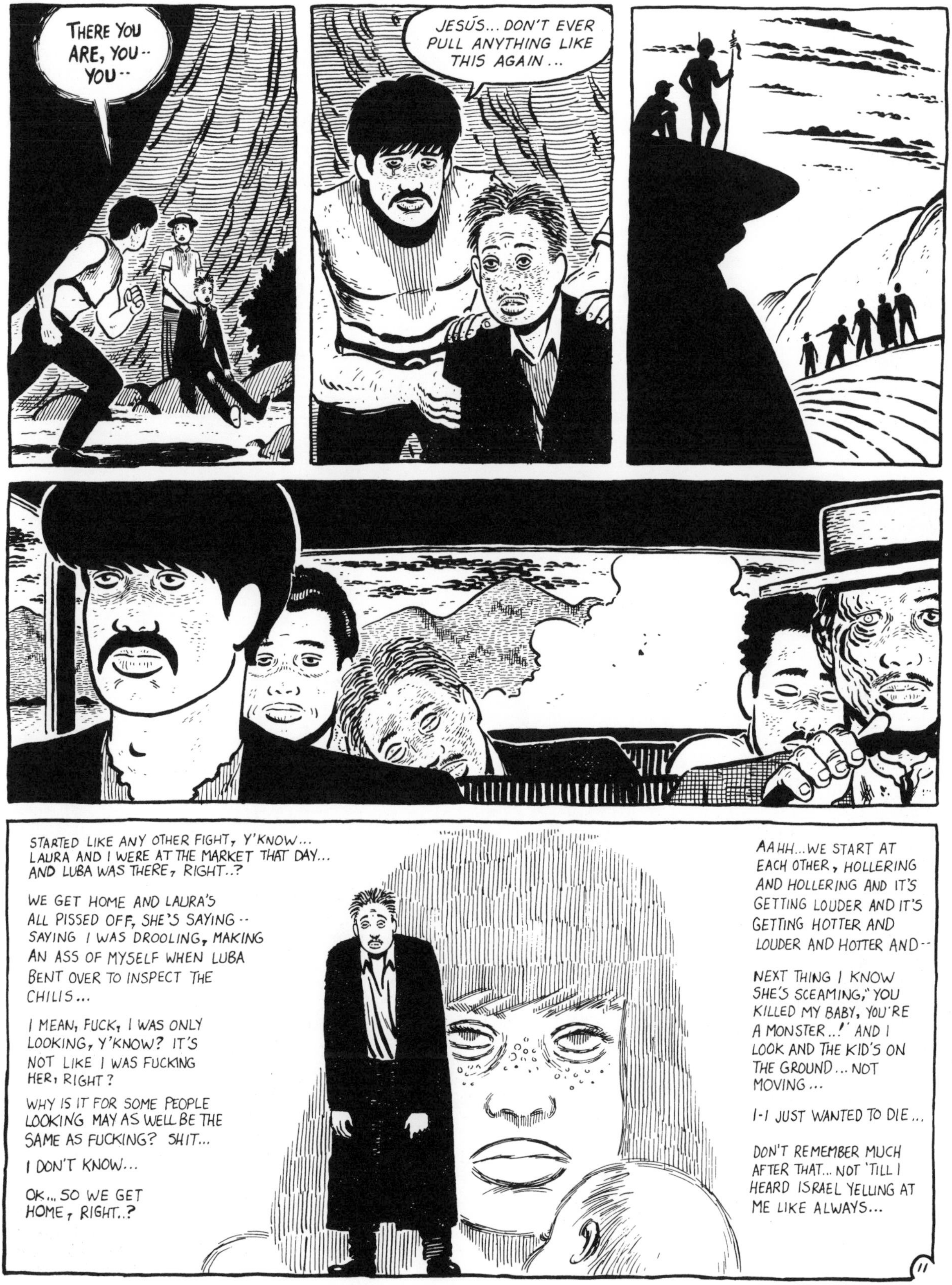

THERE YOU ARE, YOU-- YOU--
JESÚS... DON'T EVER PULL ANYTHING LIKE THIS AGAIN...
STARTED LIKE ANY OTHER FIGHT, Y'KNOW... LAURA AND I WERE AT THE MARKET THAT DAY... AND LUBA WAS THERE, RIGHT..?
WE GET HOME AND LAURA'S ALL PISSED OFF, SHE'S SAYING-- SAYING I WAS DROOLING, MAKING AN ASS OF MYSELF WHEN LUBA BENT OVER TO INSPECT THE CHILIS...
I MEAN, FUCK, I WAS ONLY LOOKING, Y'KNOW? IT'S NOT LIKE I WAS FUCKING HER, RIGHT?
WHY IS IT FOR SOME PEOPLE LOOKING MAY AS WELL BE THE SAME AS FUCKING? SHIT...
I DON'T KNOW...
OK... SO WE GET HOME, RIGHT..?
AAHH... WE START AT EACH OTHER, HOLLERING AND HOLLERING AND IT'S GETTING LOUDER AND IT'S GETTING HOTTER AND LOUDER AND HOTTER AND--
NEXT THING I KNOW SHE'S SCEAMING, "YOU KILLED MY BABY, YOU'RE A MONSTER..!' AND I LOOK AND THE KID'S ON THE GROUND... NOT MOVING...
I-I JUST WANTED TO DIE...
DON'T REMEMBER MUCH AFTER THAT... NOT 'TILL I HEARD ISRAEL YELLING AT ME LIKE ALWAYS...
11

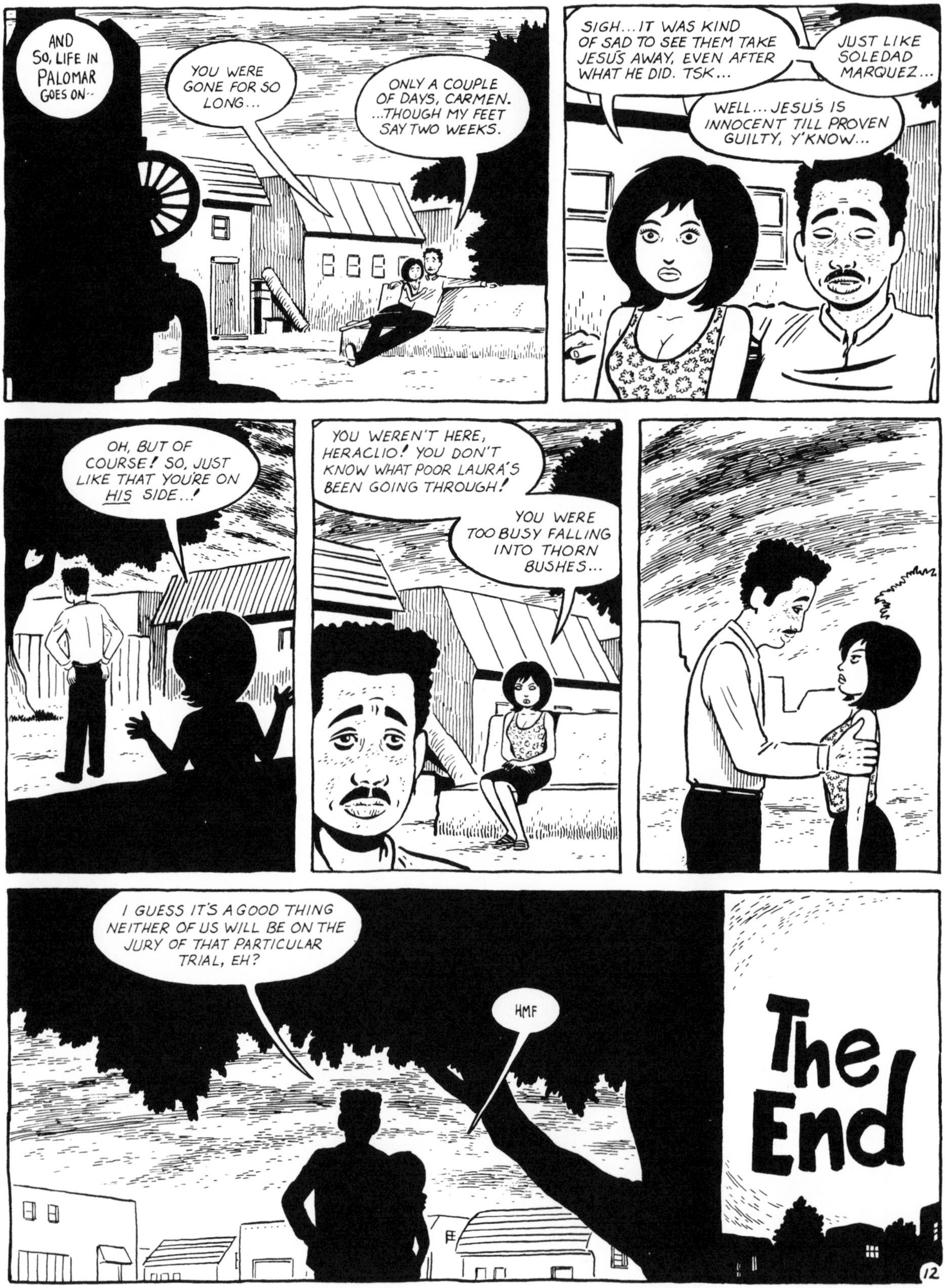
AND SO, LIFE IN PALOMAR GOES ON--
YOU WERE GONE FOR SO LONG...
ONLY A COUPLE OF DAYS, CARMEN. ...THOUGH MY FEET SAY TWO WEEKS.
SIGH... IT WAS KIND OF SAD TO SEE THEM TAKE JESÚS AWAY, EVEN AFTER WHAT HE DID. TSK...
JUST LIKE SOLEDAD MARQUEZ...
WELL... JESÚS IS INNOCENT TILL PROVEN GUILTY, Y'KNOW...
OH, BUT OF COURSE! SO, JUST LIKE THAT YOU'RE ON HIS SIDE...!
YOU WEREN'T HERE, HERACLIO! YOU DON'T KNOW WHAT POOR LAURA'S BEEN GOING THROUGH!
YOU WERE TOO BUSY FALLING INTO THORN BUSHES...
I GUESS IT'S A GOOD THING NEITHER OF US WILL BE ON THE JURY OF THAT PARTICULAR TRIAL, EH?
HMF
The End
12

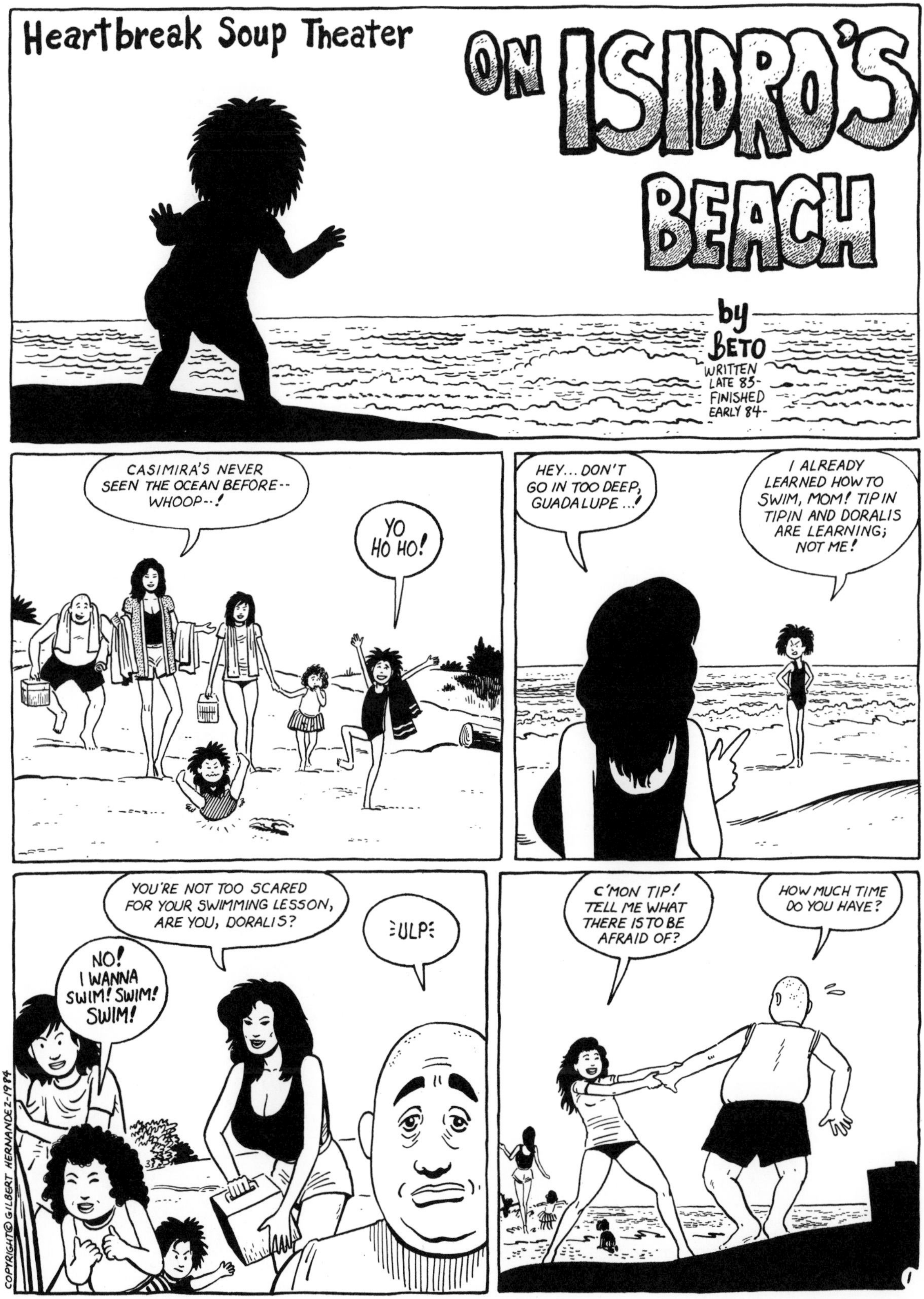
Heartbreak Soup Theater
ON ISIDRO'S BEACH
by BETO
WRITTEN LATE 83- FINISHED EARLY 84-
CASIMIRA'S NEVER SEEN THE OCEAN BEFORE-- WHOOP--!
YO HO HO!
HEY... DON'T GO IN TOO DEEP, GUADALUPE...!
I ALREADY LEARNED HOW TO SWIM, MOM! TIPIN TIPIN AND DORALIS ARE LEARNING; NOT ME!
YOU'RE NOT TOO SCARED FOR YOUR SWIMMING LESSON, ARE YOU, DORALIS?
NO! I WANNA SWIM! SWIM! SWIM!
ULP
COPYRIGHT© GILBERT HERNANDEZ-1984
C'MON TIP! TELL ME WHAT THERE IS TO BE AFRAID OF?
HOW MUCH TIME DO YOU HAVE?
1

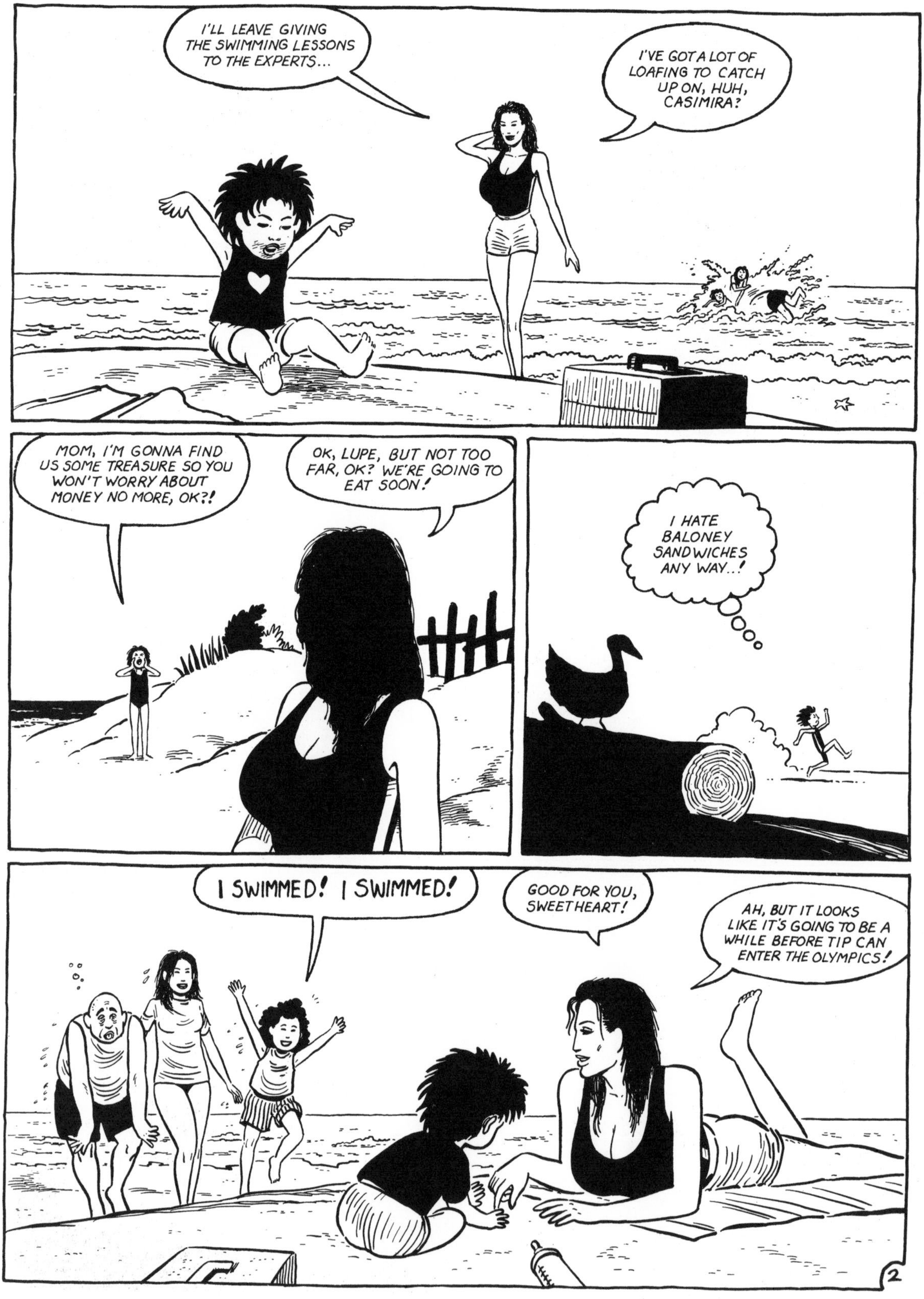
I'LL LEAVE GIVING THE SWIMMING LESSONS TO THE EXPERTS...
I'VE GOT A LOT OF LOAFING TO CATCH UP ON, HUH, CASIMIRA?
MOM, I'M GONNA FIND US SOME TREASURE SO YOU WON'T WORRY ABOUT MONEY NO MORE, OK?!
OK, LUPE, BUT NOT TOO FAR, OK? WE'RE GOING TO EAT SOON!
I HATE BALONEY SANDWICHES ANY WAY..!
I SWIMMED! I SWIMMED!
GOOD FOR YOU, SWEETHEART!
AH, BUT IT LOOKS LIKE IT'S GOING TO BE A WHILE BEFORE TIP CAN ENTER THE OLYMPICS!
2

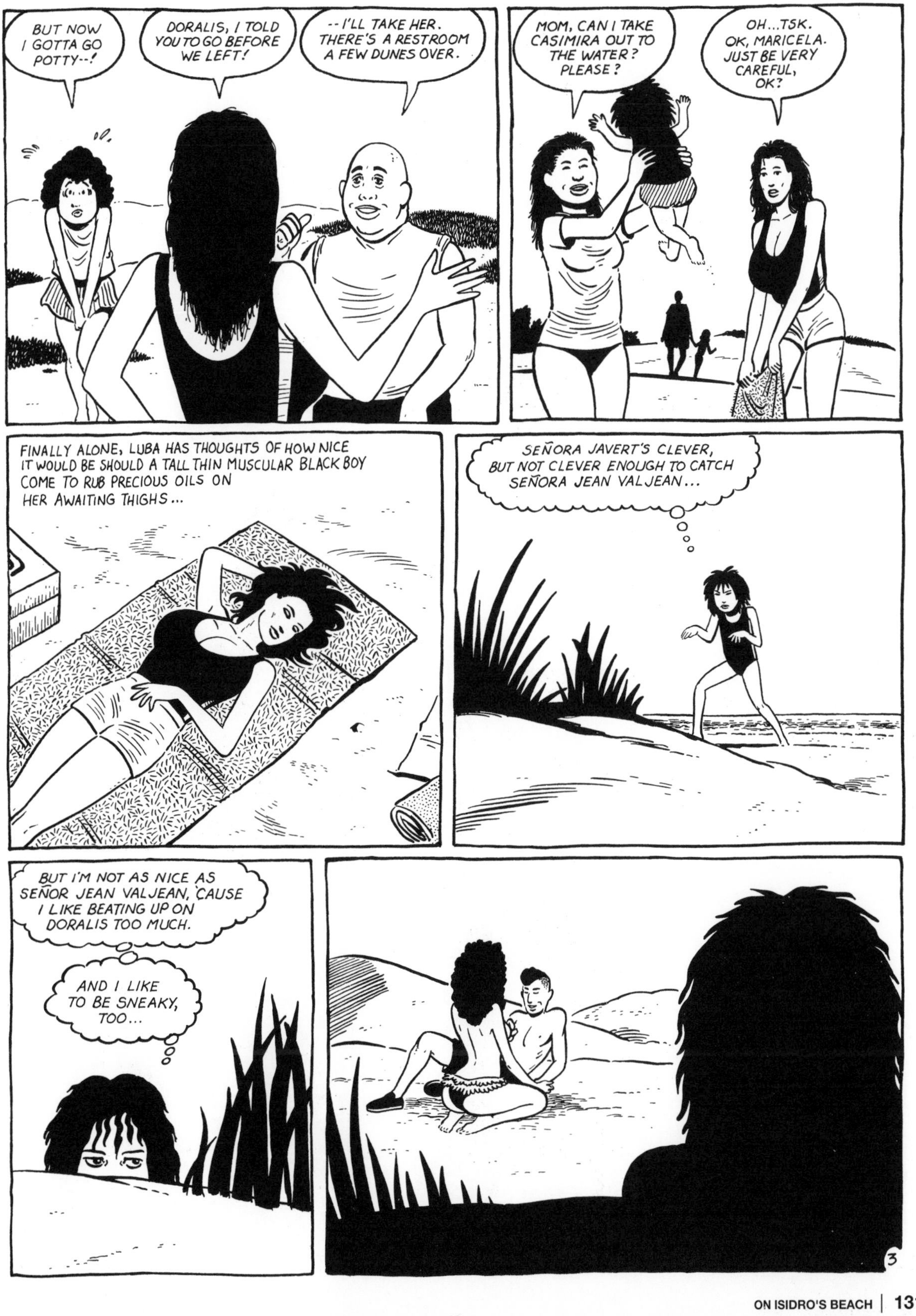
BUT NOW I GOTTA GO POTTY--!
DORALIS, I TOLD YOU TO GO BEFORE WE LEFT!
--I'LL TAKE HER. THERE'S A RESTROOM A FEW DUNES OVER.
MOM, CAN I TAKE CASIMIRA OUT TO THE WATER? PLEASE?
OH...TSK. OK, MARICELA. JUST BE VERY CAREFUL, OK?
FINALLY ALONE, LUBA HAS THOUGHTS OF HOW NICE IT WOULD BE SHOULD A TALL THIN MUSCULAR BLACK BOY COME TO RUB PRECIOUS OILS ON HER AWAITING THIGHS...
SEÑORA JAVERT'S CLEVER, BUT NOT CLEVER ENOUGH TO CATCH SEÑORA JEAN VALJEAN...
BUT I'M NOT AS NICE AS SEÑOR JEAN VALJEAN, 'CAUSE I LIKE BEATING UP ON DORALIS TOO MUCH.
AND I LIKE TO BE SNEAKY, TOO...
3

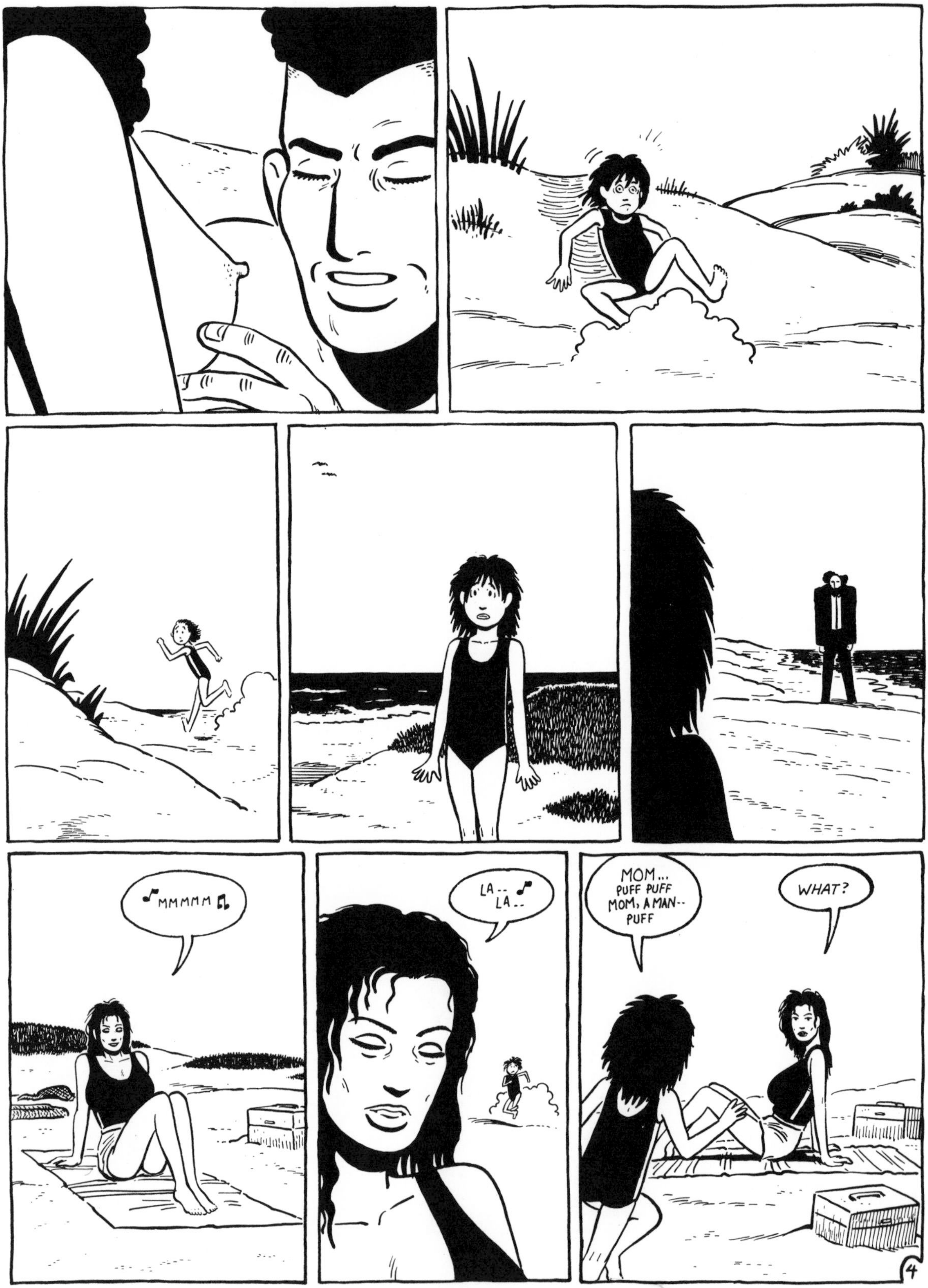
MMMMM
LA-- LA--
MOM... PUFF PUFF MOM, A MAN-- PUFF
WHAT?
4

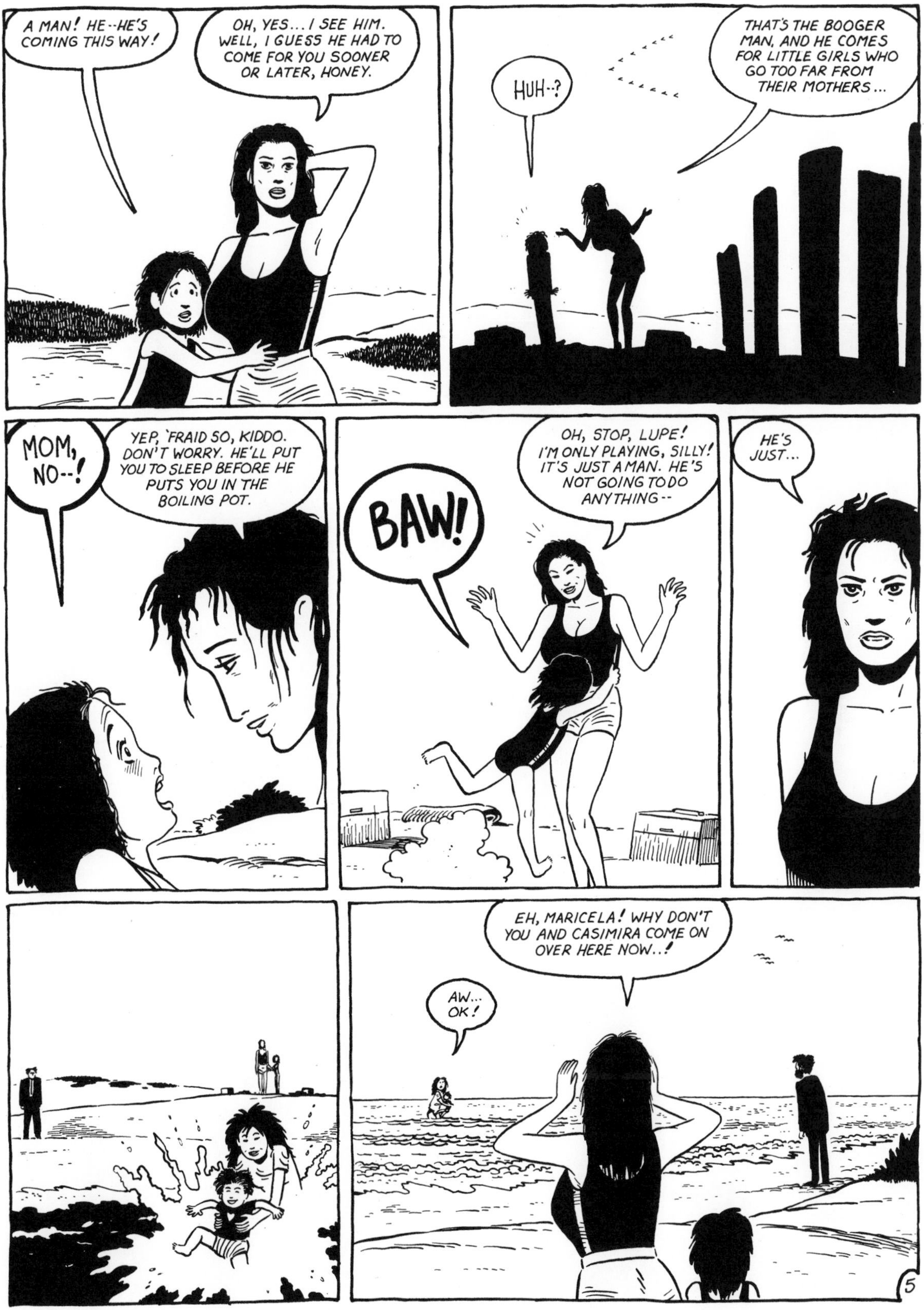
A MAN! HE--HE'S COMING THIS WAY!
OH, YES... I SEE HIM. WELL, I GUESS HE HAD TO COME FOR YOU SOONER OR LATER, HONEY.
HUH--?
THAT'S THE BOOGER MAN, AND HE COMES FOR LITTLE GIRLS WHO GO TOO FAR FROM THEIR MOTHERS...
MOM, NO--!
YEP, 'FRAID SO, KIDDO. DON'T WORRY. HE'LL PUT YOU TO SLEEP BEFORE HE PUTS YOU IN THE BOILING POT.
BAW!
OH, STOP, LUPE! I'M ONLY PLAYING, SILLY! IT'S JUST A MAN. HE'S NOT GOING TO DO ANYTHING--
HE'S JUST...
EH, MARICELA! WHY DON'T YOU AND CASIMIRA COME ON OVER HERE NOW..!
AW... OK!
5

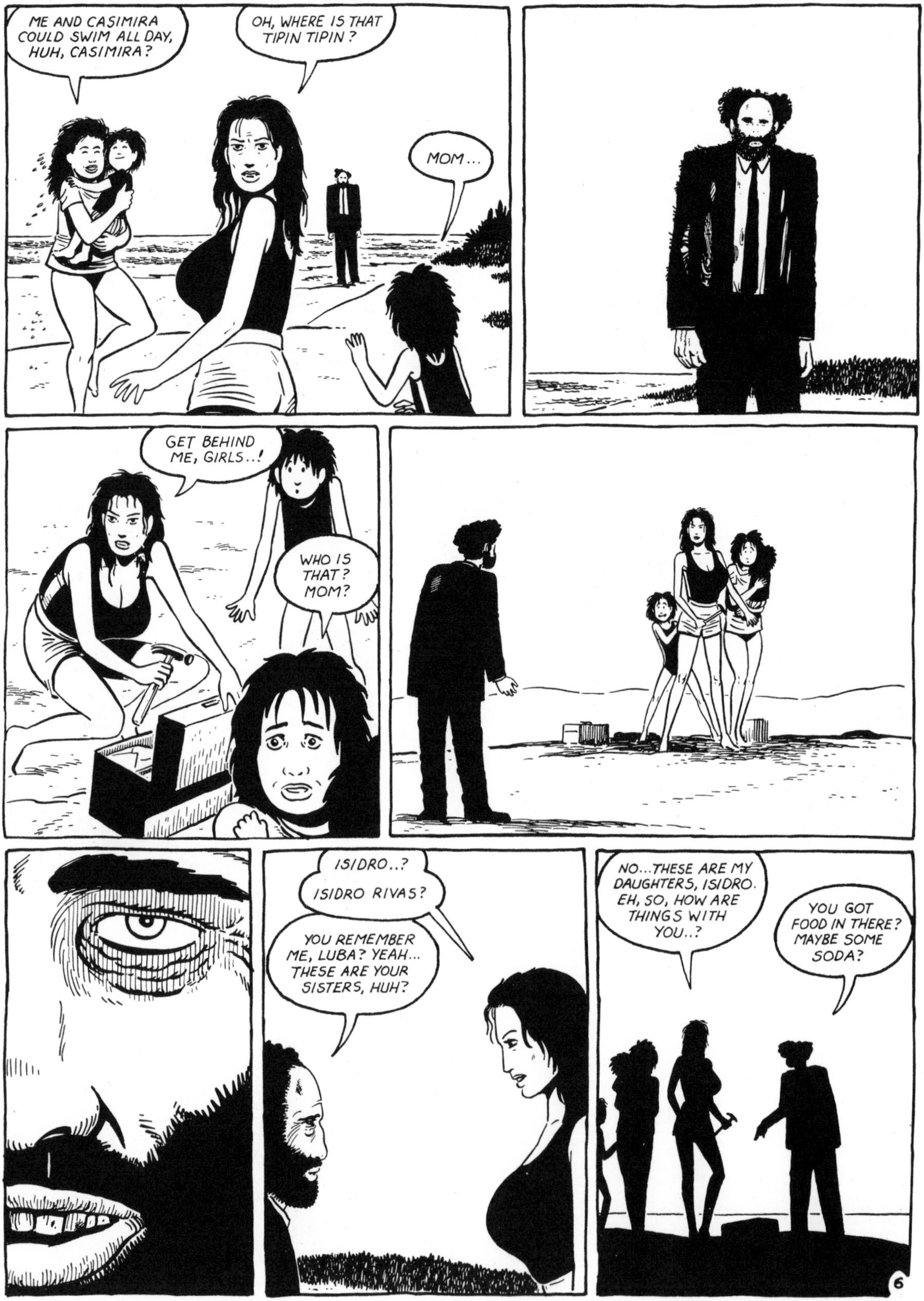
ME AND CASIMIRA COULD SWIM ALL DAY, HUH, CASIMIRA?
OH, WHERE IS THAT TIPIN TIPIN?
MOM...
GET BEHIND ME, GIRLS..!
WHO IS THAT? MOM?
ISIDRO..?
ISIDRO RIVAS?
YOU REMEMBER ME, LUBA? YEAH... THESE ARE YOUR SISTERS, HUH?
NO...THESE ARE MY DAUGHTERS, ISIDRO. EH, SO, HOW ARE THINGS WITH YOU..?
YOU GOT FOOD IN THERE? MAYBE SOME SODA?
6

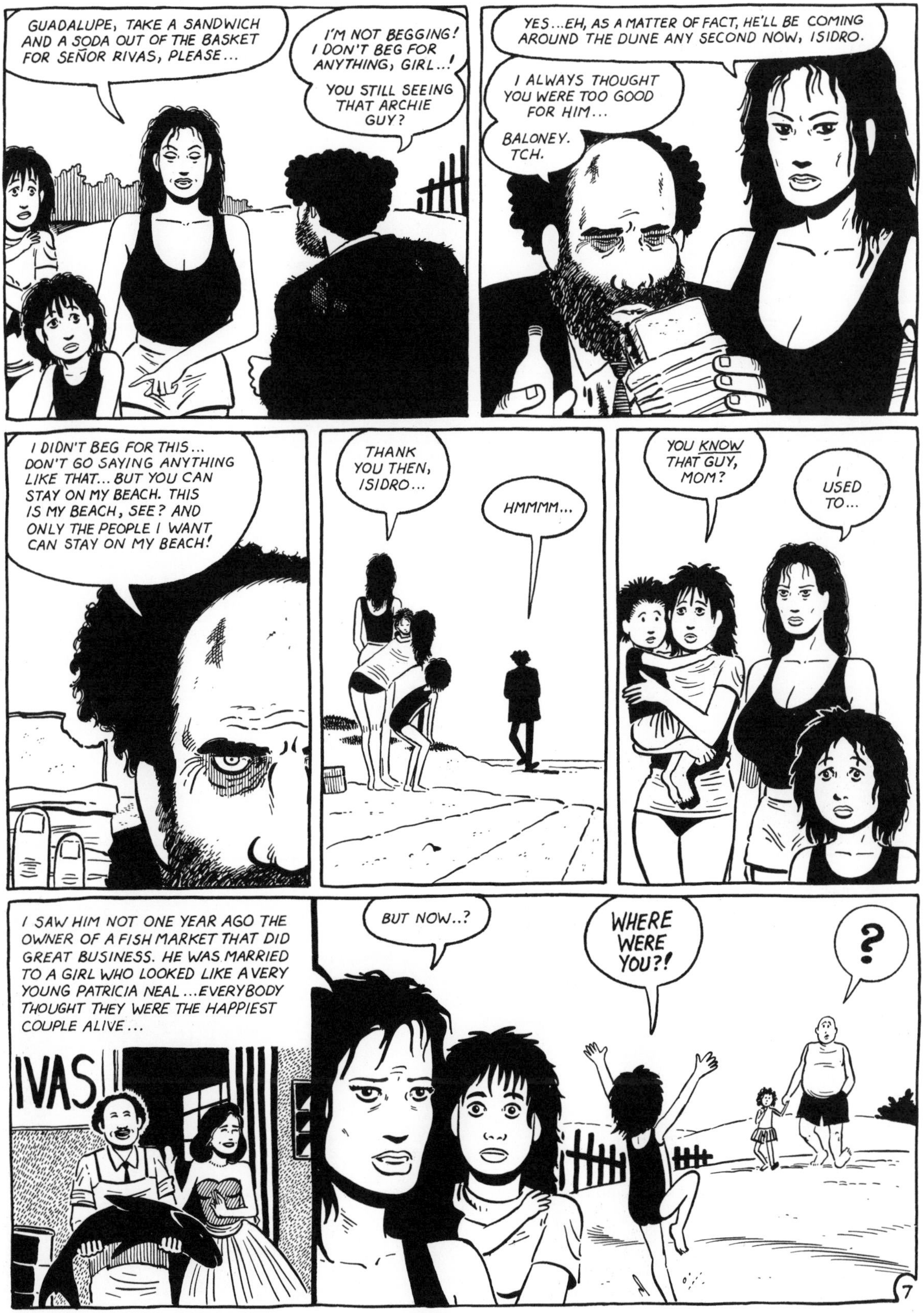
GUADALUPE, TAKE A SANDWICH AND A SODA OUT OF THE BASKET FOR SEÑOR RIVAS, PLEASE...
I'M NOT BEGGING! I DON'T BEG FOR ANYTHING, GIRL...!
YOU STILL SEEING THAT ARCHIE GUY?
YES...EH, AS A MATTER OF FACT, HE'LL BE COMING AROUND THE DUNE ANY SECOND NOW, ISIDRO.
I ALWAYS THOUGHT YOU WERE TOO GOOD FOR HIM...
BALONEY. TCH.
I DIDN'T BEG FOR THIS... DON'T GO SAYING ANYTHING LIKE THAT... BUT YOU CAN STAY ON MY BEACH. THIS IS MY BEACH, SEE? AND ONLY THE PEOPLE I WANT CAN STAY ON MY BEACH!
THANK YOU THEN, ISIDRO...
HMMMM...
YOU KNOW THAT GUY, MOM?
I USED TO...
I SAW HIM NOT ONE YEAR AGO THE OWNER OF A FISH MARKET THAT DID GREAT BUSINESS. HE WAS MARRIED TO A GIRL WHO LOOKED LIKE A VERY YOUNG PATRICIA NEAL...EVERYBODY THOUGHT THEY WERE THE HAPPIEST COUPLE ALIVE...
IVAS
BUT NOW..?
WHERE WERE YOU?!
?
7

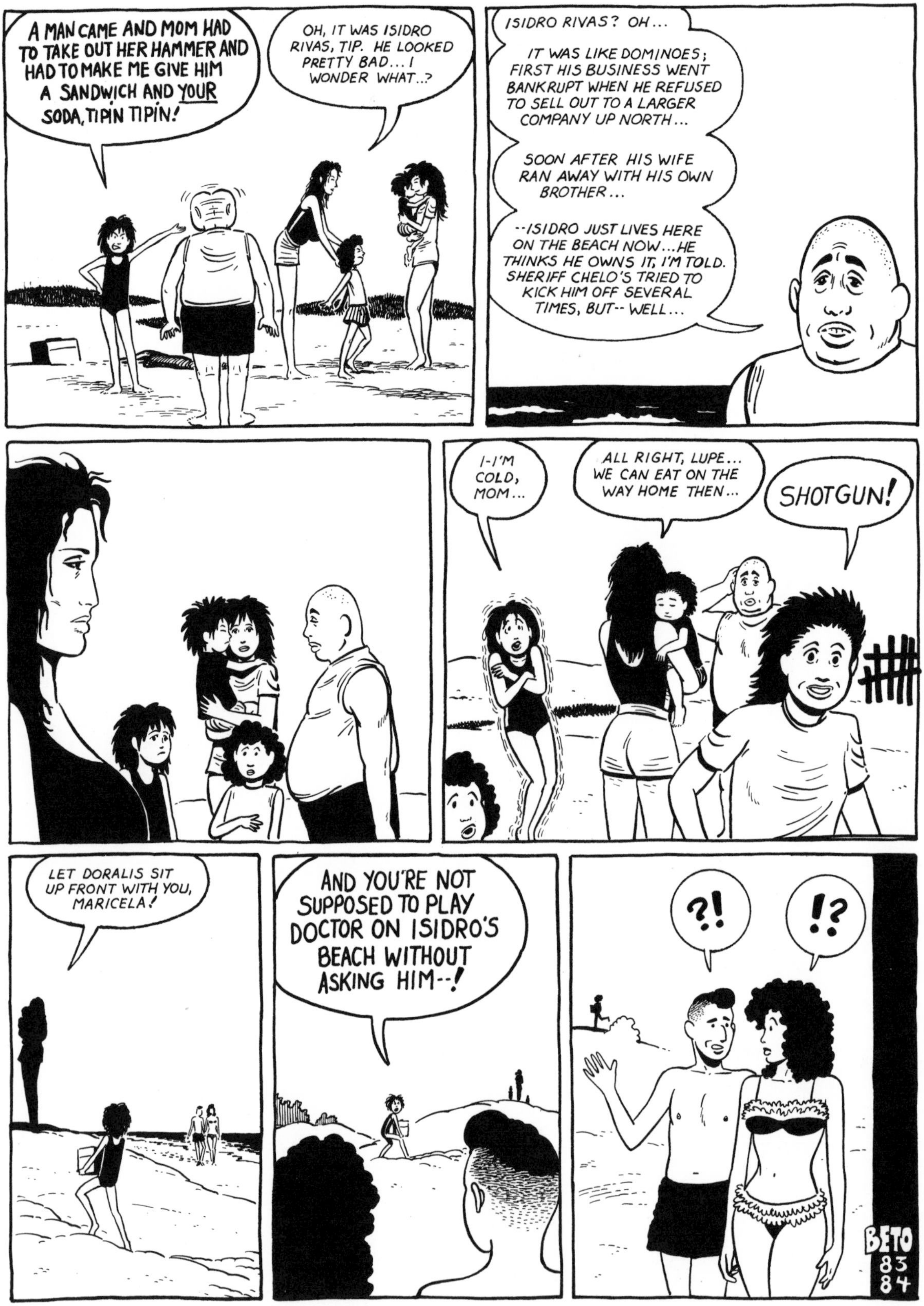
A MAN CAME AND MOM HAD TO TAKE OUT HER HAMMER AND HAD TO MAKE ME GIVE HIM A SANDWICH AND YOUR SODA, TIPIN TIPIN!
OH, IT WAS ISIDRO RIVAS, TIP. HE LOOKED PRETTY BAD... I WONDER WHAT..?
ISIDRO RIVAS? OH...
IT WAS LIKE DOMINOES; FIRST HIS BUSINESS WENT BANKRUPT WHEN HE REFUSED TO SELL OUT TO A LARGER COMPANY UP NORTH...
SOON AFTER HIS WIFE RAN AWAY WITH HIS OWN BROTHER...
--ISIDRO JUST LIVES HERE ON THE BEACH NOW...HE THINKS HE OWNS IT, I'M TOLD. SHERIFF CHELO'S TRIED TO KICK HIM OFF SEVERAL TIMES, BUT-- WELL...
I-I'M COLD, MOM...
ALL RIGHT, LUPE... WE CAN EAT ON THE WAY HOME THEN...
SHOTGUN!
LET DORALIS SIT UP FRONT WITH YOU, MARICELA!
AND YOU'RE NOT SUPPOSED TO PLAY DOCTOR ON ISIDRO'S BEACH WITHOUT ASKING HIM--!
?!
!?
BETO 83 84

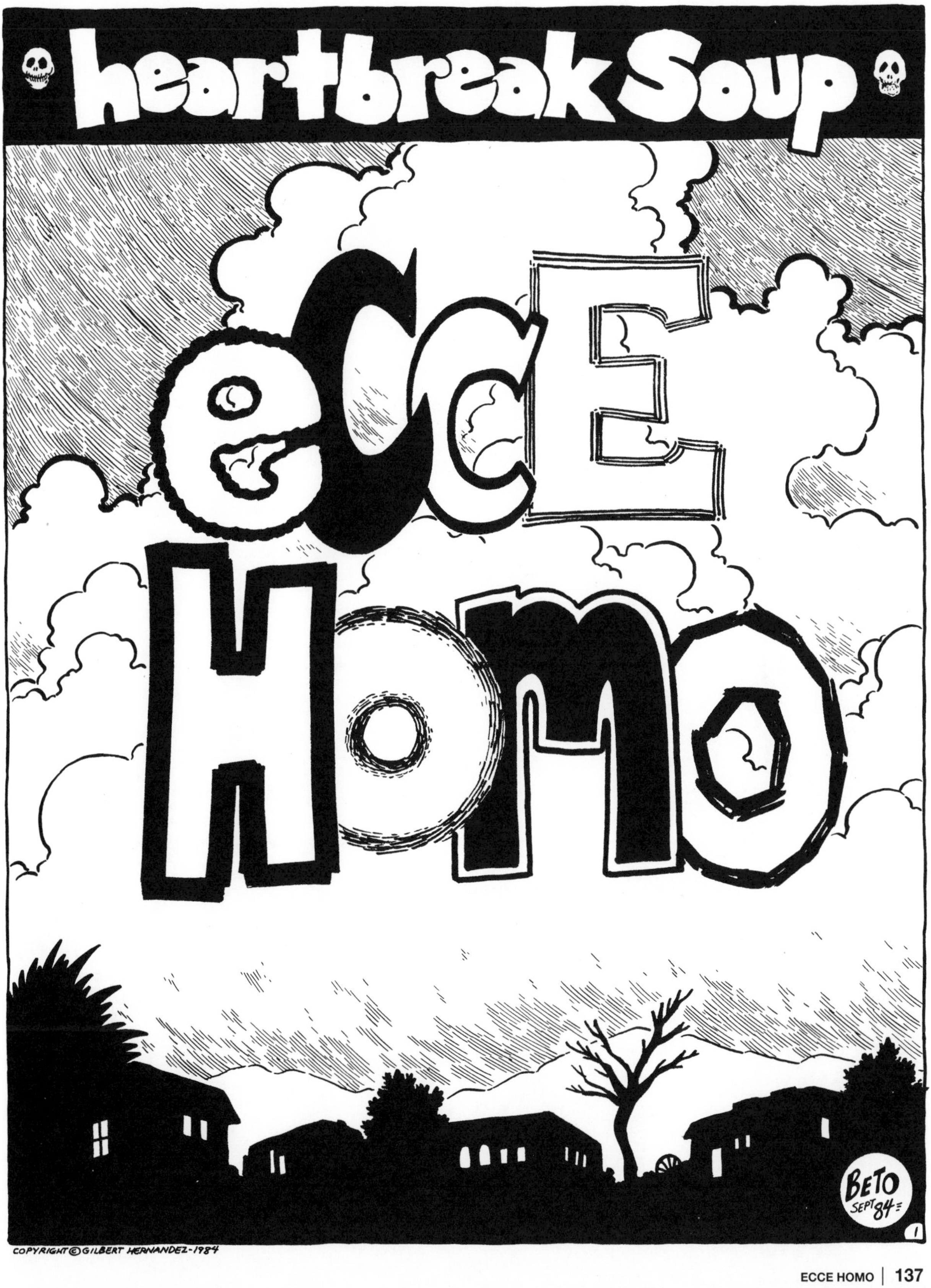
heartbreak Soup
eCCE
HOMO
BETO
SEPT 84
1

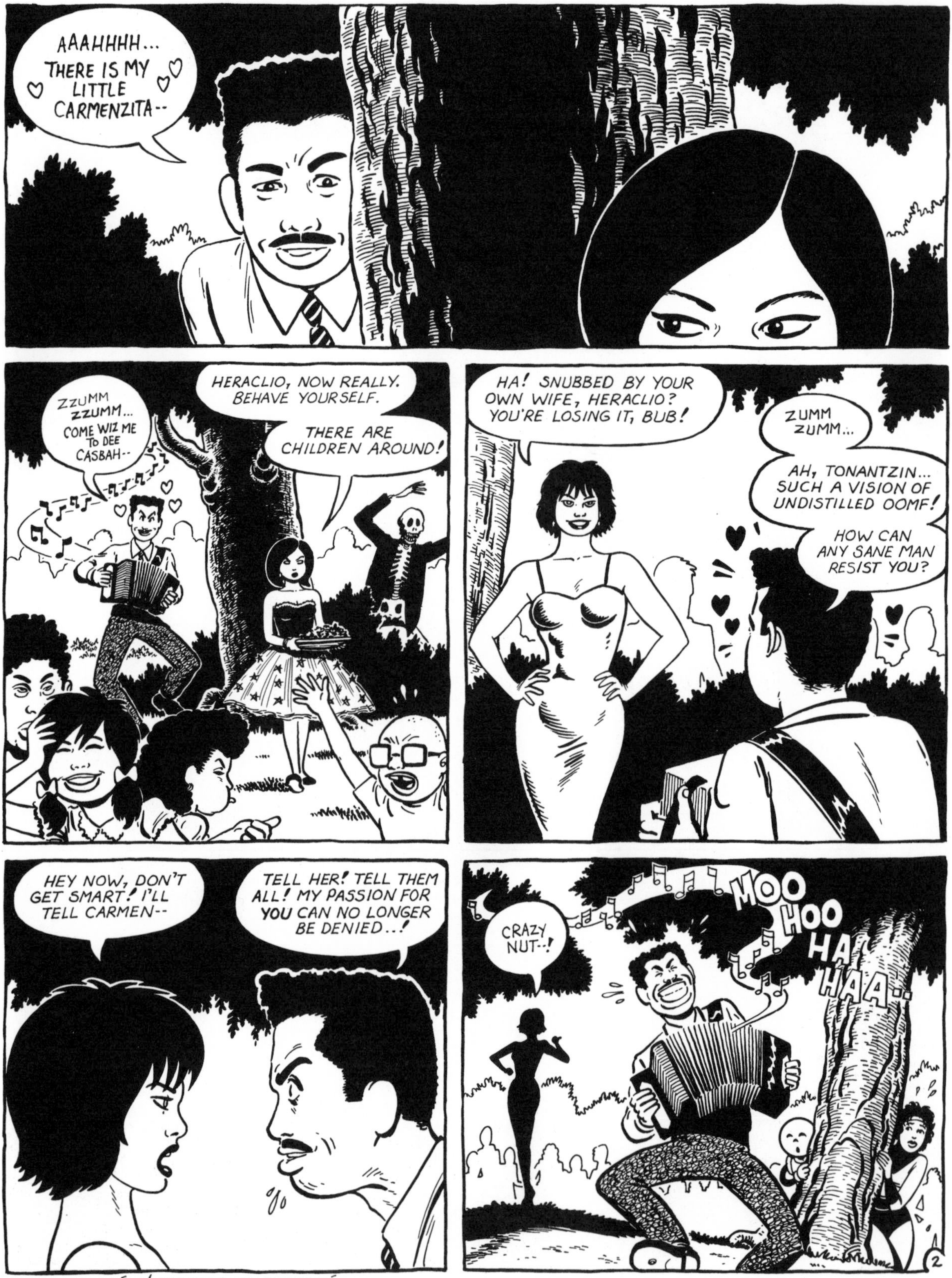
AAAHHHH... THERE IS MY LITTLE CARMENZITA--
ZZUMM ZZUMM... COME WIZ ME TO DEE CASBAH--
HERACLIO, NOW REALLY. BEHAVE YOURSELF.
THERE ARE CHILDREN AROUND!
HA! SNUBBED BY YOUR OWN WIFE, HERACLIO? YOU'RE LOSING IT, BUB!
ZUMM ZUMM...
AH, TONANTZIN... SUCH A VISION OF UNDISTILLED OOMF!
HOW CAN ANY SANE MAN RESIST YOU?
HEY NOW, DON'T GET SMART! I'LL TELL CARMEN--
TELL HER! TELL THEM ALL! MY PASSION FOR YOU CAN NO LONGER BE DENIED..!
CRAZY NUT--!
MOO HOO HA HAA..
2

HERACLIO: AIR-AWK-LEO / TONANTZIN: TOE-NONT-ZEEN

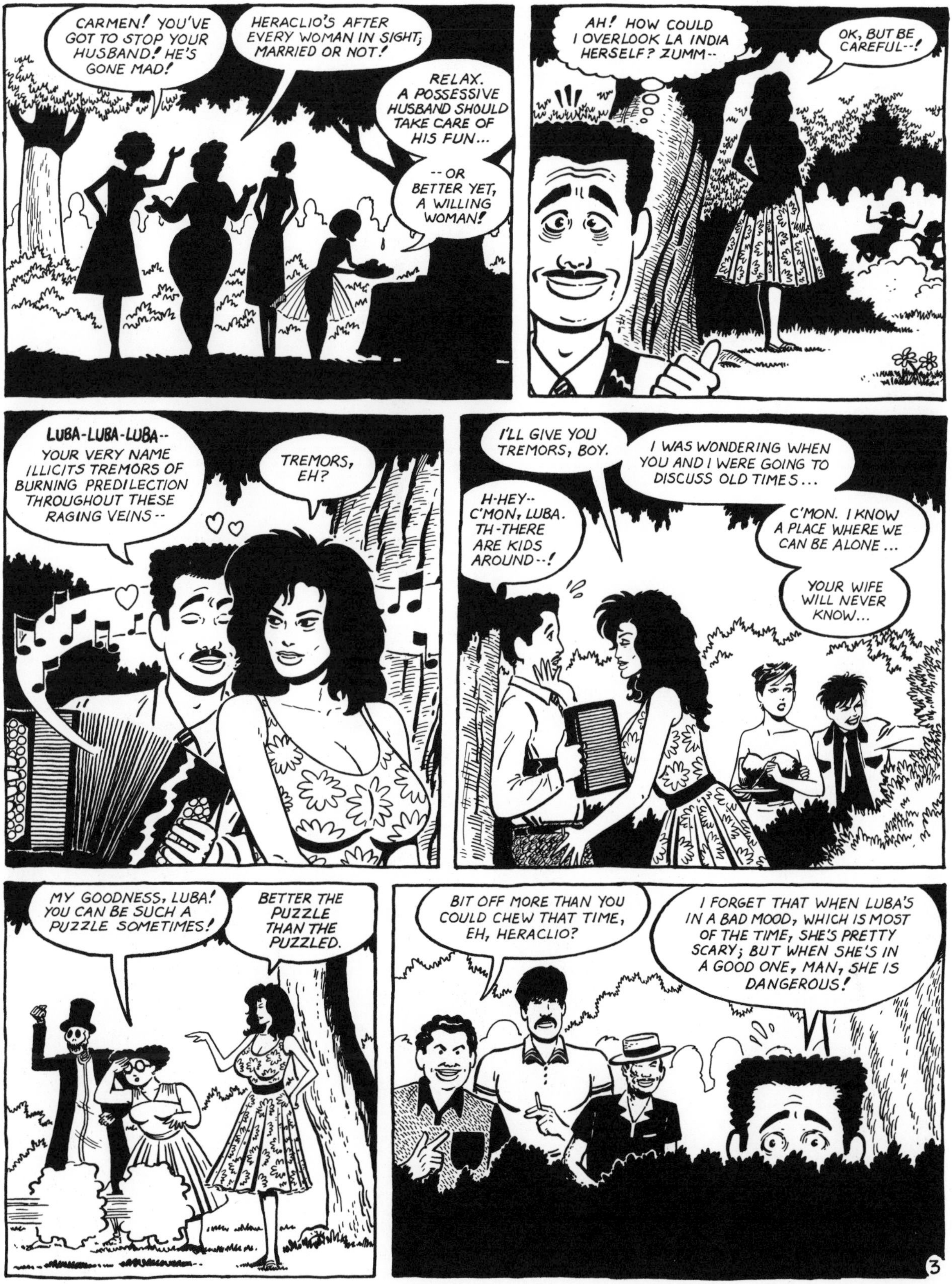
CARMEN! YOU'VE GOT TO STOP YOUR HUSBAND! HE'S GONE MAD!
HERACLIO'S AFTER EVERY WOMAN IN SIGHT; MARRIED OR NOT!
RELAX. A POSSESSIVE HUSBAND SHOULD TAKE CARE OF HIS FUN...
--OR BETTER YET, A WILLING WOMAN!
AH! HOW COULD I OVERLOOK LA INDIA HERSELF? ZUMM--
OK, BUT BE CAREFUL--!
LUBA-LUBA-LUBA-- YOUR VERY NAME ILLICITS TREMORS OF BURNING PREDILECTION THROUGHOUT THESE RAGING VEINS--
TREMORS, EH?
I'LL GIVE YOU TREMORS, BOY.
I WAS WONDERING WHEN YOU AND I WERE GOING TO DISCUSS OLD TIMES...
H-HEY-- C'MON, LUBA. TH-THERE ARE KIDS AROUND--!
C'MON. I KNOW A PLACE WHERE WE CAN BE ALONE...
YOUR WIFE WILL NEVER KNOW...
MY GOODNESS, LUBA! YOU CAN BE SUCH A PUZZLE SOMETIMES!
BETTER THE PUZZLE THAN THE PUZZLED.
BIT OFF MORE THAN YOU COULD CHEW THAT TIME, EH, HERACLIO?
I FORGET THAT WHEN LUBA'S IN A BAD MOOD, WHICH IS MOST OF THE TIME, SHE'S PRETTY SCARY; BUT WHEN SHE'S IN A GOOD ONE, MAN, SHE IS DANGEROUS!
3

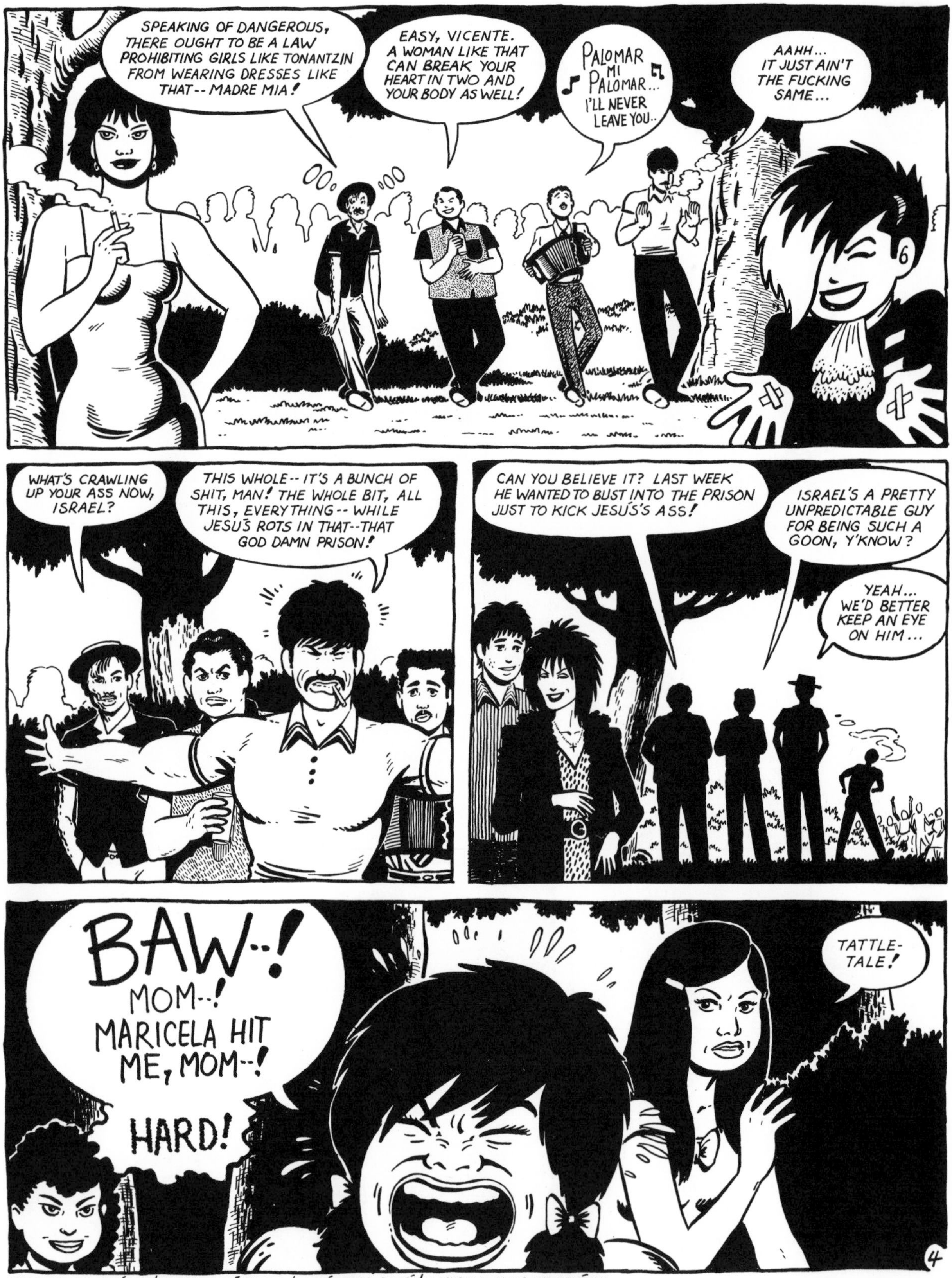
SPEAKING OF DANGEROUS, THERE OUGHT TO BE A LAW PROHIBITING GIRLS LIKE TONANTZIN FROM WEARING DRESSES LIKE THAT-- MADRE MIA!
EASY, VICENTE. A WOMAN LIKE THAT CAN BREAK YOUR HEART IN TWO AND YOUR BODY AS WELL!
PALOMAR MI PALOMAR... I'LL NEVER LEAVE YOU..
AAHH... IT JUST AIN'T THE FUCKING SAME...
WHAT'S CRAWLING UP YOUR ASS NOW, ISRAEL?
THIS WHOLE-- IT'S A BUNCH OF SHIT, MAN! THE WHOLE BIT, ALL THIS, EVERYTHING-- WHILE JESÚS ROTS IN THAT--THAT GOD DAMN PRISON!
CAN YOU BELIEVE IT? LAST WEEK HE WANTED TO BUST INTO THE PRISON JUST TO KICK JESÚS'S ASS!
ISRAEL'S A PRETTY UNPREDICTABLE GUY FOR BEING SUCH A GOON, Y'KNOW?
YEAH... WE'D BETTER KEEP AN EYE ON HIM...
BAW--! MOM--! MARICELA HIT ME, MOM--! HARD!
TATTLE-TALE!
4

VICENTE: VEE-SEN-TEH / ISRAEL: EES-RYE-EL / JESÚS: HEH-SOOS / MARICELA: MARR-EE-SELL-AH

ALL RIGHT, GUADALUPE... TSK. MARICELA, COME HERE!

BOO HOO... SNIFF...

OH, SHIT. THIS IS IT. I'M DEAD. AND IN FRONT OF EVERYBODY!

TSK! LUPE ONLY WANTED TO BE WITH YOU AND YOUR FRIENDS! GO ON, DEMOÑA! GO ON WITH YOUR FRIENDS, BUT BEHAVE, MARICELA!

O·OK, MOM...

I DON'T BELIEVE IT! SHE DIDN'T SMACK YOU!

LET'S GET OUT OF HERE BEFORE SHE CHANGES HER MIND!

LUCKY!

GONNA TAKE CARE OF MARICELA WHEN YOU GET HOME, LUBA?

PIPO! I ALMOST DIDN'T RE-COGNIZE YOU! HEY...

SERGIO, SAY HELLO TO SEÑORA LUBA...

NOW ISN'T HE THE LADY-KILLER AL-READY!

H·HELLO...

GIRL, YOU LOOK LIKE A MILLION BUCKS! AND YOUR HUSBAND GATO..?

SWEET HEART, WHY DON'T YOU GO PLAY WHILE SEÑORA LUBA AND MOTHER HAVE A LITTLE TALK?

GOD, BUT HE LOOKS SO MUCH LIKE HIS FATHER MANUEL....HOW DOES GATO FEEL..?

WELL, GATO HATED MANUEL, YOU KNOW... BUT HE ACCEPTS SERGIO.. NOW. I, EH, HAVE ALREADY TOLD SERGIO THAT HIS REAL FATHER WAS KILLED, BUT I'M NOT SURE HE UNDERSTANDS.

HI UGLY

HI UGLY

5

GUADALUPE: GWAH-DAH-LOO-PEH / DEMOÑA (DEMON GIRL): DE-MOE-NYUH / PIPO: PEE-POE / SERGIO: SAIR-HEE-O / GATO: GAH-TOE / MANUEL: MON-WELL

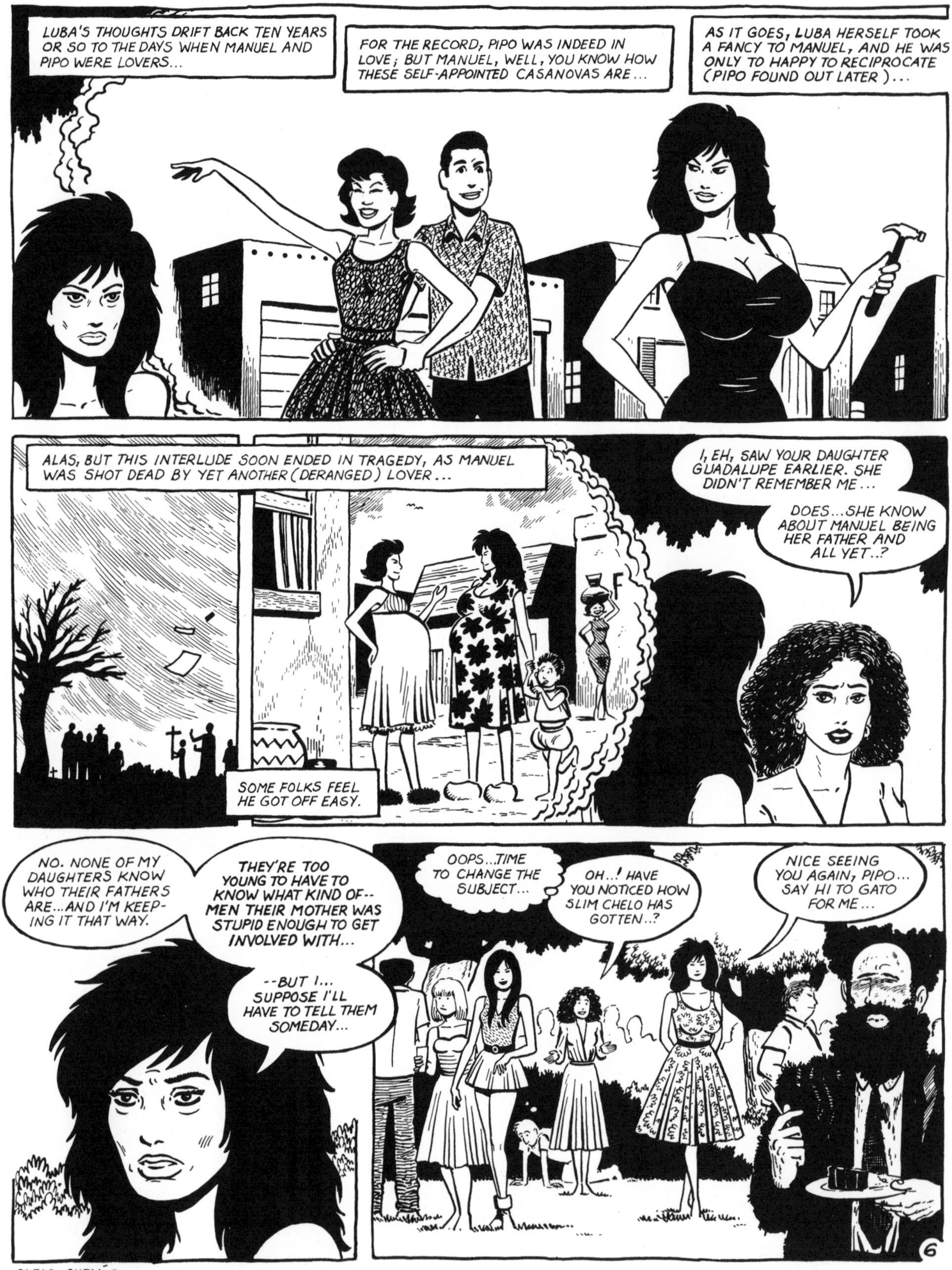
LUBA'S THOUGHTS DRIFT BACK TEN YEARS OR SO TO THE DAYS WHEN MANUEL AND PIPO WERE LOVERS...
FOR THE RECORD, PIPO WAS INDEED IN LOVE; BUT MANUEL, WELL, YOU KNOW HOW THESE SELF-APPOINTED CASANOVAS ARE...
AS IT GOES, LUBA HERSELF TOOK A FANCY TO MANUEL, AND HE WAS ONLY TO HAPPY TO RECIPROCATE (PIPO FOUND OUT LATER)...
ALAS, BUT THIS INTERLUDE SOON ENDED IN TRAGEDY, AS MANUEL WAS SHOT DEAD BY YET ANOTHER (DERANGED) LOVER...
SOME FOLKS FEEL HE GOT OFF EASY.
I, EH, SAW YOUR DAUGHTER GUADALUPE EARLIER. SHE DIDN'T REMEMBER ME...
DOES...SHE KNOW ABOUT MANUEL BEING HER FATHER AND ALL YET..?
NO. NONE OF MY DAUGHTERS KNOW WHO THEIR FATHERS ARE...AND I'M KEEPING IT THAT WAY.
THEY'RE TOO YOUNG TO HAVE TO KNOW WHAT KIND OF-- MEN THEIR MOTHER WAS STUPID ENOUGH TO GET INVOLVED WITH...
--BUT I... SUPPOSE I'LL HAVE TO TELL THEM SOMEDAY...
OOPS...TIME TO CHANGE THE SUBJECT...
OH..! HAVE YOU NOTICED HOW SLIM CHELO HAS GOTTEN..?
NICE SEEING YOU AGAIN, PIPO... SAY HI TO GATO FOR ME...
6

CHELO: CHELL-O

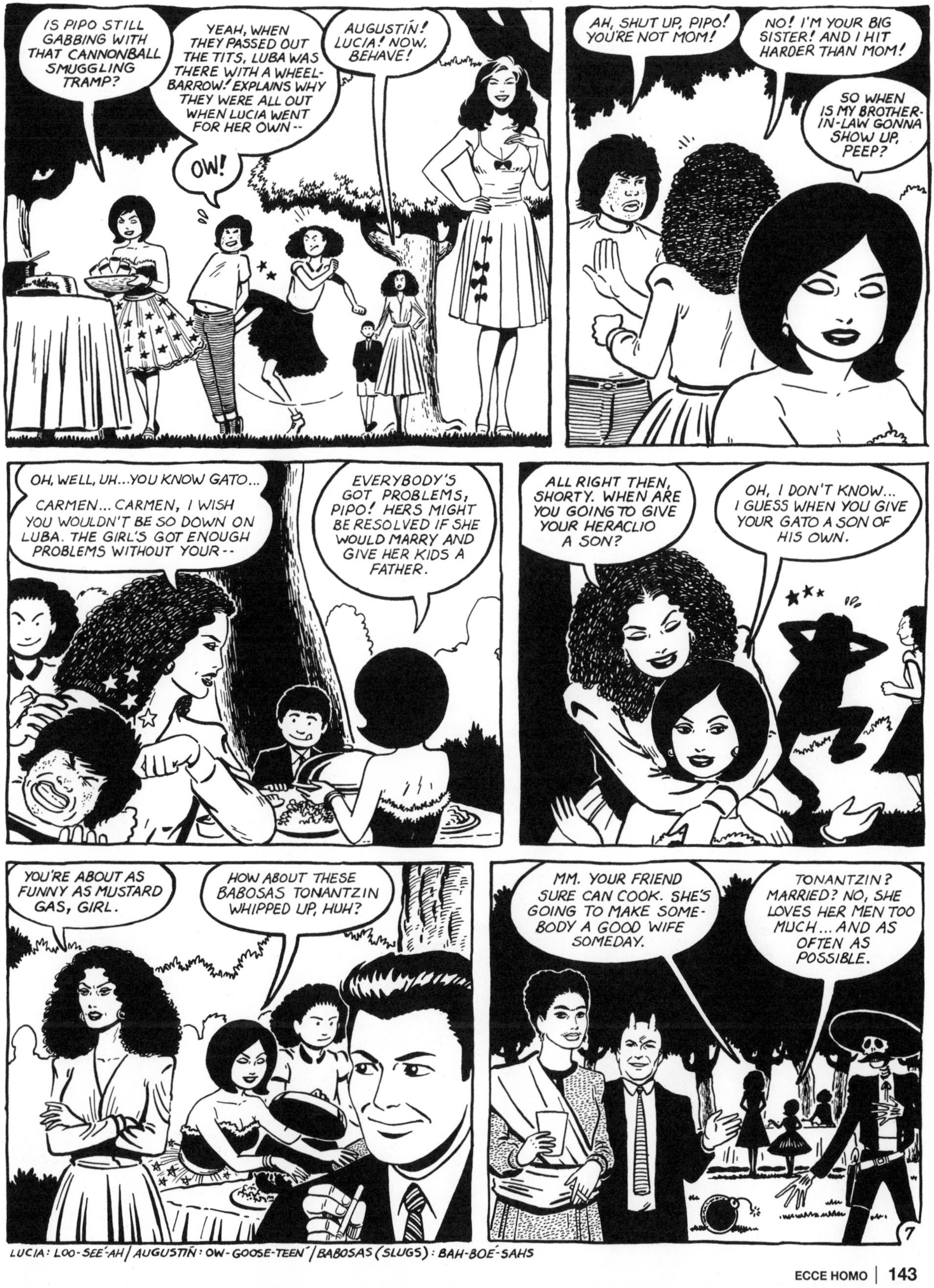
IS PIPO STILL GABBING WITH THAT CANNONBALL SMUGGLING TRAMP?
YEAH, WHEN THEY PASSED OUT THE TITS, LUBA WAS THERE WITH A WHEEL-BARROW! EXPLAINS WHY THEY WERE ALL OUT WHEN LUCIA WENT FOR HER OWN --
OW!
AUGUSTÍN! LUCIA! NOW, BEHAVE!
AH, SHUT UP, PIPO! YOU'RE NOT MOM!
NO! I'M YOUR BIG SISTER! AND I HIT HARDER THAN MOM!
SO WHEN IS MY BROTHER-IN-LAW GONNA SHOW UP, PEEP?
OH, WELL, UH...YOU KNOW GATO...
CARMEN... CARMEN, I WISH YOU WOULDN'T BE SO DOWN ON LUBA. THE GIRL'S GOT ENOUGH PROBLEMS WITHOUT YOUR --
EVERYBODY'S GOT PROBLEMS, PIPO! HERS MIGHT BE RESOLVED IF SHE WOULD MARRY AND GIVE HER KIDS A FATHER.
ALL RIGHT THEN, SHORTY. WHEN ARE YOU GOING TO GIVE YOUR HERACLIO A SON?
OH, I DON'T KNOW... I GUESS WHEN YOU GIVE YOUR GATO A SON OF HIS OWN.
YOU'RE ABOUT AS FUNNY AS MUSTARD GAS, GIRL.
HOW ABOUT THESE BABOSAS TONANTZIN WHIPPED UP, HUH?
MM. YOUR FRIEND SURE CAN COOK. SHE'S GOING TO MAKE SOME-BODY A GOOD WIFE SOMEDAY.
TONANTZIN? MARRIED? NO, SHE LOVES HER MEN TOO MUCH... AND AS OFTEN AS POSSIBLE.
7

LUCIA: LOO-SEE'-AH / AUGUSTÍN: OW-GOOSE-TEEN' / BABOSAS (SLUGS): BAH-BOÉ-SAHS

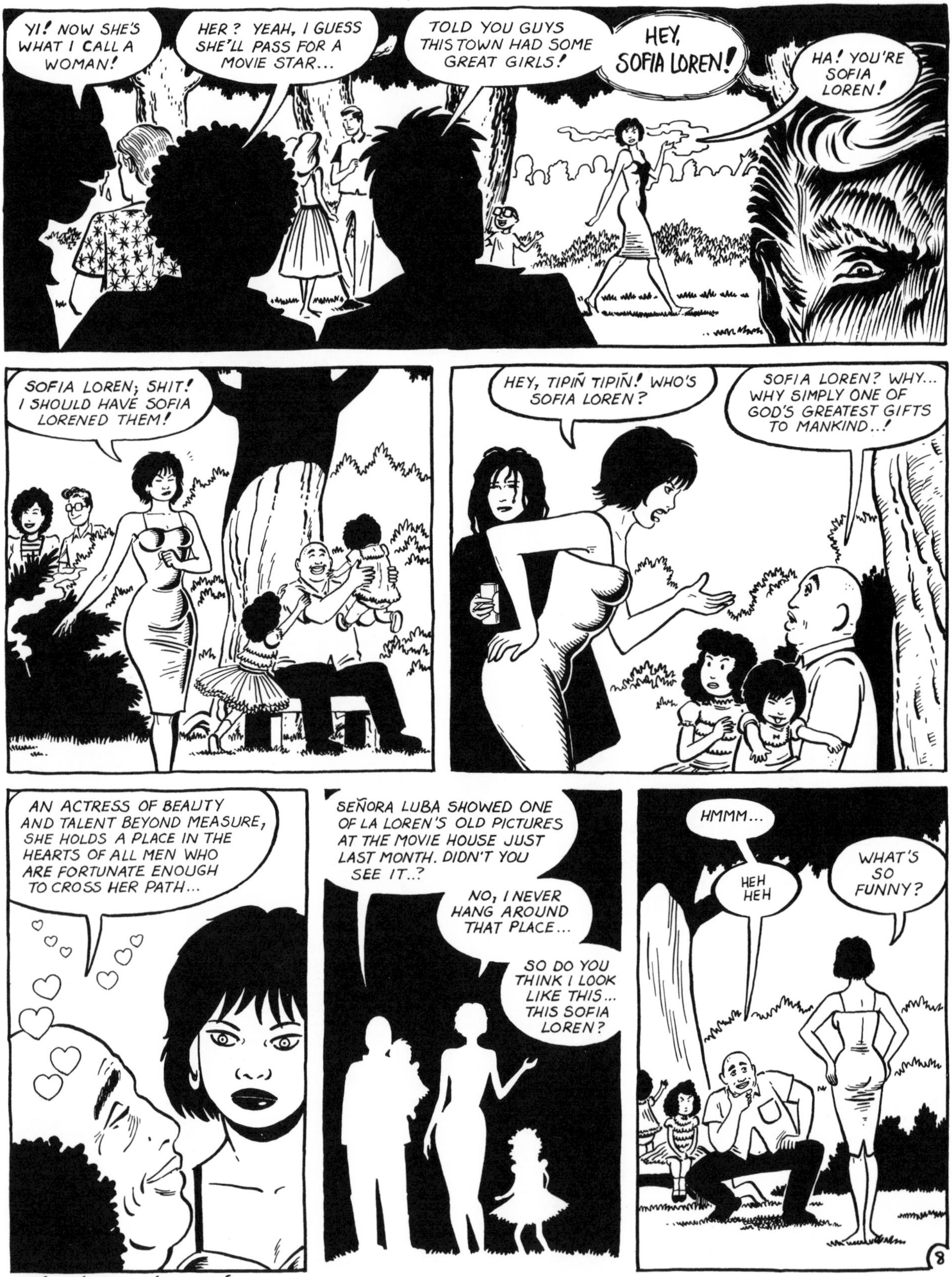
YI! NOW SHE'S WHAT I CALL A WOMAN!
HER? YEAH, I GUESS SHE'LL PASS FOR A MOVIE STAR...
TOLD YOU GUYS THIS TOWN HAD SOME GREAT GIRLS!
HEY, SOFIA LOREN!
HA! YOU'RE SOFIA LOREN!
SOFIA LOREN; SHIT! I SHOULD HAVE SOFIA LORENED THEM!
HEY, TIPIÑ TIPIÑ! WHO'S SOFIA LOREN?
SOFIA LOREN? WHY... WHY SIMPLY ONE OF GOD'S GREATEST GIFTS TO MANKIND...!
AN ACTRESS OF BEAUTY AND TALENT BEYOND MEASURE, SHE HOLDS A PLACE IN THE HEARTS OF ALL MEN WHO ARE FORTUNATE ENOUGH TO CROSS HER PATH...
SEÑORA LUBA SHOWED ONE OF LA LOREN'S OLD PICTURES AT THE MOVIE HOUSE JUST LAST MONTH. DIDN'T YOU SEE IT..?
NO, I NEVER HANG AROUND THAT PLACE...
SO DO YOU THINK I LOOK LIKE THIS... THIS SOFIA LOREN?
HMMM...
HEH HEH
WHAT'S SO FUNNY?
8

TIPIÑ TIPIÑ: TEE-PEEN' TEE-PEEN'

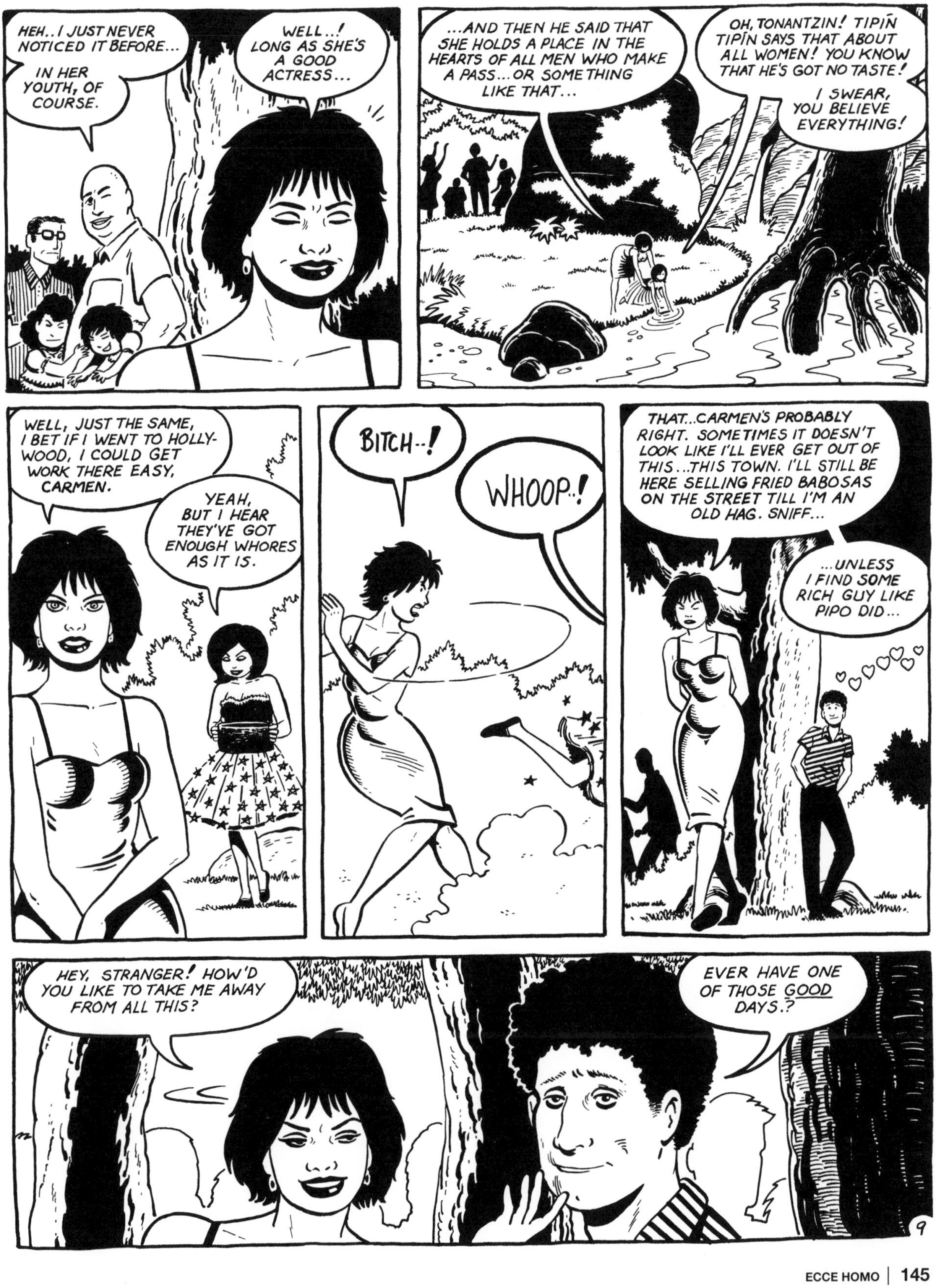
HEH.. I JUST NEVER NOTICED IT BEFORE...
IN HER YOUTH, OF COURSE.
WELL..! LONG AS SHE'S A GOOD ACTRESS...
...AND THEN HE SAID THAT SHE HOLDS A PLACE IN THE HEARTS OF ALL MEN WHO MAKE A PASS...OR SOMETHING LIKE THAT...
OH, TONANTZIN! TIPÍN TIPÍN SAYS THAT ABOUT ALL WOMEN! YOU KNOW THAT HE'S GOT NO TASTE!
I SWEAR, YOU BELIEVE EVERYTHING!
WELL, JUST THE SAME, I BET IF I WENT TO HOLLYWOOD, I COULD GET WORK THERE EASY, CARMEN.
YEAH, BUT I HEAR THEY'VE GOT ENOUGH WHORES AS IT IS.
BITCH..!
WHOOP..!
THAT...CARMEN'S PROBABLY RIGHT. SOMETIMES IT DOESN'T LOOK LIKE I'LL EVER GET OUT OF THIS...THIS TOWN. I'LL STILL BE HERE SELLING FRIED BABOSAS ON THE STREET TILL I'M AN OLD HAG. SNIFF...
...UNLESS I FIND SOME RICH GUY LIKE PIPO DID...
HEY, STRANGER! HOW'D YOU LIKE TO TAKE ME AWAY FROM ALL THIS?
EVER HAVE ONE OF THOSE GOOD DAYS.?
9

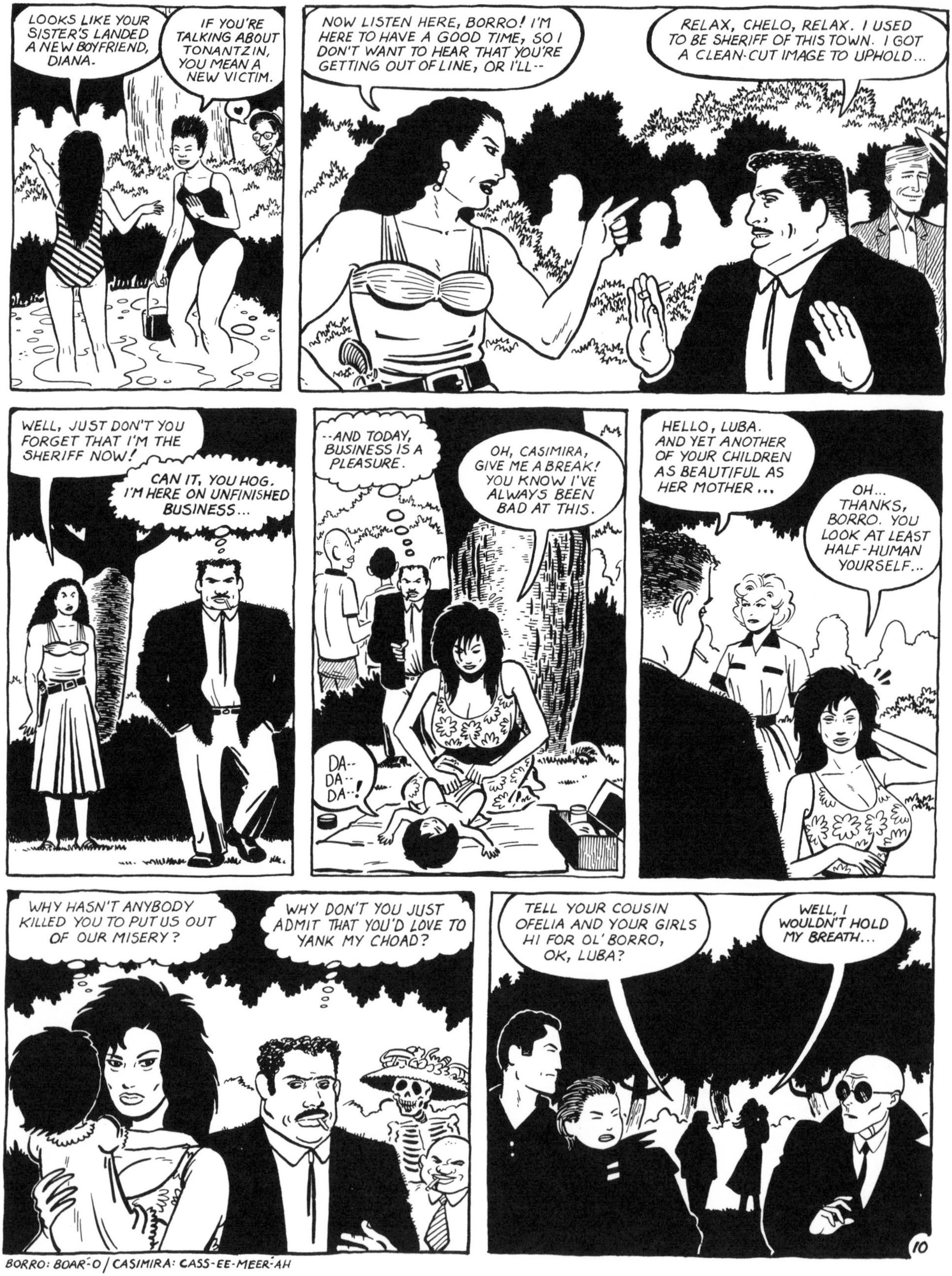
LOOKS LIKE YOUR SISTER'S LANDED A NEW BOYFRIEND, DIANA.
IF YOU'RE TALKING ABOUT TONANTZIN, YOU MEAN A NEW VICTIM.
NOW LISTEN HERE, BORRO! I'M HERE TO HAVE A GOOD TIME, SO I DON'T WANT TO HEAR THAT YOU'RE GETTING OUT OF LINE, OR I'LL--
RELAX, CHELO, RELAX. I USED TO BE SHERIFF OF THIS TOWN. I GOT A CLEAN-CUT IMAGE TO UPHOLD...
WELL, JUST DON'T YOU FORGET THAT I'M THE SHERIFF NOW!
CAN IT, YOU HOG. I'M HERE ON UNFINISHED BUSINESS...
--AND TODAY, BUSINESS IS A PLEASURE.
OH, CASIMIRA, GIVE ME A BREAK! YOU KNOW I'VE ALWAYS BEEN BAD AT THIS.
DA-- DA-- DA--!
HELLO, LUBA. AND YET ANOTHER OF YOUR CHILDREN AS BEAUTIFUL AS HER MOTHER...
OH... THANKS, BORRO. YOU LOOK AT LEAST HALF-HUMAN YOURSELF...
WHY HASN'T ANYBODY KILLED YOU TO PUT US OUT OF OUR MISERY?
WHY DON'T YOU JUST ADMIT THAT YOU'D LOVE TO YANK MY CHOAD?
TELL YOUR COUSIN OFELIA AND YOUR GIRLS HI FOR OL' BORRO, OK, LUBA?
WELL, I WOULDN'T HOLD MY BREATH...
10

BORRO: BOAR-O / CASIMIRA: CASS-EE-MEER-AH

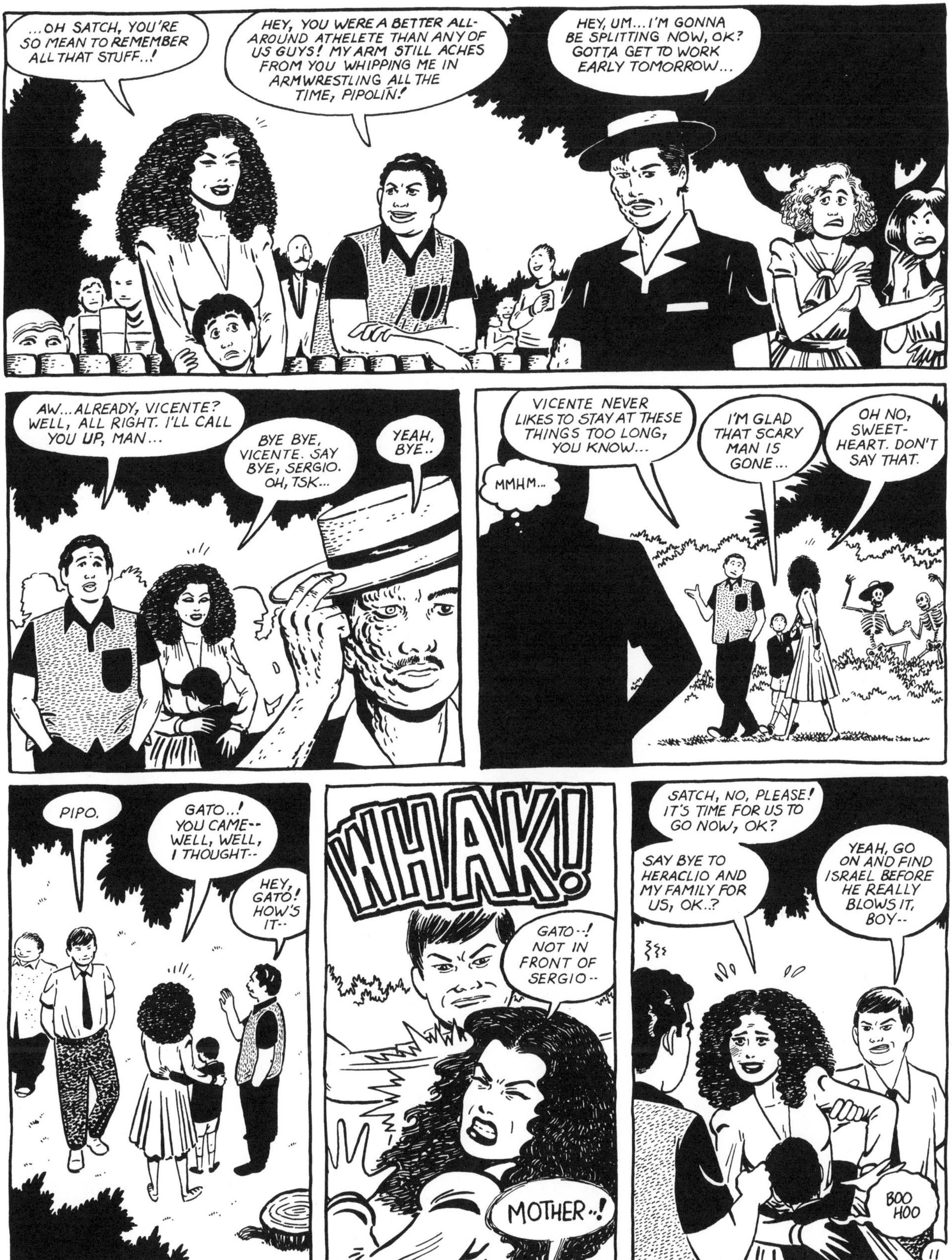
...OH SATCH, YOU'RE SO MEAN TO REMEMBER ALL THAT STUFF..!
HEY, YOU WERE A BETTER ALL-AROUND ATHELETE THAN ANY OF US GUYS! MY ARM STILL ACHES FROM YOU WHIPPING ME IN ARMWRESTLING ALL THE TIME, PIPOLÍN!
HEY, UM... I'M GONNA BE SPLITTING NOW, OK? GOTTA GET TO WORK EARLY TOMORROW...
AW... ALREADY, VICENTE? WELL, ALL RIGHT. I'LL CALL YOU UP, MAN...
BYE BYE, VICENTE. SAY BYE, SERGIO. OH, TSK...
YEAH, BYE..
VICENTE NEVER LIKES TO STAY AT THESE THINGS TOO LONG, YOU KNOW...
MMHM...
I'M GLAD THAT SCARY MAN IS GONE...
OH NO, SWEET-HEART. DON'T SAY THAT.
PIPO.
GATO..! YOU CAME-- WELL, WELL, I THOUGHT--
HEY, GATO! HOW'S IT--
WHAK!
GATO--! NOT IN FRONT OF SERGIO--
MOTHER--!
SATCH, NO, PLEASE! IT'S TIME FOR US TO GO NOW, OK?
SAY BYE TO HERACLIO AND MY FAMILY FOR US, OK..?
YEAH, GO ON AND FIND ISRAEL BEFORE HE REALLY BLOWS IT, BOY--
BOO HOO
11

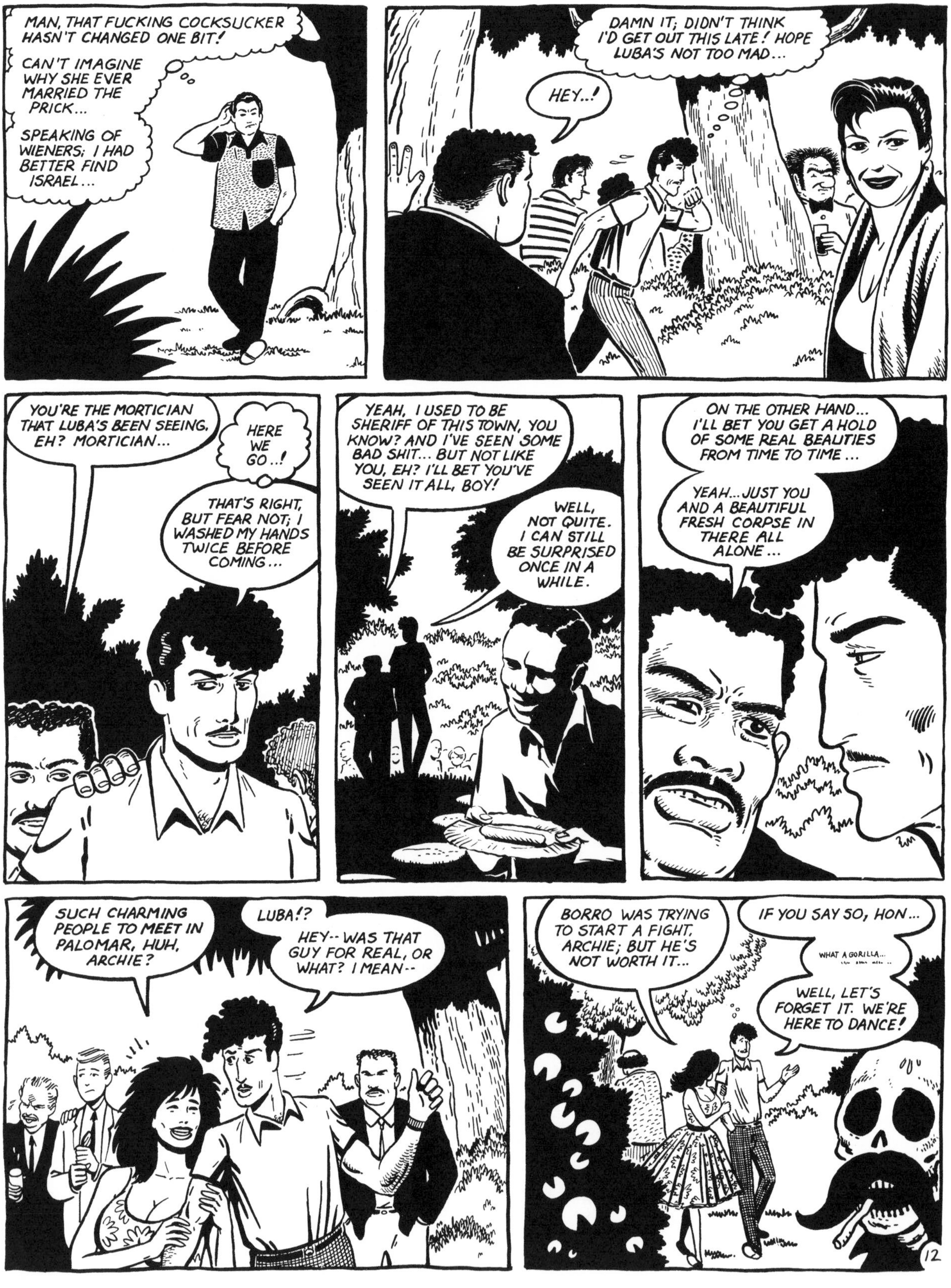
MAN, THAT FUCKING COCKSUCKER HASN'T CHANGED ONE BIT!
CAN'T IMAGINE WHY SHE EVER MARRIED THE PRICK...
SPEAKING OF WIENERS; I HAD BETTER FIND ISRAEL...
DAMN IT; DIDN'T THINK I'D GET OUT THIS LATE! HOPE LUBA'S NOT TOO MAD...
HEY..!
YOU'RE THE MORTICIAN THAT LUBA'S BEEN SEEING, EH? MORTICIAN...
HERE WE GO..!
THAT'S RIGHT, BUT FEAR NOT; I WASHED MY HANDS TWICE BEFORE COMING...
YEAH, I USED TO BE SHERIFF OF THIS TOWN, YOU KNOW? AND I'VE SEEN SOME BAD SHIT... BUT NOT LIKE YOU, EH? I'LL BET YOU'VE SEEN IT ALL, BOY!
WELL, NOT QUITE. I CAN STILL BE SURPRISED ONCE IN A WHILE.
ON THE OTHER HAND... I'LL BET YOU GET A HOLD OF SOME REAL BEAUTIES FROM TIME TO TIME...
YEAH... JUST YOU AND A BEAUTIFUL FRESH CORPSE IN THERE ALL ALONE...
SUCH CHARMING PEOPLE TO MEET IN PALOMAR, HUH, ARCHIE?
LUBA!?
HEY-- WAS THAT GUY FOR REAL, OR WHAT? I MEAN--
BORRO WAS TRYING TO START A FIGHT, ARCHIE; BUT HE'S NOT WORTH IT...
IF YOU SAY SO, HON...
WHAT A GORILLA...
WELL, LET'S FORGET IT. WE'RE HERE TO DANCE!
12

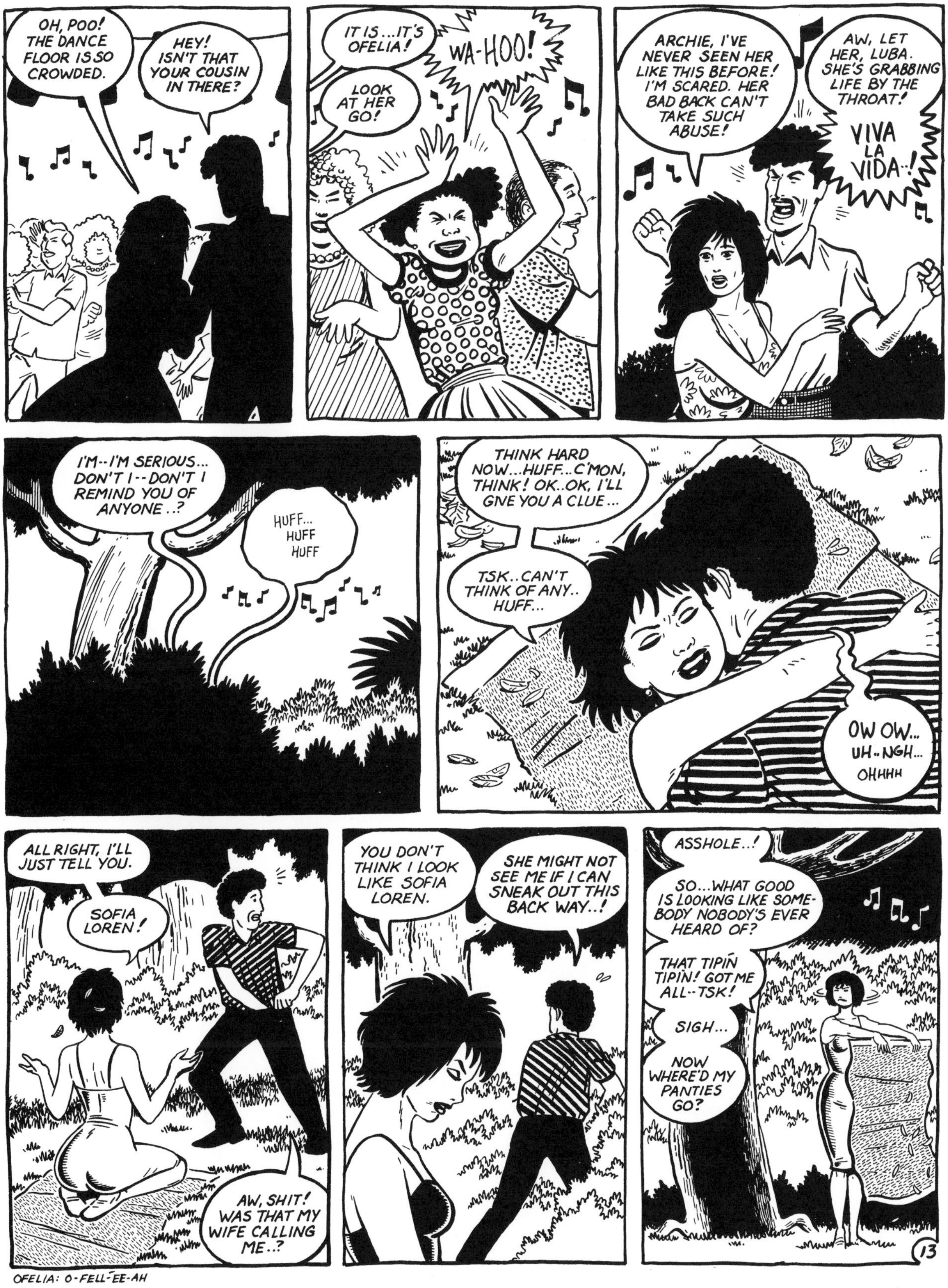
OH, POO! THE DANCE FLOOR IS SO CROWDED.
HEY! ISN'T THAT YOUR COUSIN IN THERE?
IT IS...IT'S OFELIA!
LOOK AT HER GO!
WA-HOO!
ARCHIE, I'VE NEVER SEEN HER LIKE THIS BEFORE! I'M SCARED. HER BAD BACK CAN'T TAKE SUCH ABUSE!
AW, LET HER, LUBA. SHE'S GRABBING LIFE BY THE THROAT!
VIVA LA VIDA..!
I'M--I'M SERIOUS... DON'T I--DON'T I REMIND YOU OF ANYONE..?
HUFF... HUFF HUFF
THINK HARD NOW...HUFF...C'MON, THINK! OK..OK, I'LL GIVE YOU A CLUE...
TSK..CAN'T THINK OF ANY.. HUFF...
OW OW... UH..NGH... OHHHH
ALL RIGHT, I'LL JUST TELL YOU.
SOFIA LOREN!
AW, SHIT! WAS THAT MY WIFE CALLING ME..?
YOU DON'T THINK I LOOK LIKE SOFIA LOREN.
SHE MIGHT NOT SEE ME IF I CAN SNEAK OUT THIS BACK WAY..!
ASSHOLE..!
SO...WHAT GOOD IS LOOKING LIKE SOMEBODY NOBODY'S EVER HEARD OF?
THAT TIPÍN TIPÍN! GOT ME ALL--TSK!
SIGH...
NOW WHERE'D MY PANTIES GO?
13

OFELIA: O-FELL-EE-AH

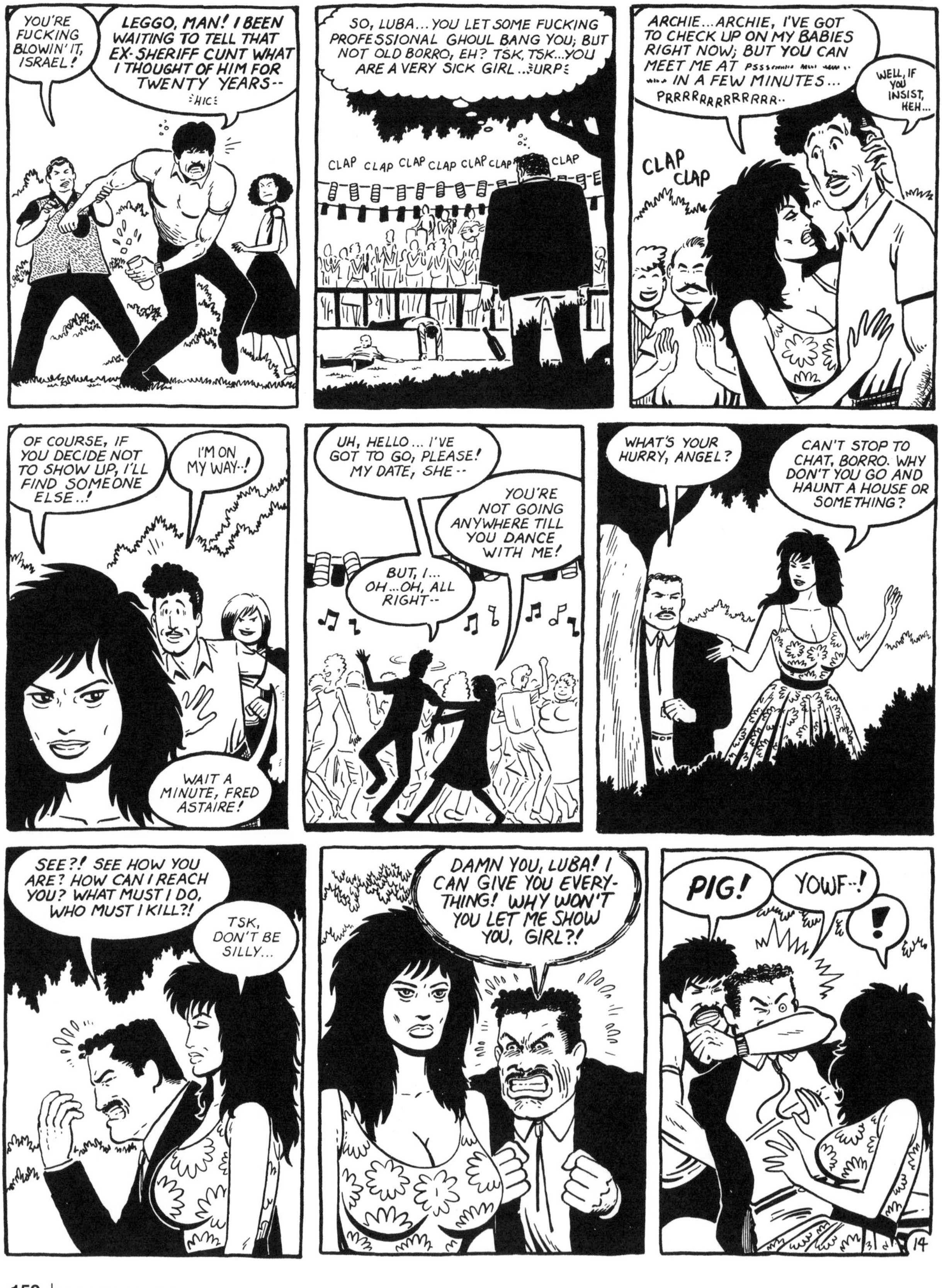
YOU'RE FUCKING BLOWIN' IT, ISRAEL!
LEGGO, MAN! I BEEN WAITING TO TELL THAT EX-SHERIFF CUNT WHAT I THOUGHT OF HIM FOR TWENTY YEARS--
HIC
SO, LUBA... YOU LET SOME FUCKING PROFESSIONAL GHOUL BANG YOU; BUT NOT OLD BORRO, EH? TSK, TSK... YOU ARE A VERY SICK GIRL... URP
CLAP CLAP CLAP CLAP CLAP CLAP CLAP
ARCHIE... ARCHIE, I'VE GOT TO CHECK UP ON MY BABIES RIGHT NOW; BUT YOU CAN MEET ME AT PSSS... IN A FEW MINUTES... PRRRRRRRRRRRR..
WELL, IF YOU INSIST, HEH...
CLAP CLAP
OF COURSE, IF YOU DECIDE NOT TO SHOW UP, I'LL FIND SOMEONE ELSE..!
I'M ON MY WAY..!
WAIT A MINUTE, FRED ASTAIRE!
UH, HELLO... I'VE GOT TO GO, PLEASE! MY DATE, SHE--
YOU'RE NOT GOING ANYWHERE TILL YOU DANCE WITH ME!
BUT, I... OH... OH, ALL RIGHT--
WHAT'S YOUR HURRY, ANGEL?
CAN'T STOP TO CHAT, BORRO. WHY DON'T YOU GO AND HAUNT A HOUSE OR SOMETHING?
SEE?! SEE HOW YOU ARE? HOW CAN I REACH YOU? WHAT MUST I DO, WHO MUST I KILL?!
TSK, DON'T BE SILLY...
DAMN YOU, LUBA! I CAN GIVE YOU EVERY-THING! WHY WON'T YOU LET ME SHOW YOU, GIRL?!
PIG!
YOWF--!
!
14

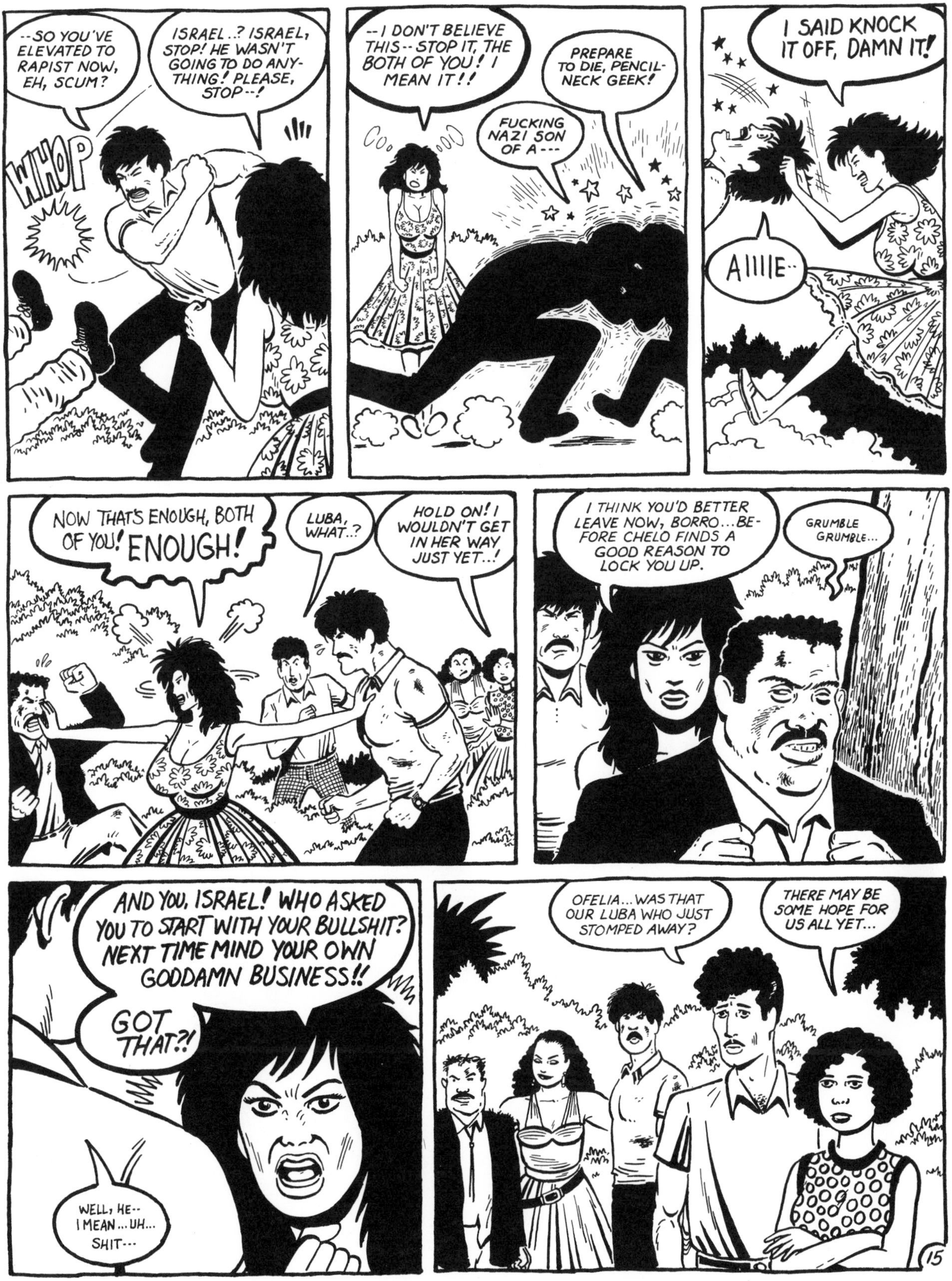
--SO YOU'VE ELEVATED TO RAPIST NOW, EH, SCUM?
ISRAEL..? ISRAEL, STOP! HE WASN'T GOING TO DO ANYTHING! PLEASE, STOP--!
WHOP
--I DON'T BELIEVE THIS--STOP IT, THE BOTH OF YOU! I MEAN IT!!
PREPARE TO DIE, PENCIL-NECK GEEK!
FUCKING NAZI SON OF A---
I SAID KNOCK IT OFF, DAMN IT!
AIIIIE..
NOW THAT'S ENOUGH, BOTH OF YOU! ENOUGH!
LUBA, WHAT..?
HOLD ON! I WOULDN'T GET IN HER WAY JUST YET..!
I THINK YOU'D BETTER LEAVE NOW, BORRO... BEFORE CHELO FINDS A GOOD REASON TO LOCK YOU UP.
GRUMBLE GRUMBLE...
AND YOU, ISRAEL! WHO ASKED YOU TO START WITH YOUR BULLSHIT? NEXT TIME MIND YOUR OWN GODDAMN BUSINESS!!
GOT THAT?!
WELL, HE-- I MEAN... UH... SHIT---
OFELIA... WAS THAT OUR LUBA WHO JUST STOMPED AWAY?
THERE MAY BE SOME HOPE FOR US ALL YET...
15

THERE GOES MARTIN EL LOCO AGAIN. WHERE DOES HE COME UP WITH THESE THINGS?

WHEN'S THE BEAST!

WELL, WITH THE MONEY HIS FATHER HAS LEFT HIM, MARTIN OFTEN VISITS THE STATES...

MARTIN TAKES A PLANE TO HOLLYWOOD, AND THEN RENTS A HOTEL ROOM. HE SPENDS HIS WHOLE TIME THERE WATCHING A TELEVISION SET.

THEN HE COMES HOME TO TELL US WHAT THE UNITED STATES IS LIKE.

HUH..!

POO! PWOAT!

MATTER OF FACT, I THINK HE'S LEAVING AGAIN NEXT WEEK, TONANTZIN.

HEY MARTÍN! WAIT UP!

I DIDN'T DO NUTHIN'!

HUH! MY BIG SISTER'S AFTER MARTIN NOW, EH? WHAT IS IT? THE OLDER YOU GET, THE MORE HARD UP, OR WHAT?

TSK TSK. DIANA, DIANA...

WHEN YOU'RE ALL GROWN UP YOU'LL SEE THAT AN ADULT IS MORE WILLING TO ACCEPT THE DIFFERENCES WITHIN US ALL, HOWEVER UNPLEASANT OR ENDEARING.

YEAH? TELL YOU WHAT, TIPIN TIPIN...

IF YOU EVER COME ACROSS AN ADULT IN MY TOWN, LET ME KNOW, OK?

?

HEY, YOU TWO! KNOCK IT OFF!

END

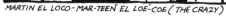

MARTIN EL LOCO - MAR-TEEN EL LOE-COE (THE CRAZY)

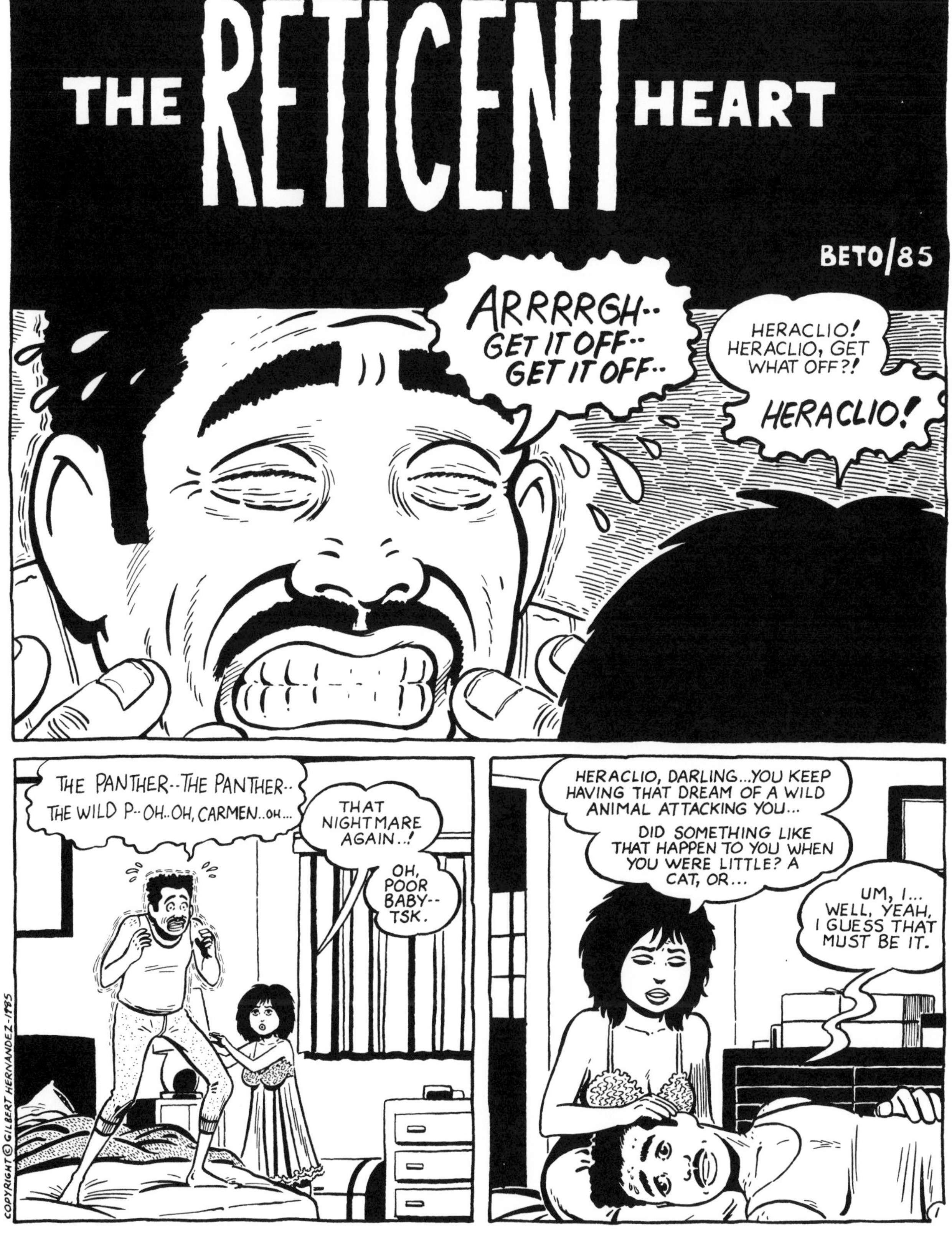
THE RETICENT HEART
BETO/85
ARRRRGH.. GET IT OFF.. GET IT OFF..
HERACLIO! HERACLIO, GET WHAT OFF?! HERACLIO!
THE PANTHER--THE PANTHER.. THE WILD P..OH..OH, CARMEN..OH...
THAT NIGHTMARE AGAIN..!
OH, POOR BABY--TSK.
COPYRIGHT © GILBERT HERNANDEZ-1985
HERACLIO, DARLING...YOU KEEP HAVING THAT DREAM OF A WILD ANIMAL ATTACKING YOU...
DID SOMETHING LIKE THAT HAPPEN TO YOU WHEN YOU WERE LITTLE? A CAT, OR...
UM, I... WELL, YEAH, I GUESS THAT MUST BE IT.

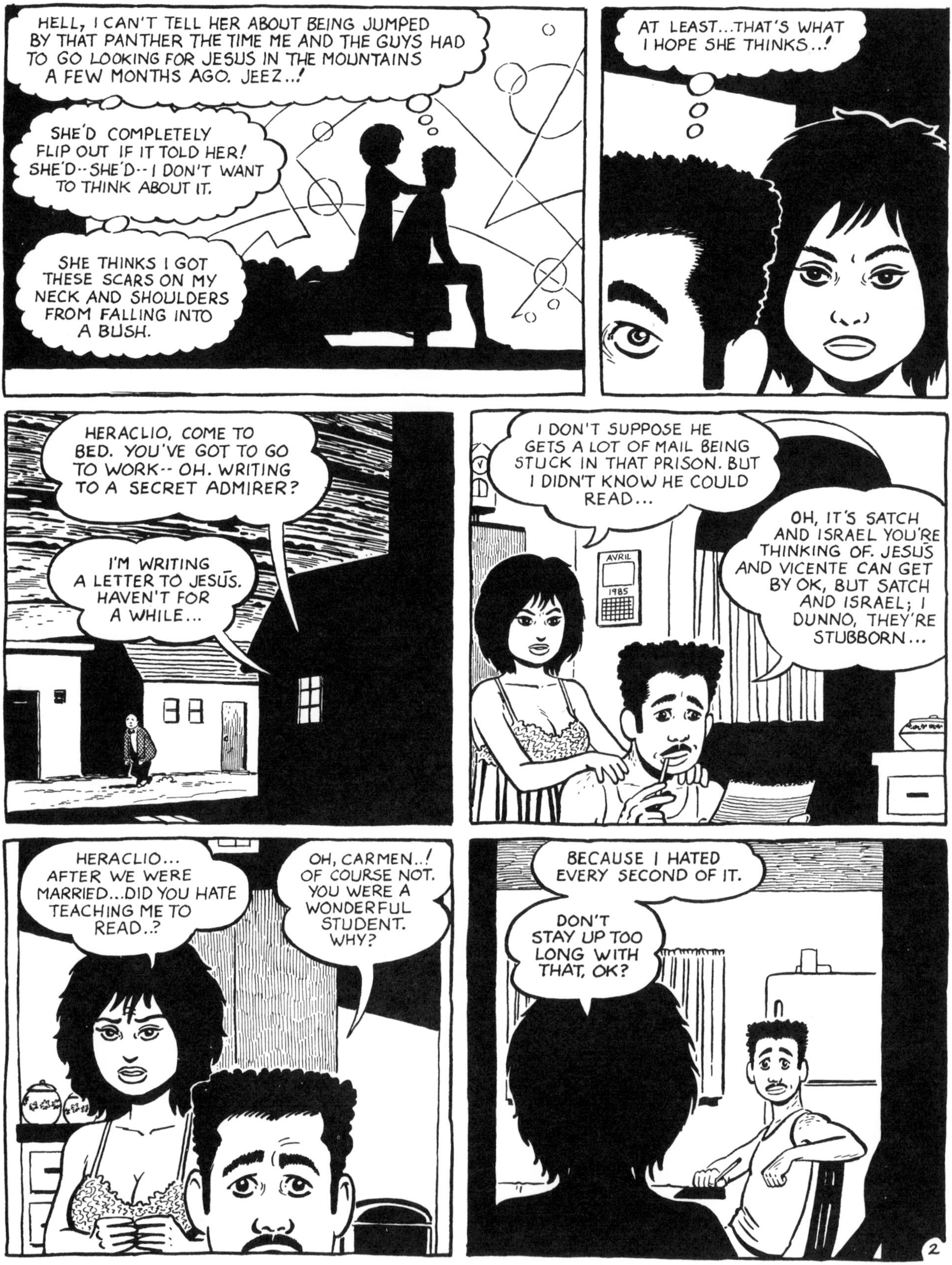
HELL, I CAN'T TELL HER ABOUT BEING JUMPED BY THAT PANTHER THE TIME ME AND THE GUYS HAD TO GO LOOKING FOR JESUS IN THE MOUNTAINS A FEW MONTHS AGO. JEEZ..!
SHE'D COMPLETELY FLIP OUT IF IT TOLD HER! SHE'D--SHE'D--I DON'T WANT TO THINK ABOUT IT.
SHE THINKS I GOT THESE SCARS ON MY NECK AND SHOULDERS FROM FALLING INTO A BUSH.
AT LEAST...THAT'S WHAT I HOPE SHE THINKS..!
HERACLIO, COME TO BED. YOU'VE GOT TO GO TO WORK-- OH. WRITING TO A SECRET ADMIRER?
I'M WRITING A LETTER TO JESÚS. HAVEN'T FOR A WHILE...
I DON'T SUPPOSE HE GETS A LOT OF MAIL BEING STUCK IN THAT PRISON. BUT I DIDN'T KNOW HE COULD READ...
AVRIL
1985
OH, IT'S SATCH AND ISRAEL YOU'RE THINKING OF. JESÚS AND VICENTE CAN GET BY OK, BUT SATCH AND ISRAEL; I DUNNO, THEY'RE STUBBORN...
HERACLIO... AFTER WE WERE MARRIED...DID YOU HATE TEACHING ME TO READ..?
OH, CARMEN..! OF COURSE NOT. YOU WERE A WONDERFUL STUDENT. WHY?
BECAUSE I HATED EVERY SECOND OF IT.
DON'T STAY UP TOO LONG WITH THAT, OK?
2

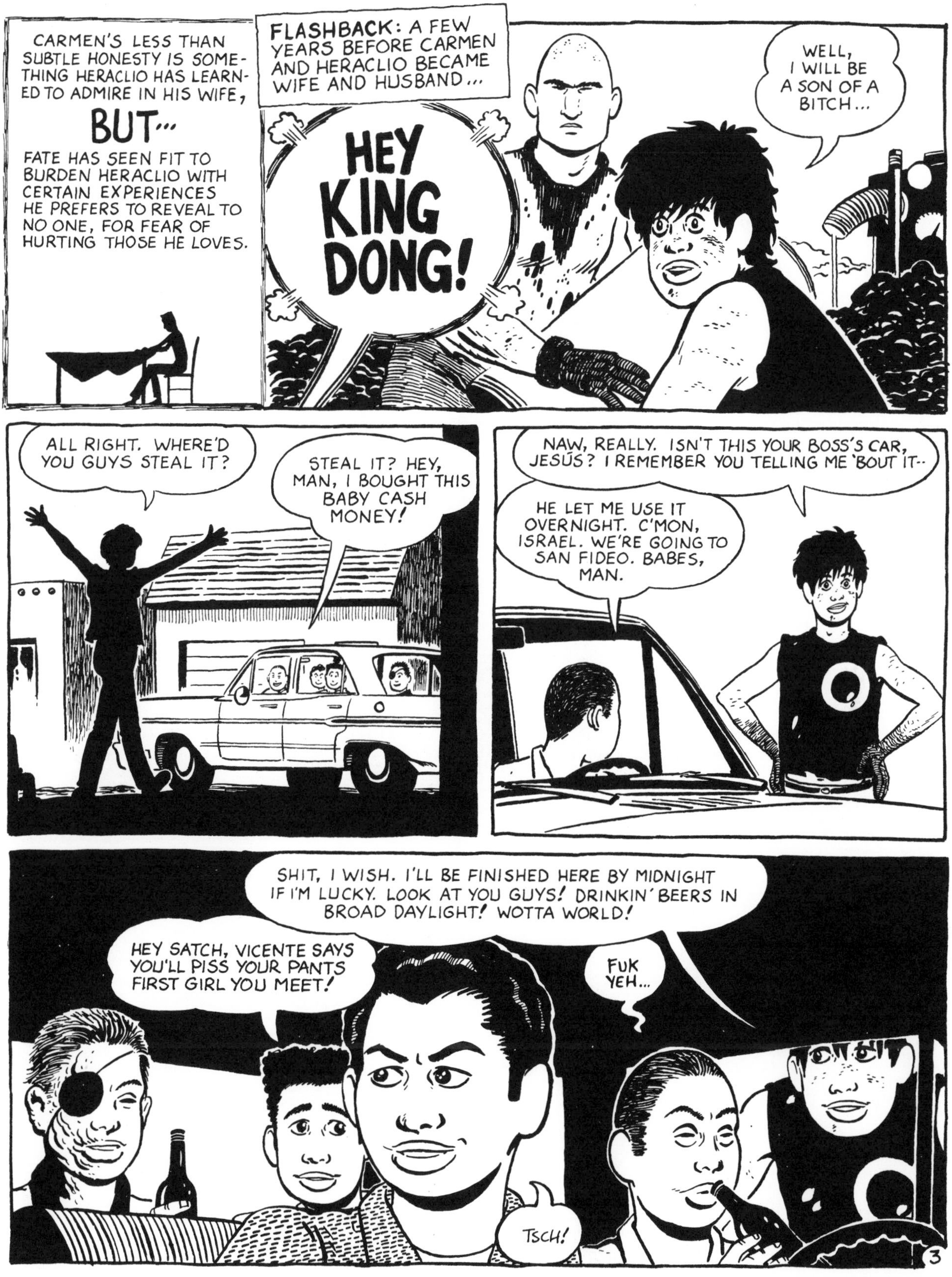
CARMEN'S LESS THAN SUBTLE HONESTY IS SOMETHING HERACLIO HAS LEARNED TO ADMIRE IN HIS WIFE,
BUT...
FATE HAS SEEN FIT TO BURDEN HERACLIO WITH CERTAIN EXPERIENCES HE PREFERS TO REVEAL TO NO ONE, FOR FEAR OF HURTING THOSE HE LOVES.
FLASHBACK: A FEW YEARS BEFORE CARMEN AND HERACLIO BECAME WIFE AND HUSBAND...
HEY KING DONG!
WELL, I WILL BE A SON OF A BITCH...
ALL RIGHT. WHERE'D YOU GUYS STEAL IT?
STEAL IT? HEY, MAN, I BOUGHT THIS BABY CASH MONEY!
NAW, REALLY. ISN'T THIS YOUR BOSS'S CAR, JESÚS? I REMEMBER YOU TELLING ME 'BOUT IT--
HE LET ME USE IT OVERNIGHT. C'MON, ISRAEL. WE'RE GOING TO SAN FIDEO. BABES, MAN.
SHIT, I WISH. I'LL BE FINISHED HERE BY MIDNIGHT IF I'M LUCKY. LOOK AT YOU GUYS! DRINKIN' BEERS IN BROAD DAYLIGHT! WOTTA WORLD!
HEY SATCH, VICENTE SAYS YOU'LL PISS YOUR PANTS FIRST GIRL YOU MEET!
FUK YEH...
TSCH!
3

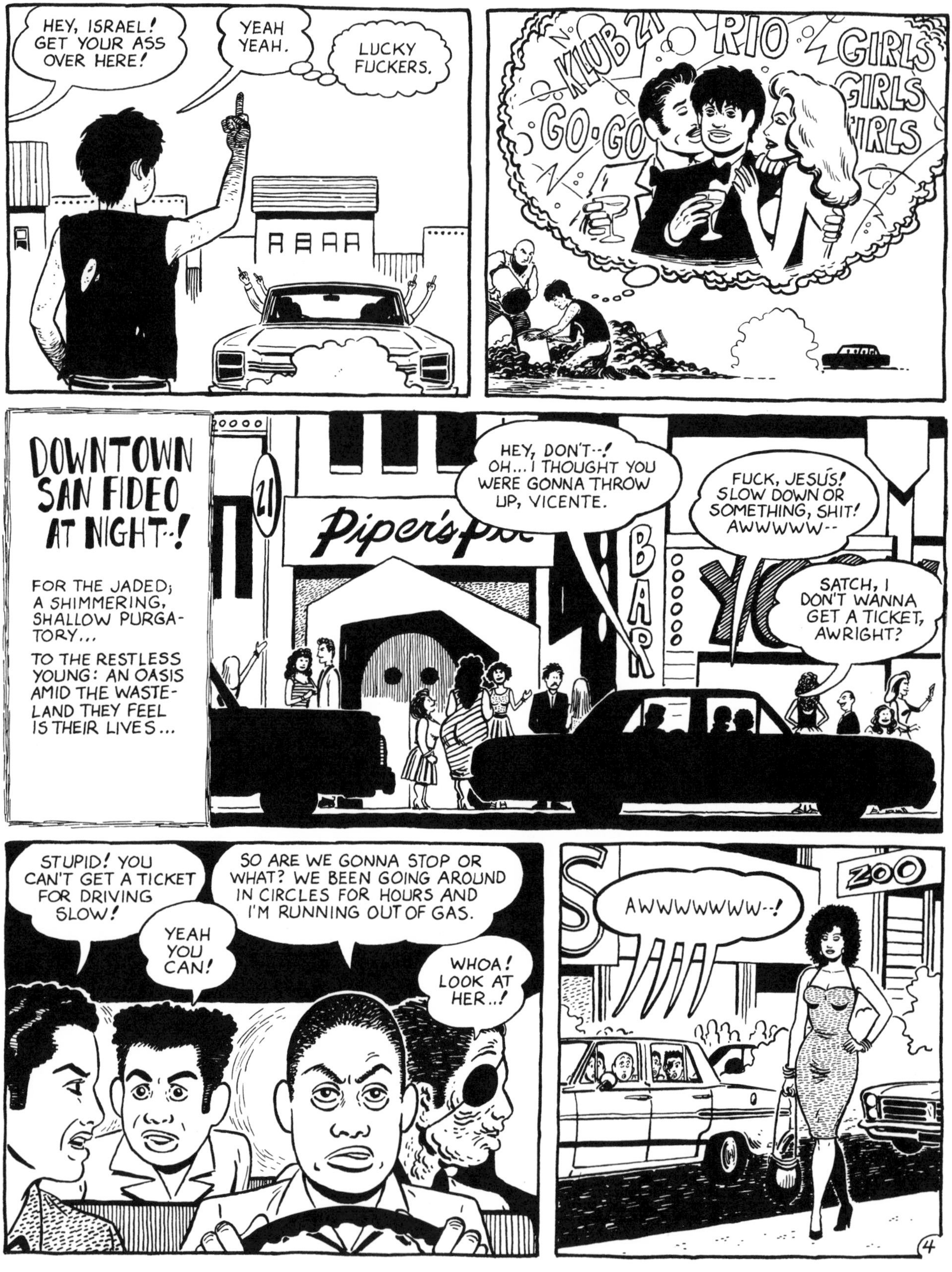
HEY, ISRAEL! GET YOUR ASS OVER HERE!
YEAH YEAH.
LUCKY FUCKERS.
KLUB 21
RIO
GIRLS GIRLS GIRLS
GO-GO
DOWNTOWN SAN FIDEO AT NIGHT--!
FOR THE JADED; A SHIMMERING, SHALLOW PURGATORY...
TO THE RESTLESS YOUNG: AN OASIS AMID THE WASTELAND THEY FEEL IS THEIR LIVES...
21
Piper's
BAR
HEY, DON'T--! OH... I THOUGHT YOU WERE GONNA THROW UP, VICENTE.
FUCK, JESÚS! SLOW DOWN OR SOMETHING, SHIT! AWWWWW--
SATCH, I DON'T WANNA GET A TICKET, AWRIGHT?
STUPID! YOU CAN'T GET A TICKET FOR DRIVING SLOW!
YEAH YOU CAN!
SO ARE WE GONNA STOP OR WHAT? WE BEEN GOING AROUND IN CIRCLES FOR HOURS AND I'M RUNNING OUT OF GAS.
WHOA! LOOK AT HER..!
ZOO
AWWWWWWW--!
4

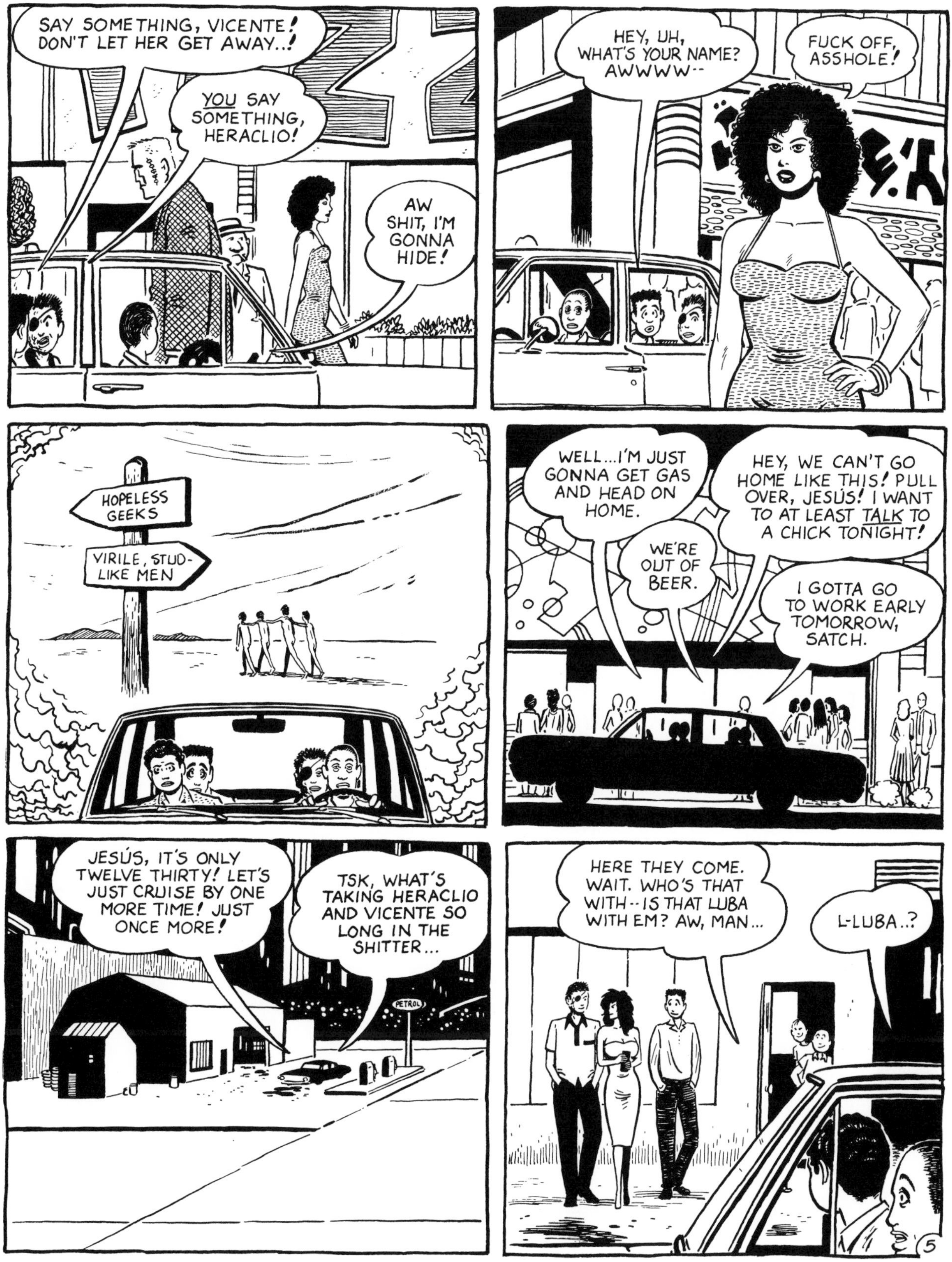
SAY SOMETHING, VICENTE! DON'T LET HER GET AWAY..!
YOU SAY SOMETHING, HERACLIO!
AW SHIT, I'M GONNA HIDE!
HEY, UH, WHAT'S YOUR NAME? AWWWW--
FUCK OFF, ASSHOLE!
HOPELESS GEEKS
VIRILE, STUD-LIKE MEN
WELL...I'M JUST GONNA GET GAS AND HEAD ON HOME.
WE'RE OUT OF BEER.
HEY, WE CAN'T GO HOME LIKE THIS! PULL OVER, JESÚS! I WANT TO AT LEAST TALK TO A CHICK TONIGHT!
I GOTTA GO TO WORK EARLY TOMORROW, SATCH.
JESÚS, IT'S ONLY TWELVE THIRTY! LET'S JUST CRUISE BY ONE MORE TIME! JUST ONCE MORE!
TSK, WHAT'S TAKING HERACLIO AND VICENTE SO LONG IN THE SHITTER...
PETROL
HERE THEY COME. WAIT. WHO'S THAT WITH--IS THAT LUBA WITH EM? AW, MAN...
L-LUBA..?
5

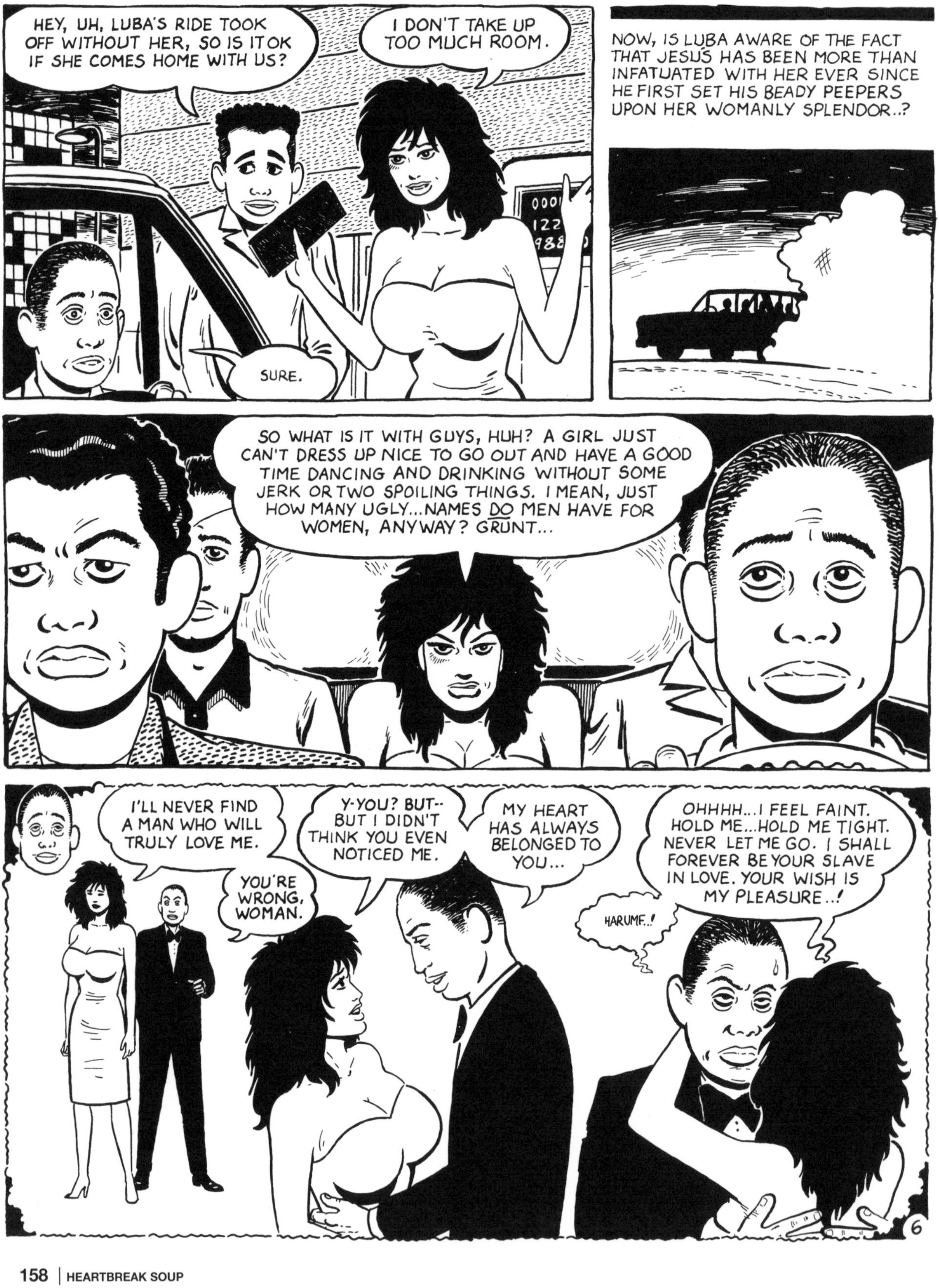
HEY, UH, LUBA'S RIDE TOOK OFF WITHOUT HER, SO IS IT OK IF SHE COMES HOME WITH US?
I DON'T TAKE UP TOO MUCH ROOM.
SURE.
NOW, IS LUBA AWARE OF THE FACT THAT JESÚS HAS BEEN MORE THAN INFATUATED WITH HER EVER SINCE HE FIRST SET HIS BEADY PEEPERS UPON HER WOMANLY SPLENDOR..?
SO WHAT IS IT WITH GUYS, HUH? A GIRL JUST CAN'T DRESS UP NICE TO GO OUT AND HAVE A GOOD TIME DANCING AND DRINKING WITHOUT SOME JERK OR TWO SPOILING THINGS. I MEAN, JUST HOW MANY UGLY...NAMES DO MEN HAVE FOR WOMEN, ANYWAY? GRUNT...
I'LL NEVER FIND A MAN WHO WILL TRULY LOVE ME.
YOU'RE WRONG, WOMAN.
Y-YOU? BUT-- BUT I DIDN'T THINK YOU EVEN NOTICED ME.
MY HEART HAS ALWAYS BELONGED TO YOU...
OHHHH...I FEEL FAINT. HOLD ME...HOLD ME TIGHT. NEVER LET ME GO. I SHALL FOREVER BE YOUR SLAVE IN LOVE. YOUR WISH IS MY PLEASURE..!
HARUMF..!
6

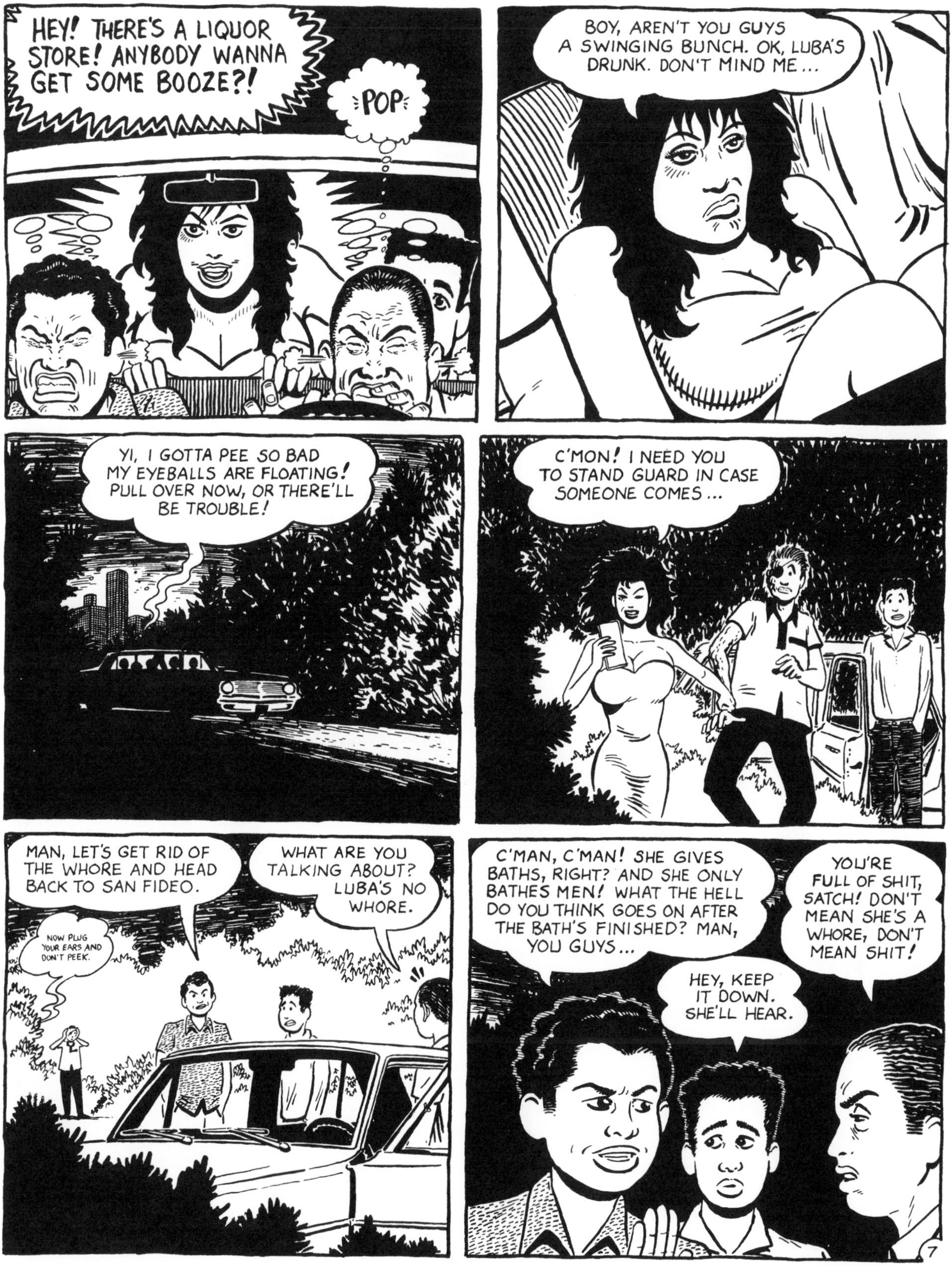
HEY! THERE'S A LIQUOR STORE! ANYBODY WANNA GET SOME BOOZE?!
POP
BOY, AREN'T YOU GUYS A SWINGING BUNCH. OK, LUBA'S DRUNK. DON'T MIND ME...
YI, I GOTTA PEE SO BAD MY EYEBALLS ARE FLOATING! PULL OVER NOW, OR THERE'LL BE TROUBLE!
C'MON! I NEED YOU TO STAND GUARD IN CASE SOMEONE COMES...
MAN, LET'S GET RID OF THE WHORE AND HEAD BACK TO SAN FIDEO.
WHAT ARE YOU TALKING ABOUT? LUBA'S NO WHORE.
NOW PLUG YOUR EARS AND DON'T PEEK.
C'MAN, C'MAN! SHE GIVES BATHS, RIGHT? AND SHE ONLY BATHES MEN! WHAT THE HELL DO YOU THINK GOES ON AFTER THE BATH'S FINISHED? MAN, YOU GUYS...
YOU'RE FULL OF SHIT, SATCH! DON'T MEAN SHE'S A WHORE, DON'T MEAN SHIT!
HEY, KEEP IT DOWN. SHE'LL HEAR.
7

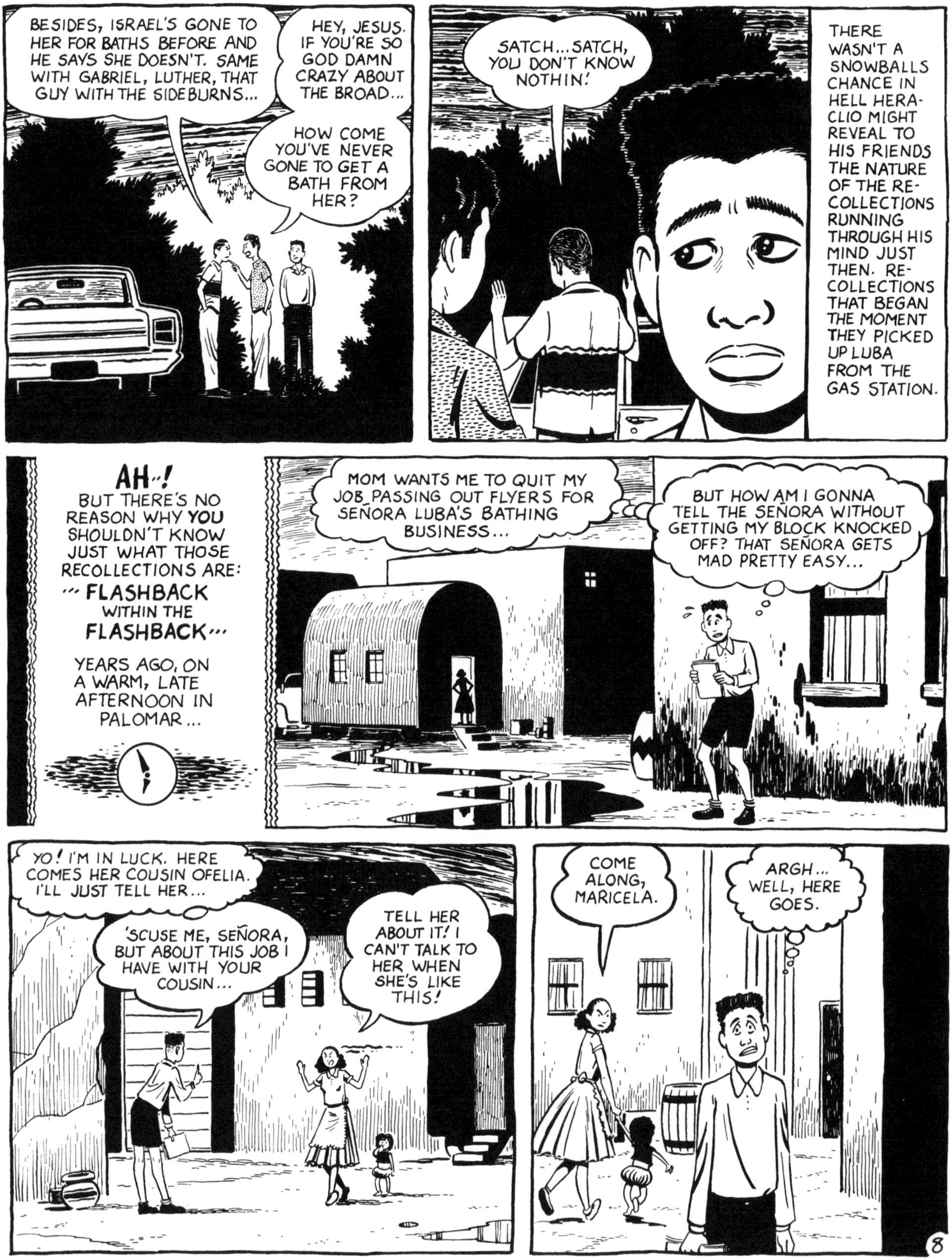
BESIDES, ISRAEL'S GONE TO HER FOR BATHS BEFORE AND HE SAYS SHE DOESN'T. SAME WITH GABRIEL, LUTHER, THAT GUY WITH THE SIDEBURNS...
HEY, JESUS. IF YOU'RE SO GOD DAMN CRAZY ABOUT THE BROAD...
HOW COME YOU'VE NEVER GONE TO GET A BATH FROM HER?
SATCH...SATCH, YOU DON'T KNOW NOTHIN'!
THERE WASN'T A SNOWBALLS CHANCE IN HELL HERACLIO MIGHT REVEAL TO HIS FRIENDS THE NATURE OF THE RECOLLECTIONS RUNNING THROUGH HIS MIND JUST THEN. RECOLLECTIONS THAT BEGAN THE MOMENT THEY PICKED UP LUBA FROM THE GAS STATION.
AH..! BUT THERE'S NO REASON WHY YOU SHOULDN'T KNOW JUST WHAT THOSE RECOLLECTIONS ARE:
...FLASHBACK WITHIN THE FLASHBACK...
YEARS AGO, ON A WARM, LATE AFTERNOON IN PALOMAR...
MOM WANTS ME TO QUIT MY JOB PASSING OUT FLYERS FOR SEÑORA LUBA'S BATHING BUSINESS...
BUT HOW AM I GONNA TELL THE SEÑORA WITHOUT GETTING MY BLOCK KNOCKED OFF? THAT SEÑORA GETS MAD PRETTY EASY...
YO! I'M IN LUCK. HERE COMES HER COUSIN OFELIA. I'LL JUST TELL HER...
'SCUSE ME, SEÑORA, BUT ABOUT THIS JOB I HAVE WITH YOUR COUSIN...
TELL HER ABOUT IT! I CAN'T TALK TO HER WHEN SHE'S LIKE THIS!
COME ALONG, MARICELA.
ARGH... WELL, HERE GOES.
8

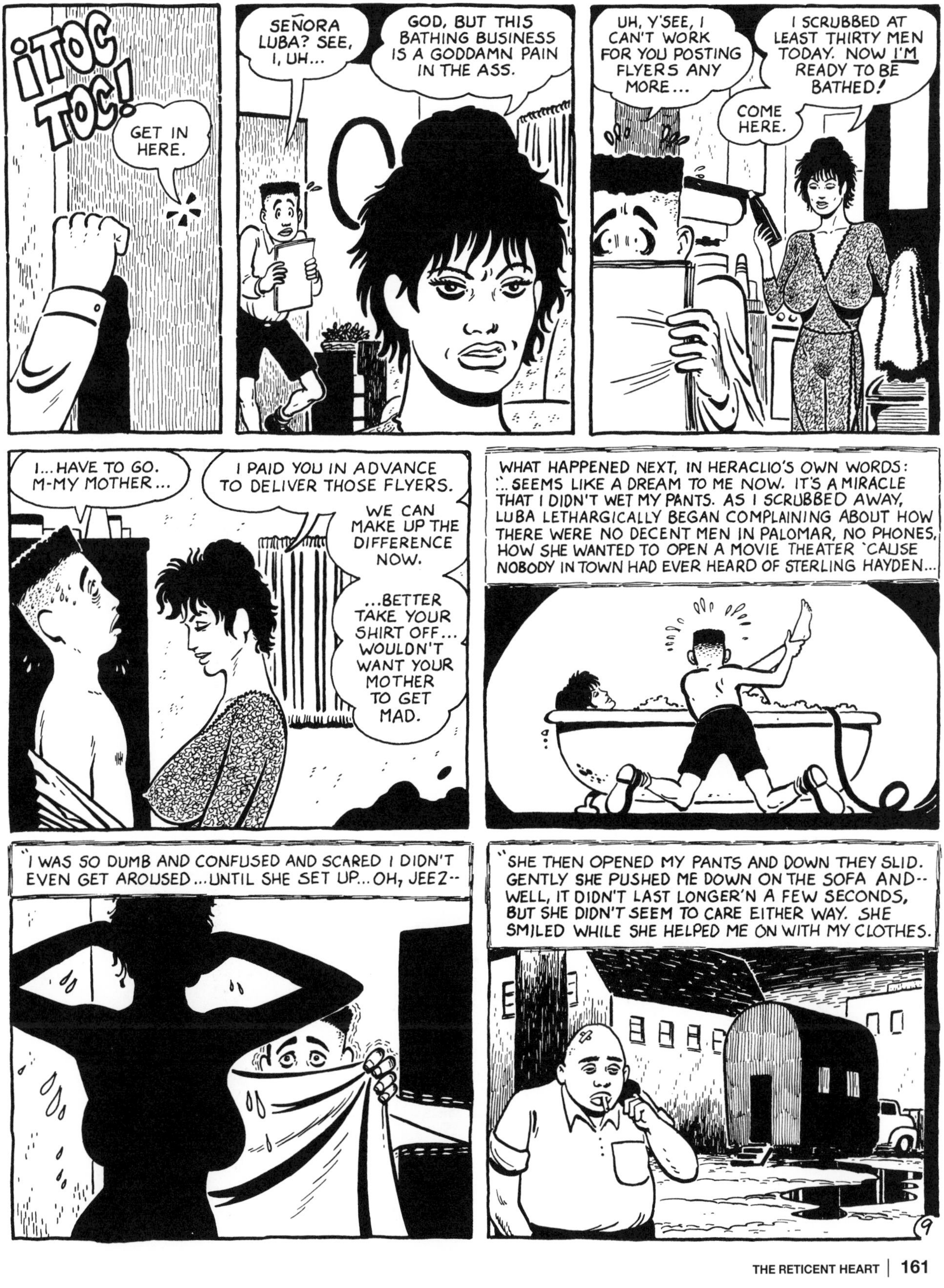
¡TOC TOC!
GET IN HERE.
SEÑORA LUBA? SEE, I, UH...
GOD, BUT THIS BATHING BUSINESS IS A GODDAMN PAIN IN THE ASS.
UH, Y'SEE, I CAN'T WORK FOR YOU POSTING FLYERS ANY MORE...
I SCRUBBED AT LEAST THIRTY MEN TODAY. NOW I'M READY TO BE BATHED!
COME HERE.
I... HAVE TO GO. M-MY MOTHER...
I PAID YOU IN ADVANCE TO DELIVER THOSE FLYERS.
WE CAN MAKE UP THE DIFFERENCE NOW.
...BETTER TAKE YOUR SHIRT OFF... WOULDN'T WANT YOUR MOTHER TO GET MAD.
WHAT HAPPENED NEXT, IN HERACLIO'S OWN WORDS: "...SEEMS LIKE A DREAM TO ME NOW. IT'S A MIRACLE THAT I DIDN'T WET MY PANTS. AS I SCRUBBED AWAY, LUBA LETHARGICALLY BEGAN COMPLAINING ABOUT HOW THERE WERE NO DECENT MEN IN PALOMAR, NO PHONES, HOW SHE WANTED TO OPEN A MOVIE THEATER 'CAUSE NOBODY IN TOWN HAD EVER HEARD OF STERLING HAYDEN...
"I WAS SO DUMB AND CONFUSED AND SCARED I DIDN'T EVEN GET AROUSED... UNTIL SHE SET UP... OH, JEEZ--
"SHE THEN OPENED MY PANTS AND DOWN THEY SLID. GENTLY SHE PUSHED ME DOWN ON THE SOFA AND-- WELL, IT DIDN'T LAST LONGER'N A FEW SECONDS, BUT SHE DIDN'T SEEM TO CARE EITHER WAY. SHE SMILED WHILE SHE HELPED ME ON WITH MY CLOTHES.
9

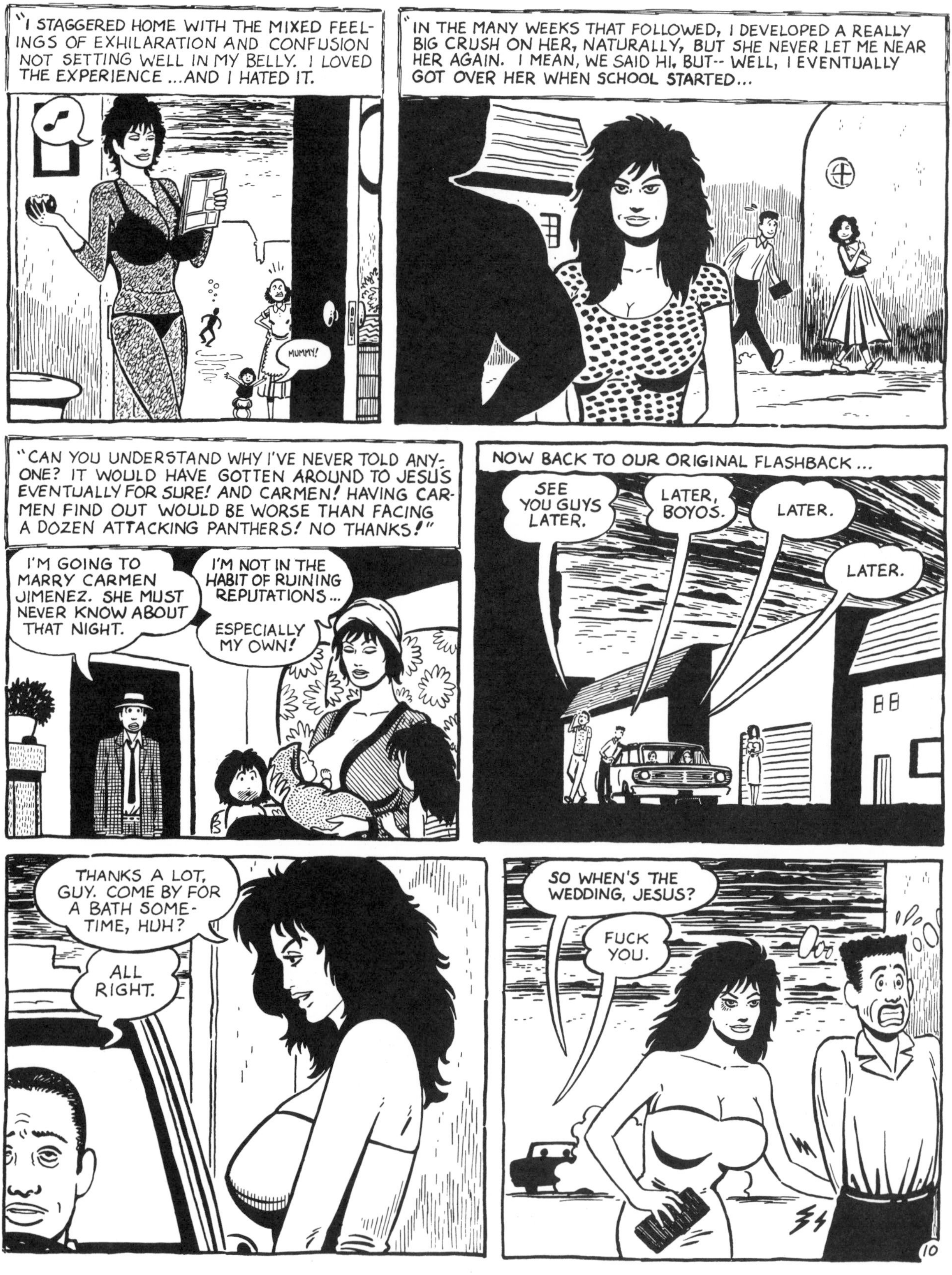
"I STAGGERED HOME WITH THE MIXED FEELINGS OF EXHILARATION AND CONFUSION NOT SETTING WELL IN MY BELLY. I LOVED THE EXPERIENCE ...AND I HATED IT.
MUMMY!
"IN THE MANY WEEKS THAT FOLLOWED, I DEVELOPED A REALLY BIG CRUSH ON HER, NATURALLY, BUT SHE NEVER LET ME NEAR HER AGAIN. I MEAN, WE SAID HI, BUT-- WELL, I EVENTUALLY GOT OVER HER WHEN SCHOOL STARTED...
"CAN YOU UNDERSTAND WHY I'VE NEVER TOLD ANYONE? IT WOULD HAVE GOTTEN AROUND TO JESUS EVENTUALLY FOR SURE! AND CARMEN! HAVING CARMEN FIND OUT WOULD BE WORSE THAN FACING A DOZEN ATTACKING PANTHERS! NO THANKS!"
I'M GOING TO MARRY CARMEN JIMENEZ. SHE MUST NEVER KNOW ABOUT THAT NIGHT.
I'M NOT IN THE HABIT OF RUINING REPUTATIONS...
ESPECIALLY MY OWN!
NOW BACK TO OUR ORIGINAL FLASHBACK...
SEE YOU GUYS LATER.
LATER, BOYOS.
LATER.
LATER.
THANKS A LOT, GUY. COME BY FOR A BATH SOMETIME, HUH?
ALL RIGHT.
SO WHEN'S THE WEDDING, JESUS?
FUCK YOU.
10

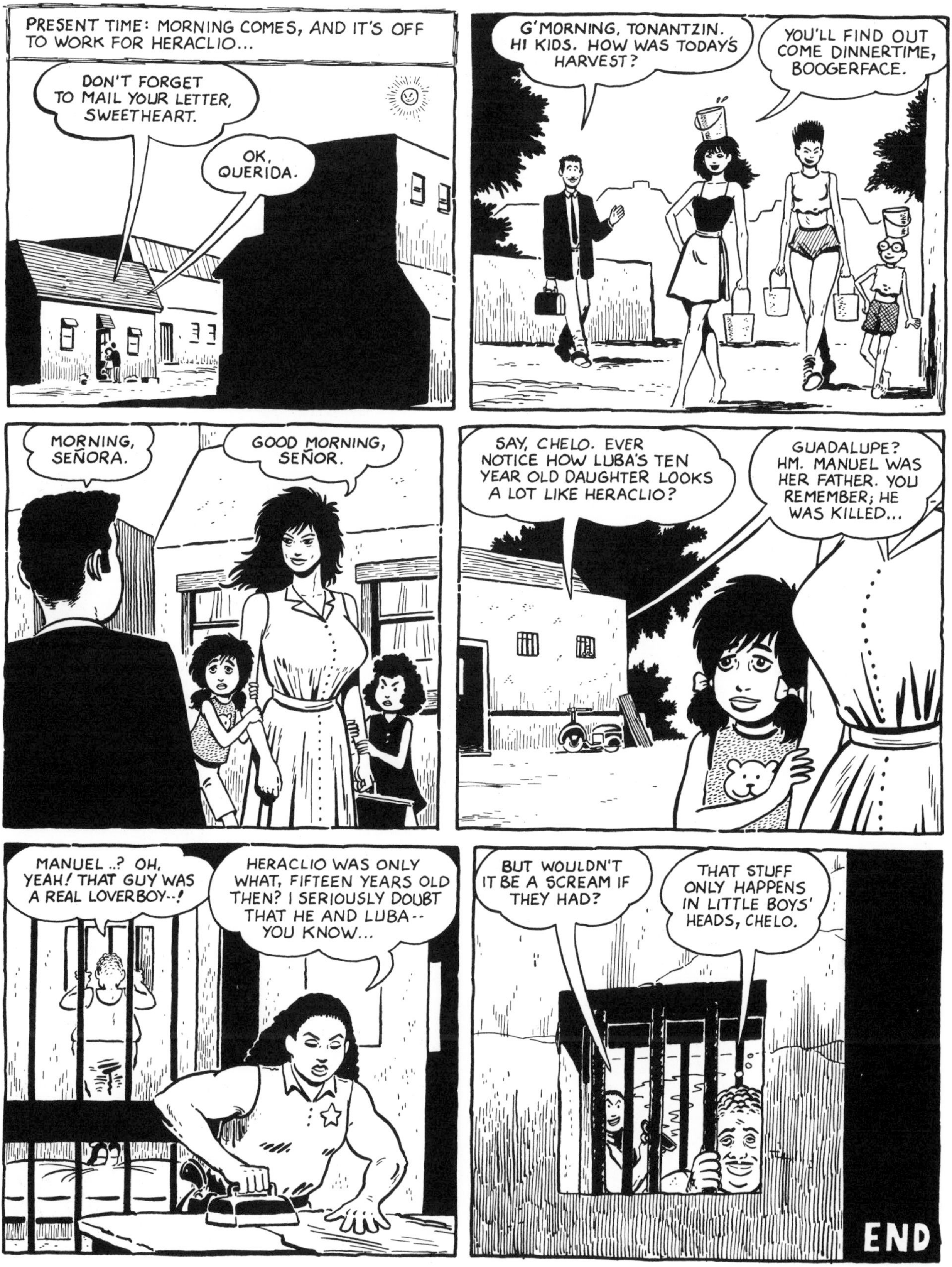
PRESENT TIME: MORNING COMES, AND IT'S OFF TO WORK FOR HERACLIO...
DON'T FORGET TO MAIL YOUR LETTER, SWEETHEART.
OK, QUERIDA.
G'MORNING, TONANTZIN. HI KIDS. HOW WAS TODAY'S HARVEST?
YOU'LL FIND OUT COME DINNERTIME, BOOGERFACE.
MORNING, SEÑORA.
GOOD MORNING, SEÑOR.
SAY, CHELO. EVER NOTICE HOW LUBA'S TEN YEAR OLD DAUGHTER LOOKS A LOT LIKE HERACLIO?
GUADALUPE? HM. MANUEL WAS HER FATHER. YOU REMEMBER; HE WAS KILLED...
MANUEL ..? OH, YEAH! THAT GUY WAS A REAL LOVERBOY--!
HERACLIO WAS ONLY WHAT, FIFTEEN YEARS OLD THEN? I SERIOUSLY DOUBT THAT HE AND LUBA-- YOU KNOW...
BUT WOULDN'T IT BE A SCREAM IF THEY HAD?
THAT STUFF ONLY HAPPENS IN LITTLE BOYS' HEADS, CHELO.
END

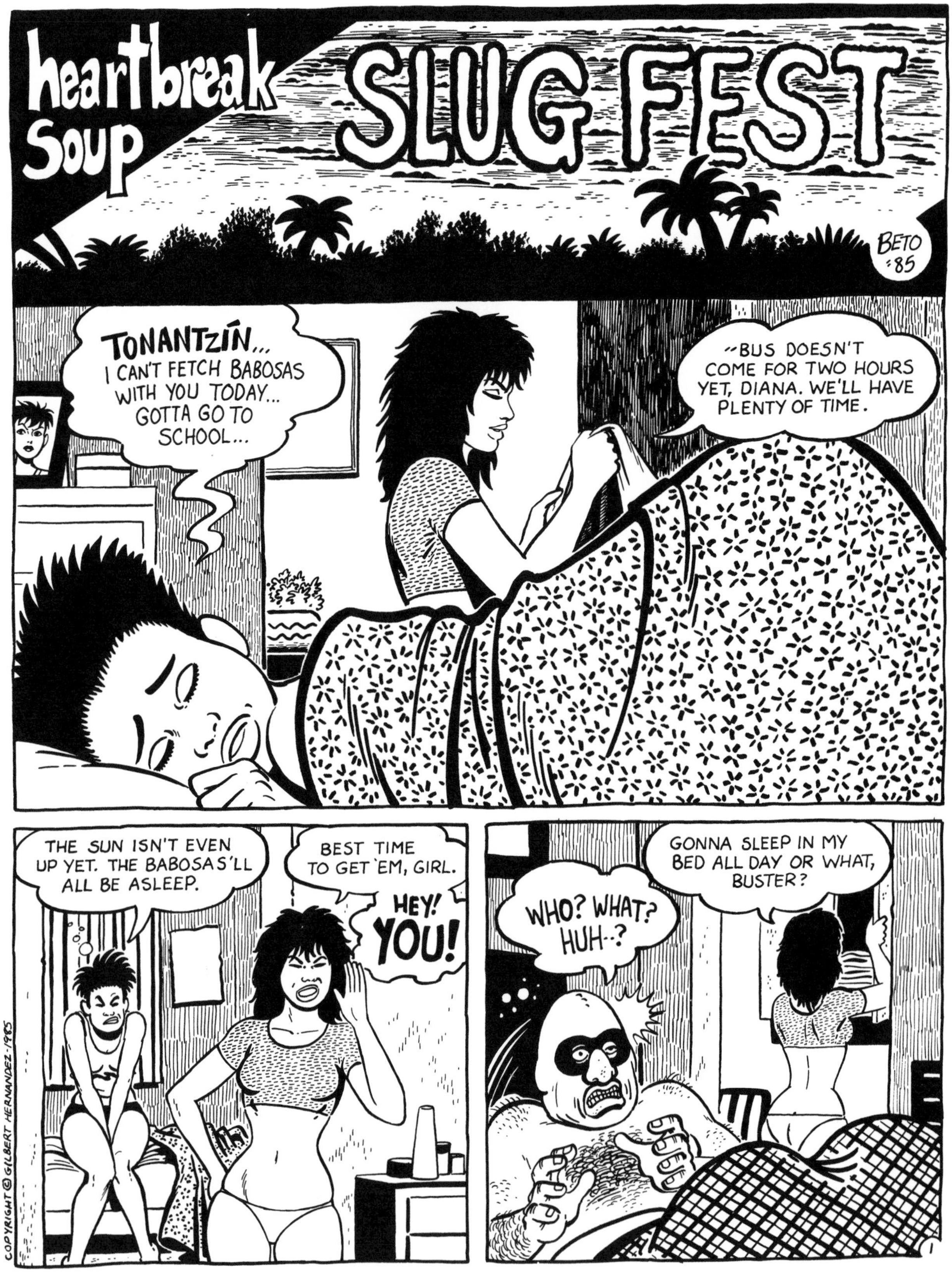
heartbreak Soup
SLUG FEST
BETO '85
TONANTZÍN... I CAN'T FETCH BABOSAS WITH YOU TODAY... GOTTA GO TO SCHOOL...
--BUS DOESN'T COME FOR TWO HOURS YET, DIANA. WE'LL HAVE PLENTY OF TIME.
THE SUN ISN'T EVEN UP YET. THE BABOSA'S'LL ALL BE ASLEEP.
BEST TIME TO GET 'EM, GIRL.
HEY! YOU!
COPYRIGHT © GILBERT HERNANDEZ · 1985
GONNA SLEEP IN MY BED ALL DAY OR WHAT, BUSTER?
WHO? WHAT? HUH..?
1

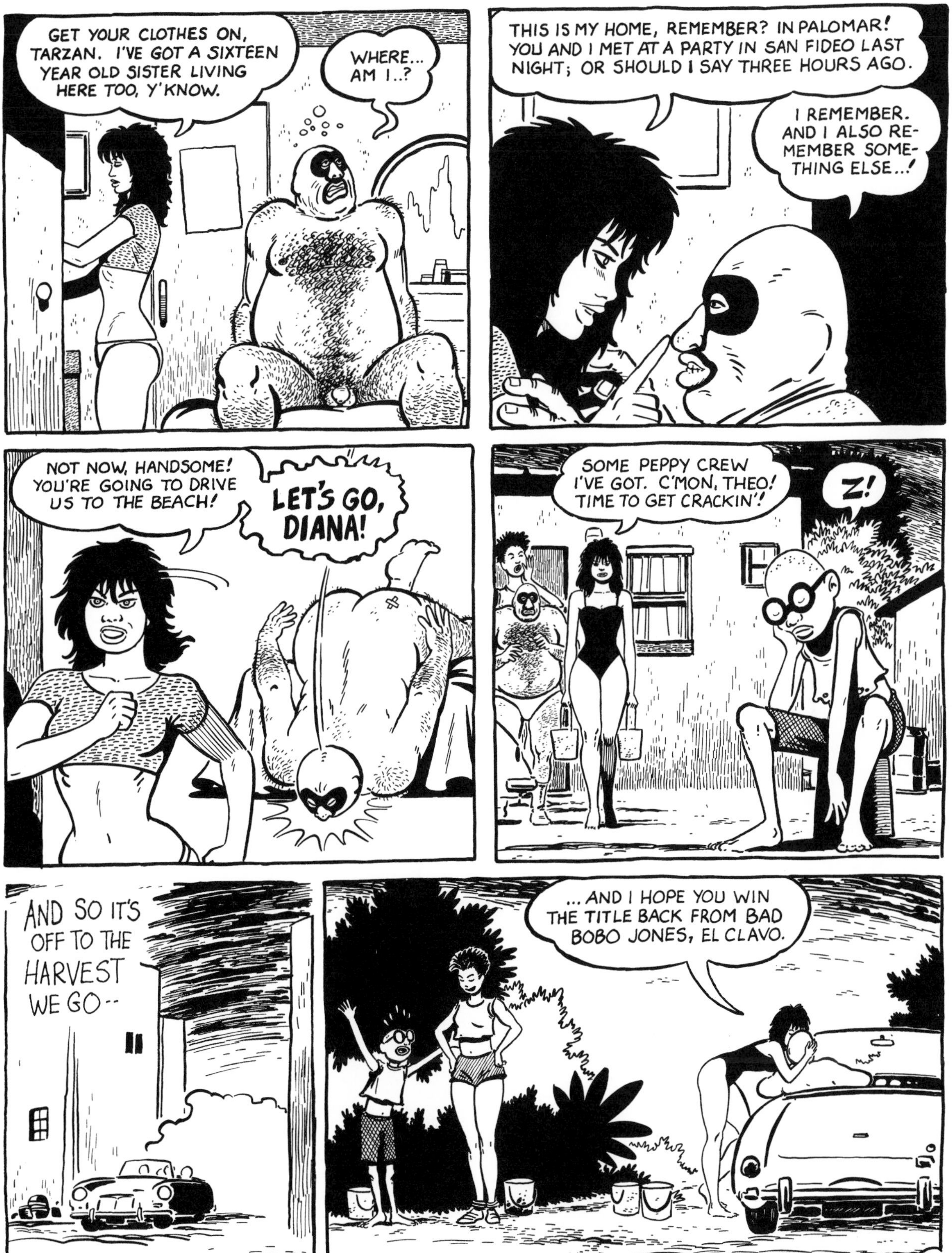
GET YOUR CLOTHES ON, TARZAN. I'VE GOT A SIXTEEN YEAR OLD SISTER LIVING HERE TOO, Y'KNOW.
WHERE... AM I..?
THIS IS MY HOME, REMEMBER? IN PALOMAR! YOU AND I MET AT A PARTY IN SAN FIDEO LAST NIGHT; OR SHOULD I SAY THREE HOURS AGO.
I REMEMBER. AND I ALSO REMEMBER SOMETHING ELSE..!
NOT NOW, HANDSOME! YOU'RE GOING TO DRIVE US TO THE BEACH!
LET'S GO, DIANA!
SOME PEPPY CREW I'VE GOT. C'MON, THEO! TIME TO GET CRACKIN'!
Z!
AND SO IT'S OFF TO THE HARVEST WE GO--
...AND I HOPE YOU WIN THE TITLE BACK FROM BAD BOBO JONES, EL CLAVO.
2
CLAVO-SPIKE

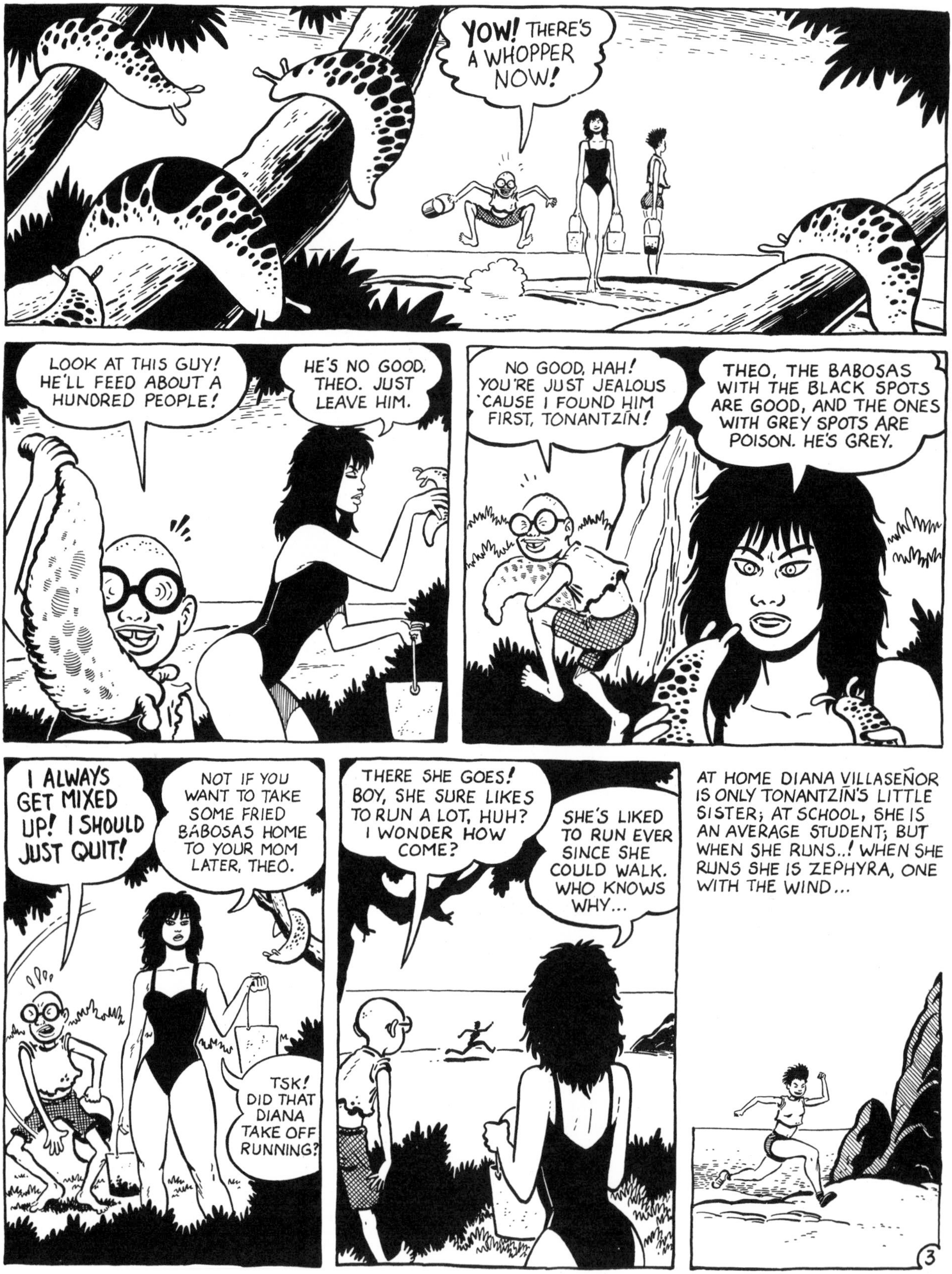
YOW! THERE'S A WHOPPER NOW!
LOOK AT THIS GUY! HE'LL FEED ABOUT A HUNDRED PEOPLE!
HE'S NO GOOD, THEO. JUST LEAVE HIM.
NO GOOD, HAH! YOU'RE JUST JEALOUS 'CAUSE I FOUND HIM FIRST, TONANTZÍN!
THEO, THE BABOSAS WITH THE BLACK SPOTS ARE GOOD, AND THE ONES WITH GREY SPOTS ARE POISON. HE'S GREY.
I ALWAYS GET MIXED UP! I SHOULD JUST QUIT!
NOT IF YOU WANT TO TAKE SOME FRIED BABOSAS HOME TO YOUR MOM LATER, THEO.
TSK! DID THAT DIANA TAKE OFF RUNNING?
THERE SHE GOES! BOY, SHE SURE LIKES TO RUN A LOT, HUH? I WONDER HOW COME?
SHE'S LIKED TO RUN EVER SINCE SHE COULD WALK. WHO KNOWS WHY...
AT HOME DIANA VILLASEÑOR IS ONLY TONANTZÍN'S LITTLE SISTER; AT SCHOOL, SHE IS AN AVERAGE STUDENT; BUT WHEN SHE RUNS..! WHEN SHE RUNS SHE IS ZEPHYRA, ONE WITH THE WIND...
3

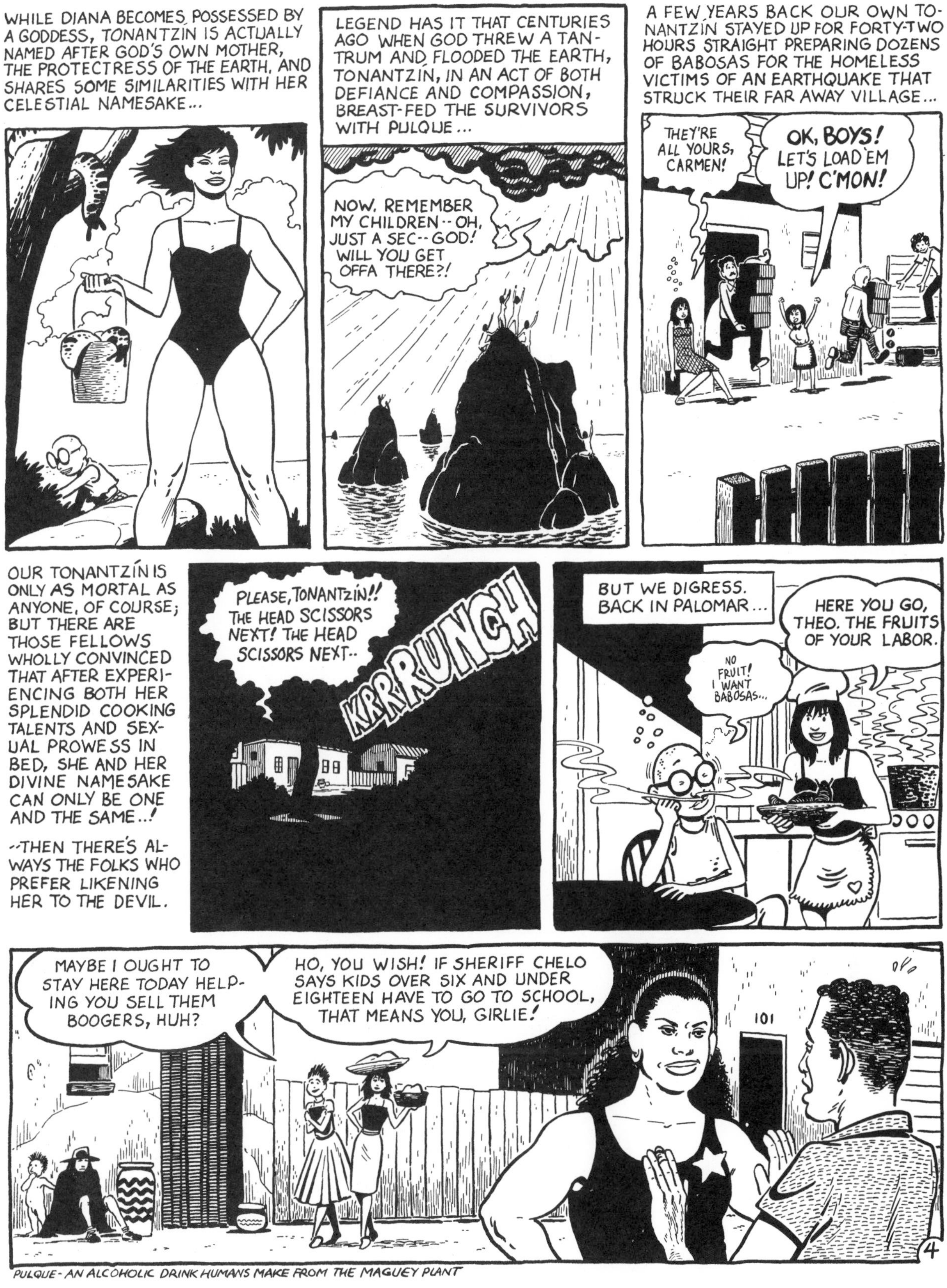
WHILE DIANA BECOMES POSSESSED BY A GODDESS, TONANTZÍN IS ACTUALLY NAMED AFTER GOD'S OWN MOTHER, THE PROTECTRESS OF THE EARTH, AND SHARES SOME SIMILARITIES WITH HER CELESTIAL NAMESAKE...
LEGEND HAS IT THAT CENTURIES AGO WHEN GOD THREW A TANTRUM AND FLOODED THE EARTH, TONANTZÍN, IN AN ACT OF BOTH DEFIANCE AND COMPASSION, BREAST-FED THE SURVIVORS WITH PULQUE...
NOW, REMEMBER MY CHILDREN--OH, JUST A SEC--GOD! WILL YOU GET OFFA THERE?!
A FEW YEARS BACK OUR OWN TONANTZÍN STAYED UP FOR FORTY-TWO HOURS STRAIGHT PREPARING DOZENS OF BABOSAS FOR THE HOMELESS VICTIMS OF AN EARTHQUAKE THAT STRUCK THEIR FAR AWAY VILLAGE...
THEY'RE ALL YOURS, CARMEN!
OK, BOYS! LET'S LOAD 'EM UP! C'MON!
OUR TONANTZÍN IS ONLY AS MORTAL AS ANYONE, OF COURSE; BUT THERE ARE THOSE FELLOWS WHOLLY CONVINCED THAT AFTER EXPERIENCING BOTH HER SPLENDID COOKING TALENTS AND SEXUAL PROWESS IN BED, SHE AND HER DIVINE NAMESAKE CAN ONLY BE ONE AND THE SAME...!
--THEN THERE'S ALWAYS THE FOLKS WHO PREFER LIKENING HER TO THE DEVIL.
PLEASE, TONANTZÍN!! THE HEAD SCISSORS NEXT! THE HEAD SCISSORS NEXT..
KRRRUNCH
BUT WE DIGRESS. BACK IN PALOMAR...
HERE YOU GO, THEO. THE FRUITS OF YOUR LABOR.
NO FRUIT! I WANT BABOSAS...
MAYBE I OUGHT TO STAY HERE TODAY HELPING YOU SELL THEM BOOGERS, HUH?
HO, YOU WISH! IF SHERIFF CHELO SAYS KIDS OVER SIX AND UNDER EIGHTEEN HAVE TO GO TO SCHOOL, THAT MEANS YOU, GIRLIE!
101
4

PULQUE - AN ALCOHOLIC DRINK HUMANS MAKE FROM THE MAGUEY PLANT

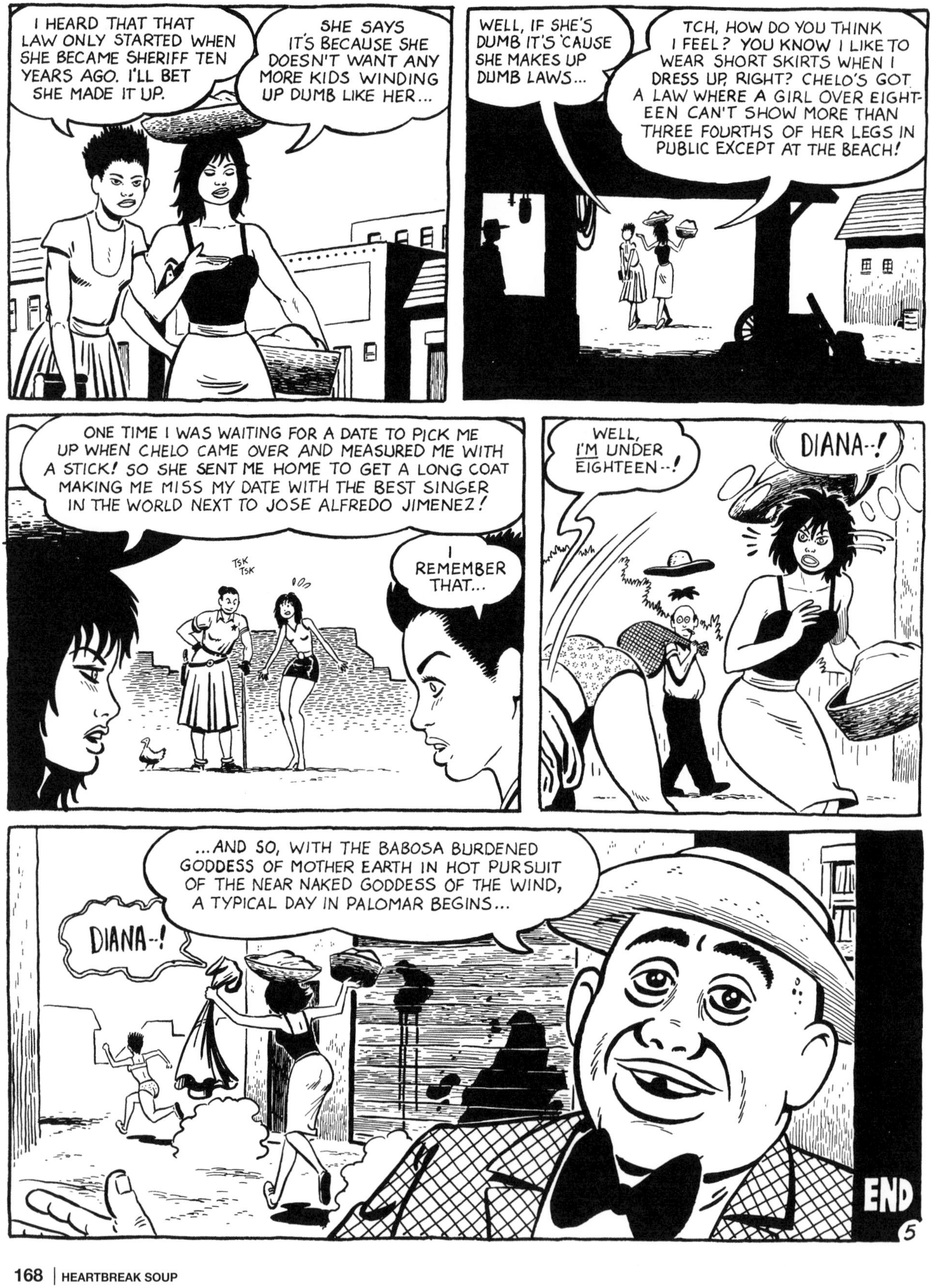
I HEARD THAT THAT LAW ONLY STARTED WHEN SHE BECAME SHERIFF TEN YEARS AGO. I'LL BET SHE MADE IT UP.
SHE SAYS IT'S BECAUSE SHE DOESN'T WANT ANY MORE KIDS WINDING UP DUMB LIKE HER...
WELL, IF SHE'S DUMB IT'S 'CAUSE SHE MAKES UP DUMB LAWS...
TCH, HOW DO YOU THINK I FEEL? YOU KNOW I LIKE TO WEAR SHORT SKIRTS WHEN I DRESS UP, RIGHT? CHELO'S GOT A LAW WHERE A GIRL OVER EIGHTEEN CAN'T SHOW MORE THAN THREE FOURTHS OF HER LEGS IN PUBLIC EXCEPT AT THE BEACH!
ONE TIME I WAS WAITING FOR A DATE TO PICK ME UP WHEN CHELO CAME OVER AND MEASURED ME WITH A STICK! SO SHE SENT ME HOME TO GET A LONG COAT MAKING ME MISS MY DATE WITH THE BEST SINGER IN THE WORLD NEXT TO JOSE ALFREDO JIMENEZ!
TSK TSK
I REMEMBER THAT...
WELL, I'M UNDER EIGHTEEN--!
DIANA--!
...AND SO, WITH THE BABOSA BURDENED GODDESS OF MOTHER EARTH IN HOT PURSUIT OF THE NEAR NAKED GODDESS OF THE WIND, A TYPICAL DAY IN PALOMAR BEGINS...
DIANA--!
END
5

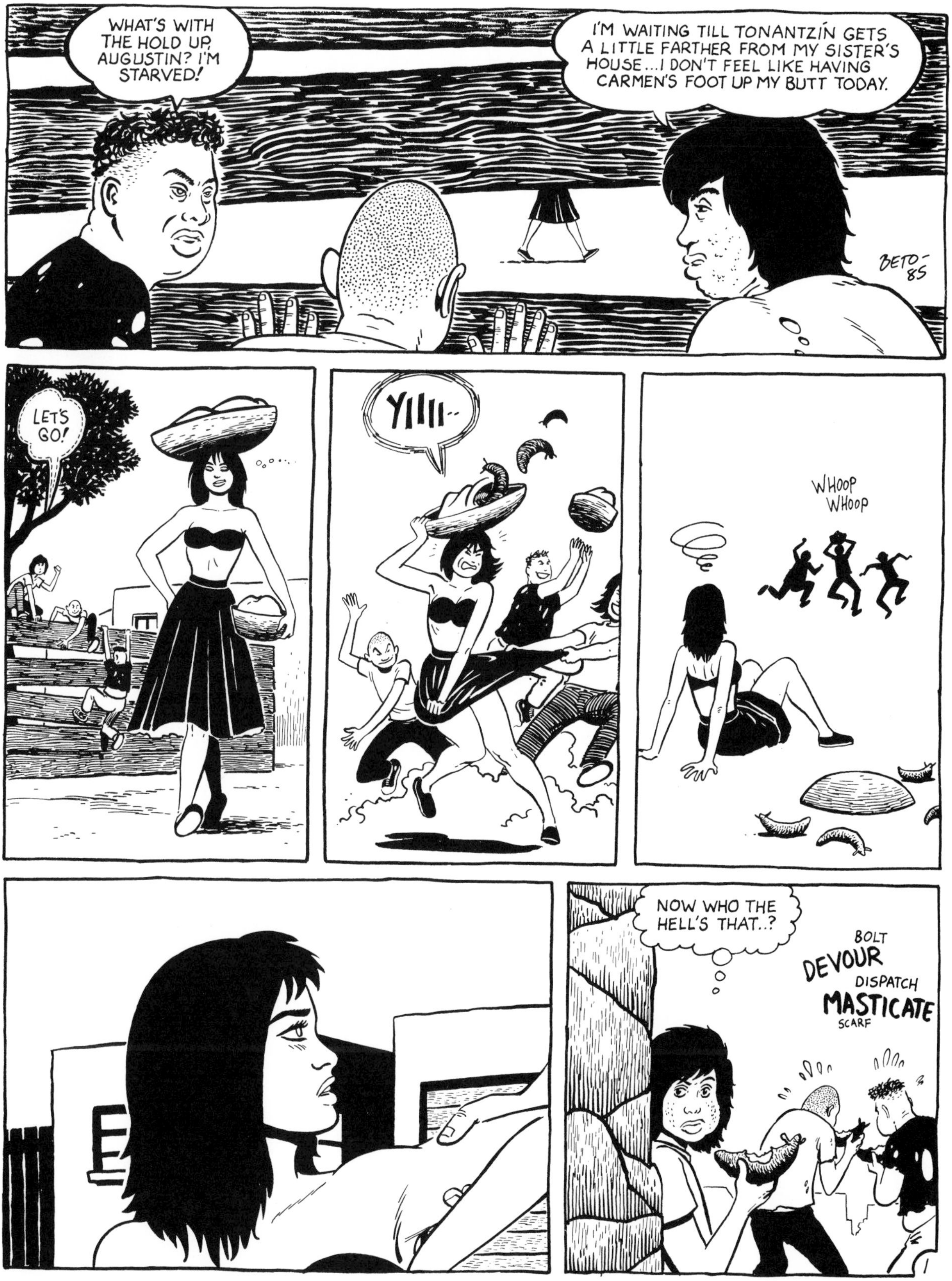

WHAT'S WITH THE HOLD UP, AUGUSTIN? I'M STARVED!
I'M WAITING TILL TONANTZÍN GETS A LITTLE FARTHER FROM MY SISTER'S HOUSE...I DON'T FEEL LIKE HAVING CARMEN'S FOOT UP MY BUTT TODAY.
BETO-85
LET'S GO!
YIIII--
WHOOP WHOOP
NOW WHO THE HELL'S THAT..?
BOLT
DEVOUR
DISPATCH
MASTICATE
SCARF

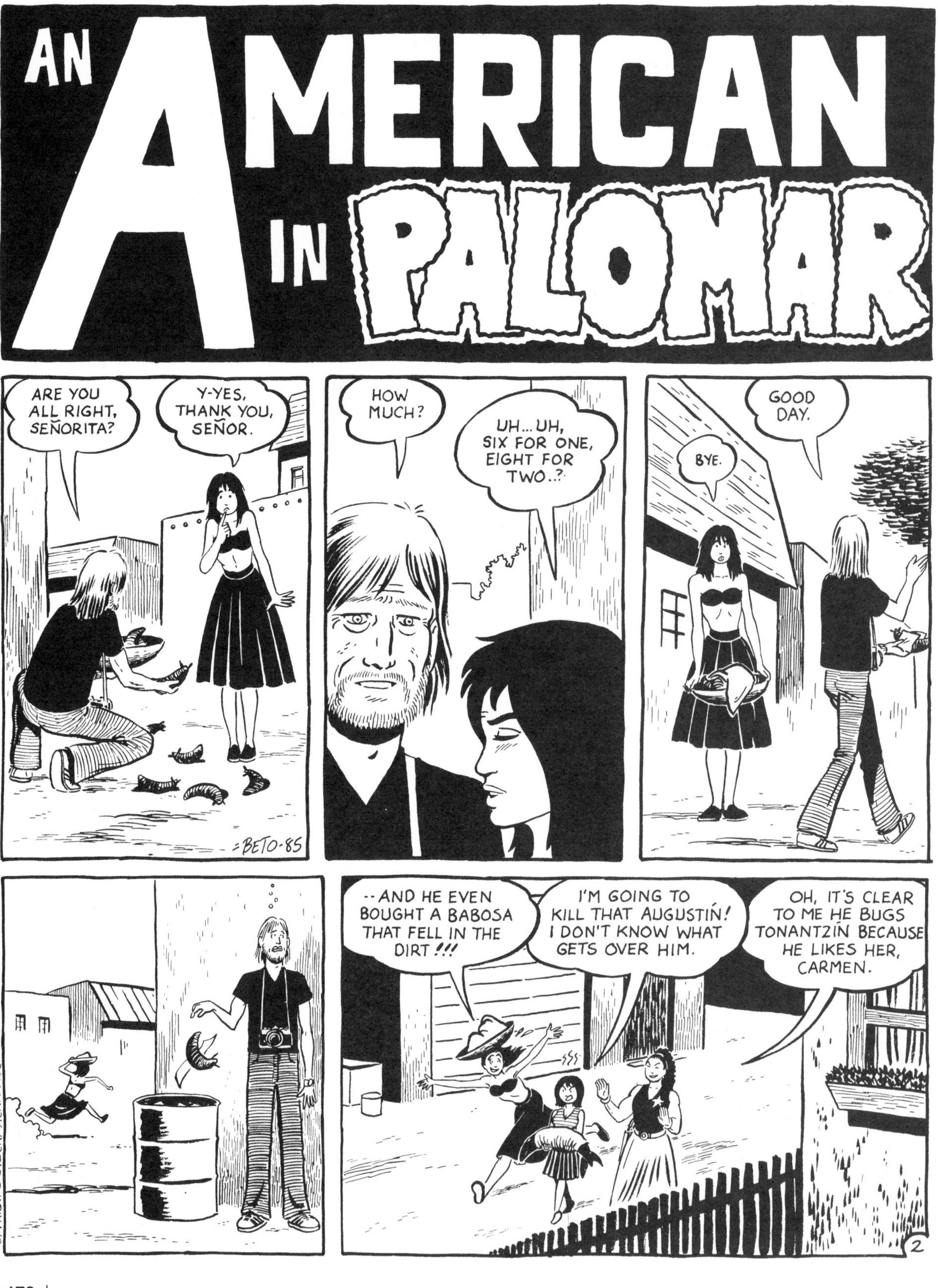
AN AMERICAN IN PALOMAR
ARE YOU ALL RIGHT, SEÑORITA?
Y-YES, THANK YOU, SEÑOR.
BETO·85
HOW MUCH?
UH... UH, SIX FOR ONE, EIGHT FOR TWO..?
GOOD DAY.
BYE.
COPYRIGHT © GILBERT HERNANDEZ · 1985
--AND HE EVEN BOUGHT A BABOSA THAT FELL IN THE DIRT!!!
I'M GOING TO KILL THAT AUGUSTÍN! I DON'T KNOW WHAT GETS OVER HIM.
OH, IT'S CLEAR TO ME HE BUGS TONANTZÍN BECAUSE HE LIKES HER, CARMEN.
2

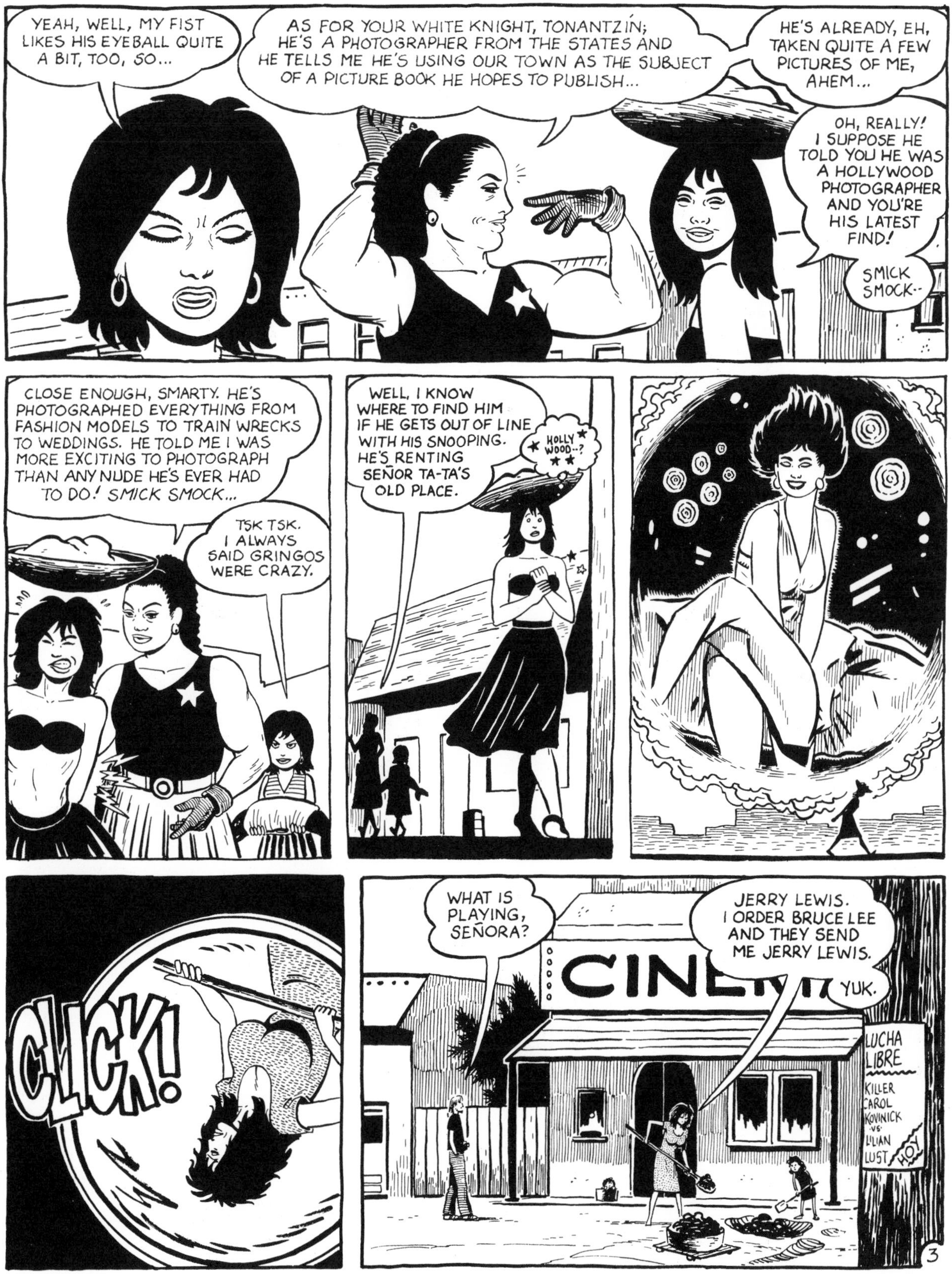
YEAH, WELL, MY FIST LIKES HIS EYEBALL QUITE A BIT, TOO, SO...
AS FOR YOUR WHITE KNIGHT, TONANTZÍN; HE'S A PHOTOGRAPHER FROM THE STATES AND HE TELLS ME HE'S USING OUR TOWN AS THE SUBJECT OF A PICTURE BOOK HE HOPES TO PUBLISH...
HE'S ALREADY, EH, TAKEN QUITE A FEW PICTURES OF ME, AHEM...
OH, REALLY! I SUPPOSE HE TOLD YOU HE WAS A HOLLYWOOD PHOTOGRAPHER AND YOU'RE HIS LATEST FIND!
SMICK SMOCK..
CLOSE ENOUGH, SMARTY. HE'S PHOTOGRAPHED EVERYTHING FROM FASHION MODELS TO TRAIN WRECKS TO WEDDINGS. HE TOLD ME I WAS MORE EXCITING TO PHOTOGRAPH THAN ANY NUDE HE'S EVER HAD TO DO! SMICK SMOCK...
TSK TSK. I ALWAYS SAID GRINGOS WERE CRAZY.
WELL, I KNOW WHERE TO FIND HIM IF HE GETS OUT OF LINE WITH HIS SNOOPING. HE'S RENTING SEÑOR TA-TA'S OLD PLACE.
HOLLY WOOD--?
CLICK!
WHAT IS PLAYING, SEÑORA?
JERRY LEWIS. I ORDER BRUCE LEE AND THEY SEND ME JERRY LEWIS.
YUK.
CINE
LUCHA LIBRE
KILLER CAROL KOVINICK VS. LILIAN LUST
HOY
3

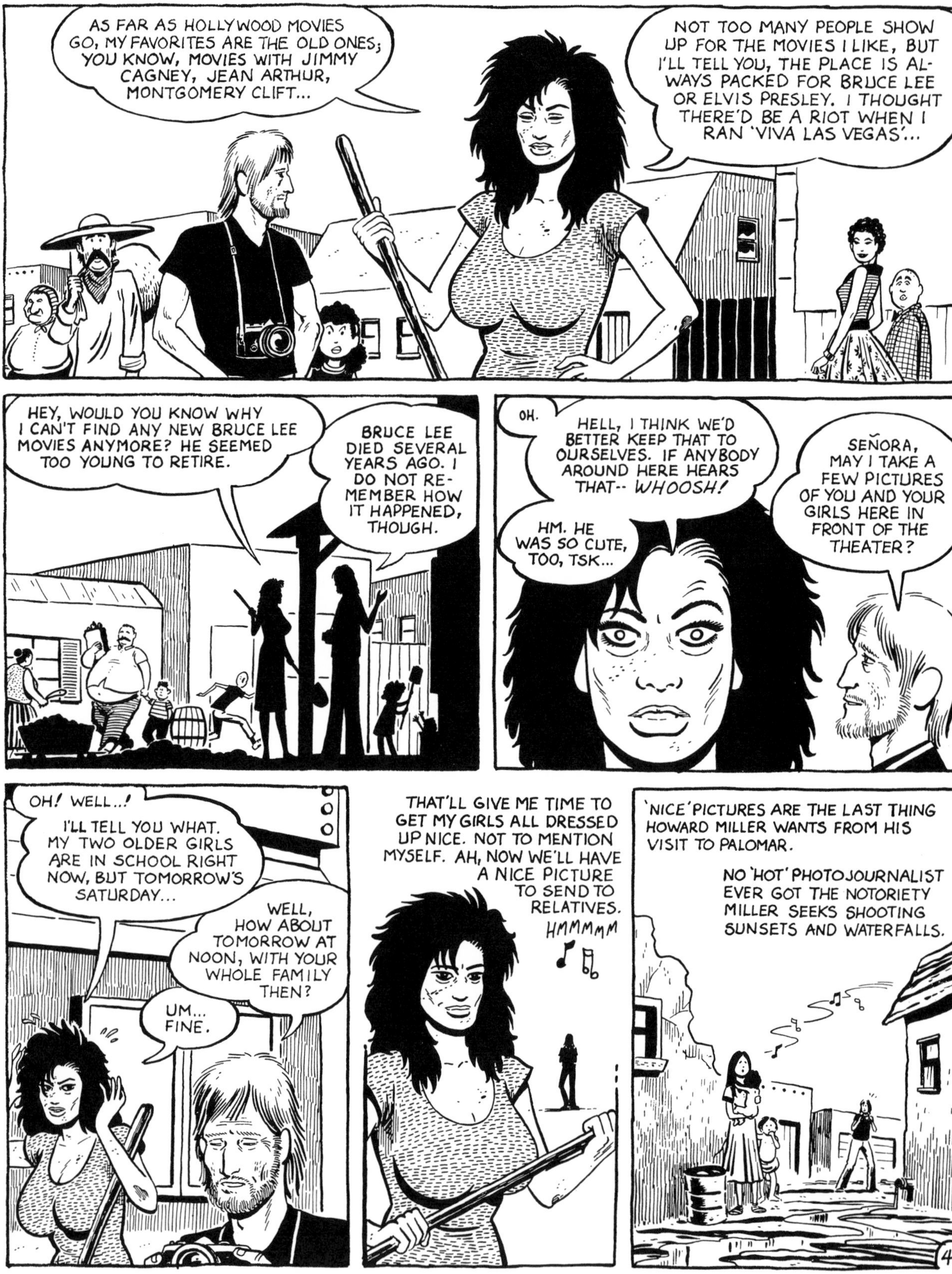
AS FAR AS HOLLYWOOD MOVIES GO, MY FAVORITES ARE THE OLD ONES; YOU KNOW, MOVIES WITH JIMMY CAGNEY, JEAN ARTHUR, MONTGOMERY CLIFT...
NOT TOO MANY PEOPLE SHOW UP FOR THE MOVIES I LIKE, BUT I'LL TELL YOU, THE PLACE IS ALWAYS PACKED FOR BRUCE LEE OR ELVIS PRESLEY. I THOUGHT THERE'D BE A RIOT WHEN I RAN 'VIVA LAS VEGAS'...
HEY, WOULD YOU KNOW WHY I CAN'T FIND ANY NEW BRUCE LEE MOVIES ANYMORE? HE SEEMED TOO YOUNG TO RETIRE.
BRUCE LEE DIED SEVERAL YEARS AGO. I DO NOT REMEMBER HOW IT HAPPENED, THOUGH.
OH.
HM. HE WAS SO CUTE, TOO, TSK...
HELL, I THINK WE'D BETTER KEEP THAT TO OURSELVES. IF ANYBODY AROUND HERE HEARS THAT-- WHOOSH!
SEÑORA, MAY I TAKE A FEW PICTURES OF YOU AND YOUR GIRLS HERE IN FRONT OF THE THEATER?
OH! WELL...!
I'LL TELL YOU WHAT. MY TWO OLDER GIRLS ARE IN SCHOOL RIGHT NOW, BUT TOMORROW'S SATURDAY...
WELL, HOW ABOUT TOMORROW AT NOON, WITH YOUR WHOLE FAMILY THEN?
UM... FINE.
THAT'LL GIVE ME TIME TO GET MY GIRLS ALL DRESSED UP NICE. NOT TO MENTION MYSELF. AH, NOW WE'LL HAVE A NICE PICTURE TO SEND TO RELATIVES.
HMMMMM
'NICE' PICTURES ARE THE LAST THING HOWARD MILLER WANTS FROM HIS VISIT TO PALOMAR.
NO 'HOT' PHOTOJOURNALIST EVER GOT THE NOTORIETY MILLER SEEKS SHOOTING SUNSETS AND WATERFALLS.
4

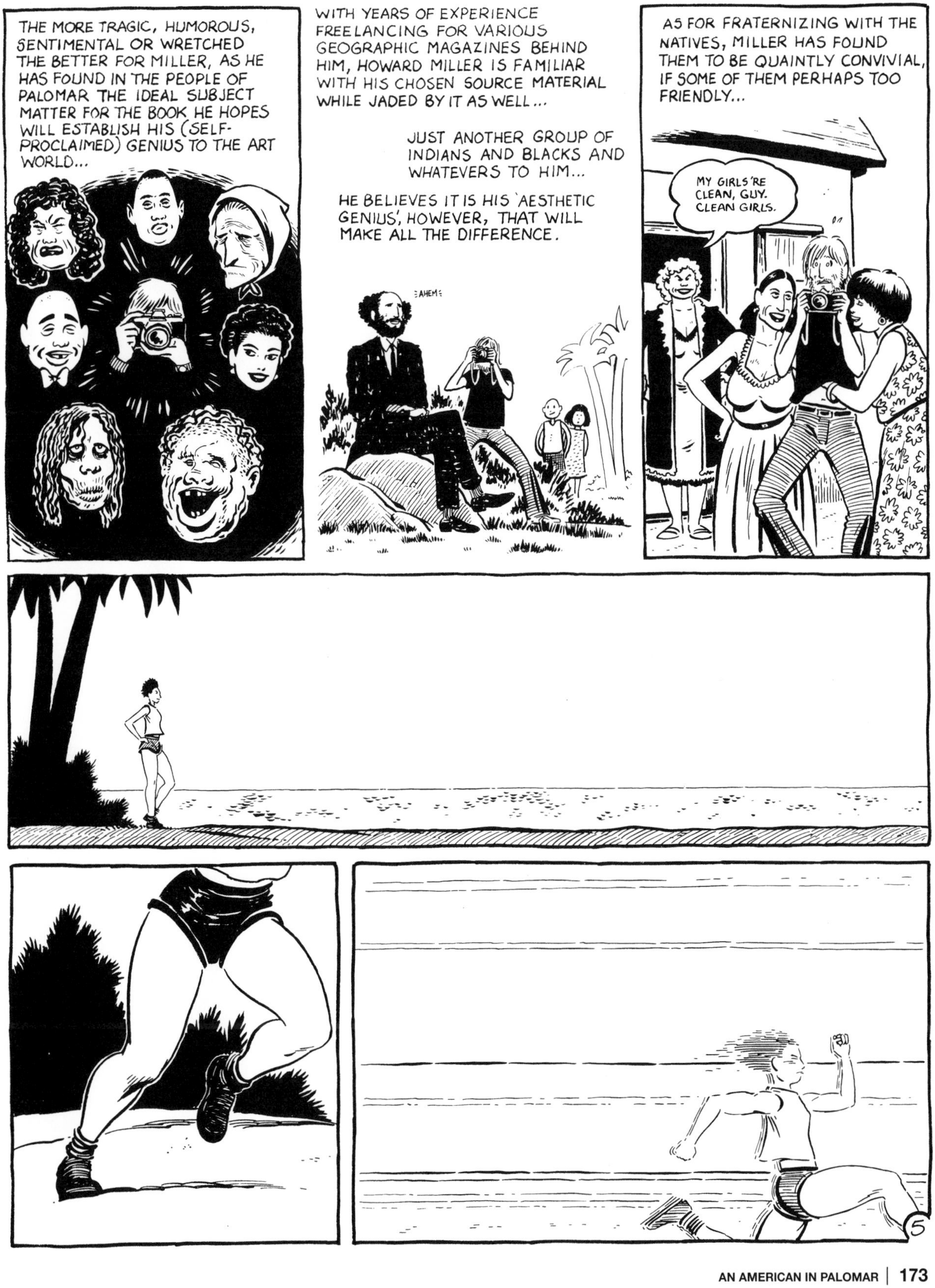
THE MORE TRAGIC, HUMOROUS, SENTIMENTAL OR WRETCHED THE BETTER FOR MILLER, AS HE HAS FOUND IN THE PEOPLE OF PALOMAR THE IDEAL SUBJECT MATTER FOR THE BOOK HE HOPES WILL ESTABLISH HIS (SELF-PROCLAIMED) GENIUS TO THE ART WORLD...
WITH YEARS OF EXPERIENCE FREELANCING FOR VARIOUS GEOGRAPHIC MAGAZINES BEHIND HIM, HOWARD MILLER IS FAMILIAR WITH HIS CHOSEN SOURCE MATERIAL WHILE JADED BY IT AS WELL...
JUST ANOTHER GROUP OF INDIANS AND BLACKS AND WHATEVERS TO HIM...
HE BELIEVES IT IS HIS 'AESTHETIC GENIUS', HOWEVER, THAT WILL MAKE ALL THE DIFFERENCE.
AHEM
AS FOR FRATERNIZING WITH THE NATIVES, MILLER HAS FOUND THEM TO BE QUAINTLY CONVIVIAL, IF SOME OF THEM PERHAPS TOO FRIENDLY...
MY GIRLS'RE CLEAN, GUY. CLEAN GIRLS.
5

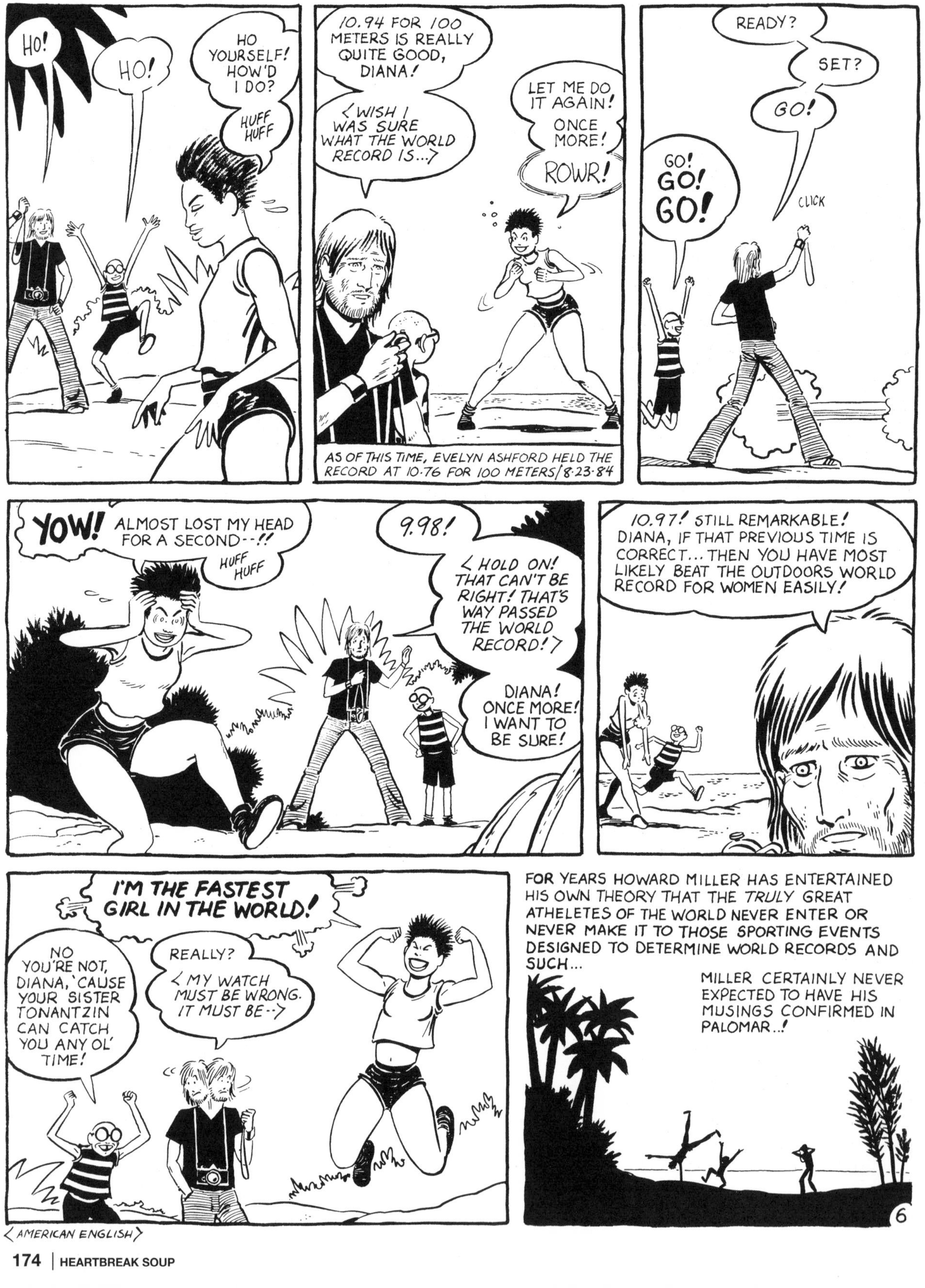
HO!
HO!
HO YOURSELF! HOW'D I DO?
HUFF HUFF
10.94 FOR 100 METERS IS REALLY QUITE GOOD, DIANA!
< WISH I WAS SURE WHAT THE WORLD RECORD IS... >
LET ME DO IT AGAIN! ONCE MORE!
ROWR!
AS OF THIS TIME, EVELYN ASHFORD HELD THE RECORD AT 10.76 FOR 100 METERS / 8·23·84
READY?
SET?
GO!
GO! GO! GO!
CLICK
YOW! ALMOST LOST MY HEAD FOR A SECOND--!!
HUFF HUFF
9.98!
< HOLD ON! THAT CAN'T BE RIGHT! THAT'S WAY PASSED THE WORLD RECORD! >
DIANA! ONCE MORE! I WANT TO BE SURE!
10.97! STILL REMARKABLE! DIANA, IF THAT PREVIOUS TIME IS CORRECT... THEN YOU HAVE MOST LIKELY BEAT THE OUTDOORS WORLD RECORD FOR WOMEN EASILY!
I'M THE FASTEST GIRL IN THE WORLD!
NO YOU'RE NOT, DIANA, 'CAUSE YOUR SISTER TONANTZIN CAN CATCH YOU ANY OL' TIME!
REALLY?
< MY WATCH MUST BE WRONG. IT MUST BE -- >
FOR YEARS HOWARD MILLER HAS ENTERTAINED HIS OWN THEORY THAT THE *TRULY* GREAT ATHELETES OF THE WORLD NEVER ENTER OR NEVER MAKE IT TO THOSE SPORTING EVENTS DESIGNED TO DETERMINE WORLD RECORDS AND SUCH...
MILLER CERTAINLY NEVER EXPECTED TO HAVE HIS MUSINGS CONFIRMED IN PALOMAR...!
6

< AMERICAN ENGLISH >

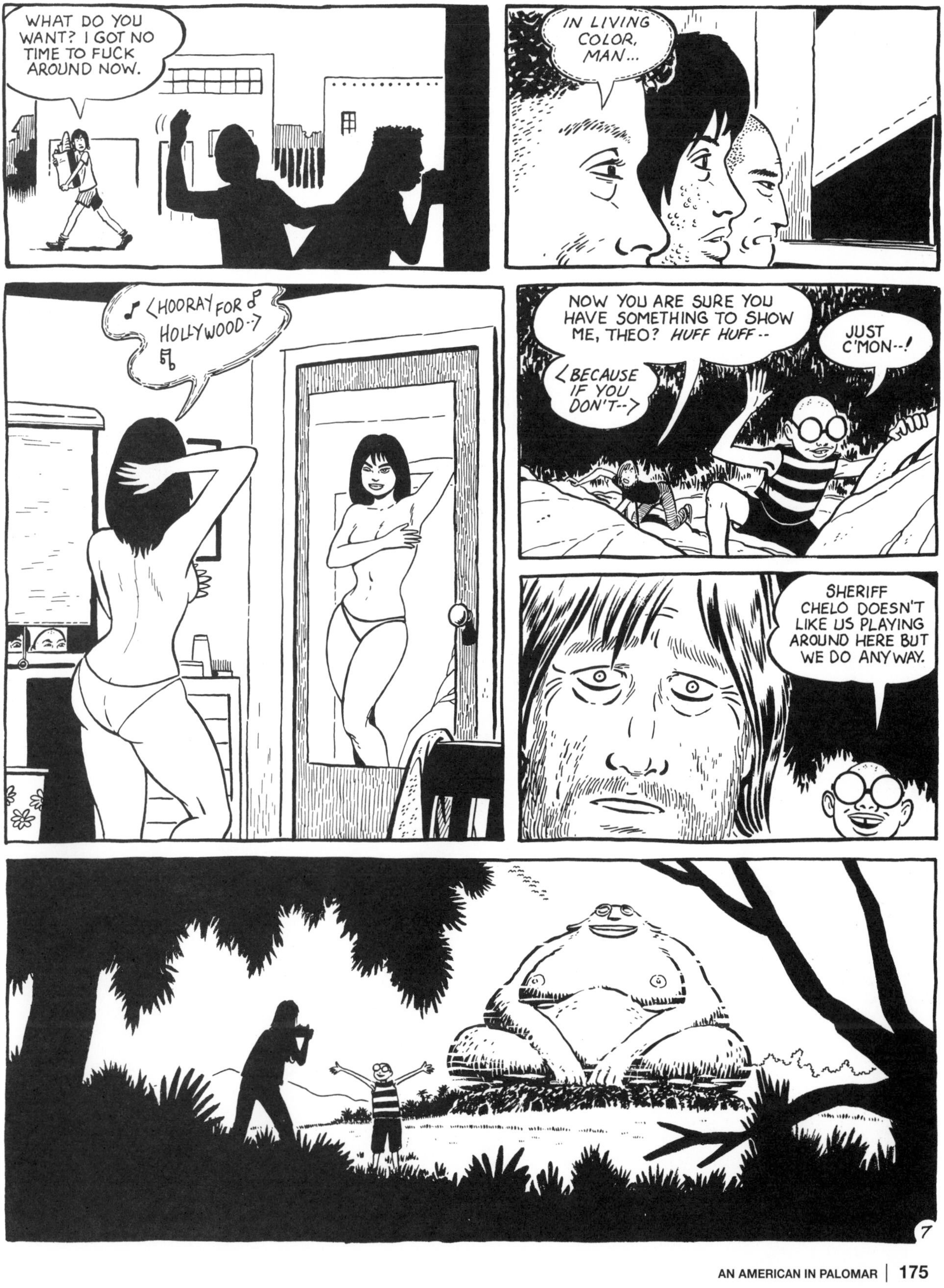
WHAT DO YOU WANT? I GOT NO TIME TO FUCK AROUND NOW.
IN LIVING COLOR, MAN...
⟨HOORAY FOR HOLLYWOOD--⟩
NOW YOU ARE SURE YOU HAVE SOMETHING TO SHOW ME, THEO? *HUFF HUFF* --
⟨BECAUSE IF YOU DON'T--⟩
JUST C'MON--!
SHERIFF CHELO DOESN'T LIKE US PLAYING AROUND HERE BUT WE DO ANYWAY.
7

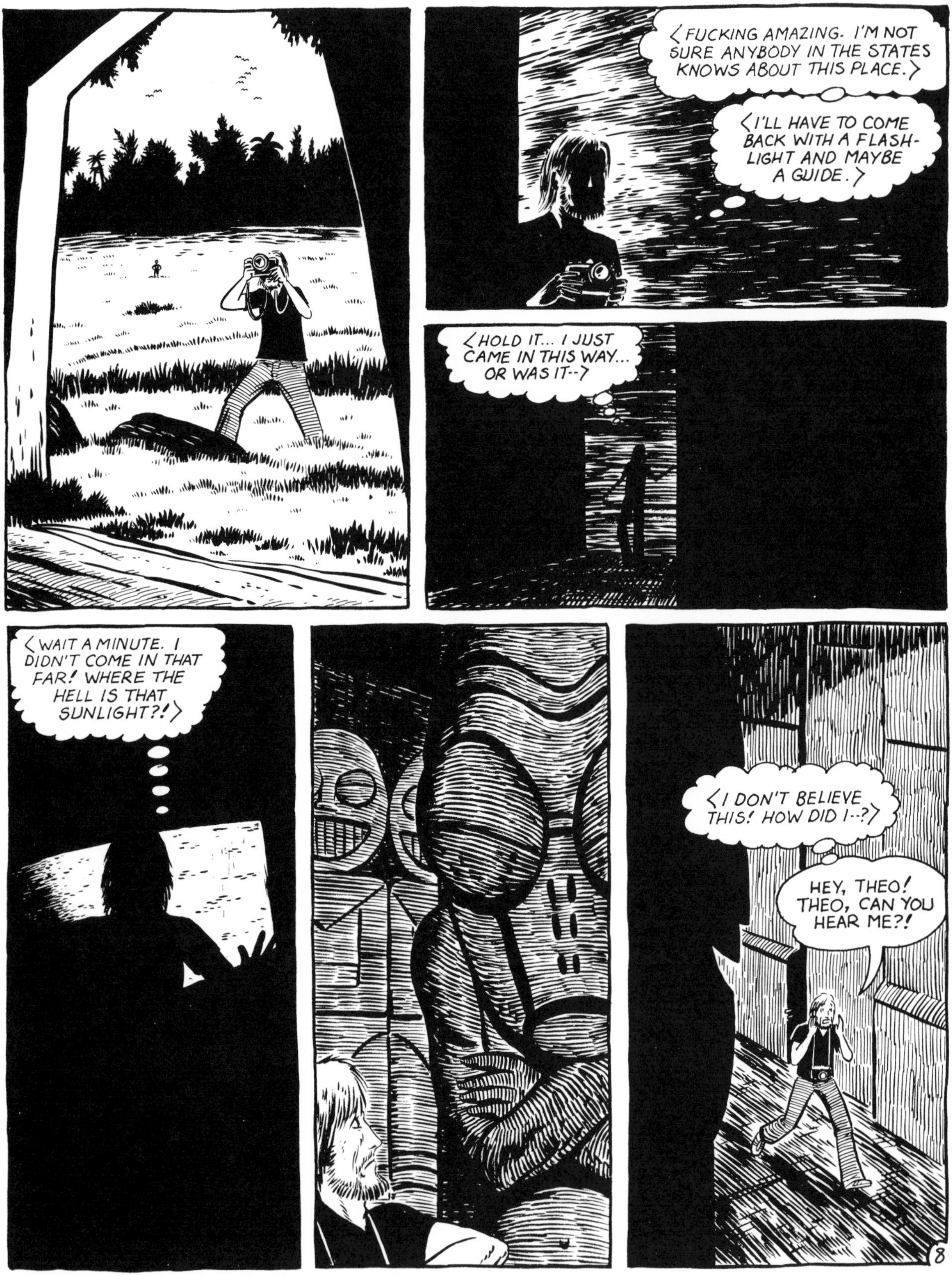
< FUCKING AMAZING. I'M NOT SURE ANYBODY IN THE STATES KNOWS ABOUT THIS PLACE. >
< I'LL HAVE TO COME BACK WITH A FLASH-LIGHT AND MAYBE A GUIDE. >
< HOLD IT... I JUST CAME IN THIS WAY... OR WAS IT-- >
< WAIT A MINUTE. I DIDN'T COME IN THAT FAR! WHERE THE HELL IS THAT SUNLIGHT?! >
< I DON'T BELIEVE THIS! HOW DID I--? >
HEY, THEO! THEO, CAN YOU HEAR ME?!
8

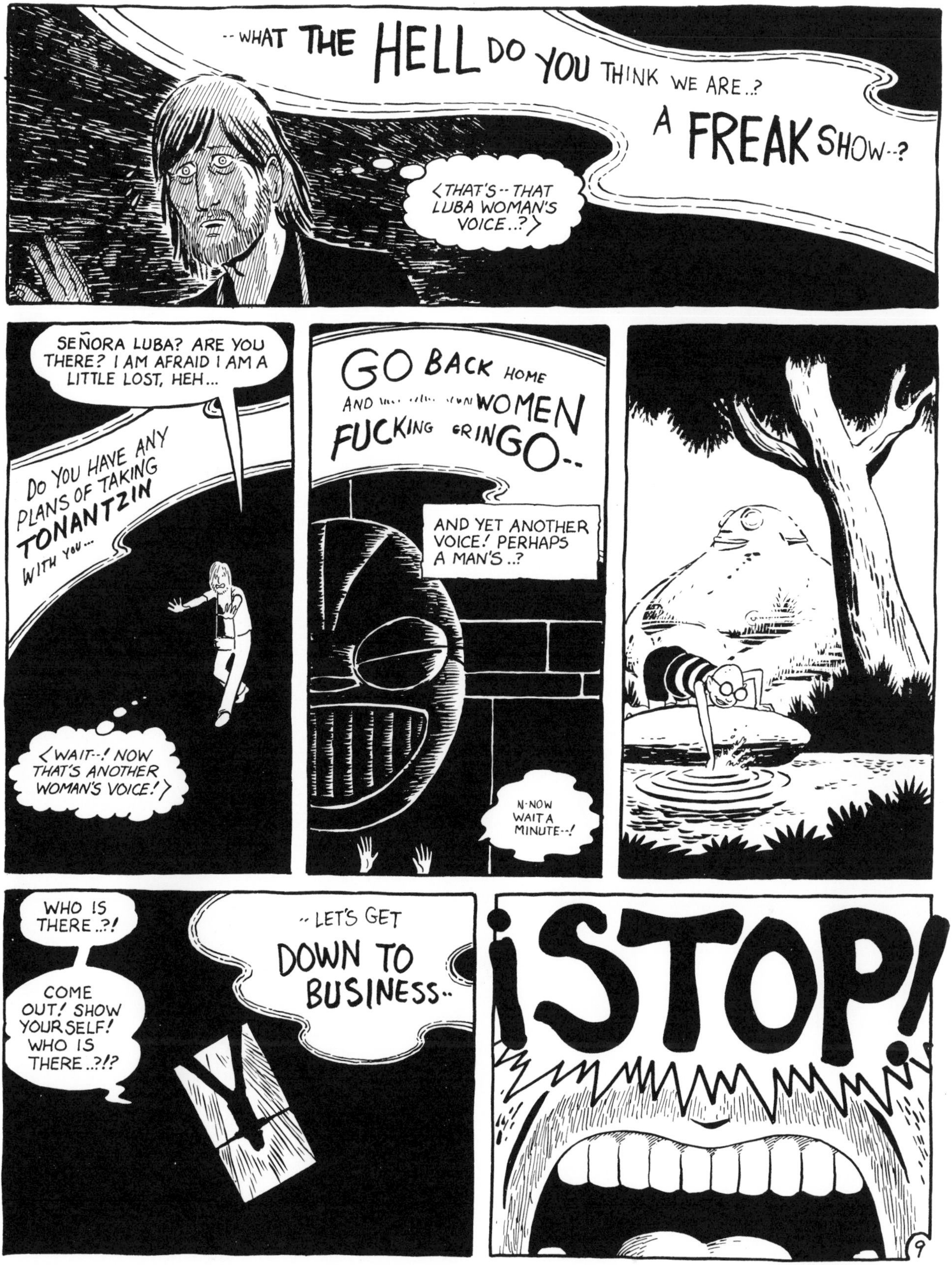
--WHAT THE HELL DO YOU THINK WE ARE..? A FREAK SHOW--?
<THAT'S--THAT LUBA WOMAN'S VOICE..?>
SEÑORA LUBA? ARE YOU THERE? I AM AFRAID I AM A LITTLE LOST, HEH...
DO YOU HAVE ANY PLANS OF TAKING TONANTZIN WITH YOU...
<WAIT--! NOW THAT'S ANOTHER WOMAN'S VOICE!>
GO BACK HOME AND
WOMEN FUCKING GRINGO--
AND YET ANOTHER VOICE! PERHAPS A MAN'S..?
N-NOW WAIT A MINUTE--!
WHO IS THERE..?!
COME OUT! SHOW YOURSELF! WHO IS THERE..?!?
--LET'S GET DOWN TO BUSINESS--
¡STOP!
9

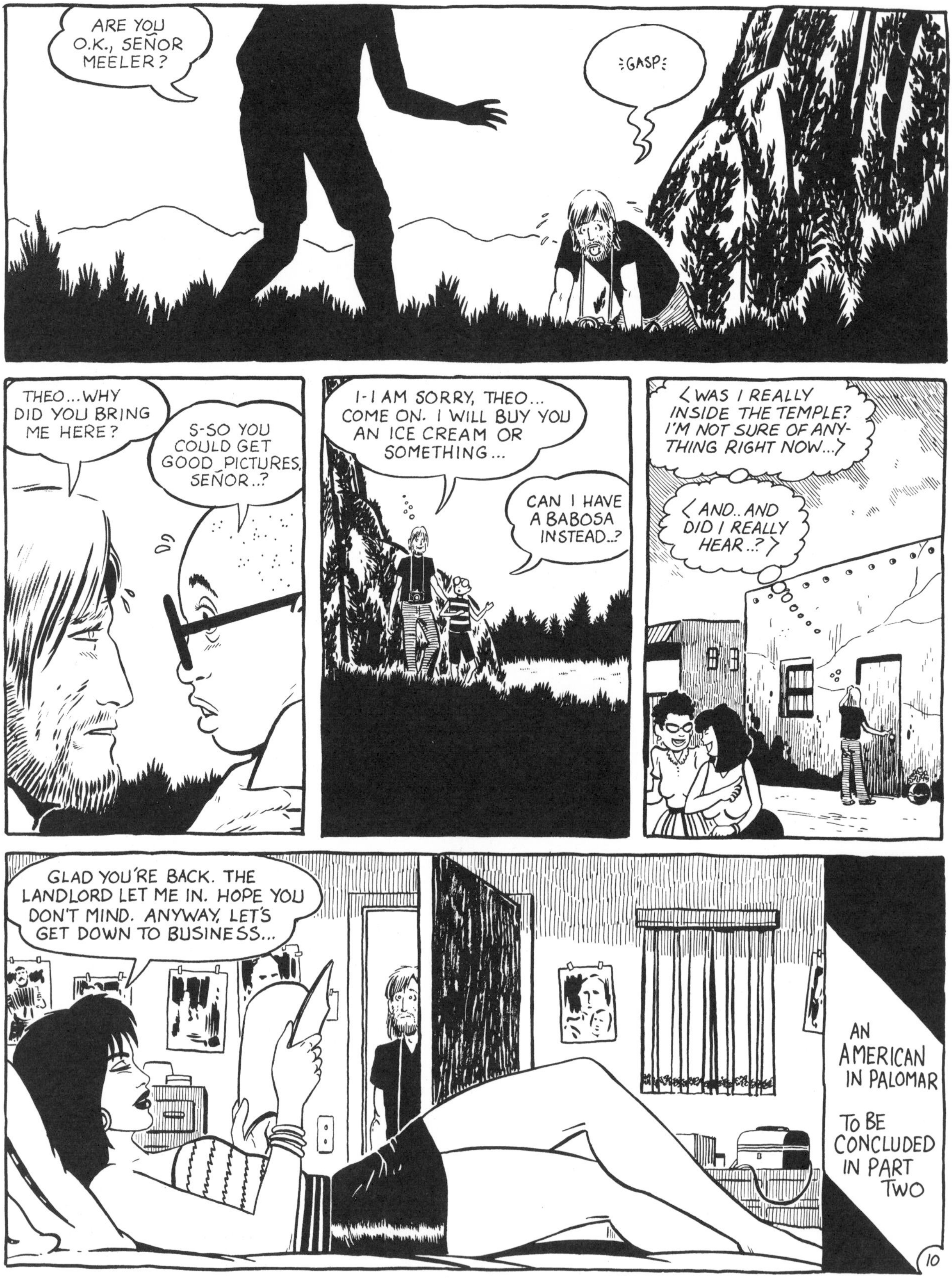
ARE YOU O.K., SEÑOR MEELER?
GASP
THEO... WHY DID YOU BRING ME HERE?
S-SO YOU COULD GET GOOD PICTURES, SEÑOR..?
I-I AM SORRY, THEO... COME ON. I WILL BUY YOU AN ICE CREAM OR SOMETHING...
CAN I HAVE A BABOSA INSTEAD..?
<WAS I REALLY INSIDE THE TEMPLE? I'M NOT SURE OF ANYTHING RIGHT NOW...>
<AND.. AND DID I REALLY HEAR..?>
GLAD YOU'RE BACK. THE LANDLORD LET ME IN. HOPE YOU DON'T MIND. ANYWAY, LET'S GET DOWN TO BUSINESS...
AN AMERICAN IN PALOMAR
TO BE CONCLUDED IN PART TWO
10

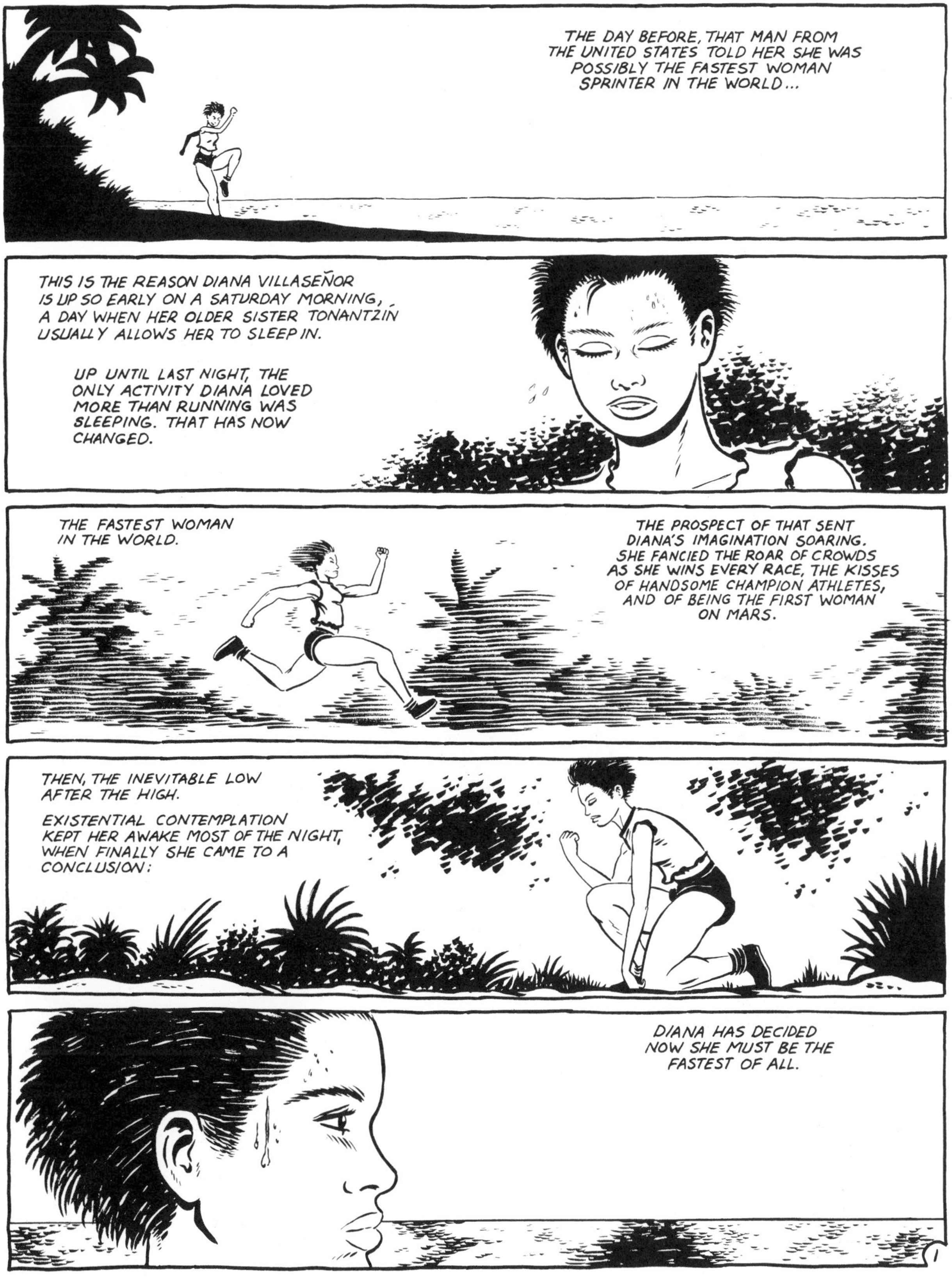
THE DAY BEFORE, THAT MAN FROM THE UNITED STATES TOLD HER SHE WAS POSSIBLY THE FASTEST WOMAN SPRINTER IN THE WORLD...
THIS IS THE REASON DIANA VILLASEÑOR IS UP SO EARLY ON A SATURDAY MORNING, A DAY WHEN HER OLDER SISTER TONANTZÍN USUALLY ALLOWS HER TO SLEEP IN.
UP UNTIL LAST NIGHT, THE ONLY ACTIVITY DIANA LOVED MORE THAN RUNNING WAS SLEEPING. THAT HAS NOW CHANGED.
THE FASTEST WOMAN IN THE WORLD.
THE PROSPECT OF THAT SENT DIANA'S IMAGINATION SOARING. SHE FANCIED THE ROAR OF CROWDS AS SHE WINS EVERY RACE, THE KISSES OF HANDSOME CHAMPION ATHLETES, AND OF BEING THE FIRST WOMAN ON MARS.
THEN, THE INEVITABLE LOW AFTER THE HIGH.
EXISTENTIAL CONTEMPLATION KEPT HER AWAKE MOST OF THE NIGHT, WHEN FINALLY SHE CAME TO A CONCLUSION:
DIANA HAS DECIDED NOW SHE MUST BE THE FASTEST OF ALL.
1

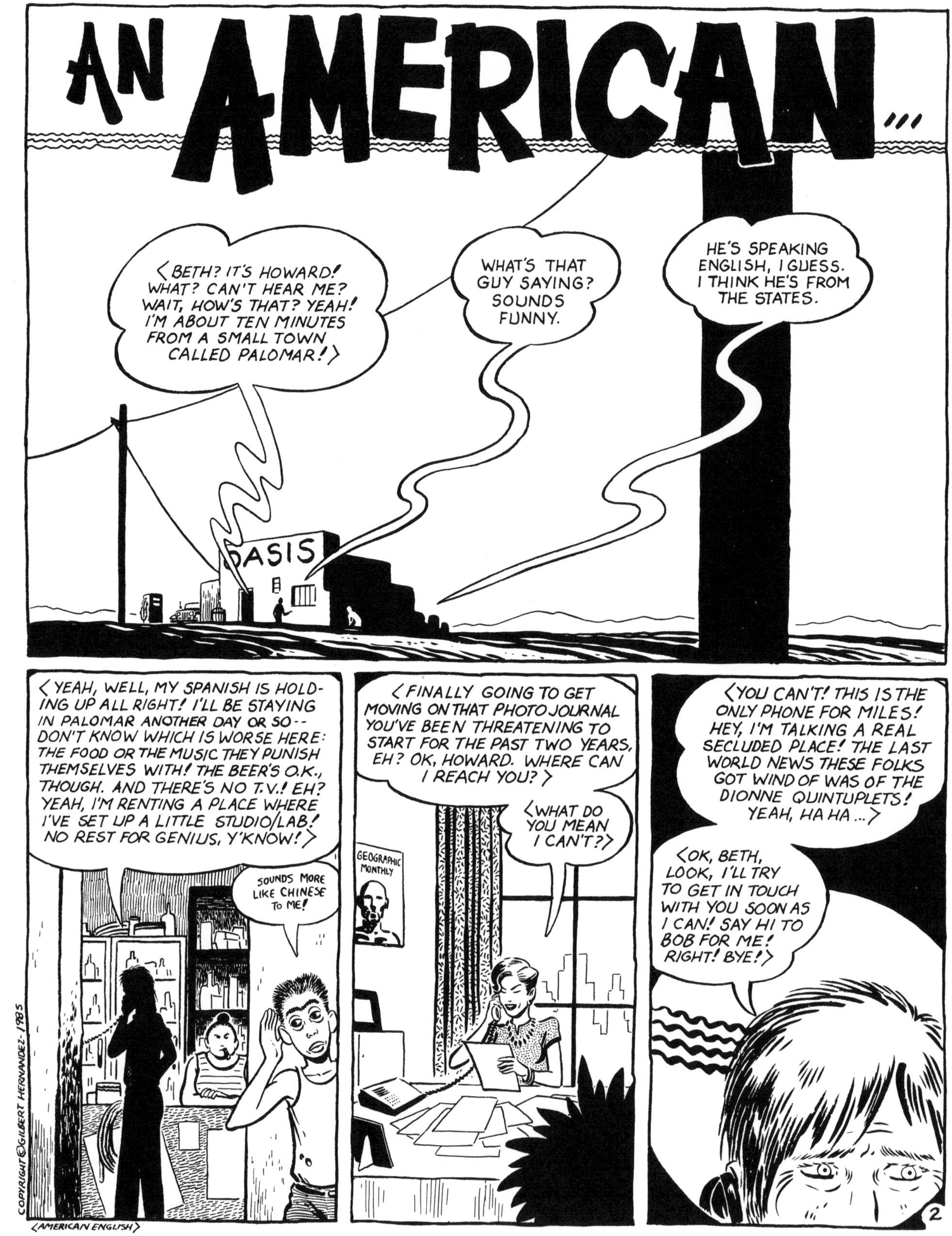

AN AMERICAN...
< BETH? IT'S HOWARD! WHAT? CAN'T HEAR ME? WAIT, HOW'S THAT? YEAH! I'M ABOUT TEN MINUTES FROM A SMALL TOWN CALLED PALOMAR! >
WHAT'S THAT GUY SAYING? SOUNDS FUNNY.
HE'S SPEAKING ENGLISH, I GUESS. I THINK HE'S FROM THE STATES.
OASIS
< YEAH, WELL, MY SPANISH IS HOLDING UP ALL RIGHT! I'LL BE STAYING IN PALOMAR ANOTHER DAY OR SO-- DON'T KNOW WHICH IS WORSE HERE: THE FOOD OR THE MUSIC THEY PUNISH THEMSELVES WITH! THE BEER'S O.K., THOUGH. AND THERE'S NO T.V.! EH? YEAH, I'M RENTING A PLACE WHERE I'VE SET UP A LITTLE STUDIO/LAB! NO REST FOR GENIUS, Y'KNOW! >
SOUNDS MORE LIKE CHINESE TO ME!
COPYRIGHT © GILBERT HERNANDEZ · 1985
< AMERICAN ENGLISH >
< FINALLY GOING TO GET MOVING ON THAT PHOTO JOURNAL YOU'VE BEEN THREATENING TO START FOR THE PAST TWO YEARS, EH? OK, HOWARD. WHERE CAN I REACH YOU? >
< WHAT DO YOU MEAN I CAN'T? >
GEOGRAPHIC MONTHLY
< YOU CAN'T! THIS IS THE ONLY PHONE FOR MILES! HEY, I'M TALKING A REAL SECLUDED PLACE! THE LAST WORLD NEWS THESE FOLKS GOT WIND OF WAS OF THE DIONNE QUINTUPLETS! YEAH, HA HA ... >
< OK, BETH, LOOK, I'LL TRY TO GET IN TOUCH WITH YOU SOON AS I CAN! SAY HI TO BOB FOR ME! RIGHT! BYE! >
2

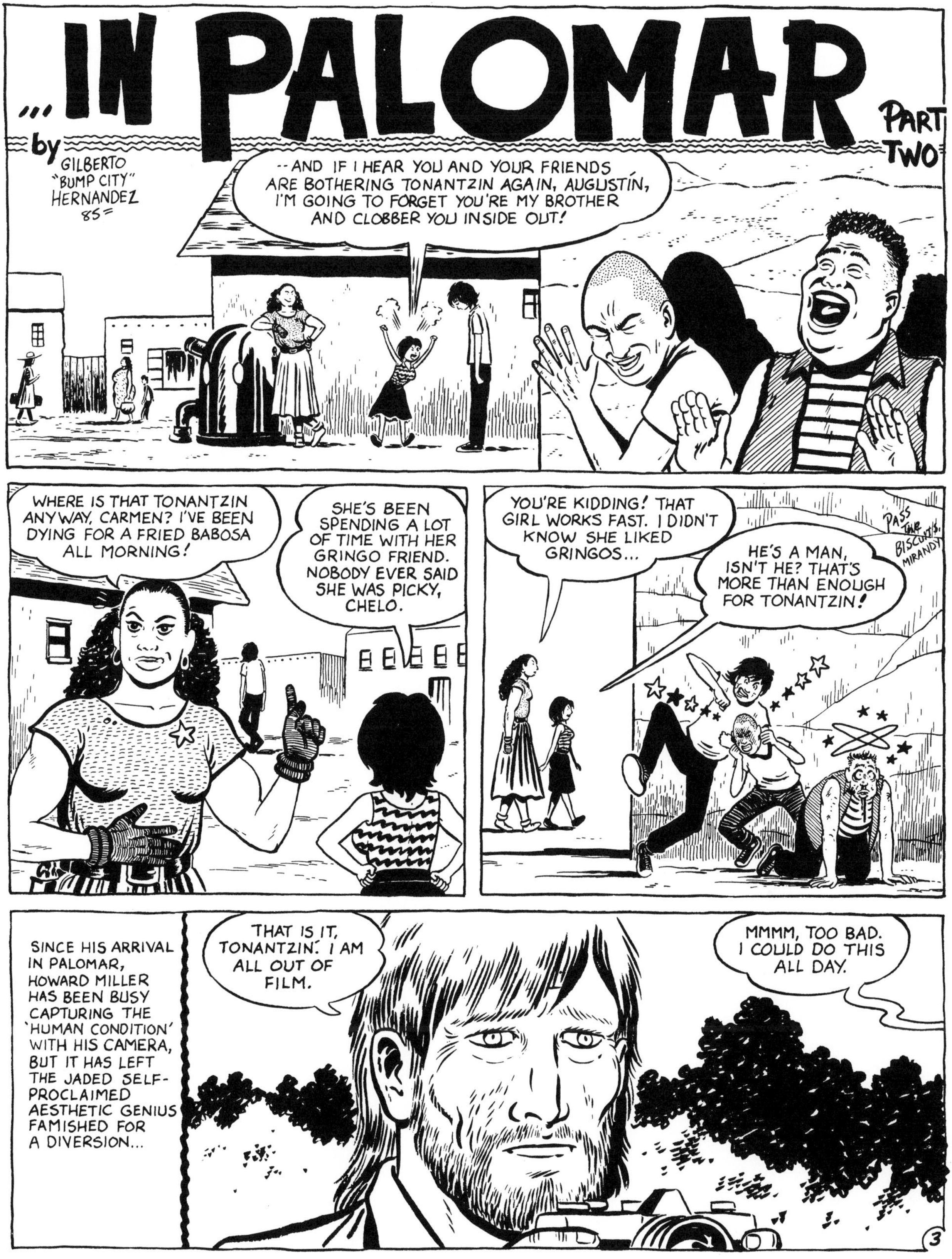
...IN PALOMAR
PART TWO
by GILBERTO "BUMP CITY" HERNANDEZ 85
--AND IF I HEAR YOU AND YOUR FRIENDS ARE BOTHERING TONANTZIN AGAIN, AUGUSTÍN, I'M GOING TO FORGET YOU'RE MY BROTHER AND CLOBBER YOU INSIDE OUT!
WHERE IS THAT TONANTZIN ANYWAY, CARMEN? I'VE BEEN DYING FOR A FRIED BABOSA ALL MORNING!
SHE'S BEEN SPENDING A LOT OF TIME WITH HER GRINGO FRIEND. NOBODY EVER SAID SHE WAS PICKY, CHELO.
YOU'RE KIDDING! THAT GIRL WORKS FAST. I DIDN'T KNOW SHE LIKED GRINGOS...
HE'S A MAN, ISN'T HE? THAT'S MORE THAN ENOUGH FOR TONANTZIN!
SINCE HIS ARRIVAL IN PALOMAR, HOWARD MILLER HAS BEEN BUSY CAPTURING THE 'HUMAN CONDITION' WITH HIS CAMERA, BUT IT HAS LEFT THE JADED SELF-PROCLAIMED AESTHETIC GENIUS FAMISHED FOR A DIVERSION...
THAT IS IT, TONANTZIN. I AM ALL OUT OF FILM.
MMMM, TOO BAD. I COULD DO THIS ALL DAY.
3

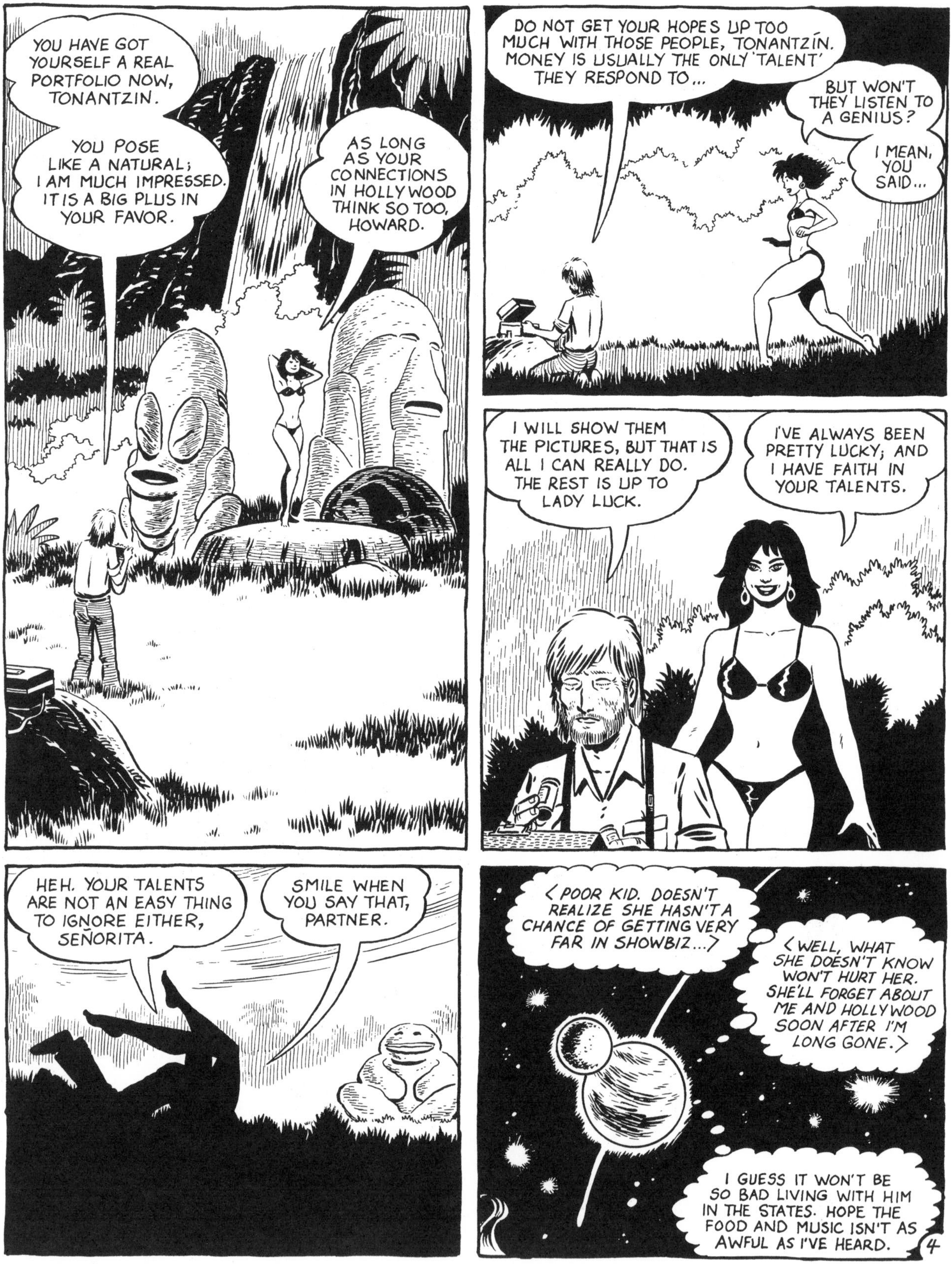
YOU HAVE GOT YOURSELF A REAL PORTFOLIO NOW, TONANTZIN.
YOU POSE LIKE A NATURAL; I AM MUCH IMPRESSED. IT IS A BIG PLUS IN YOUR FAVOR.
AS LONG AS YOUR CONNECTIONS IN HOLLYWOOD THINK SO TOO, HOWARD.
DO NOT GET YOUR HOPES UP TOO MUCH WITH THOSE PEOPLE, TONANTZÍN. MONEY IS USUALLY THE ONLY 'TALENT' THEY RESPOND TO...
BUT WON'T THEY LISTEN TO A GENIUS?
I MEAN, YOU SAID...
I WILL SHOW THEM THE PICTURES, BUT THAT IS ALL I CAN REALLY DO. THE REST IS UP TO LADY LUCK.
I'VE ALWAYS BEEN PRETTY LUCKY; AND I HAVE FAITH IN YOUR TALENTS.
HEH. YOUR TALENTS ARE NOT AN EASY THING TO IGNORE EITHER, SEÑORITA.
SMILE WHEN YOU SAY THAT, PARTNER.
< POOR KID. DOESN'T REALIZE SHE HASN'T A CHANCE OF GETTING VERY FAR IN SHOWBIZ... >
< WELL, WHAT SHE DOESN'T KNOW WON'T HURT HER. SHE'LL FORGET ABOUT ME AND HOLLYWOOD SOON AFTER I'M LONG GONE. >
I GUESS IT WON'T BE SO BAD LIVING WITH HIM IN THE STATES. HOPE THE FOOD AND MUSIC ISN'T AS AWFUL AS I'VE HEARD.
4

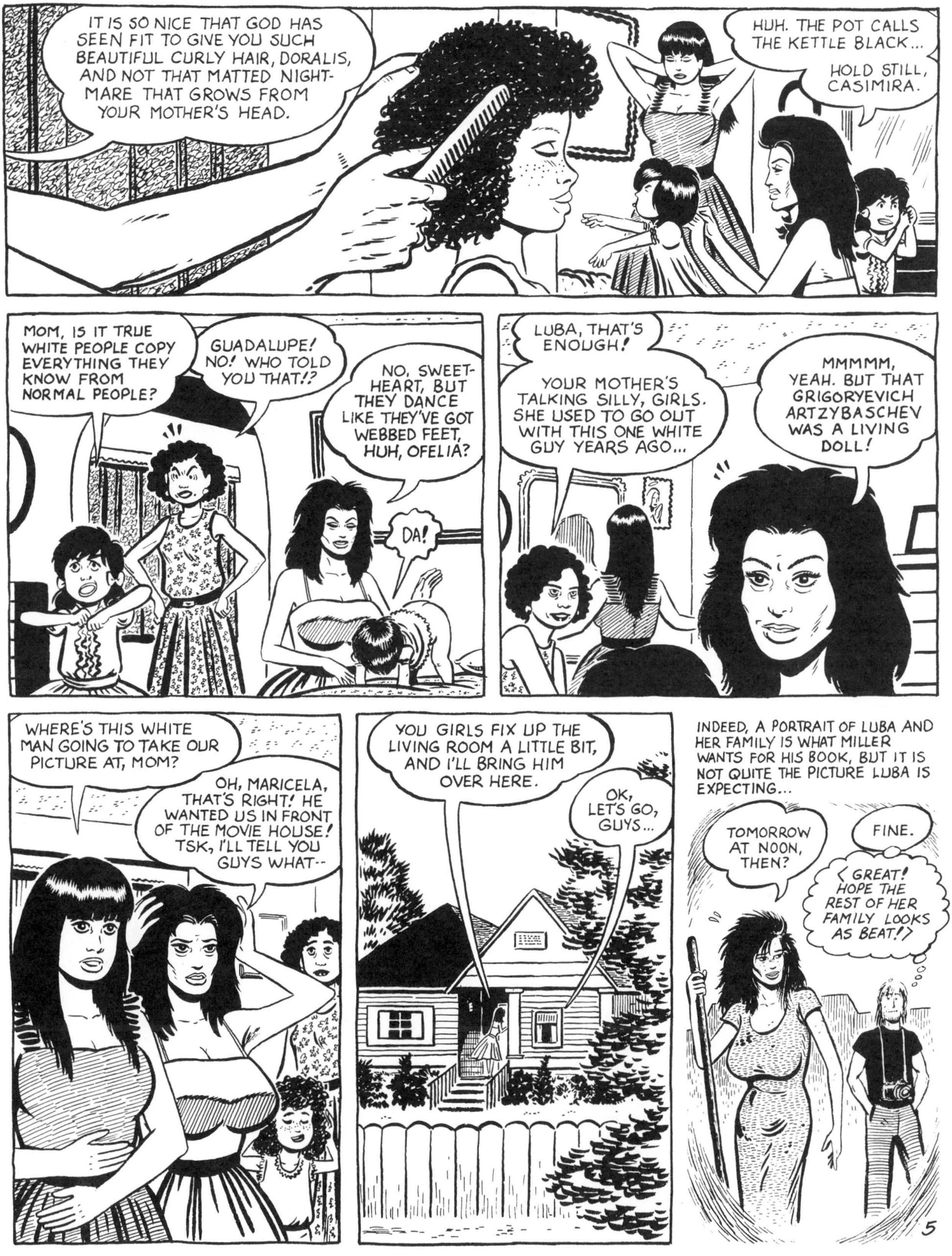
IT IS SO NICE THAT GOD HAS SEEN FIT TO GIVE YOU SUCH BEAUTIFUL CURLY HAIR, DORALIS, AND NOT THAT MATTED NIGHT-MARE THAT GROWS FROM YOUR MOTHER'S HEAD.
HUH. THE POT CALLS THE KETTLE BLACK...
HOLD STILL, CASIMIRA.
MOM, IS IT TRUE WHITE PEOPLE COPY EVERYTHING THEY KNOW FROM NORMAL PEOPLE?
GUADALUPE! NO! WHO TOLD YOU THAT!?
NO, SWEET-HEART, BUT THEY DANCE LIKE THEY'VE GOT WEBBED FEET, HUH, OFELIA?
DA!
LUBA, THAT'S ENOUGH!
YOUR MOTHER'S TALKING SILLY, GIRLS. SHE USED TO GO OUT WITH THIS ONE WHITE GUY YEARS AGO...
MMMMM, YEAH. BUT THAT GRIGORYEVICH ARTZYBASCHEV WAS A LIVING DOLL!
WHERE'S THIS WHITE MAN GOING TO TAKE OUR PICTURE AT, MOM?
OH, MARICELA, THAT'S RIGHT! HE WANTED US IN FRONT OF THE MOVIE HOUSE! TSK, I'LL TELL YOU GUYS WHAT--
YOU GIRLS FIX UP THE LIVING ROOM A LITTLE BIT, AND I'LL BRING HIM OVER HERE.
OK, LET'S GO, GUYS...
INDEED, A PORTRAIT OF LUBA AND HER FAMILY IS WHAT MILLER WANTS FOR HIS BOOK, BUT IT IS NOT QUITE THE PICTURE LUBA IS EXPECTING...
TOMORROW AT NOON, THEN?
FINE.
<GREAT! HOPE THE REST OF HER FAMILY LOOKS AS BEAT!>
5

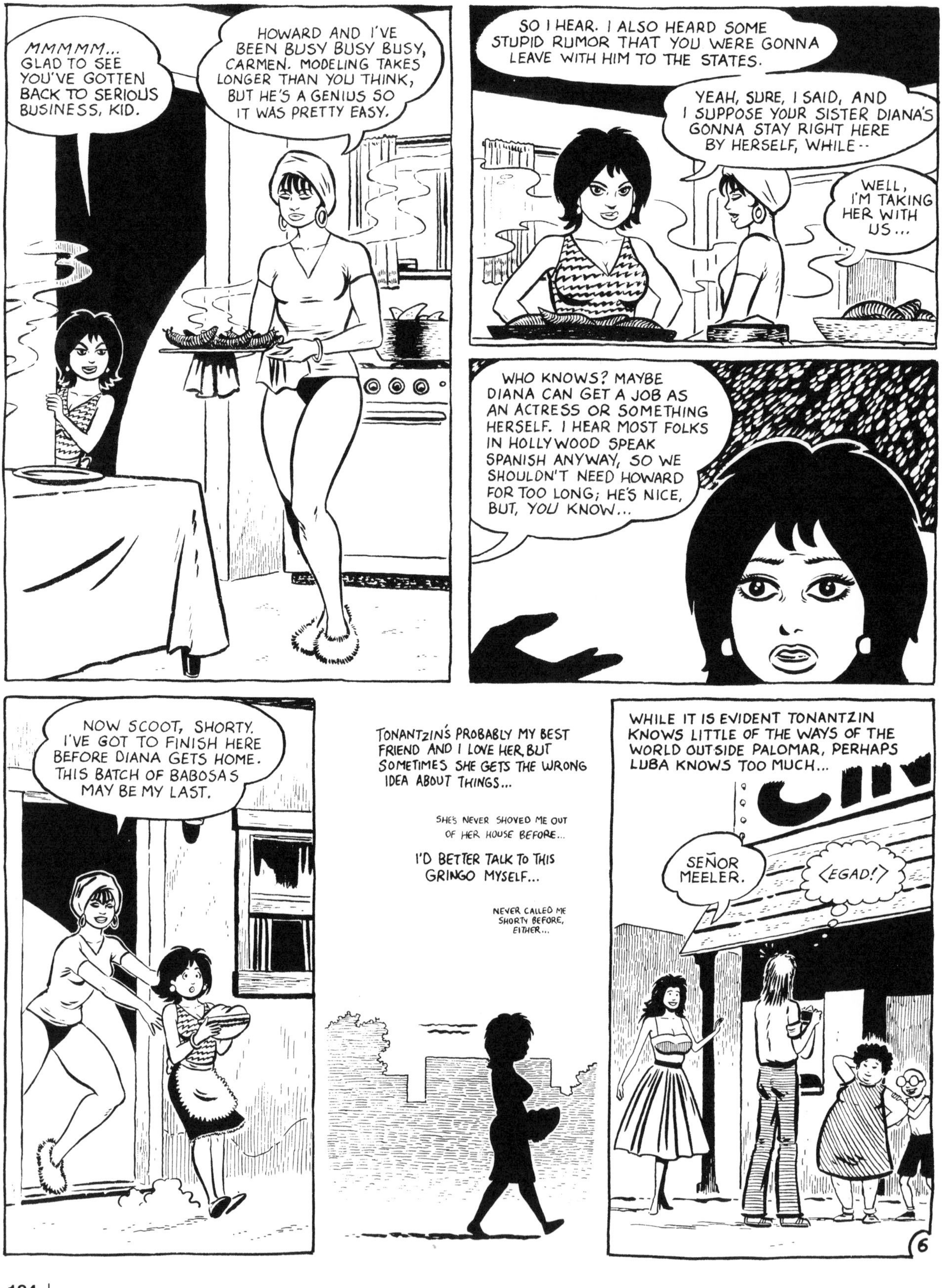
MMMMM... GLAD TO SEE YOU'VE GOTTEN BACK TO SERIOUS BUSINESS, KID.
HOWARD AND I'VE BEEN BUSY BUSY BUSY, CARMEN. MODELING TAKES LONGER THAN YOU THINK, BUT HE'S A GENIUS SO IT WAS PRETTY EASY.
SO I HEAR. I ALSO HEARD SOME STUPID RUMOR THAT YOU WERE GONNA LEAVE WITH HIM TO THE STATES.
YEAH, SURE, I SAID, AND I SUPPOSE YOUR SISTER DIANA'S GONNA STAY RIGHT HERE BY HERSELF, WHILE--
WELL, I'M TAKING HER WITH US...
WHO KNOWS? MAYBE DIANA CAN GET A JOB AS AN ACTRESS OR SOMETHING HERSELF. I HEAR MOST FOLKS IN HOLLYWOOD SPEAK SPANISH ANYWAY, SO WE SHOULDN'T NEED HOWARD FOR TOO LONG; HE'S NICE, BUT, YOU KNOW...
NOW SCOOT, SHORTY. I'VE GOT TO FINISH HERE BEFORE DIANA GETS HOME. THIS BATCH OF BABOSAS MAY BE MY LAST.
TONANTZIN'S PROBABLY MY BEST FRIEND AND I LOVE HER, BUT SOMETIMES SHE GETS THE WRONG IDEA ABOUT THINGS...
SHE'S NEVER SHOVED ME OUT OF HER HOUSE BEFORE...
I'D BETTER TALK TO THIS GRINGO MYSELF...
NEVER CALLED ME SHORTY BEFORE, EITHER...
WHILE IT IS EVIDENT TONANTZIN KNOWS LITTLE OF THE WAYS OF THE WORLD OUTSIDE PALOMAR, PERHAPS LUBA KNOWS TOO MUCH...
SEÑOR MEELER.
<EGAD!>
6

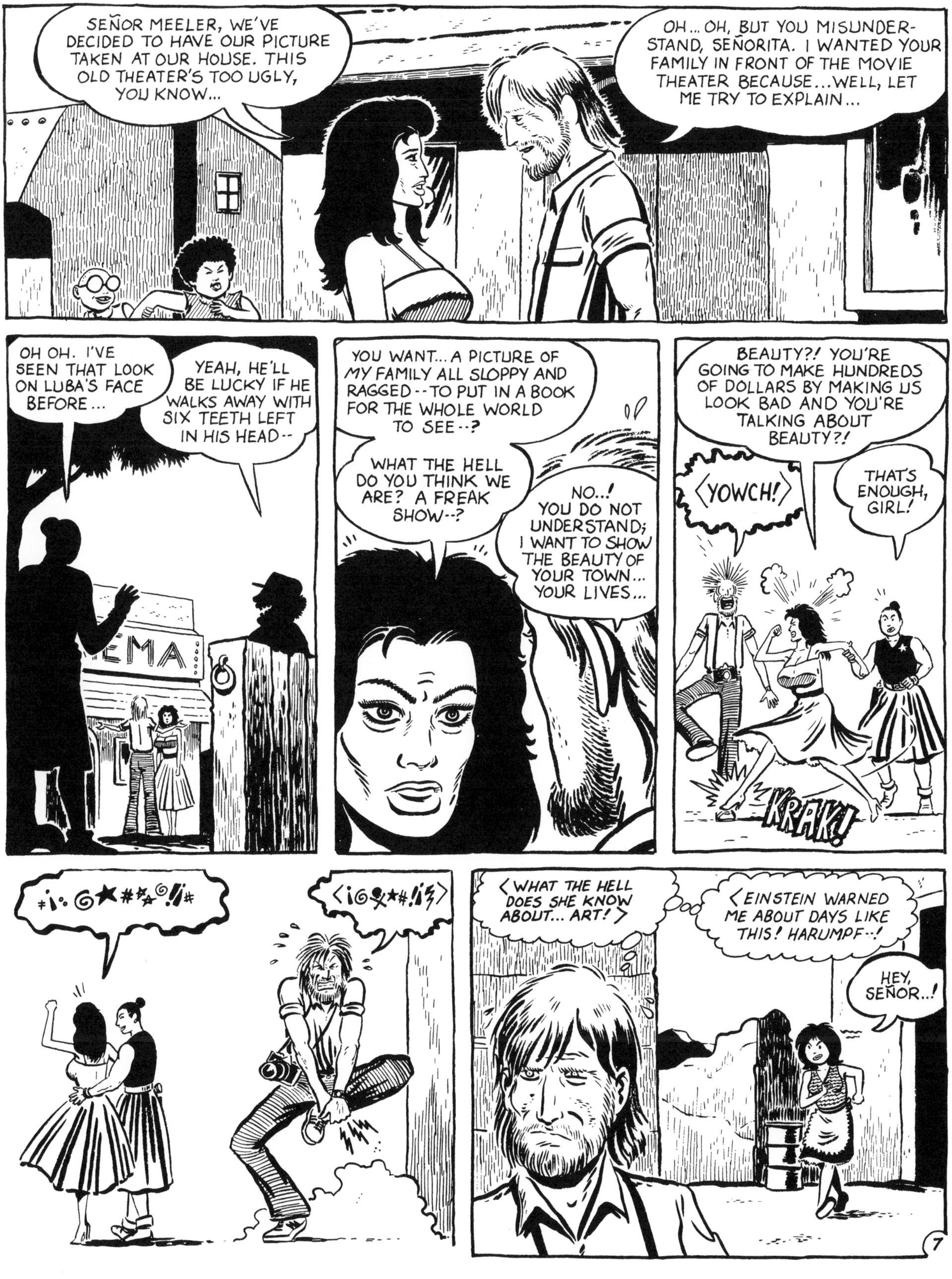
SEÑOR MEELER, WE'VE DECIDED TO HAVE OUR PICTURE TAKEN AT OUR HOUSE. THIS OLD THEATER'S TOO UGLY, YOU KNOW...
OH... OH, BUT YOU MISUNDERSTAND, SEÑORITA. I WANTED YOUR FAMILY IN FRONT OF THE MOVIE THEATER BECAUSE... WELL, LET ME TRY TO EXPLAIN...
OH OH. I'VE SEEN THAT LOOK ON LUBA'S FACE BEFORE...
YEAH, HE'LL BE LUCKY IF HE WALKS AWAY WITH SIX TEETH LEFT IN HIS HEAD--
EMA
YOU WANT... A PICTURE OF MY FAMILY ALL SLOPPY AND RAGGED--TO PUT IN A BOOK FOR THE WHOLE WORLD TO SEE--?
WHAT THE HELL DO YOU THINK WE ARE? A FREAK SHOW--?
NO..! YOU DO NOT UNDERSTAND; I WANT TO SHOW THE BEAUTY OF YOUR TOWN... YOUR LIVES...
BEAUTY?! YOU'RE GOING TO MAKE HUNDREDS OF DOLLARS BY MAKING US LOOK BAD AND YOU'RE TALKING ABOUT BEAUTY?!
⟨YOWCH!⟩
THAT'S ENOUGH, GIRL!
KRAK!
⟨WHAT THE HELL DOES SHE KNOW ABOUT... ART!⟩
⟨EINSTEIN WARNED ME ABOUT DAYS LIKE THIS! HARUMPF--!⟩
HEY, SEÑOR..!
7

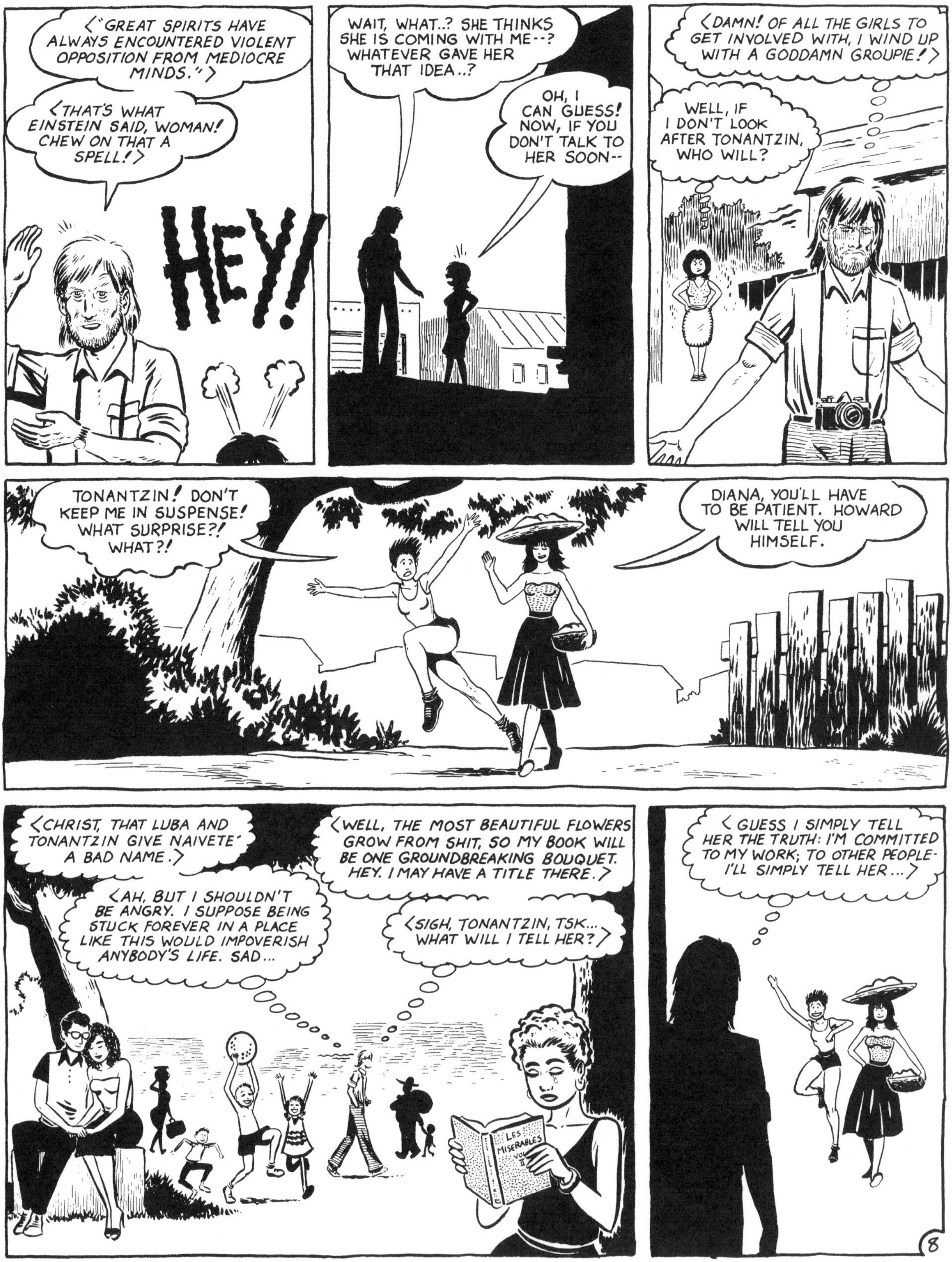

<"GREAT SPIRITS HAVE ALWAYS ENCOUNTERED VIOLENT OPPOSITION FROM MEDIOCRE MINDS.">
<THAT'S WHAT EINSTEIN SAID, WOMAN! CHEW ON THAT A SPELL!>
HEY!
WAIT, WHAT..? SHE THINKS SHE IS COMING WITH ME--? WHATEVER GAVE HER THAT IDEA..?
OH, I CAN GUESS! NOW, IF YOU DON'T TALK TO HER SOON--
<DAMN! OF ALL THE GIRLS TO GET INVOLVED WITH, I WIND UP WITH A GODDAMN GROUPIE!>
WELL, IF I DON'T LOOK AFTER TONANTZIN, WHO WILL?
TONANTZIN! DON'T KEEP ME IN SUSPENSE! WHAT SURPRISE?! WHAT?!
DIANA, YOU'LL HAVE TO BE PATIENT. HOWARD WILL TELL YOU HIMSELF.
<CHRIST, THAT LUBA AND TONANTZIN GIVE NAIVETÉ A BAD NAME.>
<WELL, THE MOST BEAUTIFUL FLOWERS GROW FROM SHIT, SO MY BOOK WILL BE ONE GROUNDBREAKING BOUQUET. HEY. I MAY HAVE A TITLE THERE.>
<AH, BUT I SHOULDN'T BE ANGRY. I SUPPOSE BEING STUCK FOREVER IN A PLACE LIKE THIS WOULD IMPOVERISH ANYBODY'S LIFE. SAD...
<SIGH, TONANTZIN, TSK... WHAT WILL I TELL HER?>
LES MISERABLES VOL II
< GUESS I SIMPLY TELL HER THE TRUTH: I'M COMMITTED TO MY WORK; TO OTHER PEOPLE- I'LL SIMPLY TELL HER...>
8

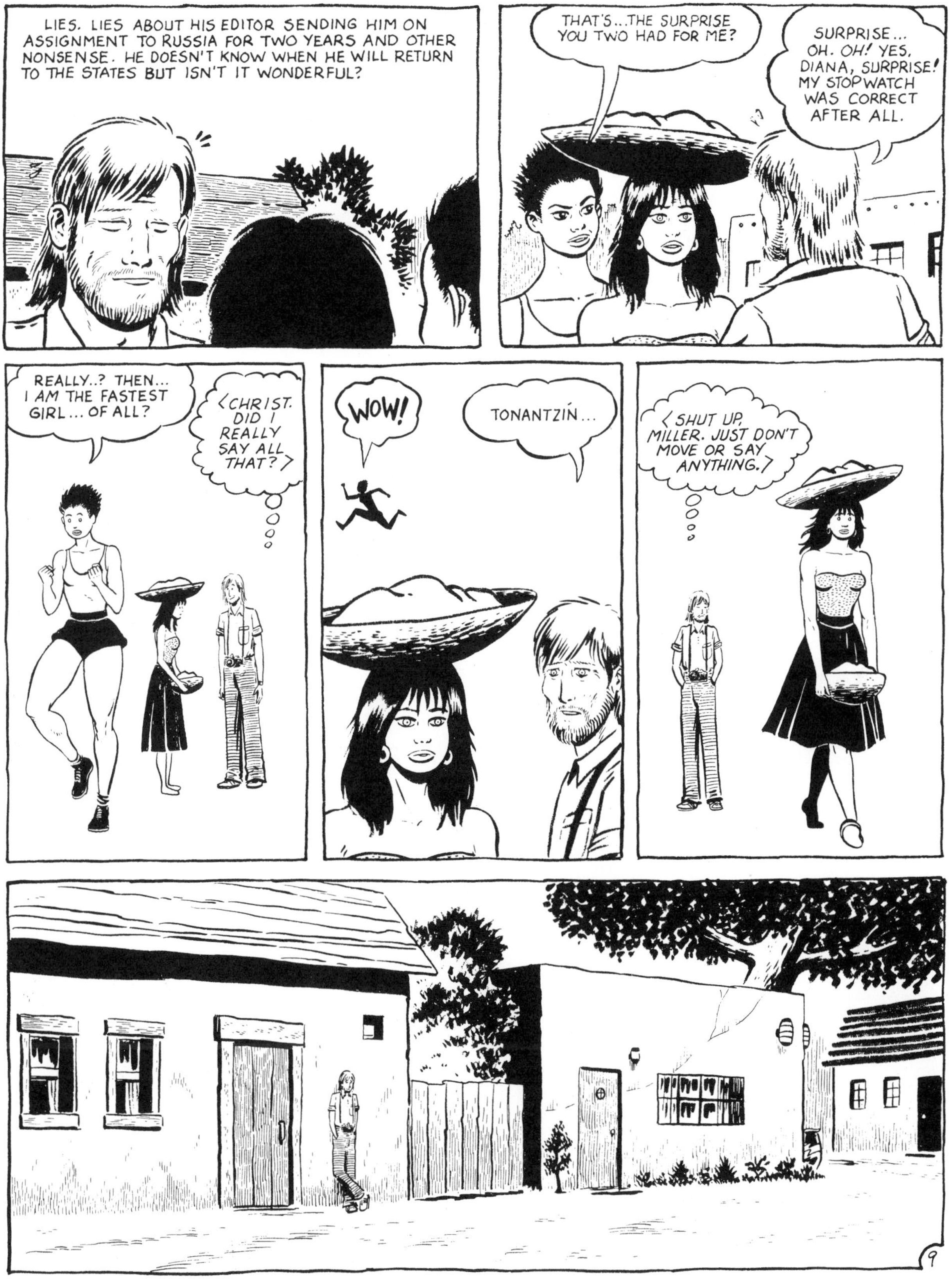
LIES. LIES ABOUT HIS EDITOR SENDING HIM ON ASSIGNMENT TO RUSSIA FOR TWO YEARS AND OTHER NONSENSE. HE DOESN'T KNOW WHEN HE WILL RETURN TO THE STATES BUT ISN'T IT WONDERFUL?
THAT'S... THE SURPRISE YOU TWO HAD FOR ME?
SURPRISE... OH. *OH!* YES, DIANA, SURPRISE! MY STOPWATCH WAS CORRECT AFTER ALL.
REALLY..? THEN... I AM THE FASTEST GIRL... OF ALL?
<CHRIST. DID I REALLY SAY ALL THAT?>
WOW!
TONANTZÍN...
<SHUT UP, MILLER. JUST DON'T MOVE OR SAY ANYTHING.>
9

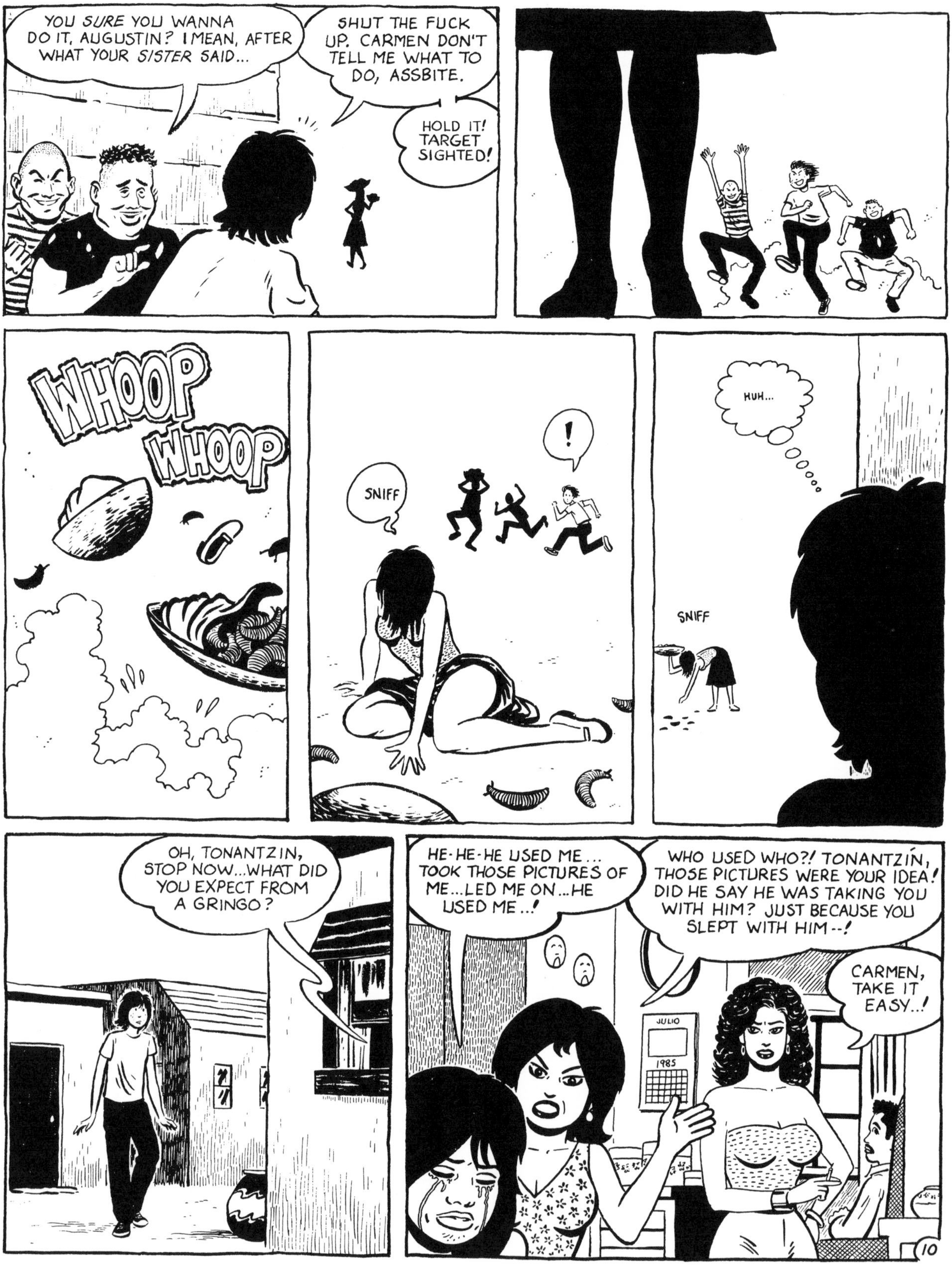

YOU SURE YOU WANNA DO IT, AUGUSTIN? I MEAN, AFTER WHAT YOUR SISTER SAID...
SHUT THE FUCK UP. CARMEN DON'T TELL ME WHAT TO DO, ASSBITE.
HOLD IT! TARGET SIGHTED!
WHOOP WHOOP
SNIFF
!
HUH...
SNIFF
OH, TONANTZIN, STOP NOW...WHAT DID YOU EXPECT FROM A GRINGO?
HE-HE-HE USED ME... TOOK THOSE PICTURES OF ME...LED ME ON...HE USED ME...!
WHO USED WHO?! TONANTZÍN, THOSE PICTURES WERE YOUR IDEA! DID HE SAY HE WAS TAKING YOU WITH HIM? JUST BECAUSE YOU SLEPT WITH HIM--!
CARMEN, TAKE IT EASY...!
JULIO
1985
10

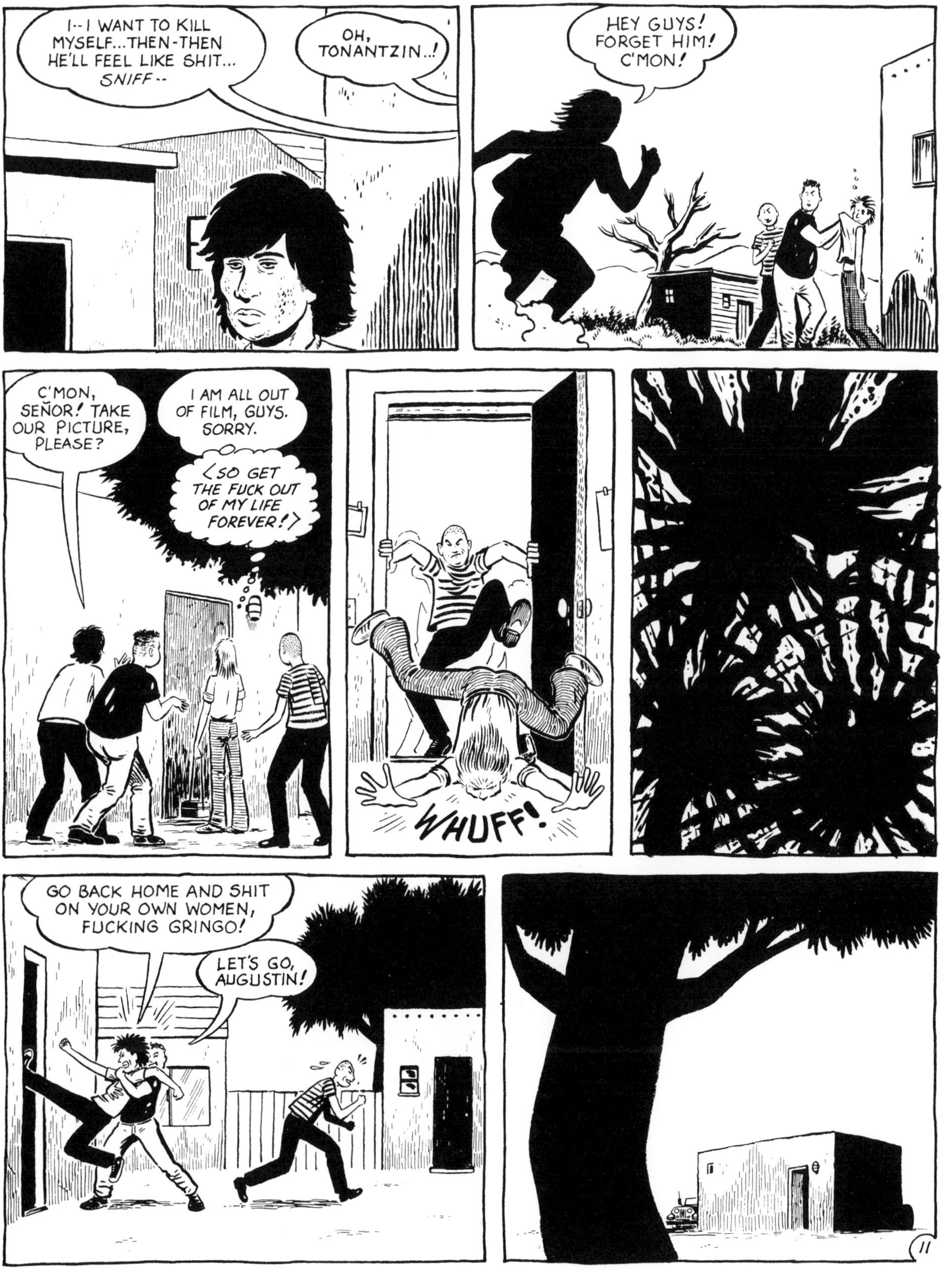
I-- I WANT TO KILL MYSELF... THEN-THEN HE'LL FEEL LIKE SHIT... SNIFF--
OH, TONANTZIN..!
HEY GUYS! FORGET HIM! C'MON!
C'MON, SEÑOR! TAKE OUR PICTURE, PLEASE?
I AM ALL OUT OF FILM, GUYS. SORRY.
<SO GET THE FUCK OUT OF MY LIFE FOREVER!>
WHUFF!
GO BACK HOME AND SHIT ON YOUR OWN WOMEN, FUCKING GRINGO!
LET'S GO, AUGUSTIN!
11

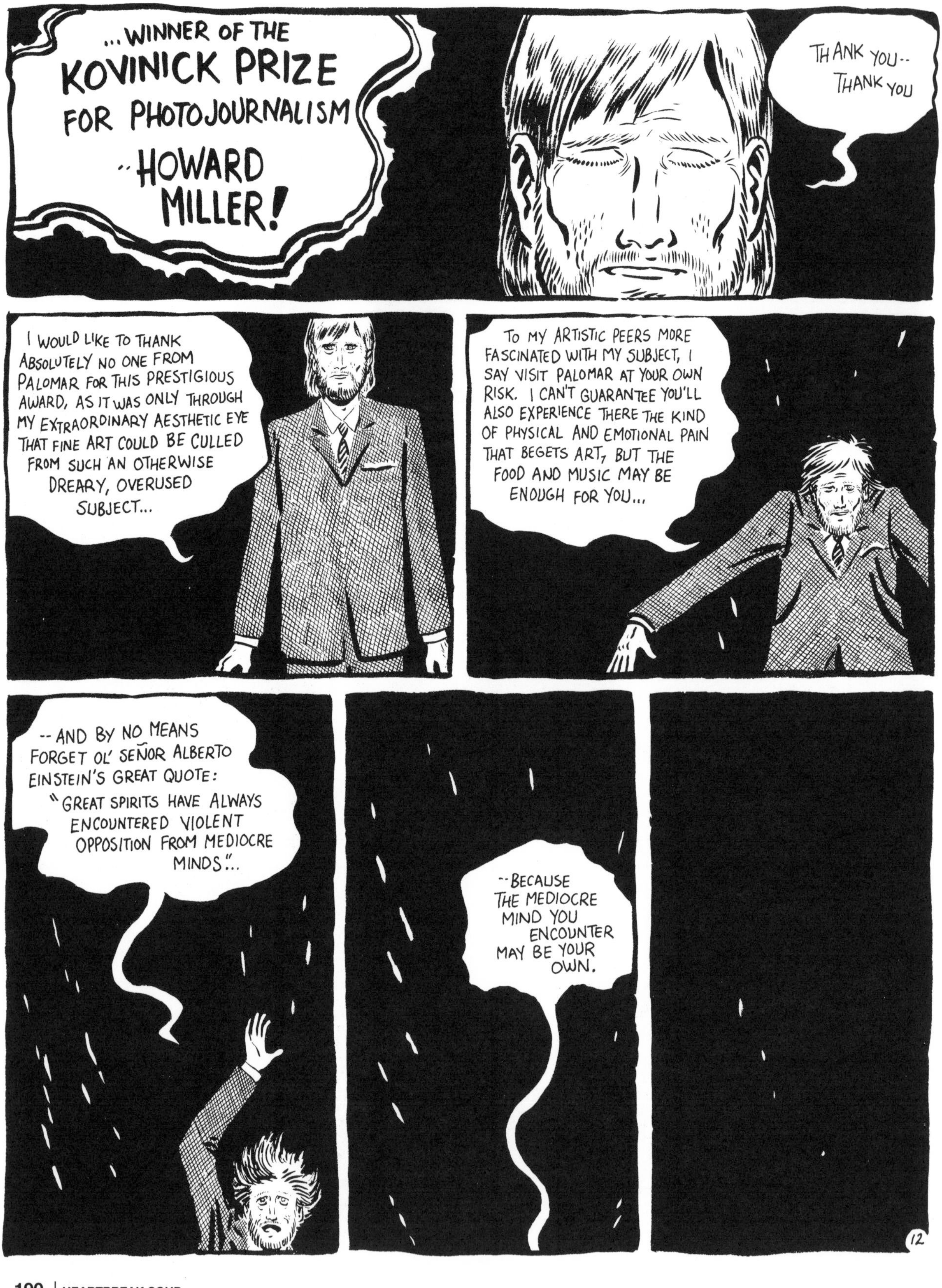
...WINNER OF THE KOVINICK PRIZE FOR PHOTOJOURNALISM ..HOWARD MILLER!
THANK YOU.. THANK YOU
I WOULD LIKE TO THANK ABSOLUTELY NO ONE FROM PALOMAR FOR THIS PRESTIGIOUS AWARD, AS IT WAS ONLY THROUGH MY EXTRAORDINARY AESTHETIC EYE THAT FINE ART COULD BE CULLED FROM SUCH AN OTHERWISE DREARY, OVERUSED SUBJECT...
TO MY ARTISTIC PEERS MORE FASCINATED WITH MY SUBJECT, I SAY VISIT PALOMAR AT YOUR OWN RISK. I CAN'T GUARANTEE YOU'LL ALSO EXPERIENCE THERE THE KIND OF PHYSICAL AND EMOTIONAL PAIN THAT BEGETS ART, BUT THE FOOD AND MUSIC MAY BE ENOUGH FOR YOU...
--AND BY NO MEANS FORGET OL' SEÑOR ALBERTO EINSTEIN'S GREAT QUOTE: "GREAT SPIRITS HAVE ALWAYS ENCOUNTERED VIOLENT OPPOSITION FROM MEDIOCRE MINDS."..
--BECAUSE THE MEDIOCRE MIND YOU ENCOUNTER MAY BE YOUR OWN.
12

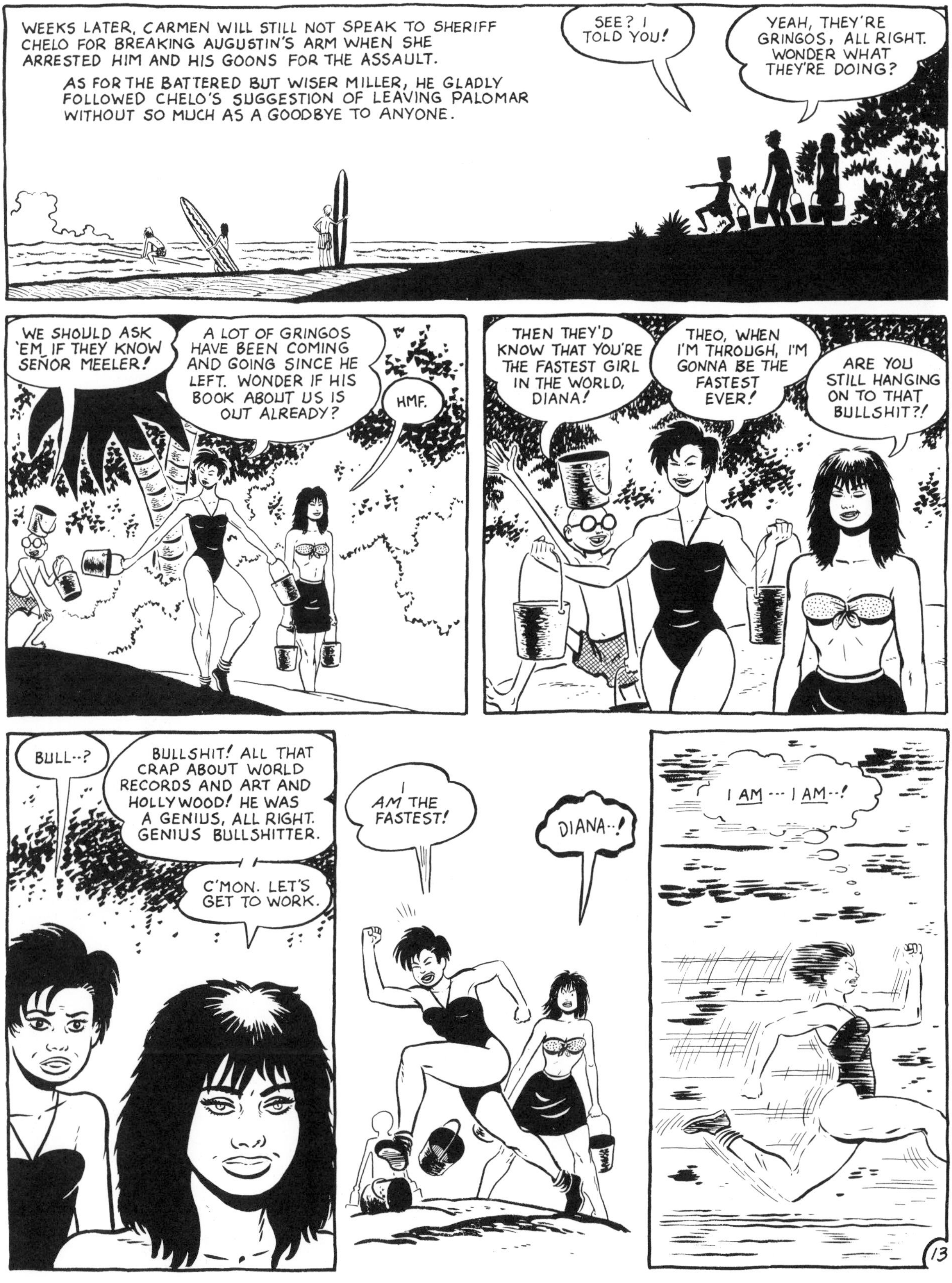
WEEKS LATER, CARMEN WILL STILL NOT SPEAK TO SHERIFF CHELO FOR BREAKING AUGUSTIN'S ARM WHEN SHE ARRESTED HIM AND HIS GOONS FOR THE ASSAULT.
AS FOR THE BATTERED BUT WISER MILLER, HE GLADLY FOLLOWED CHELO'S SUGGESTION OF LEAVING PALOMAR WITHOUT SO MUCH AS A GOODBYE TO ANYONE.
SEE? I TOLD YOU!
YEAH, THEY'RE GRINGOS, ALL RIGHT. WONDER WHAT THEY'RE DOING?
WE SHOULD ASK 'EM IF THEY KNOW SEÑOR MEELER!
A LOT OF GRINGOS HAVE BEEN COMING AND GOING SINCE HE LEFT. WONDER IF HIS BOOK ABOUT US IS OUT ALREADY?
HMF.
THEN THEY'D KNOW THAT YOU'RE THE FASTEST GIRL IN THE WORLD, DIANA!
THEO, WHEN I'M THROUGH, I'M GONNA BE THE FASTEST EVER!
ARE YOU STILL HANGING ON TO THAT BULLSHIT?!
BULL--?
BULLSHIT! ALL THAT CRAP ABOUT WORLD RECORDS AND ART AND HOLLYWOOD! HE WAS A GENIUS, ALL RIGHT. GENIUS BULLSHITTER.
C'MON. LET'S GET TO WORK.
I AM THE FASTEST!
DIANA--!
I AM --- I AM--!
13

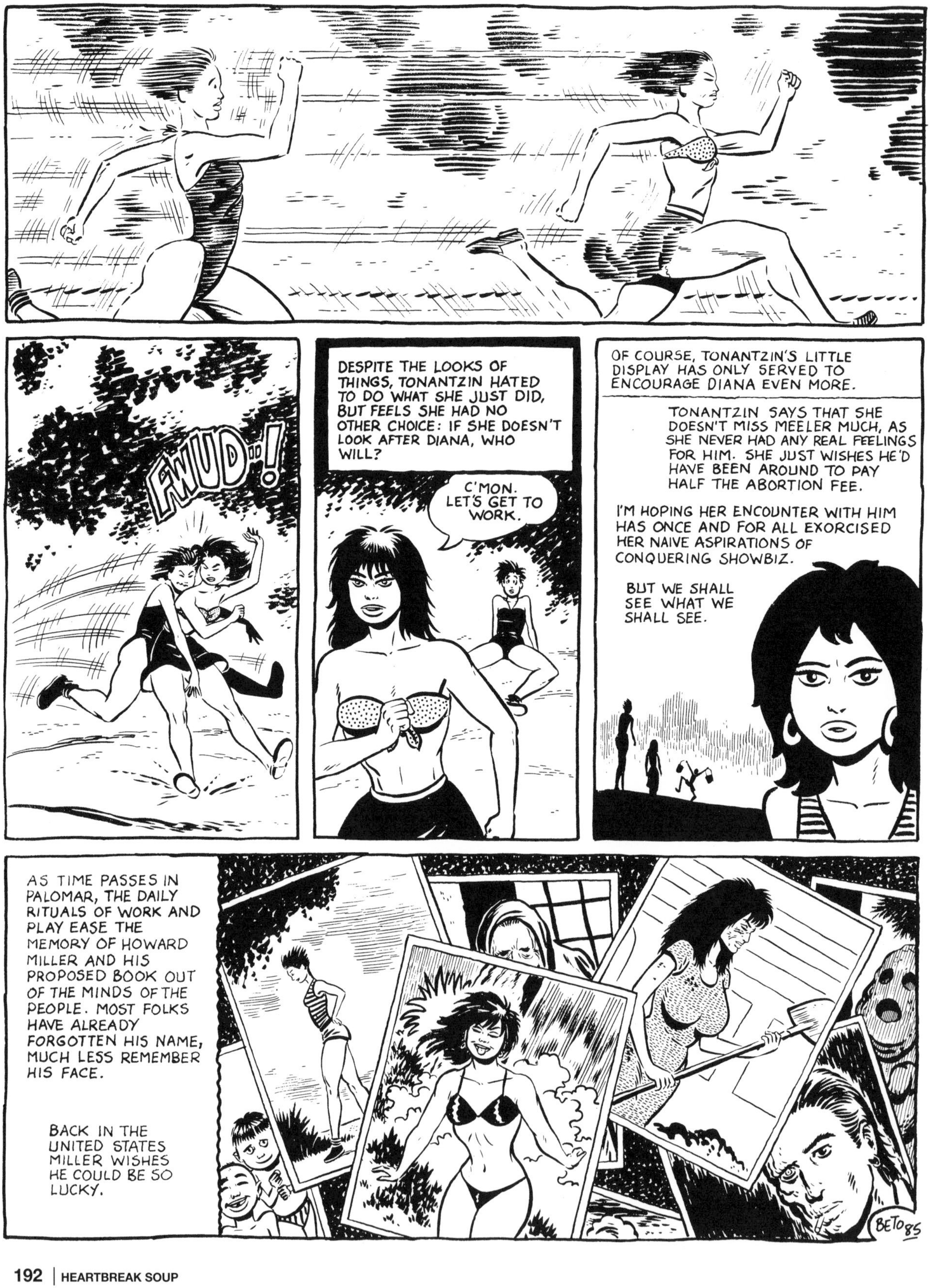
FWUD!
DESPITE THE LOOKS OF THINGS, TONANTZIN HATED TO DO WHAT SHE JUST DID, BUT FEELS SHE HAD NO OTHER CHOICE: IF SHE DOESN'T LOOK AFTER DIANA, WHO WILL?
C'MON. LET'S GET TO WORK.
OF COURSE, TONANTZIN'S LITTLE DISPLAY HAS ONLY SERVED TO ENCOURAGE DIANA EVEN MORE.
TONANTZIN SAYS THAT SHE DOESN'T MISS MEELER MUCH, AS SHE NEVER HAD ANY REAL FEELINGS FOR HIM. SHE JUST WISHES HE'D HAVE BEEN AROUND TO PAY HALF THE ABORTION FEE.
I'M HOPING HER ENCOUNTER WITH HIM HAS ONCE AND FOR ALL EXORCISED HER NAIVE ASPIRATIONS OF CONQUERING SHOWBIZ.
BUT WE SHALL SEE WHAT WE SHALL SEE.
AS TIME PASSES IN PALOMAR, THE DAILY RITUALS OF WORK AND PLAY EASE THE MEMORY OF HOWARD MILLER AND HIS PROPOSED BOOK OUT OF THE MINDS OF THE PEOPLE. MOST FOLKS HAVE ALREADY FORGOTTEN HIS NAME, MUCH LESS REMEMBER HIS FACE.
BACK IN THE UNITED STATES MILLER WISHES HE COULD BE SO LUCKY.
BETO 85

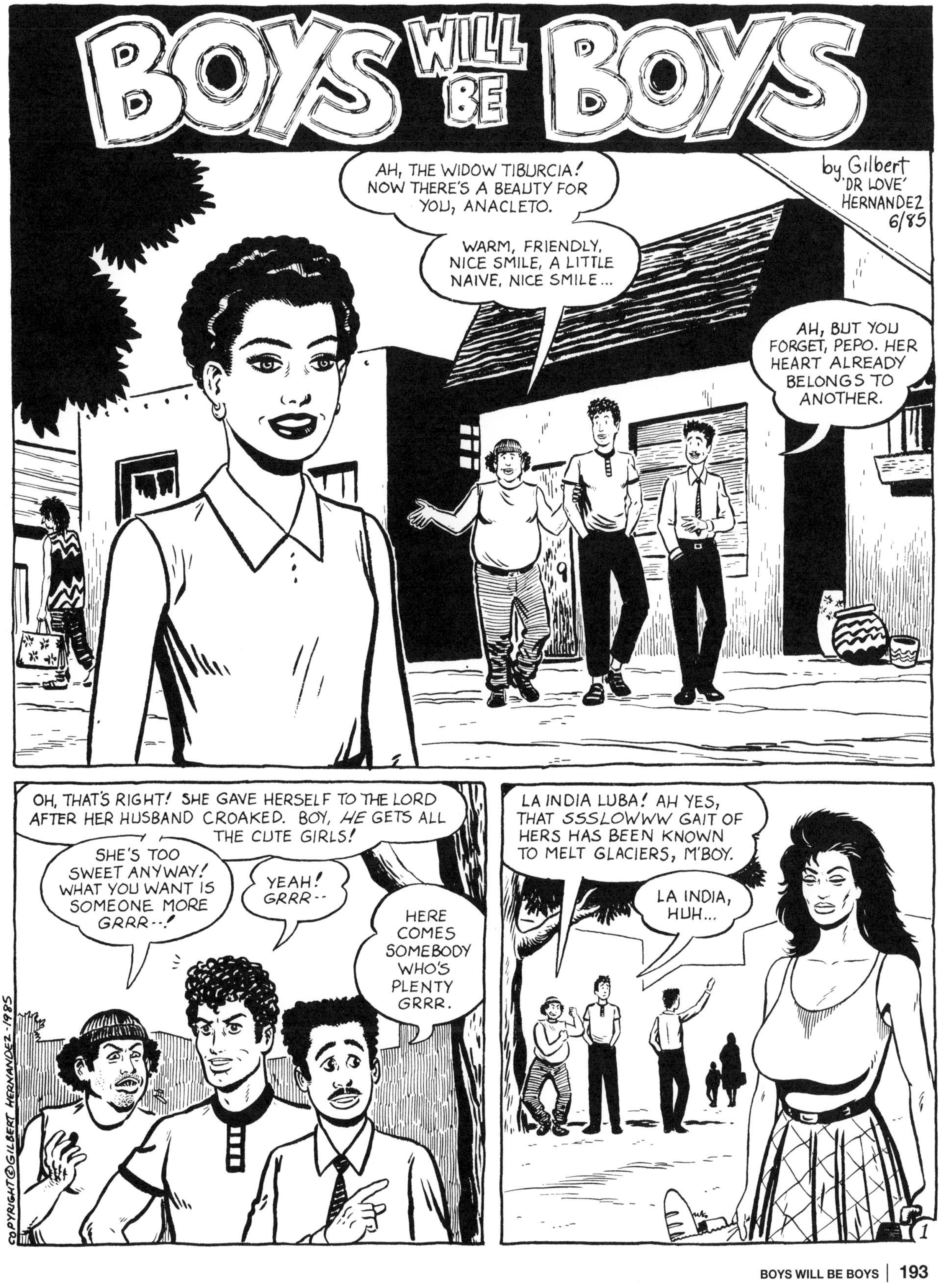
BOYS WILL BE BOYS
by Gilbert 'DR LOVE' HERNANDEZ 6/85
AH, THE WIDOW TIBURCIA! NOW THERE'S A BEAUTY FOR YOU, ANACLETO.
WARM, FRIENDLY, NICE SMILE, A LITTLE NAIVE, NICE SMILE...
AH, BUT YOU FORGET, PEPO. HER HEART ALREADY BELONGS TO ANOTHER.
OH, THAT'S RIGHT! SHE GAVE HERSELF TO THE LORD AFTER HER HUSBAND CROAKED. BOY, *HE* GETS ALL THE CUTE GIRLS!
SHE'S TOO SWEET ANYWAY! WHAT YOU WANT IS SOMEONE MORE GRRR--!
YEAH! GRRR--
HERE COMES SOMEBODY WHO'S PLENTY GRRR.
COPYRIGHT © GILBERT HERNANDEZ · 1985
LA INDIA LUBA! AH YES, THAT *SSSLOWWW* GAIT OF HERS HAS BEEN KNOWN TO MELT GLACIERS, M'BOY.
LA INDIA, HUH...
1

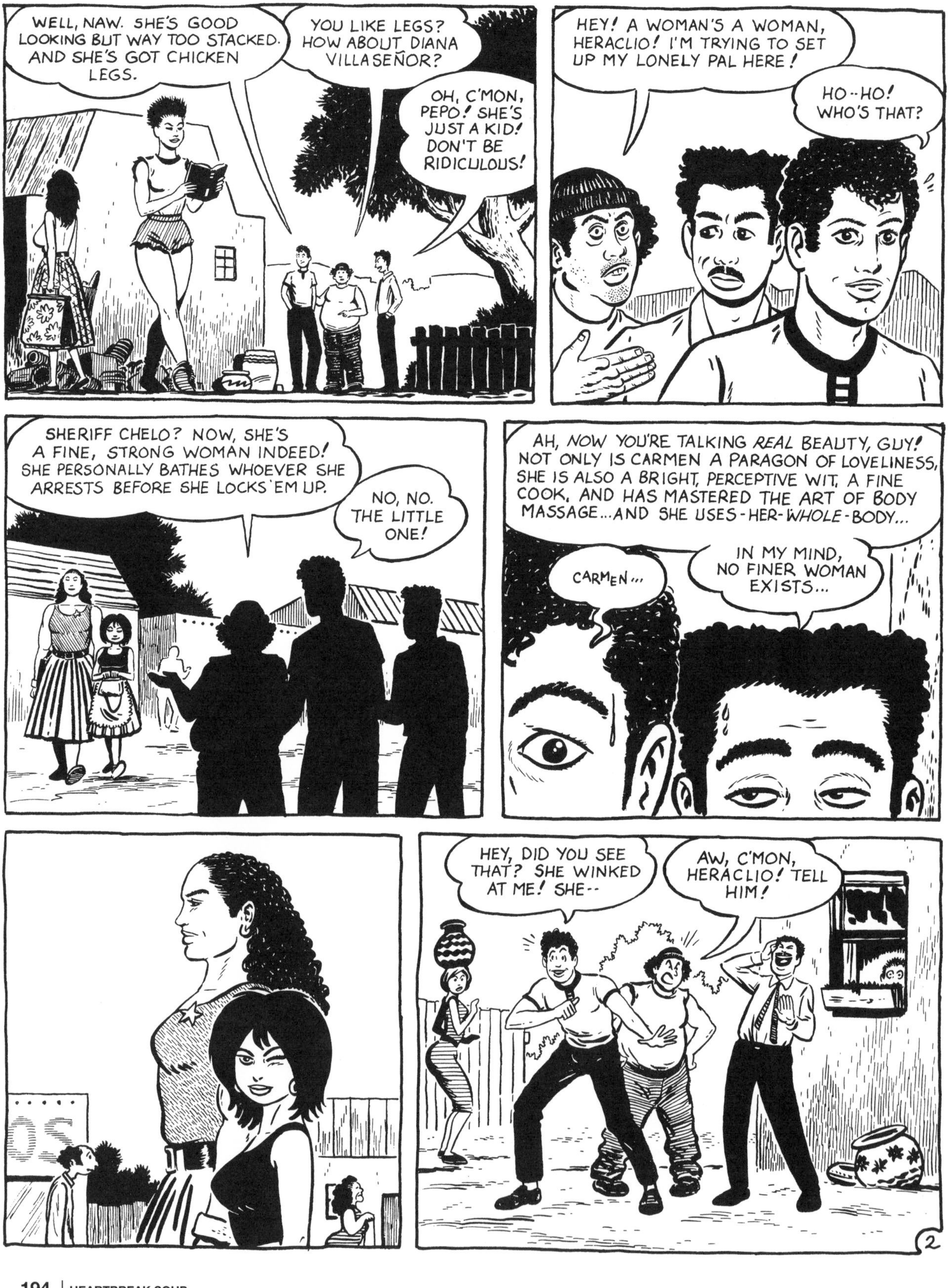
WELL, NAW. SHE'S GOOD LOOKING BUT WAY TOO STACKED. AND SHE'S GOT CHICKEN LEGS.
YOU LIKE LEGS? HOW ABOUT DIANA VILLASEÑOR?
OH, C'MON, PEPO! SHE'S JUST A KID! DON'T BE RIDICULOUS!
HEY! A WOMAN'S A WOMAN, HERACLIO! I'M TRYING TO SET UP MY LONELY PAL HERE!
HO--HO! WHO'S THAT?
SHERIFF CHELO? NOW, SHE'S A FINE, STRONG WOMAN INDEED! SHE PERSONALLY BATHES WHOEVER SHE ARRESTS BEFORE SHE LOCKS 'EM UP.
NO, NO. THE LITTLE ONE!
AH, NOW YOU'RE TALKING REAL BEAUTY, GUY! NOT ONLY IS CARMEN A PARAGON OF LOVELINESS, SHE IS ALSO A BRIGHT, PERCEPTIVE WIT, A FINE COOK, AND HAS MASTERED THE ART OF BODY MASSAGE...AND SHE USES-HER-WHOLE-BODY...
CARMEN...
IN MY MIND, NO FINER WOMAN EXISTS...
HEY, DID YOU SEE THAT? SHE WINKED AT ME! SHE--
AW, C'MON, HERACLIO! TELL HIM!
2

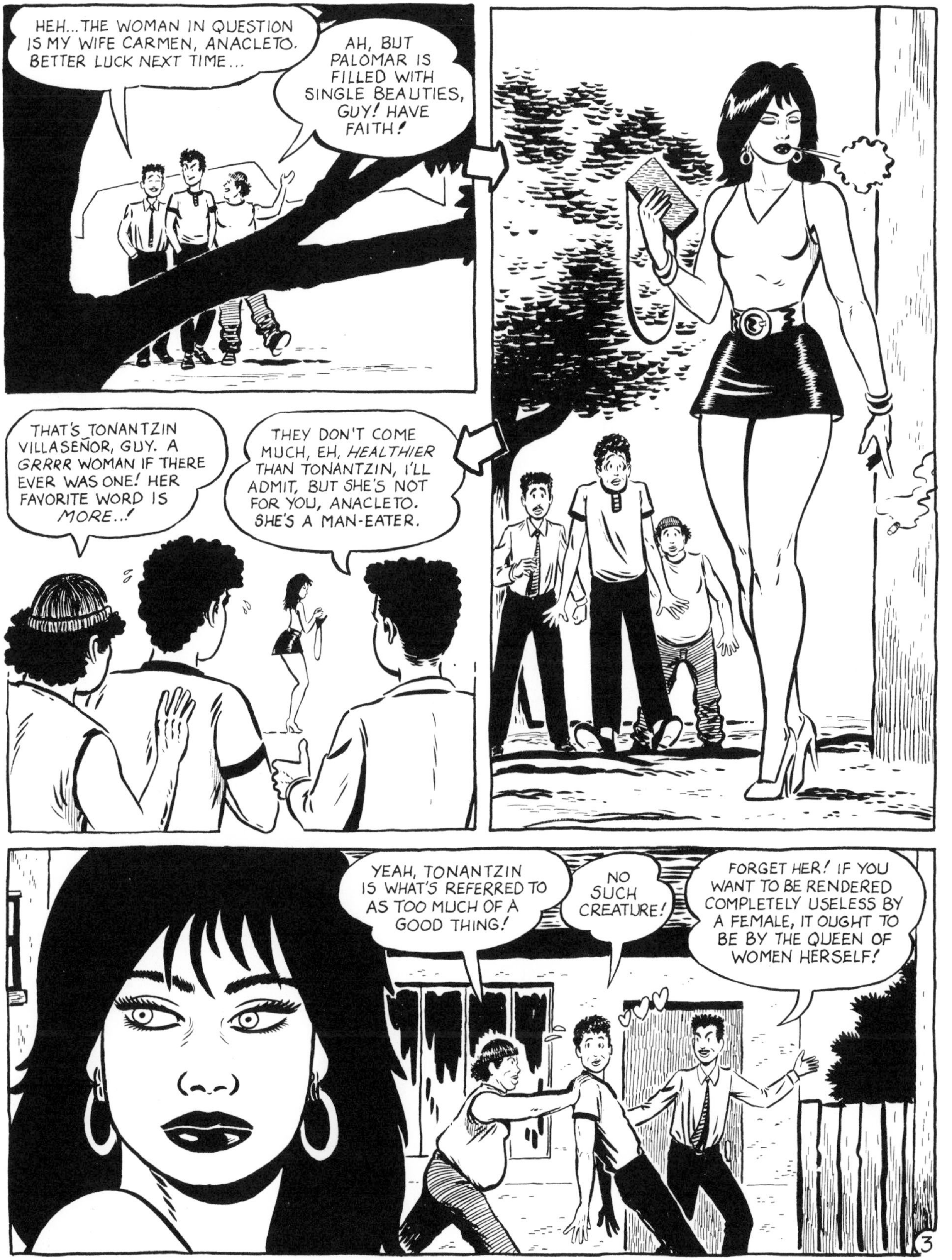
HEH...THE WOMAN IN QUESTION IS MY WIFE CARMEN, ANACLETO. BETTER LUCK NEXT TIME...
AH, BUT PALOMAR IS FILLED WITH SINGLE BEAUTIES, GUY! HAVE FAITH!
THAT'S TONANTZIN VILLASEÑOR, GUY. A *GRRRR* WOMAN IF THERE EVER WAS ONE! HER FAVORITE WORD IS *MORE*..!
THEY DON'T COME MUCH, EH, *HEALTHIER* THAN TONANTZIN, I'LL ADMIT, BUT SHE'S NOT FOR YOU, ANACLETO. SHE'S A MAN-EATER.
YEAH, TONANTZIN IS WHAT'S REFERRED TO AS TOO MUCH OF A GOOD THING!
NO SUCH CREATURE!
FORGET HER! IF YOU WANT TO BE RENDERED COMPLETELY USELESS BY A FEMALE, IT OUGHT TO BE BY THE QUEEN OF WOMEN HERSELF!
3

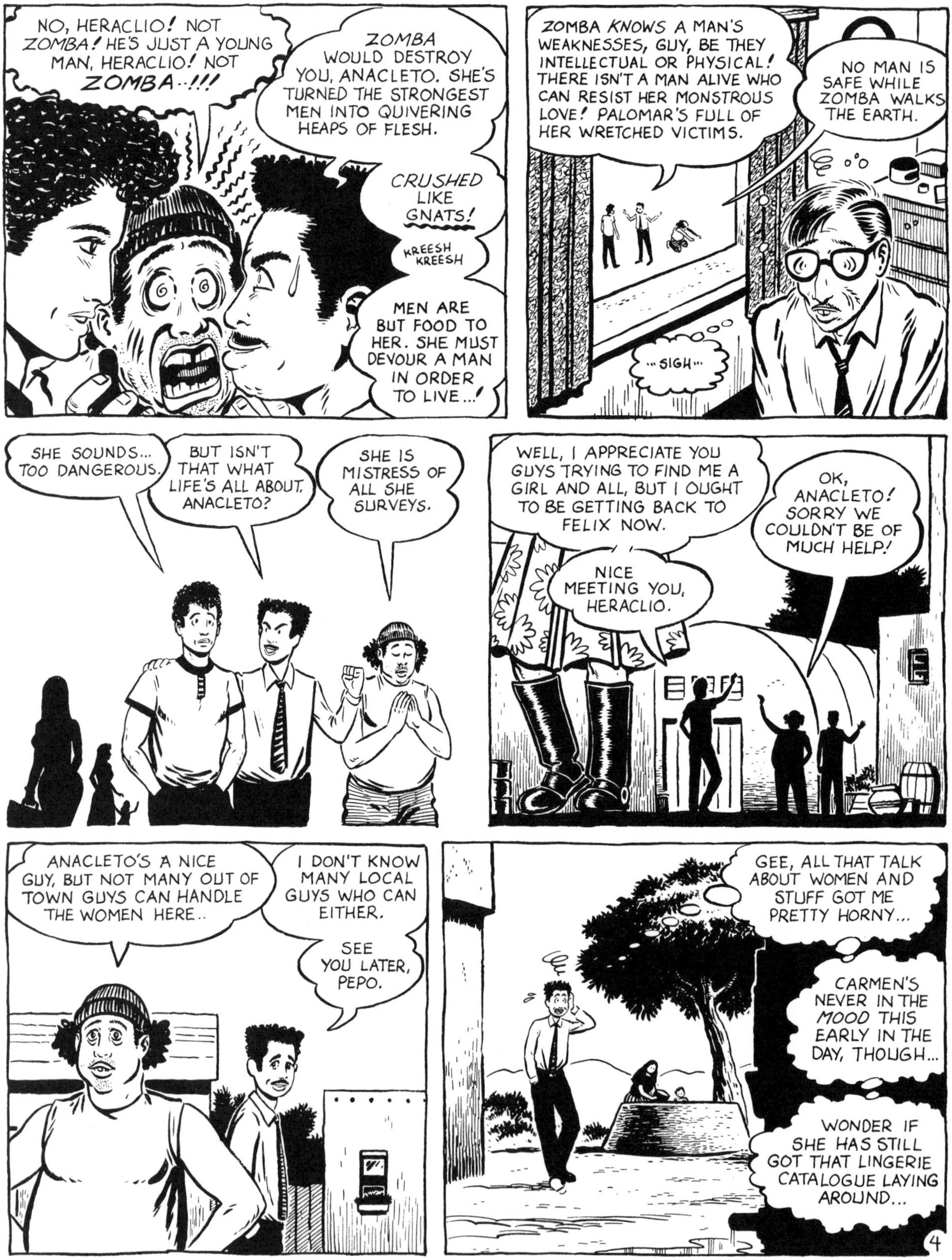
NO, HERACLIO! NOT ZOMBA! HE'S JUST A YOUNG MAN, HERACLIO! NOT ZOMBA..!!!
ZOMBA WOULD DESTROY YOU, ANACLETO. SHE'S TURNED THE STRONGEST MEN INTO QUIVERING HEAPS OF FLESH.
CRUSHED LIKE GNATS!
KREESH KREESH
MEN ARE BUT FOOD TO HER. SHE MUST DEVOUR A MAN IN ORDER TO LIVE...!
ZOMBA KNOWS A MAN'S WEAKNESSES, GUY, BE THEY INTELLECTUAL OR PHYSICAL! THERE ISN'T A MAN ALIVE WHO CAN RESIST HER MONSTROUS LOVE! PALOMAR'S FULL OF HER WRETCHED VICTIMS.
NO MAN IS SAFE WHILE ZOMBA WALKS THE EARTH.
...SIGH...
SHE SOUNDS... TOO DANGEROUS.
BUT ISN'T THAT WHAT LIFE'S ALL ABOUT, ANACLETO?
SHE IS MISTRESS OF ALL SHE SURVEYS.
WELL, I APPRECIATE YOU GUYS TRYING TO FIND ME A GIRL AND ALL, BUT I OUGHT TO BE GETTING BACK TO FELIX NOW.
NICE MEETING YOU, HERACLIO.
OK, ANACLETO! SORRY WE COULDN'T BE OF MUCH HELP!
ANACLETO'S A NICE GUY, BUT NOT MANY OUT OF TOWN GUYS CAN HANDLE THE WOMEN HERE..
I DON'T KNOW MANY LOCAL GUYS WHO CAN EITHER.
SEE YOU LATER, PEPO.
GEE, ALL THAT TALK ABOUT WOMEN AND STUFF GOT ME PRETTY HORNY...
CARMEN'S NEVER IN THE MOOD THIS EARLY IN THE DAY, THOUGH...
WONDER IF SHE HAS STILL GOT THAT LINGERIE CATALOGUE LAYING AROUND...
4

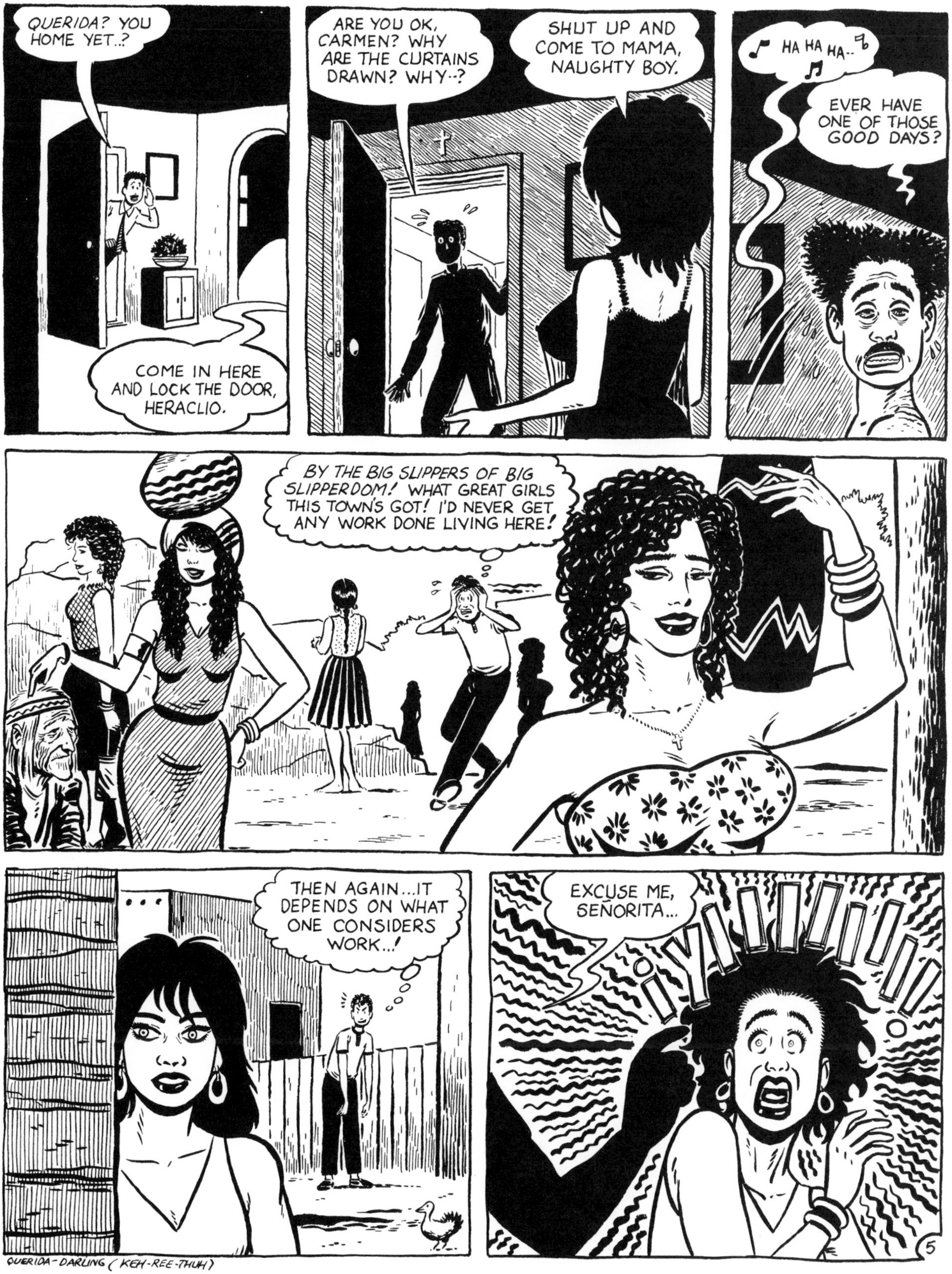
QUERIDA? YOU HOME YET..?
COME IN HERE AND LOCK THE DOOR, HERACLIO.
ARE YOU OK, CARMEN? WHY ARE THE CURTAINS DRAWN? WHY..?
SHUT UP AND COME TO MAMA, NAUGHTY BOY.
HA HA HA..
EVER HAVE ONE OF THOSE GOOD DAYS?
BY THE BIG SLIPPERS OF BIG SLIPPERDOM! WHAT GREAT GIRLS THIS TOWN'S GOT! I'D NEVER GET ANY WORK DONE LIVING HERE!
THEN AGAIN...IT DEPENDS ON WHAT ONE CONSIDERS WORK...!
EXCUSE ME, SEÑORITA...
¡YIIIIIII!
5
QUERIDA - DARLING (KEH-REE-THUH)

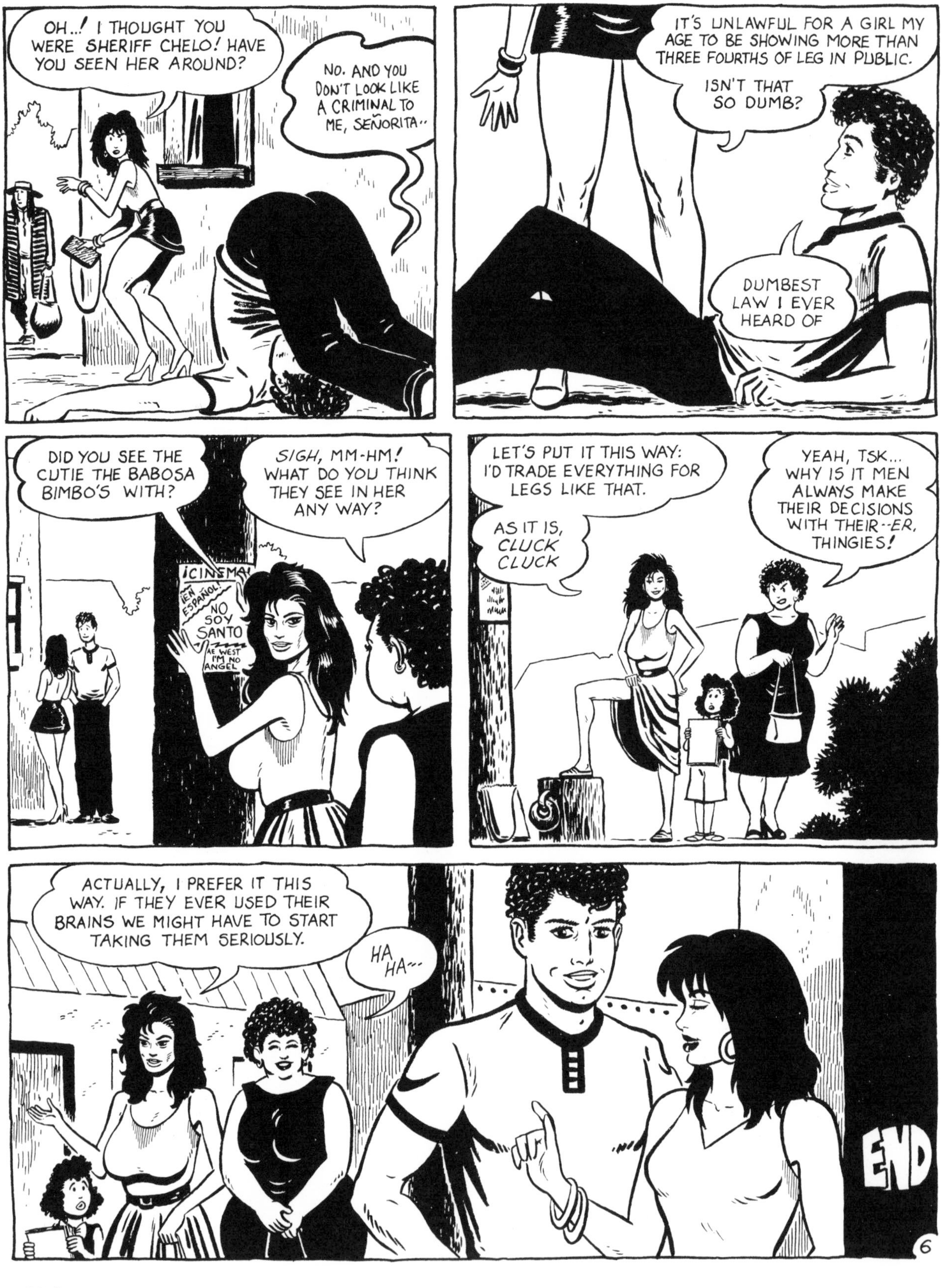
OH..! I THOUGHT YOU WERE SHERIFF CHELO! HAVE YOU SEEN HER AROUND?
NO. AND YOU DON'T LOOK LIKE A CRIMINAL TO ME, SEÑORITA..
IT'S UNLAWFUL FOR A GIRL MY AGE TO BE SHOWING MORE THAN THREE FOURTHS OF LEG IN PUBLIC.
ISN'T THAT SO DUMB?
DUMBEST LAW I EVER HEARD OF
DID YOU SEE THE CUTIE THE BABOSA BIMBO'S WITH?
SIGH, MM-HM! WHAT DO YOU THINK THEY SEE IN HER ANY WAY?
¡CINEMA!
¡EN ESPAÑOL!
NO SOY SANTO
MAE WEST I'M NO ANGEL
LET'S PUT IT THIS WAY: I'D TRADE EVERYTHING FOR LEGS LIKE THAT.
AS IT IS, CLUCK CLUCK
YEAH, TSK... WHY IS IT MEN ALWAYS MAKE THEIR DECISIONS WITH THEIR--ER, THINGIES!
ACTUALLY, I PREFER IT THIS WAY. IF THEY EVER USED THEIR BRAINS WE MIGHT HAVE TO START TAKING THEM SERIOUSLY.
HA HA...
END
6

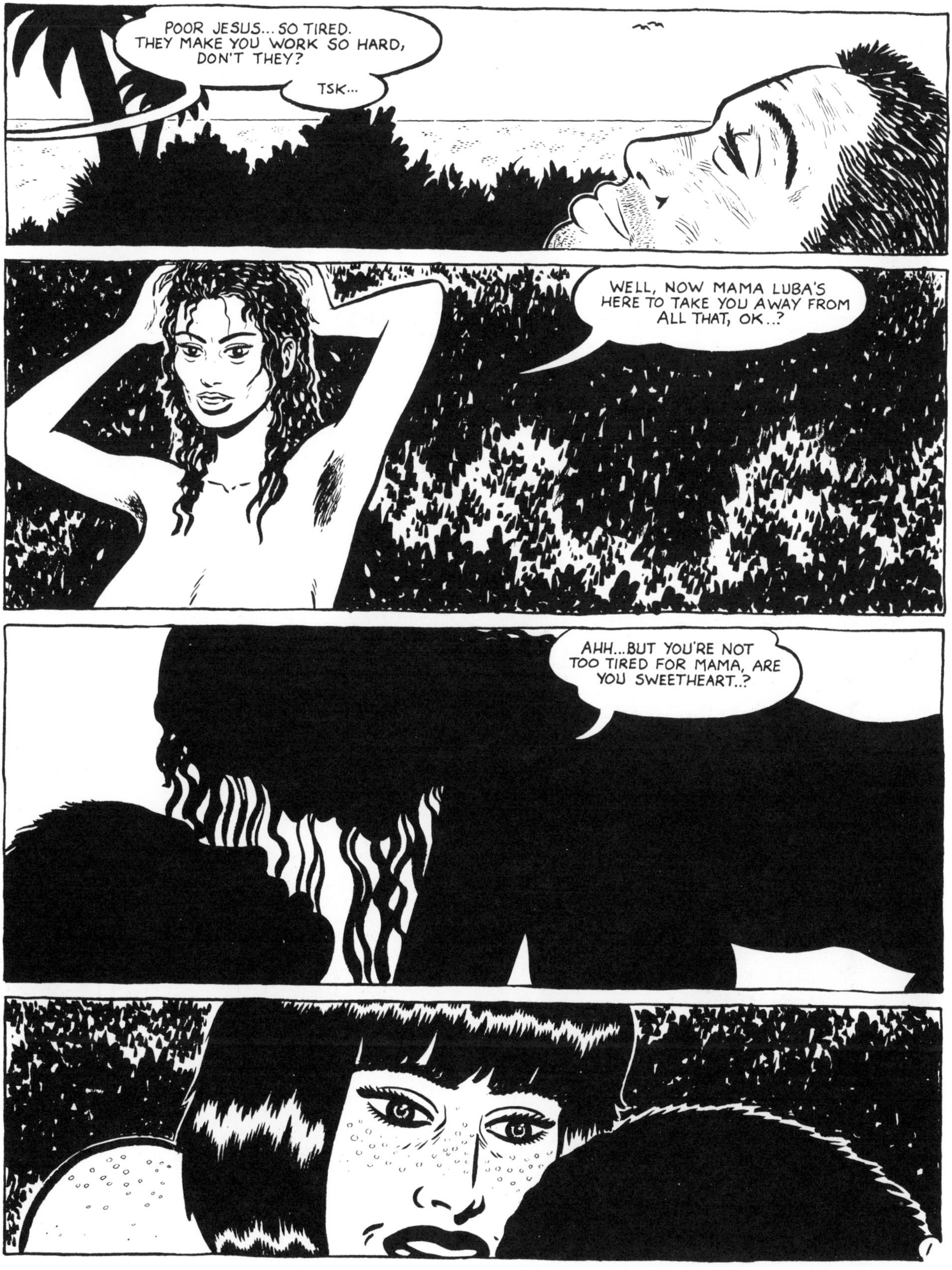
POOR JESUS... SO TIRED. THEY MAKE YOU WORK SO HARD, DON'T THEY?
TSK...
WELL, NOW MAMA LUBA'S HERE TO TAKE YOU AWAY FROM ALL THAT, OK..?
AHH...BUT YOU'RE NOT TOO TIRED FOR MAMA, ARE YOU SWEETHEART..?

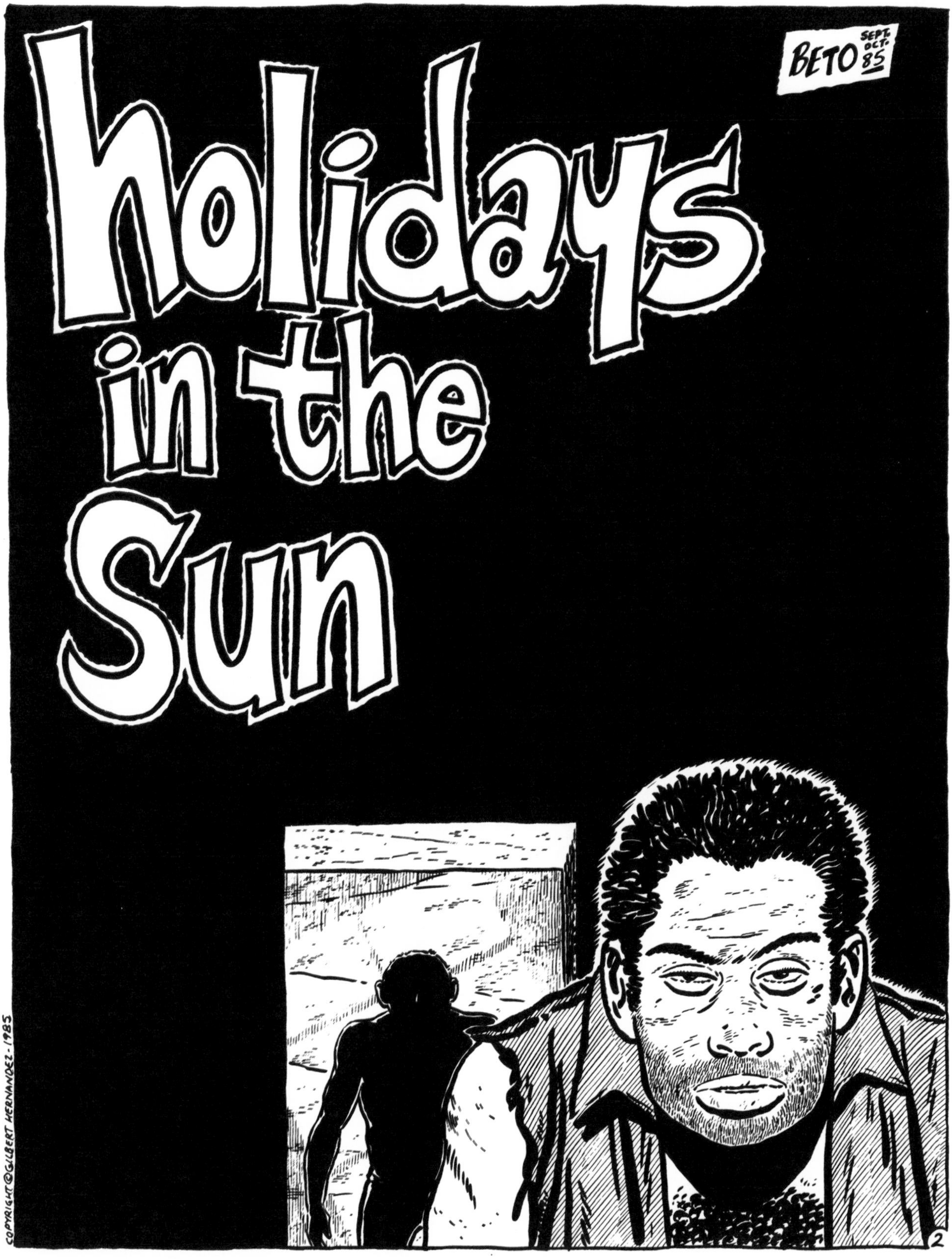
holidays in the Sun
BETO SEPT. OCT. 85
2

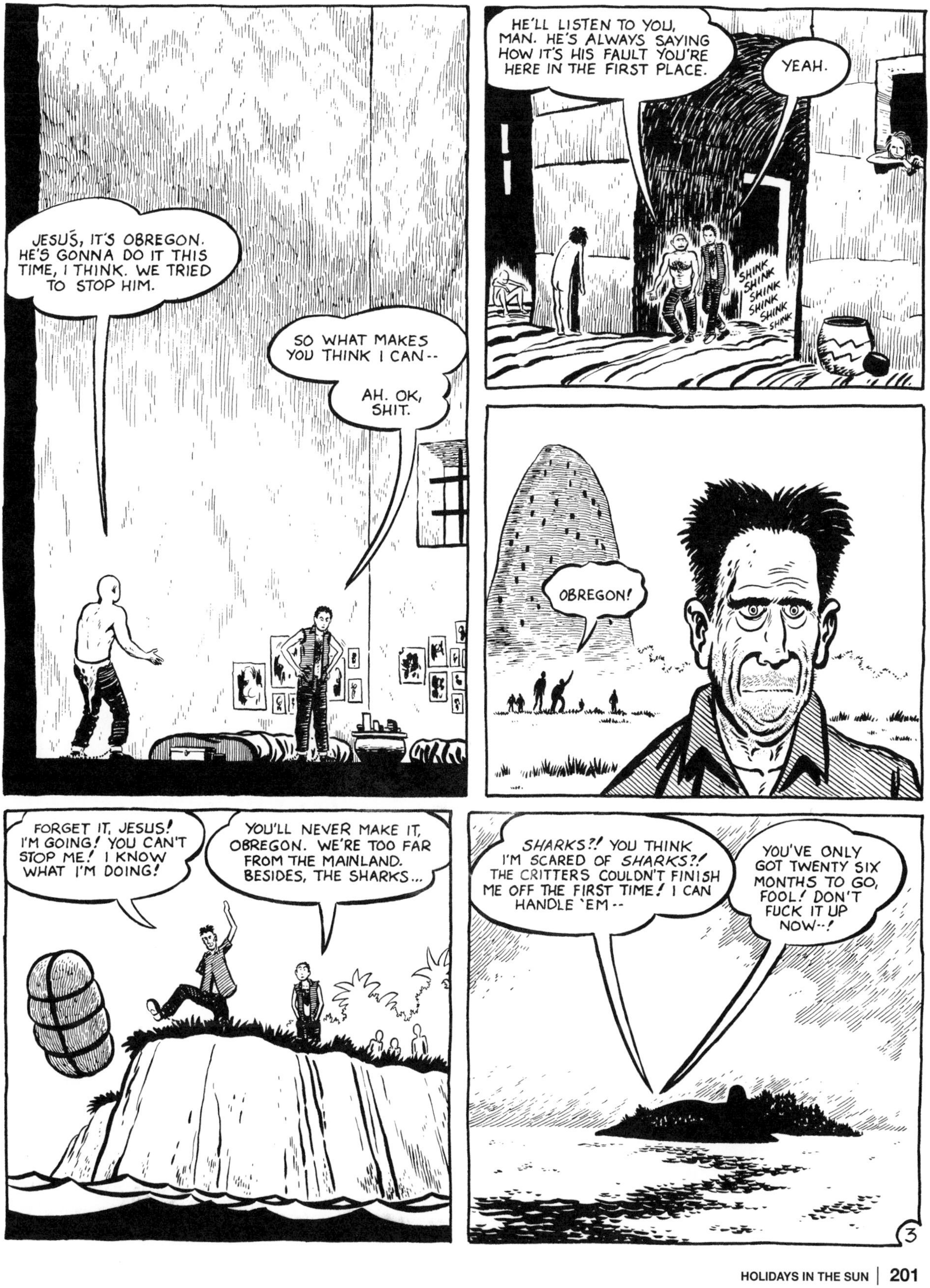
JESUS, IT'S OBREGON. HE'S GONNA DO IT THIS TIME, I THINK. WE TRIED TO STOP HIM.
SO WHAT MAKES YOU THINK I CAN--
AH. OK, SHIT.
HE'LL LISTEN TO YOU, MAN. HE'S ALWAYS SAYING HOW IT'S HIS FAULT YOU'RE HERE IN THE FIRST PLACE.
YEAH.
SHINK SHINK SHINK SHINK SHINK SHINK
OBREGON!
FORGET IT, JESUS! I'M GOING! YOU CAN'T STOP ME! I KNOW WHAT I'M DOING!
YOU'LL NEVER MAKE IT, OBREGON. WE'RE TOO FAR FROM THE MAINLAND. BESIDES, THE SHARKS...
SHARKS?! YOU THINK I'M SCARED OF SHARKS?! THE CRITTERS COULDN'T FINISH ME OFF THE FIRST TIME! I CAN HANDLE 'EM--
YOU'VE ONLY GOT TWENTY SIX MONTHS TO GO, FOOL! DON'T FUCK IT UP NOW--!
3

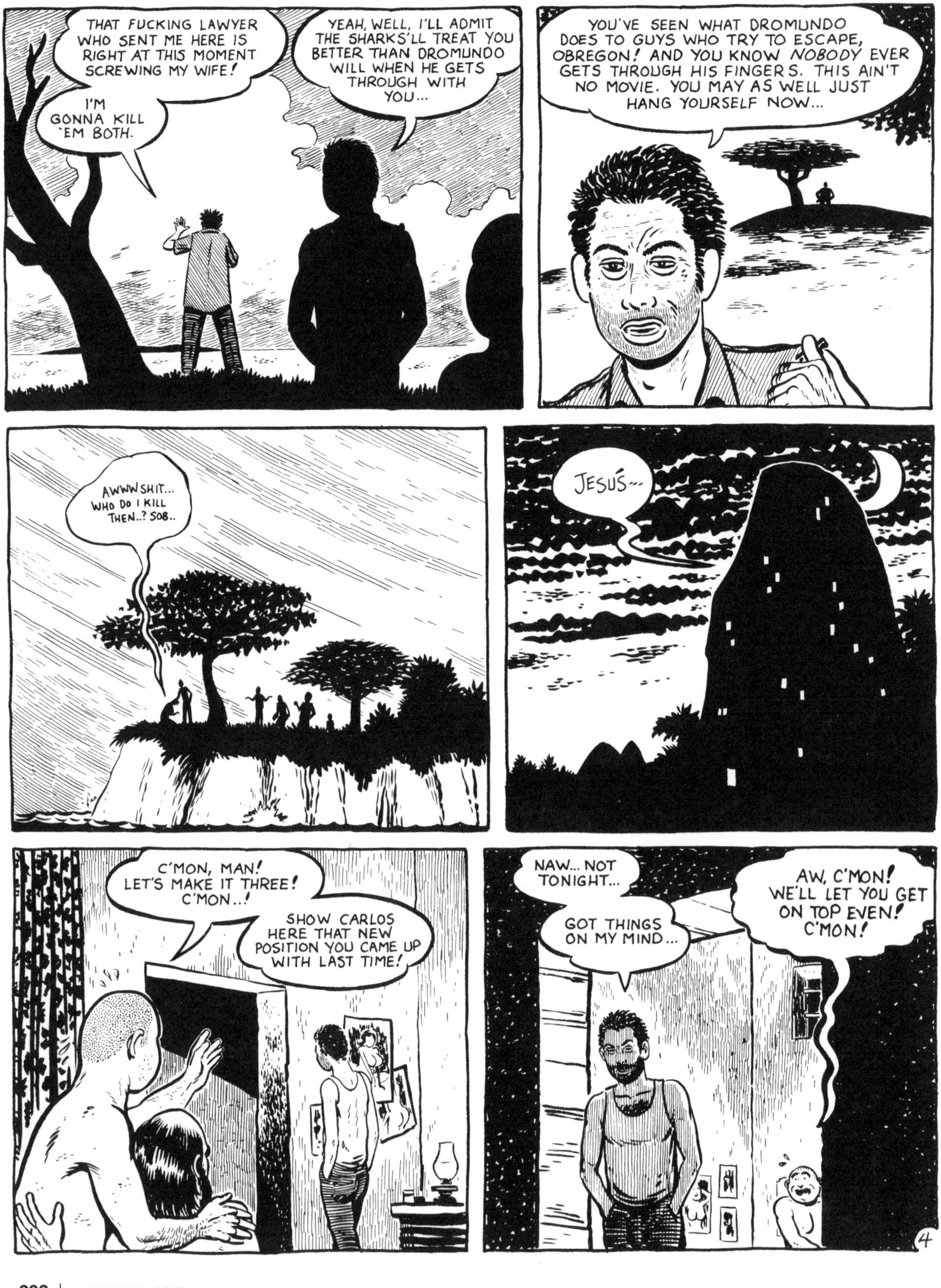
THAT FUCKING LAWYER WHO SENT ME HERE IS RIGHT AT THIS MOMENT SCREWING MY WIFE!
I'M GONNA KILL 'EM BOTH.
YEAH, WELL, I'LL ADMIT THE SHARKS'LL TREAT YOU BETTER THAN DROMUNDO WILL WHEN HE GETS THROUGH WITH YOU...
YOU'VE SEEN WHAT DROMUNDO DOES TO GUYS WHO TRY TO ESCAPE, OBREGON! AND YOU KNOW NOBODY EVER GETS THROUGH HIS FINGERS. THIS AIN'T NO MOVIE. YOU MAY AS WELL JUST HANG YOURSELF NOW...
AWWW SHIT... WHO DO I KILL THEN..? SOB..
JESÚS...
C'MON, MAN! LET'S MAKE IT THREE! C'MON...!
SHOW CARLOS HERE THAT NEW POSITION YOU CAME UP WITH LAST TIME!
NAW... NOT TONIGHT...
GOT THINGS ON MY MIND...
AW, C'MON! WE'LL LET YOU GET ON TOP EVEN! C'MON!
4

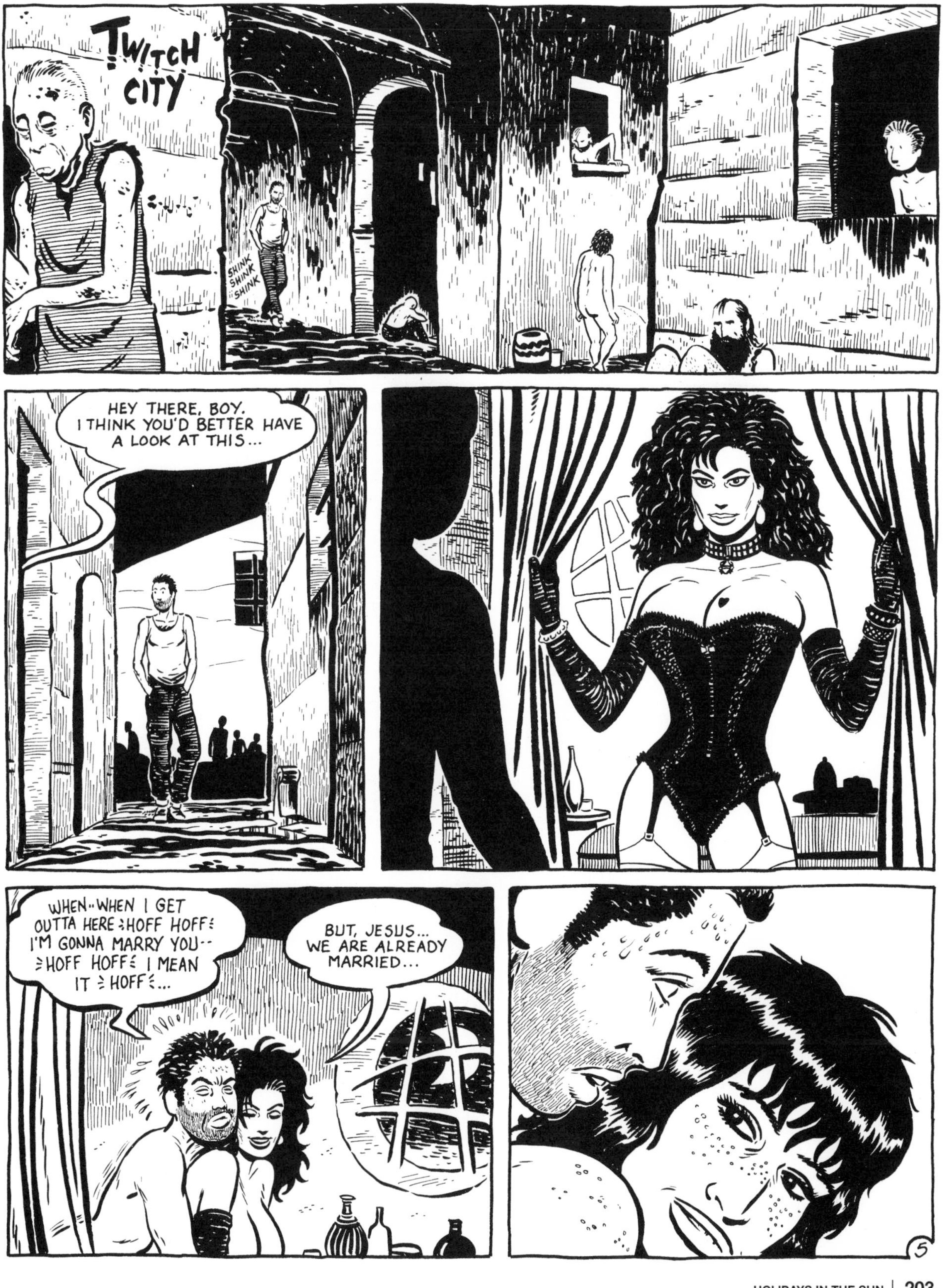
TWITCH CITY
SHINK SHINK SHINK
HEY THERE, BOY. I THINK YOU'D BETTER HAVE A LOOK AT THIS...
WHEN.. WHEN I GET OUTTA HERE ≥HOFF HOFF≤ I'M GONNA MARRY YOU-- ≥HOFF HOFF≤ I MEAN IT ≥HOFF≤...
BUT, JESUS... WE ARE ALREADY MARRIED...
5

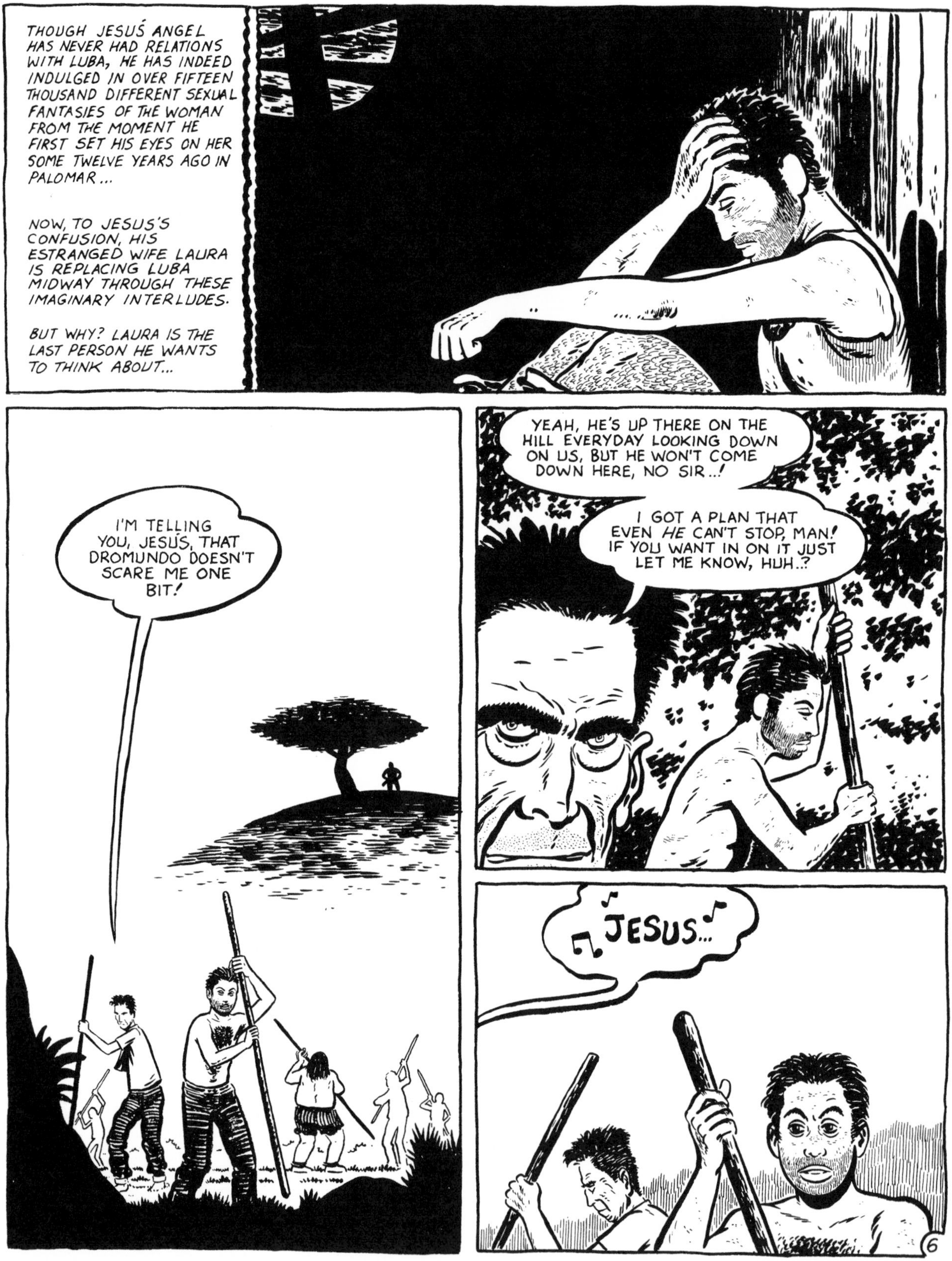
THOUGH JESÚS ANGEL HAS NEVER HAD RELATIONS WITH LUBA, HE HAS INDEED INDULGED IN OVER FIFTEEN THOUSAND DIFFERENT SEXUAL FANTASIES OF THE WOMAN FROM THE MOMENT HE FIRST SET HIS EYES ON HER SOME TWELVE YEARS AGO IN PALOMAR...
NOW, TO JESUS'S CONFUSION, HIS ESTRANGED WIFE LAURA IS REPLACING LUBA MIDWAY THROUGH THESE IMAGINARY INTERLUDES.
BUT WHY? LAURA IS THE LAST PERSON HE WANTS TO THINK ABOUT...
I'M TELLING YOU, JESÚS, THAT DROMUNDO DOESN'T SCARE ME ONE BIT!
YEAH, HE'S UP THERE ON THE HILL EVERYDAY LOOKING DOWN ON US, BUT HE WON'T COME DOWN HERE, NO SIR..!
I GOT A PLAN THAT EVEN *HE* CAN'T STOP, MAN! IF YOU WANT IN ON IT JUST LET ME KNOW, HUH..?
JESUS...
6

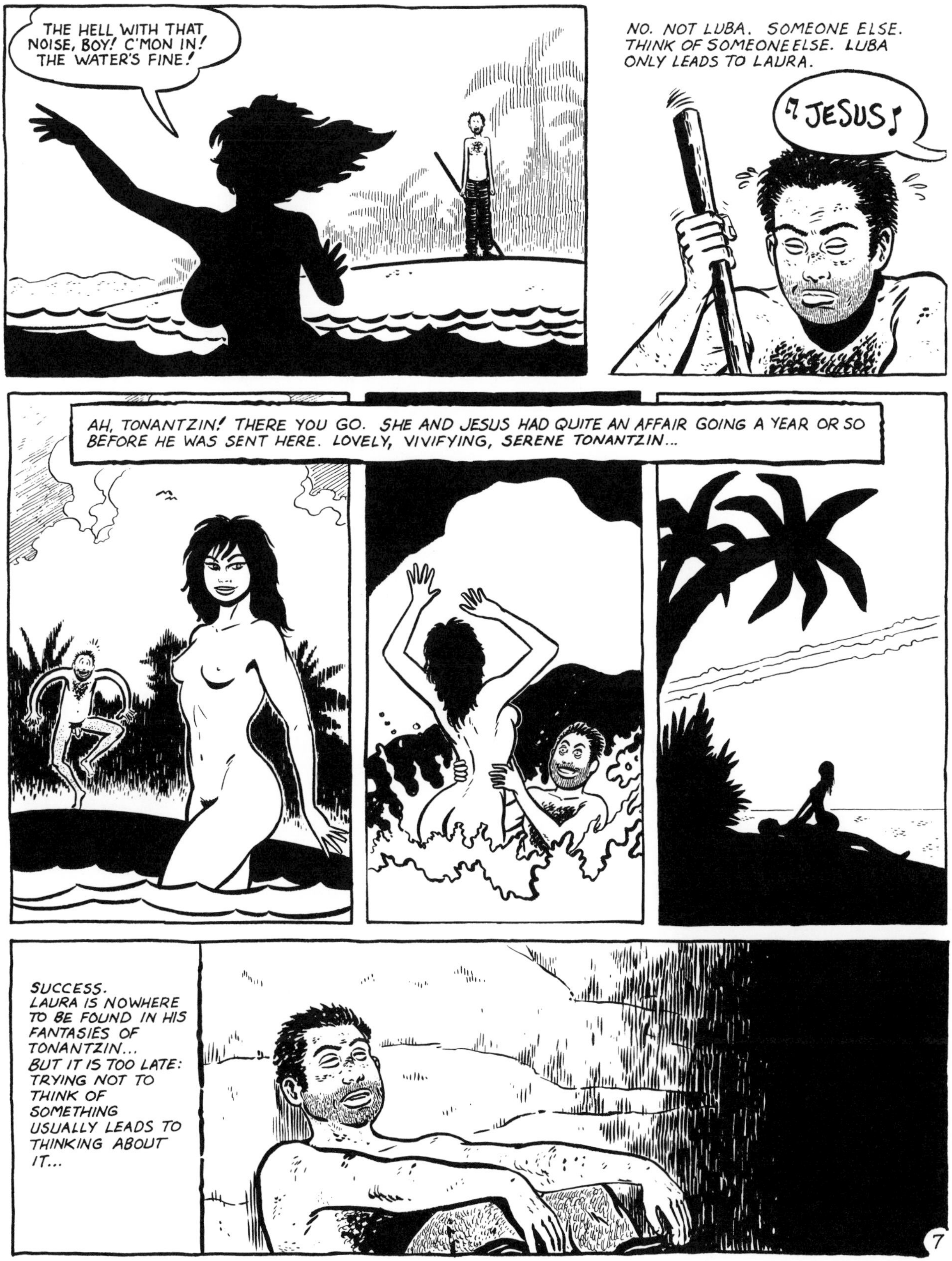
THE HELL WITH THAT NOISE, BOY! C'MON IN! THE WATER'S FINE!
NO. NOT LUBA. SOMEONE ELSE. THINK OF SOMEONE ELSE. LUBA ONLY LEADS TO LAURA.
♫ JESUS ♫
AH, TONANTZIN! THERE YOU GO. SHE AND JESUS HAD QUITE AN AFFAIR GOING A YEAR OR SO BEFORE HE WAS SENT HERE. LOVELY, VIVIFYING, SERENE TONANTZIN...
SUCCESS. LAURA IS NOWHERE TO BE FOUND IN HIS FANTASIES OF TONANTZIN... BUT IT IS TOO LATE: TRYING NOT TO THINK OF SOMETHING USUALLY LEADS TO THINKING ABOUT IT...
7

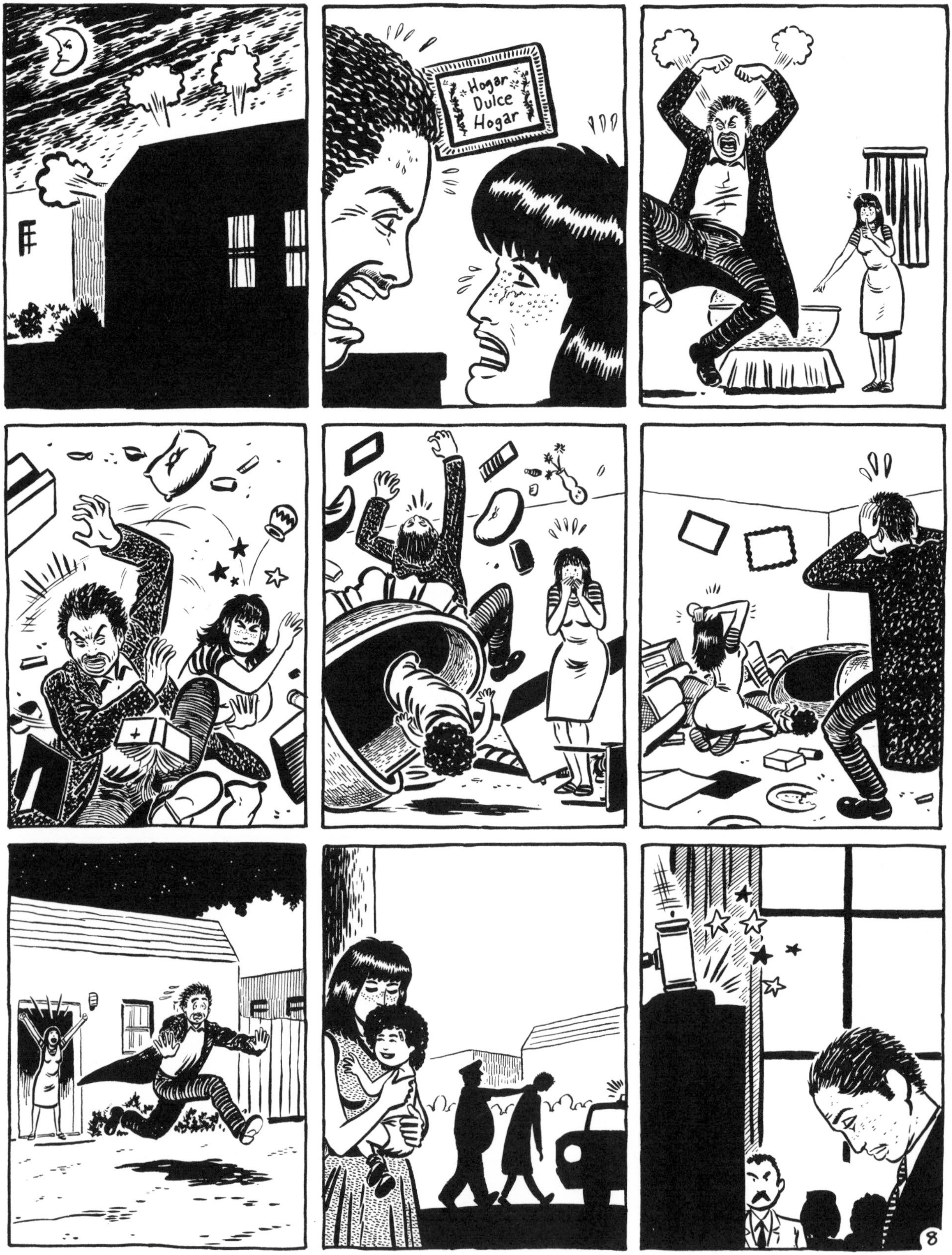
Hogar
Dulce
Hogar
8

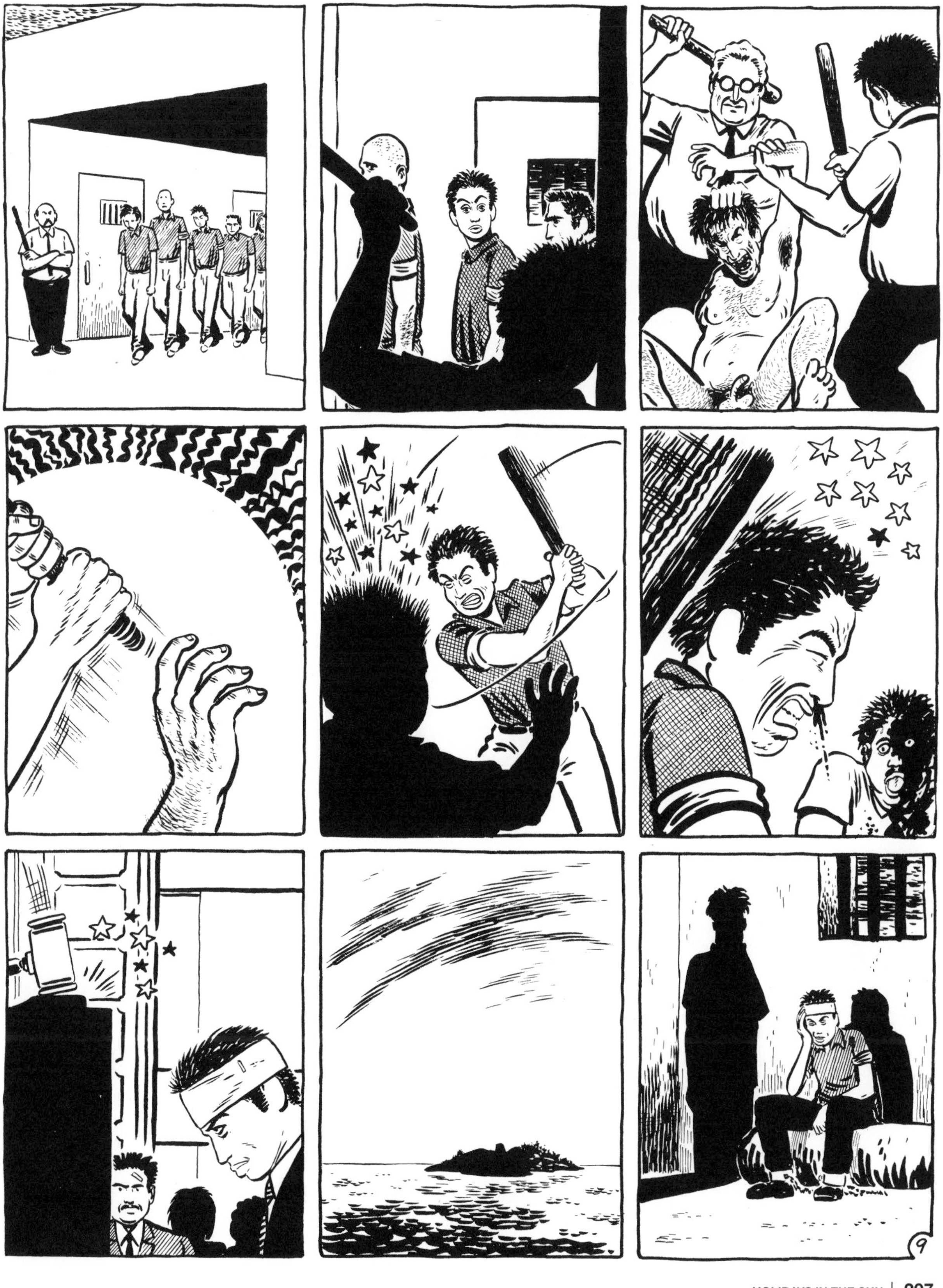
9

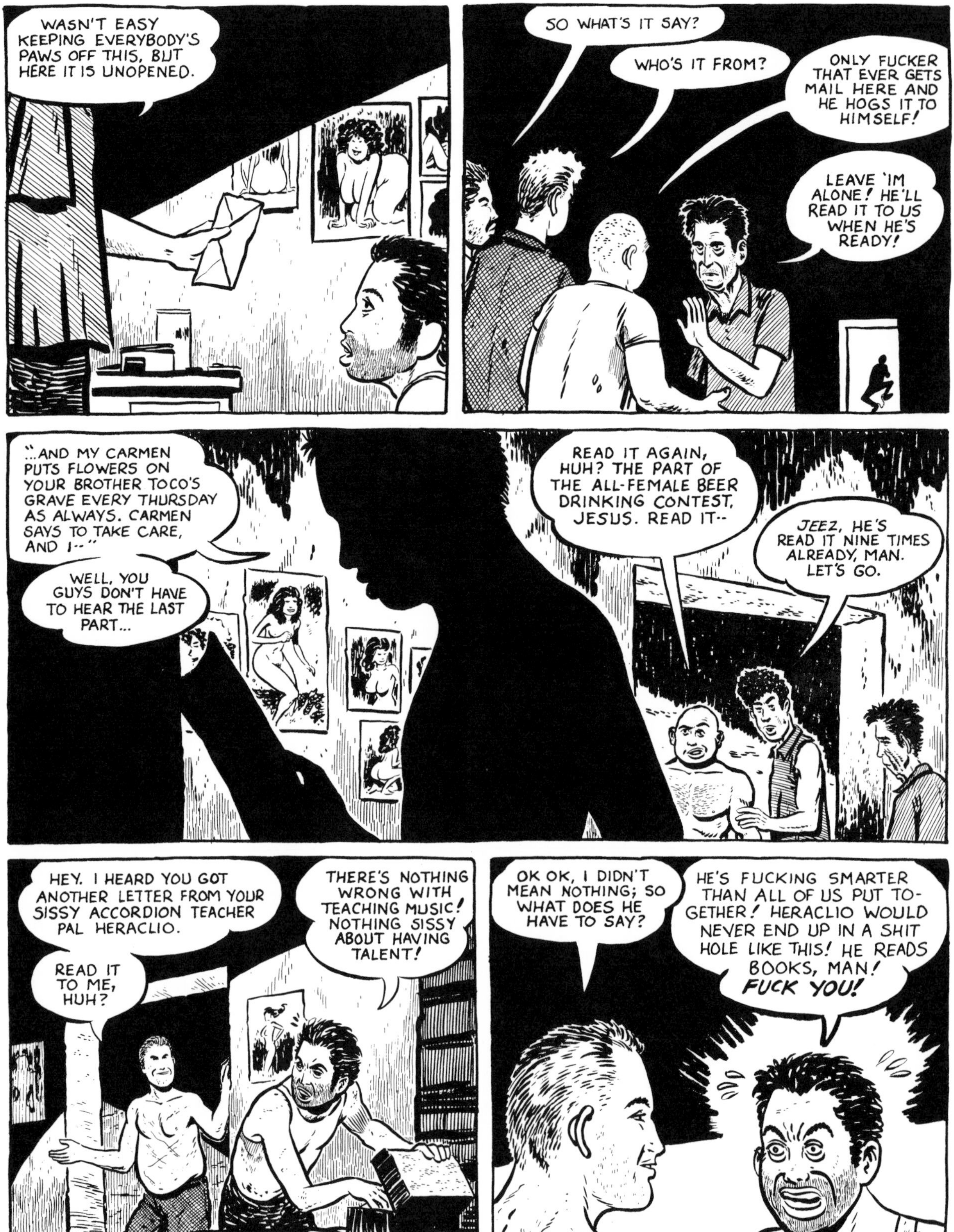
WASN'T EASY KEEPING EVERYBODY'S PAWS OFF THIS, BUT HERE IT IS UNOPENED.
SO WHAT'S IT SAY?
WHO'S IT FROM?
ONLY FUCKER THAT EVER GETS MAIL HERE AND HE HOGS IT TO HIMSELF!
LEAVE 'IM ALONE! HE'LL READ IT TO US WHEN HE'S READY!
"...AND MY CARMEN PUTS FLOWERS ON YOUR BROTHER TOCO'S GRAVE EVERY THURSDAY AS ALWAYS. CARMEN SAYS TO TAKE CARE, AND I--"
WELL, YOU GUYS DON'T HAVE TO HEAR THE LAST PART...
READ IT AGAIN, HUH? THE PART OF THE ALL-FEMALE BEER DRINKING CONTEST, JESUS. READ IT--
JEEZ, HE'S READ IT NINE TIMES ALREADY, MAN. LET'S GO.
HEY. I HEARD YOU GOT ANOTHER LETTER FROM YOUR SISSY ACCORDION TEACHER PAL HERACLIO.
READ IT TO ME, HUH?
THERE'S NOTHING WRONG WITH TEACHING MUSIC! NOTHING SISSY ABOUT HAVING TALENT!
OK OK, I DIDN'T MEAN NOTHING; SO WHAT DOES HE HAVE TO SAY?
HE'S FUCKING SMARTER THAN ALL OF US PUT TOGETHER! HERACLIO WOULD NEVER END UP IN A SHIT HOLE LIKE THIS! HE READS BOOKS, MAN! FUCK YOU!
10

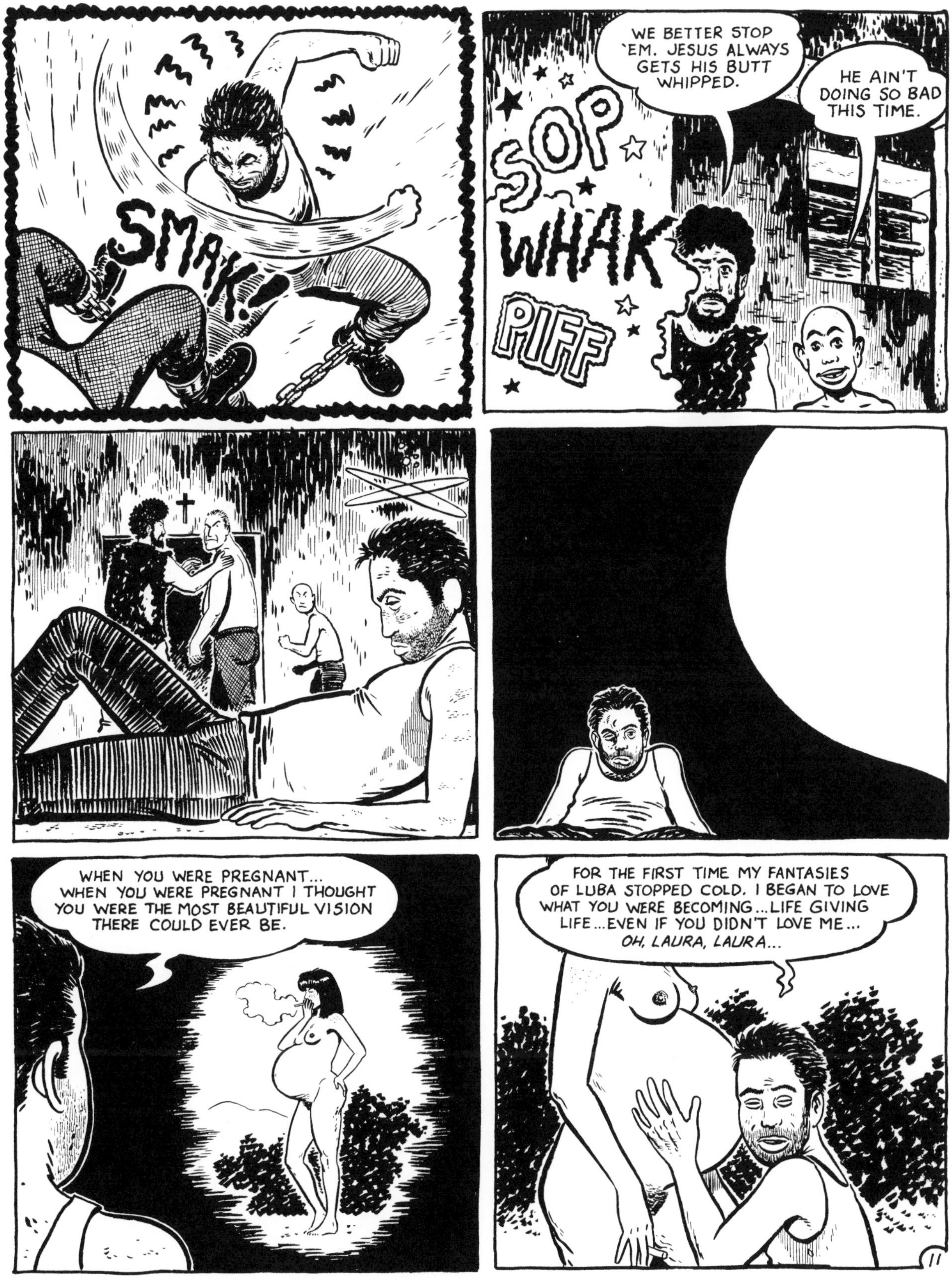
SMAK!
WE BETTER STOP 'EM. JESUS ALWAYS GETS HIS BUTT WHIPPED.
HE AIN'T DOING SO BAD THIS TIME.
SOP
WHAK
PIFF
WHEN YOU WERE PREGNANT... WHEN YOU WERE PREGNANT I THOUGHT YOU WERE THE MOST BEAUTIFUL VISION THERE COULD EVER BE.
FOR THE FIRST TIME MY FANTASIES OF LUBA STOPPED COLD. I BEGAN TO LOVE WHAT YOU WERE BECOMING...LIFE GIVING LIFE...EVEN IF YOU DIDN'T LOVE ME... *OH, LAURA, LAURA...*
11

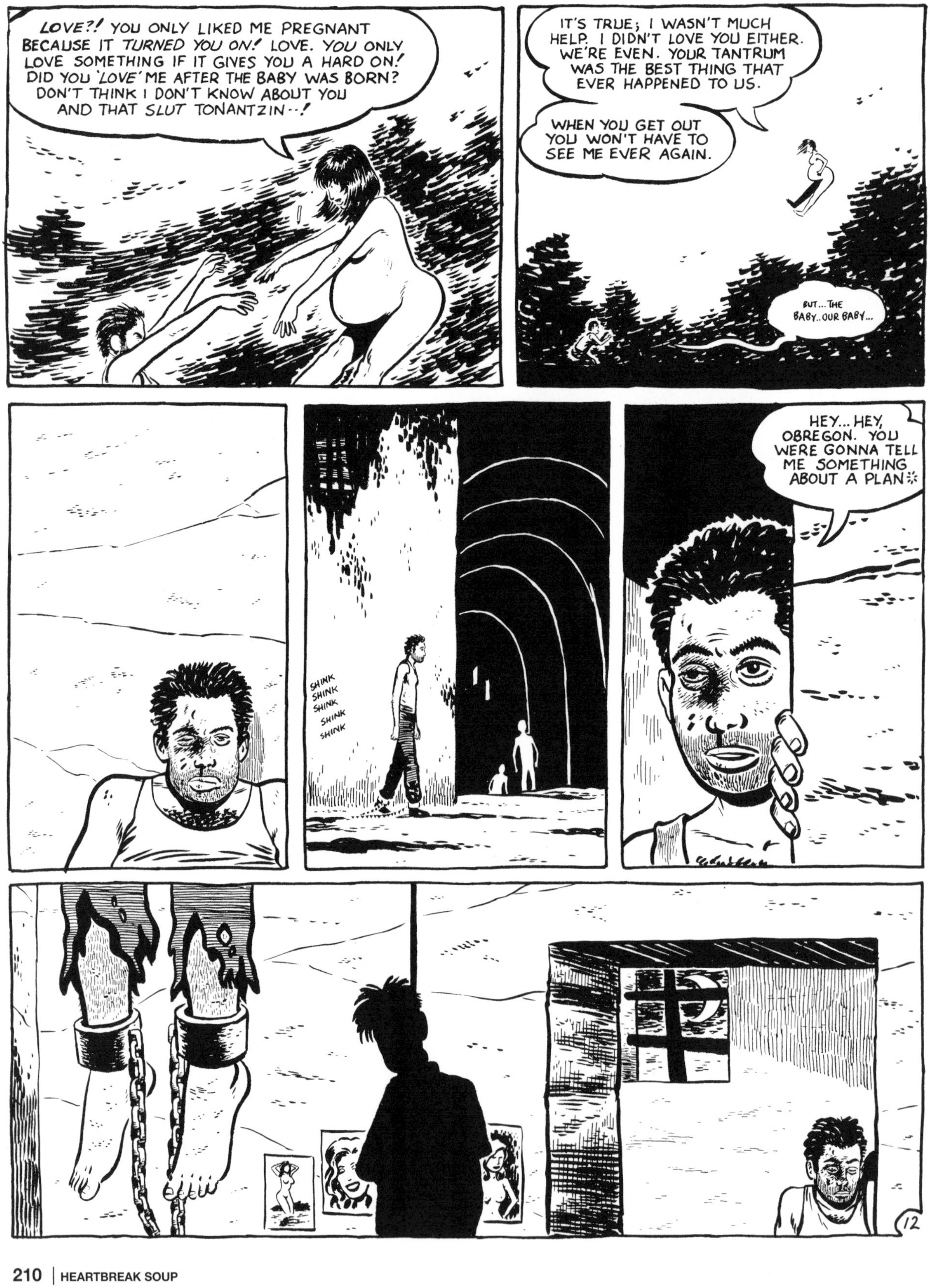
LOVE?! YOU ONLY LIKED ME PREGNANT BECAUSE IT TURNED YOU ON! LOVE. YOU ONLY LOVE SOMETHING IF IT GIVES YOU A HARD ON! DID YOU 'LOVE' ME AFTER THE BABY WAS BORN? DON'T THINK I DON'T KNOW ABOUT YOU AND THAT SLUT TONANTZIN--!
!
IT'S TRUE; I WASN'T MUCH HELP. I DIDN'T LOVE YOU EITHER. WE'RE EVEN. YOUR TANTRUM WAS THE BEST THING THAT EVER HAPPENED TO US.
WHEN YOU GET OUT YOU WON'T HAVE TO SEE ME EVER AGAIN.
BUT... THE BABY.. OUR BABY...
SHINK SHINK SHINK SHINK SHINK
HEY... HEY, OBREGON. YOU WERE GONNA TELL ME SOMETHING ABOUT A PLAN
12

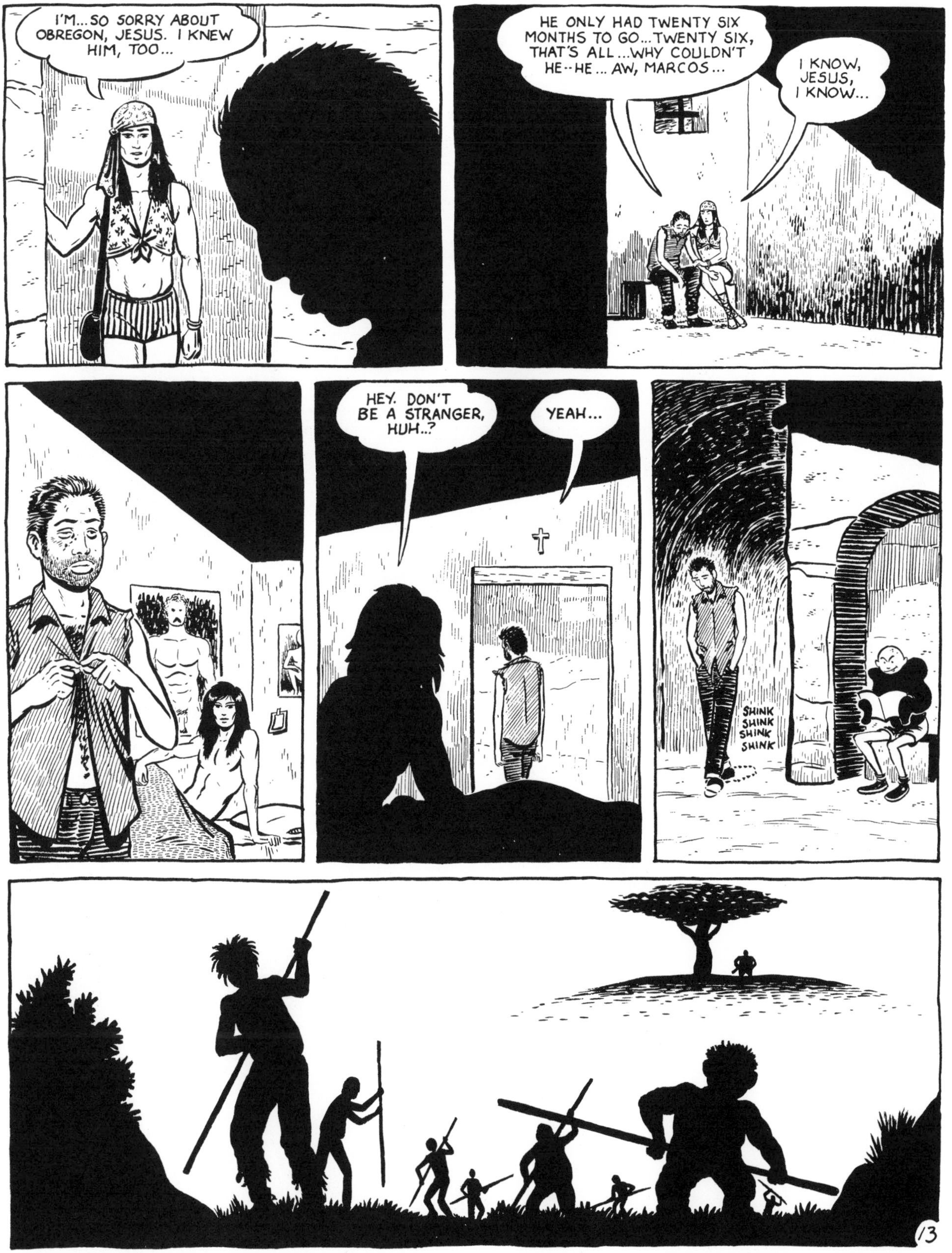
I'M...SO SORRY ABOUT OBREGON, JESUS. I KNEW HIM, TOO...
HE ONLY HAD TWENTY SIX MONTHS TO GO...TWENTY SIX, THAT'S ALL...WHY COULDN'T HE--HE... AW, MARCOS...
I KNOW, JESUS, I KNOW...
HEY. DON'T BE A STRANGER, HUH..?
YEAH...
SHINK
SHINK
SHINK
SHINK
13

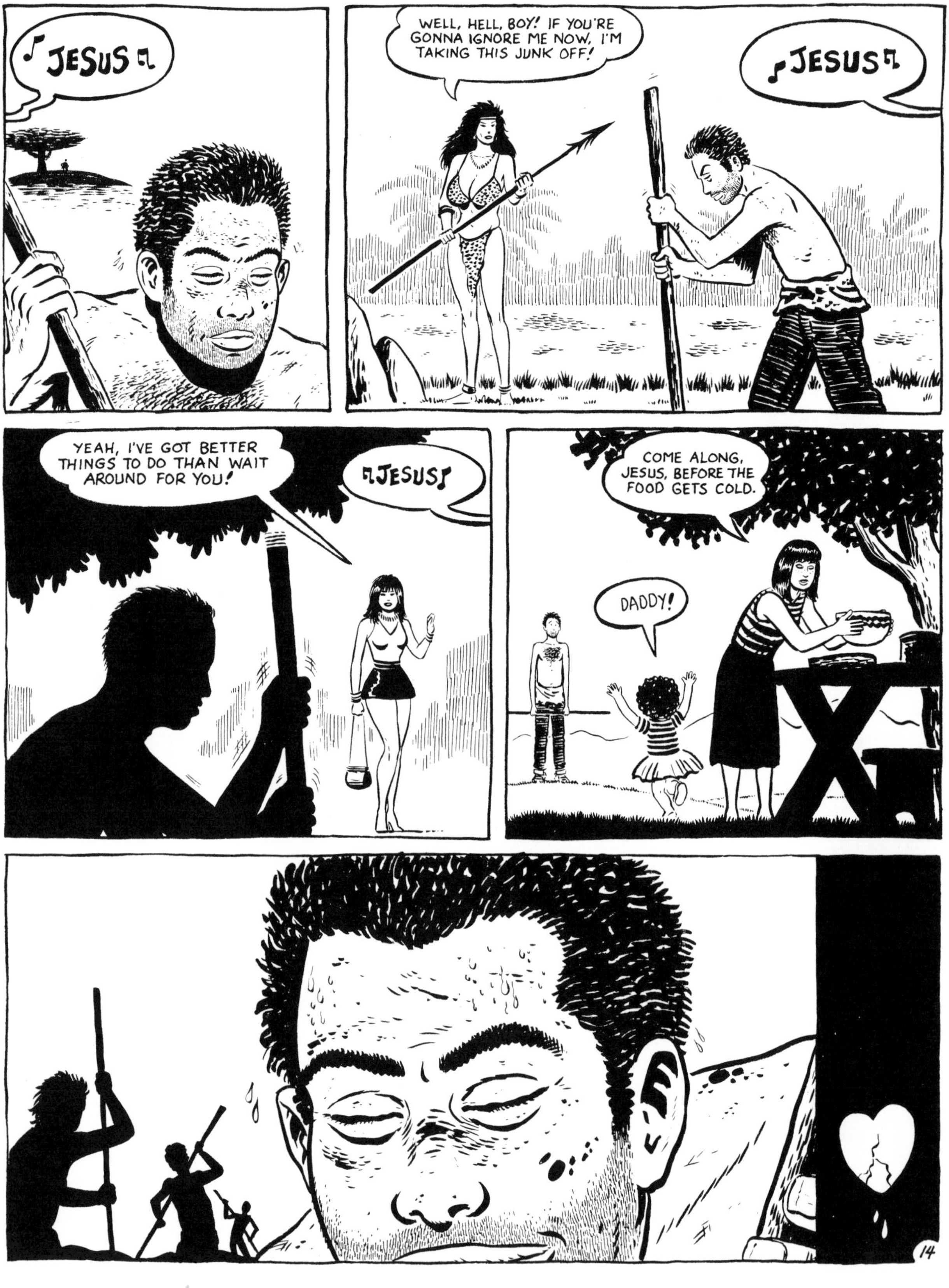
JESUS
WELL, HELL, BOY! IF YOU'RE GONNA IGNORE ME NOW, I'M TAKING THIS JUNK OFF!
JESUS
YEAH, I'VE GOT BETTER THINGS TO DO THAN WAIT AROUND FOR YOU!
JESUS!
COME ALONG, JESUS, BEFORE THE FOOD GETS COLD.
DADDY!
14

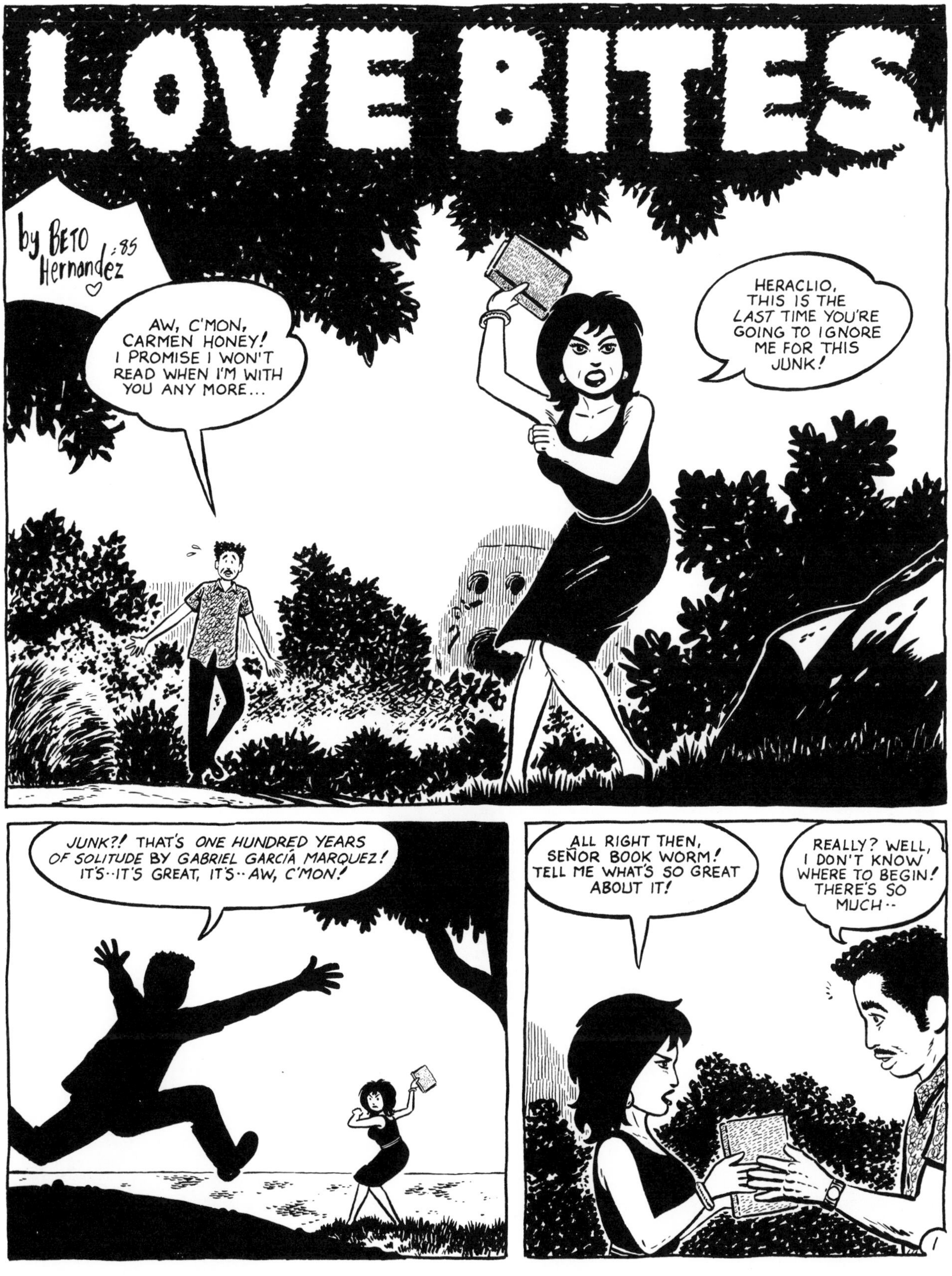
LOVE BITES
by BETO Hernandez '85
AW, C'MON, CARMEN HONEY! I PROMISE I WON'T READ WHEN I'M WITH YOU ANY MORE...
HERACLIO, THIS IS THE LAST TIME YOU'RE GOING TO IGNORE ME FOR THIS JUNK!
JUNK?! THAT'S ONE HUNDRED YEARS OF SOLITUDE BY GABRIEL GARCÍA MARQUEZ! IT'S··IT'S GREAT, IT'S··AW, C'MON!
ALL RIGHT THEN, SEÑOR BOOK WORM! TELL ME WHAT'S SO GREAT ABOUT IT!
REALLY? WELL, I DON'T KNOW WHERE TO BEGIN! THERE'S SO MUCH··
1

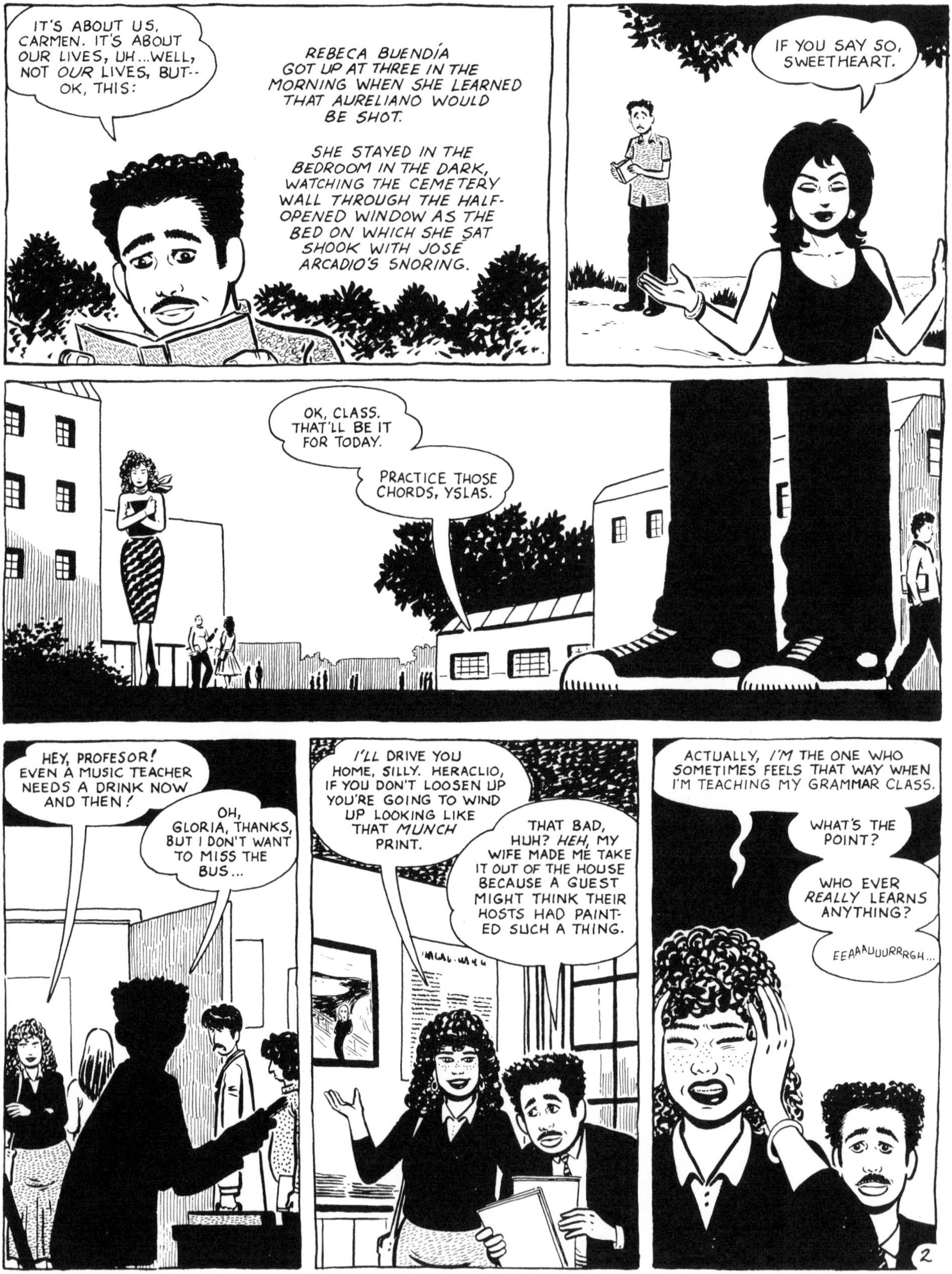

IT'S ABOUT US, CARMEN. IT'S ABOUT OUR LIVES, UH...WELL, NOT OUR LIVES, BUT-- OK, THIS:
REBECA BUENDÍA GOT UP AT THREE IN THE MORNING WHEN SHE LEARNED THAT AURELIANO WOULD BE SHOT.
SHE STAYED IN THE BEDROOM IN THE DARK, WATCHING THE CEMETERY WALL THROUGH THE HALF-OPENED WINDOW AS THE BED ON WHICH SHE SAT SHOOK WITH JOSÉ ARCADIO'S SNORING.
IF YOU SAY SO, SWEETHEART.
OK, CLASS. THAT'LL BE IT FOR TODAY.
PRACTICE THOSE CHORDS, YSLAS.
HEY, PROFESOR! EVEN A MUSIC TEACHER NEEDS A DRINK NOW AND THEN!
OH, GLORIA, THANKS, BUT I DON'T WANT TO MISS THE BUS...
I'LL DRIVE YOU HOME, SILLY. HERACLIO, IF YOU DON'T LOOSEN UP YOU'RE GOING TO WIND UP LOOKING LIKE THAT MUNCH PRINT.
THAT BAD, HUH? HEH, MY WIFE MADE ME TAKE IT OUT OF THE HOUSE BECAUSE A GUEST MIGHT THINK THEIR HOSTS HAD PAINTED SUCH A THING.
ACTUALLY, I'M THE ONE WHO SOMETIMES FEELS THAT WAY WHEN I'M TEACHING MY GRAMMAR CLASS.
WHAT'S THE POINT?
WHO EVER REALLY LEARNS ANYTHING?
EEAAAUUURRRGH...
2

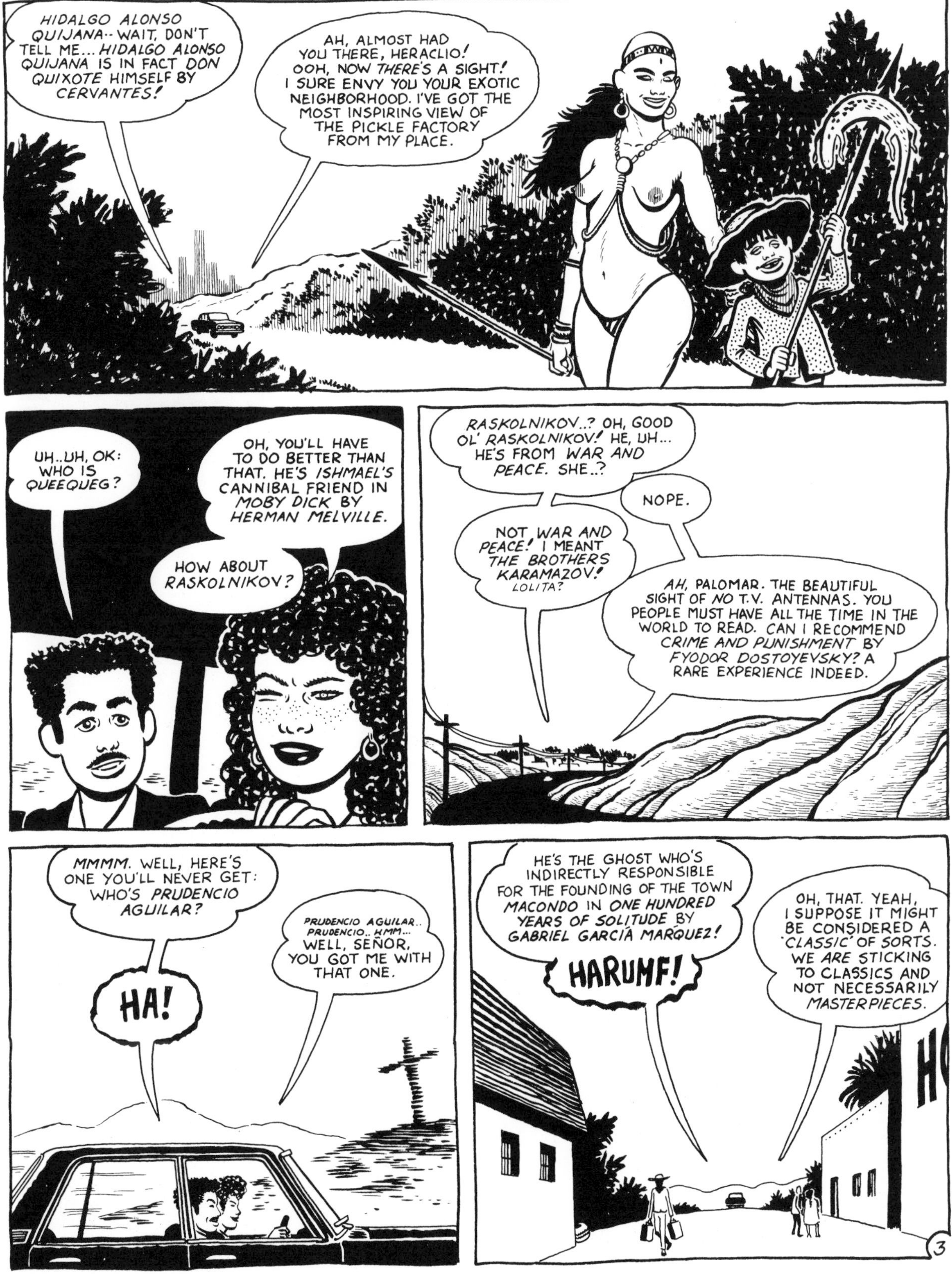

HIDALGO ALONSO QUIJANA.. WAIT, DON'T TELL ME... HIDALGO ALONSO QUIJANA IS IN FACT DON QUIXOTE HIMSELF BY CERVANTES!
AH, ALMOST HAD YOU THERE, HERACLIO! OOH, NOW THERE'S A SIGHT! I SURE ENVY YOU YOUR EXOTIC NEIGHBORHOOD. I'VE GOT THE MOST INSPIRING VIEW OF THE PICKLE FACTORY FROM MY PLACE.
UH..UH, OK: WHO IS QUEEQUEG?
OH, YOU'LL HAVE TO DO BETTER THAN THAT. HE'S ISHMAEL'S CANNIBAL FRIEND IN MOBY DICK BY HERMAN MELVILLE.
HOW ABOUT RASKOLNIKOV?
RASKOLNIKOV..? OH, GOOD OL' RASKOLNIKOV! HE, UH... HE'S FROM WAR AND PEACE. SHE..?
NOPE.
NOT WAR AND PEACE! I MEANT THE BROTHERS KARAMAZOV! LOLITA?
AH, PALOMAR. THE BEAUTIFUL SIGHT OF NO T.V. ANTENNAS. YOU PEOPLE MUST HAVE ALL THE TIME IN THE WORLD TO READ. CAN I RECOMMEND CRIME AND PUNISHMENT BY FYODOR DOSTOYEVSKY? A RARE EXPERIENCE INDEED.
MMMM. WELL, HERE'S ONE YOU'LL NEVER GET: WHO'S PRUDENCIO AGUILAR?
HA!
PRUDENCIO AGUILAR.. PRUDENCIO.. HMM... WELL, SEÑOR, YOU GOT ME WITH THAT ONE.
HE'S THE GHOST WHO'S INDIRECTLY RESPONSIBLE FOR THE FOUNDING OF THE TOWN MACONDO IN ONE HUNDRED YEARS OF SOLITUDE BY GABRIEL GARCÍA MARQUEZ!
HARUMF!
OH, THAT. YEAH, I SUPPOSE IT MIGHT BE CONSIDERED A 'CLASSIC' OF SORTS. WE ARE STICKING TO CLASSICS AND NOT NECESSARILY MASTERPIECES.
HO
3

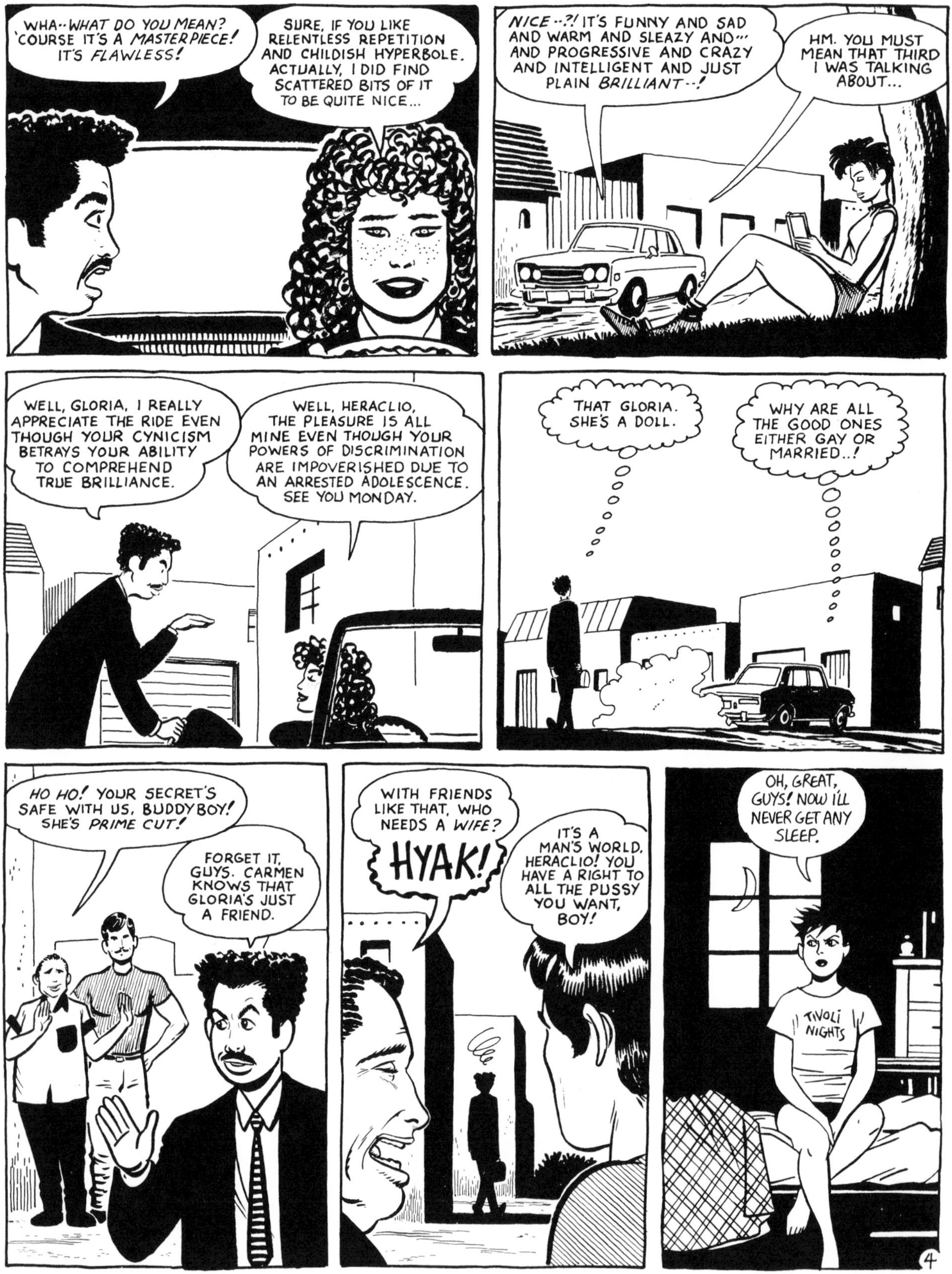
WHA-- WHAT DO YOU MEAN? 'COURSE IT'S A MASTERPIECE! IT'S FLAWLESS!
SURE, IF YOU LIKE RELENTLESS REPETITION AND CHILDISH HYPERBOLE. ACTUALLY, I DID FIND SCATTERED BITS OF IT TO BE QUITE NICE...
NICE--?! IT'S FUNNY AND SAD AND WARM AND SLEAZY AND... AND PROGRESSIVE AND CRAZY AND INTELLIGENT AND JUST PLAIN BRILLIANT--!
HM. YOU MUST MEAN THAT THIRD I WAS TALKING ABOUT...
WELL, GLORIA, I REALLY APPRECIATE THE RIDE EVEN THOUGH YOUR CYNICISM BETRAYS YOUR ABILITY TO COMPREHEND TRUE BRILLIANCE.
WELL, HERACLIO, THE PLEASURE IS ALL MINE EVEN THOUGH YOUR POWERS OF DISCRIMINATION ARE IMPOVERISHED DUE TO AN ARRESTED ADOLESCENCE. SEE YOU MONDAY.
THAT GLORIA. SHE'S A DOLL.
WHY ARE ALL THE GOOD ONES EITHER GAY OR MARRIED..!
HO HO! YOUR SECRET'S SAFE WITH US, BUDDY BOY! SHE'S PRIME CUT!
FORGET IT, GUYS. CARMEN KNOWS THAT GLORIA'S JUST A FRIEND.
WITH FRIENDS LIKE THAT, WHO NEEDS A WIFE?
HYAK!
IT'S A MAN'S WORLD, HERACLIO! YOU HAVE A RIGHT TO ALL THE PUSSY YOU WANT, BOY!
OH, GREAT, GUYS! NOW I'LL NEVER GET ANY SLEEP.
TIVOLI NIGHTS
4

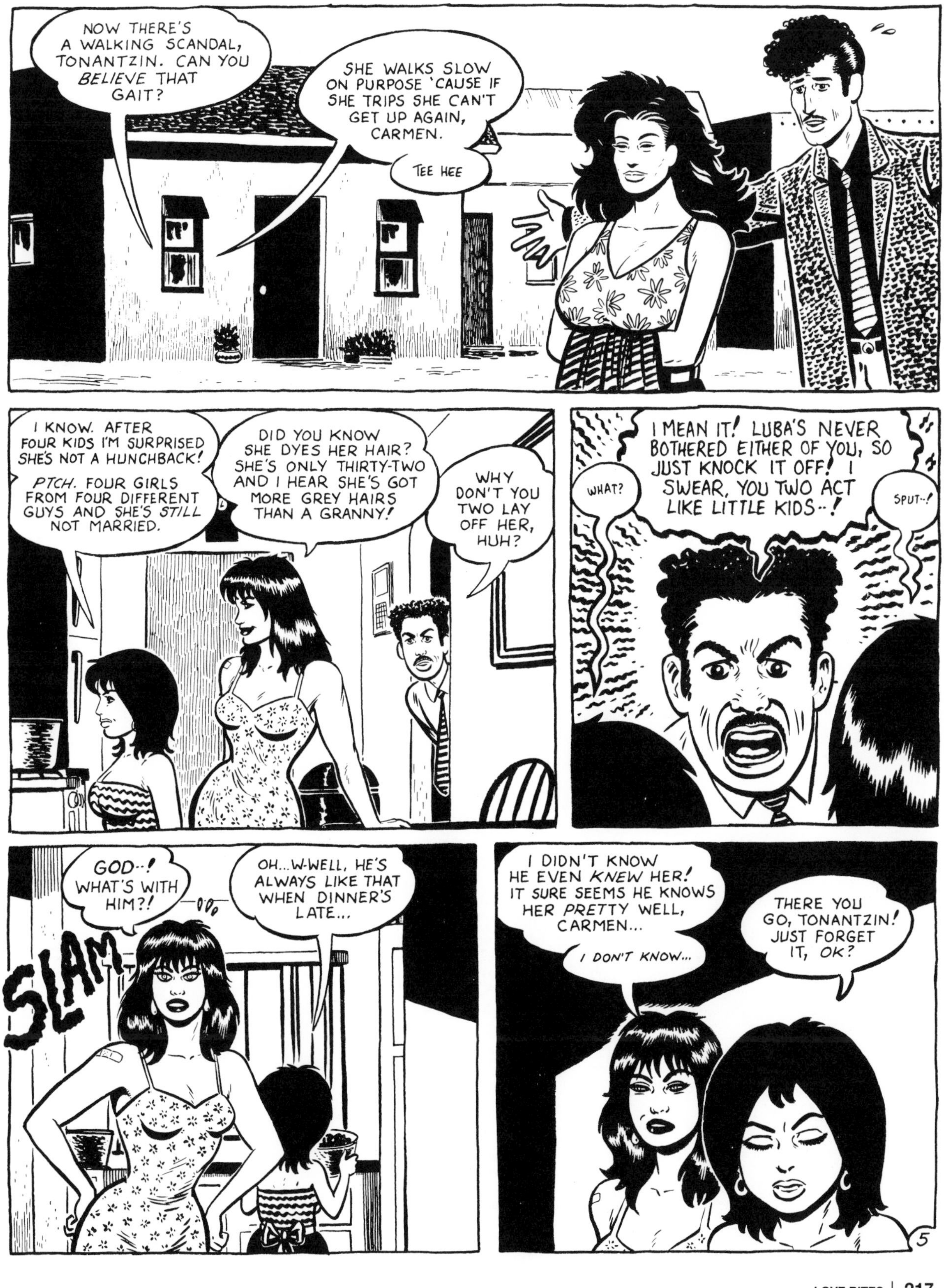
NOW THERE'S A WALKING SCANDAL, TONANTZIN. CAN YOU *BELIEVE* THAT GAIT?
SHE WALKS SLOW ON PURPOSE 'CAUSE IF SHE TRIPS SHE CAN'T GET UP AGAIN, CARMEN.
TEE HEE
I KNOW. AFTER FOUR KIDS I'M SURPRISED SHE'S NOT A HUNCHBACK!
PTCH. FOUR GIRLS FROM FOUR DIFFERENT GUYS AND SHE'S *STILL* NOT MARRIED.
DID YOU KNOW SHE DYES HER HAIR? SHE'S ONLY THIRTY-TWO AND I HEAR SHE'S GOT MORE GREY HAIRS THAN A GRANNY!
WHY DON'T YOU TWO LAY OFF HER, HUH?
WHAT?
I MEAN IT! LUBA'S NEVER BOTHERED EITHER OF YOU, SO JUST KNOCK IT OFF! I SWEAR, YOU TWO ACT LIKE LITTLE KIDS--!
SPUT--!
GOD--! WHAT'S WITH HIM?!
OH...W-WELL, HE'S ALWAYS LIKE THAT WHEN DINNER'S LATE...
SLAM
I DIDN'T KNOW HE EVEN *KNEW* HER! IT SURE SEEMS HE KNOWS HER *PRETTY* WELL, CARMEN...
I DON'T KNOW...
THERE YOU GO, TONANTZIN! JUST FORGET IT, *OK?*
5

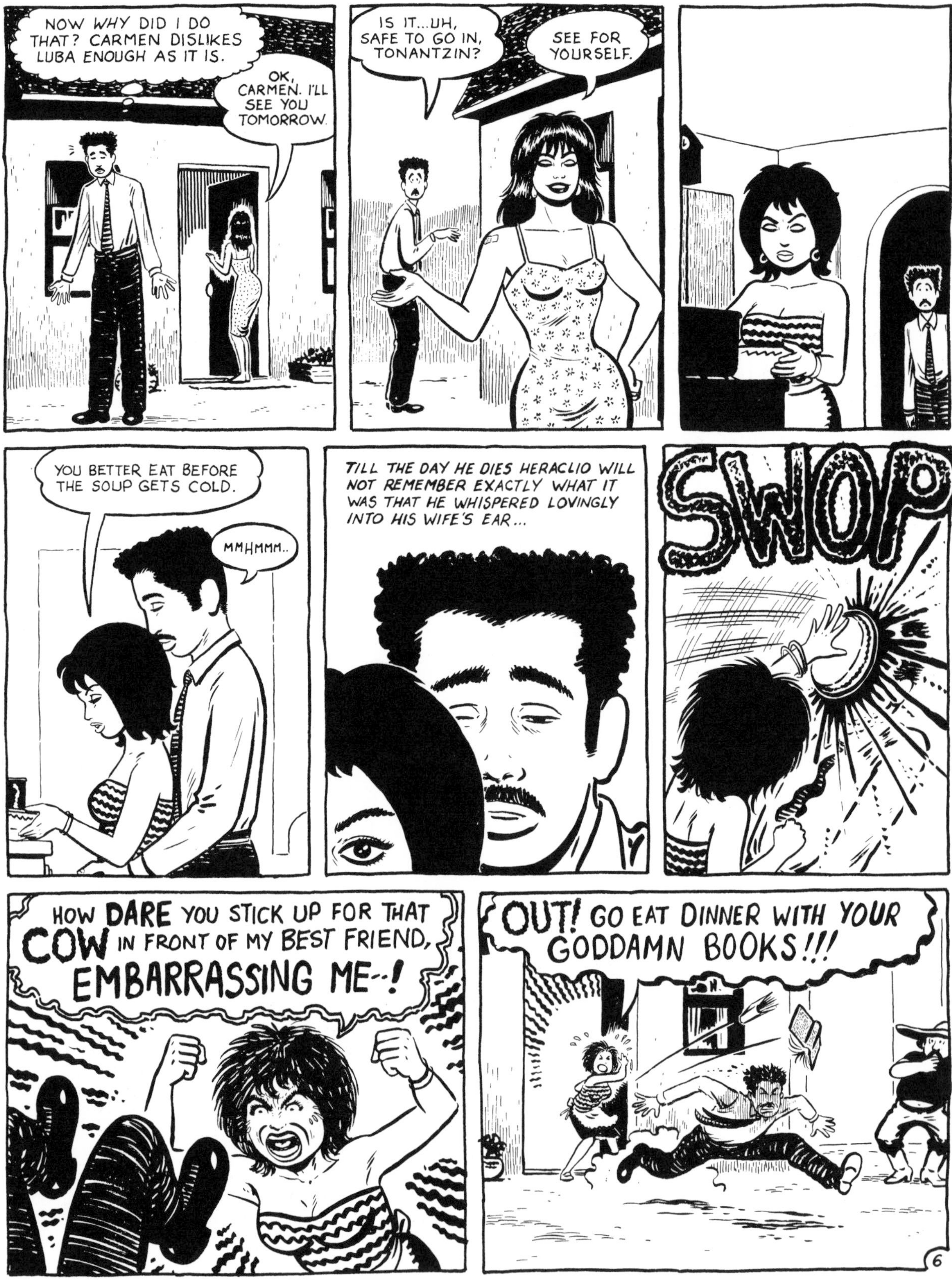
NOW WHY DID I DO THAT? CARMEN DISLIKES LUBA ENOUGH AS IT IS.
OK, CARMEN. I'LL SEE YOU TOMORROW.
IS IT...UH, SAFE TO GO IN, TONANTZIN?
SEE FOR YOURSELF.
YOU BETTER EAT BEFORE THE SOUP GETS COLD.
MMHMMM..
TILL THE DAY HE DIES HERACLIO WILL NOT REMEMBER EXACTLY WHAT IT WAS THAT HE WHISPERED LOVINGLY INTO HIS WIFE'S EAR...
SWOP
HOW DARE YOU STICK UP FOR THAT COW IN FRONT OF MY BEST FRIEND, EMBARRASSING ME--!
OUT! GO EAT DINNER WITH YOUR GODDAMN BOOKS!!!
6

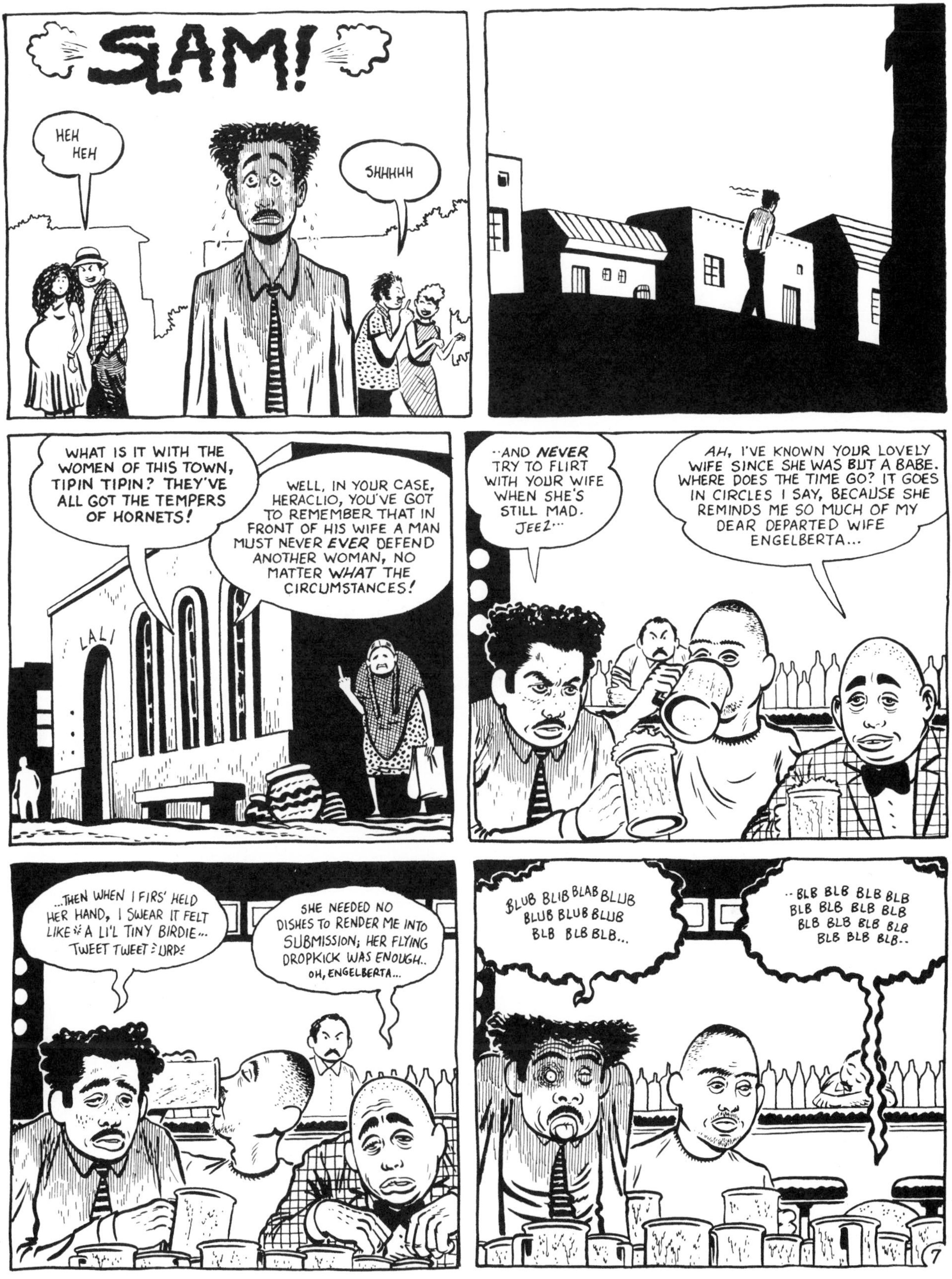
SLAM!
HEH HEH
SHHHHH
WHAT IS IT WITH THE WOMEN OF THIS TOWN, TIPIN TIPIN? THEY'VE ALL GOT THE TEMPERS OF HORNETS!
WELL, IN YOUR CASE, HERACLIO, YOU'VE GOT TO REMEMBER THAT IN FRONT OF HIS WIFE A MAN MUST NEVER EVER DEFEND ANOTHER WOMAN, NO MATTER WHAT THE CIRCUMSTANCES!
LALI
..AND NEVER TRY TO FLIRT WITH YOUR WIFE WHEN SHE'S STILL MAD. JEEZ...
AH, I'VE KNOWN YOUR LOVELY WIFE SINCE SHE WAS BUT A BABE. WHERE DOES THE TIME GO? IT GOES IN CIRCLES I SAY, BECAUSE SHE REMINDS ME SO MUCH OF MY DEAR DEPARTED WIFE ENGELBERTA...
...THEN WHEN I FIRS' HELD HER HAND, I SWEAR IT FELT LIKE A LI'L TINY BIRDIE... TWEET TWEET URP
SHE NEEDED NO DISHES TO RENDER ME INTO SUBMISSION; HER FLYING DROPKICK WAS ENOUGH.. OH, ENGELBERTA...
BLUB BLIB BLAB BLUB BLUB BLUB BLUB BLB BLB BLB...
..BLB BLB BLB BLB BLB BLB BLB BLB BLB BLB BLB BLB BLB BLB BLB..
7

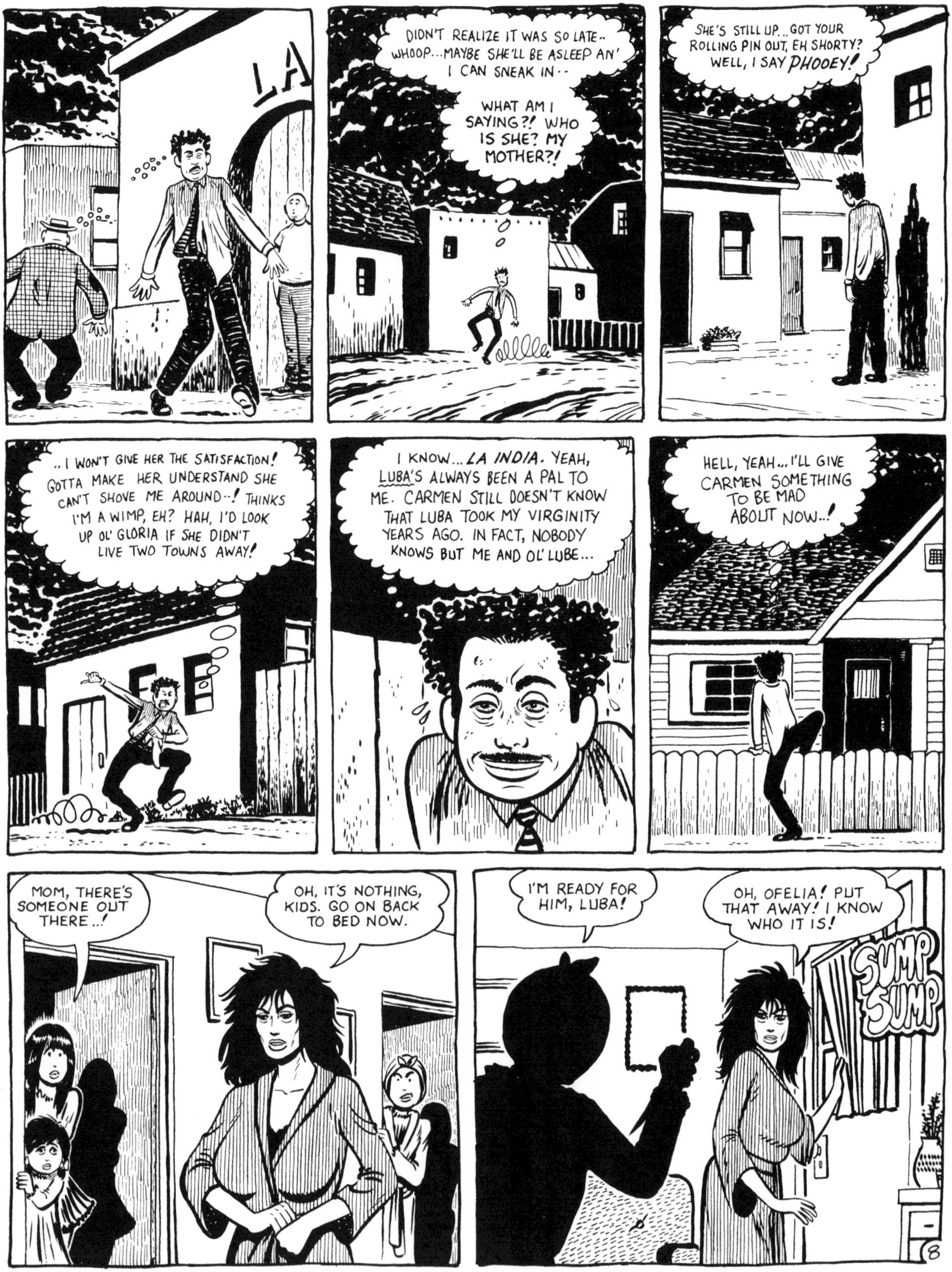
LA
DIDN'T REALIZE IT WAS SO LATE.. WHOOP...MAYBE SHE'LL BE ASLEEP AN' I CAN SNEAK IN..
WHAT AM I SAYING?! WHO IS SHE? MY MOTHER?!
SHE'S STILL UP...GOT YOUR ROLLING PIN OUT, EH SHORTY? WELL, I SAY PHOOEY!
..I WON'T GIVE HER THE SATISFACTION! GOTTA MAKE HER UNDERSTAND SHE CAN'T SHOVE ME AROUND..! THINKS I'M A WIMP, EH? HAH, I'D LOOK UP OL' GLORIA IF SHE DIDN'T LIVE TWO TOWNS AWAY!
I KNOW... LA INDIA. YEAH, LUBA'S ALWAYS BEEN A PAL TO ME. CARMEN STILL DOESN'T KNOW THAT LUBA TOOK MY VIRGINITY YEARS AGO. IN FACT, NOBODY KNOWS BUT ME AND OL' LUBE...
HELL, YEAH...I'LL GIVE CARMEN SOMETHING TO BE MAD ABOUT NOW...!
MOM, THERE'S SOMEONE OUT THERE...!
OH, IT'S NOTHING, KIDS. GO ON BACK TO BED NOW.
I'M READY FOR HIM, LUBA!
OH, OFELIA! PUT THAT AWAY! I KNOW WHO IT IS!
SUMP SUMP
8

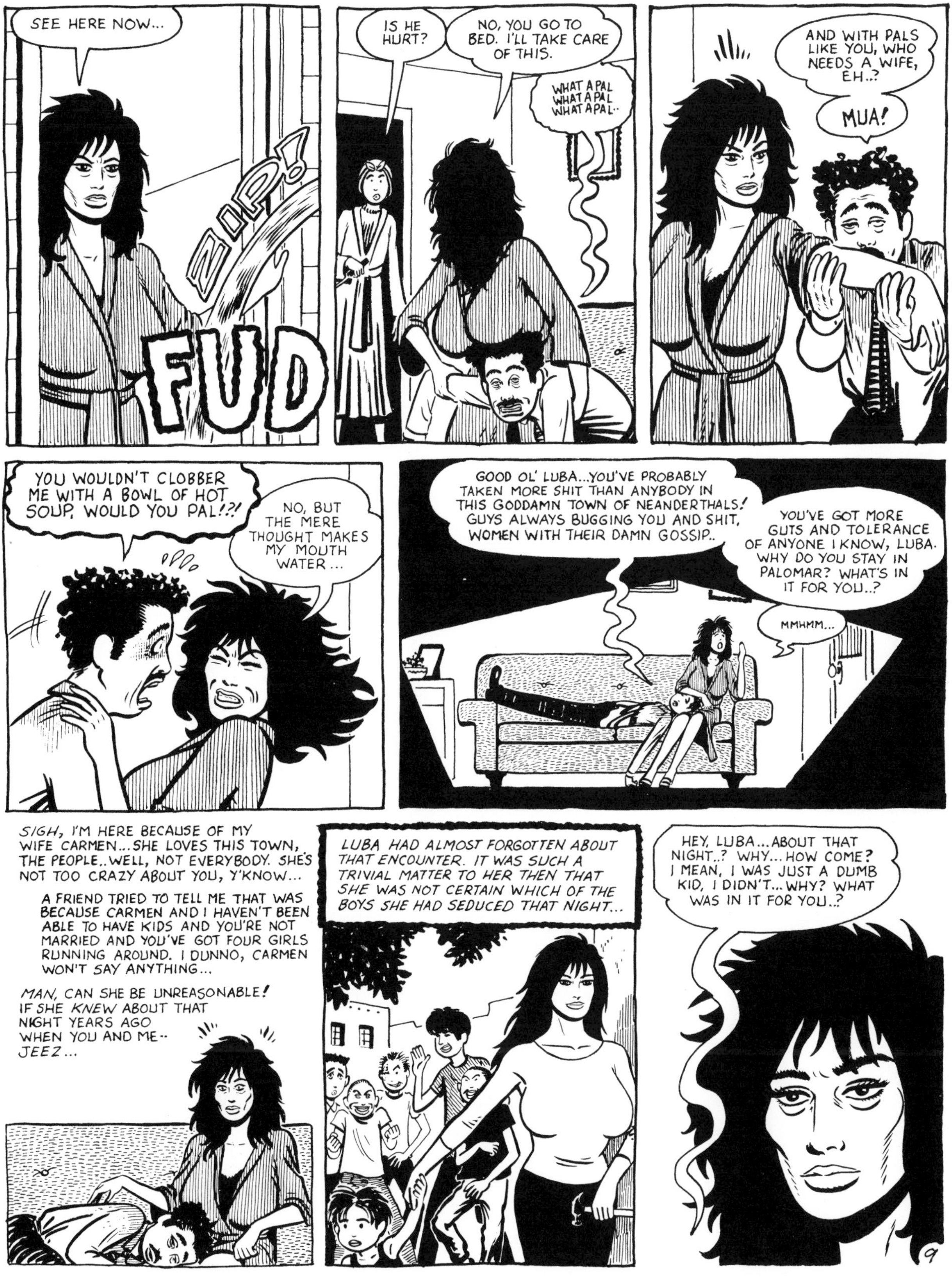
SEE HERE NOW...
ZIP!
FUD
IS HE HURT?
NO, YOU GO TO BED. I'LL TAKE CARE OF THIS.
WHAT A PAL WHAT A PAL WHAT A PAL..
AND WITH PALS LIKE YOU, WHO NEEDS A WIFE, EH..?
MUA!
YOU WOULDN'T CLOBBER ME WITH A BOWL OF HOT SOUP, WOULD YOU PAL!?!
NO, BUT THE MERE THOUGHT MAKES MY MOUTH WATER...
GOOD OL' LUBA...YOU'VE PROBABLY TAKEN MORE SHIT THAN ANYBODY IN THIS GODDAMN TOWN OF NEANDERTHALS! GUYS ALWAYS BUGGING YOU AND SHIT, WOMEN WITH THEIR DAMN GOSSIP..
YOU'VE GOT MORE GUTS AND TOLERANCE OF ANYONE I KNOW, LUBA. WHY DO YOU STAY IN PALOMAR? WHAT'S IN IT FOR YOU..?
MMHMM...
SIGH, I'M HERE BECAUSE OF MY WIFE CARMEN... SHE LOVES THIS TOWN, THE PEOPLE.. WELL, NOT EVERYBODY. SHE'S NOT TOO CRAZY ABOUT YOU, Y'KNOW...
A FRIEND TRIED TO TELL ME THAT WAS BECAUSE CARMEN AND I HAVEN'T BEEN ABLE TO HAVE KIDS AND YOU'RE NOT MARRIED AND YOU'VE GOT FOUR GIRLS RUNNING AROUND. I DUNNO, CARMEN WON'T SAY ANYTHING...
MAN, CAN SHE BE UNREASONABLE! IF SHE KNEW ABOUT THAT NIGHT YEARS AGO WHEN YOU AND ME.. JEEZ...
LUBA HAD ALMOST FORGOTTEN ABOUT THAT ENCOUNTER. IT WAS SUCH A TRIVIAL MATTER TO HER THEN THAT SHE WAS NOT CERTAIN WHICH OF THE BOYS SHE HAD SEDUCED THAT NIGHT...
HEY, LUBA... ABOUT THAT NIGHT..? WHY... HOW COME? I MEAN, I WAS JUST A DUMB KID, I DIDN'T... WHY? WHAT WAS IN IT FOR YOU..?
9

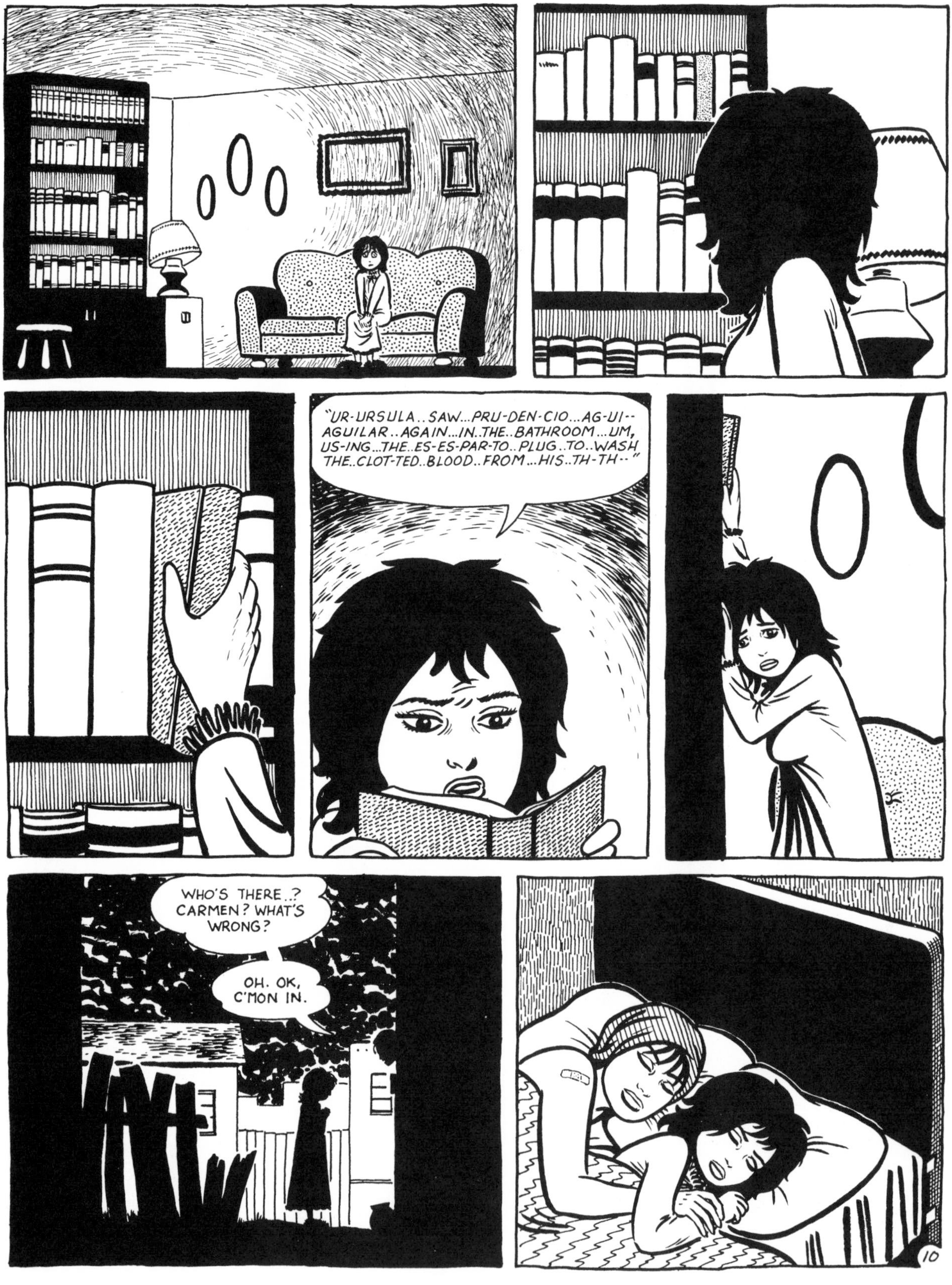
"UR-URSULA..SAW...PRU-DEN-CIO...AG-UI--AGUILAR..AGAIN...IN..THE..BATHROOM...UM, US-ING...THE..ES-ES-PAR-TO..PLUG..TO..WASH THE..CLOT-TED..BLOOD..FROM...HIS..TH-TH--"
WHO'S THERE..? CARMEN? WHAT'S WRONG?
OH. OK, C'MON IN.
10

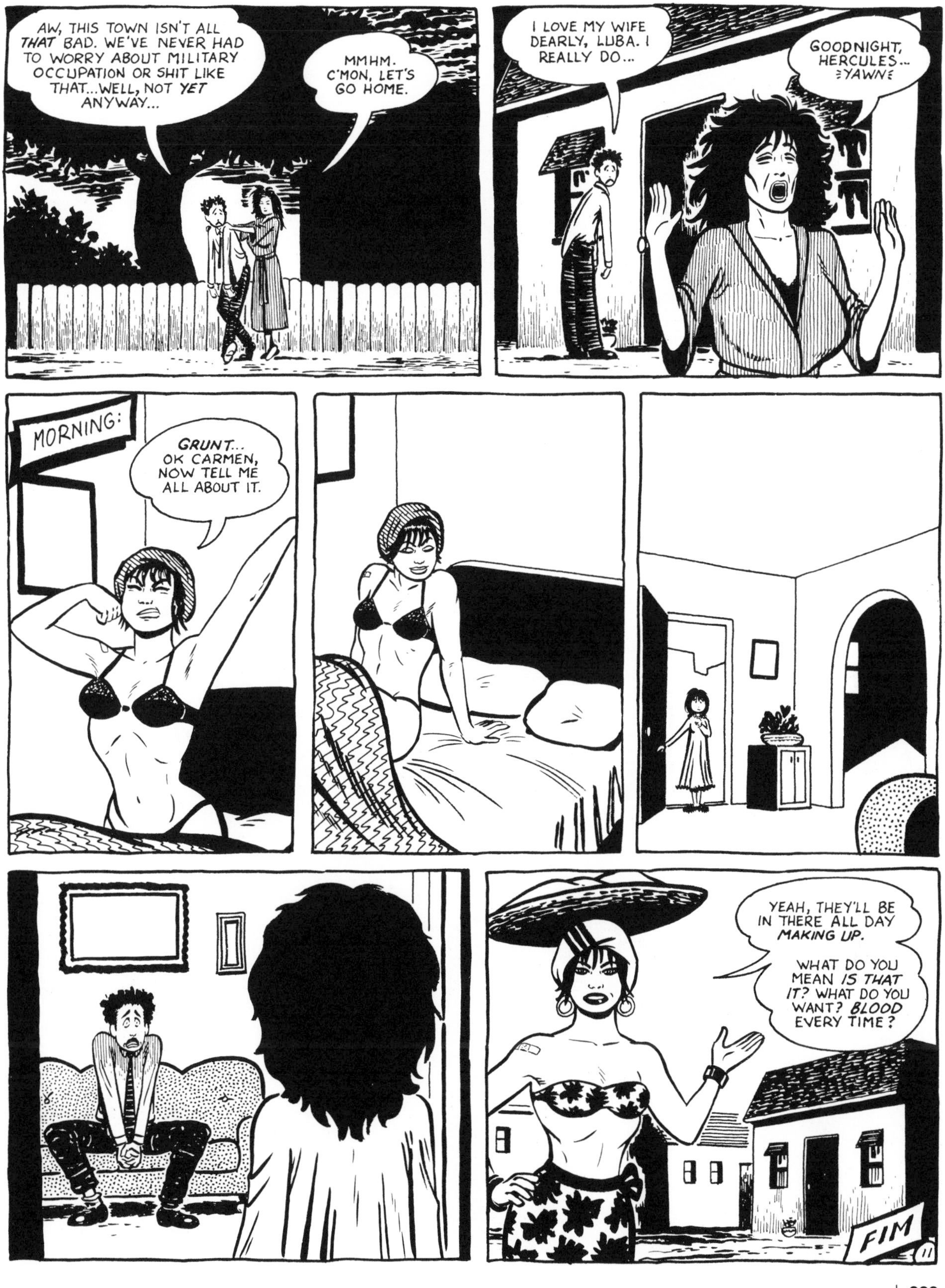
AW, THIS TOWN ISN'T ALL THAT BAD. WE'VE NEVER HAD TO WORRY ABOUT MILITARY OCCUPATION OR SHIT LIKE THAT...WELL, NOT YET ANYWAY...
MMHM. C'MON, LET'S GO HOME.
I LOVE MY WIFE DEARLY, LUBA. I REALLY DO...
GOODNIGHT, HERCULES... YAWN
MORNING:
GRUNT... OK CARMEN, NOW TELL ME ALL ABOUT IT.
YEAH, THEY'LL BE IN THERE ALL DAY MAKING UP.
WHAT DO YOU MEAN IS THAT IT? WHAT DO YOU WANT? BLOOD EVERY TIME?
FIM
11

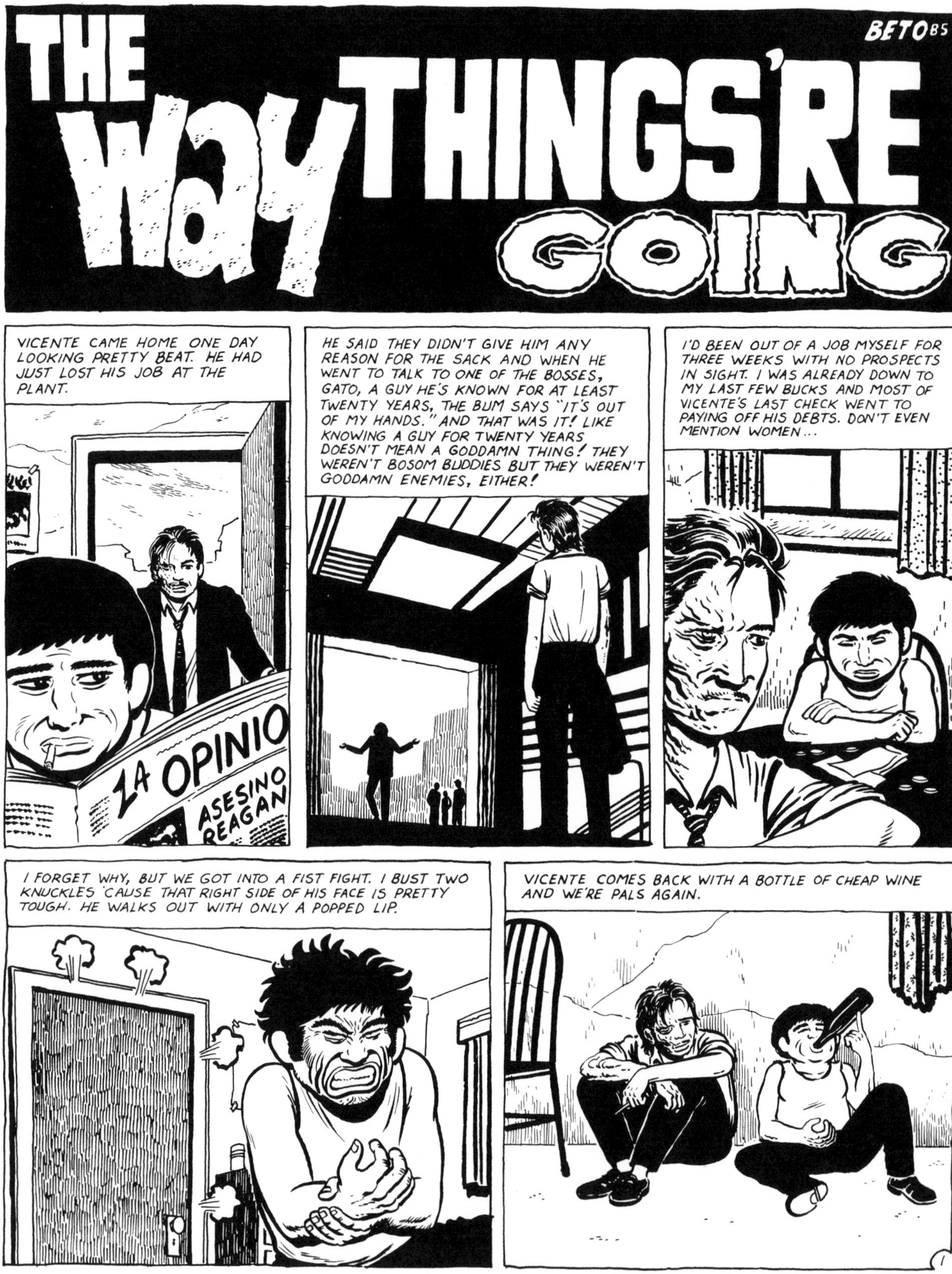
THE WAY THINGS'RE GOING
BETO 85
VICENTE CAME HOME ONE DAY LOOKING PRETTY BEAT. HE HAD JUST LOST HIS JOB AT THE PLANT.
LA OPINIO
ASESINO REAGAN
HE SAID THEY DIDN'T GIVE HIM ANY REASON FOR THE SACK AND WHEN HE WENT TO TALK TO ONE OF THE BOSSES, GATO, A GUY HE'S KNOWN FOR AT LEAST TWENTY YEARS, THE BUM SAYS "IT'S OUT OF MY HANDS." AND THAT WAS IT! LIKE KNOWING A GUY FOR TWENTY YEARS DOESN'T MEAN A GODDAMN THING! THEY WEREN'T BOSOM BUDDIES BUT THEY WEREN'T GODDAMN ENEMIES, EITHER!
I'D BEEN OUT OF A JOB MYSELF FOR THREE WEEKS WITH NO PROSPECTS IN SIGHT. I WAS ALREADY DOWN TO MY LAST FEW BUCKS AND MOST OF VICENTE'S LAST CHECK WENT TO PAYING OFF HIS DEBTS. DON'T EVEN MENTION WOMEN...
I FORGET WHY, BUT WE GOT INTO A FIST FIGHT. I BUST TWO KNUCKLES 'CAUSE THAT RIGHT SIDE OF HIS FACE IS PRETTY TOUGH. HE WALKS OUT WITH ONLY A POPPED LIP.
VICENTE COMES BACK WITH A BOTTLE OF CHEAP WINE AND WE'RE PALS AGAIN.
1

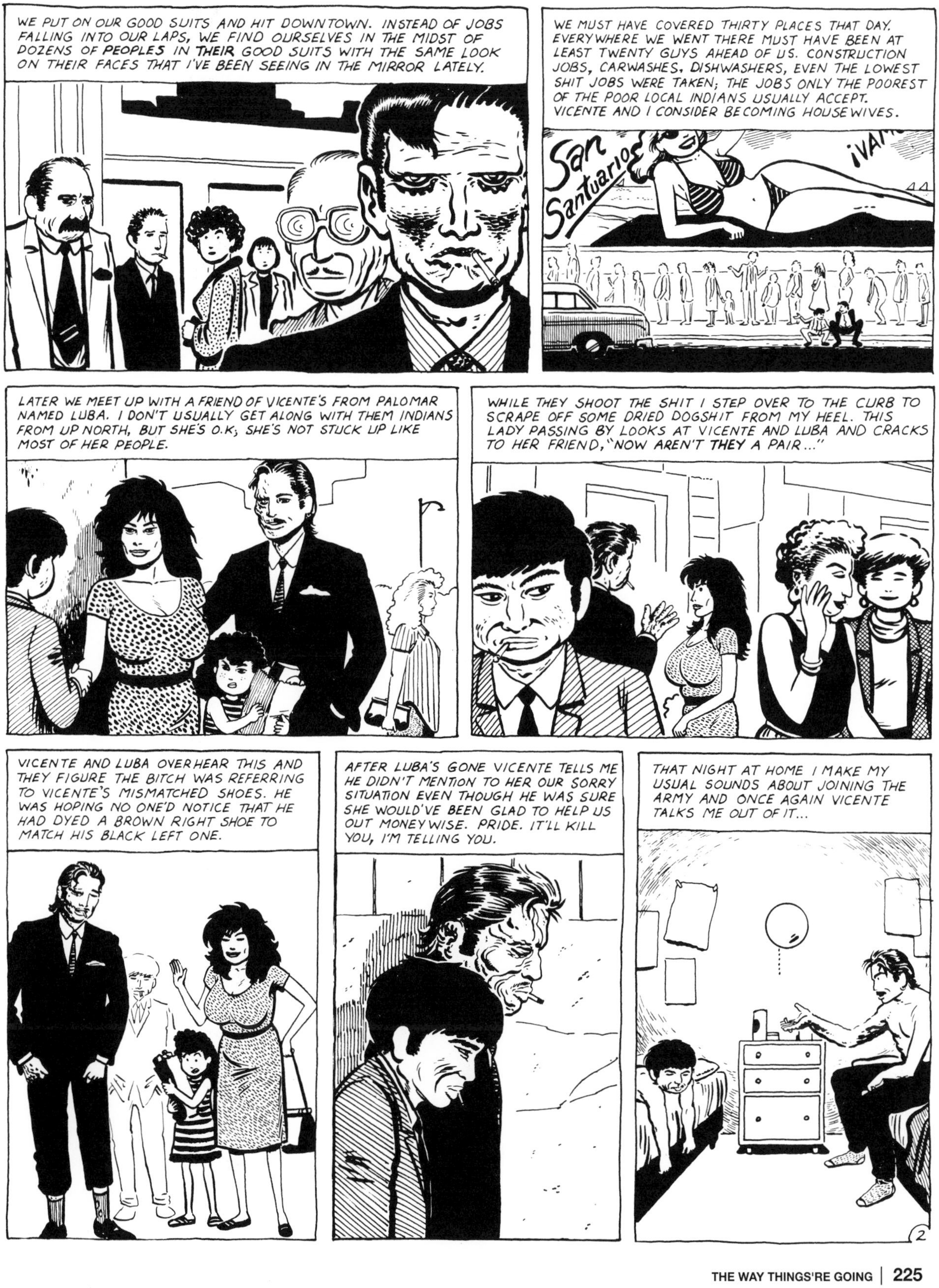
WE PUT ON OUR GOOD SUITS AND HIT DOWNTOWN. INSTEAD OF JOBS FALLING INTO OUR LAPS, WE FIND OURSELVES IN THE MIDST OF DOZENS OF **PEOPLES** IN **THEIR** GOOD SUITS WITH THE SAME LOOK ON THEIR FACES THAT I'VE BEEN SEEING IN THE MIRROR LATELY.
WE MUST HAVE COVERED THIRTY PLACES THAT DAY. EVERYWHERE WE WENT THERE MUST HAVE BEEN AT LEAST TWENTY GUYS AHEAD OF US. CONSTRUCTION JOBS, CARWASHES, DISHWASHERS, EVEN THE LOWEST SHIT JOBS WERE TAKEN; THE JOBS ONLY THE POOREST OF THE POOR LOCAL INDIANS USUALLY ACCEPT. VICENTE AND I CONSIDER BECOMING HOUSEWIVES.
San Santuario
LATER WE MEET UP WITH A FRIEND OF VICENTE'S FROM PALOMAR NAMED LUBA. I DON'T USUALLY GET ALONG WITH THEM INDIANS FROM UP NORTH, BUT SHE'S O.K.; SHE'S NOT STUCK UP LIKE MOST OF HER PEOPLE.
WHILE THEY SHOOT THE SHIT I STEP OVER TO THE CURB TO SCRAPE OFF SOME DRIED DOGSHIT FROM MY HEEL. THIS LADY PASSING BY LOOKS AT VICENTE AND LUBA AND CRACKS TO HER FRIEND, "NOW AREN'T **THEY** A PAIR..."
VICENTE AND LUBA OVERHEAR THIS AND THEY FIGURE THE BITCH WAS REFERRING TO VICENTE'S MISMATCHED SHOES. HE WAS HOPING NO ONE'D NOTICE THAT HE HAD DYED A BROWN RIGHT SHOE TO MATCH HIS BLACK LEFT ONE.
AFTER LUBA'S GONE VICENTE TELLS ME HE DIDN'T MENTION TO HER OUR SORRY SITUATION EVEN THOUGH HE WAS SURE SHE WOULD'VE BEEN GLAD TO HELP US OUT MONEYWISE. PRIDE. IT'LL KILL YOU, I'M TELLING YOU.
THAT NIGHT AT HOME I MAKE MY USUAL SOUNDS ABOUT JOINING THE ARMY AND ONCE AGAIN VICENTE TALKS ME OUT OF IT...
2

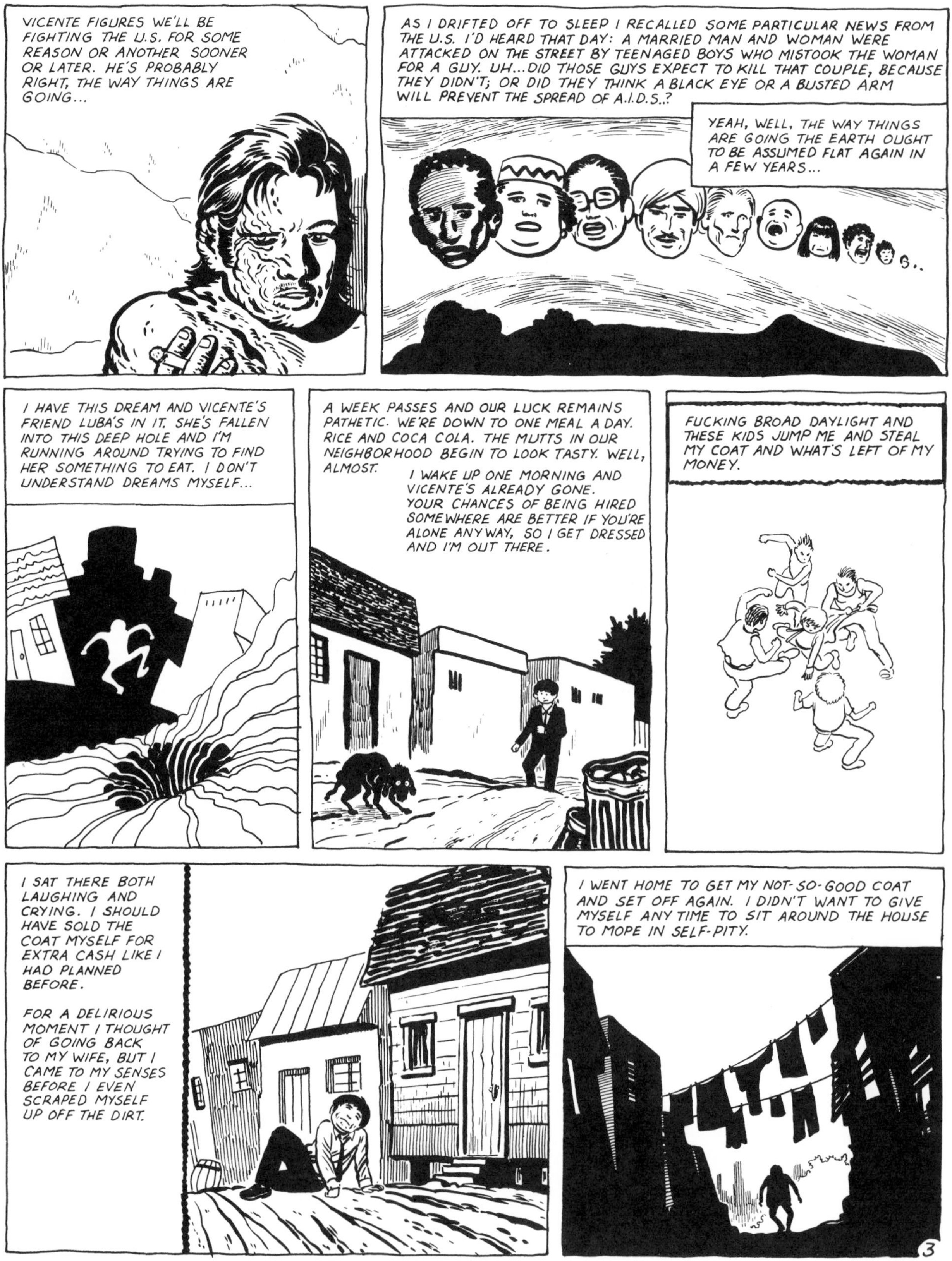
VICENTE FIGURES WE'LL BE FIGHTING THE U.S. FOR SOME REASON OR ANOTHER SOONER OR LATER. HE'S PROBABLY RIGHT, THE WAY THINGS ARE GOING...
AS I DRIFTED OFF TO SLEEP I RECALLED SOME PARTICULAR NEWS FROM THE U.S. I'D HEARD THAT DAY: A MARRIED MAN AND WOMAN WERE ATTACKED ON THE STREET BY TEENAGED BOYS WHO MISTOOK THE WOMAN FOR A GUY. UH...DID THOSE GUYS EXPECT TO KILL THAT COUPLE, BECAUSE THEY DIDN'T; OR DID THEY THINK A BLACK EYE OR A BUSTED ARM WILL PREVENT THE SPREAD OF A.I.D.S..?
YEAH, WELL, THE WAY THINGS ARE GOING THE EARTH OUGHT TO BE ASSUMED FLAT AGAIN IN A FEW YEARS...
I HAVE THIS DREAM AND VICENTE'S FRIEND LUBA'S IN IT. SHE'S FALLEN INTO THIS DEEP HOLE AND I'M RUNNING AROUND TRYING TO FIND HER SOMETHING TO EAT. I DON'T UNDERSTAND DREAMS MYSELF...
A WEEK PASSES AND OUR LUCK REMAINS PATHETIC. WE'RE DOWN TO ONE MEAL A DAY. RICE AND COCA COLA. THE MUTTS IN OUR NEIGHBORHOOD BEGIN TO LOOK TASTY. WELL, ALMOST.
I WAKE UP ONE MORNING AND VICENTE'S ALREADY GONE. YOUR CHANCES OF BEING HIRED SOMEWHERE ARE BETTER IF YOU'RE ALONE ANYWAY, SO I GET DRESSED AND I'M OUT THERE.
FUCKING BROAD DAYLIGHT AND THESE KIDS JUMP ME AND STEAL MY COAT AND WHAT'S LEFT OF MY MONEY.
I SAT THERE BOTH LAUGHING AND CRYING. I SHOULD HAVE SOLD THE COAT MYSELF FOR EXTRA CASH LIKE I HAD PLANNED BEFORE.
FOR A DELIRIOUS MOMENT I THOUGHT OF GOING BACK TO MY WIFE, BUT I CAME TO MY SENSES BEFORE I EVEN SCRAPED MYSELF UP OFF THE DIRT.
I WENT HOME TO GET MY NOT-SO-GOOD COAT AND SET OFF AGAIN. I DIDN'T WANT TO GIVE MYSELF ANY TIME TO SIT AROUND THE HOUSE TO MOPE IN SELF-PITY.
3

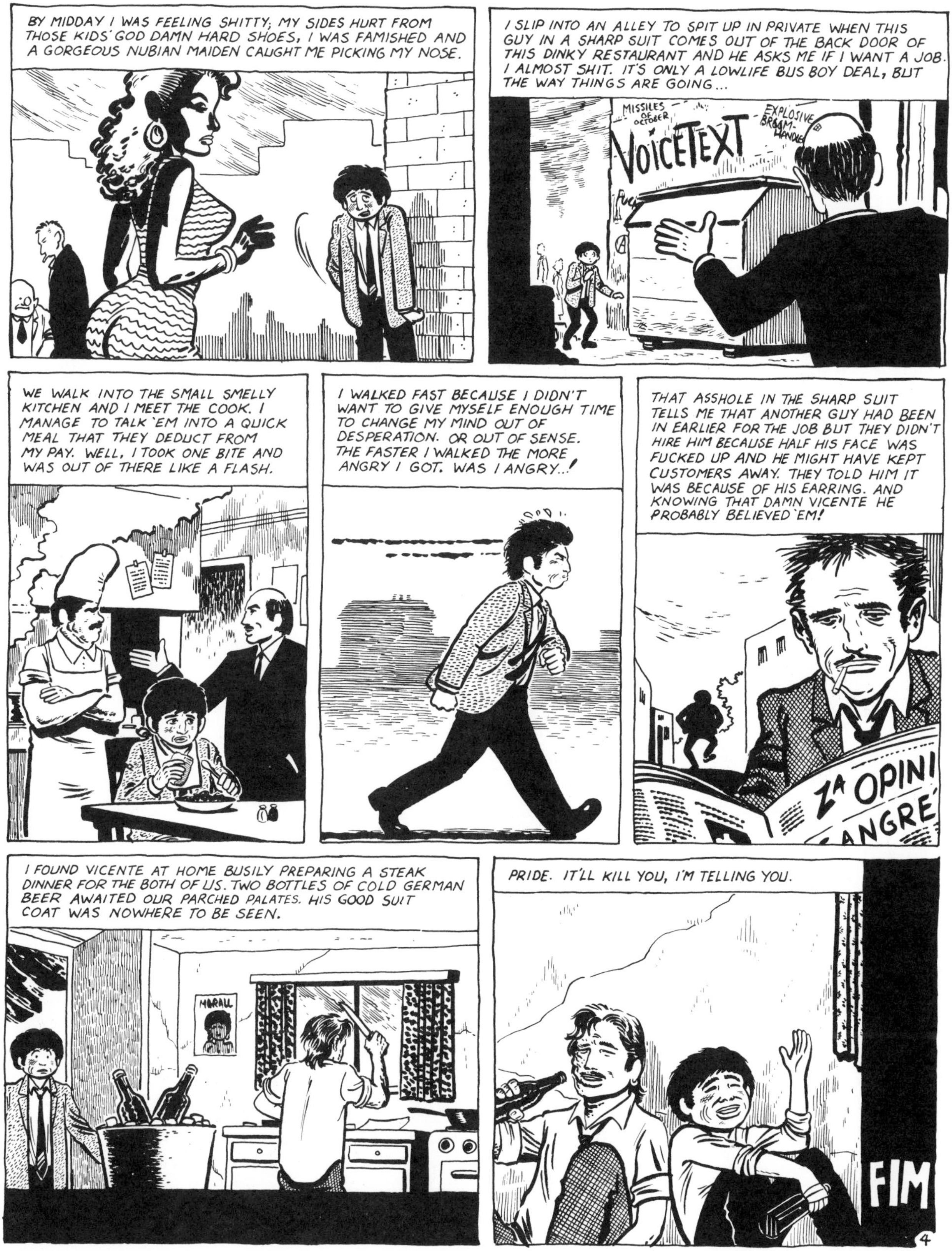
BY MIDDAY I WAS FEELING SHITTY; MY SIDES HURT FROM THOSE KIDS' GOD DAMN HARD SHOES, I WAS FAMISHED AND A GORGEOUS NUBIAN MAIDEN CAUGHT ME PICKING MY NOSE.
I SLIP INTO AN ALLEY TO SPIT UP IN PRIVATE WHEN THIS GUY IN A SHARP SUIT COMES OUT OF THE BACK DOOR OF THIS DINKY RESTAURANT AND HE ASKS ME IF I WANT A JOB. I ALMOST SHIT. IT'S ONLY A LOWLIFE BUS BOY DEAL, BUT THE WAY THINGS ARE GOING...
MISSILES OF OCTOBER
VOICETEXT
EXPLOSIVE BROOM-HANDLE
WE WALK INTO THE SMALL SMELLY KITCHEN AND I MEET THE COOK. I MANAGE TO TALK 'EM INTO A QUICK MEAL THAT THEY DEDUCT FROM MY PAY. WELL, I TOOK ONE BITE AND WAS OUT OF THERE LIKE A FLASH.
I WALKED FAST BECAUSE I DIDN'T WANT TO GIVE MYSELF ENOUGH TIME TO CHANGE MY MIND OUT OF DESPERATION. OR OUT OF SENSE. THE FASTER I WALKED THE MORE ANGRY I GOT. WAS I ANGRY..!
THAT ASSHOLE IN THE SHARP SUIT TELLS ME THAT ANOTHER GUY HAD BEEN IN EARLIER FOR THE JOB BUT THEY DIDN'T HIRE HIM BECAUSE HALF HIS FACE WAS FUCKED UP AND HE MIGHT HAVE KEPT CUSTOMERS AWAY. THEY TOLD HIM IT WAS BECAUSE OF HIS EARRING. AND KNOWING THAT DAMN VICENTE HE PROBABLY BELIEVED 'EM!
OPINI
ANGRE
I FOUND VICENTE AT HOME BUSILY PREPARING A STEAK DINNER FOR THE BOTH OF US. TWO BOTTLES OF COLD GERMAN BEER AWAITED OUR PARCHED PALATES. HIS GOOD SUIT COAT WAS NOWHERE TO BE SEEN.
PRIDE. IT'LL KILL YOU, I'M TELLING YOU.
FIM
4

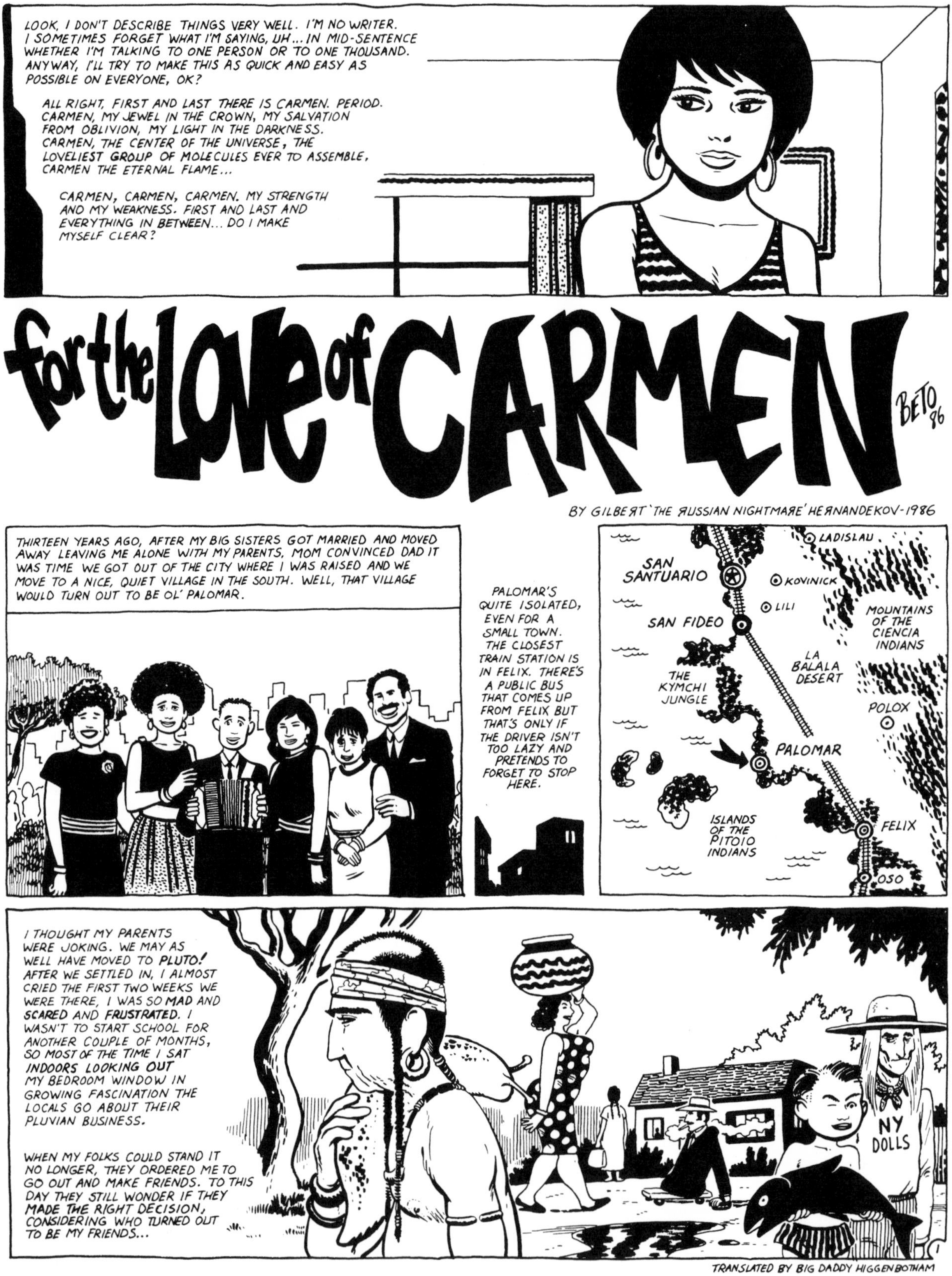
LOOK, I DON'T DESCRIBE THINGS VERY WELL. I'M NO WRITER. I SOMETIMES FORGET WHAT I'M SAYING, UH... IN MID-SENTENCE WHETHER I'M TALKING TO ONE PERSON OR TO ONE THOUSAND. ANYWAY, I'LL TRY TO MAKE THIS AS QUICK AND EASY AS POSSIBLE ON EVERYONE, OK?
ALL RIGHT, FIRST AND LAST THERE IS CARMEN. PERIOD. CARMEN, MY JEWEL IN THE CROWN, MY SALVATION FROM OBLIVION, MY LIGHT IN THE DARKNESS. CARMEN, THE CENTER OF THE UNIVERSE, THE LOVELIEST GROUP OF MOLECULES EVER TO ASSEMBLE, CARMEN THE ETERNAL FLAME...
CARMEN, CARMEN, CARMEN. MY STRENGTH AND MY WEAKNESS. FIRST AND LAST AND EVERYTHING IN BETWEEN... DO I MAKE MYSELF CLEAR?
for the LOVE of CARMEN
BETO 86
BY GILBERT 'THE RUSSIAN NIGHTMARE' HERNANDEKOV-1986
THIRTEEN YEARS AGO, AFTER MY BIG SISTERS GOT MARRIED AND MOVED AWAY LEAVING ME ALONE WITH MY PARENTS, MOM CONVINCED DAD IT WAS TIME WE GOT OUT OF THE CITY WHERE I WAS RAISED AND WE MOVE TO A NICE, QUIET VILLAGE IN THE SOUTH. WELL, THAT VILLAGE WOULD TURN OUT TO BE OL' PALOMAR.
PALOMAR'S QUITE ISOLATED, EVEN FOR A SMALL TOWN. THE CLOSEST TRAIN STATION IS IN FELIX. THERE'S A PUBLIC BUS THAT COMES UP FROM FELIX BUT THAT'S ONLY IF THE DRIVER ISN'T TOO LAZY AND PRETENDS TO FORGET TO STOP HERE.
LADISLAU
SAN SANTUARIO
KOVINICK
LILI
SAN FIDEO
MOUNTAINS OF THE CIENCIA INDIANS
LA BALALA DESERT
THE KYMCHI JUNGLE
POLOX
PALOMAR
ISLANDS OF THE PITOIO INDIANS
FELIX
OSO
I THOUGHT MY PARENTS WERE JOKING. WE MAY AS WELL HAVE MOVED TO PLUTO! AFTER WE SETTLED IN, I ALMOST CRIED THE FIRST TWO WEEKS WE WERE THERE, I WAS SO MAD AND SCARED AND FRUSTRATED. I WASN'T TO START SCHOOL FOR ANOTHER COUPLE OF MONTHS, SO MOST OF THE TIME I SAT INDOORS LOOKING OUT MY BEDROOM WINDOW IN GROWING FASCINATION THE LOCALS GO ABOUT THEIR PLUVIAN BUSINESS.
WHEN MY FOLKS COULD STAND IT NO LONGER, THEY ORDERED ME TO GO OUT AND MAKE FRIENDS. TO THIS DAY THEY STILL WONDER IF THEY MADE THE RIGHT DECISION, CONSIDERING WHO TURNED OUT TO BE MY FRIENDS...
NY DOLLS
1
TRANSLATED BY BIG DADDY HIGGENBOTHAM

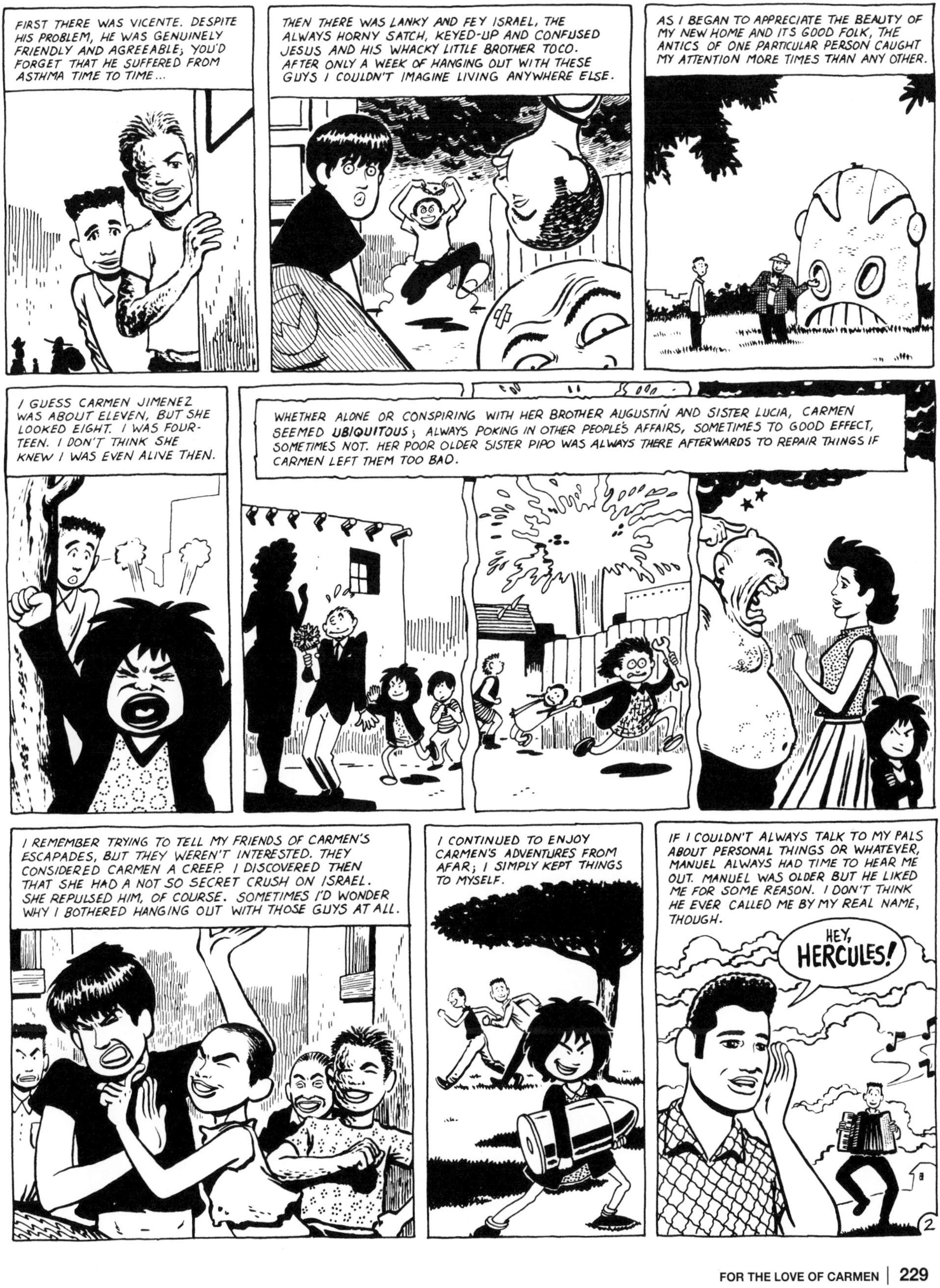
FIRST THERE WAS VICENTE. DESPITE HIS PROBLEM, HE WAS GENUINELY FRIENDLY AND AGREEABLE; YOU'D FORGET THAT HE SUFFERED FROM ASTHMA TIME TO TIME...
THEN THERE WAS LANKY AND FEY ISRAEL, THE ALWAYS HORNY SATCH, KEYED-UP AND CONFUSED JESUS AND HIS WHACKY LITTLE BROTHER TOCO. AFTER ONLY A WEEK OF HANGING OUT WITH THESE GUYS I COULDN'T IMAGINE LIVING ANYWHERE ELSE.
AS I BEGAN TO APPRECIATE THE BEAUTY OF MY NEW HOME AND ITS GOOD FOLK, THE ANTICS OF ONE PARTICULAR PERSON CAUGHT MY ATTENTION MORE TIMES THAN ANY OTHER.
I GUESS CARMEN JIMENEZ WAS ABOUT ELEVEN, BUT SHE LOOKED EIGHT. I WAS FOURTEEN. I DON'T THINK SHE KNEW I WAS EVEN ALIVE THEN.
WHETHER ALONE OR CONSPIRING WITH HER BROTHER AUGUSTÍN AND SISTER LUCIA, CARMEN SEEMED UBIQUITOUS; ALWAYS POKING IN OTHER PEOPLE'S AFFAIRS, SOMETIMES TO GOOD EFFECT, SOMETIMES NOT. HER POOR OLDER SISTER PIPO WAS ALWAYS THERE AFTERWARDS TO REPAIR THINGS IF CARMEN LEFT THEM TOO BAD.
I REMEMBER TRYING TO TELL MY FRIENDS OF CARMEN'S ESCAPADES, BUT THEY WEREN'T INTERESTED. THEY CONSIDERED CARMEN A CREEP. I DISCOVERED THEN THAT SHE HAD A NOT SO SECRET CRUSH ON ISRAEL. SHE REPULSED HIM, OF COURSE. SOMETIMES I'D WONDER WHY I BOTHERED HANGING OUT WITH THOSE GUYS AT ALL.
I CONTINUED TO ENJOY CARMEN'S ADVENTURES FROM AFAR; I SIMPLY KEPT THINGS TO MYSELF.
IF I COULDN'T ALWAYS TALK TO MY PALS ABOUT PERSONAL THINGS OR WHATEVER, MANUEL ALWAYS HAD TIME TO HEAR ME OUT. MANUEL WAS OLDER BUT HE LIKED ME FOR SOME REASON. I DON'T THINK HE EVER CALLED ME BY MY REAL NAME, THOUGH.
HEY, HERCULES!
2

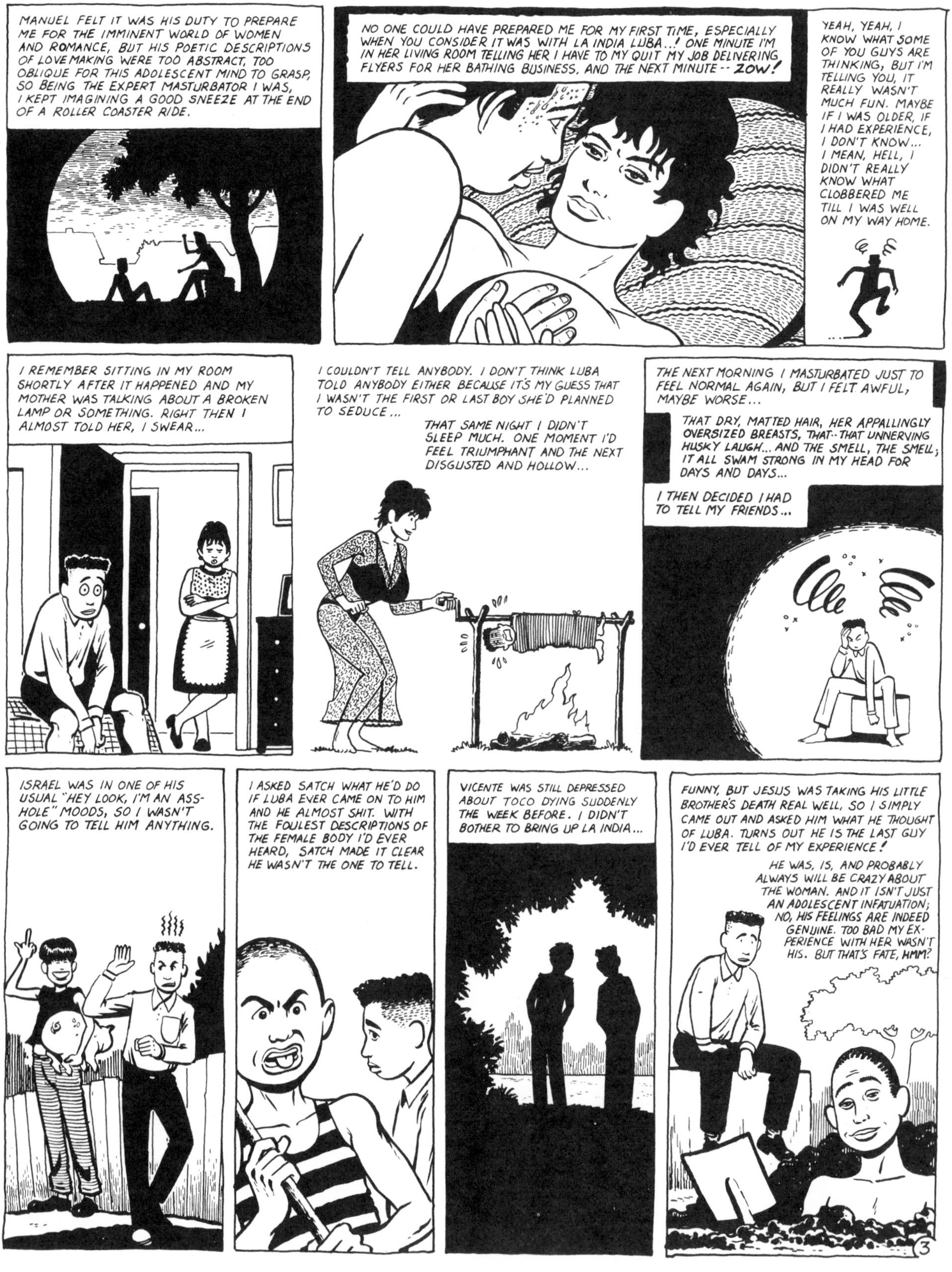

MANUEL FELT IT WAS HIS DUTY TO PREPARE ME FOR THE IMMINENT WORLD OF WOMEN AND ROMANCE, BUT HIS POETIC DESCRIPTIONS OF LOVE MAKING WERE TOO ABSTRACT, TOO OBLIQUE FOR THIS ADOLESCENT MIND TO GRASP, SO BEING THE EXPERT MASTURBATOR I WAS, I KEPT IMAGINING A GOOD SNEEZE AT THE END OF A ROLLER COASTER RIDE.
NO ONE COULD HAVE PREPARED ME FOR MY FIRST TIME, ESPECIALLY WHEN YOU CONSIDER IT WAS WITH LA INDIA LUBA...! ONE MINUTE I'M IN HER LIVING ROOM TELLING HER I HAVE TO MY QUIT MY JOB DELIVERING FLYERS FOR HER BATHING BUSINESS, AND THE NEXT MINUTE -- ZOW!
YEAH, YEAH, I KNOW WHAT SOME OF YOU GUYS ARE THINKING, BUT I'M TELLING YOU, IT REALLY WASN'T MUCH FUN. MAYBE IF I WAS OLDER, IF I HAD EXPERIENCE, I DON'T KNOW... I MEAN, HELL, I DIDN'T REALLY KNOW WHAT CLOBBERED ME TILL I WAS WELL ON MY WAY HOME.
I REMEMBER SITTING IN MY ROOM SHORTLY AFTER IT HAPPENED AND MY MOTHER WAS TALKING ABOUT A BROKEN LAMP OR SOMETHING. RIGHT THEN I ALMOST TOLD HER, I SWEAR...
I COULDN'T TELL ANYBODY. I DON'T THINK LUBA TOLD ANYBODY EITHER BECAUSE IT'S MY GUESS THAT I WASN'T THE FIRST OR LAST BOY SHE'D PLANNED TO SEDUCE...
THAT SAME NIGHT I DIDN'T SLEEP MUCH. ONE MOMENT I'D FEEL TRIUMPHANT AND THE NEXT DISGUSTED AND HOLLOW...
THE NEXT MORNING I MASTURBATED JUST TO FEEL NORMAL AGAIN, BUT I FELT AWFUL, MAYBE WORSE...
THAT DRY, MATTED HAIR, HER APPALLINGLY OVERSIZED BREASTS, THAT-- THAT UNNERVING HUSKY LAUGH... AND THE SMELL, THE SMELL; IT ALL SWAM STRONG IN MY HEAD FOR DAYS AND DAYS...
I THEN DECIDED I HAD TO TELL MY FRIENDS...
ISRAEL WAS IN ONE OF HIS USUAL "HEY LOOK, I'M AN ASS-HOLE" MOODS, SO I WASN'T GOING TO TELL HIM ANYTHING.
I ASKED SATCH WHAT HE'D DO IF LUBA EVER CAME ON TO HIM AND HE ALMOST SHIT. WITH THE FOULEST DESCRIPTIONS OF THE FEMALE BODY I'D EVER HEARD, SATCH MADE IT CLEAR HE WASN'T THE ONE TO TELL.
VICENTE WAS STILL DEPRESSED ABOUT TOCO DYING SUDDENLY THE WEEK BEFORE. I DIDN'T BOTHER TO BRING UP LA INDIA...
FUNNY, BUT JESUS WAS TAKING HIS LITTLE BROTHER'S DEATH REAL WELL, SO I SIMPLY CAME OUT AND ASKED HIM WHAT HE THOUGHT OF LUBA. TURNS OUT HE IS THE LAST GUY I'D EVER TELL OF MY EXPERIENCE!
HE WAS, IS, AND PROBABLY ALWAYS WILL BE CRAZY ABOUT THE WOMAN. AND IT ISN'T JUST AN ADOLESCENT INFATUATION; NO, HIS FEELINGS ARE INDEED GENUINE. TOO BAD MY EX-PERIENCE WITH HER WASN'T HIS. BUT THAT'S FATE, HMM?
3

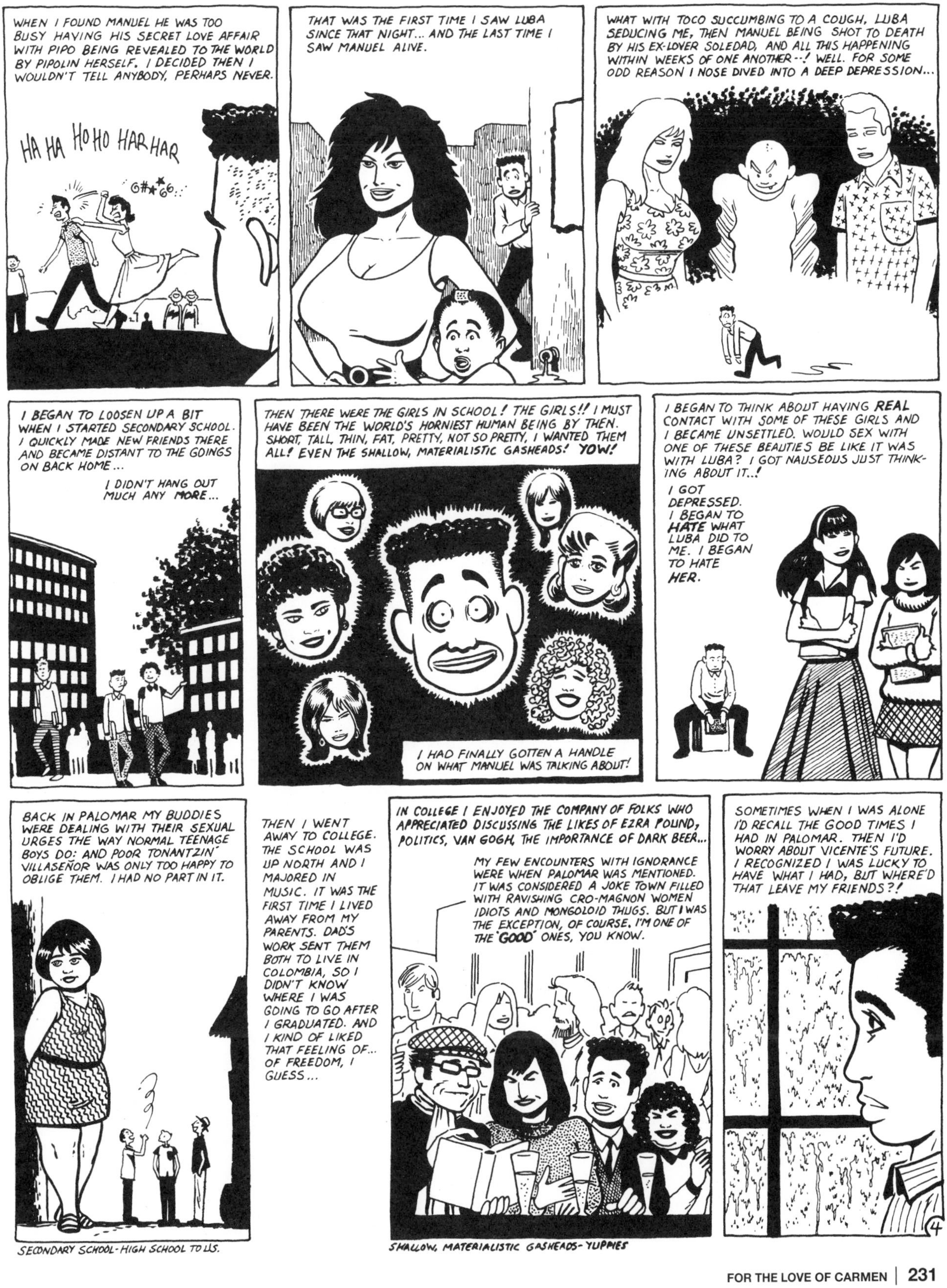
WHEN I FOUND MANUEL HE WAS TOO BUSY HAVING HIS SECRET LOVE AFFAIR WITH PIPO BEING REVEALED TO THE WORLD BY PIPOLIN HERSELF. I DECIDED THEN I WOULDN'T TELL ANYBODY, PERHAPS NEVER.
HA HA HO HO HAR HAR
THAT WAS THE FIRST TIME I SAW LUBA SINCE THAT NIGHT... AND THE LAST TIME I SAW MANUEL ALIVE.
WHAT WITH TOCO SUCCUMBING TO A COUGH, LUBA SEDUCING ME, THEN MANUEL BEING SHOT TO DEATH BY HIS EX-LOVER SOLEDAD, AND ALL THIS HAPPENING WITHIN WEEKS OF ONE ANOTHER--! WELL. FOR SOME ODD REASON I NOSE DIVED INTO A DEEP DEPRESSION...
I BEGAN TO LOOSEN UP A BIT WHEN I STARTED SECONDARY SCHOOL. I QUICKLY MADE NEW FRIENDS THERE AND BECAME DISTANT TO THE GOINGS ON BACK HOME...
I DIDN'T HANG OUT MUCH ANY MORE...
THEN THERE WERE THE GIRLS IN SCHOOL! THE GIRLS!! I MUST HAVE BEEN THE WORLD'S HORNIEST HUMAN BEING BY THEN. SHORT, TALL, THIN, FAT, PRETTY, NOT SO PRETTY, I WANTED THEM ALL! EVEN THE SHALLOW, MATERIALISTIC GASHEADS! YOW!
I HAD FINALLY GOTTEN A HANDLE ON WHAT MANUEL WAS TALKING ABOUT!
I BEGAN TO THINK ABOUT HAVING REAL CONTACT WITH SOME OF THESE GIRLS AND I BECAME UNSETTLED. WOULD SEX WITH ONE OF THESE BEAUTIES BE LIKE IT WAS WITH LUBA? I GOT NAUSEOUS JUST THINKING ABOUT IT..!
I GOT DEPRESSED. I BEGAN TO HATE WHAT LUBA DID TO ME. I BEGAN TO HATE HER.
BACK IN PALOMAR MY BUDDIES WERE DEALING WITH THEIR SEXUAL URGES THE WAY NORMAL TEENAGE BOYS DO: AND POOR TONANTZIN VILLASEÑOR WAS ONLY TOO HAPPY TO OBLIGE THEM. I HAD NO PART IN IT.
THEN I WENT AWAY TO COLLEGE. THE SCHOOL WAS UP NORTH AND I MAJORED IN MUSIC. IT WAS THE FIRST TIME I LIVED AWAY FROM MY PARENTS. DAD'S WORK SENT THEM BOTH TO LIVE IN COLOMBIA, SO I DIDN'T KNOW WHERE I WAS GOING TO GO AFTER I GRADUATED. AND I KIND OF LIKED THAT FEELING OF... OF FREEDOM, I GUESS...
IN COLLEGE I ENJOYED THE COMPANY OF FOLKS WHO APPRECIATED DISCUSSING THE LIKES OF EZRA POUND, POLITICS, VAN GOGH, THE IMPORTANCE OF DARK BEER...
MY FEW ENCOUNTERS WITH IGNORANCE WERE WHEN PALOMAR WAS MENTIONED. IT WAS CONSIDERED A JOKE TOWN FILLED WITH RAVISHING CRO-MAGNON WOMEN IDIOTS AND MONGOLOID THUGS. BUT I WAS THE EXCEPTION, OF COURSE. I'M ONE OF THE 'GOOD' ONES, YOU KNOW.
SOMETIMES WHEN I WAS ALONE I'D RECALL THE GOOD TIMES I HAD IN PALOMAR. THEN I'D WORRY ABOUT VICENTE'S FUTURE. I RECOGNIZED I WAS LUCKY TO HAVE WHAT I HAD, BUT WHERE'D THAT LEAVE MY FRIENDS?!
4
SECONDARY SCHOOL-HIGH SCHOOL TO US.
SHALLOW, MATERIALISTIC GASHEADS-YUPPIES

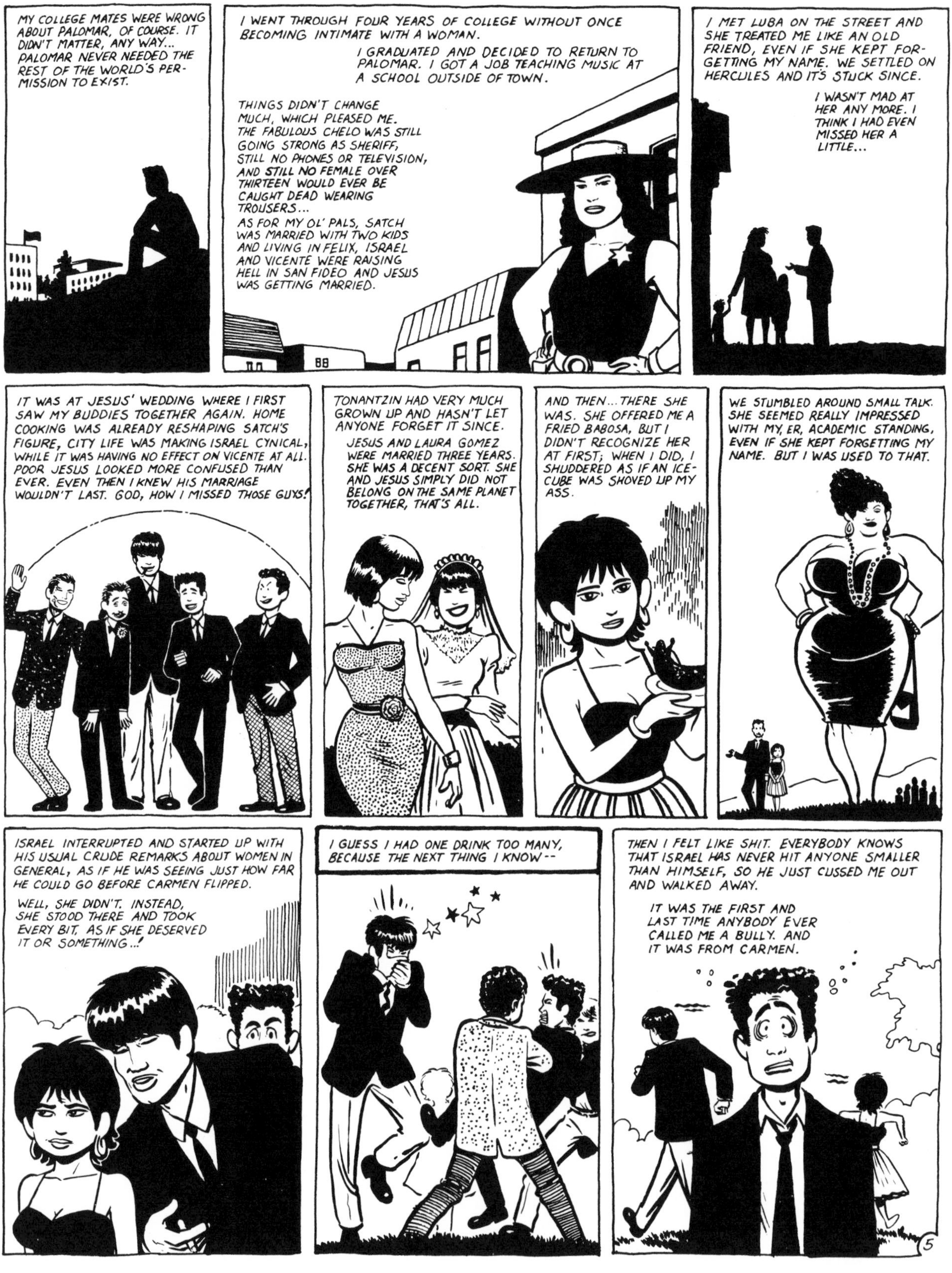
MY COLLEGE MATES WERE WRONG ABOUT PALOMAR, OF COURSE. IT DIDN'T MATTER, ANY WAY... PALOMAR NEVER NEEDED THE REST OF THE WORLD'S PERMISSION TO EXIST.
I WENT THROUGH FOUR YEARS OF COLLEGE WITHOUT ONCE BECOMING INTIMATE WITH A WOMAN.
I GRADUATED AND DECIDED TO RETURN TO PALOMAR. I GOT A JOB TEACHING MUSIC AT A SCHOOL OUTSIDE OF TOWN.
THINGS DIDN'T CHANGE MUCH, WHICH PLEASED ME. THE FABULOUS CHELO WAS STILL GOING STRONG AS SHERIFF, STILL NO PHONES OR TELEVISION, AND STILL NO FEMALE OVER THIRTEEN WOULD EVER BE CAUGHT DEAD WEARING TROUSERS...
AS FOR MY OL' PALS, SATCH WAS MARRIED WITH TWO KIDS AND LIVING IN FELIX, ISRAEL AND VICENTE WERE RAISING HELL IN SAN FIDEO AND JESUS WAS GETTING MARRIED.
I MET LUBA ON THE STREET AND SHE TREATED ME LIKE AN OLD FRIEND, EVEN IF SHE KEPT FORGETTING MY NAME. WE SETTLED ON HERCULES AND IT'S STUCK SINCE.
I WASN'T MAD AT HER ANY MORE. I THINK I HAD EVEN MISSED HER A LITTLE...
IT WAS AT JESUS' WEDDING WHERE I FIRST SAW MY BUDDIES TOGETHER AGAIN. HOME COOKING WAS ALREADY RESHAPING SATCH'S FIGURE, CITY LIFE WAS MAKING ISRAEL CYNICAL, WHILE IT WAS HAVING NO EFFECT ON VICENTE AT ALL. POOR JESUS LOOKED MORE CONFUSED THAN EVER. EVEN THEN I KNEW HIS MARRIAGE WOULDN'T LAST. GOD, HOW I MISSED THOSE GUYS!
TONANTZIN HAD VERY MUCH GROWN UP AND HASN'T LET ANYONE FORGET IT SINCE.
JESUS AND LAURA GOMEZ WERE MARRIED THREE YEARS. SHE WAS A DECENT SORT. SHE AND JESUS SIMPLY DID NOT BELONG ON THE SAME PLANET TOGETHER, THAT'S ALL.
AND THEN... THERE SHE WAS. SHE OFFERED ME A FRIED BABOSA, BUT I DIDN'T RECOGNIZE HER AT FIRST; WHEN I DID, I SHUDDERED AS IF AN ICE-CUBE WAS SHOVED UP MY ASS.
WE STUMBLED AROUND SMALL TALK. SHE SEEMED REALLY IMPRESSED WITH MY, ER, ACADEMIC STANDING, EVEN IF SHE KEPT FORGETTING MY NAME. BUT I WAS USED TO THAT.
ISRAEL INTERRUPTED AND STARTED UP WITH HIS USUAL CRUDE REMARKS ABOUT WOMEN IN GENERAL, AS IF HE WAS SEEING JUST HOW FAR HE COULD GO BEFORE CARMEN FLIPPED.
WELL, SHE DIDN'T. INSTEAD, SHE STOOD THERE AND TOOK EVERY BIT, AS IF SHE DESERVED IT OR SOMETHING...!
I GUESS I HAD ONE DRINK TOO MANY, BECAUSE THE NEXT THING I KNOW--
THEN I FELT LIKE SHIT. EVERYBODY KNOWS THAT ISRAEL HAS NEVER HIT ANYONE SMALLER THAN HIMSELF, SO HE JUST CUSSED ME OUT AND WALKED AWAY.
IT WAS THE FIRST AND LAST TIME ANYBODY EVER CALLED ME A BULLY. AND IT WAS FROM CARMEN.
5

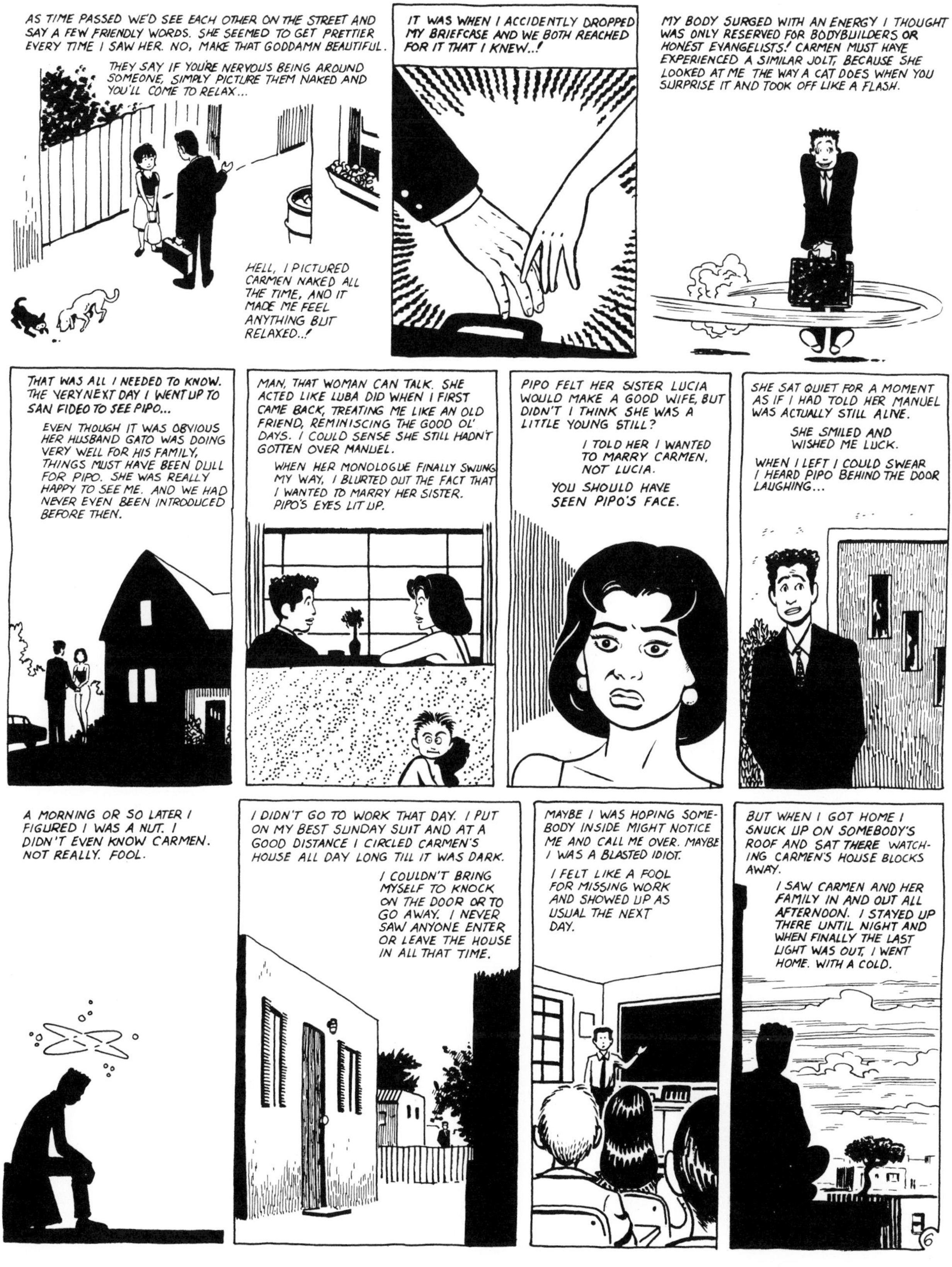
AS TIME PASSED WE'D SEE EACH OTHER ON THE STREET AND SAY A FEW FRIENDLY WORDS. SHE SEEMED TO GET PRETTIER EVERY TIME I SAW HER. NO, MAKE THAT GODDAMN BEAUTIFUL.
THEY SAY IF YOU'RE NERVOUS BEING AROUND SOMEONE, SIMPLY PICTURE THEM NAKED AND YOU'LL COME TO RELAX...
HELL, I PICTURED CARMEN NAKED ALL THE TIME, AND IT MADE ME FEEL ANYTHING BUT RELAXED..!
IT WAS WHEN I ACCIDENTLY DROPPED MY BRIEFCASE AND WE BOTH REACHED FOR IT THAT I KNEW..!
MY BODY SURGED WITH AN ENERGY I THOUGHT WAS ONLY RESERVED FOR BODYBUILDERS OR HONEST EVANGELISTS! CARMEN MUST HAVE EXPERIENCED A SIMILAR JOLT, BECAUSE SHE LOOKED AT ME THE WAY A CAT DOES WHEN YOU SURPRISE IT AND TOOK OFF LIKE A FLASH.
THAT WAS ALL I NEEDED TO KNOW. THE VERY NEXT DAY I WENT UP TO SAN FIDEO TO SEE PIPO...
EVEN THOUGH IT WAS OBVIOUS HER HUSBAND GATO WAS DOING VERY WELL FOR HIS FAMILY, THINGS MUST HAVE BEEN DULL FOR PIPO. SHE WAS REALLY HAPPY TO SEE ME. AND WE HAD NEVER EVEN BEEN INTRODUCED BEFORE THEN.
MAN, THAT WOMAN CAN TALK. SHE ACTED LIKE LUBA DID WHEN I FIRST CAME BACK, TREATING ME LIKE AN OLD FRIEND, REMINISCING THE GOOD OL' DAYS. I COULD SENSE SHE STILL HADN'T GOTTEN OVER MANUEL.
WHEN HER MONOLOGUE FINALLY SWUNG MY WAY, I BLURTED OUT THE FACT THAT I WANTED TO MARRY HER SISTER. PIPO'S EYES LIT UP.
PIPO FELT HER SISTER LUCIA WOULD MAKE A GOOD WIFE, BUT DIDN'T I THINK SHE WAS A LITTLE YOUNG STILL?
I TOLD HER I WANTED TO MARRY CARMEN, NOT LUCIA.
YOU SHOULD HAVE SEEN PIPO'S FACE.
SHE SAT QUIET FOR A MOMENT AS IF I HAD TOLD HER MANUEL WAS ACTUALLY STILL ALIVE.
SHE SMILED AND WISHED ME LUCK.
WHEN I LEFT I COULD SWEAR I HEARD PIPO BEHIND THE DOOR LAUGHING...
A MORNING OR SO LATER I FIGURED I WAS A NUT. I DIDN'T EVEN KNOW CARMEN. NOT REALLY. FOOL.
I DIDN'T GO TO WORK THAT DAY. I PUT ON MY BEST SUNDAY SUIT AND AT A GOOD DISTANCE I CIRCLED CARMEN'S HOUSE ALL DAY LONG TILL IT WAS DARK.
I COULDN'T BRING MYSELF TO KNOCK ON THE DOOR OR TO GO AWAY. I NEVER SAW ANYONE ENTER OR LEAVE THE HOUSE IN ALL THAT TIME.
MAYBE I WAS HOPING SOMEBODY INSIDE MIGHT NOTICE ME AND CALL ME OVER. MAYBE I WAS A BLASTED IDIOT.
I FELT LIKE A FOOL FOR MISSING WORK AND SHOWED UP AS USUAL THE NEXT DAY.
BUT WHEN I GOT HOME I SNUCK UP ON SOMEBODY'S ROOF AND SAT THERE WATCHING CARMEN'S HOUSE BLOCKS AWAY.
I SAW CARMEN AND HER FAMILY IN AND OUT ALL AFTERNOON. I STAYED UP THERE UNTIL NIGHT AND WHEN FINALLY THE LAST LIGHT WAS OUT, I WENT HOME. WITH A COLD.
6

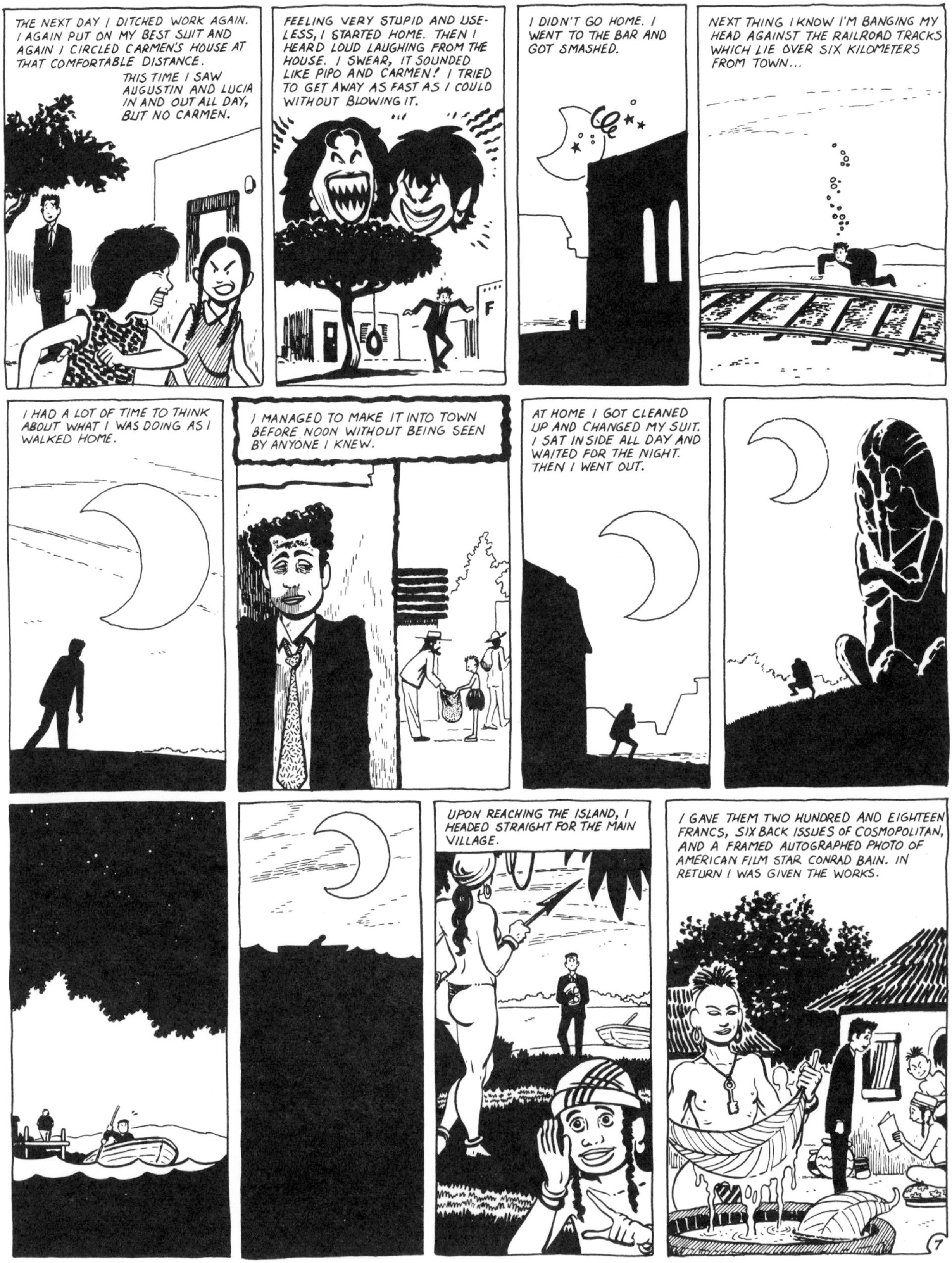
THE NEXT DAY I DITCHED WORK AGAIN. I AGAIN PUT ON MY BEST SUIT AND AGAIN I CIRCLED CARMEN'S HOUSE AT THAT COMFORTABLE DISTANCE.
THIS TIME I SAW AUGUSTIN AND LUCIA IN AND OUT ALL DAY, BUT NO CARMEN.
FEELING VERY STUPID AND USELESS, I STARTED HOME. THEN I HEARD LOUD LAUGHING FROM THE HOUSE. I SWEAR, IT SOUNDED LIKE PIPO AND CARMEN! I TRIED TO GET AWAY AS FAST AS I COULD WITHOUT BLOWING IT.
F
I DIDN'T GO HOME. I WENT TO THE BAR AND GOT SMASHED.
NEXT THING I KNOW I'M BANGING MY HEAD AGAINST THE RAILROAD TRACKS WHICH LIE OVER SIX KILOMETERS FROM TOWN...
I HAD A LOT OF TIME TO THINK ABOUT WHAT I WAS DOING AS I WALKED HOME.
I MANAGED TO MAKE IT INTO TOWN BEFORE NOON WITHOUT BEING SEEN BY ANYONE I KNEW.
AT HOME I GOT CLEANED UP AND CHANGED MY SUIT. I SAT INSIDE ALL DAY AND WAITED FOR THE NIGHT. THEN I WENT OUT.
UPON REACHING THE ISLAND, I HEADED STRAIGHT FOR THE MAIN VILLAGE.
I GAVE THEM TWO HUNDRED AND EIGHTEEN FRANCS, SIX BACK ISSUES OF COSMOPOLITAN, AND A FRAMED AUTOGRAPHED PHOTO OF AMERICAN FILM STAR CONRAD BAIN. IN RETURN I WAS GIVEN THE WORKS.
7

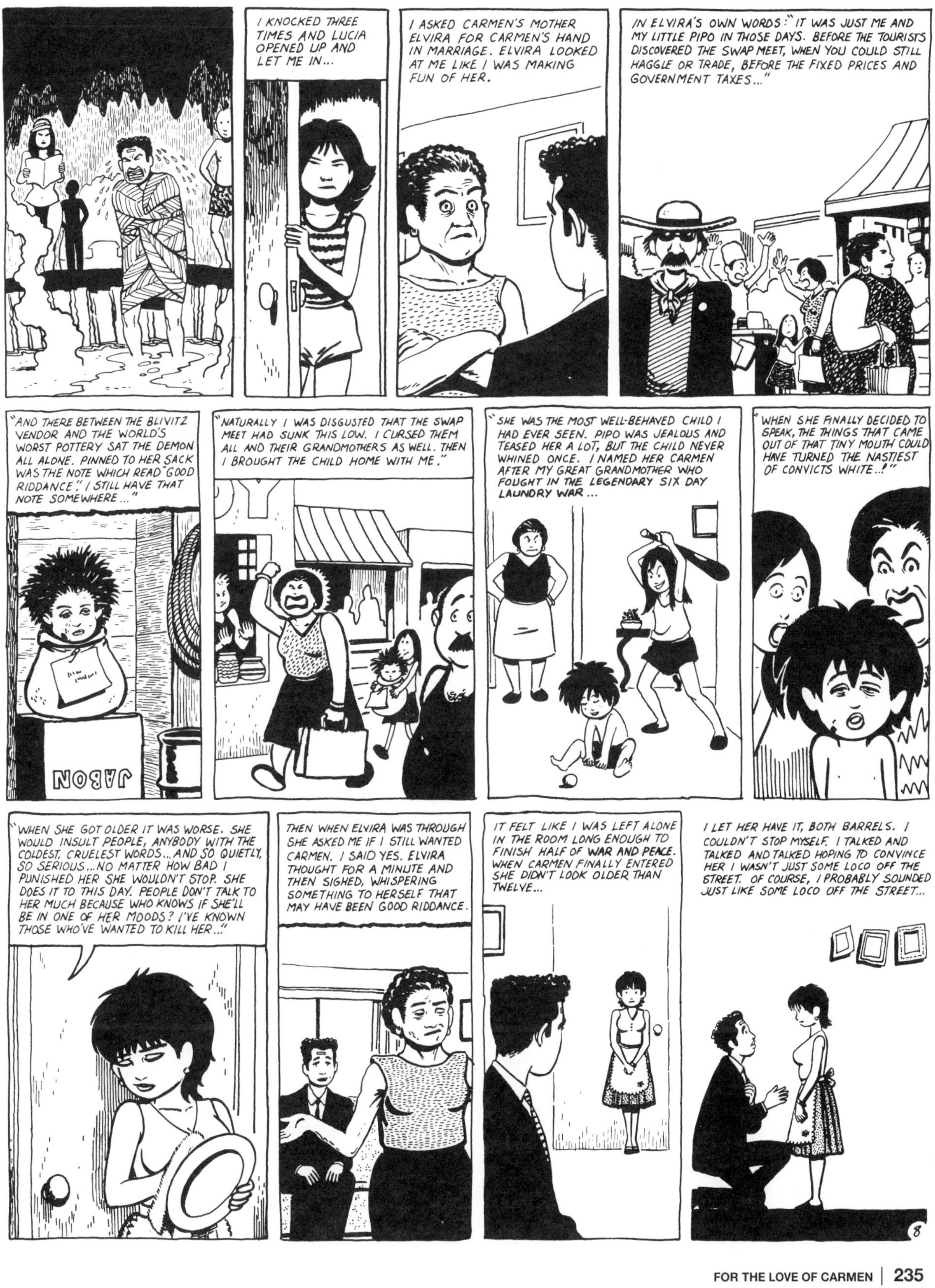
I KNOCKED THREE TIMES AND LUCIA OPENED UP AND LET ME IN...
I ASKED CARMEN'S MOTHER ELVIRA FOR CARMEN'S HAND IN MARRIAGE. ELVIRA LOOKED AT ME LIKE I WAS MAKING FUN OF HER.
IN ELVIRA'S OWN WORDS: "IT WAS JUST ME AND MY LITTLE PIPO IN THOSE DAYS. BEFORE THE TOURISTS DISCOVERED THE SWAP MEET, WHEN YOU COULD STILL HAGGLE OR TRADE, BEFORE THE FIXED PRICES AND GOVERNMENT TAXES..."
"AND THERE BETWEEN THE BLIVITZ VENDOR AND THE WORLD'S WORST POTTERY SAT THE DEMON ALL ALONE. PINNED TO HER SACK WAS THE NOTE WHICH READ "GOOD RIDDANCE". I STILL HAVE THAT NOTE SOMEWHERE..."
JABON
"NATURALLY I WAS DISGUSTED THAT THE SWAP MEET HAD SUNK THIS LOW. I CURSED THEM ALL AND THEIR GRANDMOTHERS AS WELL. THEN I BROUGHT THE CHILD HOME WITH ME."
"SHE WAS THE MOST WELL-BEHAVED CHILD I HAD EVER SEEN. PIPO WAS JEALOUS AND TEASED HER A LOT, BUT THE CHILD NEVER WHINED ONCE. I NAMED HER CARMEN AFTER MY GREAT GRANDMOTHER WHO FOUGHT IN THE LEGENDARY SIX DAY LAUNDRY WAR...
"WHEN SHE FINALLY DECIDED TO SPEAK, THE THINGS THAT CAME OUT OF THAT TINY MOUTH COULD HAVE TURNED THE NASTIEST OF CONVICTS WHITE..!"
"WHEN SHE GOT OLDER IT WAS WORSE. SHE WOULD INSULT PEOPLE, ANYBODY WITH THE COLDEST, CRUELEST WORDS... AND SO QUIETLY, SO SERIOUS... NO MATTER HOW BAD I PUNISHED HER SHE WOULDN'T STOP. SHE DOES IT TO THIS DAY. PEOPLE DON'T TALK TO HER MUCH BECAUSE WHO KNOWS IF SHE'LL BE IN ONE OF HER MOODS? I'VE KNOWN THOSE WHO'VE WANTED TO KILL HER..."
THEN WHEN ELVIRA WAS THROUGH SHE ASKED ME IF I STILL WANTED CARMEN. I SAID YES. ELVIRA THOUGHT FOR A MINUTE AND THEN SIGHED, WHISPERING SOMETHING TO HERSELF THAT MAY HAVE BEEN GOOD RIDDANCE.
IT FELT LIKE I WAS LEFT ALONE IN THE ROOM LONG ENOUGH TO FINISH HALF OF WAR AND PEACE. WHEN CARMEN FINALLY ENTERED SHE DIDN'T LOOK OLDER THAN TWELVE...
I LET HER HAVE IT, BOTH BARRELS. I COULDN'T STOP MYSELF. I TALKED AND TALKED AND TALKED HOPING TO CONVINCE HER I WASN'T JUST SOME LOCO OFF THE STREET. OF COURSE, I PROBABLY SOUNDED JUST LIKE SOME LOCO OFF THE STREET...
8

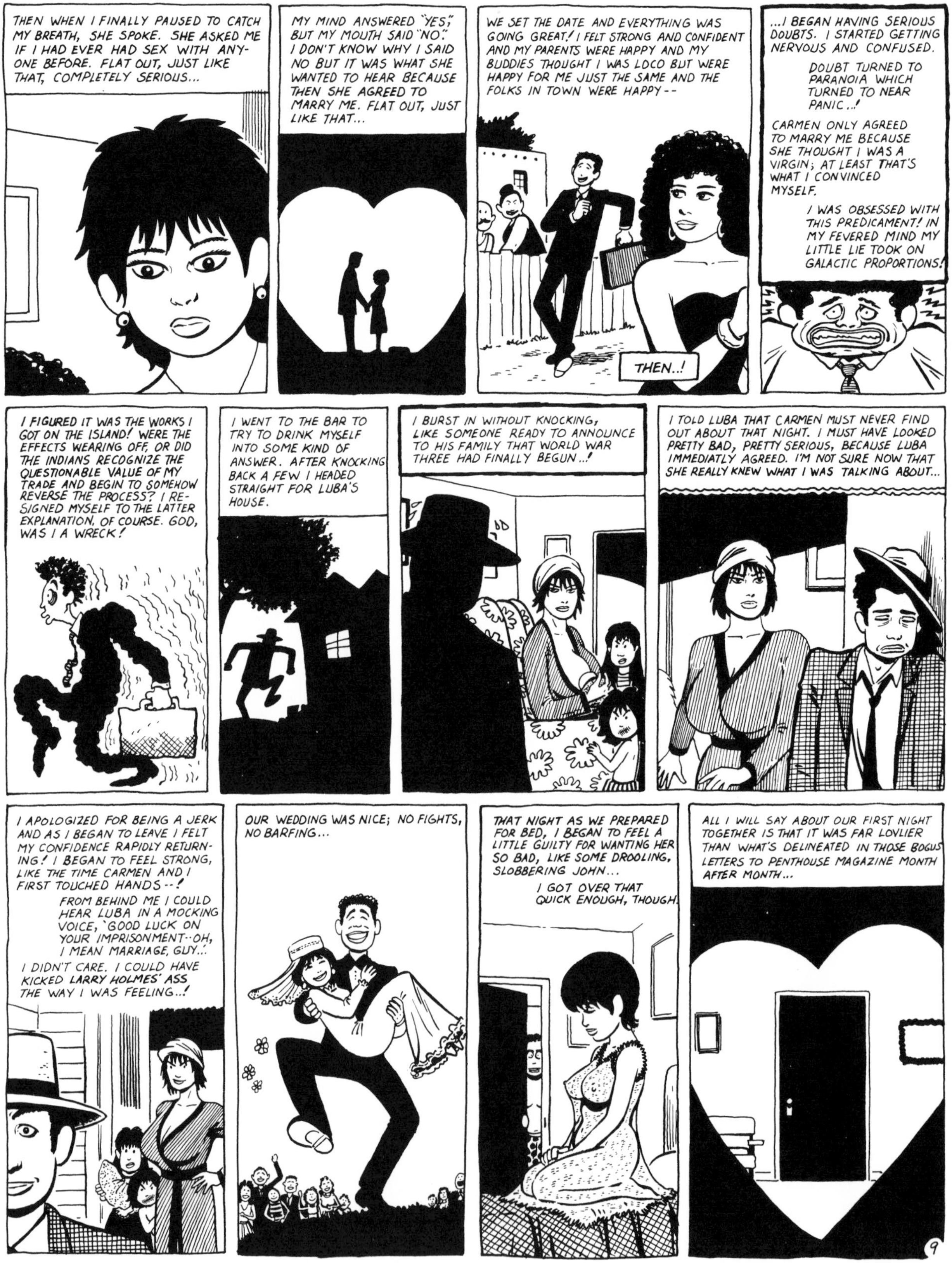
THEN WHEN I FINALLY PAUSED TO CATCH MY BREATH, SHE SPOKE. SHE ASKED ME IF I HAD EVER HAD SEX WITH ANYONE BEFORE. FLAT OUT, JUST LIKE THAT, COMPLETELY SERIOUS...
MY MIND ANSWERED "YES," BUT MY MOUTH SAID "NO." I DON'T KNOW WHY I SAID NO BUT IT WAS WHAT SHE WANTED TO HEAR BECAUSE THEN SHE AGREED TO MARRY ME. FLAT OUT, JUST LIKE THAT...
WE SET THE DATE AND EVERYTHING WAS GOING GREAT! I FELT STRONG AND CONFIDENT AND MY PARENTS WERE HAPPY AND MY BUDDIES THOUGHT I WAS LOCO BUT WERE HAPPY FOR ME JUST THE SAME AND THE FOLKS IN TOWN WERE HAPPY--
THEN..!
...I BEGAN HAVING SERIOUS DOUBTS. I STARTED GETTING NERVOUS AND CONFUSED.
DOUBT TURNED TO PARANOIA WHICH TURNED TO NEAR PANIC..!
CARMEN ONLY AGREED TO MARRY ME BECAUSE SHE THOUGHT I WAS A VIRGIN; AT LEAST THAT'S WHAT I CONVINCED MYSELF.
I WAS OBSESSED WITH THIS PREDICAMENT! IN MY FEVERED MIND MY LITTLE LIE TOOK ON GALACTIC PROPORTIONS!
I FIGURED IT WAS THE WORKS I GOT ON THE ISLAND! WERE THE EFFECTS WEARING OFF, OR DID THE INDIANS RECOGNIZE THE QUESTIONABLE VALUE OF MY TRADE AND BEGIN TO SOMEHOW REVERSE THE PROCESS? I RESIGNED MYSELF TO THE LATTER EXPLANATION, OF COURSE. GOD, WAS I A WRECK!
I WENT TO THE BAR TO TRY TO DRINK MYSELF INTO SOME KIND OF ANSWER. AFTER KNOCKING BACK A FEW I HEADED STRAIGHT FOR LUBA'S HOUSE.
I BURST IN WITHOUT KNOCKING, LIKE SOMEONE READY TO ANNOUNCE TO HIS FAMILY THAT WORLD WAR THREE HAD FINALLY BEGUN...!
I TOLD LUBA THAT CARMEN MUST NEVER FIND OUT ABOUT THAT NIGHT. I MUST HAVE LOOKED PRETTY BAD, PRETTY SERIOUS, BECAUSE LUBA IMMEDIATLY AGREED. I'M NOT SURE NOW THAT SHE REALLY KNEW WHAT I WAS TALKING ABOUT...
I APOLOGIZED FOR BEING A JERK AND AS I BEGAN TO LEAVE I FELT MY CONFIDENCE RAPIDLY RETURNING! I BEGAN TO FEEL STRONG, LIKE THE TIME CARMEN AND I FIRST TOUCHED HANDS--!
FROM BEHIND ME I COULD HEAR LUBA IN A MOCKING VOICE, "GOOD LUCK ON YOUR IMPRISONMENT..OH, I MEAN MARRIAGE, GUY..."
I DIDN'T CARE. I COULD HAVE KICKED LARRY HOLMES' ASS THE WAY I WAS FEELING...!
OUR WEDDING WAS NICE; NO FIGHTS, NO BARFING...
THAT NIGHT AS WE PREPARED FOR BED, I BEGAN TO FEEL A LITTLE GUILTY FOR WANTING HER SO BAD, LIKE SOME DROOLING, SLOBBERING JOHN...
I GOT OVER THAT QUICK ENOUGH, THOUGH.
ALL I WILL SAY ABOUT OUR FIRST NIGHT TOGETHER IS THAT IT WAS FAR LOVLIER THAN WHAT'S DELINEATED IN THOSE BOGUS LETTERS TO PENTHOUSE MAGAZINE MONTH AFTER MONTH...
9

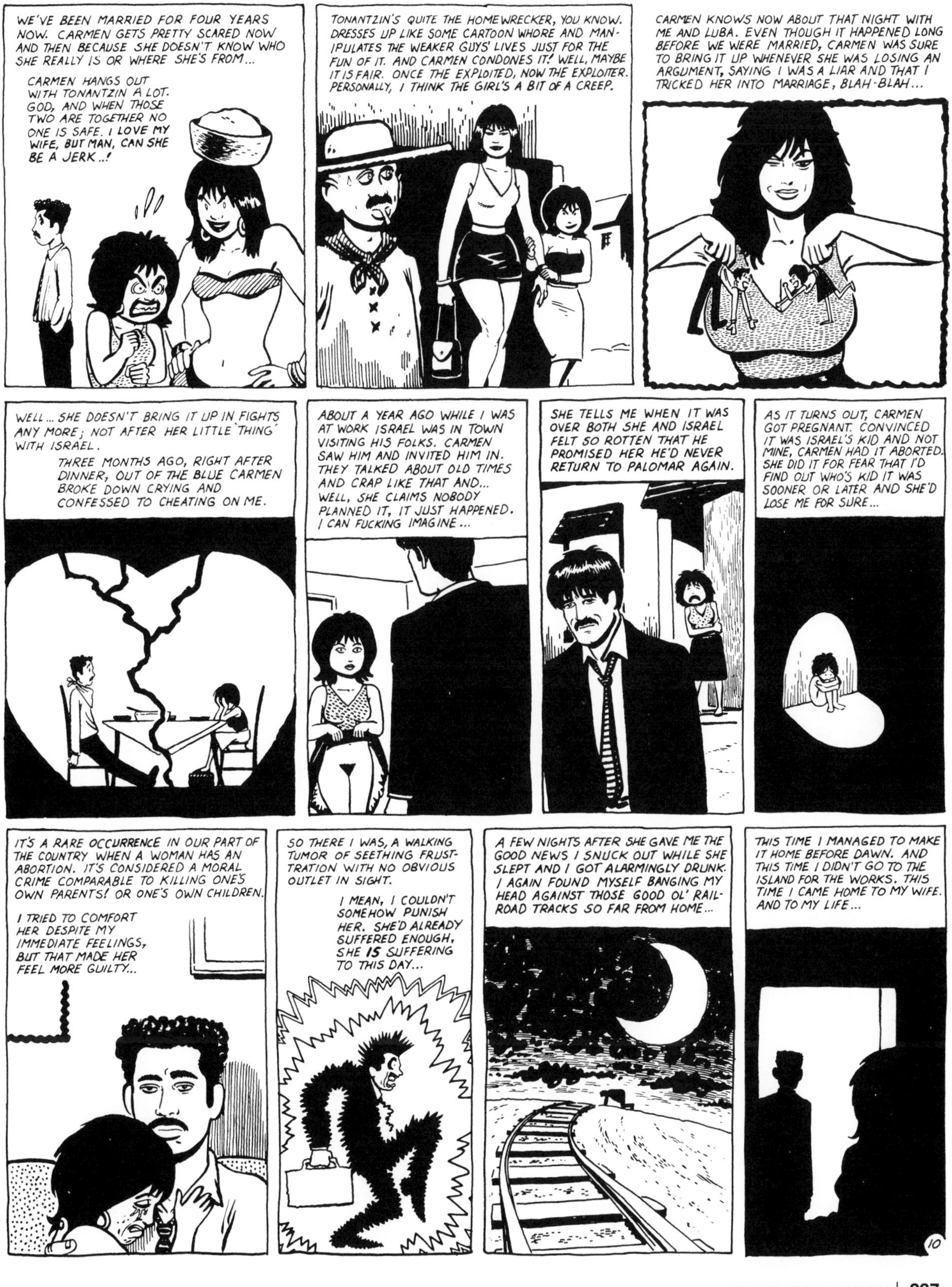
WE'VE BEEN MARRIED FOR FOUR YEARS NOW. CARMEN GETS PRETTY SCARED NOW AND THEN BECAUSE SHE DOESN'T KNOW WHO SHE REALLY IS OR WHERE SHE'S FROM...
CARMEN HANGS OUT WITH TONANTZIN A LOT. GOD, AND WHEN THOSE TWO ARE TOGETHER NO ONE IS SAFE. I LOVE MY WIFE, BUT MAN, CAN SHE BE A JERK..!
TONANTZIN'S QUITE THE HOMEWRECKER, YOU KNOW. DRESSES UP LIKE SOME CARTOON WHORE AND MANIPULATES THE WEAKER GUYS' LIVES JUST FOR THE FUN OF IT. AND CARMEN CONDONES IT! WELL, MAYBE IT IS FAIR. ONCE THE EXPLOITED, NOW THE EXPLOITER. PERSONALLY, I THINK THE GIRL'S A BIT OF A CREEP.
CARMEN KNOWS NOW ABOUT THAT NIGHT WITH ME AND LUBA. EVEN THOUGH IT HAPPENED LONG BEFORE WE WERE MARRIED, CARMEN WAS SURE TO BRING IT UP WHENEVER SHE WAS LOSING AN ARGUMENT, SAYING I WAS A LIAR AND THAT I TRICKED HER INTO MARRIAGE, BLAH-BLAH...
WELL... SHE DOESN'T BRING IT UP IN FIGHTS ANY MORE; NOT AFTER HER LITTLE 'THING' WITH ISRAEL.
THREE MONTHS AGO, RIGHT AFTER DINNER, OUT OF THE BLUE CARMEN BROKE DOWN CRYING AND CONFESSED TO CHEATING ON ME.
ABOUT A YEAR AGO WHILE I WAS AT WORK ISRAEL WAS IN TOWN VISITING HIS FOLKS. CARMEN SAW HIM AND INVITED HIM IN. THEY TALKED ABOUT OLD TIMES AND CRAP LIKE THAT AND... WELL, SHE CLAIMS NOBODY PLANNED IT, IT JUST HAPPENED. I CAN FUCKING IMAGINE...
SHE TELLS ME WHEN IT WAS OVER BOTH SHE AND ISRAEL FELT SO ROTTEN THAT HE PROMISED HER HE'D NEVER RETURN TO PALOMAR AGAIN.
AS IT TURNS OUT, CARMEN GOT PREGNANT. CONVINCED IT WAS ISRAEL'S KID AND NOT MINE, CARMEN HAD IT ABORTED. SHE DID IT FOR FEAR THAT I'D FIND OUT WHO'S KID IT WAS SOONER OR LATER AND SHE'D LOSE ME FOR SURE...
IT'S A RARE OCCURRENCE IN OUR PART OF THE COUNTRY WHEN A WOMAN HAS AN ABORTION. IT'S CONSIDERED A MORAL CRIME COMPARABLE TO KILLING ONE'S OWN PARENTS! OR ONE'S OWN CHILDREN.
I TRIED TO COMFORT HER DESPITE MY IMMEDIATE FEELINGS, BUT THAT MADE HER FEEL MORE GUILTY...
SO THERE I WAS, A WALKING TUMOR OF SEETHING FRUSTRATION WITH NO OBVIOUS OUTLET IN SIGHT.
I MEAN, I COULDN'T SOMEHOW PUNISH HER. SHE'D ALREADY SUFFERED ENOUGH. SHE IS SUFFERING TO THIS DAY...
A FEW NIGHTS AFTER SHE GAVE ME THE GOOD NEWS I SNUCK OUT WHILE SHE SLEPT AND I GOT ALARMINGLY DRUNK. I AGAIN FOUND MYSELF BANGING MY HEAD AGAINST THOSE GOOD OL' RAILROAD TRACKS SO FAR FROM HOME...
THIS TIME I MANAGED TO MAKE IT HOME BEFORE DAWN. AND THIS TIME I DIDN'T GO TO THE ISLAND FOR THE WORKS. THIS TIME I CAME HOME TO MY WIFE. AND TO MY LIFE...
10

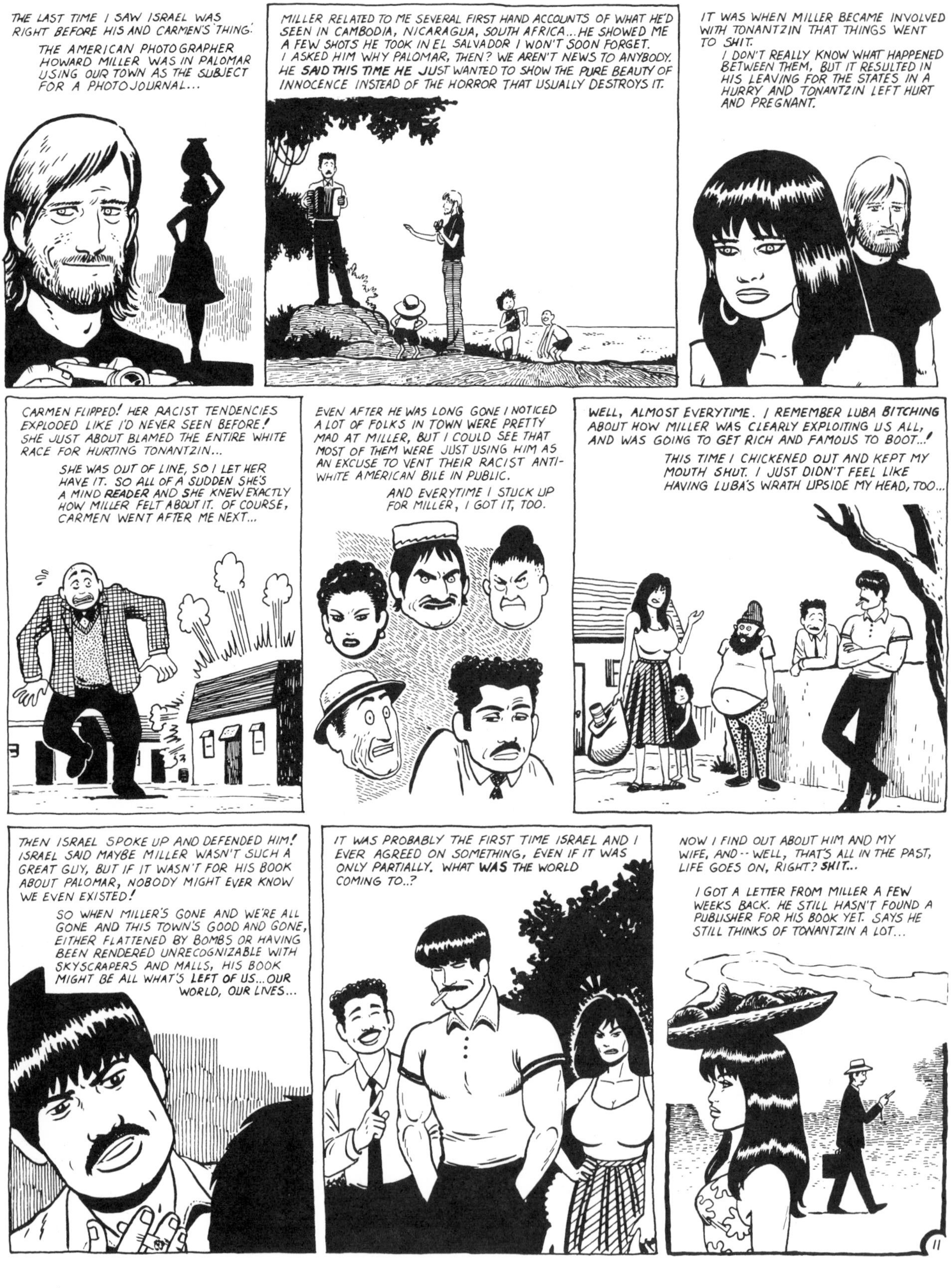

THE LAST TIME I SAW ISRAEL WAS RIGHT BEFORE HIS AND CARMEN'S 'THING'.
THE AMERICAN PHOTOGRAPHER HOWARD MILLER WAS IN PALOMAR USING OUR TOWN AS THE SUBJECT FOR A PHOTOJOURNAL...
MILLER RELATED TO ME SEVERAL FIRST HAND ACCOUNTS OF WHAT HE'D SEEN IN CAMBODIA, NICARAGUA, SOUTH AFRICA... HE SHOWED ME A FEW SHOTS HE TOOK IN EL SALVADOR I WON'T SOON FORGET. I ASKED HIM WHY PALOMAR, THEN? WE AREN'T NEWS TO ANYBODY. HE SAID THIS TIME HE JUST WANTED TO SHOW THE PURE BEAUTY OF INNOCENCE INSTEAD OF THE HORROR THAT USUALLY DESTROYS IT.
IT WAS WHEN MILLER BECAME INVOLVED WITH TONANTZIN THAT THINGS WENT TO SHIT.
I DON'T REALLY KNOW WHAT HAPPENED BETWEEN THEM, BUT IT RESULTED IN HIS LEAVING FOR THE STATES IN A HURRY AND TONANTZIN LEFT HURT AND PREGNANT.
CARMEN FLIPPED! HER RACIST TENDENCIES EXPLODED LIKE I'D NEVER SEEN BEFORE! SHE JUST ABOUT BLAMED THE ENTIRE WHITE RACE FOR HURTING TONANTZIN...
SHE WAS OUT OF LINE, SO I LET HER HAVE IT. SO ALL OF A SUDDEN SHE'S A MIND READER AND SHE KNEW EXACTLY HOW MILLER FELT ABOUT IT. OF COURSE, CARMEN WENT AFTER ME NEXT...
EVEN AFTER HE WAS LONG GONE I NOTICED A LOT OF FOLKS IN TOWN WERE PRETTY MAD AT MILLER, BUT I COULD SEE THAT MOST OF THEM WERE JUST USING HIM AS AN EXCUSE TO VENT THEIR RACIST ANTI-WHITE AMERICAN BILE IN PUBLIC.
AND EVERYTIME I STUCK UP FOR MILLER, I GOT IT, TOO.
WELL, ALMOST EVERYTIME. I REMEMBER LUBA BITCHING ABOUT HOW MILLER WAS CLEARLY EXPLOITING US ALL, AND WAS GOING TO GET RICH AND FAMOUS TO BOOT...!
THIS TIME I CHICKENED OUT AND KEPT MY MOUTH SHUT. I JUST DIDN'T FEEL LIKE HAVING LUBA'S WRATH UPSIDE MY HEAD, TOO...
THEN ISRAEL SPOKE UP AND DEFENDED HIM! ISRAEL SAID MAYBE MILLER WASN'T SUCH A GREAT GUY, BUT IF IT WASN'T FOR HIS BOOK ABOUT PALOMAR, NOBODY MIGHT EVER KNOW WE EVEN EXISTED!
SO WHEN MILLER'S GONE AND WE'RE ALL GONE AND THIS TOWN'S GOOD AND GONE, EITHER FLATTENED BY BOMBS OR HAVING BEEN RENDERED UNRECOGNIZABLE WITH SKYSCRAPERS AND MALLS, HIS BOOK MIGHT BE ALL WHAT'S LEFT OF US... OUR WORLD, OUR LIVES...
IT WAS PROBABLY THE FIRST TIME ISRAEL AND I EVER AGREED ON SOMETHING, EVEN IF IT WAS ONLY PARTIALLY. WHAT WAS THE WORLD COMING TO..?
NOW I FIND OUT ABOUT HIM AND MY WIFE, AND -- WELL, THAT'S ALL IN THE PAST, LIFE GOES ON, RIGHT? SHIT...
I GOT A LETTER FROM MILLER A FEW WEEKS BACK. HE STILL HASN'T FOUND A PUBLISHER FOR HIS BOOK YET. SAYS HE STILL THINKS OF TONANTZIN A LOT...
11

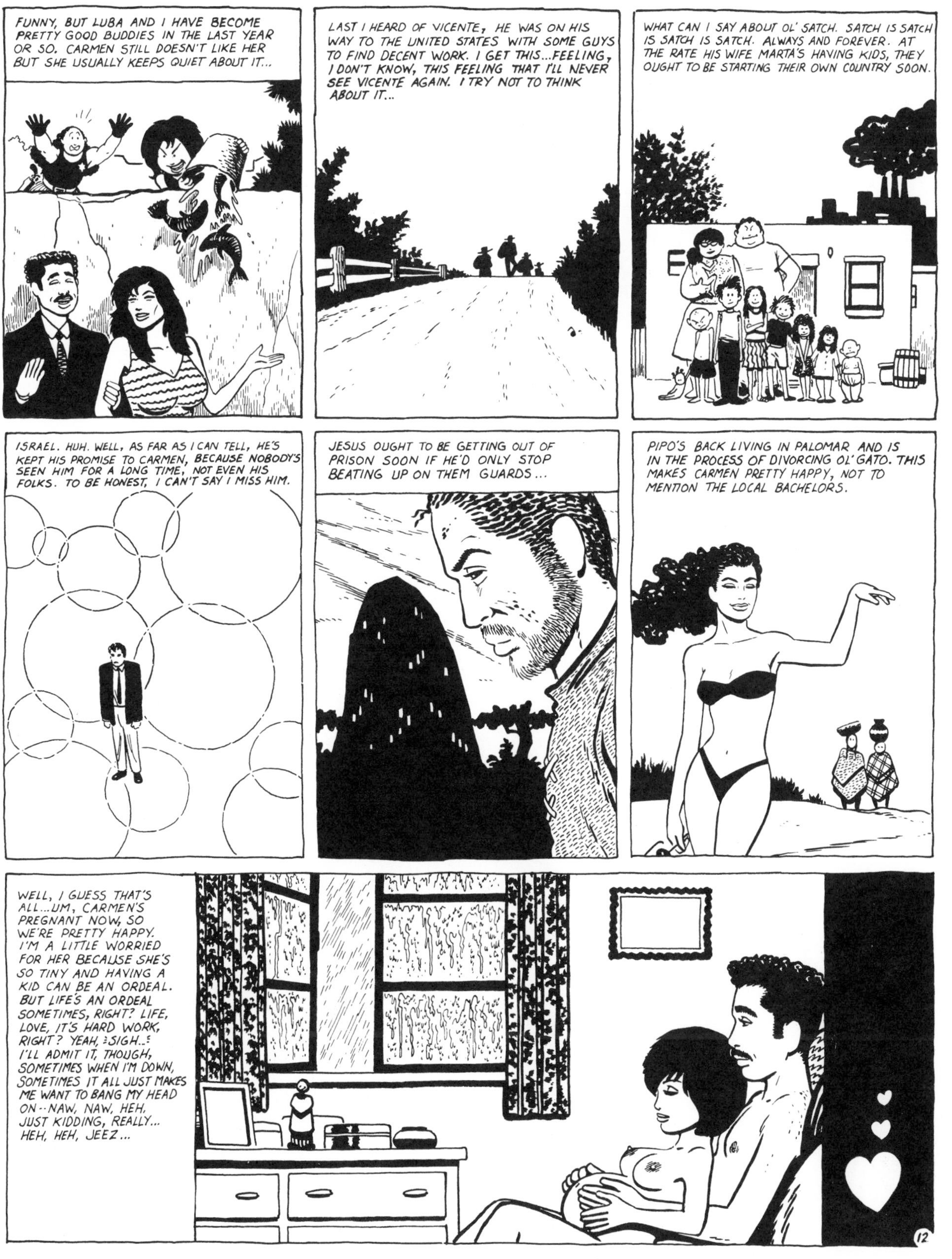
FUNNY, BUT LUBA AND I HAVE BECOME PRETTY GOOD BUDDIES IN THE LAST YEAR OR SO. CARMEN STILL DOESN'T LIKE HER BUT SHE USUALLY KEEPS QUIET ABOUT IT...
LAST I HEARD OF VICENTE, HE WAS ON HIS WAY TO THE UNITED STATES WITH SOME GUYS TO FIND DECENT WORK. I GET THIS...FEELING, I DON'T KNOW, THIS FEELING THAT I'LL NEVER SEE VICENTE AGAIN. I TRY NOT TO THINK ABOUT IT...
WHAT CAN I SAY ABOUT OL' SATCH. SATCH IS SATCH IS SATCH IS SATCH. ALWAYS AND FOREVER. AT THE RATE HIS WIFE MARTA'S HAVING KIDS, THEY OUGHT TO BE STARTING THEIR OWN COUNTRY SOON.
ISRAEL. HUH. WELL, AS FAR AS I CAN TELL, HE'S KEPT HIS PROMISE TO CARMEN, BECAUSE NOBODY'S SEEN HIM FOR A LONG TIME, NOT EVEN HIS FOLKS. TO BE HONEST, I CAN'T SAY I MISS HIM.
JESUS OUGHT TO BE GETTING OUT OF PRISON SOON IF HE'D ONLY STOP BEATING UP ON THEM GUARDS...
PIPO'S BACK LIVING IN PALOMAR AND IS IN THE PROCESS OF DIVORCING OL' GATO. THIS MAKES CARMEN PRETTY HAPPY, NOT TO MENTION THE LOCAL BACHELORS.
WELL, I GUESS THAT'S ALL...UM, CARMEN'S PREGNANT NOW, SO WE'RE PRETTY HAPPY. I'M A LITTLE WORRIED FOR HER BECAUSE SHE'S SO TINY AND HAVING A KID CAN BE AN ORDEAL. BUT LIFE'S AN ORDEAL SOMETIMES, RIGHT? LIFE, LOVE, IT'S HARD WORK, RIGHT? YEAH, :SIGH..: I'LL ADMIT IT, THOUGH, SOMETIMES WHEN I'M DOWN, SOMETIMES IT ALL JUST MAKES ME WANT TO BANG MY HEAD ON--NAW, NAW, HEH, JUST KIDDING, REALLY... HEH, HEH, JEEZ...
12

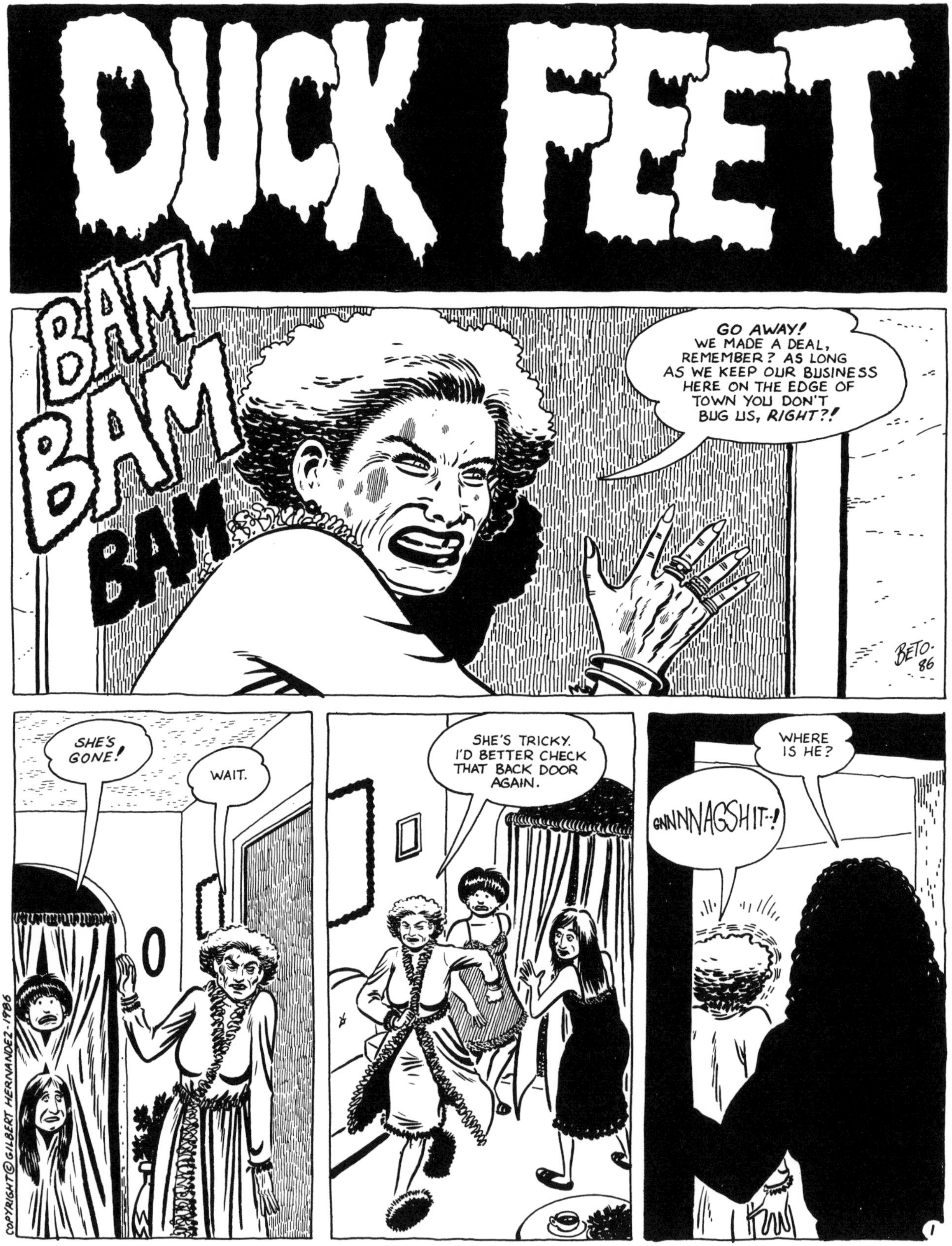
DUCK FEET
BAM BAM BAM
GO AWAY! WE MADE A DEAL, REMEMBER? AS LONG AS WE KEEP OUR BUSINESS HERE ON THE EDGE OF TOWN YOU DON'T BUG US, RIGHT?!
BETO-86
SHE'S GONE!
WAIT.
COPYRIGHT © GILBERT HERNANDEZ-1986
SHE'S TRICKY. I'D BETTER CHECK THAT BACK DOOR AGAIN.
WHERE IS HE?
GNNNNAGSHIT-!
1

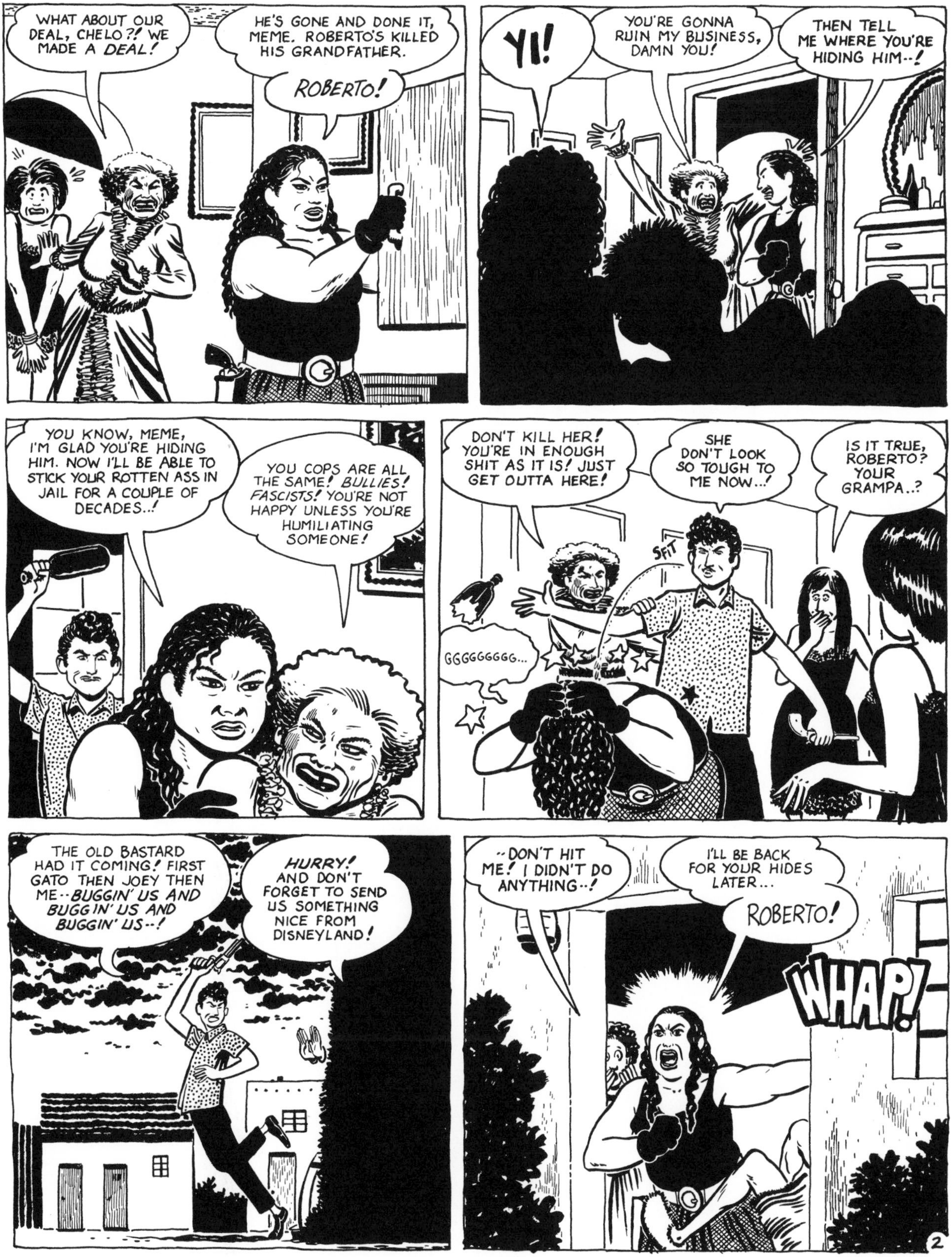
WHAT ABOUT OUR DEAL, CHELO?! WE MADE A DEAL!
HE'S GONE AND DONE IT, MEME. ROBERTO'S KILLED HIS GRANDFATHER.
ROBERTO!
YI!
YOU'RE GONNA RUIN MY BUSINESS, DAMN YOU!
THEN TELL ME WHERE YOU'RE HIDING HIM--!
YOU KNOW, MEME, I'M GLAD YOU'RE HIDING HIM. NOW I'LL BE ABLE TO STICK YOUR ROTTEN ASS IN JAIL FOR A COUPLE OF DECADES..!
YOU COPS ARE ALL THE SAME! BULLIES! FASCISTS! YOU'RE NOT HAPPY UNLESS YOU'RE HUMILIATING SOMEONE!
DON'T KILL HER! YOU'RE IN ENOUGH SHIT AS IT IS! JUST GET OUTTA HERE!
SHE DON'T LOOK SO TOUGH TO ME NOW...!
IS IT TRUE, ROBERTO? YOUR GRAMPA..?
SFIT
GGGGGGGGG...
THE OLD BASTARD HAD IT COMING! FIRST GATO THEN JOEY THEN ME--BUGGIN' US AND BUGGIN' US AND BUGGIN' US--!
HURRY! AND DON'T FORGET TO SEND US SOMETHING NICE FROM DISNEYLAND!
--DON'T HIT ME! I DIDN'T DO ANYTHING--!
I'LL BE BACK FOR YOUR HIDES LATER...
ROBERTO!
WHAP!
2

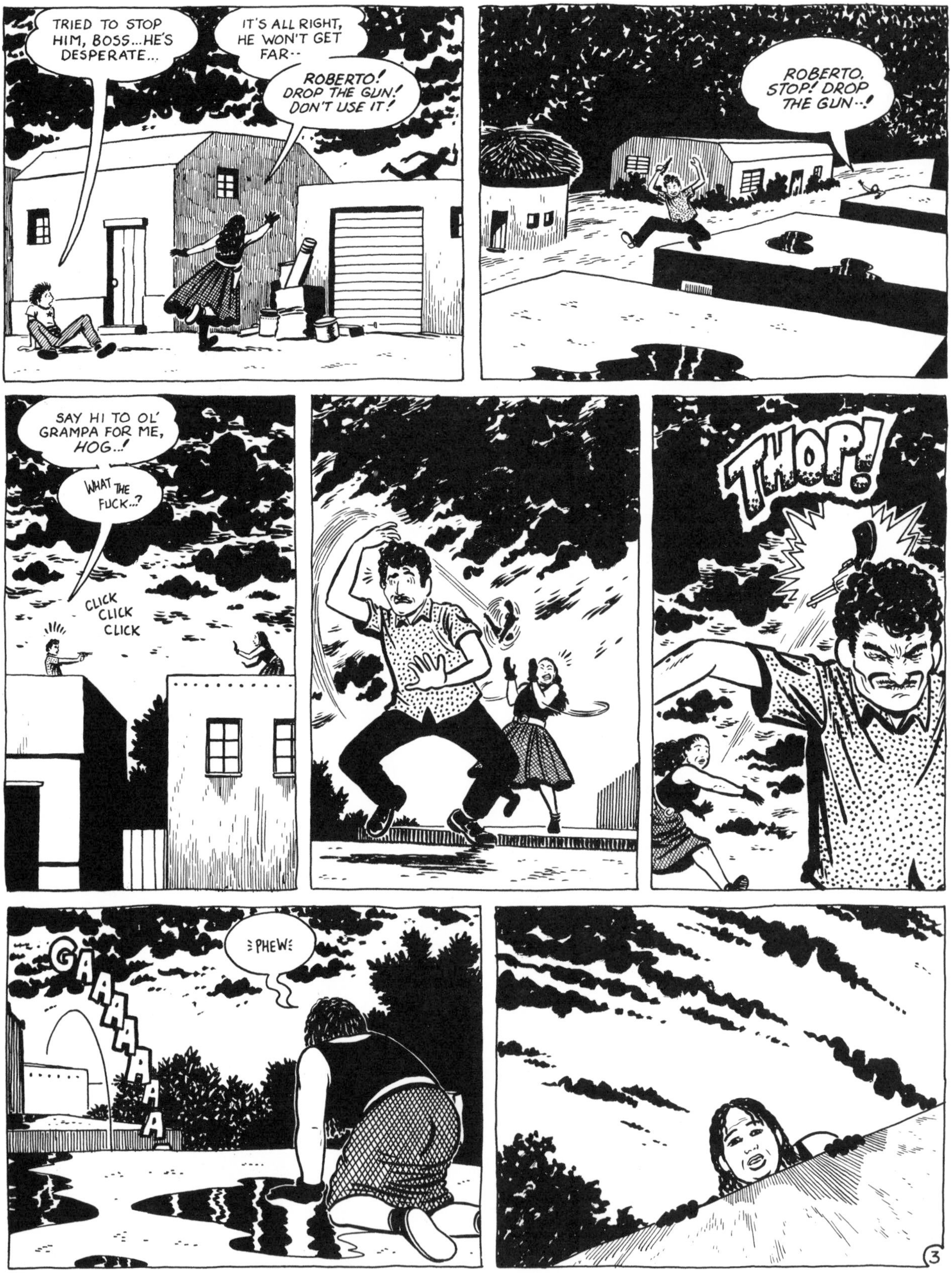
TRIED TO STOP HIM, BOSS...HE'S DESPERATE...
IT'S ALL RIGHT, HE WON'T GET FAR--
ROBERTO! DROP THE GUN! DON'T USE IT!
ROBERTO, STOP! DROP THE GUN--!
SAY HI TO OL' GRAMPA FOR ME, HOG...!
WHAT THE FUCK...?
CLICK CLICK CLICK
THOP!
GAAAAAAAA
PHEW
3

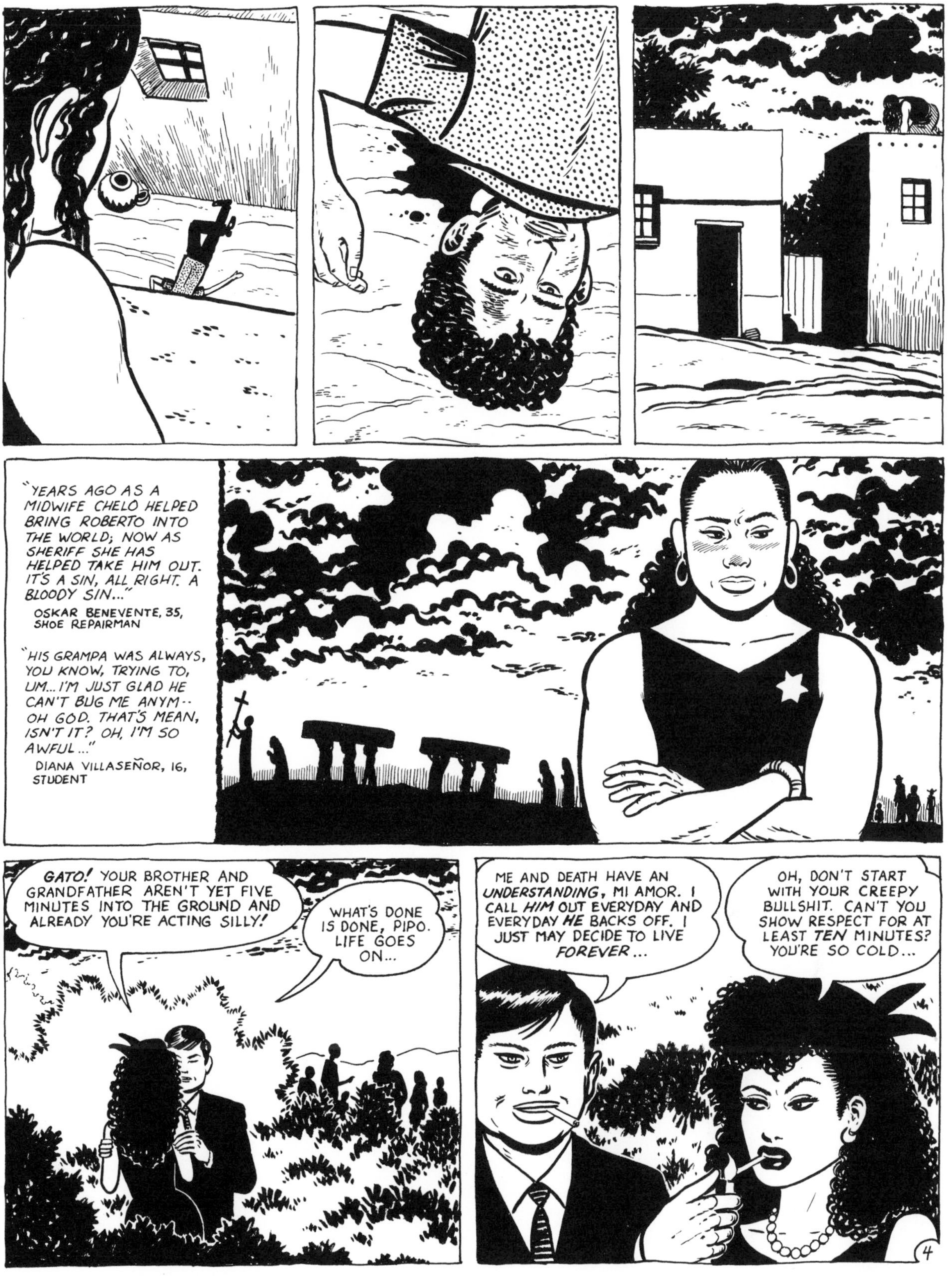
"YEARS AGO AS A MIDWIFE CHELO HELPED BRING ROBERTO INTO THE WORLD; NOW AS SHERIFF SHE HAS HELPED TAKE HIM OUT. IT'S A SIN, ALL RIGHT. A BLOODY SIN..."
OSKAR BENEVENTE, 35, SHOE REPAIRMAN
"HIS GRAMPA WAS ALWAYS, YOU KNOW, TRYING TO, UM... I'M JUST GLAD HE CAN'T BUG ME ANYM-- OH GOD. THAT'S MEAN, ISN'T IT? OH, I'M SO AWFUL..."
DIANA VILLASEÑOR, 16, STUDENT
GATO! YOUR BROTHER AND GRANDFATHER AREN'T YET FIVE MINUTES INTO THE GROUND AND ALREADY YOU'RE ACTING SILLY!
WHAT'S DONE IS DONE, PIPO. LIFE GOES ON...
ME AND DEATH HAVE AN UNDERSTANDING, MI AMOR. I CALL HIM OUT EVERYDAY AND EVERYDAY HE BACKS OFF. I JUST MAY DECIDE TO LIVE FOREVER...
OH, DON'T START WITH YOUR CREEPY BULLSHIT. CAN'T YOU SHOW RESPECT FOR AT LEAST TEN MINUTES? YOU'RE SO COLD...
4

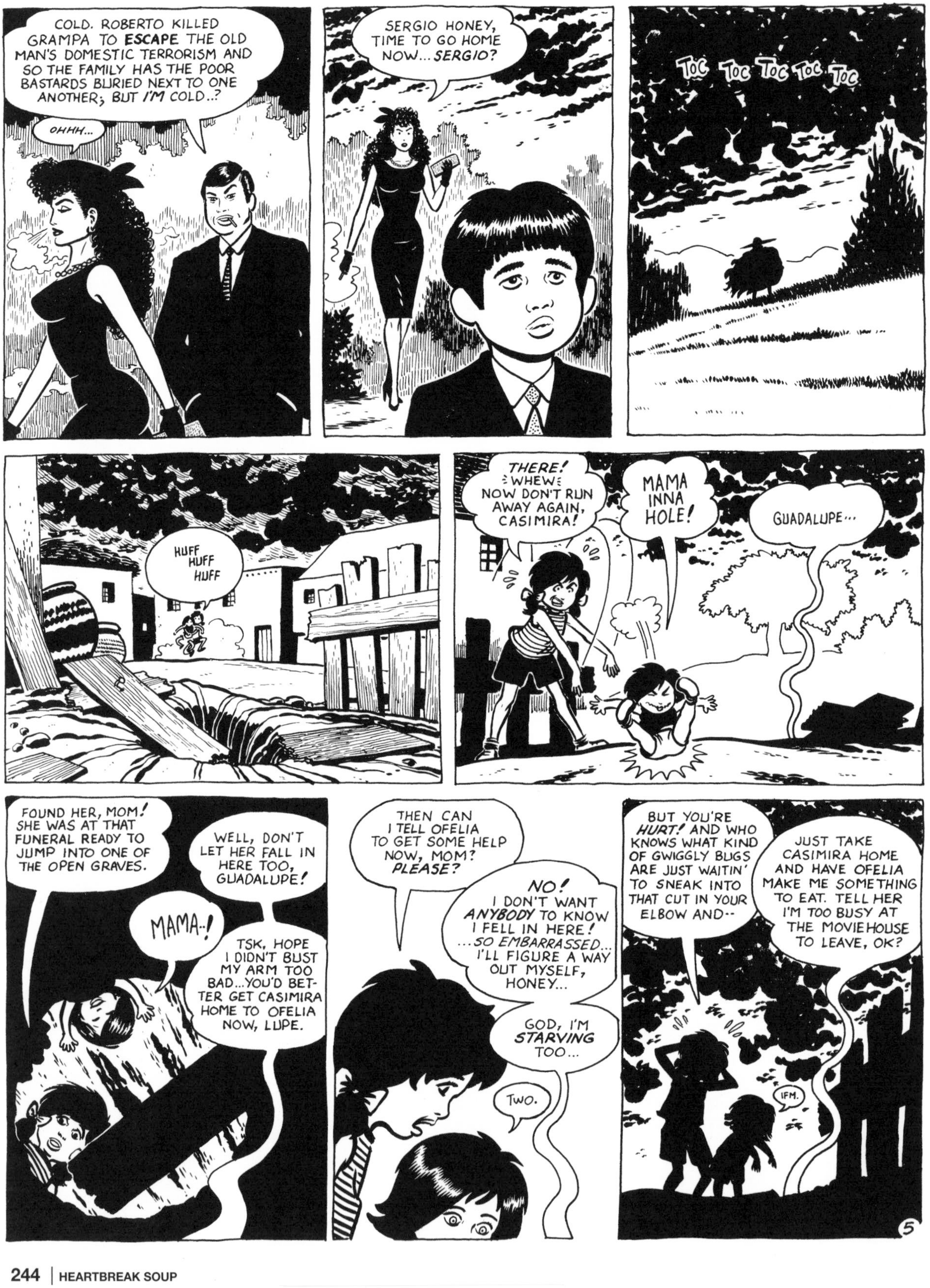
COLD. ROBERTO KILLED GRAMPA TO **ESCAPE** THE OLD MAN'S DOMESTIC TERRORISM AND SO THE FAMILY HAS THE POOR BASTARDS BURIED NEXT TO ONE ANOTHER; BUT *I'M* COLD..?
OHHH...
SERGIO HONEY, TIME TO GO HOME NOW... *SERGIO?*
TOC TOC TOC TOC TOC
HUFF HUFF HUFF
THERE! WHEW NOW DON'T RUN AWAY AGAIN, CASIMIRA!
MAMA INNA HOLE!
GUADALUPE...
FOUND HER, MOM! SHE WAS AT THAT FUNERAL READY TO JUMP INTO ONE OF THE OPEN GRAVES.
WELL, DON'T LET HER FALL IN HERE TOO, GUADALUPE!
MAMA..!
TSK, HOPE I DIDN'T BUST MY ARM TOO BAD...YOU'D BETTER GET CASIMIRA HOME TO OFELIA NOW, LUPE.
THEN CAN I TELL OFELIA TO GET SOME HELP NOW, MOM? *PLEASE?*
NO! I DON'T WANT *ANYBODY* TO KNOW I FELL IN HERE! ...*SO EMBARRASSED*... I'LL FIGURE A WAY OUT MYSELF, HONEY...
GOD, I'M *STARVING* TOO...
TWO.
BUT YOU'RE *HURT!* AND WHO KNOWS WHAT KIND OF GWIGGLY BUGS ARE JUST WAITIN' TO SNEAK INTO THAT CUT IN YOUR ELBOW AND--
JUST TAKE CASIMIRA HOME AND HAVE OFELIA MAKE ME SOMETHING TO EAT. TELL HER I'M TOO BUSY AT THE MOVIEHOUSE TO LEAVE, OK?
IFM.
5

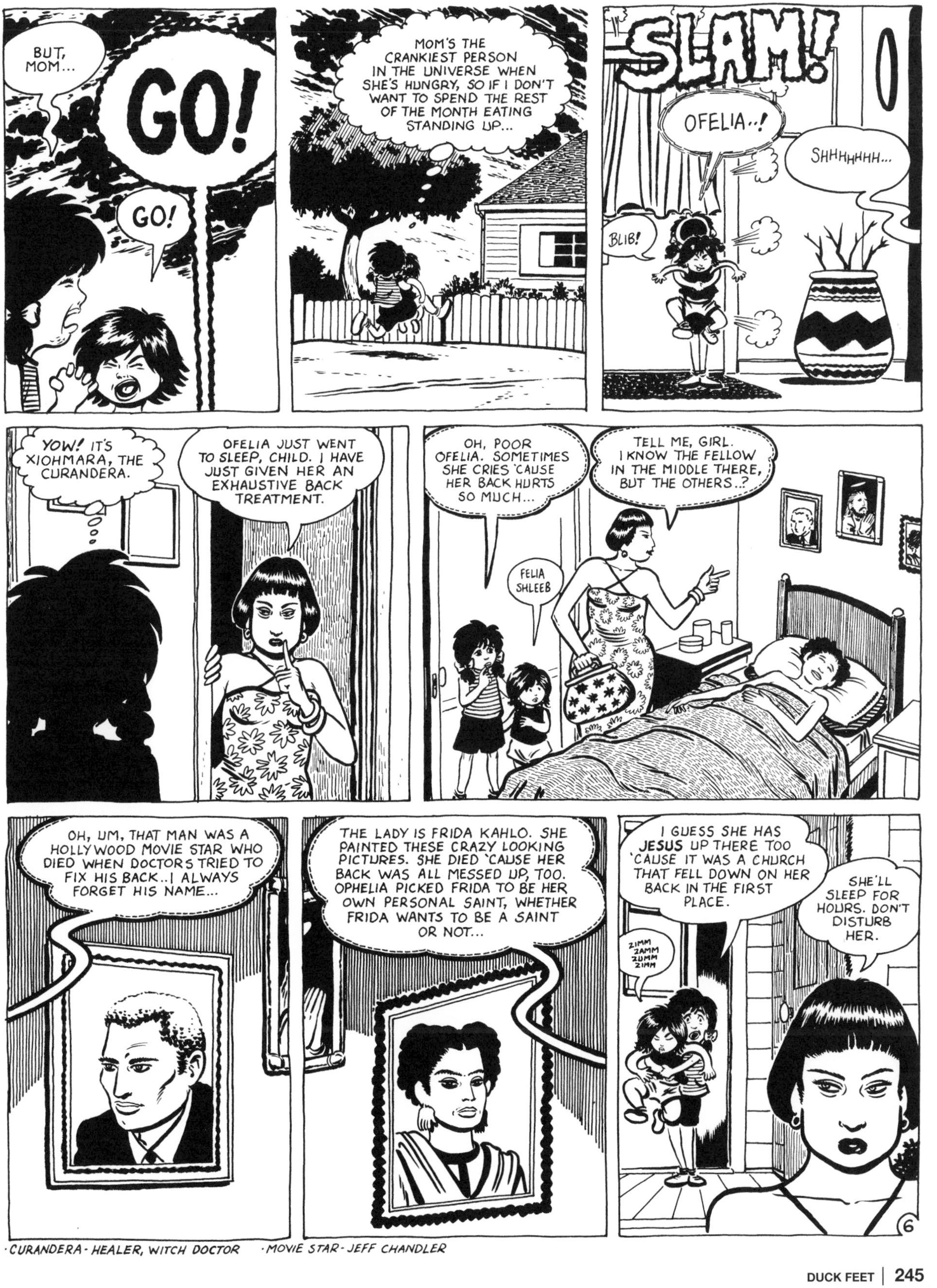
BUT, MOM...
GO!
GO!
MOM'S THE CRANKIEST PERSON IN THE UNIVERSE WHEN SHE'S HUNGRY, SO IF I DON'T WANT TO SPEND THE REST OF THE MONTH EATING STANDING UP...
SLAM!
OFELIA..!
SHHHHHHH...
BLIB!
YOW! IT'S XIOHMARA, THE CURANDERA.
OFELIA JUST WENT TO SLEEP, CHILD. I HAVE JUST GIVEN HER AN EXHAUSTIVE BACK TREATMENT.
OH, POOR OFELIA. SOMETIMES SHE CRIES 'CAUSE HER BACK HURTS SO MUCH...
TELL ME, GIRL. I KNOW THE FELLOW IN THE MIDDLE THERE, BUT THE OTHERS..?
FELIA SHLEEB
OH, UM, THAT MAN WAS A HOLLYWOOD MOVIE STAR WHO DIED WHEN DOCTORS TRIED TO FIX HIS BACK..I ALWAYS FORGET HIS NAME...
THE LADY IS FRIDA KAHLO. SHE PAINTED THESE CRAZY LOOKING PICTURES. SHE DIED 'CAUSE HER BACK WAS ALL MESSED UP, TOO. OPHELIA PICKED FRIDA TO BE HER OWN PERSONAL SAINT, WHETHER FRIDA WANTS TO BE A SAINT OR NOT...
I GUESS SHE HAS JESUS UP THERE TOO 'CAUSE IT WAS A CHURCH THAT FELL DOWN ON HER BACK IN THE FIRST PLACE.
ZIMM ZAMM ZUMM ZIMM
SHE'LL SLEEP FOR HOURS. DON'T DISTURB HER.
6

·CURANDERA - HEALER, WITCH DOCTOR ·MOVIE STAR - JEFF CHANDLER

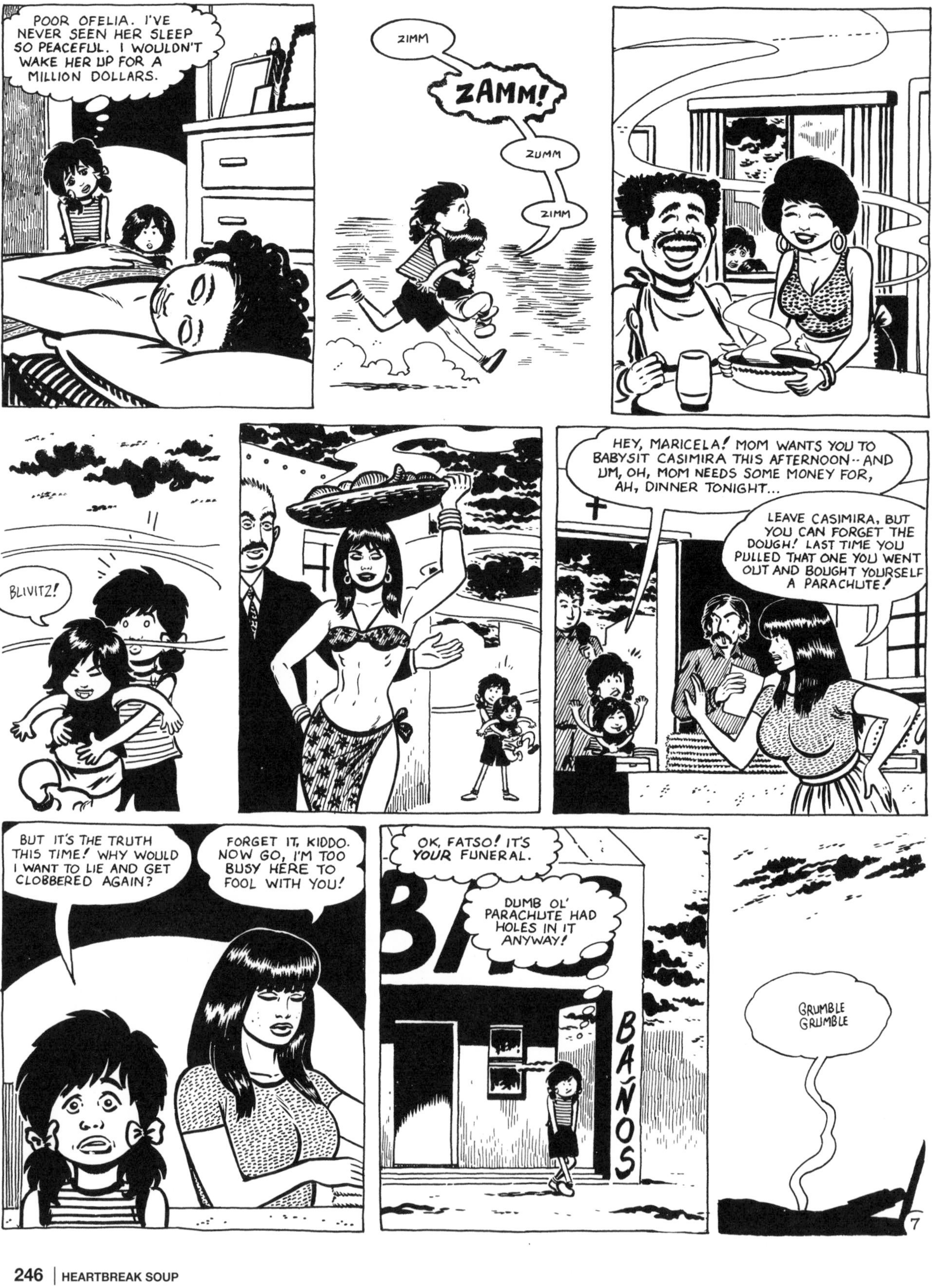

POOR OFELIA. I'VE NEVER SEEN HER SLEEP SO PEACEFUL. I WOULDN'T WAKE HER UP FOR A MILLION DOLLARS.
ZIMM
ZAMM!
ZUMM
ZIMM
BLIVITZ!
HEY, MARICELA! MOM WANTS YOU TO BABYSIT CASIMIRA THIS AFTERNOON-- AND UM, OH, MOM NEEDS SOME MONEY FOR, AH, DINNER TONIGHT...
LEAVE CASIMIRA, BUT YOU CAN FORGET THE DOUGH! LAST TIME YOU PULLED THAT ONE YOU WENT OUT AND BOUGHT YOURSELF A PARACHUTE!
BUT IT'S THE TRUTH THIS TIME! WHY WOULD I WANT TO LIE AND GET CLOBBERED AGAIN?
FORGET IT, KIDDO. NOW GO, I'M TOO BUSY HERE TO FOOL WITH YOU!
OK, FATSO! IT'S YOUR FUNERAL.
DUMB OL' PARACHUTE HAD HOLES IN IT ANYWAY!
BAÑOS
GRUMBLE GRUMBLE
7

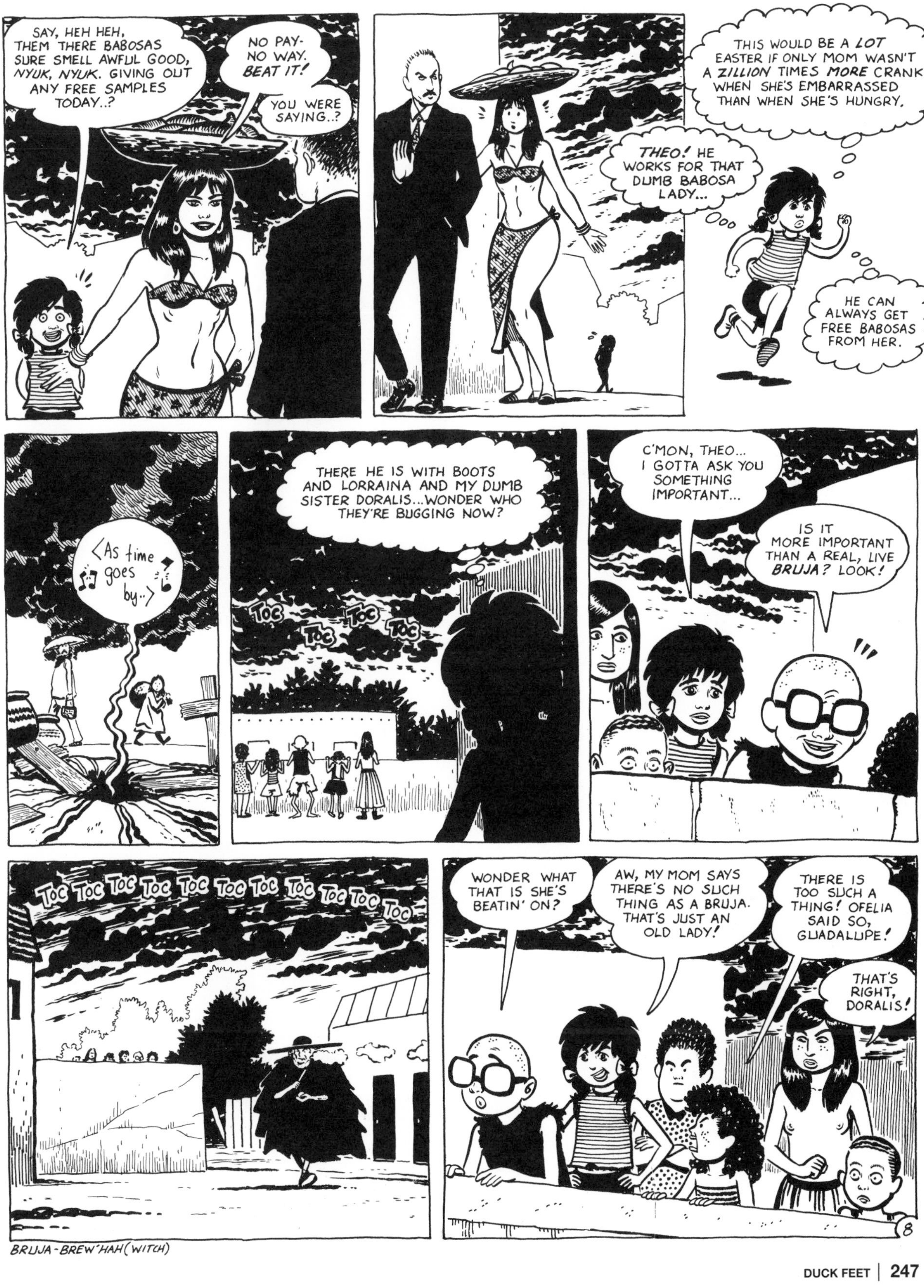
SAY, HEH HEH, THEM THERE BABOSAS SURE SMELL AWFUL GOOD, NYUK, NYUK. GIVING OUT ANY FREE SAMPLES TODAY..?
NO PAY- NO WAY. BEAT IT!
YOU WERE SAYING..?
THIS WOULD BE A LOT EASIER IF ONLY MOM WASN'T A ZILLION TIMES MORE CRANKY WHEN SHE'S EMBARRASSED THAN WHEN SHE'S HUNGRY.
THEO! HE WORKS FOR THAT DUMB BABOSA LADY...
HE CAN ALWAYS GET FREE BABOSAS FROM HER.
<As time goes by..>
THERE HE IS WITH BOOTS AND LORRAINA AND MY DUMB SISTER DORALIS...WONDER WHO THEY'RE BUGGING NOW?
TOC TOC TOC TOC
C'MON, THEO... I GOTTA ASK YOU SOMETHING IMPORTANT...
IS IT MORE IMPORTANT THAN A REAL, LIVE BRUJA? LOOK!
TOC TOC TOC TOC TOC TOC TOC TOC TOC TOC TOC
WONDER WHAT THAT IS SHE'S BEATIN' ON?
AW, MY MOM SAYS THERE'S NO SUCH THING AS A BRUJA. THAT'S JUST AN OLD LADY!
THERE IS TOO SUCH A THING! OFELIA SAID SO, GUADALUPE!
THAT'S RIGHT, DORALIS!
8

BRUJA - BREW'HAH (WITCH)

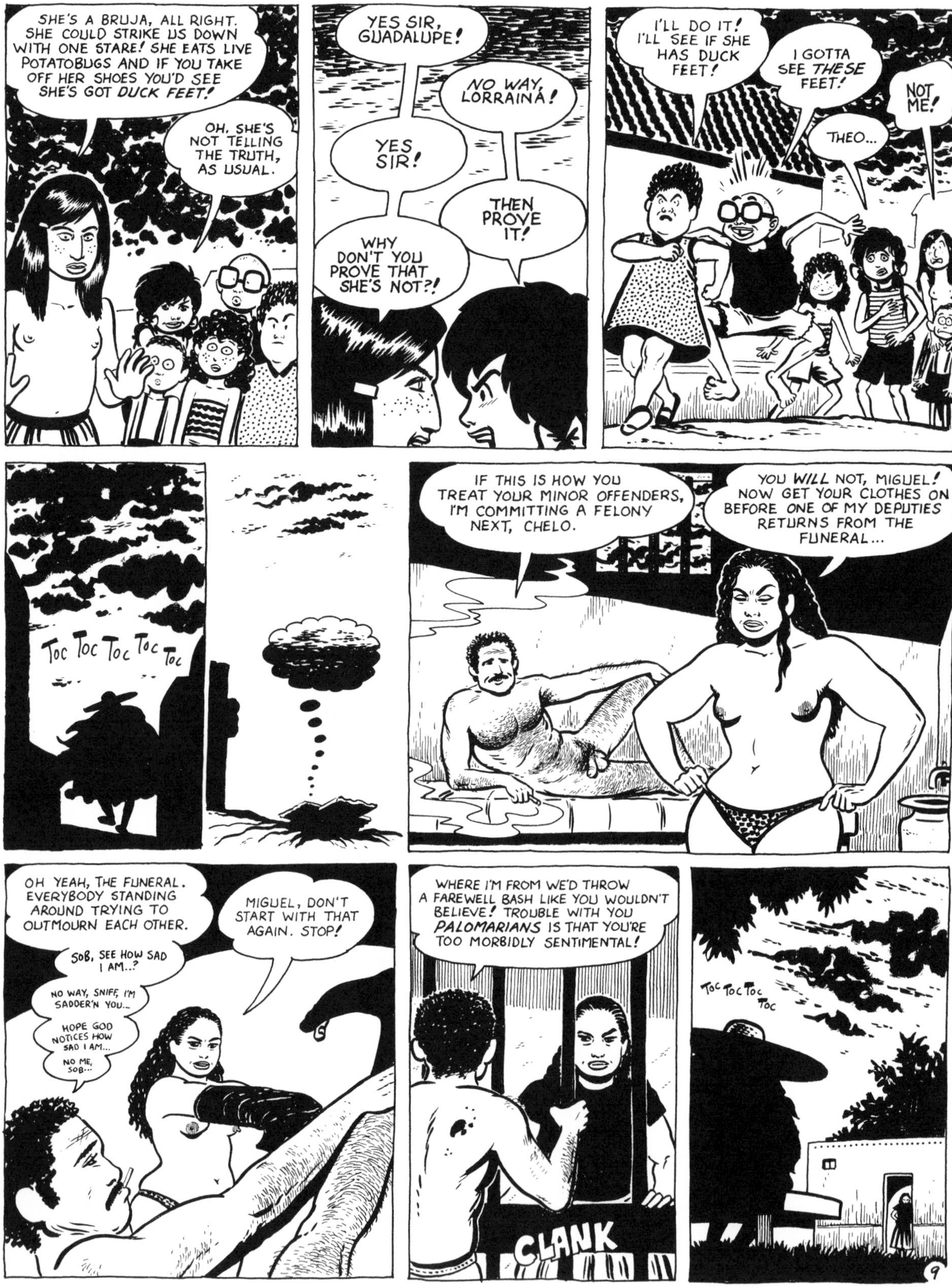
SHE'S A BRUJA, ALL RIGHT. SHE COULD STRIKE US DOWN WITH ONE STARE! SHE EATS LIVE POTATOBUGS AND IF YOU TAKE OFF HER SHOES YOU'D SEE SHE'S GOT DUCK FEET!
OH, SHE'S NOT TELLING THE TRUTH, AS USUAL.
YES SIR, GUADALUPE!
YES SIR!
WHY DON'T YOU PROVE THAT SHE'S NOT?!
NO WAY, LORRAINA!
THEN PROVE IT!
I'LL DO IT! I'LL SEE IF SHE HAS DUCK FEET!
I GOTTA SEE THESE FEET!
THEO...
NOT ME!
TOC TOC TOC TOC TOC
IF THIS IS HOW YOU TREAT YOUR MINOR OFFENDERS, I'M COMMITTING A FELONY NEXT, CHELO.
YOU WILL NOT, MIGUEL! NOW GET YOUR CLOTHES ON BEFORE ONE OF MY DEPUTIES RETURNS FROM THE FUNERAL...
OH YEAH, THE FUNERAL. EVERYBODY STANDING AROUND TRYING TO OUTMOURN EACH OTHER.
SOB, SEE HOW SAD I AM..?
NO WAY, SNIFF, I'M SADDER'N YOU...
HOPE GOD NOTICES HOW SAD I AM...
NO ME, SOB...
MIGUEL, DON'T START WITH THAT AGAIN. STOP!
WHERE I'M FROM WE'D THROW A FAREWELL BASH LIKE YOU WOULDN'T BELIEVE! TROUBLE WITH YOU PALOMARIANS IS THAT YOU'RE TOO MORBIDLY SENTIMENTAL!
CLANK
TOC TOC TOC TOC
9

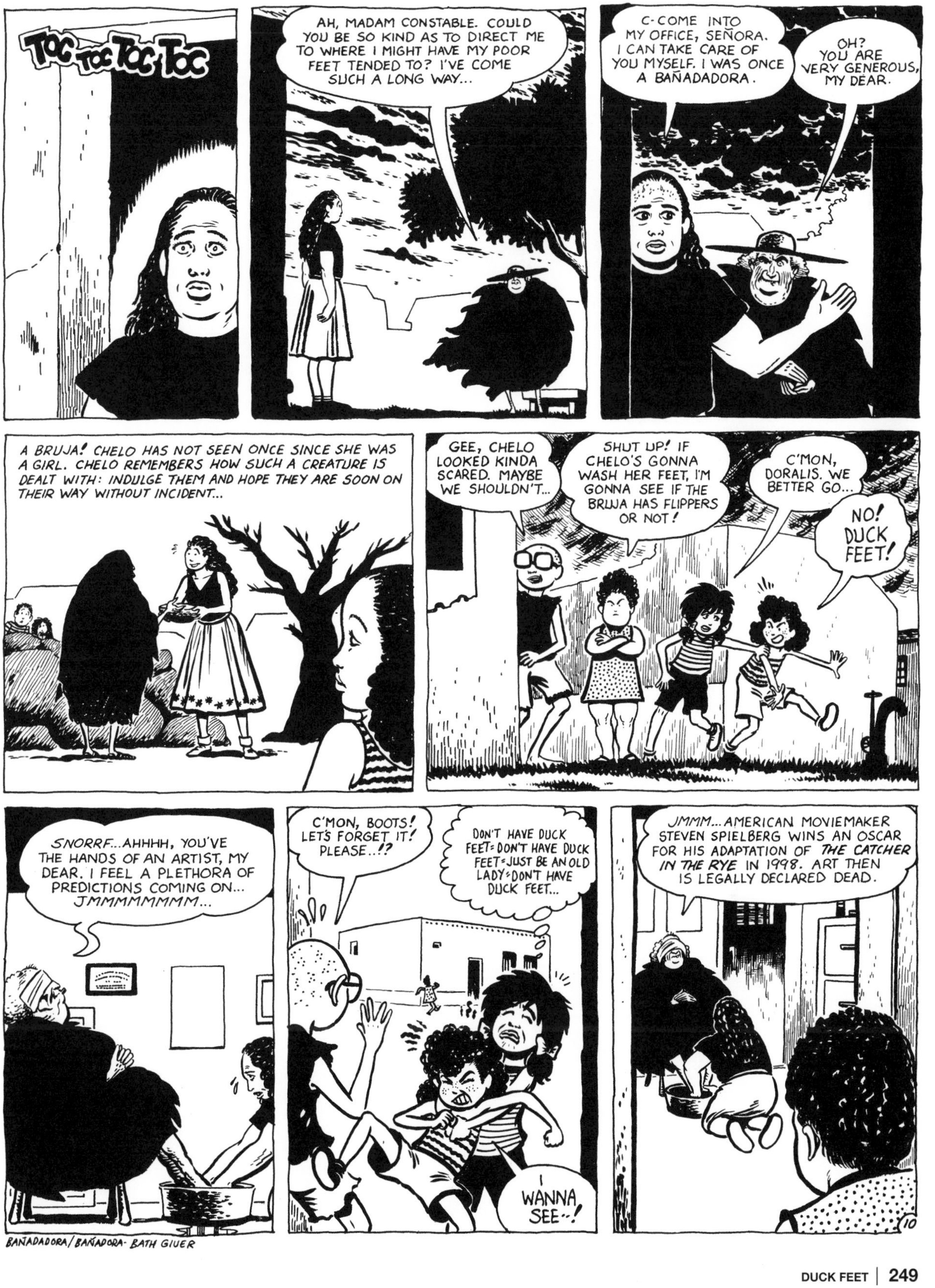
TOC TOC TOC TOC
AH, MADAM CONSTABLE. COULD YOU BE SO KIND AS TO DIRECT ME TO WHERE I MIGHT HAVE MY POOR FEET TENDED TO? I'VE COME SUCH A LONG WAY...
C-COME INTO MY OFFICE, SEÑORA. I CAN TAKE CARE OF YOU MYSELF. I WAS ONCE A BAÑADADORA.
OH? YOU ARE VERY GENEROUS, MY DEAR.
A BRUJA! CHELO HAS NOT SEEN ONCE SINCE SHE WAS A GIRL. CHELO REMEMBERS HOW SUCH A CREATURE IS DEALT WITH: INDULGE THEM AND HOPE THEY ARE SOON ON THEIR WAY WITHOUT INCIDENT...
GEE, CHELO LOOKED KINDA SCARED. MAYBE WE SHOULDN'T...
SHUT UP! IF CHELO'S GONNA WASH HER FEET, I'M GONNA SEE IF THE BRUJA HAS FLIPPERS OR NOT!
C'MON, DORALIS. WE BETTER GO...
NO! DUCK FEET!
SNORRF...AHHHH, YOU'VE THE HANDS OF AN ARTIST, MY DEAR. I FEEL A PLETHORA OF PREDICTIONS COMING ON... JMMMMMMMM...
C'MON, BOOTS! LET'S FORGET IT! PLEASE..!?
DON'T HAVE DUCK FEET= DON'T HAVE DUCK FEET= JUST BE AN OLD LADY= DON'T HAVE DUCK FEET...
I WANNA SEE..!
JMMM... AMERICAN MOVIEMAKER STEVEN SPIELBERG WINS AN OSCAR FOR HIS ADAPTATION OF THE CATCHER IN THE RYE IN 1998. ART THEN IS LEGALLY DECLARED DEAD.
10

BAÑADADORA/BAÑADORA- BATH GIVER

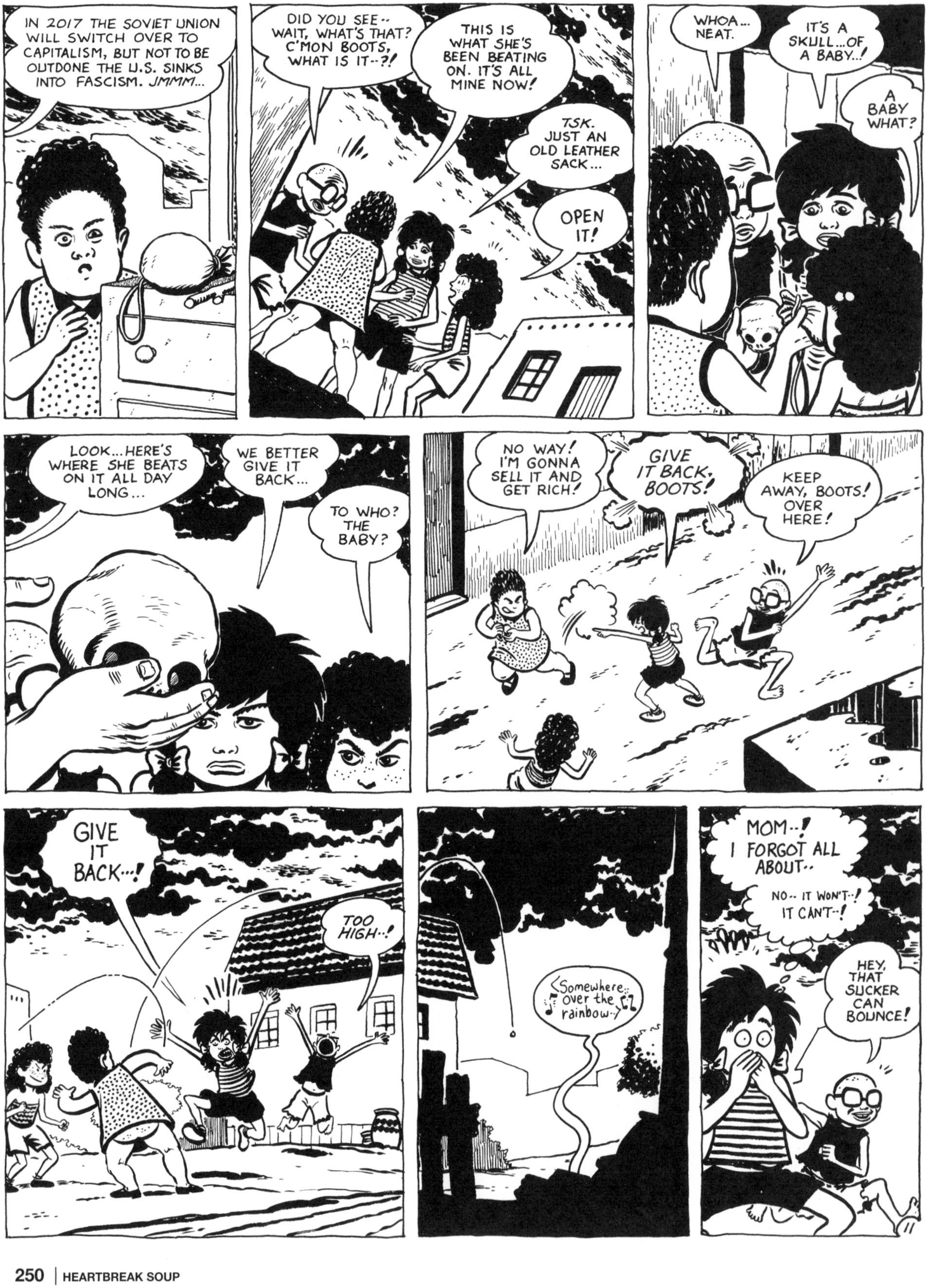
IN 2017 THE SOVIET UNION WILL SWITCH OVER TO CAPITALISM, BUT NOT TO BE OUTDONE THE U.S. SINKS INTO FASCISM. JMMM...
DID YOU SEE-- WAIT, WHAT'S THAT? C'MON BOOTS, WHAT IS IT--?!
THIS IS WHAT SHE'S BEEN BEATING ON. IT'S ALL MINE NOW!
TSK. JUST AN OLD LEATHER SACK...
OPEN IT!
WHOA... NEAT.
IT'S A SKULL...OF A BABY..!
A BABY WHAT?
LOOK...HERE'S WHERE SHE BEATS ON IT ALL DAY LONG...
WE BETTER GIVE IT BACK...
TO WHO? THE BABY?
NO WAY! I'M GONNA SELL IT AND GET RICH!
GIVE IT BACK, BOOTS!
KEEP AWAY, BOOTS! OVER HERE!
GIVE IT BACK--!
TOO HIGH--!
Somewhere over the rainbow--
MOM--! I FORGOT ALL ABOUT--
NO-- IT WON'T--! IT CAN'T--!
HEY, THAT SUCKER CAN BOUNCE!
11

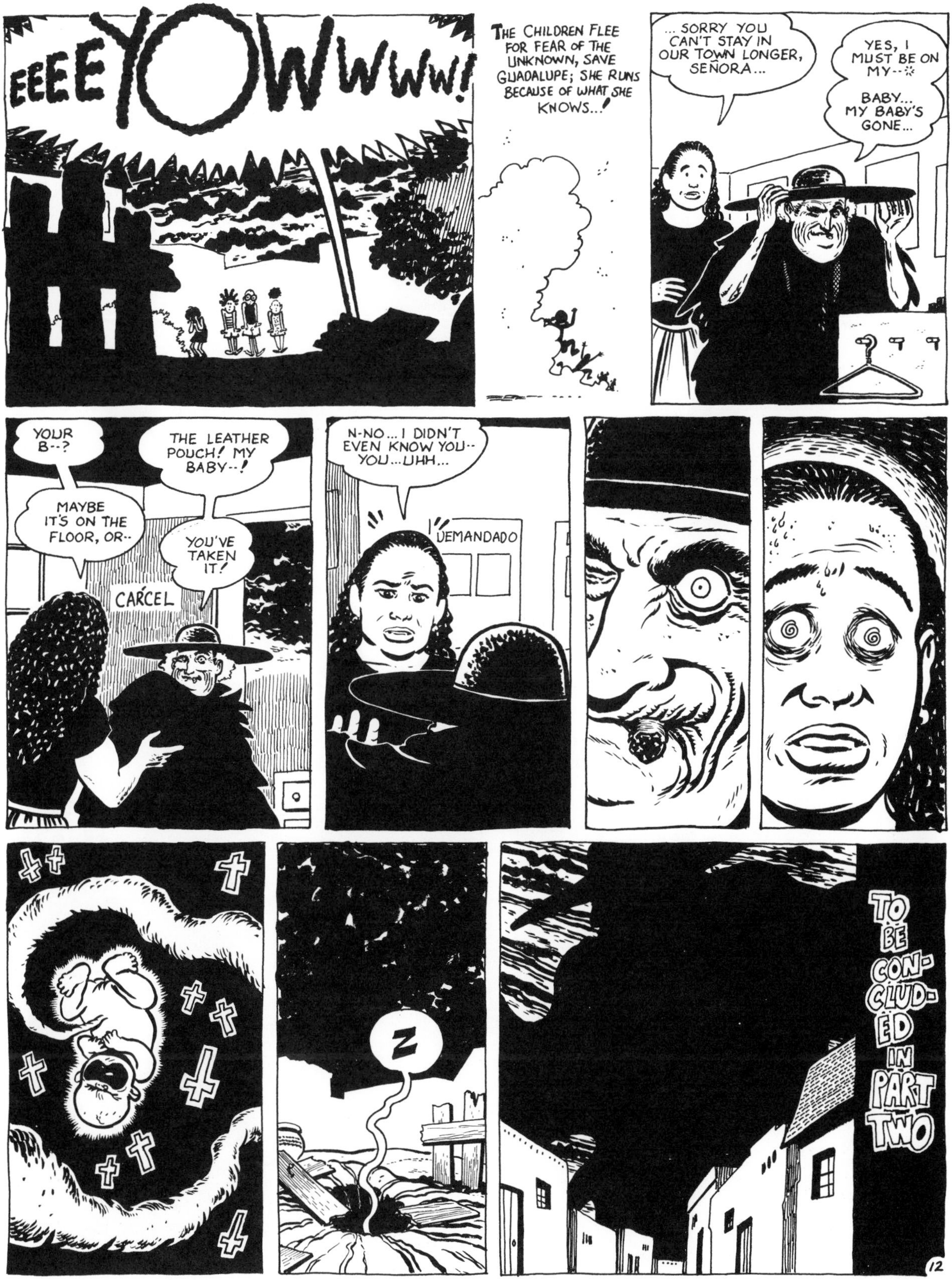
EEEEYOWWWW!
THE CHILDREN FLEE FOR FEAR OF THE UNKNOWN, SAVE GUADALUPE; SHE RUNS BECAUSE OF WHAT SHE KNOWS...!
... SORRY YOU CAN'T STAY IN OUR TOWN LONGER, SEÑORA...
YES, I MUST BE ON MY--
BABY... MY BABY'S GONE...
YOUR B--?
THE LEATHER POUCH! MY BABY--!
MAYBE IT'S ON THE FLOOR, OR--
YOU'VE TAKEN IT!
CARCEL
N-NO... I DIDN'T EVEN KNOW YOU-- YOU... UHH...
DEMANDADO
Z
TO BE CON-CLUD-ED IN PART TWO
12

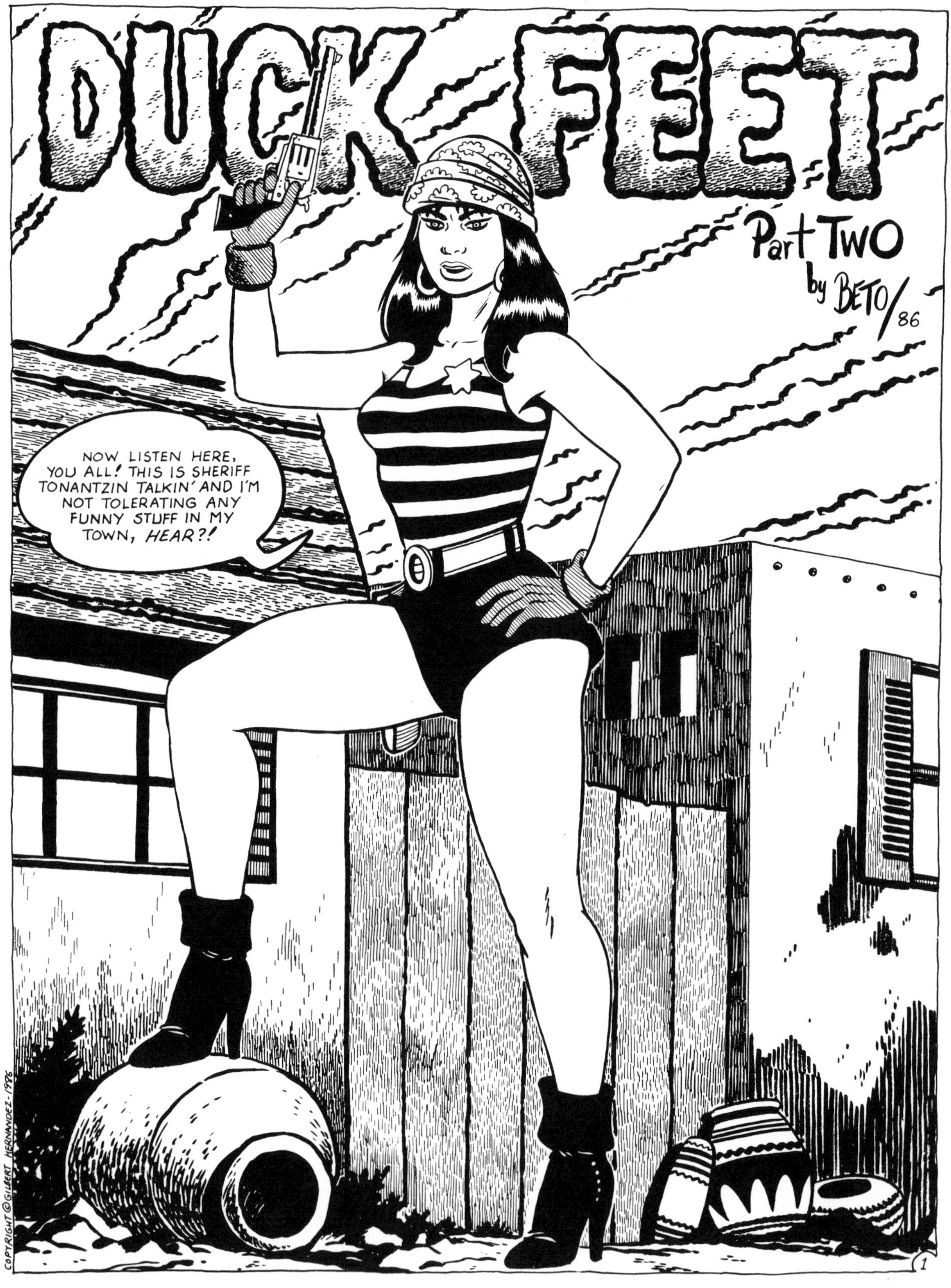
DUCK FEET
Part TWO
by BETO/86
NOW LISTEN HERE, YOU ALL! THIS IS SHERIFF TONANTZIN TALKIN' AND I'M NOT TOLERATING ANY FUNNY STUFF IN MY TOWN, HEAR?!
COPYRIGHT © GILBERT HERNANDEZ - 1986
1

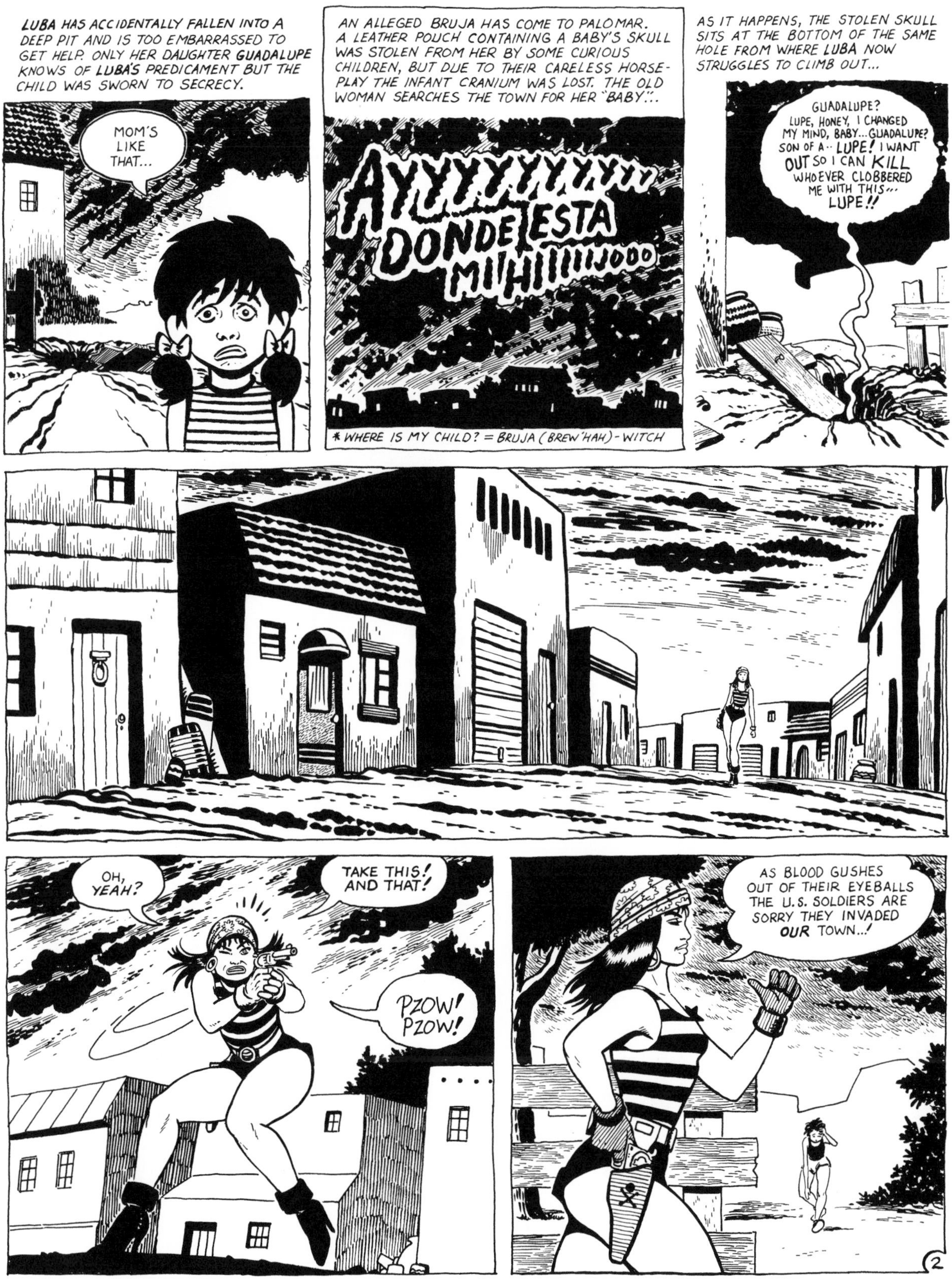
LUBA HAS ACCIDENTALLY FALLEN INTO A DEEP PIT AND IS TOO EMBARRASSED TO GET HELP. ONLY HER DAUGHTER GUADALUPE KNOWS OF LUBA'S PREDICAMENT BUT THE CHILD WAS SWORN TO SECRECY.
MOM'S LIKE THAT...
AN ALLEGED BRUJA HAS COME TO PALOMAR. A LEATHER POUCH CONTAINING A BABY'S SKULL WAS STOLEN FROM HER BY SOME CURIOUS CHILDREN, BUT DUE TO THEIR CARELESS HORSE-PLAY THE INFANT CRANIUM WAS LOST. THE OLD WOMAN SEARCHES THE TOWN FOR HER "BABY"...
AYYYYYYYYYY DONDE ESTA MI HIIIIIJOOO
* WHERE IS MY CHILD? = BRUJA (BREW'HAH) - WITCH
AS IT HAPPENS, THE STOLEN SKULL SITS AT THE BOTTOM OF THE SAME HOLE FROM WHERE LUBA NOW STRUGGLES TO CLIMB OUT...
GUADALUPE? LUPE, HONEY, I CHANGED MY MIND, BABY... GUADALUPE? SON OF A.. LUPE! I WANT OUT SO I CAN KILL WHOEVER CLOBBERED ME WITH THIS... LUPE!!
OH, YEAH?
TAKE THIS! AND THAT!
PZOW! PZOW!
AS BLOOD GUSHES OUT OF THEIR EYEBALLS THE U.S. SOLDIERS ARE SORRY THEY INVADED OUR TOWN...!
2

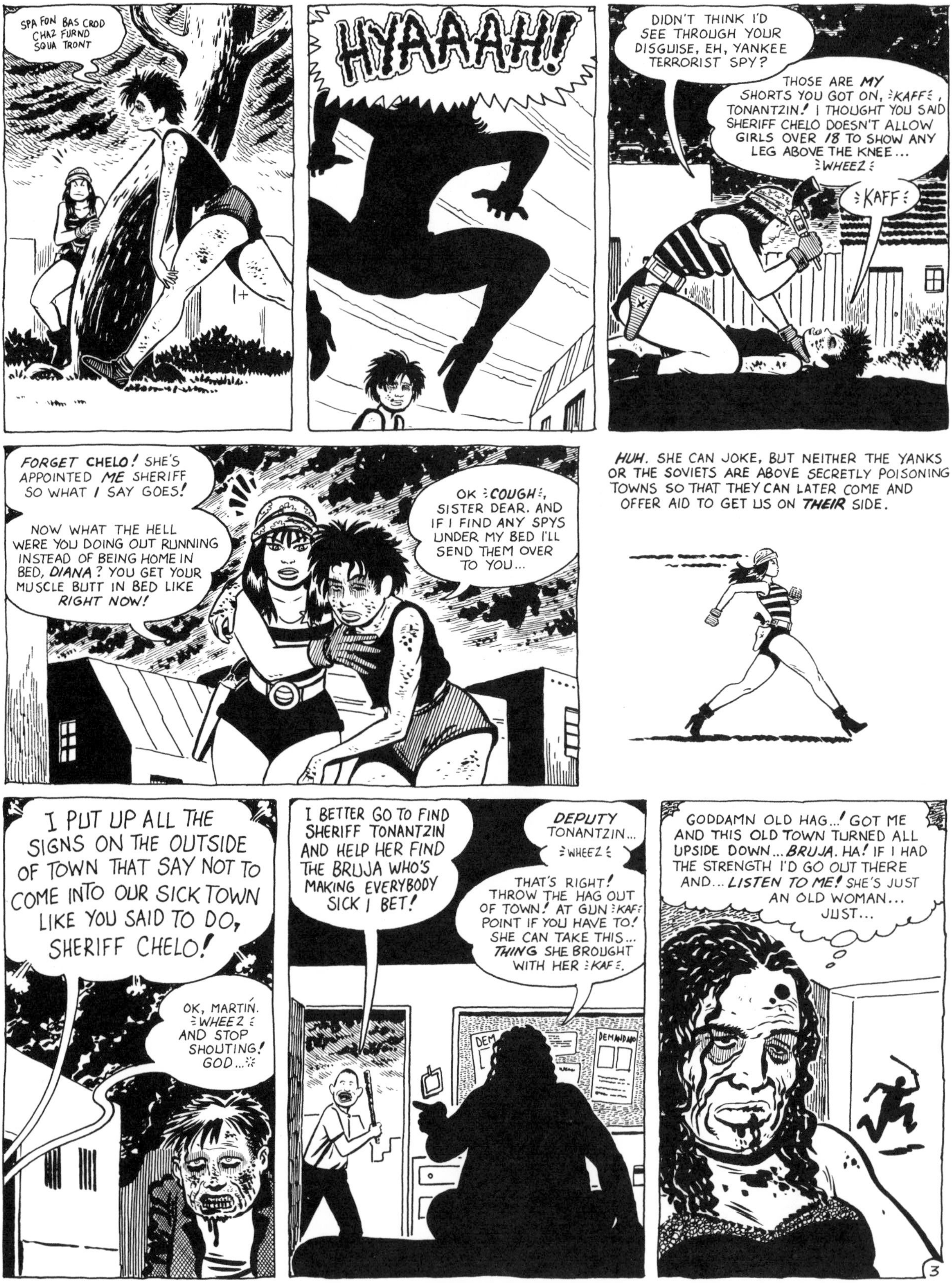
SPA FON BAS CROD CHAZ FURND SQUA TRONT
HYAAAH!
DIDN'T THINK I'D SEE THROUGH YOUR DISGUISE, EH, YANKEE TERRORIST SPY?
THOSE ARE MY SHORTS YOU GOT ON, KAFF, TONANTZIN! I THOUGHT YOU SAID SHERIFF CHELO DOESN'T ALLOW GIRLS OVER 18 TO SHOW ANY LEG ABOVE THE KNEE... WHEEZ
KAFF
FORGET CHELO! SHE'S APPOINTED ME SHERIFF SO WHAT I SAY GOES!
NOW WHAT THE HELL WERE YOU DOING OUT RUNNING INSTEAD OF BEING HOME IN BED, DIANA? YOU GET YOUR MUSCLE BUTT IN BED LIKE RIGHT NOW!
OK COUGH, SISTER DEAR. AND IF I FIND ANY SPYS UNDER MY BED I'LL SEND THEM OVER TO YOU...
HUH. SHE CAN JOKE, BUT NEITHER THE YANKS OR THE SOVIETS ARE ABOVE SECRETLY POISONING TOWNS SO THAT THEY CAN LATER COME AND OFFER AID TO GET US ON THEIR SIDE.
I PUT UP ALL THE SIGNS ON THE OUTSIDE OF TOWN THAT SAY NOT TO COME INTO OUR SICK TOWN LIKE YOU SAID TO DO, SHERIFF CHELO!
OK, MARTÍN. WHEEZ AND STOP SHOUTING! GOD...
I BETTER GO TO FIND SHERIFF TONANTZIN AND HELP HER FIND THE BRUJA WHO'S MAKING EVERYBODY SICK I BET!
DEPUTY TONANTZIN... WHEEZ
THAT'S RIGHT! THROW THE HAG OUT OF TOWN! AT GUN KAF POINT IF YOU HAVE TO! SHE CAN TAKE THIS... THING SHE BROUGHT WITH HER KAF.
GODDAMN OLD HAG...! GOT ME AND THIS OLD TOWN TURNED ALL UPSIDE DOWN... BRUJA. HA! IF I HAD THE STRENGTH I'D GO OUT THERE AND... LISTEN TO ME! SHE'S JUST AN OLD WOMAN... JUST...
3

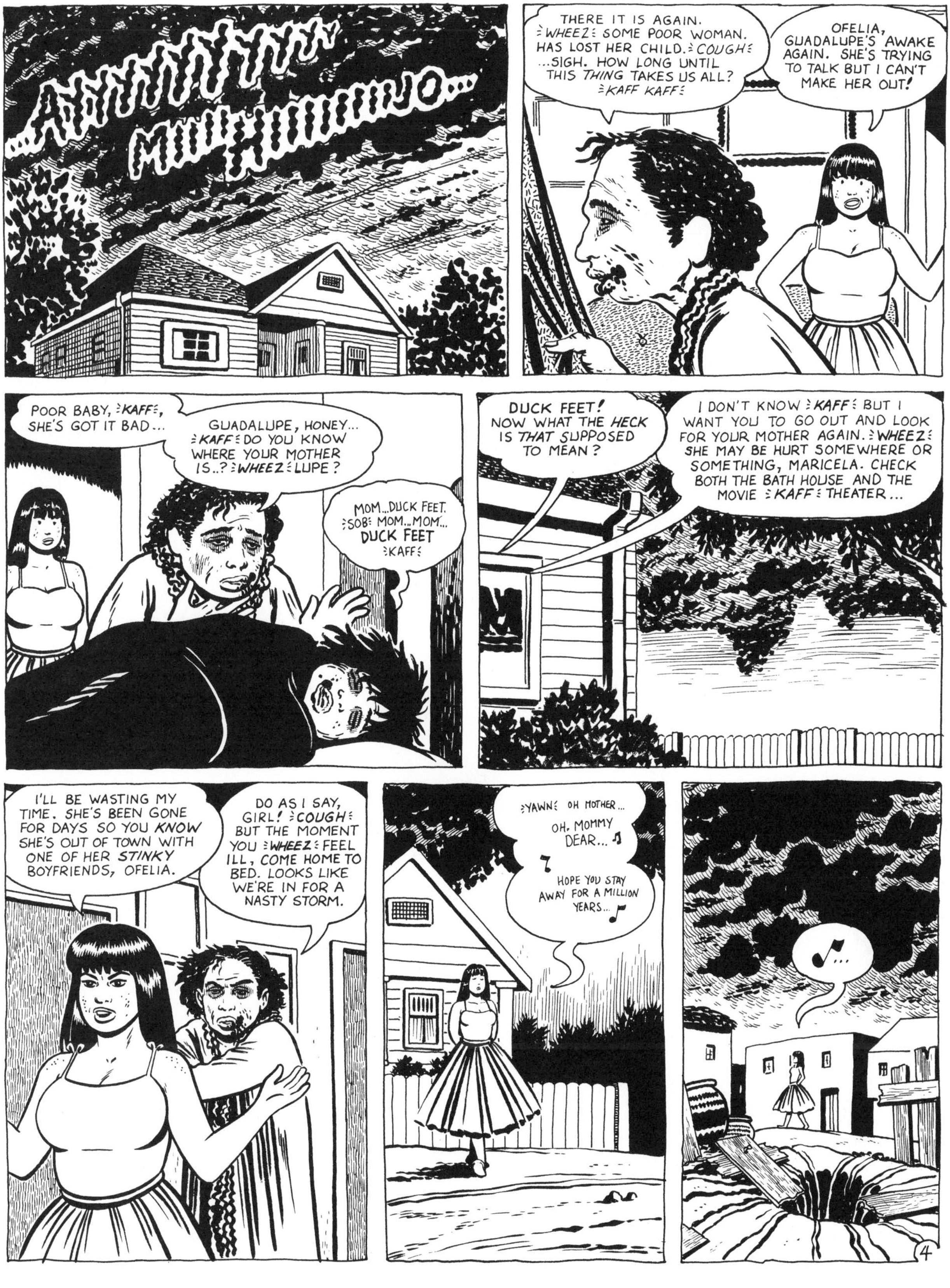

...AYYYYYYYYY... MIIIHIIIIIIJO...
THERE IT IS AGAIN. ≷WHEEZ≷ SOME POOR WOMAN. HAS LOST HER CHILD. ≷COUGH≷ ...SIGH. HOW LONG UNTIL THIS THING TAKES US ALL? ≷KAFF KAFF≷
OFELIA, GUADALUPE'S AWAKE AGAIN. SHE'S TRYING TO TALK BUT I CAN'T MAKE HER OUT!
POOR BABY, ≷KAFF≷, SHE'S GOT IT BAD...
GUADALUPE, HONEY... ≷KAFF≷ DO YOU KNOW WHERE YOUR MOTHER IS..? ≷WHEEZ≷ LUPE?
MOM...DUCK FEET. ≷SOB≷ MOM...MOM... DUCK FEET ≷KAFF≷
DUCK FEET! NOW WHAT THE HECK IS THAT SUPPOSED TO MEAN?
I DON'T KNOW ≷KAFF≷ BUT I WANT YOU TO GO OUT AND LOOK FOR YOUR MOTHER AGAIN. ≷WHEEZ≷ SHE MAY BE HURT SOMEWHERE OR SOMETHING, MARICELA. CHECK BOTH THE BATH HOUSE AND THE MOVIE ≷KAFF≷ THEATER...
I'LL BE WASTING MY TIME. SHE'S BEEN GONE FOR DAYS SO YOU KNOW SHE'S OUT OF TOWN WITH ONE OF HER STINKY BOYFRIENDS, OFELIA.
DO AS I SAY, GIRL! ≷COUGH≷ BUT THE MOMENT YOU ≷WHEEZ≷ FEEL ILL, COME HOME TO BED. LOOKS LIKE WE'RE IN FOR A NASTY STORM.
≷YAWN≷ OH MOTHER... OH, MOMMY DEAR... ♪
HOPE YOU STAY AWAY FOR A MILLION YEARS... ♪
♪...
4

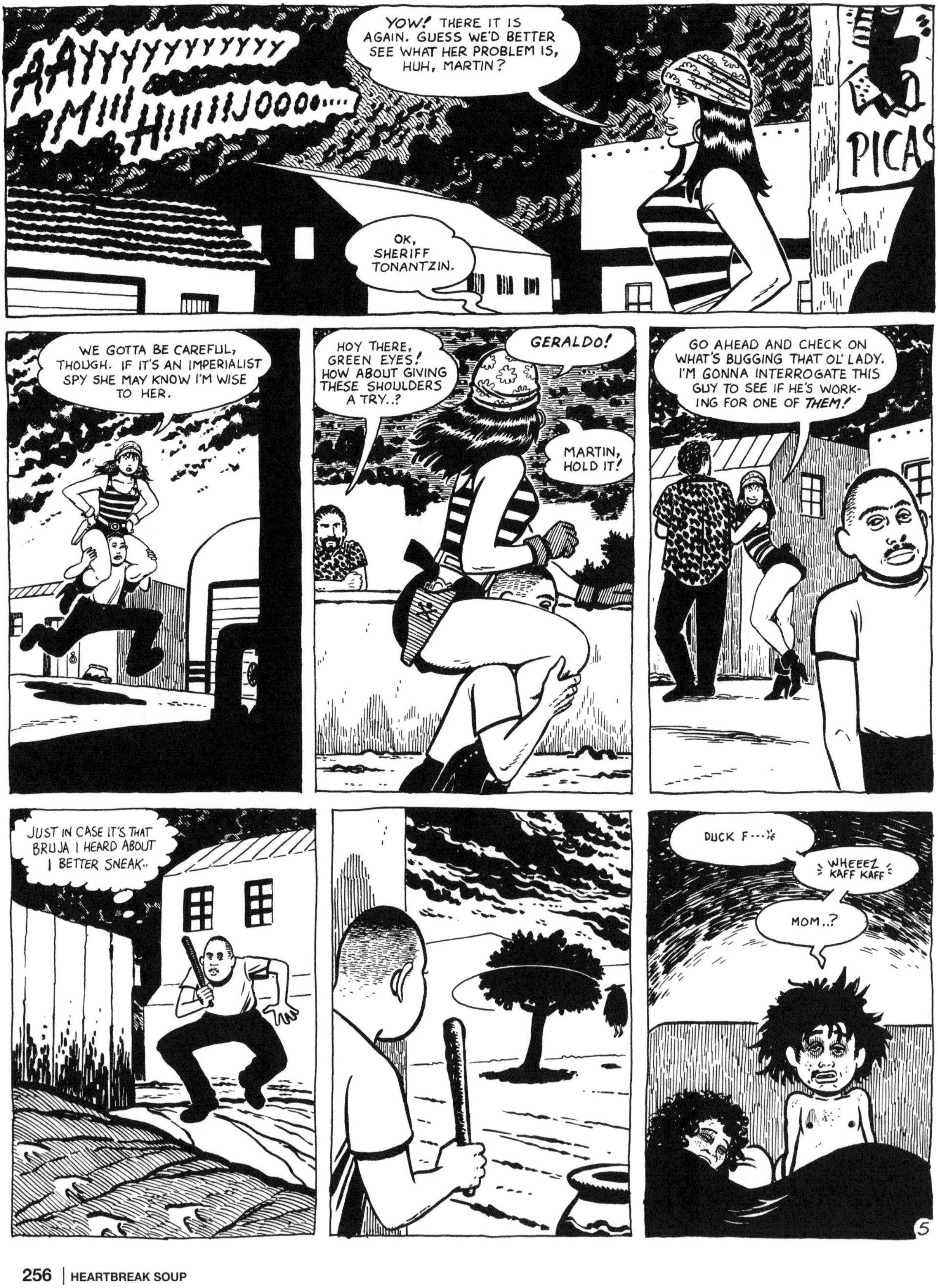
AAYYYYYYYYYYY MIIIHIIIIJOOOo....
YOW! THERE IT IS AGAIN. GUESS WE'D BETTER SEE WHAT HER PROBLEM IS, HUH, MARTIN?
OK, SHERIFF TONANTZIN.
PICAS
WE GOTTA BE CAREFUL, THOUGH. IF IT'S AN IMPERIALIST SPY SHE MAY KNOW I'M WISE TO HER.
HOY THERE, GREEN EYES! HOW ABOUT GIVING THESE SHOULDERS A TRY..?
GERALDO!
MARTIN, HOLD IT!
GO AHEAD AND CHECK ON WHAT'S BUGGING THAT OL' LADY. I'M GONNA INTERROGATE THIS GUY TO SEE IF HE'S WORKING FOR ONE OF THEM!
JUST IN CASE IT'S THAT BRUJA I HEARD ABOUT I BETTER SNEAK..
DUCK F---
WHEEEZ KAFF KAFF
MOM..?
5

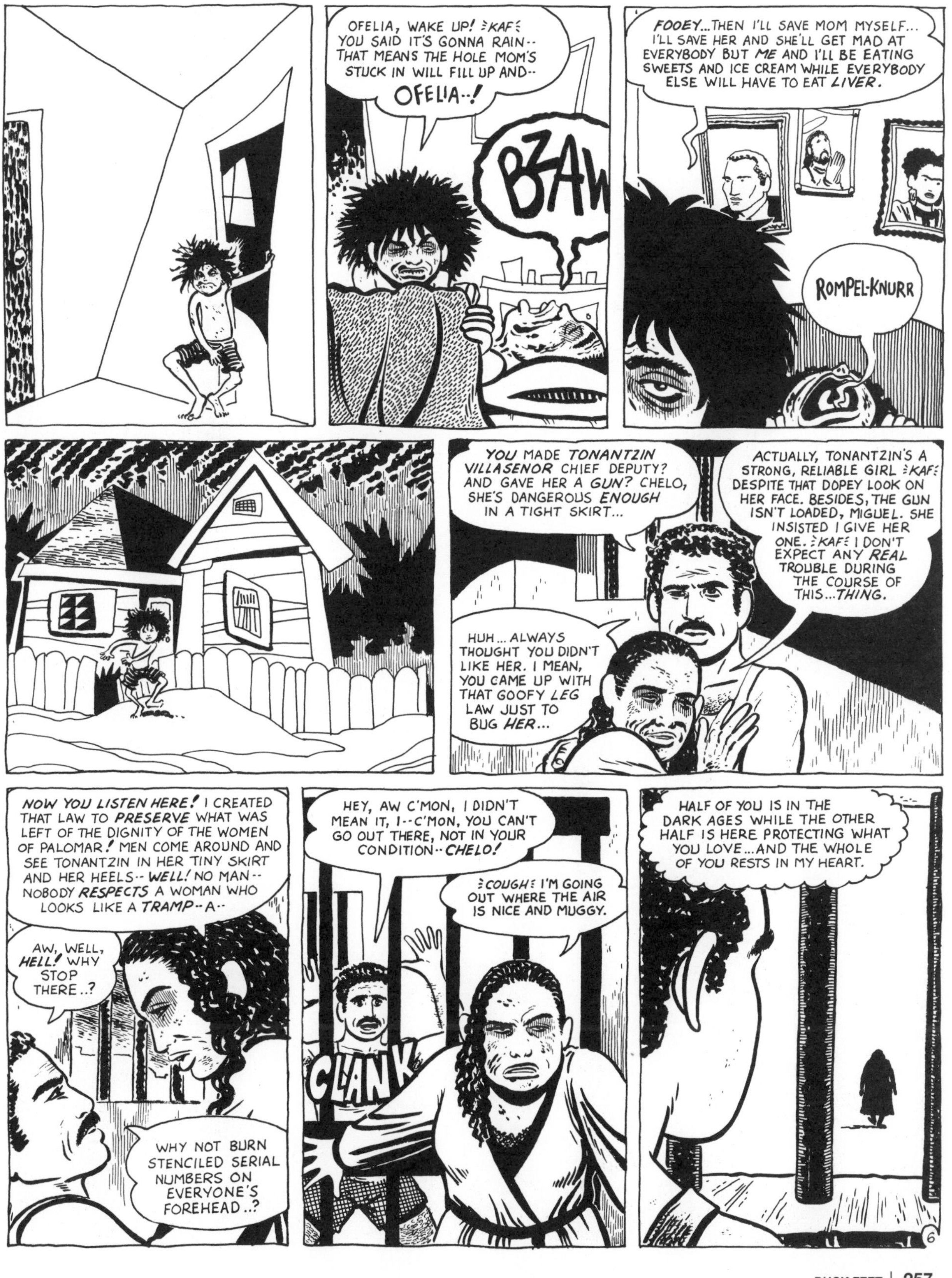
OFELIA, WAKE UP! ⁝KAF⁝ YOU SAID IT'S GONNA RAIN-- THAT MEANS THE HOLE MOM'S STUCK IN WILL FILL UP AND--
OFELIA--!
BZAW
FOOEY...THEN I'LL SAVE MOM MYSELF... I'LL SAVE HER AND SHE'LL GET MAD AT EVERYBODY BUT ME AND I'LL BE EATING SWEETS AND ICE CREAM WHILE EVERYBODY ELSE WILL HAVE TO EAT LIVER.
ROMPEL-KNURR
YOU MADE TONANTZIN VILLASENOR CHIEF DEPUTY? AND GAVE HER A GUN? CHELO, SHE'S DANGEROUS ENOUGH IN A TIGHT SKIRT...
ACTUALLY, TONANTZIN'S A STRONG, RELIABLE GIRL ⁝KAF⁝ DESPITE THAT DOPEY LOOK ON HER FACE. BESIDES, THE GUN ISN'T LOADED, MIGUEL. SHE INSISTED I GIVE HER ONE. ⁝KAF⁝ I DON'T EXPECT ANY REAL TROUBLE DURING THE COURSE OF THIS...THING.
HUH... ALWAYS THOUGHT YOU DIDN'T LIKE HER. I MEAN, YOU CAME UP WITH THAT GOOFY LEG LAW JUST TO BUG HER...
NOW YOU LISTEN HERE! I CREATED THAT LAW TO PRESERVE WHAT WAS LEFT OF THE DIGNITY OF THE WOMEN OF PALOMAR! MEN COME AROUND AND SEE TONANTZIN IN HER TINY SKIRT AND HER HEELS-- WELL! NO MAN-- NOBODY RESPECTS A WOMAN WHO LOOKS LIKE A TRAMP--A--
AW, WELL, HELL! WHY STOP THERE..?
WHY NOT BURN STENCILED SERIAL NUMBERS ON EVERYONE'S FOREHEAD..?
HEY, AW C'MON, I DIDN'T MEAN IT, I--C'MON, YOU CAN'T GO OUT THERE, NOT IN YOUR CONDITION--CHELO!
⁝COUGH⁝ I'M GOING OUT WHERE THE AIR IS NICE AND MUGGY.
CLANK
HALF OF YOU IS IN THE DARK AGES WHILE THE OTHER HALF IS HERE PROTECTING WHAT YOU LOVE...AND THE WHOLE OF YOU RESTS IN MY HEART.
6

ER, GERALDO, DIDN'T YOU SEE THE WARNING SIGNS OUTSIDE OF TOWN?

DON'T CHANGE THE SUBJECT! YOUR SHERIFF WHAT'S-ER-NAME MURDERED MY COUSIN ROBERTO ALL THE SAME! HE DIED LIKE A COMMON--LIKE A DOG IN THE STREET, LIKE-- HIS HEAD WAS TURNED COMPLETELY BACKWARDS! I WOULDN'T CALL THAT CRIB DEATH..!

YOU FORGET ROBERTO KILLED HIS GRAMPA IN THE FIRST PLACE, GERALDO...

AAAH, YOU KNOW WHAT KIND OF SWINE THE OLD MAN WAS! TREATED EVERYONE LIKE DIRT, LIKE-- HE CAME CLOSE TO MOLESTING YOUR LITTLE SISTER DIANA A FEW TIMES, AS I RECALL...

CHELO DIDN'T MEAN TO KILL YOUR COUSIN. SHE HIT HIM AND HE FELL...

OH SURE, THAT'S WHAT SHE TOLD EVERY-BODY. BUT I'VE BEEN IN AND OUT OF JAIL ALL MY LIFE AND I KNOW WHAT SHIT COPS PULL WHEN THEY THINK NOBODY IS LOOKING. COPS. PIMPS. THE POPE. THEY'RE ALL OF THE SAME BREED. TERRORISTS. KEEPING THE PEOPLE IN LINE WITH FEAR...

THAT'S CRAZY TALK! MAYBE I OUGHT TO SIT YOU IN A CELL FOR A FEW DAYS TO COOL YOU OFF!

HEH. I AM GOING TO JAIL REAL SOON. BUSTED A BOTTLE ACROSS SOME STUPID COP'S FACE AFTER HE POPPED ME FOR COKE. JUMPED BAIL.

THEY'LL FIND ME, NO PROBLEM.

AH, BUT ALL THIS SHIT ABOUT COPS AND STUFF IS OLD NEWS. `BUT THAT'S THE WAY IT IS, THE WAY IT'S ALWAYS BEEN, SO FORGET IT' THEY TELL YOU. YEAH, WELL, TELL THAT TO A BLACK KID IN SOUTH AFRICA...

HEY, WAIT! AREN'T WE STILL GONNA --AW, FORGET IT. GO TO HELL!

GOD, HOW'D A GUY WHO'D BEEN SO GOOD IN THE SACK TURN OUT TO BE SUCH A LOON? CRAZY PEOPLE GIVE ME THE SHIVERS...

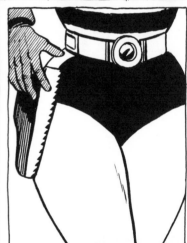

MY--MY GUN! GERALDO! DID YOU SEE WHERE I--I--

GERALDO--?

7

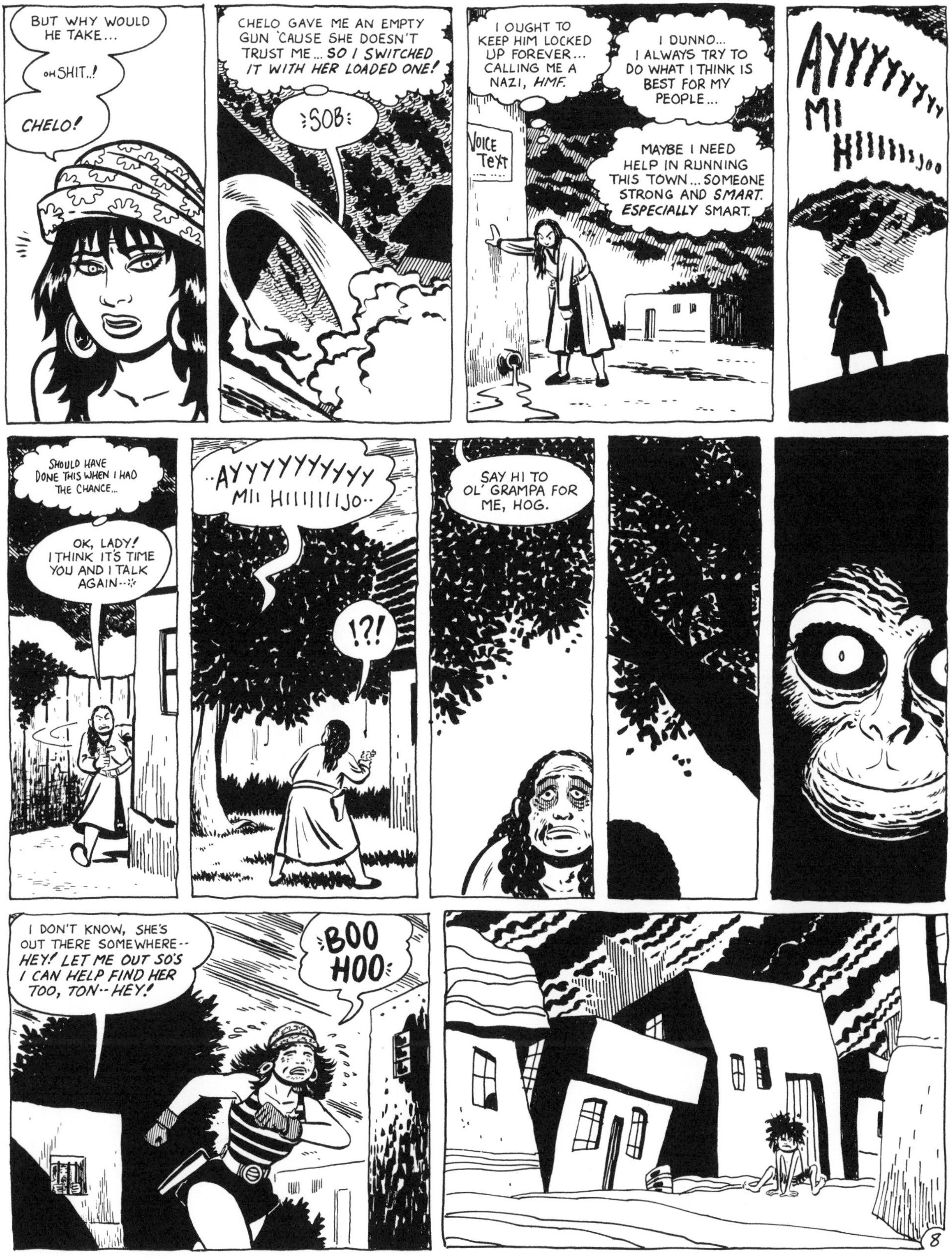

BUT WHY WOULD HE TAKE...
OH SHIT..!
CHELO!
CHELO GAVE ME AN EMPTY GUN 'CAUSE SHE DOESN'T TRUST ME... SO I SWITCHED IT WITH HER LOADED ONE!
SOB
I OUGHT TO KEEP HIM LOCKED UP FOREVER... CALLING ME A NAZI, HMF.
I DUNNO... I ALWAYS TRY TO DO WHAT I THINK IS BEST FOR MY PEOPLE...
MAYBE I NEED HELP IN RUNNING THIS TOWN... SOMEONE STRONG AND SMART. ESPECIALLY SMART.
VOICE TEXT
AYYYYYYYYYY MI HIIIIIIJOO
SHOULD HAVE DONE THIS WHEN I HAD THE CHANCE...
OK, LADY! I THINK IT'S TIME YOU AND I TALK AGAIN--
..AYYYYYYYYYY MII HIIIIIIIJO..
!?!
SAY HI TO OL' GRAMPA FOR ME, HOG.
I DON'T KNOW, SHE'S OUT THERE SOMEWHERE-- HEY! LET ME OUT SO'S I CAN HELP FIND HER TOO, TON-- HEY!
BOO HOO
8

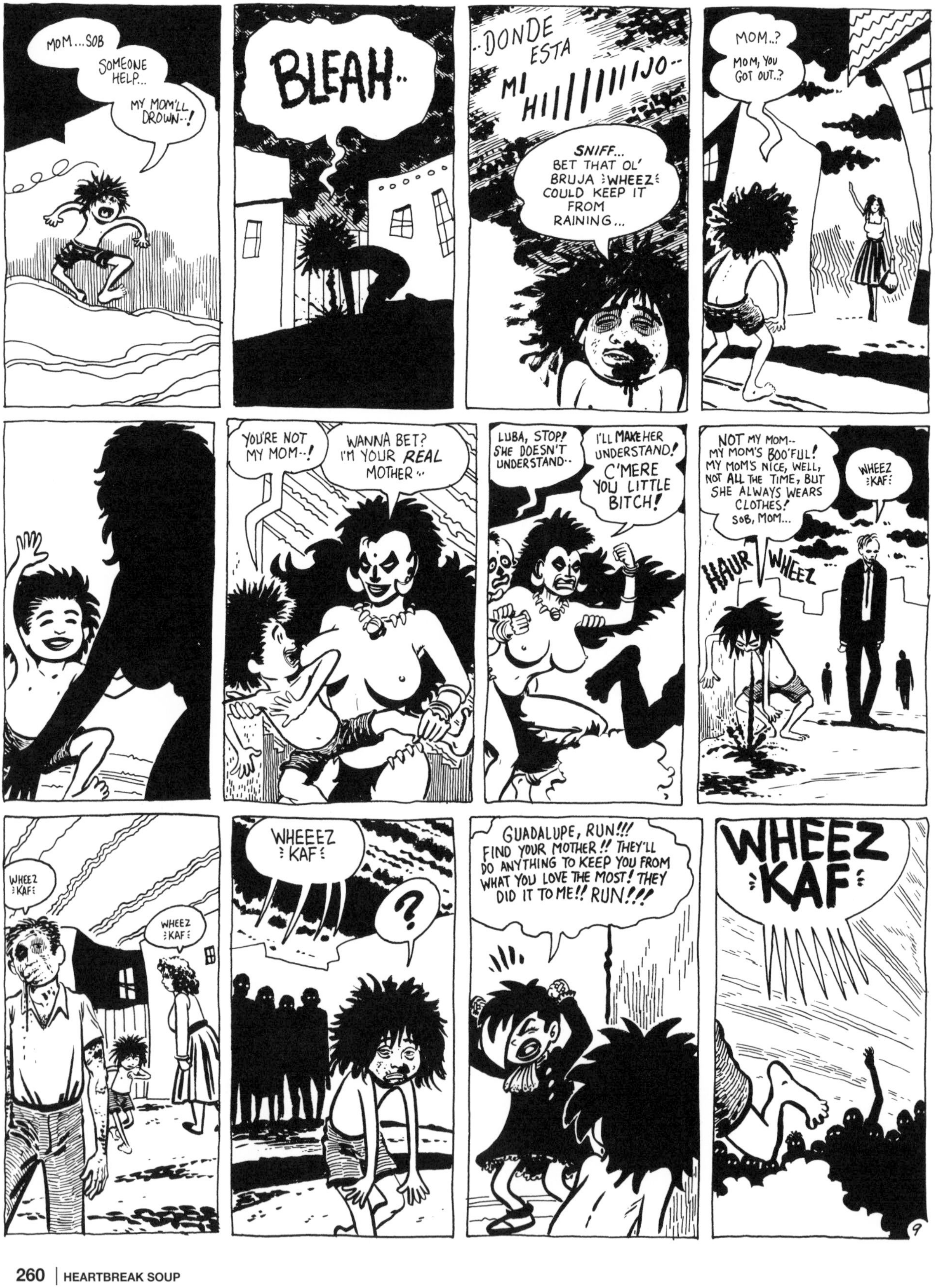

MOM...SOB
SOMEONE HELP...
MY MOM'LL DROWN--!
BLEAH..
..DONDE ESTA MI HIIIIIIIJO--
SNIFF... BET THAT OL' BRUJA WHEEZ COULD KEEP IT FROM RAINING...
MOM..?
MOM, YOU GOT OUT..?
YOU'RE NOT MY MOM--!
WANNA BET? I'M YOUR REAL MOTHER...
LUBA, STOP! SHE DOESN'T UNDERSTAND--
I'LL MAKE HER UNDERSTAND! C'MERE YOU LITTLE BITCH!
NOT MY MOM-- MY MOM'S BOO'FUL! MY MOM'S NICE, WELL, NOT ALL THE TIME, BUT SHE ALWAYS WEARS CLOTHES! SOB, MOM...
WHEEZ KAF
HAUR
WHEEZ
WHEEZ KAF
WHEEZ KAF
WHEEEZ KAF
?
GUADALUPE, RUN!!! FIND YOUR MOTHER!! THEY'LL DO ANYTHING TO KEEP YOU FROM WHAT YOU LOVE THE MOST! THEY DID IT TO ME!! RUN!!!
WHEEZ KAF
9

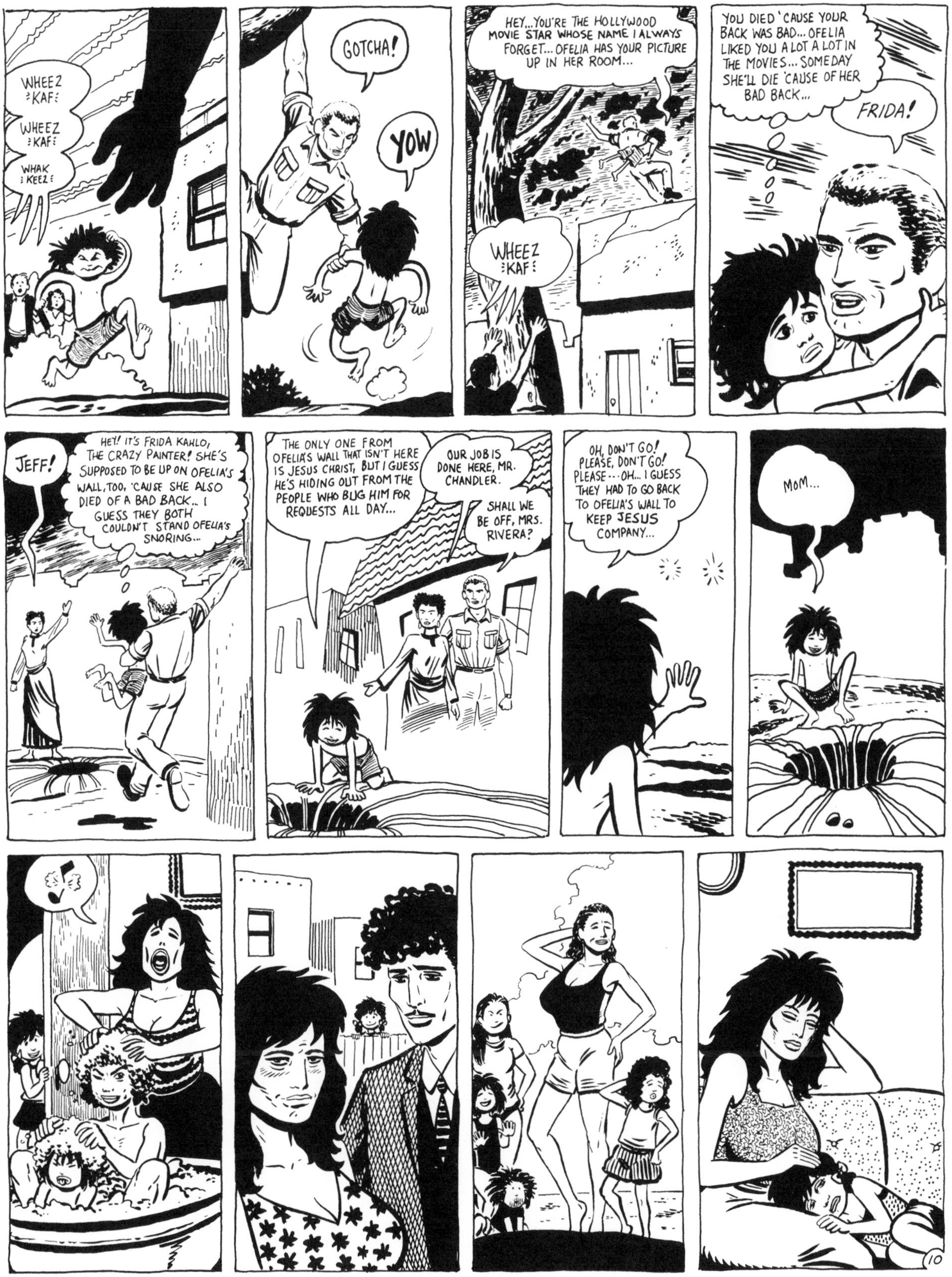

WHEEZ KAF
WHEEZ KAF
WHAK KEEZ
GOTCHA!
YOW
HEY...YOU'RE THE HOLLYWOOD MOVIE STAR WHOSE NAME I ALWAYS FORGET... OFELIA HAS YOUR PICTURE UP IN HER ROOM...
WHEEZ KAF
YOU DIED 'CAUSE YOUR BACK WAS BAD... OFELIA LIKED YOU A LOT A LOT IN THE MOVIES... SOMEDAY SHE'LL DIE 'CAUSE OF HER BAD BACK...
FRIDA!
JEFF!
HEY! IT'S FRIDA KAHLO, THE CRAZY PAINTER! SHE'S SUPPOSED TO BE UP ON OFELIA'S WALL, TOO, 'CAUSE SHE ALSO DIED OF A BAD BACK... I GUESS THEY BOTH COULDN'T STAND OFELIA'S SNORING...
THE ONLY ONE FROM OFELIA'S WALL THAT ISN'T HERE IS JESUS CHRIST, BUT I GUESS HE'S HIDING OUT FROM THE PEOPLE WHO BUG HIM FOR REQUESTS ALL DAY...
OUR JOB IS DONE HERE, MR. CHANDLER.
SHALL WE BE OFF, MRS. RIVERA?
OH, DON'T GO! PLEASE, DON'T GO! PLEASE··· OH... I GUESS THEY HAD TO GO BACK TO OFELIA'S WALL TO KEEP JESUS COMPANY...
MOM...
10

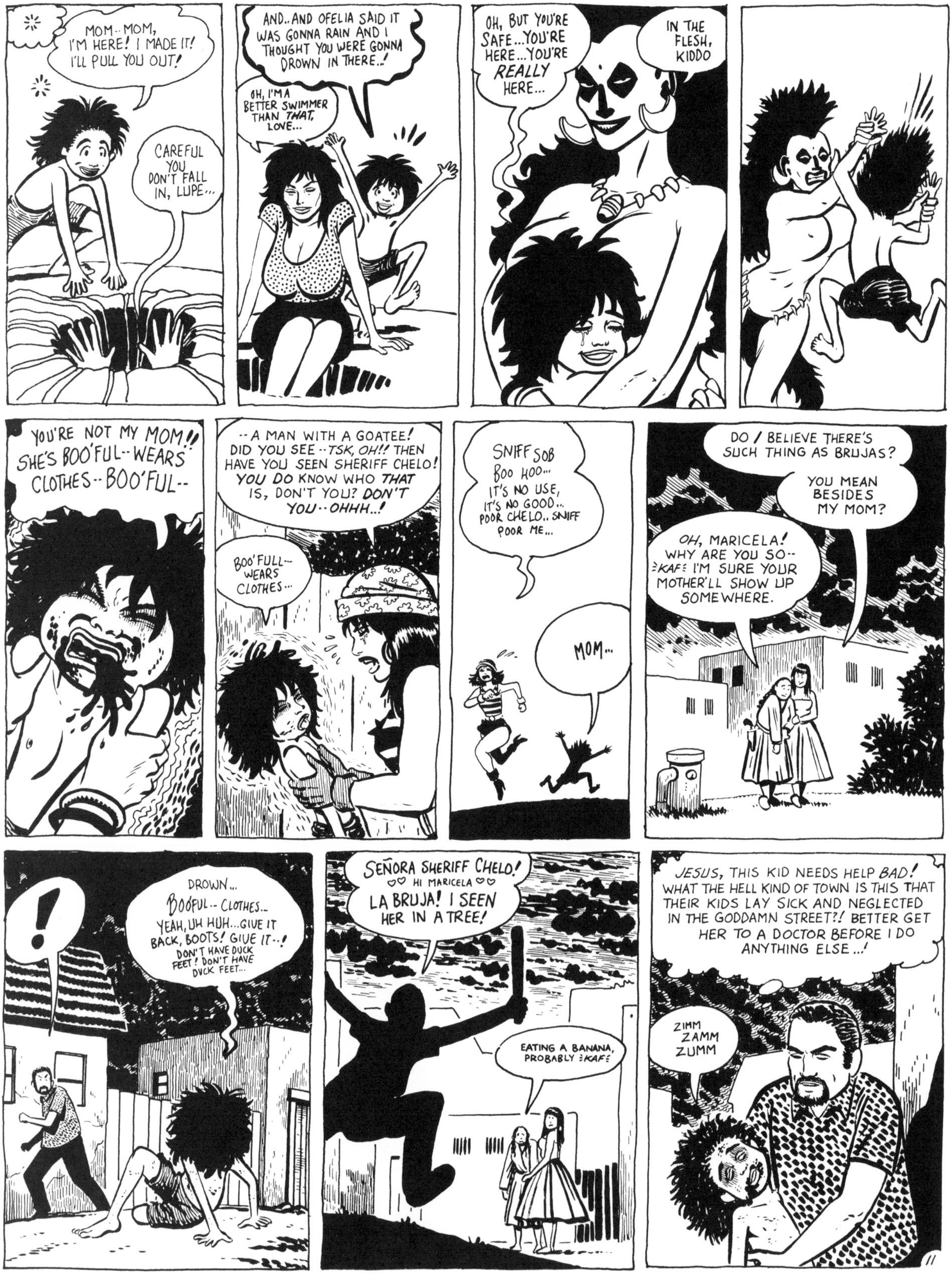

MOM--MOM, I'M HERE! I MADE IT! I'LL PULL YOU OUT!
CAREFUL YOU DON'T FALL IN, LUPE...
AND..AND OFELIA SAID IT WAS GONNA RAIN AND I THOUGHT YOU WERE GONNA DROWN IN THERE..!
OH, I'M A BETTER SWIMMER THAN THAT, LOVE...
OH, BUT YOU'RE SAFE...YOU'RE HERE...YOU'RE REALLY HERE...
IN THE FLESH, KIDDO
YOU'RE NOT MY MOM!! SHE'S BOO'FUL--WEARS CLOTHES--BOO'FUL--
--A MAN WITH A GOATEE! DID YOU SEE--TSK, OH!! THEN HAVE YOU SEEN SHERIFF CHELO! YOU DO KNOW WHO THAT IS, DON'T YOU? DON'T YOU--OHHH..!
BOO'FULL--WEARS CLOTHES...
SNIFF SOB BOO HOO... IT'S NO USE, IT'S NO GOOD.. POOR CHELO.. SNIFF POOR ME...
MOM...
DO I BELIEVE THERE'S SUCH THING AS BRUJAS?
YOU MEAN BESIDES MY MOM?
OH, MARICELA! WHY ARE YOU SO-- KAF I'M SURE YOUR MOTHER'LL SHOW UP SOMEWHERE.
!
DROWN... BOOFUL--CLOTHES... YEAH, UH HUH...GIVE IT BACK, BOOTS! GIVE IT--! DON'T HAVE DUCK FEET! DON'T HAVE DUCK FEET...
SEÑORA SHERIFF CHELO! HI MARICELA LA BRUJA! I SEEN HER IN A TREE!
EATING A BANANA, PROBABLY KAF
JESUS, THIS KID NEEDS HELP BAD! WHAT THE HELL KIND OF TOWN IS THIS THAT THEIR KIDS LAY SICK AND NEGLECTED IN THE GODDAMN STREET?! BETTER GET HER TO A DOCTOR BEFORE I DO ANYTHING ELSE...!
ZIMM ZAMM ZUMM
11

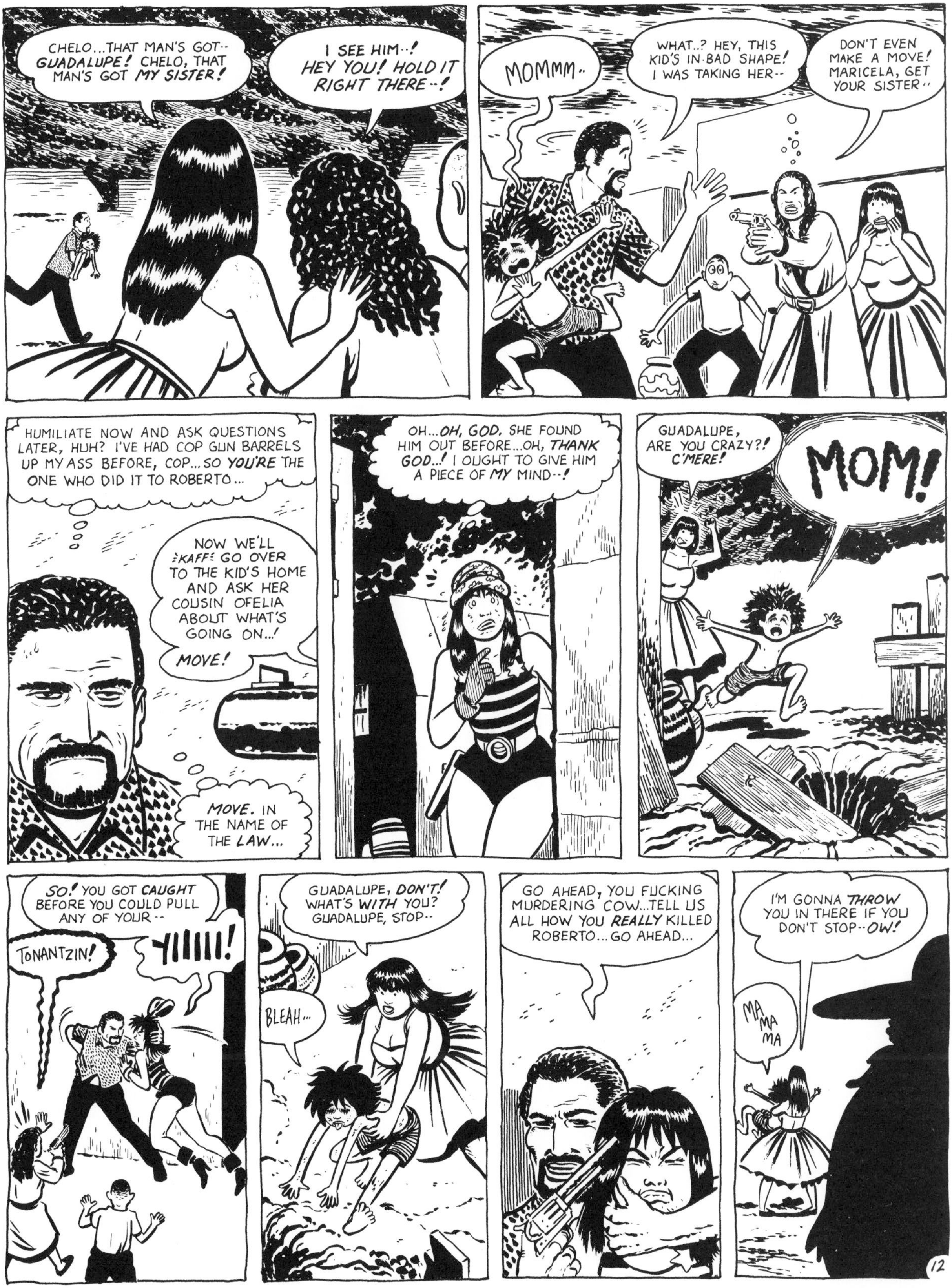
CHELO...THAT MAN'S GOT-- GUADALUPE! CHELO, THAT MAN'S GOT MY SISTER!
I SEE HIM--! HEY YOU! HOLD IT RIGHT THERE--!
MOMMM--
WHAT..? HEY, THIS KID'S IN BAD SHAPE! I WAS TAKING HER--
DON'T EVEN MAKE A MOVE! MARICELA, GET YOUR SISTER--
HUMILIATE NOW AND ASK QUESTIONS LATER, HUH? I'VE HAD COP GUN BARRELS UP MY ASS BEFORE, COP...SO YOU'RE THE ONE WHO DID IT TO ROBERTO...
NOW WE'LL *KAFF* GO OVER TO THE KID'S HOME AND ASK HER COUSIN OFELIA ABOUT WHAT'S GOING ON...!
MOVE!
MOVE. IN THE NAME OF THE LAW...
OH...OH, GOD. SHE FOUND HIM OUT BEFORE...OH, THANK GOD...! I OUGHT TO GIVE HIM A PIECE OF MY MIND--!
GUADALUPE, ARE YOU CRAZY?! C'MERE!
MOM!
SO! YOU GOT CAUGHT BEFORE YOU COULD PULL ANY OF YOUR--
TONANTZIN!
YIIIII!
GUADALUPE, DON'T! WHAT'S WITH YOU? GUADALUPE, STOP--
BLEAH...
GO AHEAD, YOU FUCKING MURDERING COW...TELL US ALL HOW YOU REALLY KILLED ROBERTO...GO AHEAD...
I'M GONNA THROW YOU IN THERE IF YOU DON'T STOP--OW!
MA MA MA
12

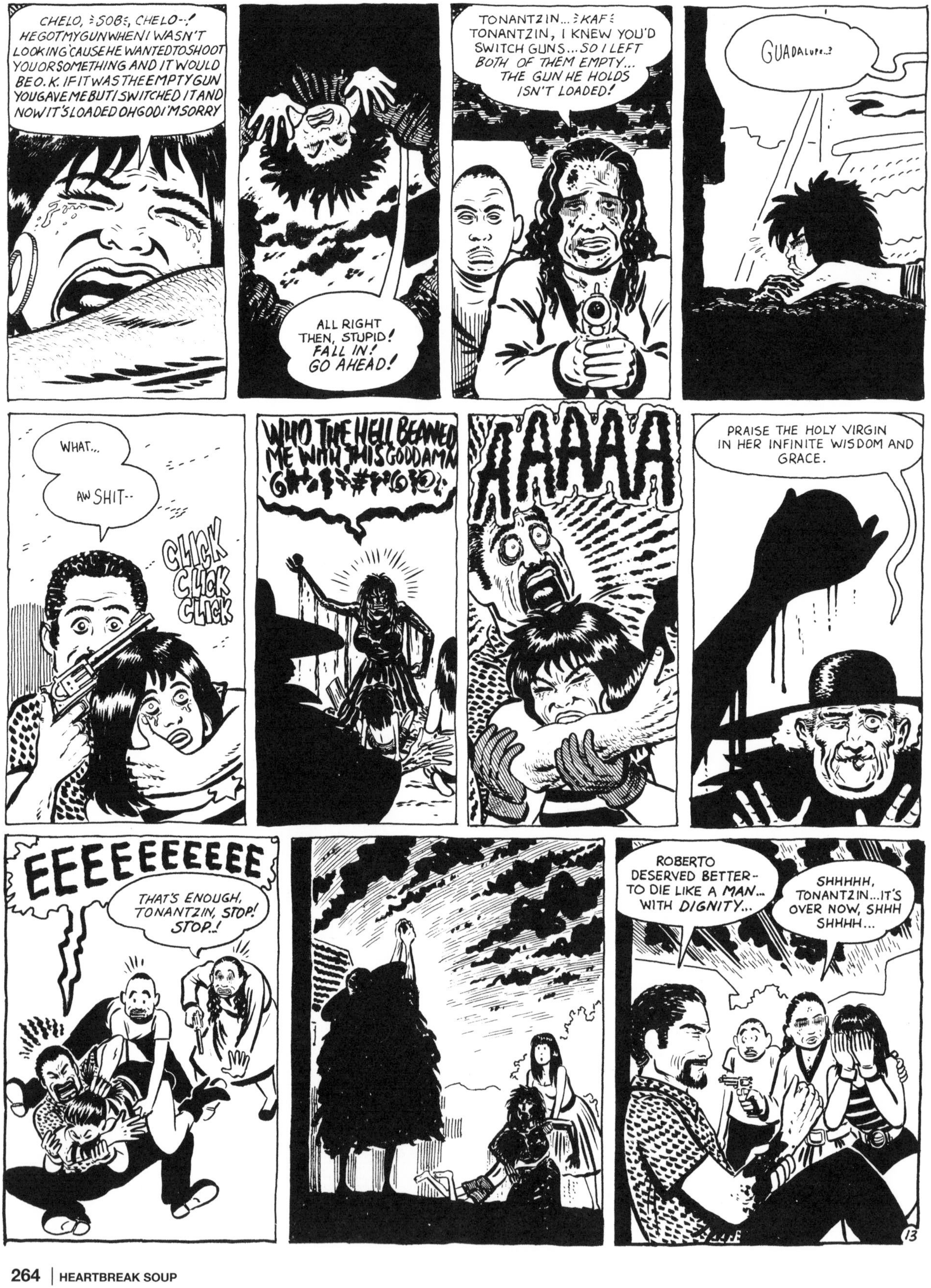
CHELO, SOB, CHELO--! HEGOTMYGUNWHENI WASN'T LOOKING'CAUSEHE WANTEDTOSHOOT YOUORSOMETHING AND IT WOULD BEO.K. IFITWASTHEEMPTYGUN YOUGAVEMEBUTI SWITCHED ITAND NOWIT'SLOADEDOHGODI'MSORRY
ALL RIGHT THEN, STUPID! FALL IN! GO AHEAD!
TONANTZIN... KAF TONANTZIN, I KNEW YOU'D SWITCH GUNS... SO I LEFT BOTH OF THEM EMPTY... THE GUN HE HOLDS ISN'T LOADED!
GUADALUPE..?
WHAT...
AW SHIT--
CLICK CLICK CLICK
WHO THE HELL BEANED ME WITH THIS GODDAMN
AAAAA
PRAISE THE HOLY VIRGIN IN HER INFINITE WISDOM AND GRACE.
EEEEEEEEEE
THAT'S ENOUGH, TONANTZIN, STOP! STOP..!
ROBERTO DESERVED BETTER-- TO DIE LIKE A MAN... WITH DIGNITY...
SHHHHH, TONANTZIN... IT'S OVER NOW, SHHH SHHHH...
13

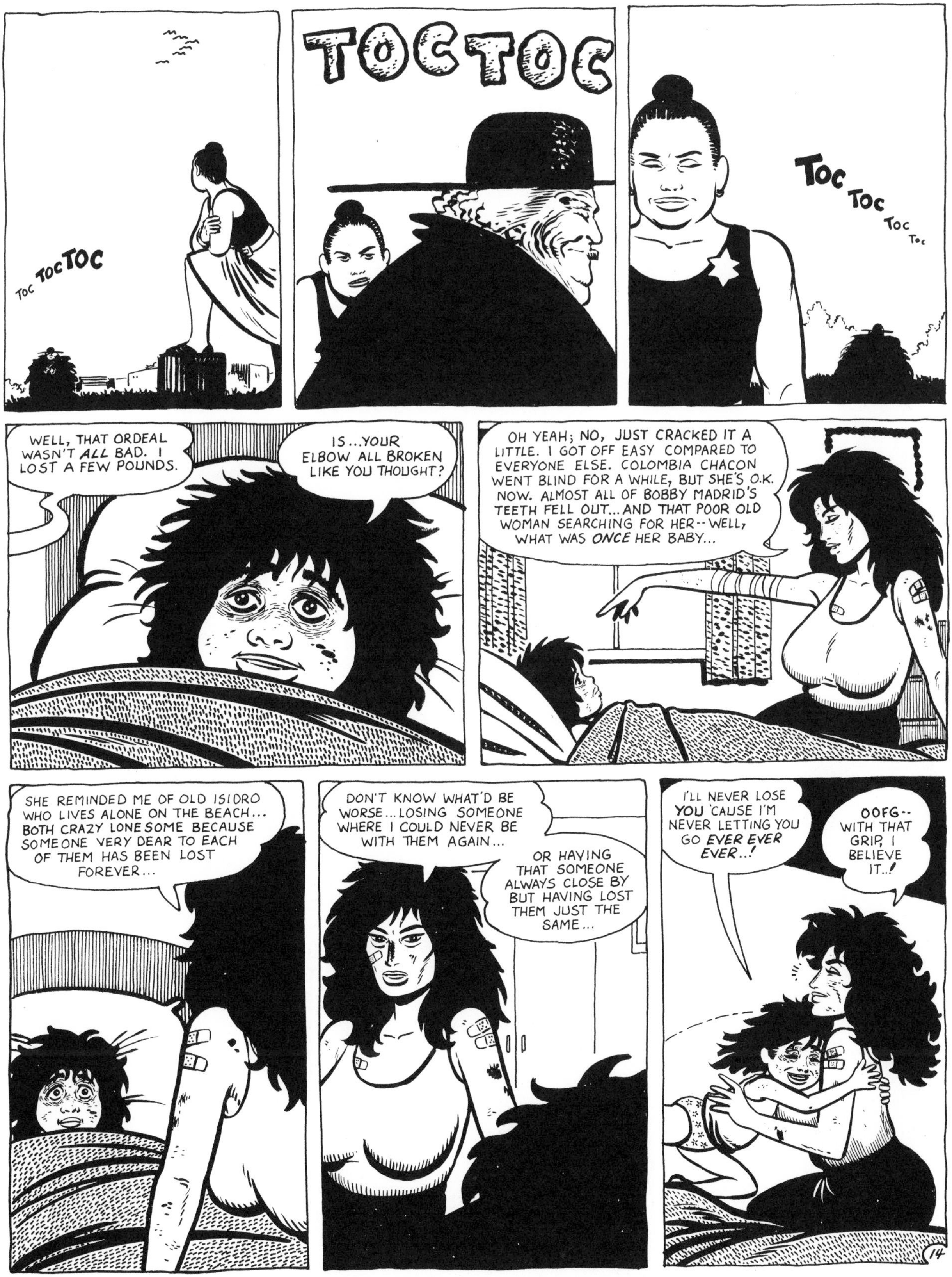
TOC TOC TOC
TOC TOC
TOC TOC TOC TOC TOC
WELL, THAT ORDEAL WASN'T ALL BAD. I LOST A FEW POUNDS.
IS...YOUR ELBOW ALL BROKEN LIKE YOU THOUGHT?
OH YEAH; NO, JUST CRACKED IT A LITTLE. I GOT OFF EASY COMPARED TO EVERYONE ELSE. COLOMBIA CHACON WENT BLIND FOR A WHILE, BUT SHE'S O.K. NOW. ALMOST ALL OF BOBBY MADRID'S TEETH FELL OUT... AND THAT POOR OLD WOMAN SEARCHING FOR HER-- WELL, WHAT WAS ONCE HER BABY...
SHE REMINDED ME OF OLD ISIDRO WHO LIVES ALONE ON THE BEACH... BOTH CRAZY LONESOME BECAUSE SOMEONE VERY DEAR TO EACH OF THEM HAS BEEN LOST FOREVER...
DON'T KNOW WHAT'D BE WORSE... LOSING SOMEONE WHERE I COULD NEVER BE WITH THEM AGAIN...
OR HAVING THAT SOMEONE ALWAYS CLOSE BY BUT HAVING LOST THEM JUST THE SAME...
I'LL NEVER LOSE YOU 'CAUSE I'M NEVER LETTING YOU GO EVER EVER EVER..!
OOFG-- WITH THAT GRIP, I BELIEVE IT..!
14

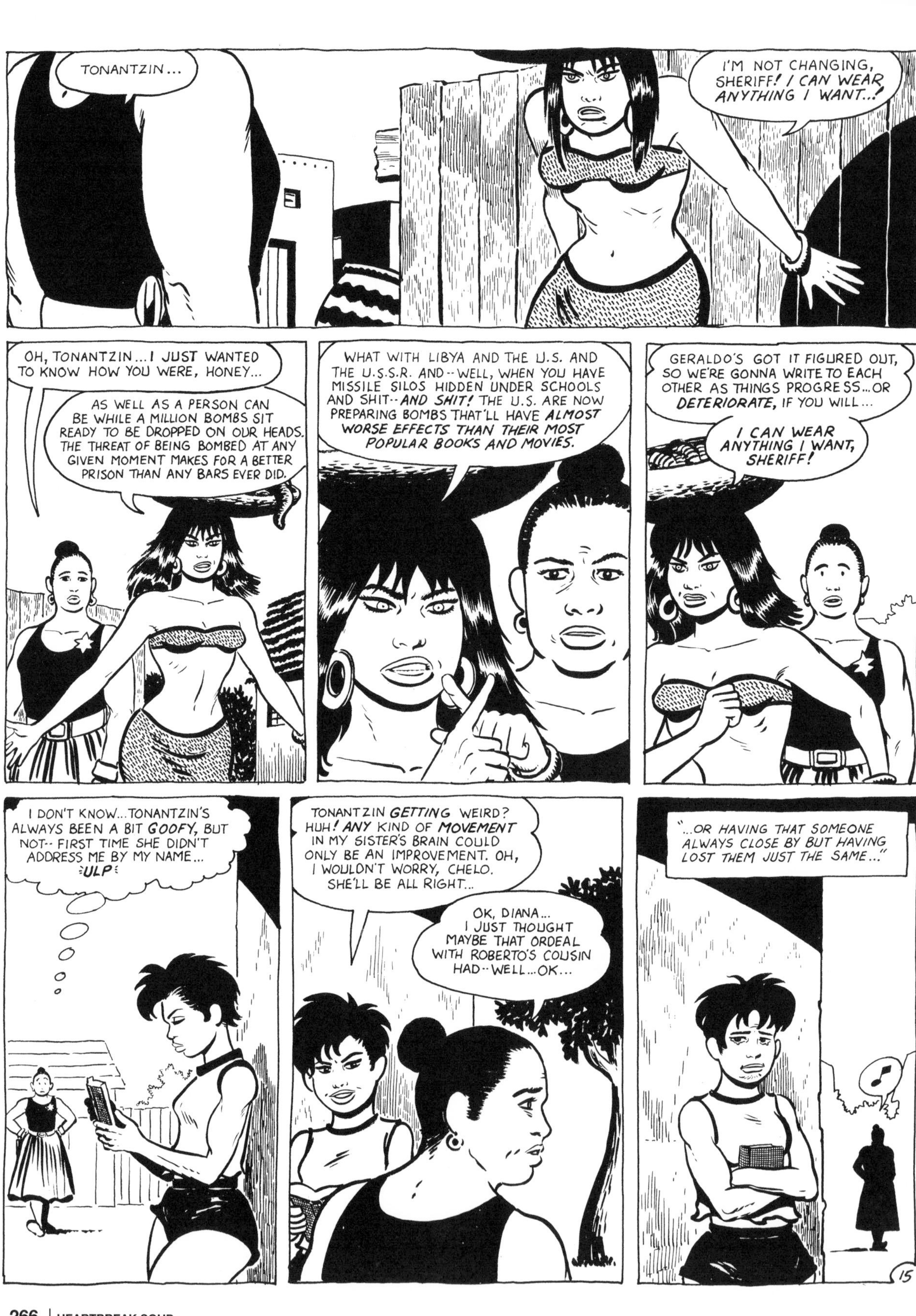
TONANTZIN...
I'M NOT CHANGING, SHERIFF! I CAN WEAR ANYTHING I WANT...!
OH, TONANTZIN... I JUST WANTED TO KNOW HOW YOU WERE, HONEY...
AS WELL AS A PERSON CAN BE WHILE A MILLION BOMBS SIT READY TO BE DROPPED ON OUR HEADS. THE THREAT OF BEING BOMBED AT ANY GIVEN MOMENT MAKES FOR A BETTER PRISON THAN ANY BARS EVER DID.
WHAT WITH LIBYA AND THE U.S. AND THE U.S.S.R. AND-- WELL, WHEN YOU HAVE MISSILE SILOS HIDDEN UNDER SCHOOLS AND SHIT-- AND SHIT! THE U.S. ARE NOW PREPARING BOMBS THAT'LL HAVE ALMOST WORSE EFFECTS THAN THEIR MOST POPULAR BOOKS AND MOVIES.
GERALDO'S GOT IT FIGURED OUT, SO WE'RE GONNA WRITE TO EACH OTHER AS THINGS PROGRESS...OR DETERIORATE, IF YOU WILL...
I CAN WEAR ANYTHING I WANT, SHERIFF!
I DON'T KNOW...TONANTZIN'S ALWAYS BEEN A BIT GOOFY, BUT NOT-- FIRST TIME SHE DIDN'T ADDRESS ME BY MY NAME... ULP
TONANTZIN GETTING WEIRD? HUH! ANY KIND OF MOVEMENT IN MY SISTER'S BRAIN COULD ONLY BE AN IMPROVEMENT. OH, I WOULDN'T WORRY, CHELO. SHE'LL BE ALL RIGHT...
OK, DIANA... I JUST THOUGHT MAYBE THAT ORDEAL WITH ROBERTO'S COUSIN HAD-- WELL...OK...
"...OR HAVING THAT SOMEONE ALWAYS CLOSE BY BUT HAVING LOST THEM JUST THE SAME..."
15

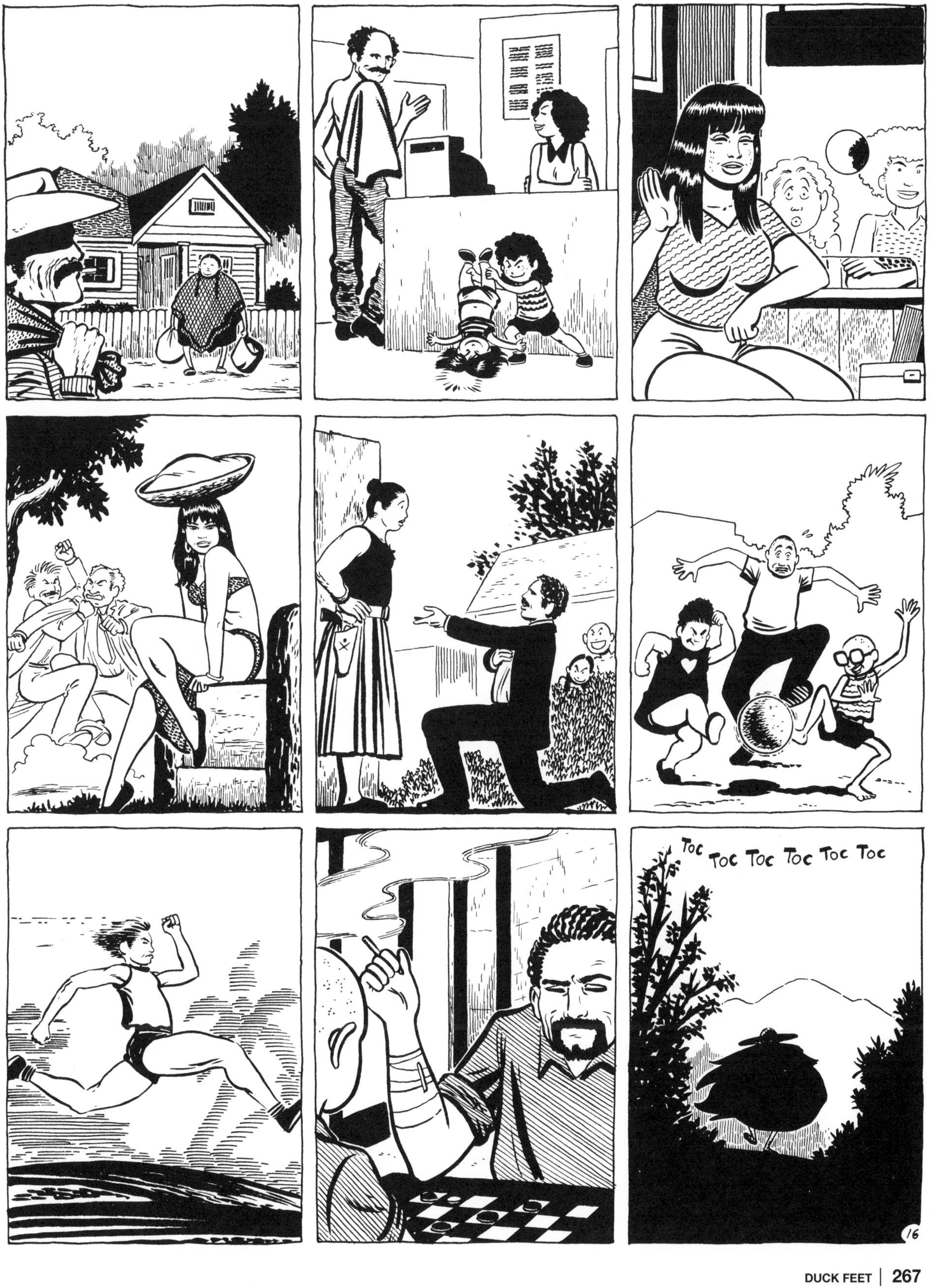
Toc Toc Toc Toc Toc Toc
16

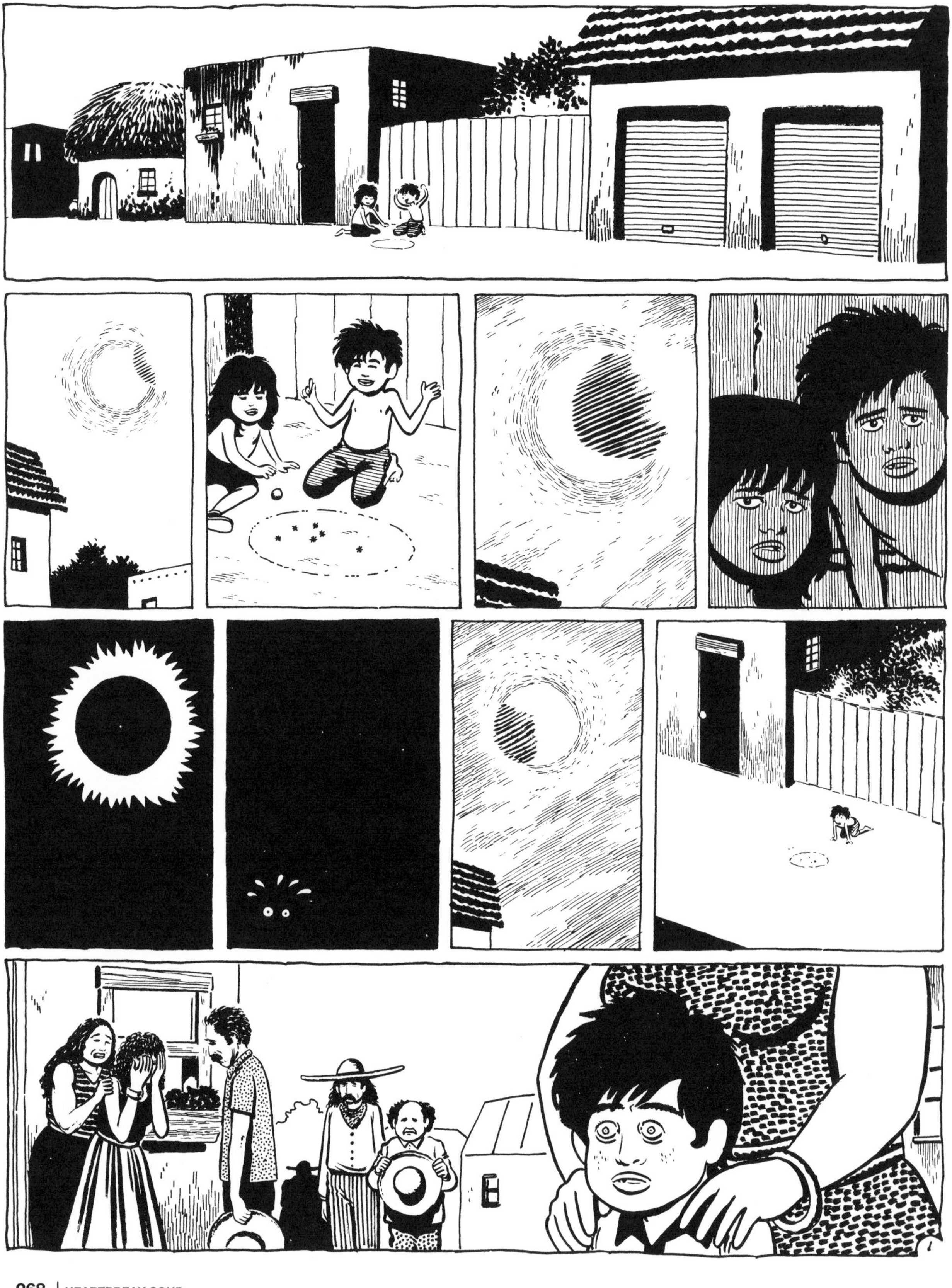

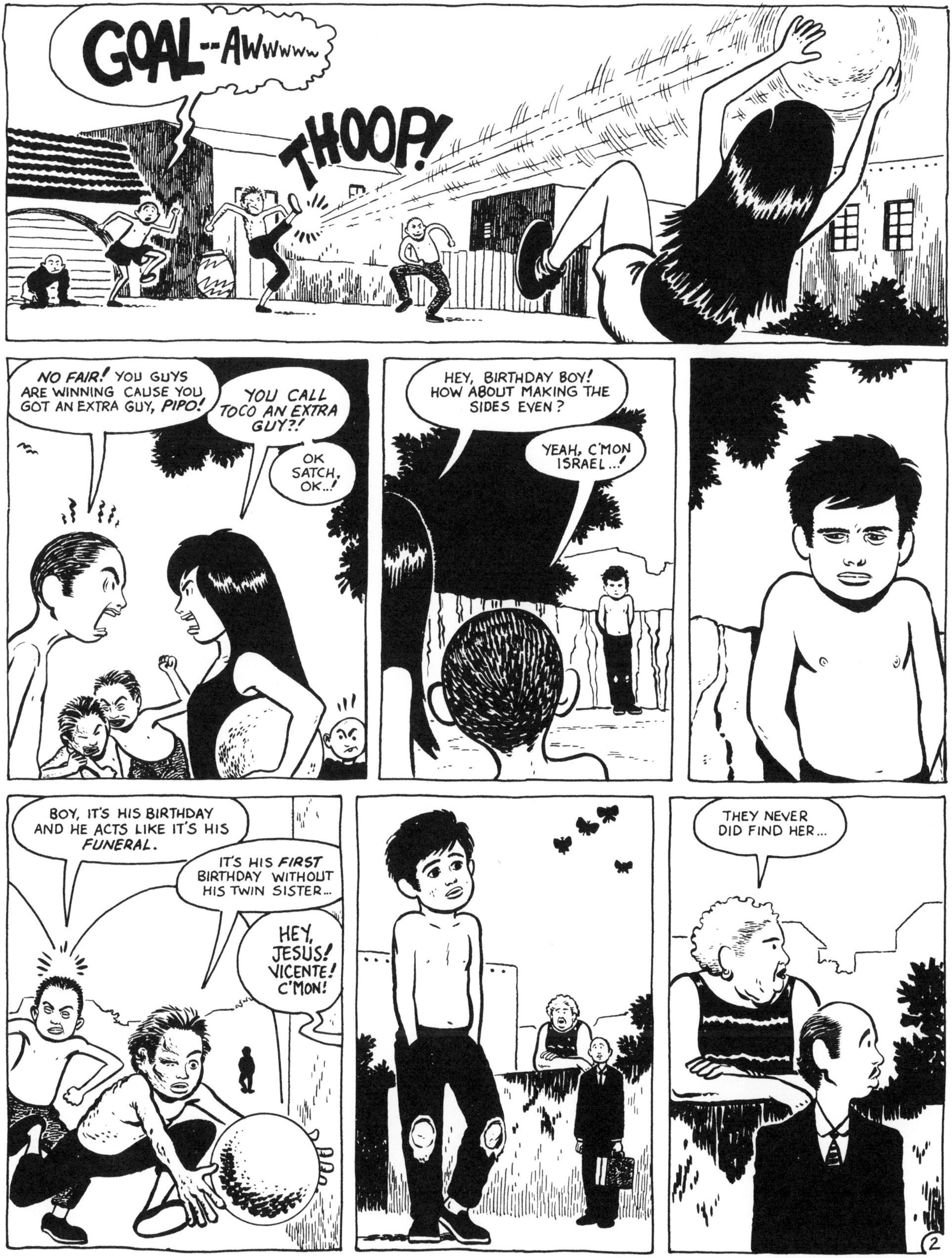
GOAL--AWWWWW
THOOP!
NO FAIR! YOU GUYS ARE WINNING CAUSE YOU GOT AN EXTRA GUY, PIPO!
YOU CALL TOCO AN EXTRA GUY?!
OK SATCH, OK..!
HEY, BIRTHDAY BOY! HOW ABOUT MAKING THE SIDES EVEN?
YEAH, C'MON ISRAEL...!
BOY, IT'S HIS BIRTHDAY AND HE ACTS LIKE IT'S HIS FUNERAL.
IT'S HIS FIRST BIRTHDAY WITHOUT HIS TWIN SISTER...
HEY, JESUS! VICENTE! C'MON!
THEY NEVER DID FIND HER...
2

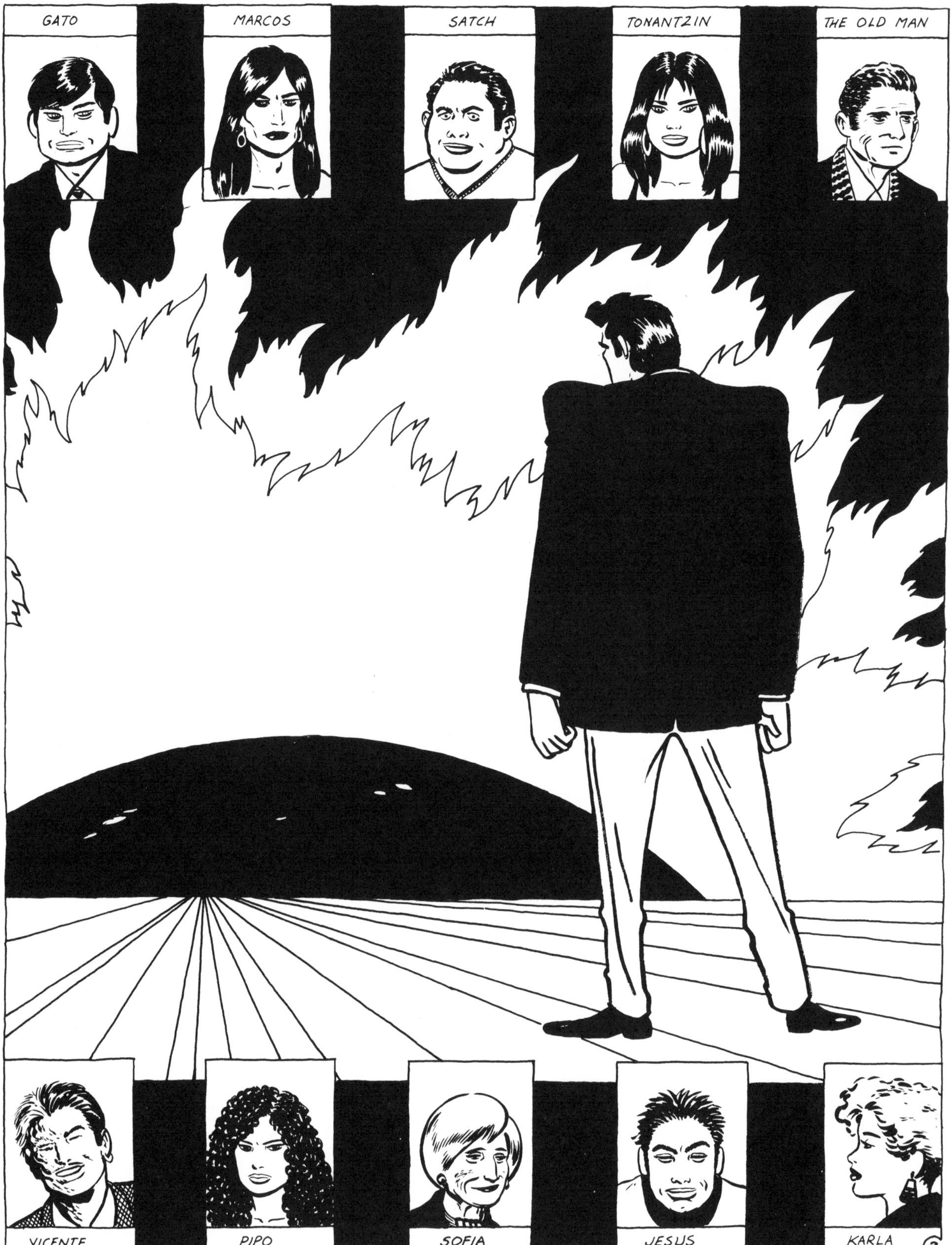
GATO
MARCOS
SATCH
TONANTZIN
THE OLD MAN
VICENTE
PIPO
SOFIA
JESUS
KARLA
3

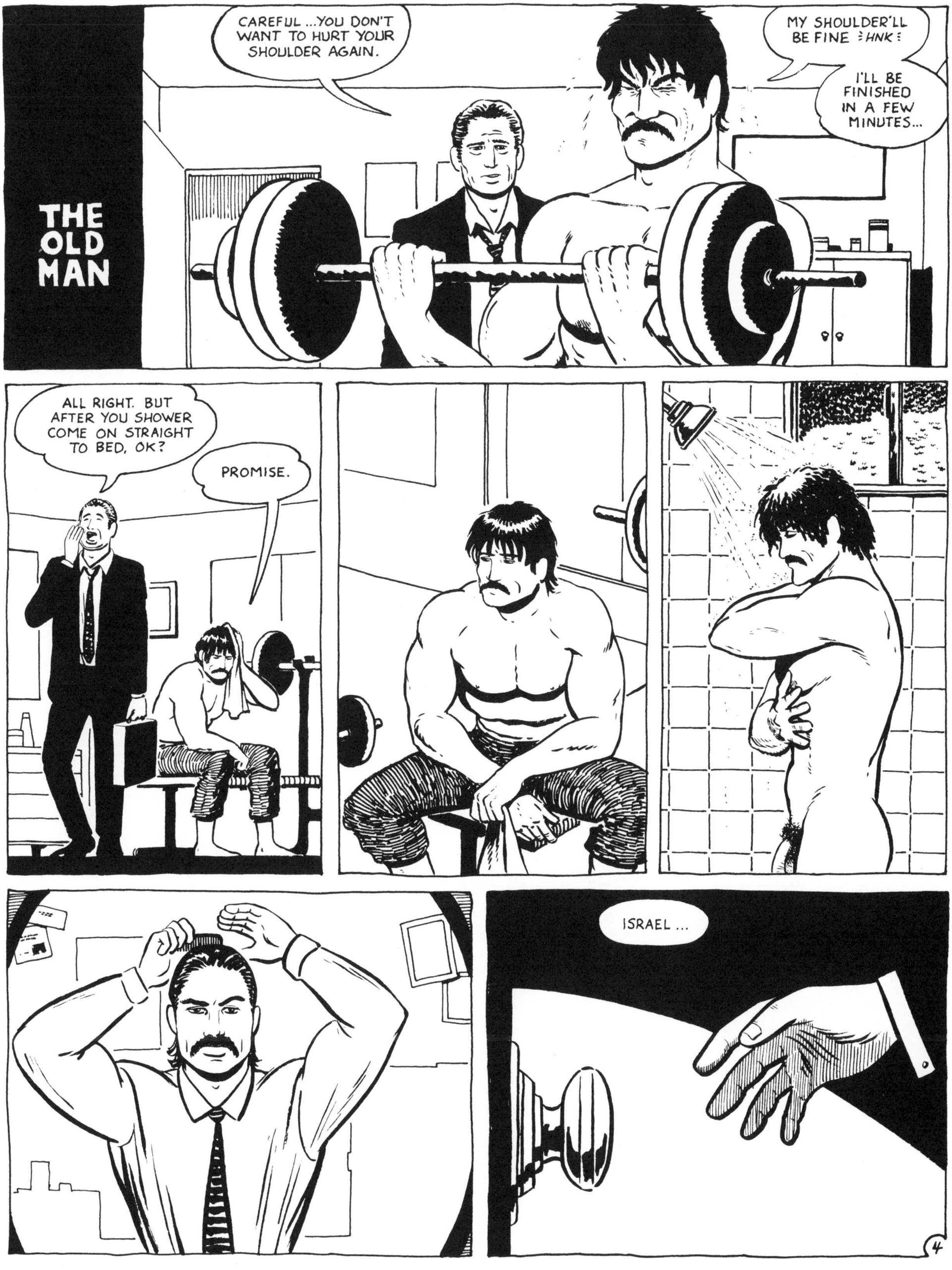
THE OLD MAN
CAREFUL ...YOU DON'T WANT TO HURT YOUR SHOULDER AGAIN.
MY SHOULDER'LL BE FINE HNK
I'LL BE FINISHED IN A FEW MINUTES...
ALL RIGHT. BUT AFTER YOU SHOWER COME ON STRAIGHT TO BED, OK?
PROMISE.
ISRAEL ...
4

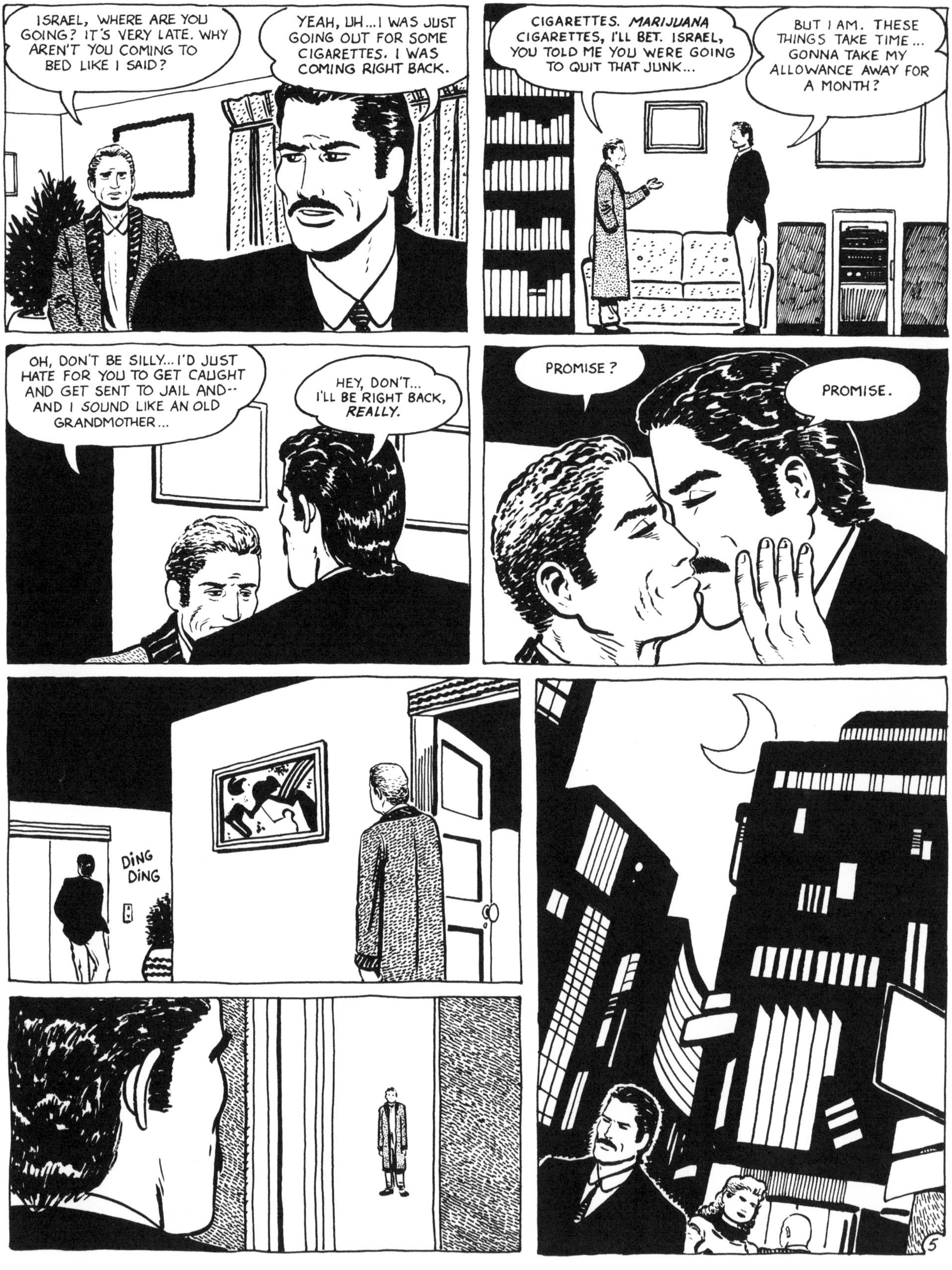

ISRAEL, WHERE ARE YOU GOING? IT'S VERY LATE. WHY AREN'T YOU COMING TO BED LIKE I SAID?
YEAH, UH... I WAS JUST GOING OUT FOR SOME CIGARETTES. I WAS COMING RIGHT BACK.
CIGARETTES. MARIJUANA CIGARETTES, I'LL BET. ISRAEL, YOU TOLD ME YOU WERE GOING TO QUIT THAT JUNK...
BUT I AM. THESE THINGS TAKE TIME... GONNA TAKE MY ALLOWANCE AWAY FOR A MONTH?
OH, DON'T BE SILLY... I'D JUST HATE FOR YOU TO GET CAUGHT AND GET SENT TO JAIL AND-- AND I SOUND LIKE AN OLD GRANDMOTHER...
HEY, DON'T... I'LL BE RIGHT BACK, REALLY.
PROMISE?
PROMISE.
DING DING
5

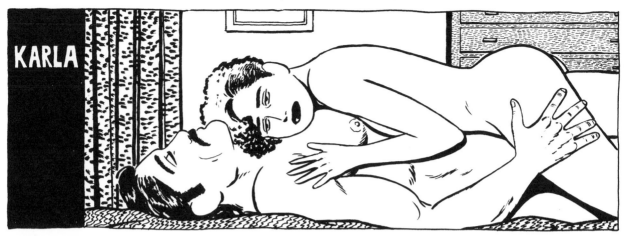

KARLA

CAN'T STAY. IS THERE ANYTHING LEFT OF MY SHIT?

YOU'RE THE ONLY ONE WHO USES THAT *JUNK*.

IT'S IN THE BOTTOM DRAWER.

I'LL TRY TO COME STAY WITH YOU NEXT WEEK.

THE OLD MAN'S GETTING SUSPICIOUS.

SNORF

RUBEN SALAS ASKED ME TO GO TO BAHIA WITH HIM, ISRAEL.

OH YEAH? HEH... ARE YOU GONNA GO?

YEAH.

YOU... COMING BACK..?

N...NO,

YOU COULD HAVE TRIED TO TALK ME OUT OF IT...

I DON'T EVEN KNOW WHERE BAHIA IS...

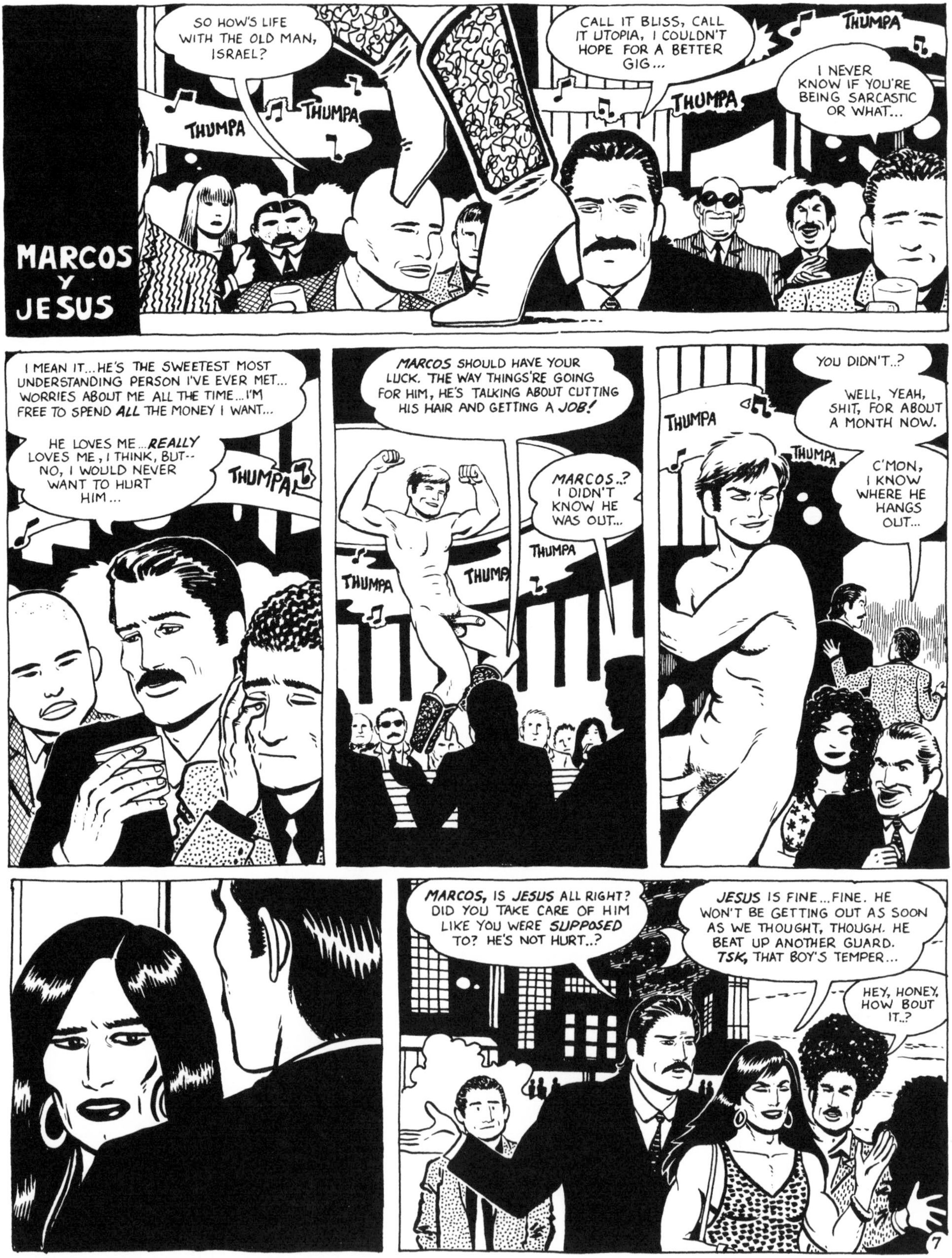
MARCOS Y JESUS
SO HOW'S LIFE WITH THE OLD MAN, ISRAEL?
THUMPA
THUMPA
CALL IT BLISS, CALL IT UTOPIA, I COULDN'T HOPE FOR A BETTER GIG...
THUMPA
THUMPA
I NEVER KNOW IF YOU'RE BEING SARCASTIC OR WHAT...
I MEAN IT... HE'S THE SWEETEST MOST UNDERSTANDING PERSON I'VE EVER MET... WORRIES ABOUT ME ALL THE TIME... I'M FREE TO SPEND ALL THE MONEY I WANT...
HE LOVES ME... REALLY LOVES ME, I THINK, BUT-- NO, I WOULD NEVER WANT TO HURT HIM...
THUMPA
MARCOS SHOULD HAVE YOUR LUCK. THE WAY THINGS'RE GOING FOR HIM, HE'S TALKING ABOUT CUTTING HIS HAIR AND GETTING A JOB!
MARCOS..? I DIDN'T KNOW HE WAS OUT...
THUMPA
THUMPA
THUMPA
YOU DIDN'T..?
WELL, YEAH, SHIT, FOR ABOUT A MONTH NOW.
THUMPA
THUMPA
C'MON, I KNOW WHERE HE HANGS OUT...
MARCOS, IS JESUS ALL RIGHT? DID YOU TAKE CARE OF HIM LIKE YOU WERE SUPPOSED TO? HE'S NOT HURT..?
JESUS IS FINE... FINE. HE WON'T BE GETTING OUT AS SOON AS WE THOUGHT, THOUGH. HE BEAT UP ANOTHER GUARD. TSK, THAT BOY'S TEMPER...
HEY, HONEY, HOW BOUT IT..?
7

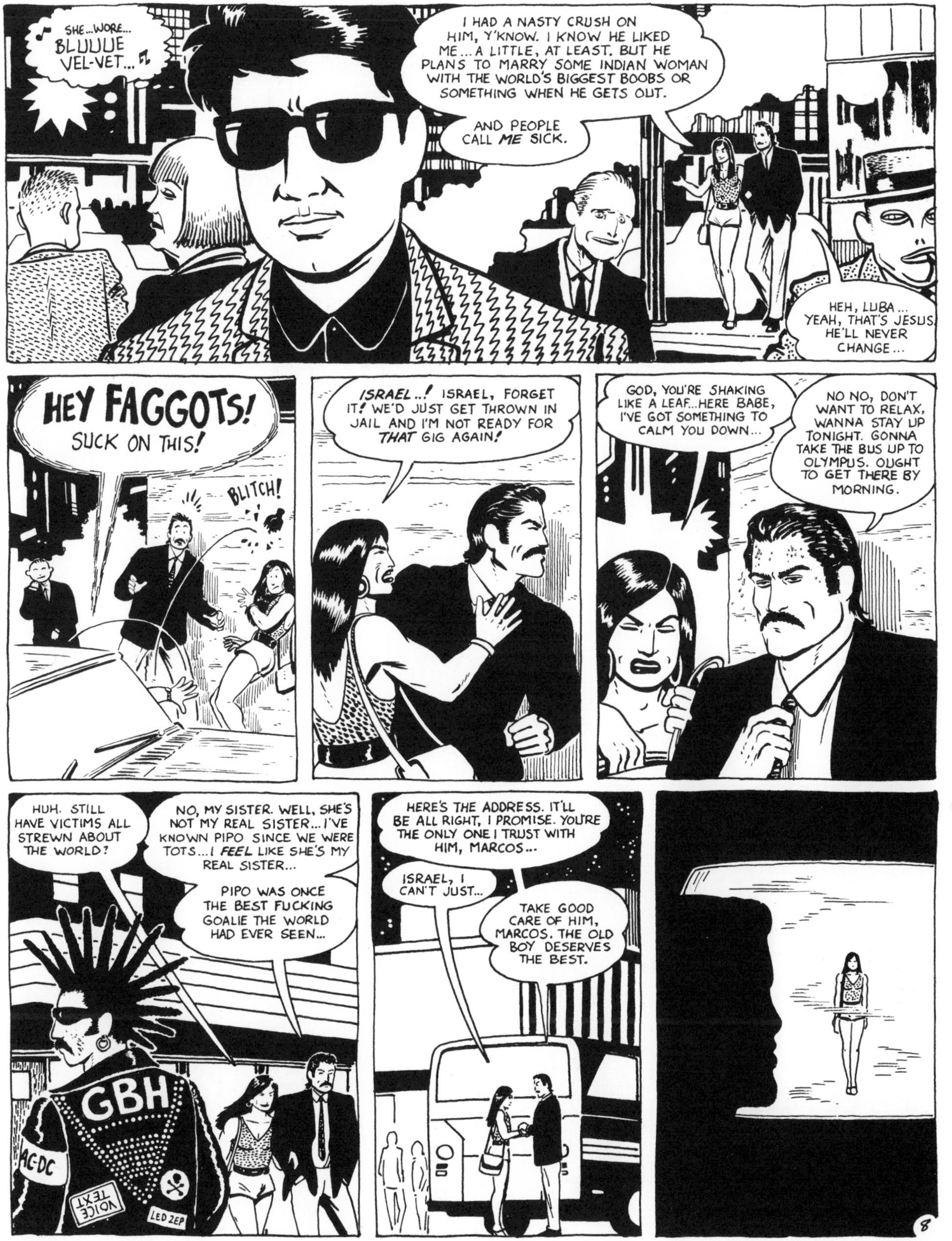

SHE...WORE... BLUUUE VEL-VET...
I HAD A NASTY CRUSH ON HIM, Y'KNOW. I KNOW HE LIKED ME... A LITTLE, AT LEAST. BUT HE PLANS TO MARRY SOME INDIAN WOMAN WITH THE WORLD'S BIGGEST BOOBS OR SOMETHING WHEN HE GETS OUT.
AND PEOPLE CALL ME SICK.
HEH, LUBA... YEAH, THAT'S JESUS. HE'LL NEVER CHANGE...
HEY FAGGOTS! SUCK ON THIS!
BLITCH!
ISRAEL..! ISRAEL, FORGET IT! WE'D JUST GET THROWN IN JAIL AND I'M NOT READY FOR THAT GIG AGAIN!
GOD, YOU'RE SHAKING LIKE A LEAF...HERE BABE, I'VE GOT SOMETHING TO CALM YOU DOWN...
NO NO, DON'T WANT TO RELAX, WANNA STAY UP TONIGHT. GONNA TAKE THE BUS UP TO OLYMPUS. OUGHT TO GET THERE BY MORNING.
HUH. STILL HAVE VICTIMS ALL STREWN ABOUT THE WORLD?
NO, MY SISTER. WELL, SHE'S NOT MY REAL SISTER... I'VE KNOWN PIPO SINCE WE WERE TOTS... I FEEL LIKE SHE'S MY REAL SISTER...
PIPO WAS ONCE THE BEST FUCKING GOALIE THE WORLD HAD EVER SEEN...
GBH
AC-DC
VOICE TEXT
LED ZEP
HERE'S THE ADDRESS. IT'LL BE ALL RIGHT, I PROMISE. YOU'RE THE ONLY ONE I TRUST WITH HIM, MARCOS...
ISRAEL, I CAN'T JUST...
TAKE GOOD CARE OF HIM, MARCOS. THE OLD BOY DESERVES THE BEST.
8

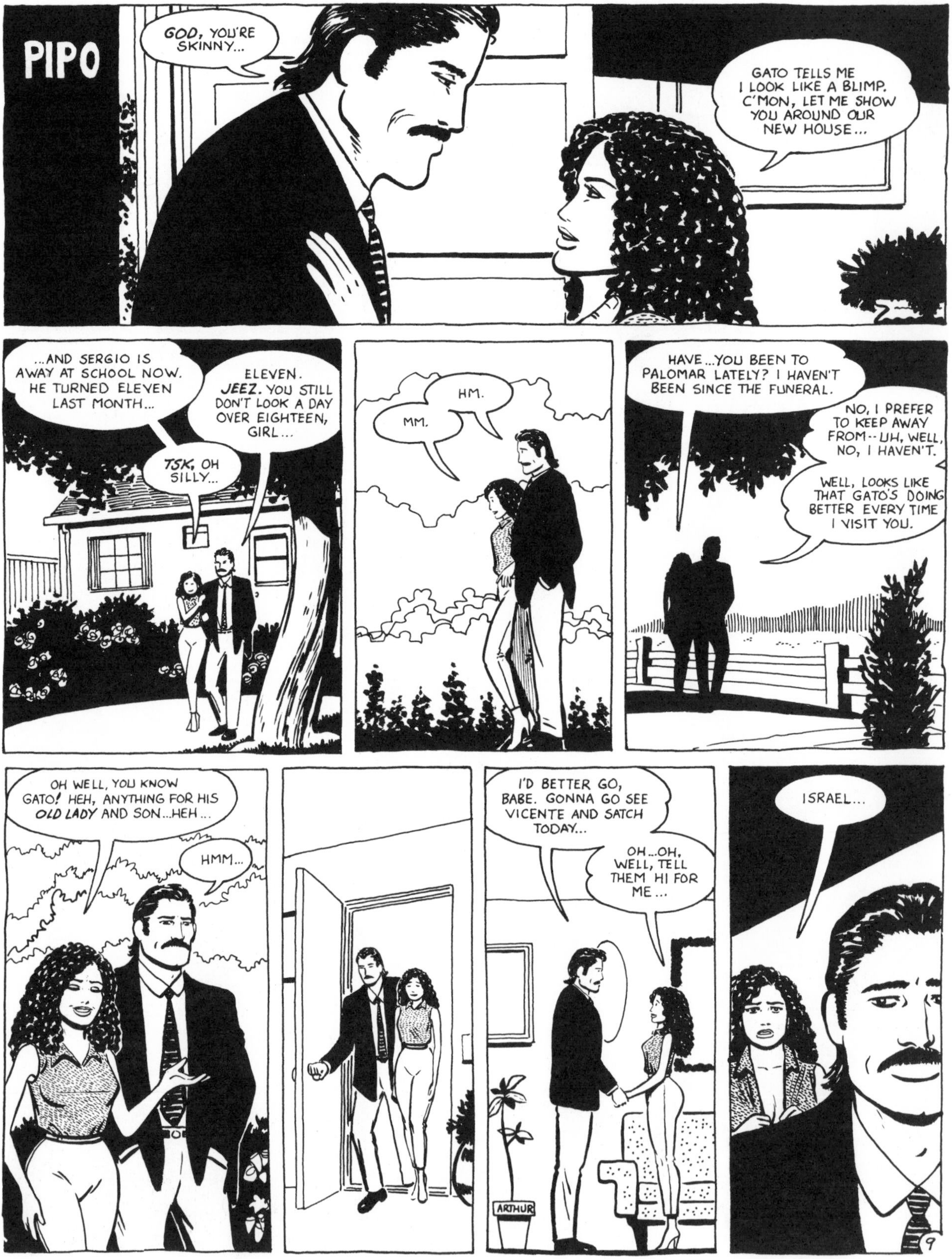
PIPO
GOD, YOU'RE SKINNY...
GATO TELLS ME I LOOK LIKE A BLIMP. C'MON, LET ME SHOW YOU AROUND OUR NEW HOUSE...
...AND SERGIO IS AWAY AT SCHOOL NOW. HE TURNED ELEVEN LAST MONTH...
ELEVEN. JEEZ. YOU STILL DON'T LOOK A DAY OVER EIGHTEEN, GIRL...
TSK, OH SILLY...
MM.
HM.
HAVE...YOU BEEN TO PALOMAR LATELY? I HAVEN'T BEEN SINCE THE FUNERAL.
NO, I PREFER TO KEEP AWAY FROM--UH, WELL, NO, I HAVEN'T.
WELL, LOOKS LIKE THAT GATO'S DOING BETTER EVERY TIME I VISIT YOU.
OH WELL, YOU KNOW GATO! HEH, ANYTHING FOR HIS OLD LADY AND SON...HEH...
HMM...
I'D BETTER GO, BABE. GONNA GO SEE VICENTE AND SATCH TODAY...
OH...OH, WELL, TELL THEM HI FOR ME...
ARTHUR
ISRAEL...
9

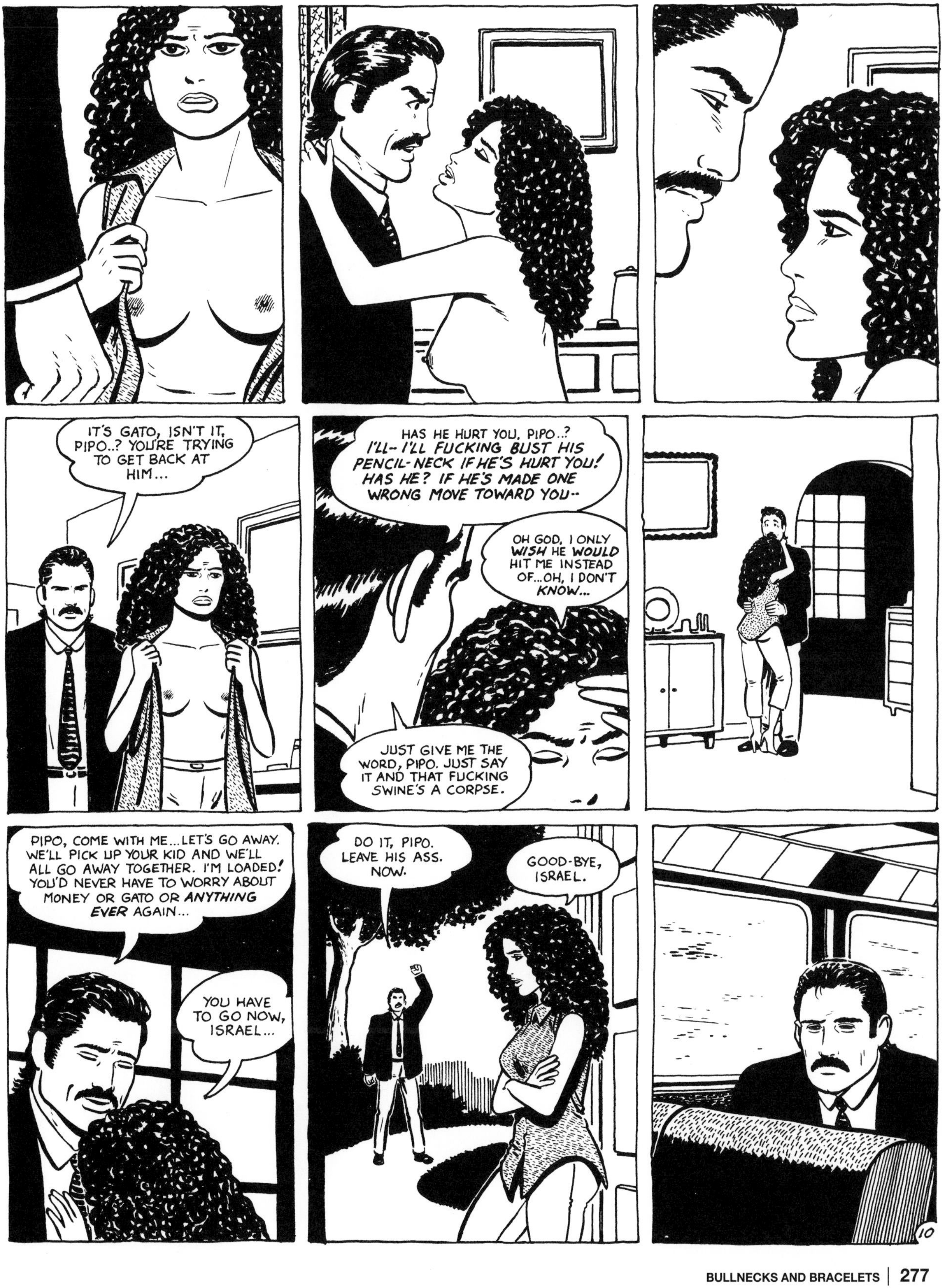
IT'S GATO, ISN'T IT, PIPO..? YOU'RE TRYING TO GET BACK AT HIM...
HAS HE HURT YOU, PIPO..? I'LL-- I'LL FUCKING BUST HIS PENCIL-NECK IF HE'S HURT YOU! HAS HE? IF HE'S MADE ONE WRONG MOVE TOWARD YOU--
OH GOD, I ONLY WISH HE WOULD HIT ME INSTEAD OF...OH, I DON'T KNOW...
JUST GIVE ME THE WORD, PIPO. JUST SAY IT AND THAT FUCKING SWINE'S A CORPSE.
PIPO, COME WITH ME...LET'S GO AWAY. WE'LL PICK UP YOUR KID AND WE'LL ALL GO AWAY TOGETHER. I'M LOADED! YOU'D NEVER HAVE TO WORRY ABOUT MONEY OR GATO OR ANYTHING EVER AGAIN...
YOU HAVE TO GO NOW, ISRAEL...
DO IT, PIPO. LEAVE HIS ASS. NOW.
GOOD-BYE, ISRAEL.
10

SATCH Y VICENTE

I'M TELLING YOU, ISRAEL, VICENTE'S *GONE*. HE AND HIS BUDDY SATURNINO PULLED UP STAKES AND HEADED FOR THE STATES...

BUT WHY DIDN'T HE TELL ME. I COULD HAVE TRIED TALKING HIM OUT OF IT·· I COULD HAVE GONE WITH HIM...!

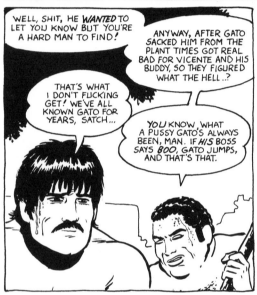

WELL, SHIT, HE *WANTED* TO LET YOU KNOW BUT YOU'RE A HARD MAN TO FIND!

ANYWAY, AFTER GATO SACKED HIM FROM THE PLANT TIMES GOT REAL BAD FOR VICENTE AND HIS BUDDY, SO THEY FIGURED WHAT THE HELL..?

THAT'S WHAT I DON'T FUCKING GET! WE'VE ALL KNOWN GATO FOR YEARS, SATCH...

YOU KNOW, WHAT A PUSSY GATO'S ALWAYS BEEN, MAN. IF *HIS* BOSS SAYS *BOO*, GATO JUMPS, AND THAT'S THAT.

YOU BOYS LOOK LIKE YOU BOTH COULD USE A COLD ONE.

OOH, YOU'RE A DREAM, MARTA.

THANKS, MART.

YEAH... FUCKIN' VICENTE...

GUESS I'M PRETTY LUCKY WITH WHAT I GOT...DON'T MAKE TOO MUCH MONEY, BUT I GOT A GOOD WIFE, GOOD KIDS, MY OWN HOME...

WELL, TAKE CARE THEN, ISRAEL...AND THANKS AGAIN FOR THE HELP. THIS WOULD HAVE TAKEN ME A WEEK TO DO BY MYSELF...

GLAD TO HELP OUT, SATCH. SAY BYE TO MARTA FOR ME...

OH. DID ISRAEL LEAVE ALREADY? I DIDN'T SEE HIM GO...

THE *HELL* YOU DIDN'T...

STARING AT HIM LIKE HE WAS A GODDAMN SIDE OF BEEF AND YOU HADN'T EATEN FOR A MONTH·· GET INSIDE!

WHONG

AAAAAAAAA~ I'LL POISON YOUR DINNER! I WILL!

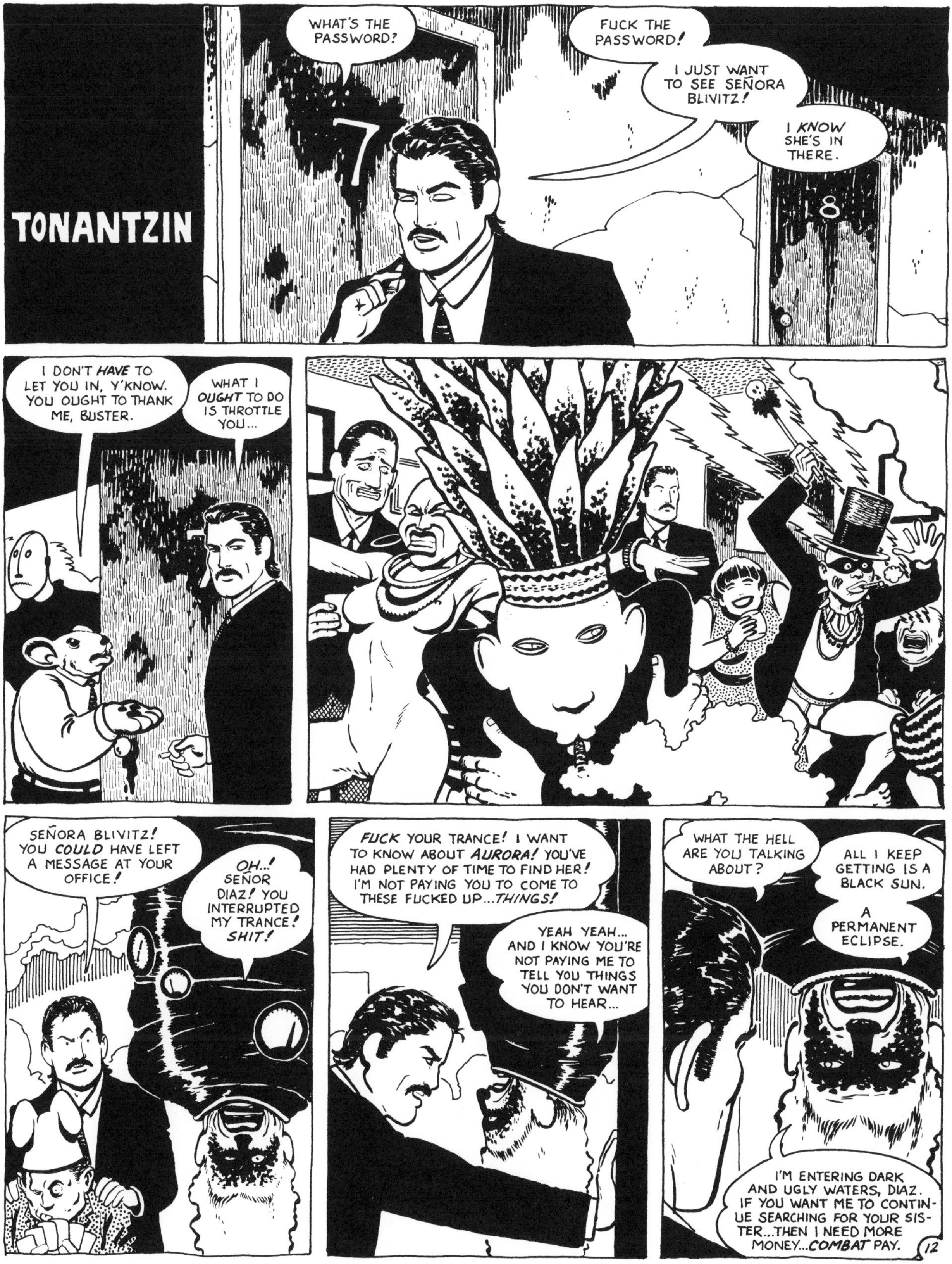
TONANTZIN
WHAT'S THE PASSWORD?
FUCK THE PASSWORD!
I JUST WANT TO SEE SEÑORA BLIVITZ!
I KNOW SHE'S IN THERE.
7
8
I DON'T HAVE TO LET YOU IN, Y'KNOW. YOU OUGHT TO THANK ME, BUSTER.
WHAT I OUGHT TO DO IS THROTTLE YOU...
SEÑORA BLIVITZ! YOU COULD HAVE LEFT A MESSAGE AT YOUR OFFICE!
OH...! SEÑOR DIAZ! YOU INTERRUPTED MY TRANCE! SHIT!
FUCK YOUR TRANCE! I WANT TO KNOW ABOUT AURORA! YOU'VE HAD PLENTY OF TIME TO FIND HER! I'M NOT PAYING YOU TO COME TO THESE FUCKED UP...THINGS!
YEAH YEAH... AND I KNOW YOU'RE NOT PAYING ME TO TELL YOU THINGS YOU DON'T WANT TO HEAR...
WHAT THE HELL ARE YOU TALKING ABOUT?
ALL I KEEP GETTING IS A BLACK SUN.
A PERMANENT ECLIPSE.
I'M ENTERING DARK AND UGLY WATERS, DIAZ. IF YOU WANT ME TO CONTINUE SEARCHING FOR YOUR SISTER...THEN I NEED MORE MONEY...COMBAT PAY.
12

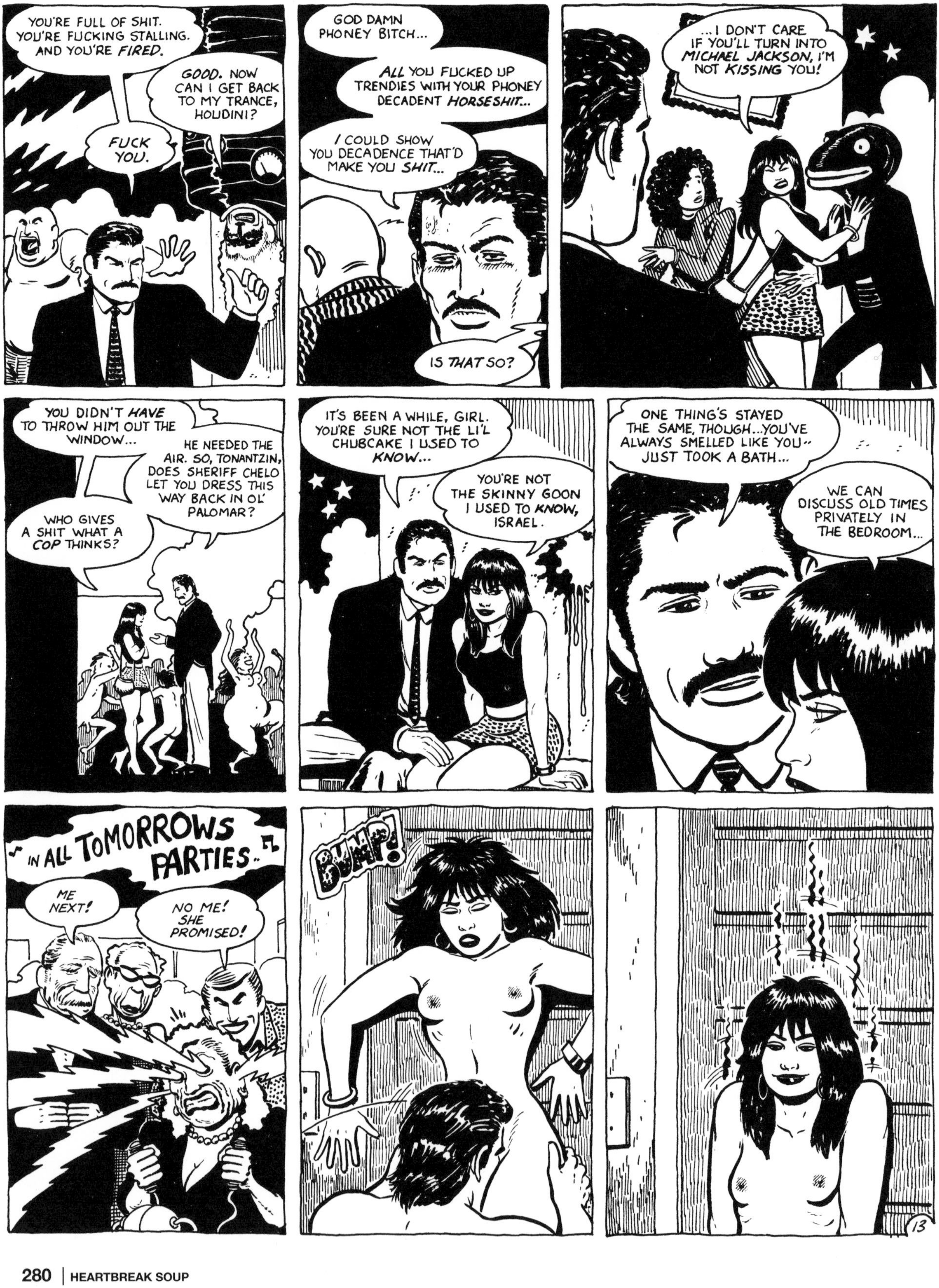
YOU'RE FULL OF SHIT. YOU'RE FUCKING STALLING. AND YOU'RE FIRED.
GOOD. NOW CAN I GET BACK TO MY TRANCE, HOUDINI?
FUCK YOU.
GOD DAMN PHONEY BITCH...
ALL YOU FUCKED UP TRENDIES WITH YOUR PHONEY DECADENT HORSESHIT...
I COULD SHOW YOU DECADENCE THAT'D MAKE YOU SHIT...
IS THAT SO?
...I DON'T CARE IF YOU'LL TURN INTO MICHAEL JACKSON, I'M NOT KISSING YOU!
YOU DIDN'T HAVE TO THROW HIM OUT THE WINDOW...
HE NEEDED THE AIR. SO, TONANTZIN, DOES SHERIFF CHELO LET YOU DRESS THIS WAY BACK IN OL' PALOMAR?
WHO GIVES A SHIT WHAT A COP THINKS?
IT'S BEEN A WHILE, GIRL. YOU'RE SURE NOT THE LI'L CHUBCAKE I USED TO KNOW...
YOU'RE NOT THE SKINNY GOON I USED TO KNOW, ISRAEL.
ONE THING'S STAYED THE SAME, THOUGH...YOU'VE ALWAYS SMELLED LIKE YOU JUST TOOK A BATH...
WE CAN DISCUSS OLD TIMES PRIVATELY IN THE BEDROOM...
IN ALL TOMORROWS PARTIES..
ME NEXT!
NO ME! SHE PROMISED!
BUMP!
13

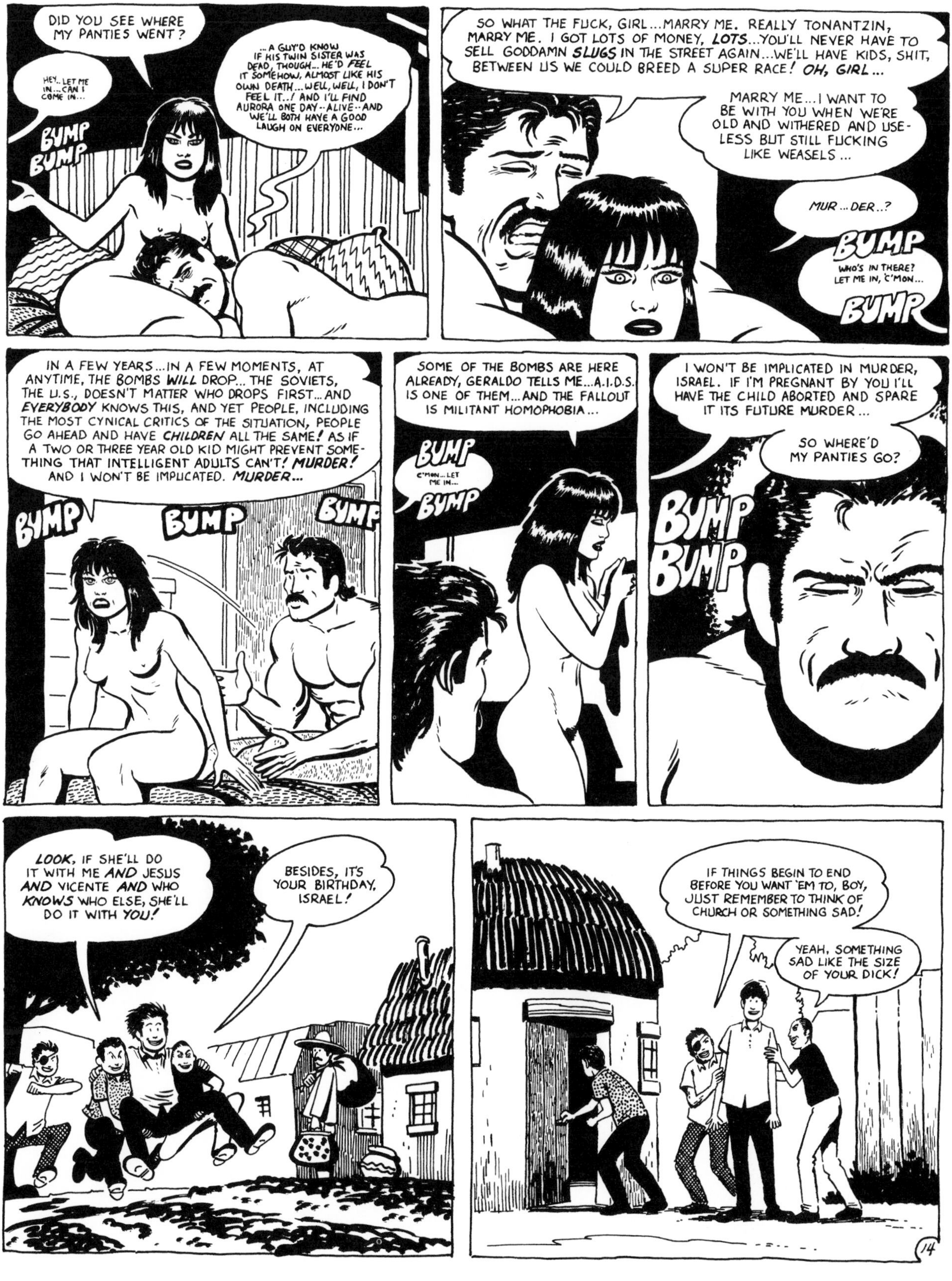
DID YOU SEE WHERE MY PANTIES WENT?
HEY.. LET ME IN... CAN I COME IN...
BUMP BUMP
...A GUY'D KNOW IF HIS TWIN SISTER WAS DEAD, THOUGH... HE'D FEEL IT SOMEHOW, ALMOST LIKE HIS OWN DEATH... WELL, WELL, I DON'T FEEL IT...! AND I'LL FIND AURORA ONE DAY--ALIVE--AND WE'LL BOTH HAVE A GOOD LAUGH ON EVERYONE...
SO WHAT THE FUCK, GIRL... MARRY ME. REALLY TONANTZIN, MARRY ME. I GOT LOTS OF MONEY, LOTS... YOU'LL NEVER HAVE TO SELL GODDAMN SLUGS IN THE STREET AGAIN... WE'LL HAVE KIDS, SHIT, BETWEEN US WE COULD BREED A SUPER RACE! OH, GIRL...
MARRY ME... I WANT TO BE WITH YOU WHEN WE'RE OLD AND WITHERED AND USELESS BUT STILL FUCKING LIKE WEASELS...
MUR... DER..?
BUMP
WHO'S IN THERE? LET ME IN, C'MON...
BUMP
IN A FEW YEARS... IN A FEW MOMENTS, AT ANYTIME, THE BOMBS WILL DROP... THE SOVIETS, THE U.S., DOESN'T MATTER WHO DROPS FIRST... AND EVERYBODY KNOWS THIS, AND YET PEOPLE, INCLUDING THE MOST CYNICAL CRITICS OF THE SITUATION, PEOPLE GO AHEAD AND HAVE CHILDREN ALL THE SAME! AS IF A TWO OR THREE YEAR OLD KID MIGHT PREVENT SOMETHING THAT INTELLIGENT ADULTS CAN'T! MURDER! AND I WON'T BE IMPLICATED. MURDER...
BUMP BUMP BUMP
SOME OF THE BOMBS ARE HERE ALREADY, GERALDO TELLS ME... A.I.D.S. IS ONE OF THEM... AND THE FALLOUT IS MILITANT HOMOPHOBIA...
BUMP
C'MON... LET ME IN...
BUMP
I WON'T BE IMPLICATED IN MURDER, ISRAEL. IF I'M PREGNANT BY YOU I'LL HAVE THE CHILD ABORTED AND SPARE IT ITS FUTURE MURDER...
SO WHERE'D MY PANTIES GO?
BUMP BUMP
LOOK, IF SHE'LL DO IT WITH ME AND JESUS AND VICENTE AND WHO KNOWS WHO ELSE, SHE'LL DO IT WITH YOU!
BESIDES, IT'S YOUR BIRTHDAY, ISRAEL!
IF THINGS BEGIN TO END BEFORE YOU WANT 'EM TO, BOY, JUST REMEMBER TO THINK OF CHURCH OR SOMETHING SAD!
YEAH, SOMETHING SAD LIKE THE SIZE OF YOUR DICK!
14

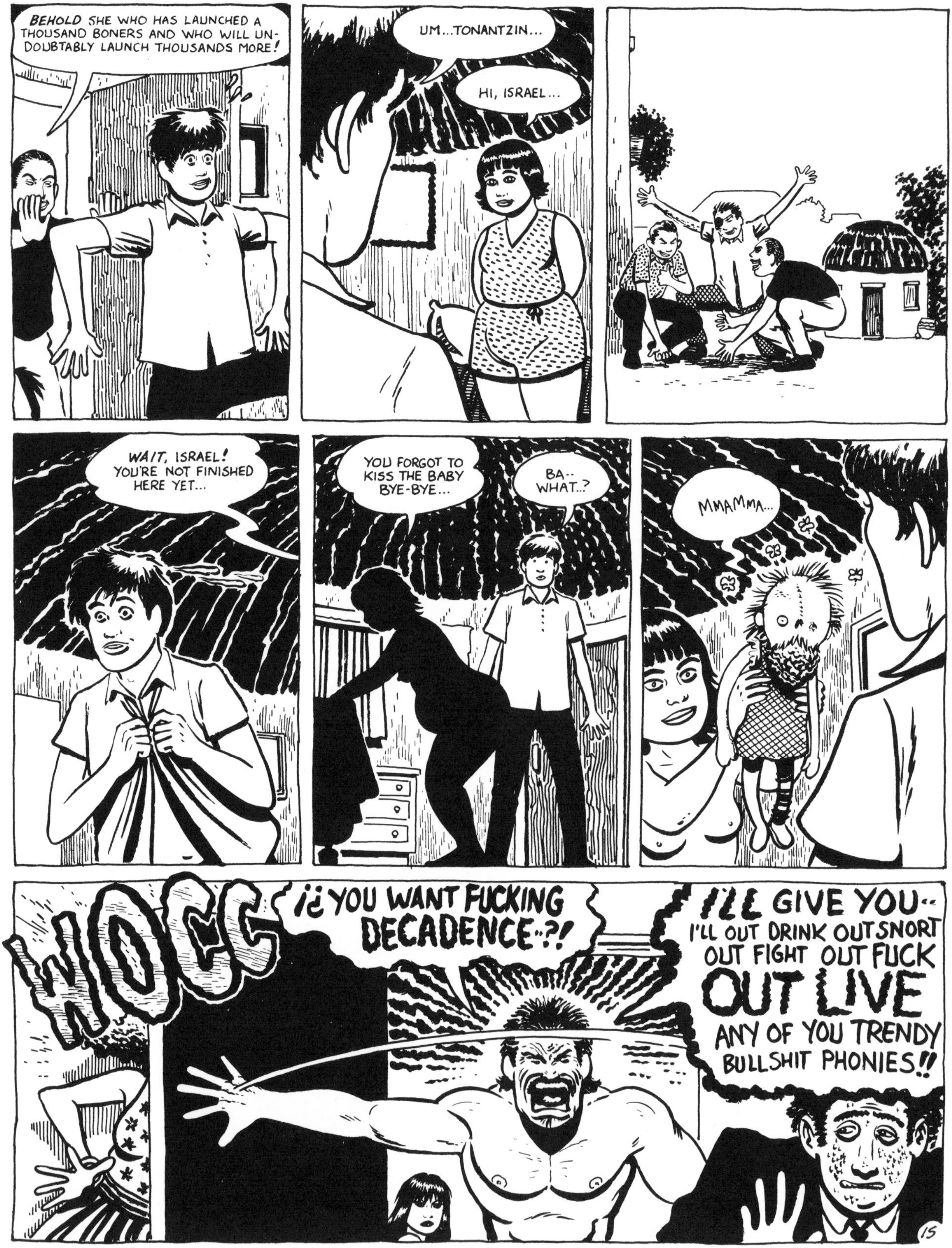

BEHOLD SHE WHO HAS LAUNCHED A THOUSAND BONERS AND WHO WILL UNDOUBTABLY LAUNCH THOUSANDS MORE!
UM...TONANTZIN...
HI, ISRAEL...
WAIT, ISRAEL! YOU'RE NOT FINISHED HERE YET...
YOU FORGOT TO KISS THE BABY BYE-BYE...
BA-- WHAT..?
MMAMMA...
WOCC
¡¿ YOU WANT FUCKING DECADENCE..?!
I'LL GIVE YOU-- I'LL OUT DRINK OUT SNORT OUT FIGHT OUT FUCK OUT LIVE ANY OF YOU TRENDY BULLSHIT PHONIES!!
15

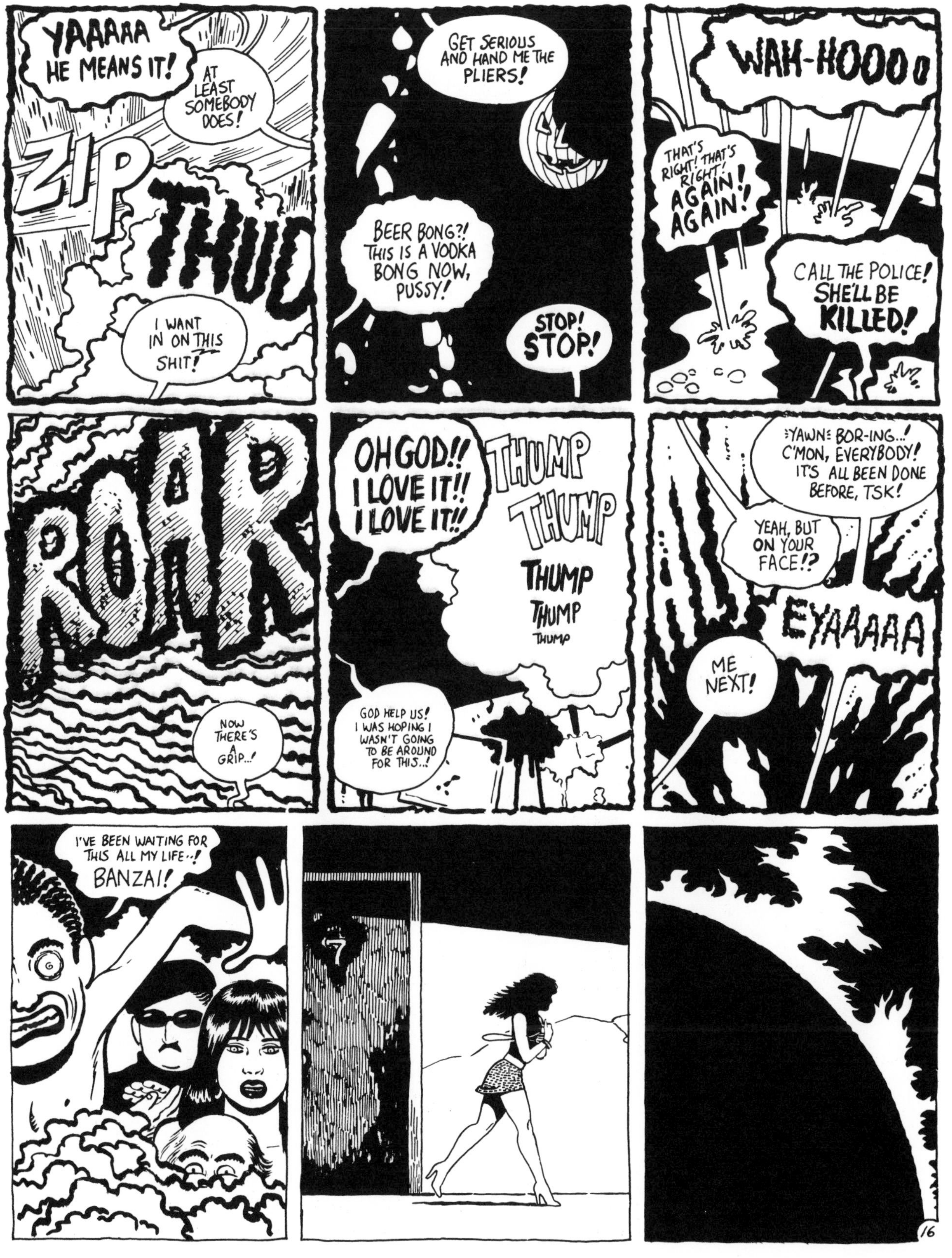
YAAAAA HE MEANS IT!
AT LEAST SOMEBODY DOES!
ZIP
THUD
I WANT IN ON THIS SHIT!
GET SERIOUS AND HAND ME THE PLIERS!
BEER BONG?! THIS IS A VODKA BONG NOW, PUSSY!
STOP! STOP!
WAH-HOOOO
THAT'S RIGHT! THAT'S RIGHT! AGAIN! AGAIN!
CALL THE POLICE! SHE'LL BE KILLED!
ROAR
NOW THERE'S A GRIP..!
OH GOD!! I LOVE IT!! I LOVE IT!!
THUMP THUMP THUMP THUMP THUMP
GOD HELP US! I WAS HOPING I WASN'T GOING TO BE AROUND FOR THIS..!
YAWN BOR-ING...! C'MON, EVERYBODY! IT'S ALL BEEN DONE BEFORE, TSK!
YEAH, BUT ON YOUR FACE!?
EYAAAAA
ME NEXT!
I'VE BEEN WAITING FOR THIS ALL MY LIFE..! BANZAI!
7
16

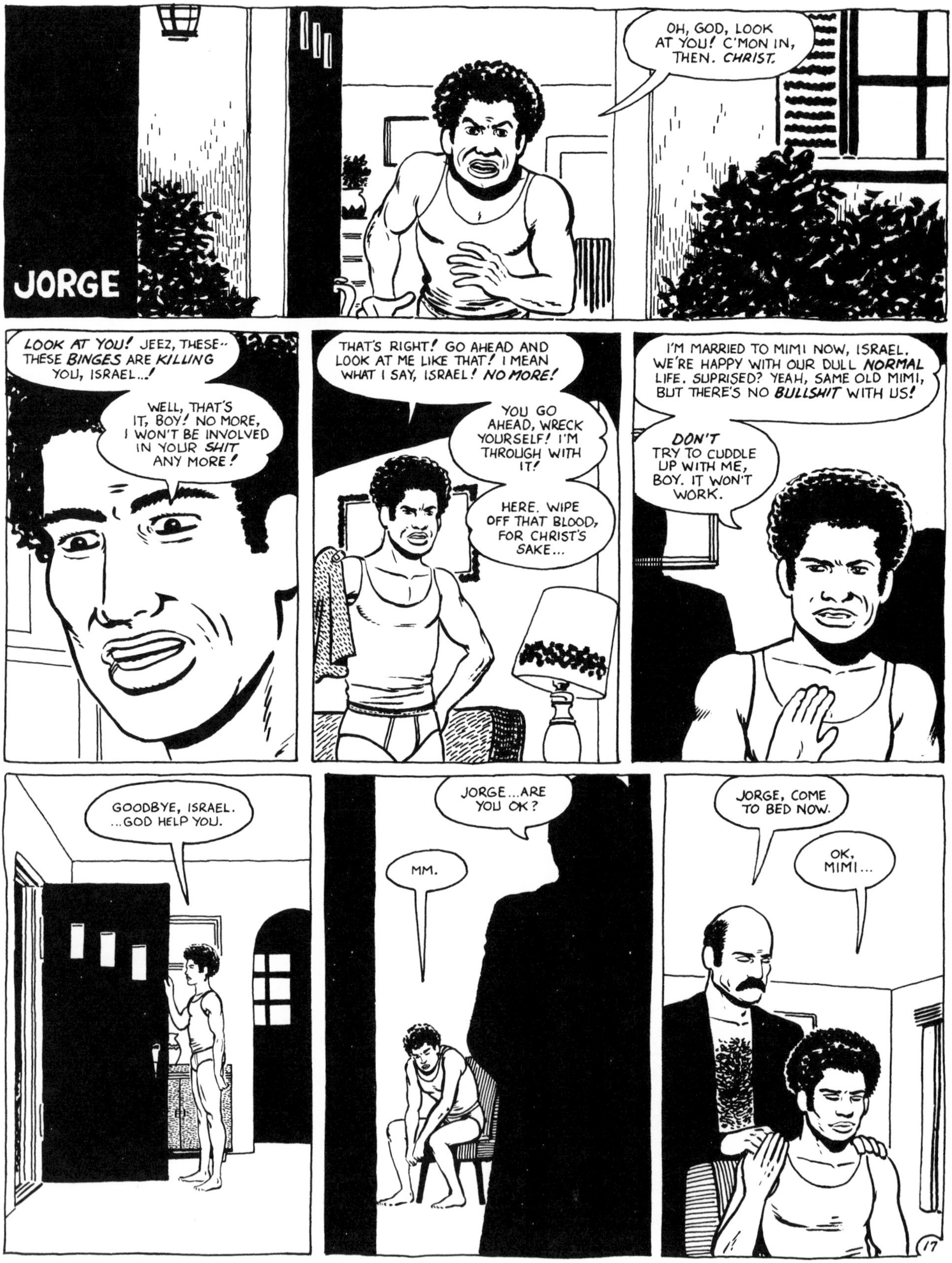
JORGE
OH, GOD, LOOK AT YOU! C'MON IN, THEN. CHRIST.
LOOK AT YOU! JEEZ, THESE.. THESE BINGES ARE KILLING YOU, ISRAEL...!
WELL, THAT'S IT, BOY! NO MORE, I WON'T BE INVOLVED IN YOUR SHIT ANY MORE!
THAT'S RIGHT! GO AHEAD AND LOOK AT ME LIKE THAT! I MEAN WHAT I SAY, ISRAEL! NO MORE!
YOU GO AHEAD, WRECK YOURSELF! I'M THROUGH WITH IT!
HERE. WIPE OFF THAT BLOOD, FOR CHRIST'S SAKE...
I'M MARRIED TO MIMI NOW, ISRAEL. WE'RE HAPPY WITH OUR DULL NORMAL LIFE. SUPRISED? YEAH, SAME OLD MIMI, BUT THERE'S NO BULLSHIT WITH US!
DON'T TRY TO CUDDLE UP WITH ME, BOY. IT WON'T WORK.
GOODBYE, ISRAEL. ...GOD HELP YOU.
JORGE...ARE YOU OK?
MM.
JORGE, COME TO BED NOW.
OK, MIMI...
17

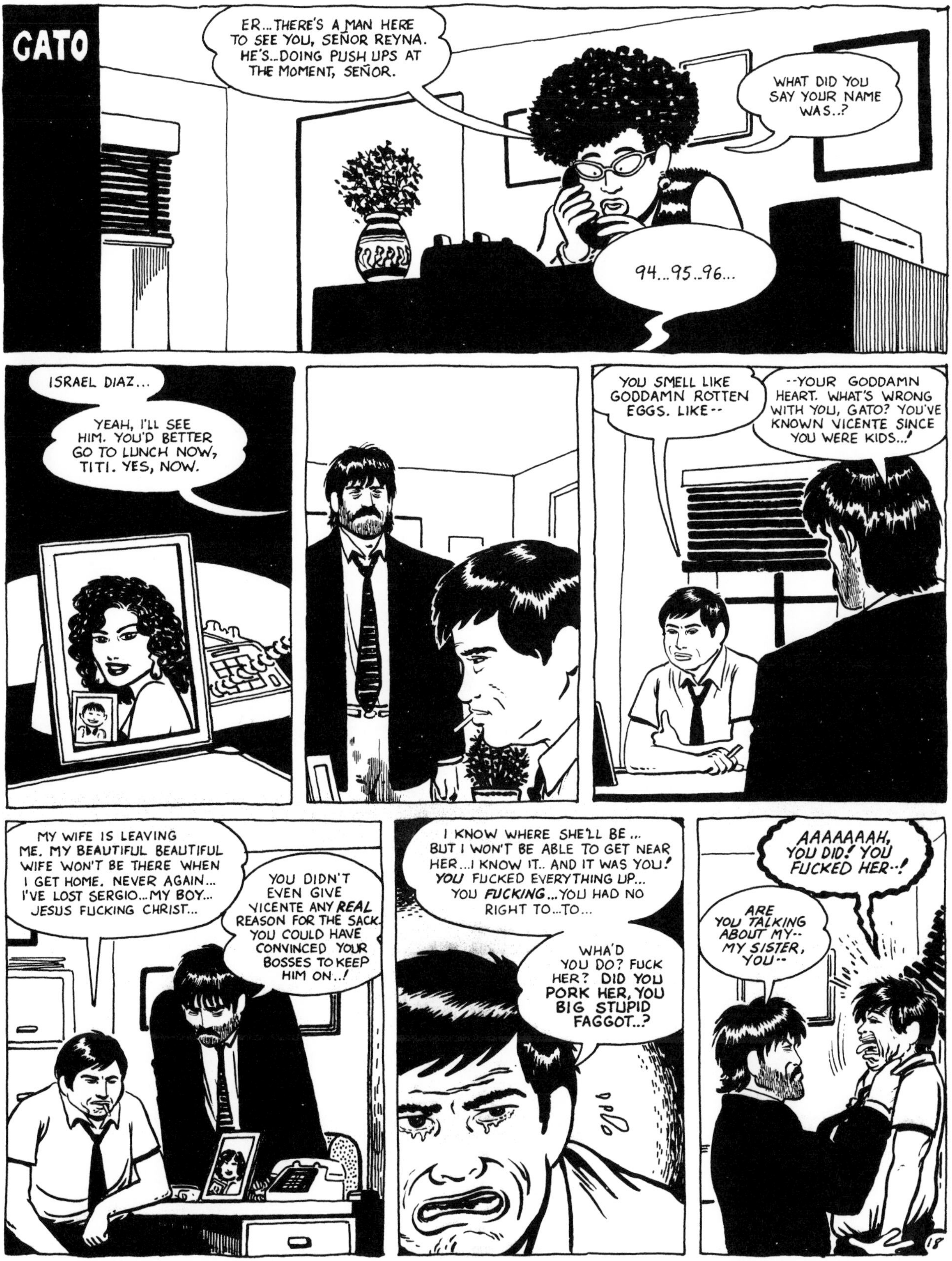
GATO
ER... THERE'S A MAN HERE TO SEE YOU, SEÑOR REYNA. HE'S...DOING PUSH UPS AT THE MOMENT, SEÑOR.
WHAT DID YOU SAY YOUR NAME WAS..?
94...95..96...
ISRAEL DIAZ...
YEAH, I'LL SEE HIM. YOU'D BETTER GO TO LUNCH NOW, TITI. YES, NOW.
YOU SMELL LIKE GODDAMN ROTTEN EGGS. LIKE--
--YOUR GODDAMN HEART. WHAT'S WRONG WITH YOU, GATO? YOU'VE KNOWN VICENTE SINCE YOU WERE KIDS...!
MY WIFE IS LEAVING ME. MY BEAUTIFUL BEAUTIFUL WIFE WON'T BE THERE WHEN I GET HOME. NEVER AGAIN... I'VE LOST SERGIO...MY BOY... JESUS FUCKING CHRIST...
YOU DIDN'T EVEN GIVE VICENTE ANY REAL REASON FOR THE SACK. YOU COULD HAVE CONVINCED YOUR BOSSES TO KEEP HIM ON..!
I KNOW WHERE SHE'LL BE... BUT I WON'T BE ABLE TO GET NEAR HER...I KNOW IT.. AND IT WAS YOU! YOU FUCKED EVERYTHING UP... YOU FUCKING...YOU HAD NO RIGHT TO...TO...
WHA'D YOU DO? FUCK HER? DID YOU PORK HER, YOU BIG STUPID FAGGOT..?
AAAAAAAH, YOU DID! YOU FUCKED HER--!
ARE YOU TALKING ABOUT MY-- MY SISTER, YOU--
18

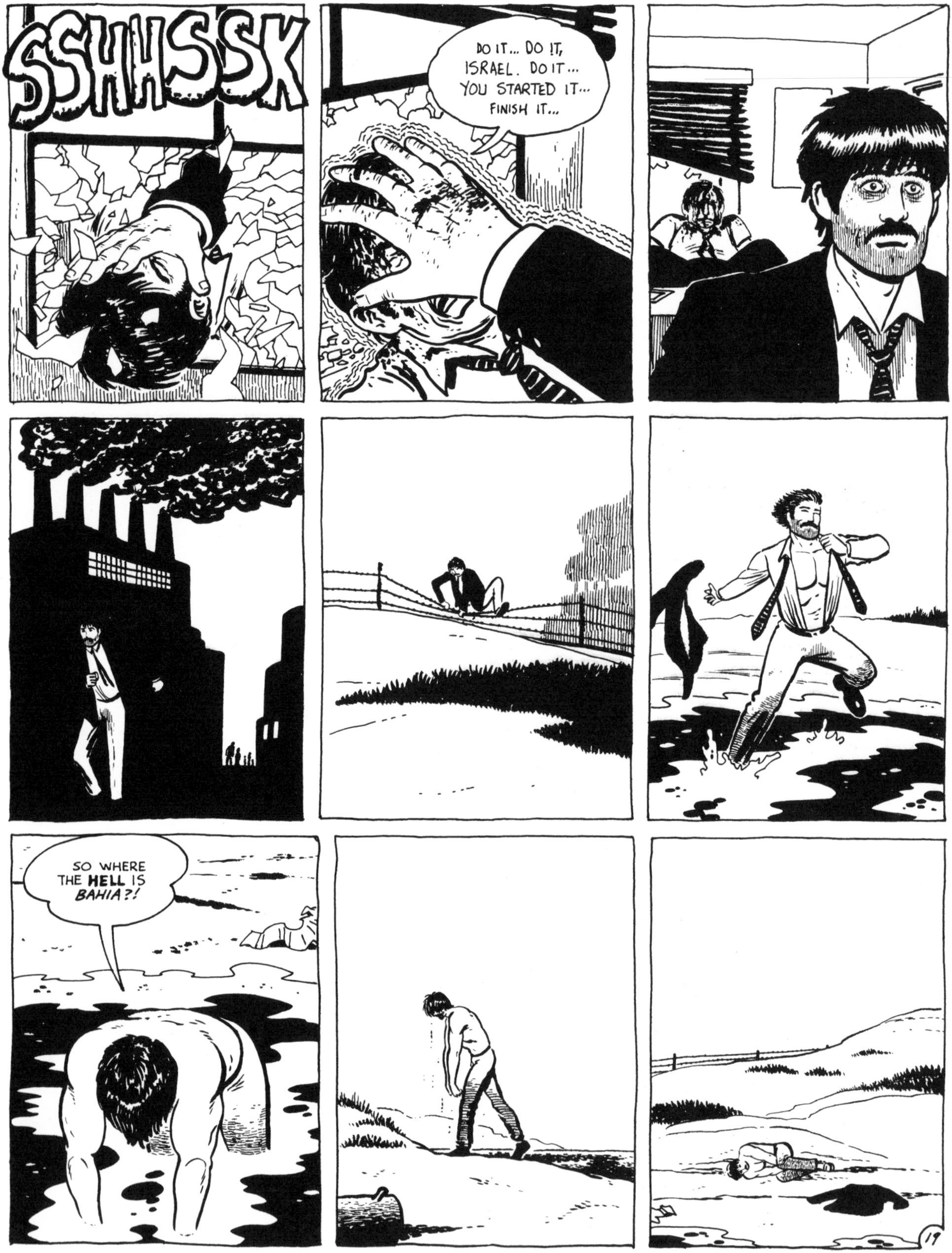
SSHSSK
DO IT... DO IT, ISRAEL. DO IT... YOU STARTED IT... FINISH IT...
SO WHERE THE **HELL** IS *BAHIA?!*
19

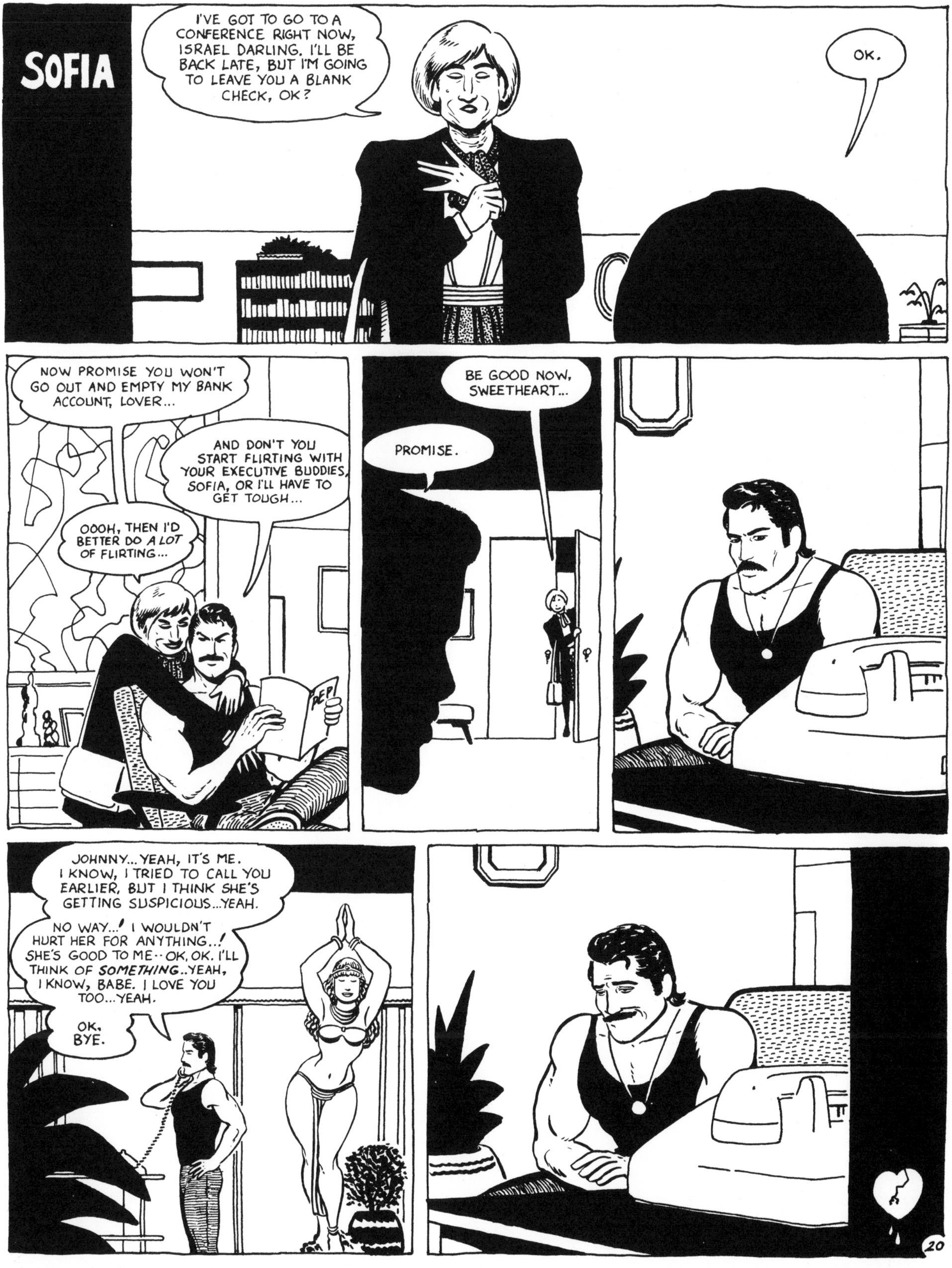
SOFIA
I'VE GOT TO GO TO A CONFERENCE RIGHT NOW, ISRAEL DARLING. I'LL BE BACK LATE, BUT I'M GOING TO LEAVE YOU A BLANK CHECK, OK?
OK.
NOW PROMISE YOU WON'T GO OUT AND EMPTY MY BANK ACCOUNT, LOVER...
AND DON'T YOU START FLIRTING WITH YOUR EXECUTIVE BUDDIES, SOFIA, OR I'LL HAVE TO GET TOUGH...
OOOH, THEN I'D BETTER DO *A LOT* OF FLIRTING...
REP
BE GOOD NOW, SWEETHEART...
PROMISE.
JOHNNY... YEAH, IT'S ME. I KNOW, I TRIED TO CALL YOU EARLIER, BUT I THINK SHE'S GETTING SUSPICIOUS... YEAH.
NO WAY...! I WOULDN'T HURT HER FOR ANYTHING...! SHE'S GOOD TO ME·· OK, OK. I'LL THINK OF *SOMETHING*.. YEAH, I KNOW, BABE. I LOVE YOU TOO... YEAH.
OK. BYE.
20

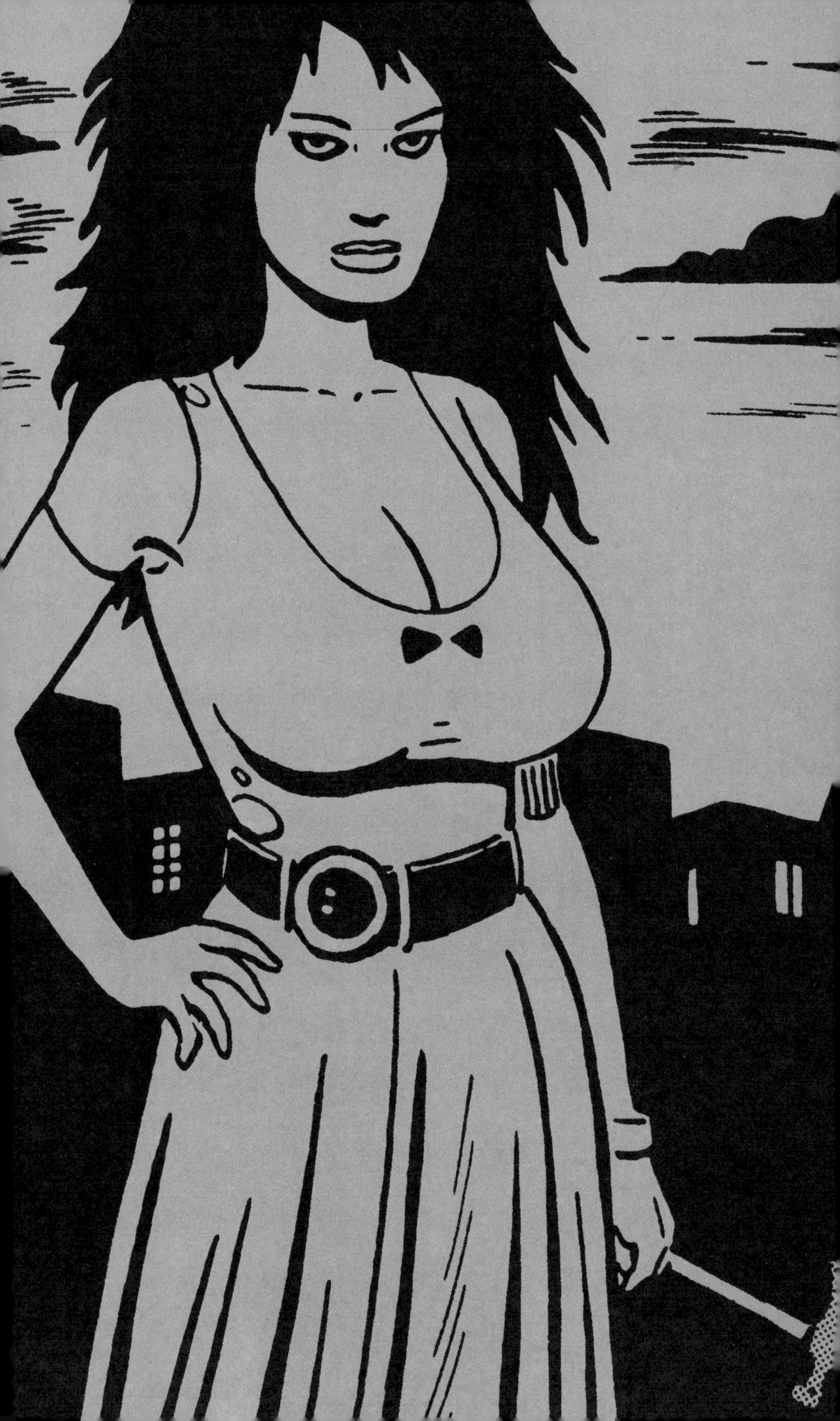

THE COMPLETE *LOVE AND ROCKETS* LIBRARY

Jaime and Gilbert Hernandez celebrated 30 years of *Love and Rockets* in 2013. This towering and beloved body of work remains a must-have for any discerning comics lover, and this comprehensive trade paperback series is the place to start.

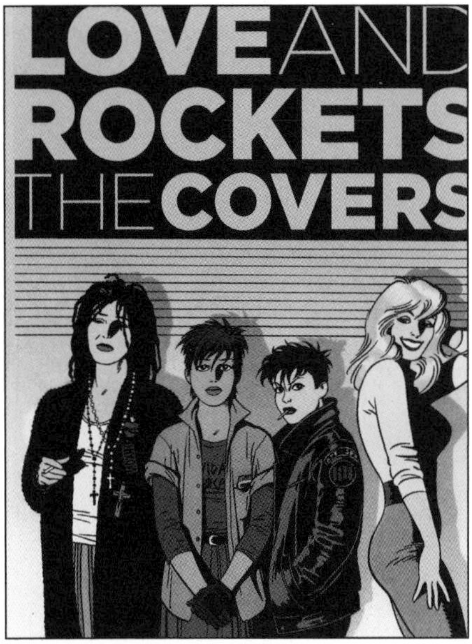
LOVE AND
ROCKETS
THE COVERS

LOVE AND ROCKETS: THE COVERS
$35.00 Hardcover ISBN 978-1-60699-598-3
A beautiful, oversized art book featuring over 120 iconic comic covers (front & back) from the first 3 decades of *Love and Rockets*, collected for the first time in full color.

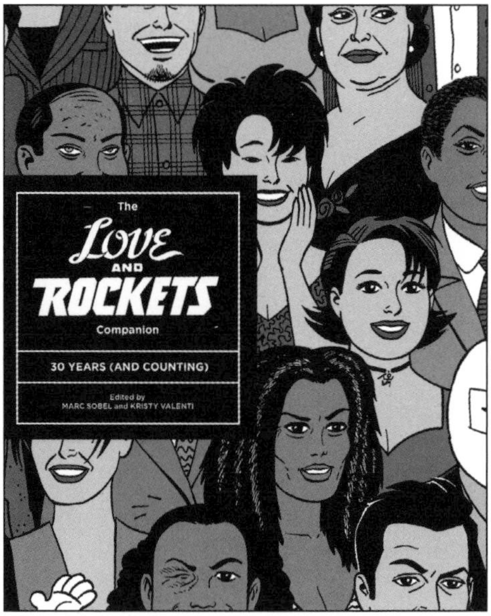
The
Love
AND
ROCKETS
Companion
30 YEARS (AND COUNTING)
Edited by
MARC SOBEL and KRISTY VALENTI

THE LOVE AND ROCKETS COMPANION
$29.99 Paperback Original ISBN 978-1-60699-579-2
An indispensable guide and massive love letter to the award-winning, world-renowned series. Interviews, family trees, timelines, unpublished art, bibliography, and more.

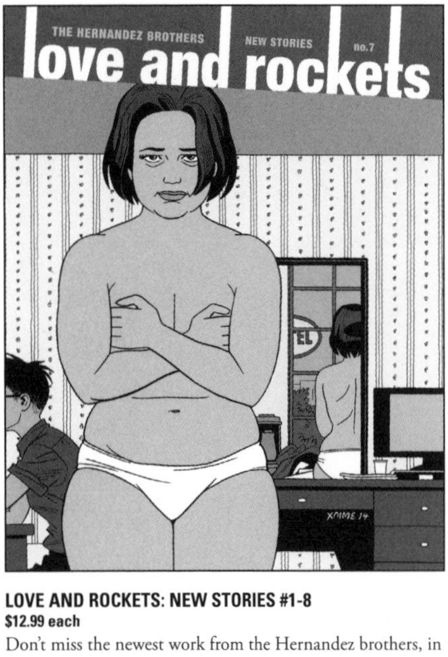
THE HERNANDEZ BROTHERS
NEW STORIES
no.7
love and rockets

LOVE AND ROCKETS: NEW STORIES #1-8
$12.99 each
Don't miss the newest work from the Hernandez brothers, in this annual series that has yet to be collected in *The Love and Rockets* Library.

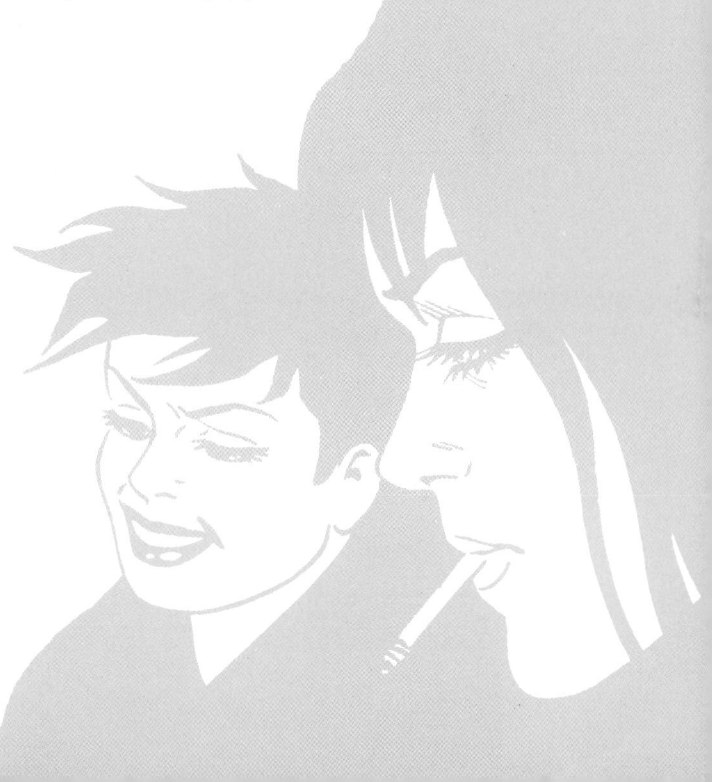